Lecture Notes in Computer Science   14440

Founding Editors

Gerhard Goos
Juris Hartmanis

The series Lecture Notes in Computer Science (LNCS), including its subseries Lecture Notes in Artificial Intelligence (LNAI) and Lecture Notes in Bioinformatics (LNBI), has established itself as a medium for the publication of new developments in computer science and information technology research, teaching, and education.

LNCS enjoys close cooperation with the computer science R & D community, the series counts many renowned academics among its volume editors and paper authors, and collaborates with prestigious societies. Its mission is to serve this international community by providing an invaluable service, mainly focused on the publication of conference and workshop proceedings and postproceedings. LNCS commenced publication in 1973.

Jian Guo · Ron Steinfeld
Editors

Advances in Cryptology – ASIACRYPT 2023

29th International Conference on the Theory
and Application of Cryptology and Information Security
Guangzhou, China, December 4–8, 2023
Proceedings, Part III

Springer

Editors
Jian Guo [iD]
Nanyang Technological University
Singapore, Singapore

Ron Steinfeld [iD]
Monash University
Melbourne, VIC, Australia

ISSN 0302-9743   ISSN 1611-3349 (electronic)
Lecture Notes in Computer Science
ISBN 978-981-99-8726-9   ISBN 978-981-99-8727-6 (eBook)
https://doi.org/10.1007/978-981-99-8727-6

This Springer imprint is published by the registered company Springer Nature Singapore Pte Ltd.
The registered company address is: 152 Beach Road, #21-01/04 Gateway East, Singapore 189721, Singapore

Paper in this product is recyclable.

Preface

The 29th Annual International Conference on the Theory and Application of Cryptology and Information Security (Asiacrypt 2023) was held in Guangzhou, China, on December 4–8, 2023. The conference covered all technical aspects of cryptology, and was sponsored by the International Association for Cryptologic Research (IACR).

We received an Asiacrypt record of 376 paper submissions from all over the world, and the Program Committee (PC) selected 106 papers for publication in the proceedings of the conference. Due to this large number of papers, the Asiacrypt 2023 program had 3 tracks.

The two program chairs were supported by the great help and excellent advice of six area chairs, selected to cover the main topic areas of the conference. The area chairs were Kai-Min Chung for Information-Theoretic and Complexity-Theoretic Cryptography, Tanja Lange for Efficient and Secure Implementations, Shengli Liu for Public-Key Cryptography Algorithms and Protocols, Khoa Nguyen for Multi-Party Computation and Zero-Knowledge, Duong Hieu Phan for Public-Key Primitives with Advanced Functionalities, and Yu Sasaki for Symmetric-Key Cryptology. Each of the area chairs helped to lead discussions together with the PC members assigned as paper discussion lead. Area chairs also helped to decide on the submissions that should be accepted from their respective areas. We are very grateful for the invaluable contribution provided by the area chairs.

To review and evaluate the submissions, while keeping the load per PC member manageable, we selected a record size PC consisting of 105 leading experts from all over the world, in all six topic areas of cryptology. The two program chairs were not allowed to submit a paper, and PC members were limited to submit one single-author paper, or at most two co-authored papers, or at most three co-authored papers all with students. Each non-PC submission was reviewed by at least three reviewers consisting of either PC members or their external sub-reviewers, while each PC member submission received at least four reviews. The strong conflict of interest rules imposed by IACR ensure that papers are not handled by PC members with a close working relationship with the authors. There were approximately 420 external reviewers, whose input was critical to the selection of papers. Submissions were anonymous and their length was limited to 30 pages excluding the bibliography and supplementary materials.

The review process was conducted using double-blind peer review. The conference operated a two-round review system with a rebuttal phase. After the reviews and first round discussions the PC selected 244 submissions to proceed to the second round and the authors were then invited to participate in an interactive rebuttal phase with the reviewers to clarify questions and concerns. The remaining 131 papers were rejected, including one desk reject. The second round involved extensive discussions by the PC members. After several weeks of additional discussions, the committee selected the final 106 papers to appear in these proceedings.

The eight volumes of the conference proceedings contain the revised versions of the 106 papers that were selected. The final revised versions of papers were not reviewed again and the authors are responsible for their contents.

The PC nominated and voted for two papers to receive the Best Paper Awards, and one paper to receive the Best Early Career Paper Award. The Best Paper Awards went to Thomas Espitau, Alexandre Wallet and Yang Yu for their paper "On Gaussian Sampling, Smoothing Parameter and Application to Signatures", and to Kaijie Jiang, Anyu Wang, Hengyi Luo, Guoxiao Liu, Yang Yu, and Xiaoyun Wang for their paper "Exploiting the Symmetry of Z^n: Randomization and the Automorphism Problem". The Best Early Career Paper Award went to Maxime Plancon for the paper "Exploiting Algebraic Structure in Probing Security". The authors of those three papers were invited to submit extended versions of their papers to the Journal of Cryptology. In addition, the program of Asiacrypt 2023 also included two invited plenary talks, also nominated and voted by the PC: one talk was given by Mehdi Tibouchi and the other by Xiaoyun Wang. The conference also featured a rump session chaired by Kang Yang and Yu Yu which contained short presentations on the latest research results of the field.

Numerous people contributed to the success of Asiacrypt 2023. We would like to thank all the authors, including those whose submissions were not accepted, for submitting their research results to the conference. We are very grateful to the area chairs, PC members and external reviewers for contributing their knowledge and expertise, and for the tremendous amount of work that was done with reading papers and contributing to the discussions. We are greatly indebted to Jian Weng and Fangguo Zhang, the General Chairs, for their efforts in organizing the event and to Kevin McCurley and Kay McKelly for their help with the website and review system. We thank the Asiacrypt 2023 advisory committee members Bart Preneel, Huaxiong Wang, Kai-Min Chung, Yu Sasaki, Dongdai Lin, Shweta Agrawal and Michel Abdalla for their valuable suggestions. We are also grateful for the helpful advice and organization material provided to us by the Eurocrypt 2023 PC co-chairs Carmit Hazay and Martijn Stam and Crypto 2023 PC co-chairs Helena Handschuh and Anna Lysyanskaya. We also thank the team at Springer for handling the publication of these conference proceedings.

December 2023   Jian Guo
                                                                                                     Ron Steinfeld

Organization

General Chairs

Jian Weng   Jinan University, China
Fangguo Zhang   Sun Yat-sen University, China

Program Committee Chairs

Jian Guo   Nanyang Technological University, Singapore
Ron Steinfeld   Monash University, Australia

Program Committee

Behzad Abdolmaleki   University of Sheffield, UK
Masayuki Abe   NTT Social Informatics Laboratories, Japan
Miguel Ambrona   Input Output Global (IOHK), Spain
Daniel Apon   MITRE Labs, USA
Shi Bai   Florida Atlantic University, USA
Gustavo Banegas   Qualcomm, France
Zhenzhen Bao   Tsinghua University, China
Andrea Basso   University of Bristol, UK
Ward Beullens   IBM Research Europe, Switzerland
Katharina Boudgoust   Aarhus University, Denmark
Matteo Campanelli   Protocol Labs, Denmark
Ignacio Cascudo   IMDEA Software Institute, Spain
Wouter Castryck   imec-COSIC, KU Leuven, Belgium
Jie Chen   East China Normal University, China
Yilei Chen   Tsinghua University, China
Jung Hee Cheon   Seoul National University and Cryptolab Inc, South Korea
Sherman S. M. Chow   Chinese University of Hong Kong, China
Kai-Min Chung   Academia Sinica, Taiwan
Michele Ciampi   University of Edinburgh, UK
Bernardo David   IT University of Copenhagen, Denmark
Yi Deng   Institute of Information Engineering, Chinese Academy of Sciences, China

Patrick Derbez	University of Rennes, France
Xiaoyang Dong	Tsinghua University, China
Rafael Dowsley	Monash University, Australia
Nico Döttling	Helmholtz Center for Information Security, Germany
Maria Eichlseder	Graz University of Technology, Austria
Muhammed F. Esgin	Monash University, Australia
Thomas Espitau	PQShield, France
Jun Furukawa	NEC Corporation, Japan
Aron Gohr	Independent Researcher, New Zealand
Junqing Gong	ECNU, China
Lorenzo Grassi	Ruhr University Bochum, Germany
Tim Güneysu	Ruhr University Bochum, Germany
Chun Guo	Shandong University, China
Siyao Guo	NYU Shanghai, China
Fuchun Guo	University of Wollongong, Australia
Mohammad Hajiabadi	University of Waterloo, Canada
Lucjan Hanzlik	CISPA Helmholtz Center for Information Security, Germany
Xiaolu Hou	Slovak University of Technology, Slovakia
Yuncong Hu	Shanghai Jiao Tong University, China
Xinyi Huang	Hong Kong University of Science and Technology (Guangzhou), China
Tibor Jager	University of Wuppertal, Germany
Elena Kirshanova	Technology Innovation Institute, UAE and I. Kant Baltic Federal University, Russia
Eyal Kushilevitz	Technion, Israel
Russell W. F. Lai	Aalto University, Finland
Tanja Lange	Eindhoven University of Technology, Netherlands
Hyung Tae Lee	Chung-Ang University, South Korea
Eik List	Nanyang Technological University, Singapore
Meicheng Liu	Institute of Information Engineering, Chinese Academy of Sciences, China
Guozhen Liu	Nanyang Technological University, Singapore
Fukang Liu	Tokyo Institute of Technology, Japan
Shengli Liu	Shanghai Jiao Tong University, China
Feng-Hao Liu	Florida Atlantic University, USA
Hemanta K. Maji	Purdue University, USA
Takahiro Matsuda	AIST, Japan
Christian Matt	Concordium, Switzerland
Tomoyuki Morimae	Kyoto University, Japan
Pierrick Méaux	University of Luxembourg, Luxembourg

Mridul Nandi   Indian Statistical Institute, Kolkata, India
María Naya-Plasencia   Inria, France
Khoa Nguyen   University of Wollongong, Australia
Ryo Nishimaki   NTT Social Informatics Laboratories, Japan
Anca Nitulescu   Protocol Labs, France
Ariel Nof   Bar Ilan University, Israel
Emmanuela Orsini   Bocconi University, Italy
Adam O'Neill   UMass Amherst, USA
Morten Øygarden   Simula UiB, Norway
Sikhar Patranabis   IBM Research, India
Alice Pellet-Mary   CNRS and University of Bordeaux, France
Edoardo Persichetti   Florida Atlantic University, USA and Sapienza
                                        University, Italy
Duong Hieu Phan   Telecom Paris, Institut Polytechnique de Paris,
                                        France
Josef Pieprzyk   Data61, CSIRO, Australia and ICS, PAS, Poland
Axel Y. Poschmann   PQShield, UAE
Thomas Prest   PQShield, France
Adeline Roux-Langlois   CNRS, GREYC, France
Amin Sakzad   Monash University, Australia
Yu Sasaki   NTT Social Informatics Laboratories, Japan
Jae Hong Seo   Hanyang University, South Korea
Yaobin Shen   UCLouvain, Belgium
Danping Shi   Institute of Information Engineering, Chinese
                                        Academy of Sciences, China
Damien Stehlé   CryptoLab, France
Bing Sun   National University of Defense Technology,
                                        China
Shi-Feng Sun   Shanghai Jiao Tong University, China
Keisuke Tanaka   Tokyo Institute of Technology, Japan
Qiang Tang   University of Sydney, Australia
Vanessa Teague   Thinking Cybersecurity Pty Ltd and the
                                        Australian National University, Australia
Jean-Pierre Tillich   Inria, Paris, France
Yosuke Todo   NTT Social Informatics Laboratories, Japan
Alexandre Wallet   University of Rennes, Inria, CNRS, IRISA,
                                        France
Meiqin Wang   Shandong University, China
Yongge Wang   UNC Charlotte, USA
Yuyu Wang   University of Electronic Science and Technology
                                        of China, China
Qingju Wang   Telecom Paris, Institut Polytechnique de Paris,
                                        France

Benjamin Wesolowski	CNRS and ENS Lyon, France
Shuang Wu	Huawei International, Singapore, Singapore
Keita Xagawa	Technology Innovation Institute, UAE
Chaoping Xing	Shanghai Jiao Tong University, China
Jun Xu	Institute of Information Engineering, Chinese Academy of Sciences, China
Takashi Yamakawa	NTT Social Informatics Laboratories, Japan
Kang Yang	State Key Laboratory of Cryptology, China
Yu Yu	Shanghai Jiao Tong University, China
Yang Yu	Tsinghua University, Beijing, China
Yupeng Zhang	University of Illinois Urbana-Champaign and Texas A&M University, USA
Liangfeng Zhang	ShanghaiTech University, China
Raymond K. Zhao	CSIRO's Data61, Australia
Hong-Sheng Zhou	Virginia Commonwealth University, USA

Additional Reviewers

Amit Agarwal
Jooyoung Lee
Léo Ackermann
Akshima
Bar Alon
Ravi Anand
Sarah Arpin
Thomas Attema
Nuttapong Attrapadung
Manuel Barbosa
Razvan Barbulescu
James Bartusek
Carsten Baum
Olivier Bernard
Tyler Besselman
Ritam Bhaumik
Jingguo Bi
Loic Bidoux
Maxime Bombar
Xavier Bonnetain
Joppe Bos
Mariana Botelho da Gama
Christina Boura
Clémence Bouvier
Ross Bowden

Pedro Branco
Lauren Brandt
Alessandro Budroni
Kevin Carrier
André Chailloux
Suvradip Chakraborty
Debasmita Chakraborty
Haokai Chang
Bhuvnesh Chaturvedi
Caicai Chen
Rongmao Chen
Mingjie Chen
Yi Chen
Megan Chen
Yu Long Chen
Xin Chen
Shiyao Chen
Long Chen
Wonhee Cho
Qiaohan Chu
Valerio Cini
James Clements
Ran Cohen
Alexandru Cojocaru
Sandro Coretti-Drayton

Anamaria Costache
Alain Couvreur
Daniele Cozzo
Hongrui Cui
Giuseppe D'Alconzo
Zhaopeng Dai
Quang Dao
Nilanjan Datta
Koen de Boer
Luca De Feo
Paola de Perthuis
Thomas Decru
Rafael del Pino
Julien Devevey
Henri Devillez
Siemen Dhooghe
Yaoling Ding
Jack Doerner
Jelle Don
Mark Douglas Schultz
Benjamin Dowling
Minxin Du
Xiaoqi Duan
Jesko Dujmovic
Moumita Dutta
Avijit Dutta
Ehsan Ebrahimi
Felix Engelmann
Reo Eriguchi
Jonathan Komada Eriksen
Andre Esser
Pouria Fallahpour
Zhiyong Fang
Antonio Faonio
Pooya Farshim
Joël Felderhoff
Jakob Feldtkeller
Weiqi Feng
Xiutao Feng
Shuai Feng
Qi Feng
Hanwen Feng
Antonio Flórez-Gutiérrez
Apostolos Fournaris
Paul Frixons

Ximing Fu
Georg Fuchsbauer
Philippe Gaborit
Rachit Garg
Robin Geelen
Riddhi Ghosal
Koustabh Ghosh
Barbara Gigerl
Niv Gilboa
Valerie Gilchrist
Emanuele Giunta
Xinxin Gong
Huijing Gong
Zheng Gong
Robert Granger
Zichen Gui
Anna Guinet
Qian Guo
Xiaojie Guo
Hosein Hadipour
Mathias Hall-Andersen
Mike Hamburg
Shuai Han
Yonglin Hao
Keisuke Hara
Keitaro Hashimoto
Le He
Brett Hemenway Falk
Minki Hhan
Taiga Hiroka
Akinori Hosoyamada
Chengan Hou
Martha Norberg Hovd
Kai Hu
Tao Huang
Zhenyu Huang
Michael Hutter
Jihun Hwang
Akiko Inoue
Tetsu Iwata
Robin Jadoul
Hansraj Jangir
Dirmanto Jap
Stanislaw Jarecki
Santos Jha

Ashwin Jha
Dingding Jia
Yanxue Jia
Lin Jiao
Daniel Jost
Antoine Joux
Jiayi Kang
Gabriel Kaptchuk
Alexander Karenin
Shuichi Katsumata
Pengzhen Ke
Mustafa Khairallah
Shahram Khazaei
Hamidreza Amini Khorasgani
Hamidreza Khoshakhlagh
Ryo Kikuchi
Jiseung Kim
Minkyu Kim
Suhri Kim
Ravi Kishore
Fuyuki Kitagawa
Susumu Kiyoshima
Michael Klooß
Alexander Koch
Sreehari Kollath
Dimitris Kolonelos
Yashvanth Kondi
Anders Konring
Woong Kook
Dimitri Koshelev
Markus Krausz
Toomas Krips
Daniel Kuijsters
Anunay Kulshrestha
Qiqi Lai
Yi-Fu Lai
Georg Land
Nathalie Lang
Mario Larangeira
Joon-Woo Lee
Keewoo Lee
Hyeonbum Lee
Changmin Lee
Charlotte Lefevre
Julia Len

Antonin Leroux
Andrea Lesavourey
Jannis Leuther
Jie Li
Shuaishuai Li
Huina Li
Yu Li
Yanan Li
Jiangtao Li
Song Song Li
Wenjie Li
Shun Li
Zengpeng Li
Xiao Liang
Wei-Kai Lin
Chengjun Lin
Chao Lin
Cong Ling
Yunhao Ling
Hongqing Liu
Jing Liu
Jiahui Liu
Qipeng Liu
Yamin Liu
Weiran Liu
Tianyi Liu
Siqi Liu
Chen-Da Liu-Zhang
Jinyu Lu
Zhenghao Lu
Stefan Lucks
Yiyuan Luo
Lixia Luo
Jack P. K. Ma
Fermi Ma
Gilles Macario-Rat
Luciano Maino
Christian Majenz
Laurane Marco
Lorenzo Martinico
Loïc Masure
John McVey
Willi Meier
Kelsey Melissaris
Bart Mennink

Charles Meyer-Hilfiger
Victor Miller
Chohong Min
Marine Minier
Arash Mirzaei
Pratyush Mishra
Tarik Moataz
Johannes Mono
Fabrice Mouhartem
Alice Murphy
Erik Mårtensson
Anne Müller
Marcel Nageler
Yusuke Naito
Barak Nehoran
Patrick Neumann
Tran Ngo
Phuong Hoa Nguyen
Ngoc Khanh Nguyen
Thi Thu Quyen Nguyen
Hai H. Nguyen
Semyon Novoselov
Julian Nowakowski
Arne Tobias Malkenes Ødegaard
Kazuma Ohara
Miyako Ohkubo
Charles Olivier-Anclin
Eran Omri
Yi Ouyang
Tapas Pal
Ying-yu Pan
Jiaxin Pan
Eugenio Paracucchi
Roberto Parisella
Jeongeun Park
Guillermo Pascual-Perez
Alain Passelègue
Octavio Perez-Kempner
Thomas Peters
Phuong Pham
Cécile Pierrot
Erik Pohle
David Pointcheval
Giacomo Pope
Christopher Portmann

Romain Poussier
Lucas Prabel
Sihang Pu
Chen Qian
Luowen Qian
Tian Qiu
Anaïs Querol
Håvard Raddum
Shahram Rasoolzadeh
Divya Ravi
Prasanna Ravi
Marc Renard
Jan Richter-Brockmann
Lawrence Roy
Paul Rösler
Sayandeep Saha
Yusuke Sakai
Niels Samwel
Paolo Santini
Maria Corte-Real Santos
Sara Sarfaraz
Santanu Sarkar
Or Sattath
Markus Schofnegger
Peter Scholl
Dominique Schröder
André Schrottenloher
Jacob Schuldt
Binanda Sengupta
Srinath Setty
Yantian Shen
Yixin Shen
Ferdinand Sibleyras
Janno Siim
Mark Simkin
Scott Simon
Animesh Singh
Nitin Singh
Sayani Sinha
Daniel Slamanig
Fang Song
Ling Song
Yongsoo Song
Jana Sotakova
Gabriele Spini

Marianna Spyrakou
Lukas Stennes
Marc Stoettinger
Chuanjie Su
Xiangyu Su
Ling Sun
Akira Takahashi
Isobe Takanori
Atsushi Takayasu
Suprita Talnikar
Benjamin Hong Meng Tan
Ertem Nusret Tas
Tadanori Teruya
Masayuki Tezuka
Sri AravindaKrishnan Thyagarajan
Song Tian
Wenlong Tian
Raphael Toledo
Junichi Tomida
Daniel Tschudi
Hikaru Tsuchida
Aleksei Udovenko
Rei Ueno
Barry Van Leeuwen
Wessel van Woerden
Frederik Vercauteren
Sulani Vidhanalage
Benedikt Wagner
Roman Walch
Hendrik Waldner
Han Wang
Luping Wang
Peng Wang
Yuntao Wang
Geng Wang
Shichang Wang
Liping Wang
Jiafan Wang
Zhedong Wang
Kunpeng Wang
Jianfeng Wang
Guilin Wang
Weiqiang Wen
Chenkai Weng
Thom Wiggers

Stella Wohnig
Harry W. H. Wong
Ivy K. Y. Woo
Yu Xia
Zejun Xiang
Yuting Xiao
Zhiye Xie
Yanhong Xu
Jiayu Xu
Lei Xu
Shota Yamada
Kazuki Yamamura
Di Yan
Qianqian Yang
Shaojun Yang
Yanjiang Yang
Li Yao
Yizhou Yao
Kenji Yasunaga
Yuping Ye
Xiuyu Ye
Zeyuan Yin
Kazuki Yoneyama
Yusuke Yoshida
Albert Yu
Quan Yuan
Chen Yuan
Tsz Hon Yuen
Aaram Yun
Riccardo Zanotto
Arantxa Zapico
Shang Zehua
Mark Zhandry
Tianyu Zhang
Zhongyi Zhang
Fan Zhang
Liu Zhang
Yijian Zhang
Shaoxuan Zhang
Zhongliang Zhang
Kai Zhang
Cong Zhang
Jiaheng Zhang
Lulu Zhang
Zhiyu Zhang

Chang-An Zhao
Yongjun Zhao
Chunhuan Zhao
Xiaotong Zhou
Zhelei Zhou

Zijian Zhou
Timo Zijlstra
Jian Zou
Ferdinando Zullo
Cong Zuo

Sponsoring Institutions

- Gold Level Sponsor: Ant Research
- Silver Level Sponsors: Sansec Technology Co., Ltd., Topsec Technologies Group
- Bronze Level Sponsors: IBM, Meta, Sangfor Technologies Inc.

Contents – Part III

Quantum Cryptanalysis

Quantum Attacks on Hash Constructions with Low Quantum Random Access Memory

Xiaoyang Dong[1,2,6,7(✉)], Shun Li[3(✉)], Phuong Pham[3(✉)], and Guoyan Zhang[4,5,7(✉)]

[1] Institute for Advanced Study, BNRist, Tsinghua University, Beijing, China
xiaoyangdong@tsinghua.edu.cn
[2] State Key Laboratory of Cryptology, P.O.Box 5159, Beijing 100878, China
[3] School of Physical and Mathematical Sciences, Nanyang Technological University, Singapore, Singapore
shun.li@ntu.edu.sg, pham0079@e.ntu.edu.sg
[4] School of Cyber Science and Technology, Shandong University, Qingdao, Shandong, China
guoyanzhang@sdu.edu.cn
[5] Key Laboratory of Cryptologic Technology and Information Security, Ministry of Education, Shandong University, Jinan, China
[6] Zhongguancun Laboratory, Beijing, China
[7] Shandong Institute of Blockchain, Jinan, China

Abstract. At ASIACRYPT 2022, Benedikt, Fischlin, and Huppert proposed the quantum herding attacks on iterative hash functions for the first time. Their attack needs exponential quantum random access memory (qRAM), more precisely $2^{0.43n}$ quantum accessible classical memory (QRACM). As the existence of large qRAM is questionable, Benedikt et al. leave an open question on building low-qRAM quantum herding attacks.

In this paper, we answer this open question by building a quantum herding attack, where the time complexity is slightly increased from Benedikt et al.'s $2^{0.43n}$ to ours $2^{0.46n}$, but it does not need qRAM anymore (abbreviated as no-qRAM). Besides, we also introduce various low-qRAM or no-qRAM quantum attacks on hash concatenation combiner, hash XOR combiner, Hash-Twice, and Zipper hash functions.

Keywords: Quantum computation · qRAM · Herding Attack · Hash Combiner

1 Introduction

Shor's seminal work [59] shows that sufficiently large quantum computers allow factorization of large numbers and computation of discrete logarithms in polynomial time, potentially dooming many public-key schemes in use today. To

© International Association for Cryptologic Research 2023
J. Guo and R. Steinfeld (Eds.): ASIACRYPT 2023, LNCS 14440, pp. 3–33, 2023.
https://doi.org/10.1007/978-981-99-8727-6_1

meet the challenges posed by quantum computers, the public-key cryptography community and standardization organizations have invested a lot of effort in the research of post-quantum public-key schemes. In particular, NIST has initiated a process to solicit, evaluate, and standardize one or more quantum-resistant public-key cryptography algorithms [55]. For symmetric cryptography, the community has also recently witnessed many important quantum cryptanalysis results [15–17,25,38,41,48] since the initial work of Kuwakado and Morii, who showed that the classically provably secure Even-Mansour cipher and the three-round Feistel network can be broken in polynomial time with the help of quantum computers [46,47]. Most of these attacks that enjoy exponential speedup rely on Simon's algorithm [60] to find a key-dependent hidden period where access to a quantum superposition oracle of key primitives is necessary. This is a fairly strong (computation) model, and its actual relevance is sometimes questioned [13]. Therefore, a more complex attack still makes sense if it does not require online queries to the superposition oracles of the keyed primitives [13,14,18,35,57].

For keyless primitives, especially hash functions, quantum attacks are easier to launch, since there is no need for online queries and all computations can be done offline. The classical algorithm finds collisions of n-bit output hash functions with time complexity $\mathcal{O}(2^{n/2})$. In the quantum setting, the BHT algorithm [20] finds collisions with a query complexity of $\mathcal{O}(2^{n/3})$ if $\mathcal{O}(2^{n/3})$ quantum random access memory (qRAM) is available. However, it is generally acknowledged that the difficulty of fabricating large qRAMs is enormous [31,32]. So quantum algorithms (even has relatively high time complexity) using less or no qRAM is desirable. At ASIACRYPT 2017, Chailloux, Naya-Plasencia and Schrottenloher first overcome the $\mathcal{O}(2^{n/2})$ classical bound without using qRAM [21]. The time complexity of the algorithm is $\mathcal{O}(2^{2n/5})$, and the classical memory is $\mathcal{O}(2^{n/5})$. Also, a quantum algorithm for the generalized birthday problem (or the k-XOR problem) in settings with and without large qRAM can be found in [33,53]. Besides the generic attacks on hash functions, the first dedicated quantum attack on hash functions was presented at EUROCRYPT 2020 by Hosoyamada and Sasaki [36], showing quantum attacks on AES-MMO and Whirlpool by exploring differentials whose probability is too low to be useful in the classical setting. Later, refined collision and preimage attacks on hash functions have been presented subsequently by Dong et al. [26–28], Flórez Gutiérrez et al. [29], Hosoyamada and Sasaki [37], Schrottenloher and Stevens [58].

The Merkle-Damgård construction [22,52] is a popular way to build hash functions, where a single compression function is iteratively called to extend the input domain from a fixed length to arbitrary length and the digest length is usually the same as that of the internal state. However, some widely deployed hash function standards (such as MD5 and SHA-1) based Merkle-Damgård construction have been broken [61–63]. Besides, Kelsey and Schneier [43] have demonstrated a generic second-preimage attack against all hash functions based on the classical Merkle-Damgård construction, when the challenge message is long. At CRYPTO 2004, Joux [40] introduced multi-collision attacks on iterated hash functions. At EUROCRYPT 2006, Kelsey and Kohno introduced the herding attack (also known as nostradamus attack) [42], in which the adversary commits to a hash value T of an iterated hash function $\mathcal{H}$, such that when later given a message prefix P, the adversary is able to find a suitable "suffix explanation" S with $\mathcal{H}(P\|S) = T$.

In order to obtain a more secure hash function, and to ensure compatibility, researchers and developers try to combine the output of two (or more) independent hash functions to provide better security in case one or even both hash functions are weak. Practical examples can be found in TLS [23] and SSL [30]. There are several common hash combiners, such as concatenation combiner [56], XOR combiner, Hash-Twice [3], and Zipper hash [50]. However, the security of these hash combiners has also been challenged. At CRYPTO 2004, Joux [40] revealed that the concatenation combiner provides at most $n/2$-bit security for collision resistance and n-bit security for preimage resistance. Leurent and Wang [49] and Dinur [24] showed that the combiners may be weaker than each hash function. Besides, various cryptanalysis results [2–4,6,8,51] have been achieved on the hash combiners.

At ASIACRYPT 2022, Benedikt, Fischlin, and Huppert [9] considered quantum nostradamus attacks on iterative hash functions for the first time, and realized attacks of complexity $\mathcal{O}(2^{3n/7})$. The attack requires exponentially large qRAM, which is inherited from the BHT algorithm [20]. Since fabricating large qRAMs is difficult to realize [31,32], Benedikt et al. [9] left open questions for building low-qRAM quantum herding attack. In 2022, Bao et al. [7] built a low-qRAM quantum herding attack based Chailloux et al.'s multi-target preimage algorithm [21]. However, we find their algorithm is flawed and incorrect when building diamond structure for herding[1]. Therefore, the question is still open. Besides the quantum herding attack, Bao et al. also gave some quantum attacks on hash XOR and concatenation combiners, including collision, preimage, and herding attacks [7].

Our Contributions

In this paper, **for the first contribution,** we answer the open question by Benedikt et al. [9] to build the first valid low-qRAM quantum herding attack on iterated hash functions. We first convert Benedikt et al.'s quantum diamond-building algorithm (it needs exponential qRAM, i.e., $2^{3n/7}$ quantum accessible classical memory (QRACM)) into an algorithm that does not need qRAM anymore. The new algorithm is highly based on Chailloux et al.'s collision finding algorithm [21] with various adaptions. In our herding attack, we choose the leaves of the diamond structure to be prefixed with r-bit zeros, then apply Chailloux et al.'s collision finding to find the linking message S such that $H(P\|S)$ hits one of the leaves of the diamond structure. Note a previous work by Bao et al. [7] also built a quantum herding attack. However, in their attack, the Chailloux et al.'s

---

[1] Please find the detailed comments on Bao et al's attacks in Appendix A and B.

multi-target preimage algorithm [21] is applied, which can not take the advantage of the ability that attacker can choose the prefixed leaves of the diamond structure.

As the Second Contribution, for the quantum preimage attack on hash XOR combiners, we introduce an efficient low-qRAM quantum algorithm to build Leurent and Wang's interchange structure [49]. Then, based on Schrottenloher and Stevens's quantum Meet-in-the-Middle attack [58], or Ambainis' element distinctness algorithm [1], or Jaques and Schrottenloher's golden collision finding algorithm [39], we propose three different low-qRAM quantum preimage attacks on hash XOR combiner. Especially, our attack based on Jaques and Schrottenloher's method [39] reduces the $2^{0.143n}$ qubits of previous attack [7] to ours $2^{0.013n}$ qubits, without quantum accessible quantum memory (QRAQM). Moreover, the time complexity is also reduced from previous $2^{0.495n}$ to ours $2^{0.493n}$.

For hash concatenation combiner, we introduce a no-qRAM quantum collision attack and a no-qRAM quantum herding attack. In [7], both attacks need $2^{0.143n}$ qubits or $2^{0.333n}$ QRAQM . However, our attacks do not need qRAM and the number of qubits needed is also of polynomial size. We also introduce quantum herding attacks on other important hash combiners, including Hash-Twice, and Zipper hash function, by exploiting their different features. All the attacks are summarized in Table 1.

Table 1. A Summary of the Attacks. QRACM: quantum accessible classical memory, QRAQM: quantum accessible quantum memory, cRAM: classical random access memory

Target	Attacks	Settings	Time	Qubits	QRACM	QRAQM	cRAM	Generic	Ref.
$\mathcal{H}$	Herding	Classical	$2^{0.67n}$	–	–	–	$2^{0.67n}$	–	[42]
		Quantum	$2^{0.43n}$	$\mathcal{O}(n)$	$2^{0.43n}$	–	–	–	[9]
		Quantum	$2^{0.46n}$	$\mathcal{O}(n)$	–	–	$2^{0.23n}$	–	Sect. 4
$\mathcal{H}_1 \oplus \mathcal{H}_2$	Preimage	Classical	$2^{0.83n}$	–	–	–	$2^{0.33n}$	2^n	[49]
		Classical	$2^{0.67n}$	–	–	–	–	2^n	[24]
		Classical	$2^{0.612n}$	–	–	–	$2^{0.61n}$	2^n	[6]
		Quantum	$2^{0.476n}$	$\mathcal{O}(n)$	–	$2^{0.333n}$	–	$2^{0.5n}$	[7]
		Quantum	$2^{0.495n}$	$2^{0.143n}$	$2^{0.033n}$	–	$2^{0.2n}$	$2^{0.5n}$	[7]
		Quantum	$2^{0.493n}$	$2^{0.013n}$	$2^{0.047n}$	–	$2^{0.2n}$	$2^{0.5n}$	Sect. 5.3
		Quantum	$2^{0.485n}$	$\mathcal{O}(n)$	$2^{0.057n}$	$2^{0.0285n}$	$2^{0.2n}$	$2^{0.5n}$	Sect. 5.3
		Quantum	$2^{0.485n}$	$\mathcal{O}(n)$	$2^{0.043n}$	$2^{0.0285n}$	$2^{0.2n}$	$2^{0.5n}$	Sect. 5.3
$\mathcal{H}_1 \| \mathcal{H}_2$	Collision	Classical	$2^{0.5n}$	–	–	–	–	2^n	[40]
		Quantum	$2^{0.333n}$	$\mathcal{O}(n)$	–	$2^{0.333n}$	–	$2^{0.67n}$	[7]
		Quantum	$2^{0.43n}$	$2^{0.143n}$	–	–	$2^{0.2n}$	$2^{0.67n}$	[7]
		Quantum	$2^{0.4n}$	$\mathcal{O}(n)$	–	–	$2^{0.2n}$	$2^{0.67n}$	Sect. 6
	Herding	Classical	$2^{0.67n}$	–	–	–	$2^{0.33n}$	–	[3]
		Quantum	$2^{0.444n}$	$\mathcal{O}(n)$	–	$2^{0.333n}$	–	–	[7]
		Quantum	$2^{0.49n}$	$2^{0.143n}$	–	–	$2^{0.2n}$	–	[7]
		Quantum	$2^{0.467n}$	$\mathcal{O}(n)$	–	–	$2^{0.2n}$	–	Sect. 7
Hash-Twice	Herding	Classical	$2^{0.667n}$	–	–	–	$2^{0.33n}$	–	[3]
		Quantum	$2^{0.467n}$	$\mathcal{O}(n)$	–	–	$2^{0.2n}$	–	Sect. 8
Zipper	Herding	Classical	$2^{0.667n}$	–	–	–	$2^{0.33n}$	–	[3]
		Quantum	$2^{0.467n}$	$\mathcal{O}(n)$	–	–	$2^{0.2n}$	–	Sect. 9

2   Preliminaries

2.1   Quantum Computation and Quantum RAM

The state of the n-qubit quantum system can be described as the unit vector $\{|i\rangle :$ $0 \le i < 2^n\}$ in $\mathbb{C}^{2^n}$ under the orthogonal basis. Quantum algorithms are typically implemented by manipulating the state of an n-qubit system through a series of unitary transformations and measurements, where all unitary transformations can be implemented as a series quantum gates in *quantum circuit models* [54]. The efficiency of a quantum algorithm is quantified based on the number of quantum gates used.

Superposition Oracles for Classical Circuit. Let the quantum oracle of a function $f : \mathbb{F}_2^m \mapsto \mathbb{F}_2^n$ be the unitary operator $\mathcal{U}_f$ that $\mathcal{U}_f |x\rangle |y\rangle = |x\rangle |y \oplus f(x)\rangle$ with $x \in \mathbb{F}_2^m$ and $y \in \mathbb{F}_2^n$. When $\mathcal{U}_f$ acts on superposition states, we have

$$\mathcal{U}_f \left(\sum_{x \in \mathbb{F}_2^n} a_i |x\rangle |y\rangle \right) = \sum_{x \in \mathbb{F}_2^n} a_i |x\rangle |y \oplus f(x)\rangle. \qquad (1)$$

Variations on Grover's Algorithm. The task is to find the labeled element from the set X. Suppose we denote the subset of labeled elements by $M \subset X$ and know the fraction of the labeled elements $\epsilon = |M|/|X|$. The classical algorithm to solve this problem needs $O(1/\epsilon)$ iterations. A quantum algorithm can be expressed as a function of two parameters.

- *Setup* operation, i.e., sampling a uniform element from X. Denote the cost (execution time) of *Setup* as $|Setup|_{RT}$.
- *Checking* operation, i.e. checking if an element is labeled. Denote the cost (execution time) of *Checking* as $|Checking|_{RT}$.

Grover's algorithm [34] is a quantum search process for finding the labeled elements, whose complexity is a function of the quantum *Setup* cost $|Setup|_{RT}$ of construction of uniform superposition of all elements from X, and the quantum *Checking* cost $|Checking|_{RT}$. The time complexity of Grover's algorithm is $\sqrt{1/\epsilon} \cdot (|Setup|_{RT} + |Checking|_{RT})$. Assuming the *Setup* and *Checking* steps are simple, Grover's algorithm can find the element $x \in M$ at a cost of $\mathcal{O}(\sqrt{1/\epsilon})$.

Grover's algorithm can also be described as a special case of quantum amplitude amplification (QAA), which is a quantum algorithm introduced by Brassard, Høyer, Mosca, and Tapp [19]. Intuitively, assuming there exists an quantum algorithm $\mathcal{A}$ to produce a superposition of the good subspace and the bad subspace of X. Let a be the initial success probability that the measurement of $\mathcal{A} |0\rangle$ is good. Let $\mathcal{B}$ be a function that classifies the outcomes of $\mathcal{A}$ as either good or bad state. Quantum Amplitude Amplification (QAA) technique achieves the same result as Grover's algorithm with a quadratic improvement. The time complexity of QAA is about

$$\sqrt{1/a} \cdot (|\mathcal{A}|_{RT} + |\mathcal{B}|_{RT}). \qquad (2)$$

Quantum Random Access Memories (qRAM) can be conceptualized as the quantum counterpart of classical random access memory (RAM). In the classic setup, RAM facilitates access (read and write operations) to memory elements in time $\mathcal{O}(1)$ regardless of storage size. Following [45,58], qRAM comes in two flavors: Quantum Accessible Classical Memory (QRACM), which enables access to classical data in quantum superposition; and Quantum Accessible Quantum Memory (QRAQM), where data is stored in quantum memory. Consider a scenario where we intend to store a list of data, denoted as $D = (x_0, x_1, \cdots, x_{2^k-1})$, with each x_i representing an n-bit data. In this context, the qRAM for accessing the data D is established as a quantum gate. This qRAM is defined through a unitary operator $U_{qRAM}(D)$, which is expressed as follows:

$$U_{qRAM}(D) : |i\rangle |x_0, x_1, \cdots, x_{2^k-1}\rangle |y\rangle \rightarrow |i\rangle |x_0, x_1, \cdots, x_{2^k-1}\rangle |y \oplus x_i\rangle,$$

Here, i takes values from the set $\{0, 1\}^k$, and y represents an n-bit value. In both QRACM and QRAQM, we assume that this gate costs $\mathcal{O}(1)$. For QRACM, i is superposed but the x_i are classical; For QRAQM, both i and x_i are superposed. For example, the BHT collision finding algorithm [20] requires QRACM, the quantum element distinctness [1] and quantum meet-in-the-middle attack [58] require QRAQM. Obviously, QRAQM is the strongest quantum memory model.

For the time being, it is unknown how a working qRAM (at least for large qRAMs) can be built. Nevertheless, this disappointing fact does not stop researchers from working in a model where large qRAMs are available, in the same spirit that people started to work on classical and quantum algorithms long before a classical or quantum computer had been built. From another perspective, the absence of large qRAMs makes it quite meaningful to conduct research in an attempt to reduce or even avoid the use of qRAM in quantum algorithms.

Quantum Element Distinctness Problem

Problem 1. Given a set $S = \{x_1, x_2, \cdots, x_N\}$, does it exist i, j such that $1 \leq i < j \leq N$ and $x_i = x_j$? If yes, return i, j.

In 2007, Ambainis proposed the quantum walk algorithm for the element distinctness problem [1] and achieved time complexity of $\mathcal{O}(N^{2/3})$ with $\mathcal{O}(N^{2/3})$ QRAQM. At SAC 2020, Jaques and Schrottenloher [39] solved the element distinctness problem (or golden collision problem by [39]) in the plain quantum circuit model (i.e., the computation is a sequence of basic quantum gates applied to a pool of qubits) in time complexity of $\mathcal{O}(N^{6/7})$ with $\mathcal{O}(N^{2/7})$ qubits without qRAM.

CNS Collision Finding Algorithm [21]. At ASIACRYPT 2017, Chailloux, Naya-Plasencia and Schrottenloher [21] introduced the first quantum collision finding algorithm without any qRAM. Their algorithm is denoted as CNS algorithm in this paper. The time complexity of the algorithm is $\mathcal{O}(2^{2n/5})$, with a classical memory of $\mathcal{O}(2^{n/5})$. The CNS algorithm is based on a quantum membership algorithm.

Definition 1. *Given a set L of 2^k n-bit strings, a classical membership oracle is a function f_L that computes: $f_L(x) = 1$ if $x \in L$ and 0 otherwise.*

A quantum membership oracle for L is an operator O_L that computes f_L:

$$O_L(|x\rangle \, |b\rangle) = |x\rangle \, |b \oplus f_L(x)\rangle \,.$$

When the set L of size 2^k is stored in some classical memory, Chailloux et al. implement the quantum operator O_L with $n2^k$ simple operations and $2n + 1$ qubits. Since in the following, the time complexity is number of queries of the compression functions of hash function, the $n2^k$ simple operations are then recorded as $\mathcal{O}(2^k)$ time complexity. The CNS collision finding algorithm can be divided into two parts, i.e., the precomputing part and the matching part.

Precomputing Part: Given a hash function h that $h(m) = T$, the CNS algorithm first builds a table L of size 2^k, where the r-bit most significant bits (MSB) of all $x \in L$ are zero, and store L in a classical memory. The way to build L is to perform 2^k times of Grover's algorithm with time complexity of $2^k \times 2^{r/2} = 2^{k+r/2}$.

The Matching Part: Apply the QAA algorithm. In the setup phase $\mathcal{A}$, the Grover's algorithm is applied to produce a superposition of m, where the r-bit MSBs of m are zero. The time of the setup phase is $|\mathcal{A}|_{RT} = 2^{r/2}$. Then, in the checking phase $\mathcal{B}$, a quantum membership algorithm is applied to classify that if m is in L or not. $|\mathcal{B}|_{RT} = 2^k$. Since the initial probability, that the measurement of $\mathcal{A}|0\rangle$ is good, is $a = \frac{2^k}{2^{n-r}}$ (since only the last $n - r$ bits should be matched). According to Eq. (2), time complexity of this part is

$$\sqrt{\frac{2^{n-r}}{2^k}} \cdot (2^{r/2} + 2^k). \tag{3}$$

Totally, the time of the CNS algorithm is

$$\sqrt{\frac{2^{n-r}}{2^k}} \cdot (2^{r/2} + 2^k) + 2^{k+r/2}. \tag{4}$$

By assigning $r = 2k = 2n/5$, the complexity given in Eq. (4) will be optimal, which is $\mathcal{O}(2^{2n/5})$. The number of qubits used is $\mathcal{O}(n)$. The classical memory is $2^{n/5}$ to store L.

In this paper, the CNS algorithm is frequently used. In several applications of our paper, only the **Matching Part** of the CNS algorithm is used with a given L, while L may be built in a different way than the **Precomputing Part** and thus have a different complexity than $2^{k+r/2}$. For example, in our quantum herding attack in Sect. 4, the time to build L is the time to build the diamond structure. Therefore, the time complexity of the **Matching Part** should be weighed against the different time complexity of constructing L. To use the CNS algorithm more flexibly, we define the **Matching Part** as $\text{CNS}_h(m, L)$ in Definition 2 for a given table L and h in the following.

Definition 2. *Let $CNS_h(m, L)$ be the matching part of CNS algorithm, which finds m so that $h(m) \in L$. Given the table L of size 2^k stored in classical memory, whose elements are prefixed with r-bit zeros, the time complexity*

$$|CNS_h(m, L)|_{RT} = \sqrt{\frac{2^{n-r}}{2^k}} \cdot (2^{r/2} + 2^k).$$

Quantum Meet-in-the-Middle Algorithm. At CRYPTO 2022, Schrottenloher and Stevens [58] applied the quantum two-list merging algorithm to build the quantum MitM attack: For a given global guess $G \in \mathbb{F}_2^g$, two small lists are computed and merged to on the fly. Suppose the two small lists are L_1 and L_2, the goal is to determine if there are elements $x \in L_1$ and $y \in L_2$ such that $x = y$ (called a solution). Let $O_{\texttt{merge}}$ be the unitary operator that

$$O_{\texttt{merge}}(|G\rangle\,|b\rangle) = |G\rangle\,|b \oplus f(G)\rangle\,, \text{where } f(G) = \begin{cases} 1 \text{ if a solution occurs} \\ 0 \text{ otherwise} \end{cases}. \quad (5)$$

Lemma 1. *[58] Assume that there exists an implementation of $O_{\texttt{merge}}$ with time complexity T. Then there is a quantum MitM attack with time complexity:*

$$(\frac{\pi}{4}2^{g/2} + 1) \times T. \quad (6)$$

The T is roughly estimated by

$$\min(|L_1|, |L_2|) + \sqrt{\max(|L_{\texttt{merge}}|, |L_1|, |L_2|))}, \quad (7)$$

where $L_{\texttt{merge}}$ is the merged list. The QRAQM needed is of size $\min(|L_1|, |L_2|)$.

2.2 Iterated Hash Constructions

Iterated hash functions $\mathcal{H}(IV, M) = T$ commonly first pad and split the message M into message blocks of fixed length, i.e., $M = m_1\|m_2\| \cdots \|m_L$. The message blocks are processed sequentially and iteratively by the compression function h, i.e., $x_i = h(x_{i-1}, m_i)$, where $x_0 = IV$ is a public value, $T = x_L$ is the n-bit digest, the chaining value $x_i \in \mathbb{F}_2^n$. Two commonly used iterated hash constructions are the Merkle-Damgård construction [22,52] and the HAIFA construction [11]. In this paper, we only consider the Merkle-Damgård construction and its extensions.

The concatenation combiner $\mathcal{H}_1(IV_1, M)\|\mathcal{H}_2(IV_2, M) = T_1\|T_2$ is one of the most studied hash combiner, which is first described by Preneel in 1993 [56]. In 2004, Joux [40] described the multi-collision attack on the $2n$-bit output hash combiner with $2^{n/2}$ time complexity for collision attack and 2^n time complexity for preimage attack. Besides the concatenation combiner, there are other constructions:

- The XOR hash combiner $\mathcal{H}_1(IV_1, M) \oplus \mathcal{H}_2(IV_2, M) = T$.
- Hash-Twice is originally defined in [3]: $\mathcal{H}_2(\mathcal{H}_1(IV, M), M) = T$ shown in Fig. 1.
- Zipper hash [50] is defined as $\mathcal{H}_2(\mathcal{H}_1(IV, M), \overleftarrow{M}) = T$ shown in Fig. 2.

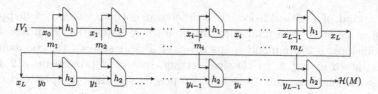

Fig. 1. Hash-Twice Construction

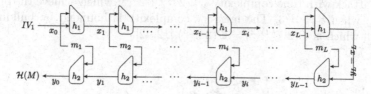

Fig. 2. Zipper Hash Construction

3 Basic Techniques and Their Quantum Versions

In this section, we give brief introductions of Joux's multi-collision technique, diamond structure (DS) and their quantum versions.

3.1 Joux's Multi-collision

At CRYPTO 2004, Joux [40] introduced an efficient method to build multi-collision on iterated hash functions. As shown in Fig. 3, started from x_0, the attacker performs t birthday attacks to find t collisions. Based on the message blocks $m_1, m_2, \cdots m_t$ and $m'_1, m'_2, \cdots m'_t$, the attacker can build 2^t collision messages pairs (denoted as $2^t\text{-}\mathcal{M}_{\mathtt{MC}}$), e.g., $(m_1\|m'_2\|\cdots\|m_t, m'_1\|m'_2\|\cdots\|m'_t,)$. The time complexity to build the 2^t collision message pairs is $t \cdot 2^{n/2}$. In quantum setting, Bao et al. [7] first applied CNS's algorithm to build Joux's multi-collision, where one collision is built in time $2^{2n/5}$. Therefore, the time to build $2^t\text{-}\mathcal{M}_{\mathtt{MC}}$ is $t \cdot 2^{2n/5}$. The quantum attack only uses a classical memory $2^{n/5}$.

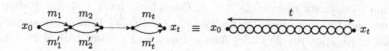

Fig. 3. Joux's multi-collision [40]

3.2 Diamond Structure and Its New Quantum Algorithm in no-QRAM setting

Kelsey and Kohno in [42] invented the diamond structure. Similar to Joux's multi-collisions and Kelsey and Schneier's expandable message [43], diamond is also a kind of multi-collision. The difference is that, instead of mapping a single starting state to a final state in the form of sequential chain like Joux's multi-collisions, a 2^t-diamond maps a set of 2^t leaf states to a common root state as shown in Fig. 4. In classical setting, several improvements [12,44] on building diamond structure have been proposed. The time complexity to build a 2^t-diamond is $\sqrt{t} \cdot 2^{\frac{n+t}{2}}$ evaluations of the compression function of the hash function. Based on the diamond structure, Kelsey and Kohno [42] introduced the herding attack with time complexity $\sqrt{t} \cdot 2^{\frac{n+t}{2}} + 2^{n-t}$, which achieve the optimal $\mathcal{O}(2^{2n/3})$ when $t = n/3$. The memory complexity is bounded by building 2^t-diamond, which is $\mathcal{O}(2^{(n+t)/2}) = \mathcal{O}(2^{2n/3})$ [12,42].

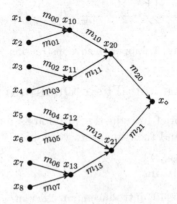

Fig. 4. 2^3-diamond [7]

Bao et al. [7] initially introduced the quantum diamond structure algorithm for both qRAM and no-qRAM scenarios. However, when we tried to replicate their algorithm, we find their no-qRAM algorithm is incorrect and for more details please refer Appendix A.

Later, at ASIACRYPT 2022, Benedikt, Fischlin, Huppert [9] presented a quantum diamond structure algorithm utilizing exponential QRACM, resulting in a time complexity of $t^{1/3} \cdot 2^{(n+2t)/3}$. Consider a level s of the 2^t-diamond structure and try to connect 2^s nodes $\{x_{s,1}, \cdots, x_{s,2^s}\}$ in a pairwise manner. Benedikt et al. split the 2^s nodes into a upper and a lower half of 2^{s-1} nodes each. For the upper half, they compute a list Y of 2^l hash evaluations $h(m_j, x_{s,i})$ with $i = 1, \cdots, 2^{s-1}$, which equally spread out over the 2^{s-1} nodes. Hence, for each node, there are $\frac{2^l}{2^{s-1}}$ hash evaluations. Store Y in QRACM, and apply Grover's algorithm to connect the first value $x_{s,2^{s-1}+1}$ of the lower half to some of these 2^l values with some message block m'. Once a connection message is found, remove the partner node from the upper half and all of its $2^l/2^{s-1}$ entries from Y. Then, add this amount of new values, again equally spread out over the remaining $2^{s-1} - 1$ values paired up, to fill the list Y up to 2^l elements again. Then connect the second node $x_{s,2^{s-1}+2}$ to Y. Continue till all 2^s nodes are connected, then proceed with the next level $s - 1$ until the entire tree is built. Benedikt et al. choose $l = \frac{n+2s}{3}$ to achieve optimal complexity to build the 2^t-diamond structure, where $s \leq t$. Therefore, the size of Y is about $2^l = 2^{\frac{n+2t}{3}}$.

To build the quantum herding attack with a 2^t-diamond structure, Benedikt et al. applied the BHT algorithm to find the M_{link} (as shown in Fig. 6). The overall complexity of the herding attack includes the complexity of building 2^t-diamond structure and finding the M_{link}, which is roughly $\mathcal{O}(2^{(n+2t)/3} + 2^{(n-t)/2})$. The optimal complexity is achieved when $t = n/7$, i.e., the optimal time complexity is $\mathcal{O}(2^{3n/7})$ with QRACM of size $\mathcal{O}(2^{(n+2t)/3}) = \mathcal{O}(2^{3n/7})$ to store Y when building 2^t-diamond structure.

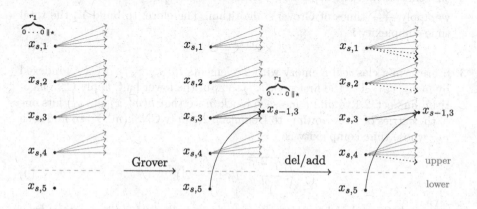

Fig. 5. Building diamond

A New no-QRAM Quantum Algorithm to Build the Diamond Structure.
In this section, we introduce a quantum algorithm to build the diamond structure in no-qRAM setting based on Benedikt et al.'s [9] method and CNS collision finding algorithm [21]. As shown in Fig. 5, again consider a level s of the 2^t-diamond structure and try to connect 2^s nodes $\{x_{s,1}, \cdots, x_{s,2^s}\}$ in a pairwise manner.

1. Begin with 2^t leaf nodes that share a common suffix of r_0 0s for the purpose of connection[2].

---

[2] Leaf nodes with r_0 0s suffix are used for the following herding attack in Sect. 4, and are not relevant to this diamond building algorithm. After a diamond is built whose leaves are suffixed with $r_0 0$, we can apply the CNS algorithm (see Definition 2) to find a linking message whose digest collides to one of those leaves. Similar techniques for constructing distinguished points (e.g., leaves suffixed with $r_0 0$) are often used in cryptanalysis, e.g., the quantum collision or preimage finding algorithm [5,10,21],

2. Let's consider a specific level $s \leq t$ of the tree where we aim to connect the 2^s nodes $\{x_{s,1}, \ldots, x_{s,2^s}\}$ pairwise. Divide the 2^s nodes into two halves, the upper half with 2^{s-1} nodes $\{x_{s,1}, \cdots, x_{s,2^{s-1}}\}$ and the lower half with 2^{s-1} nodes $\{x_{s,2^{s-1}+1}, x_{s,2^{s-1}+2}, \cdots, x_{s,2^s}\}$. For the upper half, compute a list Y of 2^l hash values $h(m_j, x_{s,i})$ with $i = 1, \cdots, 2^{s-1}$, where the r_1 MSBs of $h(m_j, x_{s,i})$ are zero. The 2^l hash values equally spread out over the 2^{s-1} nodes, with $\frac{2^l}{2^{s-1}}$ hash values for each node. Here, similar to CNS algorithm in Sect. 2.1 to build L whose elements are prefixed with r-bit zero, we also apply Grover's algorithm to build Y. For each node $x_{s,i}$ with $i = 1, \cdots, 2^{s-1}$, run Grover's algorithm to find m_j so that the r_1 MSBs of $h(m_j, x_{s,i})$ are zero. The time to find one m_j is $2^{r_1/2}$. In order to find $\frac{2^l}{2^{s-1}}$ such m_j for node $x_{s,i}$, we apply $\frac{2^l}{2^{s-1}}$ times of Grover's algorithm. Therefore, to build Y, the total time complexity is

$$2^l \times 2^{r_1/2} = 2^{l + \frac{r_1}{2}}. \tag{8}$$

3. Store Y in a classical memory with 2^l elements $(h(m_j, x_{s,i}), m_j, x_{s,i})$ indexed by $h(m_j, x_{s,i})$. For the first node $x_{s,2^{s-1}+1}$ of the lower half, apply CNS algorithm in Sect. 2.1 to find a message block m' so that $h(m', x_{s,2^{s-1}+1})$ hits one of the entries of Y. According to Definition 2, apply $\text{CNS}_h(m', Y)$ to find such m', whose time complexity is

$$\sqrt{\frac{2^{n-r_1}}{2^l}} \cdot (2^{r_1/2} + 2^l). \tag{9}$$

4. After m' is found, delete the partner node and all of its $2^l/2^{s-1}$ entries from Y. Add $2^l/2^{s-1}$ new values for Y with similar ways to Step 2 to fill Y up to 2^l elements again. Now each node of the upper half corresponds to $2^l/(2^{s-1} - 1)$ elements. Delete the first node $x_{s,2^{s-1}+1}$ from lower half. The time complexity to fill Y again is

$$2^l/2^{s-1} \times 2^{r_1/2} = 2^{l-s+1+\frac{r_1}{2}}. \tag{10}$$

5. Repeat Step 3 and Step 4 until the lower half is empty. That means all the nodes of the layer of level s have been connected pairwise.

To build the layer of level s in Step 2, 2^s nodes are divided into the upper half and the lower half, each with 2^{s-1} nodes. We are going to connect all the 2^{s-1} nodes in the lower half to the upper half. In step 3, the CNS algorithm (i.e., $\text{CNS}_h(m', Y)$) is applied to connect one node of the lower half (e.g., the first node $x_{s,2^{s-1}+1}$) to one node of the upper half by hitting one of the elements in Y. In Step 4, after the i-th node $x_{s,2^{s-1}+i}$ ($i = 1, \cdots, 2^{s-1} - 1$) in the lower half has been connected to Y, $\frac{2^l}{2^{s-1}-(i-1)}$ elements will be deleted from Y, and therefore, the same amount of new elements should be generated to fill up Y to

---

quantum k-XOR algorithm [33,53], and many classical attacks e.g. [24], to name a few. However, our Algorithm 1 is the first to apply this technique to quantum herding attack.

2^l again, whose time complexity is

$$\frac{2^l}{2^{s-1}-(i-1)} \times 2^{r_1/2}. \tag{11}$$

Since we have to connect all nodes in the lower half to the upper half, the elements in Y must be repeatedly deleted and filled up Y to 2^l for all $i = 1, 2, 3, \ldots, 2^{(s-1)} - 1$. For each i, the time to fill up Y is estimated by Eq. (11). Note that for the last node, i.e., the $i = 2^{s-1}$-th node $x_{s,2^s}$ in the lower half, we only need to apply the CNS algorithm to find a match in Y to connect the last node to the upper half, and we do not need to fill up Y again after that. Therefore, we got the component of summation in Eq. (12). Since Step 3 will be repeated for each node of the lower half, hence, $\text{CNS}_h(m', Y)$ will be repeated for 2^{s-1} times. Therefore, the total time complexity to build the layer of level s is

$$T_s = 2^l \times 2^{r_1/2} + 2^{s-1} \cdot \sqrt{\frac{2^{n-r_1}}{2^l}} \cdot (2^{r_1/2}+2^l) + \sum_{i=1}^{2^{s-1}-1} \frac{2^l}{2^{s-1}-(i-1)} \times 2^{r_1/2}. \tag{12}$$

To build the 2^t-diamond structure which includes t layers, the total time is

$$\sum_{s=t}^{1} T_s. \tag{13}$$

We could calculate

$$T_s = 2^{s-1} \cdot \sqrt{\frac{2^{n-r_1}}{2^l}} \cdot (2^{r_1/2}+2^l) + 2^l \cdot 2^{r_1/2} \cdot \sum_{j=1}^{2^{s-1}} \frac{1}{j} = 2^{s-1} \cdot \sqrt{\frac{2^{n-r_1}}{2^l}} \cdot (2^{r_1/2}+2^l) + O(s \cdot 2^{l+r_1/2})$$

using $\sum_{j=1}^{q} \frac{1}{j} \leq \ln q + c$ for the harmonic series. Then T_s could be minimized to $O(s^{1/5} \cdot 2^{(2n+4s+4)/5})$ by setting $r_1 = 2l$ and $l = \frac{n+2s+2-2\log_2 s}{5}$.

The final complexity is obtained from summing over all t levels:

$$\sum_{s=1}^{t} O(s^{1/5} \cdot 2^{(2n+4s+4)/5}) \leq O(2^{(2n+4+\log_2 t)/5} \cdot \sum_{s=1}^{t} 2^{\frac{4s}{5}})$$
$$= O(2^{(2n+4+\log_2 t)/5} \cdot 2^{\frac{4t}{5}})$$
$$= O(2^{(2n+4t+4+\log_2 t)/5}),$$

which is about $O(2^{(2n+4t)/5})$. The classical memory is dominated by $O(2^{(n+2t)/5})$ to store Y for the first layer. The number of qubits is $O(n)$.

4   Herding Attack in Quantum Settings with no-QRAM

The herding attack on iterated hash function is first given by Kelsey and Kohno [42]. In the attack, the adversary chooses a public hash value h_T, and then, she is challenged with a prefix P. Her goal is to find a suffix S such that $h_T = H(P\|S)$. At ASIACRYPT 2022, Benedikt, Fischlin, and Huppert [9] presented the quantum herding attack with $\sqrt[3]{n} \cdot 2^{3n/7}$ on iterated hash function with n-bit digest based on BHT algorithm. Their quantum attack also needs exponential qRAM inherited from the BHT algorithm [20], i.e., $2^{3n/7}$ QRACM. Therefore they left an open question on how to devise quantum herding attacks with low-qRAM. In this section, we answer the open question positively. As shown in Fig. 6, our herding attack consists in four steps:

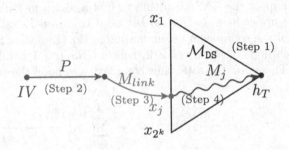

Fig. 6. Herding Attack on Iterated Hash Function [7]

– Step 1 is to build a 2^k-diamond structure. In classical herding attack by Kelsey and Kohno [42] and the quantum one by Benedikt et al. [9], the leaves x_i $(1 \leq i \leq 2^k)$ are randomly chosen. In our quantum attack, the r most significant bits (MSB) of x_i are zero. Store the leaves in D with classical memory
– Step 2 and Step 3 is to find a single block message M_{link} such that $h(P\|M_{link})$ collides with some value $x_j \in D$.
– Step 4 is to produce the message $M = P\|M_{link}\|M_j$, where M_j is a sequence of message blocks linking x_j to h_T with the diamond structure.

Our quantum herding attack is given in Algorithm 1.

Complexity. The time complexity to build the 2^k diamond structure is $k^{1/5} \cdot 2^{(2n+4k)/5}$ with a classical memory $k^{3/5} \cdot 2^{(n+2k)/5}$. The time complexity of the setup phase is $2^{r/2}$ with Grover algorithm. According to the quantum membership algorithm [21], the time complexity to implement $O_{f_L^h}$ is 2^k. For $(m, h(\bar{x}, m)) \in S_r^h$, $f_L^h(m) = 1$ holds with probability of $2^{k-(n-r)}$. Therefore, about $2^{\frac{n-r-k}{2}}$ calls of A, $A^\dagger$, $O_{f_L^h}$, $O_{f_L^h}^\dagger$ are needed to produce the correct $M_{link} = m$. Hence, the time complexity to find the M_{link} in Line 8 is $2^{\frac{n-r-k}{2}}(2^{r/2} + 2^k)$ with a classical memory 2^k to store L. Hence, the total time complexity is

$$2^{\frac{n-r-k}{2}}(2^{r/2} + 2^k) + k^{1/5} \cdot 2^{(2n+4k)/5}. \tag{15}$$

The classical memory complexity is bounded by the construction of the diamond structure, i.e., $k^{3/5} \cdot 2^{(n+2k)/5}$.

Algorithm 1: Herding Attack on Iterated Hash Function without qRAM

---

1 **Off-line precomputation:** Precompute the diamond structure using CNS quantum collision algorithm. Collect 2^k starting chaining values $D = \{x_1, x_2, \cdots, x_{2^k}\}$, where the r MSBs of $x_i \in \mathbb{F}_2^n$ are zero. The root is denoted as h_T and publish h_T.

2 **On-line precomputation:**

3 **begin**

4   Receive the challenged prefix P and compute the chaining value after absorbing the message P: $\bar{x} = \bar{H}(IV, P)$.

5   `/* Finding the linking message` M_{link} `by applying variant of CNS`
       `collision-finding algorithm:`   `*/`

6   Store $D = \{x_1, x_2, \cdots, x_{2^k}\}$ in a classical memory L.

7   Define

$$S_r^h := \{(m, h(\bar{x}, m)) : \exists z \in \{0,1\}^{n-r}, h(\bar{x}, m) = \underbrace{0 \cdots 0}_{r\ times} \| z, z \in \{0,1\}^{n-r}\},$$

    where h is the compression function with n-bit chaining value $\bar{x}$. Let $f_L^h(m) := 1$ if $\exists x' \in L$, $h(\bar{x}, m) = x'$, and $f_L^h(m) := 0$ otherwise.

8   Apply quantum amplification algorithm:

9   **begin**

10   The setup $\mathcal{A}$ is the construction of $|\phi\rangle := \frac{1}{\sqrt{|S_r^h|}} \sum_{m \in S_r^h} |m, h(\bar{x}, m)\rangle$.

11   The projector is a quantum oracle query to $O_{f_L^h}$ meaning that

$$O_{f_L^h}(|m, h(\bar{x}, m)\rangle |b\rangle) = |m, h(\bar{x}, m)\rangle |b \oplus O_{f_L^h}(m)\rangle. \qquad (14)$$

12   **end**

13   Let $M_{link} = m$ and produce the message: $M = P \| M_{link} \| M_j$, where M_j is a sequence of message blocks linking x_j to h_T following the diamond structure built before.

14 **end**

The Best-Case Complexity. The optimal complexity is to balance the three formulas, i.e., $\frac{n-k}{2}$, $\frac{n-r+k}{2}$, and $\frac{2n+4k}{5}$. When $k = n/13$ and $r = 2n/13$, the optimal complexity is achieved which results in $\mathcal{O}(2^{6n/13}) = \mathcal{O}(2^{0.46n})$ time complexity and $\mathcal{O}(2^{3n/13}) = \mathcal{O}(2^{0.23n})$ classical memory.

Remark. Bao et al. [7] also proposed a no-qRAM herding attack based on a flawed method of building the diamond structure as shown in Sect. 3.2. After correcting with our right algorithm in Sect. 3.2, Bao et al.'s no-qRAM herding attack needs a time complexity of $\mathcal{O}(2^{14n/29}) = \mathcal{O}(2^{0.48n})$ with a classical memory $\mathcal{O}(2^{7n/29}) = \mathcal{O}(2^{0.24n})$, which is inferior to our attacks. For more details, please refer to Appendix B.

5   Interchange Structure and Preimage Attack on XOR Combiners

5.1   Basic Interchange Structure Technique [49]

At EUROCRYPT 2015, Leurent and Wang [49] invented the interchange structure (IS), which is used to devise a preimage attack on the XOR combiner, i.e., $\mathcal{H}_1(IV_1, M) \oplus \mathcal{H}_2(IV_2, M) = T$. The interchange structure contains a set of messages $\mathcal{M}_{\mathrm{IS}}$ and two sets of states $\mathcal{A}$ and $\mathcal{B}$, so that for any state pair $(A_i, B_j | A_i \in \mathcal{A}, B_j \in \mathcal{B})$, the attacker can pick a message $M \in \mathcal{M}_{\mathrm{IS}}$ such that $A_i = \mathcal{H}_1(IV_1, M)$ and $B_j = \mathcal{H}_2(IV_2, M)$. Suppose there is a 2^k-interchange structure (the sizes of $\mathcal{A}$ and $\mathcal{B}$ are both 2^k). In order to reach the target value T, they select a random block m, and evaluate $L_1 = \{A_i' = h_1(A_i, m), i = 1 \cdots 2^k\}$ and $L_2 = \{B_j' = T \oplus h_2(B_j, m), j = 1 \cdots 2^k\}$, where h_1 and h_2 are the compression functions. If there is a match between the two lists L_1 and L_2, then

$$h_1(A_i, m) = T \oplus h_2(B_j, m) \Leftrightarrow \mathcal{H}_1(IV_1, M\|m) \oplus \mathcal{H}_2(IV_1, M\|m) = T. \quad (16)$$

The above technique is exactly a Meet-in-the-Middle approach. For a given m, it produce the preimage with probability 2^{2k-n} with time complexity 2^k. Therefore, to find the preimage, 2^{n-2k} m should be exhausted with a time complexity of $2^{n-2k} \times 2^k = 2^{n-k}$.

To build a 2^k-interchange structure (the sizes of $\mathcal{A}$ and $\mathcal{B}$ are both 2^k), the classical time complexity is $\tilde{O}(2^{2k+n/2})$ in [49].

5.2   Low qRAM Quantum Version of Interchange Structure

For the hash XOR combiners $\mathcal{H}_1(IV_1, M) \oplus \mathcal{H}_2(IV_2, M) = T$, the basic technique to build interchange structure is to build a single switch, which allows to jump from an already reachable pair of chains (a_i, b_k) to (a_j, b_k) as shown in Fig. 7(a).

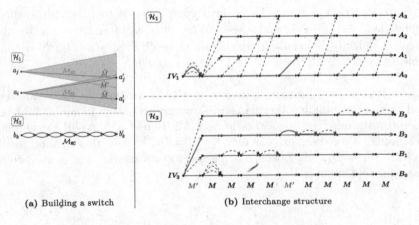

(a) Building a switch   (b) Interchange structure

Fig. 7. Interchange structure and its building block [7]

Algorithm 2: Building a Single Switch in Quantum Settings with Low qRAM

---

1 Use the quantum Joux's multi-collision algorithm to build a set $\mathcal{M}_{MC}$ of 2^t messages for h_2^* that link the starting state b_k to the same state b_k', i.e., $\forall M \in \mathcal{M}_{MC}, h_2^*(b_k, M) = b_k'$. The number of message blocks of M is t. Denote the i-th collision message blocks in Joux's multi-collision are (m_i^0, m_i^1), $1 \le i \le t$, which are stored in QRACM L_1, whose size is about $O(t \cdot n)$.

2 Given $|l_1, l_2, ..., l_t\rangle$ $1 \le i \le t$ and $l_i \in \{0, 1\}$, O_f is the quantum oracle that computes $O_f(|l_1, l_2, ..., l_t\rangle|0\rangle) = |l_1, l_2, ..., l_t\rangle|m_1^{l_1}, m_2^{l_2}, ..., m_t^{l_t}\rangle$ by accessing QRACM L_1. Therefore, we can obtain the superposition of Eq. (18)

  a) Apply Hadamard H to the first t qubits of $|0\rangle$, we get

$$\sum_{l_1, l_2, ..., l_t \in \{0, 1\}} |l_1, l_2, ..., l_t\rangle|0\rangle. \tag{17}$$

  b) Apply O_f to the superposition, we get

$$|\phi\rangle = \sum_{l_1, l_2, ..., l_t \in \{0, 1\}} |l_1, l_2, ..., l_t\rangle|m_1^{l_1}, m_2^{l_2}, ..., m_t^{l_t}\rangle. \tag{18}$$

3   `// the following lines are the CNS collision finding algorithm [21]`

4 Select 2^x $(x \le t)$ $M \in \mathcal{M}_{MC}$, where the r MSBs of $a_j' = h_1^*(a_j, M)$ are zero. Store (a_j', M) in classical memory L_2, whose size is about 2^x. Apply Grover algorithm to produce L_2 (combining with Eq. (18)) with complexity of $2^x \cdot 2^{r/2} = 2^{x+r/2}$.

5 Let $M = (m_1^{l_1}, m_2^{l_2}, ..., m_t^{l_t}) \in \mathcal{M}_{MC}$, and define $g_{L_2}^{h_1^*}(M) := 1$ if $a_i' = h_1^*(a_i, M) \in L_2$, and $g_{L_2}^{h_1^*}(M) := 0$ otherwise.   `// quantum membership checking`

6 Define

$$S_r^{h_1^*} := \{M : \exists z \in \{0,1\}^{n-r}, h_1^*(a_i, M) = \underbrace{0 \cdots 0}_{r \text{ times}} \| z, z \in \{0,1\}^{n-r}, M \in \mathcal{M}_{MC}\}.$$

7 Apply quantum amplification algorithm (QAA) to determine the collision.

  a) The setup phase of QAA is to compute the following superposition together with Eq. (18)

$$|\phi_r\rangle := \frac{1}{\sqrt{|S_r^{h_1^*}|}} \sum_{M \in S_r^{h_1^*}} |M\rangle \tag{19}$$

  b) The projector of the QAA is applying quantum oracle $O_{g_{L_2}^{h_1^*}}$, let $M = (m_1^{l_1}, m_2^{l_2}, ..., m_t^{l_t})$,

$$O_{g_{L_2}^{h_1^*}}|M\rangle|y\rangle = |M\rangle|y \oplus g_{L_2}^{h_1^*}(M)\rangle \tag{20}$$

As shown in Fig. 7(a), given the multi-collision set $\mathcal{M}_{\mathtt{MC}}$ of size 2^t, $\forall M \in \mathcal{M}_{\mathtt{MC}}$, $h_2^*(b_k, M) = b_k'$. The single switch algorithm (Alg. 2) is to find a pair $\hat{M}$, $\hat{M}' \in \mathcal{M}_{\mathtt{MC}}$, such that $h_1^*(a_j, \hat{M}) = h_1^*(a_i, \hat{M}')$.

Complexity of Algorithm 2:

- In Line 1, the time to build 2^t-$\mathcal{M}_{\mathtt{MC}}$ is $t \cdot 2^{2n/5}$, with classical memory $2^{n/5}$ by applying CNS algorithm directly.
- In Line 4, with the superposition in Eq. (18), Grover algorithm is applied to determine a $M = (m_1^{l_1}, m_2^{l_2}, ..., m_t^{l_t})$, such that the r MSBs of $h_1^*(a_j, M)$ are zero, whose time complexity is $2^{r/2}$. To find 2^x such M, the time complexity is $2^{x+r/2}$. A classical memory of size 2^x is needed to store L_2.
- In Line 7 a), the setup phase is to produce the superposition of $|\phi_r\rangle$, whose time complexity is about $2^{r/2}$.

  In Line 7 b), the projector is a quantum membership checking, whose time complexity is about 2^x. To ensure that there is at least one collision, we have $2^{t-r} \times 2^x \geq 2^{n-r}$, i.e., $t + x \geq n$. The total time complexity is

$$2^{\frac{n-r-x}{2}} \cdot (2^{r/2} + 2^x) + 2^{x+r/2} + t \cdot 2^{2n/5}. \tag{21}$$

When $x = \frac{r}{2} = \frac{n}{5}$ and $t = \frac{4n}{5}$, we get the optimal time complexity, i.e., $\mathcal{O}(\frac{4n}{5} \cdot 2^{2n/5})$. The QRACM to store L_1 is of polynomial size, which is $\mathcal{O}(t \cdot n)$. The classical memory used to store L_2 and in Line 1 is $\mathcal{O}(2^{n/5})$.

Comparison Between Our Herding Attack and the Interchange Structure Building Algorithm. The highlevel framework for herding attack (Algorithm 1) and the interchange structure (Algorithm 2) is different, but they both apply variants of CNS collision finding algorithm [21]. As shown in Sect. 2.1 of our paper, the original full CNS algorithm is divided into two parts: the **Precomputing Part** to prepare L and the **Matching Part** to find collision with L. For our herding attack, we mainly modify the **Precomputing Part** of the original CNS to prepare the diamond whose leaf nodes are then stored in L. For interchange structure, we mainly modify the **Matching Part**. It is because different from original CNS algorithm whose messages to collide with L are chosen freely, and thus an easy Hadamard transform applied to $|0\rangle^{\otimes n}$ is enough to get the quantum superposition of the messages. However, in our attack (Algorithm 2), the messages have to be chosen from the set $\mathcal{M}_{\mathtt{MC}}$ built by Joux's multi-collision algorithm. Hence, the superposition of those messages is not trivial to obtain. To deal with it, we introduce an efficient way to build this superposition and make the attack successful.

5.3   Preimage Attack on XOR Combiners with Low qRAM

In classical setting, Leurent and Wang [49] built preimage attack on the XOR combiner with an Meet-in-the-Middle approach. Leurent and Wang first built a 2^k-interchange structure (the sizes of $\mathcal{A}$ and $\mathcal{B}$ are both 2^k) as shown in Sect. 5.1.

In this section, in quantum setting, we perform three quantum attacks on XOR combiners based on three different quantum algorithms.

Attack based on Schrottenloher-Stevens' Quantum MitM Attack [58]. As shown in Sect. 5.1, the sizes of L_1 and L_2 should be equal in Leurent and Wang's classical attack to achieve the optimal time complexity. However, in quantum MitM attack, according to Eq. (7), L_1 and L_2 should be of different sizes. According to (16), the matching bits are n bits, therefore, the size of L_{merge} that contains messages satisfy (16) is very small when compared to L_1 and L_2. Actually, we only find one preimage, so that $|L_{\mathrm{merge}}|$ is about 1. Without loss of generality, we assume $|L_1|$ is bigger. Then (7) is simplified as

$$|L_2| + \sqrt{|L_1|}. \tag{22}$$

To reach an optimal balance, we choose $|L_1| = 2^{2k}$ and $|L_2| = 2^k$, so that the complexity of the quantum merging algorithm is $\mathcal{O}(2^k)$. We denote this kind of interchange structure as $(2^{2k}, 2^k)$-interchange structure, which is built by applying $2^{3k} - 1$ quantum single switches (Algorithm 2) as the following:

1. Build a single switch from (a_0, b_0) to each of (a_0, b_j) $j = 0, ..., 2^k - 1$,
2. For each j, build switches from (a_0, b_j) to all (a_i, b_j) for all $i = 0, ..., 2^{2k} - 1$,
3. To reach the chain (a_i, b_j) from (a_0, b_0), we first find the switch to jump from (a_0, b_0) to (a_0, b_j) in the first step, then find the switch to jump from (a_0, b_j) to (a_i, b_j) in the second step (see Fig. 7(b)).

The time complexity is $\mathcal{O}(\frac{4n}{5} \cdot 2^{3k+2n/5})$ with $\mathcal{O}(2^{n/5})$ classical memory to build the $(2^{2k}, 2^k)$-interchange structure.

According to Lemma 1, we first guess the message block $m \in \mathbb{F}_2^g$, and compute the two lists L_1 and L_2 with $|L_1| = 2^{2k}$ and $|L_2| = 2^k$, then build the O_{merge} with complexity $\mathcal{O}(2^k)$ according to Eq. (22). To find at least one preimage, we have $2^{g+k+2k} = 2^n$, so that $g = n - 3k$. According to Eq. (6), the time complexity of the quantum MitM attack is about $2^{\frac{n-3k}{2}} \times 2^k = 2^{\frac{n-k}{2}}$. During the quantum MitM attack, the $(2^{2k}, 2^k)$-interchange structure precomputed should be stored in QRACM, and L_2 should be stored in QRAQM. Therefore, the qRAM needed is $2^{2k}\mathrm{QRACM}+2^k\mathrm{QRAQM}$.

The overall time complexity, including the time to build $(2^{2k}, 2^k)$-interchange structure and the quantum MitM attack, is $\frac{4n}{5} \cdot 2^{3k+2n/5} + 2^{\frac{n-k}{2}}$. The optimal complexity is $2^{17n/35} = 2^{0.485n}$ by setting $k = n/35$. The classical memory is $\mathcal{O}(2^{n/5})$. The qRAM is $2^{0.0571n}\mathrm{QRACM}+2^{0.0285n}\mathrm{QRAQM}$.

We would like to thank one of the reviewers from ASIACRYPT 2023 for pointing out an error in the preliminary version of the attack based on Schrottenloher-Stevens' method [58], and also thank him for inspiring the following two attacks.

Attack Based on Ambainis' Element Distinctness Algorithm [1]. To apply Ambainis' algorithm, a $(2^k, 2^k)$-interchange structure is first prepared and stored in QRACM of size about 2^k. For a guessed message block $m \in \mathbb{F}_2^g$, we build two lists L_1 and L_2 of equal size 2^k, then apply Ambainis' quantum element distinctness algorithm to detect the collision with the time complexity of $2^{2(k+1)/3}$ and $2^{2(k+1)/3}$ QRAQM. When applying Grover's algorithm on $m \in \mathbb{F}_2^g$, the overall time complexity (including the time to build $(2^k, 2^k)$-interchange structure) to find the preimage of XOR combiner is $\frac{4n}{5} \cdot 2^{2k+2n/5} + 2^{(n-2k)/2+2(k+1)/3} \approx 2^{(2k+2n/5)} + 2^{(n/2-k/3)}$. The optimal time complexity is achieved when $k = 3n/70$, i.e., the time is $2^{(17n/35)} = 2^{(0.485n)}$, with $2^{2(k+1)/3} = 2^{0.0285n}$ QRAQM, $2^k = 2^{0.043n}$ QRACM, and $2^{n/5}$ classical memory.

Attack Based on Jaques-Schrottenloher's Golden Collision Finding Algorithm [39]. To apply Jaques-Schrottenloher's algorithm, a $(2^k, 2^k)$-interchange structure is first prepared and stored in QRACM of size about 2^k. In [7], Bao et al. applied Jaques and Schrottenloher's method [39] to find the collision between L_1 and L_2. Here we also apply this method in our attack. Note that Jaques and Schrottenloher found the single collision in a set of size N with $N^{6/7}$ time complexity and $N^{2/7}$ qubits, without QRAQM. Therefore, with a $(2^k, 2^k)$-interchange structure, the time complexity of our preimage attack on XOR combiner is $2^{(2k+2n/5)} + 2^{(n-2k)/2+6(k+1)/7} \approx 2^{2k+2n/5} + 2^{n/2-k/7}$ with $2^{2k/7}$ qubits, and $2^{0.2n}$ classical memory. The optimal time complexity is achieved when $k = 7n/150$, where the time complexity is $2^{37n/75} = 2^{0.493n}$, with $2^{n/75} = 2^{0.0133n}$ qubits, $2^k = 2^{0.047n}$ QRACM, and $2^{0.2n}$ classical memory.

In the no-QRAQM scenario, when compared our attack with the attack by Bao et al. [7], the time complexity is reduced from $2^{0.495n}$ to $2^{0.493n}$, and the number of qubits is significantly reduced from $2^{0.143n}$ to our $2^{0.0133n}$.

6   Collision Attack on Concatenation Combiners in Quantum Settings

For a hash concatenation combiner $\mathcal{H}_1(IV_1, M) \| \mathcal{H}_2(IV_2, M) = T_1 \| T_2$, the collision attack is to find two distinct M and M', so that $\mathcal{H}_1(IV_1, M) \| \mathcal{H}_2(IV_2, M) = \mathcal{H}_1(IV_1, M') \| \mathcal{H}_2(IV_2, M')$. Classically, based Joux's multi-collision method [40], the collision attack can be built in $\mathcal{O}(2^{n/2})$. Here, we introduce a new quantum collision attack on the hash combiners in Algorithm 3.

Complexity of Algorithm 3. Algorithm 3 is quite similar to Algorithm 2. When we let $t = n$, $x = 2^{n/5}$, $r = 2^{2n/5}$, the attack is optimal. The time complexity is $n \cdot 2^{2n/5}$ with a classical memory of $2^{n/5}$ and polynomial number of qubits.

Algorithm 3: Collision attack on Concatenation combiners in Quantum Settings with Low qRAM

---

1. Use the quantum Joux's multi-collision algorithm to build a set $\mathcal{M}_{MC}$ of 2^t messages for $\mathcal{H}_2$ that link the starting state IV_2 to the same state T_2, i.e., $\forall M \in \mathcal{M}_{MC}, \mathcal{H}_2(IV_2, M) = T_2$. The block length of M is t. Denote the i-th collision message blocks in Joux's multi-collision are (m_i^0, m_i^1), $1 \le i \le t$. Store (m_i^0, m_i^1) in QRACM L_1 (to be used in the construction of superposition), whose size is about $O(t \cdot n)$.

2. Given $|l_1, l_2, ..., l_t\rangle$ $1 \le i \le t$ and $l_i \in \{0, 1\}$, O_f is the quantum oracle that computes $O_f(|l_1, l_2, ..., l_t\rangle|0\rangle) = |l_1, l_2, ..., l_t\rangle|m_1^{l_1}, m_2^{l_2}, ..., m_t^{l_t}\rangle$ by accessing QRACM L_1. Therefore, we can obtain the superposition of Eq. (24)
   a) Apply Hadamard H to the first t qubits of $|0\rangle$, we get

$$\sum_{l_1, l_2, ..., l_t \in \{0,1\}} |l_1, l_2, ..., l_t\rangle|0\rangle. \tag{23}$$

   b) Apply O_f to the superposition, we get

$$|\phi\rangle = \sum_{l_1, l_2, ..., l_t \in \{0,1\}} |l_1, l_2, ..., l_t\rangle|m_1^{l_1}, m_2^{l_2}, ..., m_t^{l_t}\rangle. \tag{24}$$

3. Select 2^x $(x \le t)$ $M \in \mathcal{M}_{MC}$, where the r MSBs of $T_1 = \mathcal{H}_1(IV_1, M)$ are zero. Store (T_1, M) in classical memory L_2, whose size is about 2^x. L_2 is produced by applying Grover algorithm and combining with Eq. (24). The time complexity is $2^x \cdot 2^{r/2} = 2^{x+r/2}$.

4. Let $M = (m_1^{l_1}, m_2^{l_2}, ..., m_t^{l_t}) \in \mathcal{M}_{MC}$, and define $g_{L_2}^{\mathcal{H}_1}(M) := 1$ if $y = \mathcal{H}_1(IV_1, M) \in L_2$, and $g_{L_2}^{\mathcal{H}_1}(M) := 0$ otherwise. /* The quantum membership algorithm.   */

5. Define $S_r^{\mathcal{H}_1} := \{M : \exists z \in \{0, 1\}^{n-r}, \mathcal{H}_1(IV_1, M) = \underbrace{0 \cdots 0}_{r \text{ times}} \| z, z \in \{0, 1\}^{n-r}, M \in \mathcal{M}_{MC}\}$.

6. /* Run a variant of CNS algorithm. Apply quantum amplification algorithm (QAA).   */

7. The setup phase of QAA is the construction

$$|\phi_r\rangle := \frac{1}{\sqrt{|S_r^{\mathcal{H}_1}|}} \sum_{x \in S_r^{\mathcal{H}_1}} |M\rangle \tag{25}$$

8. The projector of the QAA is applying quantum oracle $O_{g_{L_2}^{\mathcal{H}_1}}$, let $M = (m_1^{l_1}, m_2^{l_2}, ..., m_t^{l_t})$,

$$O_{g_{L_2}^{\mathcal{H}_1}}|M\rangle|y\rangle = |M\rangle|y \oplus g_{L_2}^{\mathcal{H}_1}(M)\rangle \tag{26}$$

7 Herding Attack on Concatenation Combiners in Quantum Setting

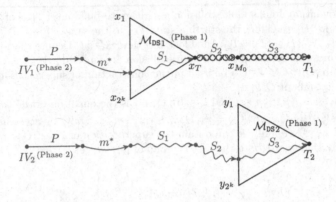

Fig. 8. Herding Attack on Concatenation Combiners in quantum settings [7]

The herding attack on concatenation combiners in quantum settings is given in Fig. 8 and Algorithm 4. In the off-line precomputation phase (Line 2 to 6), two diamond structures $\mathcal{M}_{DS1}$ and $\mathcal{M}_{DS2}$ are built, two Joux's multi-collisions $\mathcal{M}_{MC_s}$ and $\mathcal{M}_{MC_\ell}$ are built. The root node of $\mathcal{M}_{DS1}$ is x_T. The 2^t-Joux's multi-collision $\mathcal{M}_{MC_s}$ links x_T to x_{M_0}. Then the $2^{k \cdot \frac{4n}{5}}$-Joux's multi-collision $\mathcal{M}_{MC_\ell}$ is built to link x_{M_0} and T_1. After that, 2^k-diamond $\mathcal{M}_{DS2}$ is built. Here, we only apply the CNS collision finding algorithm to build the diamond without using the method given in Sect. 3.2. This is because, in the diamond building algorithm given in Sect. 3.2, one has to frequently apply Grover's algorithm to find message blocks to fill up Y to 2^l. For herding attack on MD hash (Algorithm 1), the message blocks are freely chosen. Therefore, the superposition of the message for Grover's algorithm is easy to generate, and a trivial Hadamard transformation on $|0\rangle^{\otimes n}$ is enough. However, when building the 2^k-diamond $\mathcal{M}_{DS2}$, those message blocks have to be selected from a prefixed message set constructed by Joux's multi-collision algorithm, i.e., $\mathcal{M}_{MC_\ell}$. To frequently build the superposition of messages from $\mathcal{M}_{MC_\ell}$ for applying Grover's algorithm is not easy. Therefore, we use the trivial method that only uses CNS collision finding algorithm here. Since there are $2^k - 1$ collisions in a 2^k-diamond, $2^k - 1$ times of CNS algorithm are needed to build the diamond. To build the 2^k-diamond $\mathcal{M}_{DS1}$, we can freely use diamond building algorithm in Sect. 3.2 or apply CNS algorithm trivially, since the time to build $\mathcal{M}_{MC_\ell}$ already bound the complexity, we just choose CNS algorithm trivially to build $\mathcal{M}_{DS1}$ without increasing the overall complexity. Similar reason also prevents us from applying diamond building algorithm given in Sect. 3.2 to Algorithm 5.

Algorithm 4: Quantum Herding Attack on Concatenation Combiners with low qRAM

---

1 **Off-line precomputation:**
2 **begin**
3 $\quad$ Build a diamond $\mathcal{M}_{DS1}$ for $\mathcal{H}_1$, which starts from 2^k states $D_1 = \{x_i\}_1^{2^k}$, where the r MSBs of $x_i \in \mathbb{F}_2^n$ are zero. To build $\mathcal{M}_{DS1}$, we do not use the method given in Section 3.2, but only use CNS algorithm to build each collision until the root x_T is derived. Totally, $2^{k-1} + 2^{k-2} + \cdots + 1 = 2^k - 1$ times of CNS are applied with time complexity $2^{k+2n/5}$ and memory complexity of $2^{n/5}$. The root is x_T. From the hash value x_T, build a 2^t-Joux's multi-collision $\mathcal{M}_{MC_s}$, in which all messages map x_T to a state x_{M_0}. Continue to build a $2^{k \cdot \frac{4n}{5}}$-Joux's multi-collision $\mathcal{M}_{MC_\ell}$ (consists of k fragments and each fragment is of length $4n/5$) on $\mathcal{H}_1$ from the starting state x_{M_0} and mapping to the state T_1. Denote the terminal states of each of the k fragments of $\mathcal{M}_{MC_\ell}$ by x_{M_i} for i from 1 to k (note that $x_{M_k} = T_1$).
4 $\quad$ Build a diamond $\mathcal{M}_{DS2}$ for $\mathcal{H}_2$, which starts from 2^k states $D_2 = \{y_i\}_1^{2^k}$, where the r MSBs of $y_i \in \mathbb{F}_2^n$ are zero.. The messages used to building $\mathcal{M}_{DS2}$ are all chosen from the set $\mathcal{M}_{MC_\ell}$. For example, the messages mapping the first layer of 2^k states to the 2^{k-1} states in $\mathcal{M}_{DS2}$ are chosen from the set of $2^{4n/5}$ messages in the first fragment of $\mathcal{M}_{MC_\ell}$ mapping x_{M_0} to x_{M_1}. To build $\mathcal{M}_{DS2}$, we do not use the method given in Section 3.2, but only apply $2^k - 1$ times CNS algorithm variant given by Algorithm 2 to find $2^k - 1$ collisions in $\mathcal{M}_{MC_\ell}$. Note that Algorithm 2 is exactly the method to find two messages from a set of multi-collisions that make two states collides (as shown in Figure 7(a)). The time to build $\mathcal{M}_{DS2}$ is $O(2^{k+2n/5})$ with a classical memory $2^{n/5}$.
5 $\quad$ Commit $T_1 \| T_2$ to the public.
6 **end**
7 **On-line phase:**
8 **begin**
9 $\quad$ Receive the challenged prefix P and compute the internal chaining value $x_P = h_1^*(IV_1, P)$ and $y_P = h_2^*(IV_2, P)$.
10 $\quad$ /* Finding the linking message m^* by applying variant of CNS collision-finding algorithm: $\quad\quad\quad\quad$ */
11 $\quad$ Store D_1 in a classical memory L_1.
12 $\quad$ Apply Line 6 to 12 of Algorithm 1 to determine linking message m^* that maps x_P to one of the leaf state x_j of $\mathcal{M}_{DS1}$, and retrieve the message S_1 that link the leaf x_j to the root x_T.
13 $\quad$ Compute $y_T = h_2^*(IV_2, P \| m^* \| S_1)$.
14 $\quad$ /* Finding the linking message S_2 by applying variant of CNS collision-finding algorithm: $\quad\quad\quad\quad$ */
15 $\quad$ Store D_2 in a classical memory L_2.
16 $\quad$ Apply CNS algorithm variant given by Algorithm 2 to find $S_2 \in \mathcal{M}_{MC_s}$, which maps y_T to one of the leaf state y_j of $\mathcal{M}_{DS2}$, and retrieve the message S_3 that link the leaf y_j to the root T_2.
17 $\quad$ $M = P \| m^* \| S_1 \| S_2 \| S_3$ is the returned message.
18 **end**

Algorithm 5: Quantum Herding attack on Zipper Hash with Low qRAM

---

1 **Off-line phase: begin**

2   Build a $2^{k \cdot \frac{4n}{5}}$-Joux's multi-collision $\mathcal{M}_{MC1}$ (consists of k fragments and each fragment is of length $4n/5$) that link IV and x_{M_0}. Denote the terminal states of each of the k fragments of $\mathcal{M}_{MC1}$ by x_{M_i} for i from $k-1$ to 0.

3   Build 2^t-Joux's multi-collision $\mathcal{M}_{MC2}$ from x_{M_0} to $\bar{x}$.

4   Build $\mathcal{M}_{DS}$, which starts from 2^k leaf states $D = \{y_i\}_1^{2^k}$ to the root state h_T, where the r MSBs of $y_i \in \mathbb{F}_2^n$ are zero. Similar to Line 4 of Algorithm 4, we apply $2^k - 1$ times of Algorithm 2 to build $\mathcal{M}_{DS}$, which needs $2^{k+2n/5}$ time and $2^{n/5}$ memory.

5   Commit h_T.

6 **end**

7 **On-line phase: begin**

8   Given the suffix S, compute $\bar{y} = h_2^*(h_1^*(\bar{x}, S), \overleftarrow{S})$.

9   Apply the variant of CNS to find the $m^* \in \mathcal{M}_{MC2}$ to connect $\bar{y}$ with the y_j one of the leaf states of $\mathcal{M}_{DS}$, and retrieve the corresponding message $S_1 \in \mathcal{M}_{MC2}$.

10   Output the message $S_1 \| m^* \| S$.

11 **end**

Complexity of Algorithm 4.

- In the off-line precompuation phase (Line 2 to 6), the time complexity to build $\mathcal{M}_{DS1}$, $\mathcal{M}_{MC_s}$, $\mathcal{M}_{MC_\ell}$, and $\mathcal{M}_{DS2}$ is

$$2^{k+2n/5} + t \cdot 2^{2n/5} + 4nk/5 \cdot 2^{2n/5} + 2^{k+2n/5} \approx 2^{k+2n/5},$$

  where $t = \mathcal{O}(n)$.
- In the online phase (Line 8 to 18), the time to find m^* and S_2 are both $2^{\frac{n-r-k}{2}}(2^{r/2} + 2^k)$.

Therefore, the overall optimal time complexity of Algorithm 4 is $\mathcal{O}(2^{7n/15})$ by balancing the off-line and on-line computation phases and assigning $k = n/15$, $r = 2k$, and $t = n$. The memory cost is dominated by building Joux's multi-collision with CNS, i.e., $\mathcal{O}(2^{n/5})$ classical memory.

8 Quantum Herding Attack on Hash-Twice

The attack on Hash-Twice shares the fundamental ideas of the attack on the concatenation combiners, as depicted in Fig. 9. The attacker selects T_2 as their commitment and subsequently faces a challenge involving an unknown prefix P. The attack is the same to the attack on concatenation combiner. Please see Algorithm 4 for details. The only difference is that the IV_2 is replaced by T_1. Therefore, the overall optimal time complexity is also $\mathcal{O}(2^{7n/15})$ with a classical memory of $\mathcal{O}(2^{n/5})$.

9 Quantum Herding Attack on Zipper Hash

As stated by Andreeva et al. [3], the traditional herding attack with a prefix P can not be applied to Zipper Hash. Therefore, Andreeva et al. [3] gave a variant of the herding attack, where the challenge is placed at the end: as shown in Fig. 10, the adversary commits to a hash value h_T, then she is challenged with a suffix S, and has to produce $S_1 \| m^*$ such that $\mathcal{H}(IV, S_1 \| m^* \| S) = h_T$. The complexity of Andreeva et al.'s classical attack is $\mathcal{O}(2^{2n/3})$.

In this section, we introduce a quantum version Andreeva et al.'s attack in Algorithm 5. The complexity of the off-line phase dominated by building $\mathcal{M}_{DS}$, which is about $\mathcal{O}(2^{k+2n/5})$. The on-line phase is $2^{\frac{n-r-k}{2}} \cdot (2^{r/2} + 2^k)$ with $t = n$. Let $k = \frac{n}{15}$, $r = 2k$, the optimal complexity is achieved to be $2^{7n/15}$. The memory is $2^{n/5}$.

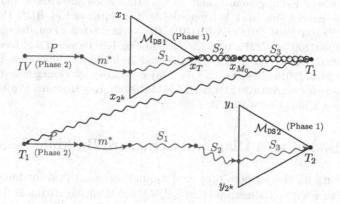

Fig. 9. Herding attack on Hash-Twice

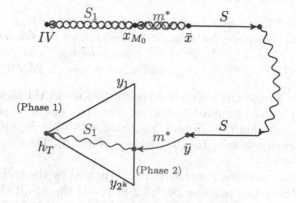

Fig. 10. Herding attack on Zipper Hash

Conclusion

This paper evaluated the quantum attacks on iterated hash functions and various important hash combiners. Most of the attacks do not need qRAM anymore, and the quantum preimage attack on hash XOR combiner is improved by significantly reducing the number of qubits from previous $2^{0.143n}$ to the current $2^{0.013n}$. Since the existence of large qRAM is still questionable, building quantum attacks with low-qRAM is of more practical relevance. Since for hash functions, the attackers do not need online superposition queries, quantum attacks on hash functions are more friendly than on other keyed primitives like block ciphers. Therefore, exploring the quantum attacks on hash functions is of more practical relevance.

Acknowledgements. We thank the anonymous reviewers of ASIACRYPT 2023 for their insightful comments, and a special thanks to our shepherd for providing so much wonderful guidance and co-inventing some algorithms that greatly improved the paper. This work is supported by the National Key R&D Program of China (2022YFB2702804, 2018YFA0704701), the Natural Science Foundation of China (62272257, 62302250, 62072270, 62072207), Shandong Key Research and Development Program (2020ZLYS09), the Major Scientific and Technological Innovation Project of Shandong, China (2019JZZY010133), the Major Program of Guangdong Basic and Applied Research (2019B030302008, 2022A1515140090), Key Research Project of Zhejiang Province, China (2023C01025).

A   On Bao et al.'s Diamond Structure Building Algorithm

In [7, Section 3.3], the authors proposed a quantum algorithm for building diamond structure with exponential large QRAQM in their Algorithm 2. After that, they try to study the no-qRAM version. However, they only give the following sentences for their no-qRAM algorithm [7, Page 12]:

> "In Scenario R2, the time complexity to find a collision is of $(2^{(n-t)})^{2/5}$ computations. Therefore, building a 2^t-diamond structure requires $\mathcal{O}(t^{(2/3)} \cdot 2^t \cdot 2^{(2(n-t)/5)}) = \mathcal{O}(t^{2/3} \cdot 2^{(2n+3t)/5})$ computations, with $\mathcal{O}(t^{2/3} \cdot 2^t \cdot 2^{(n-t)/5}) = \mathcal{O}(t^{2/3} \cdot 2^{(n+4t)/5})$ classical memory. (see [7, Page 12])"

The authors do not give concrete steps for this no-qRAM algorithm. After communicating with the authors, we know that they just estimated the time complexity by replacing the Grover's algorithm with CNS algorithm [21] and use classical memory to store the data instead of qRAM. They do not give the concrete steps at all.

However, the conversion is not trivial as estimated by the authors of [7]. In fact, we use almost two pages in Sect. 3.2 to reveal the no-qRAM algorithm. When we try to rebuild the steps with CNS collision algorithm [21] for building diamond, we find the final time complexity is $2^{(2n+4t)/5}$, which is different from the time $2^{(2n+3t)/5}$ claimed in [7]. Then, we communicated with the authors of [7] again, and they admitted our steps and time evaluation are correct.

Since the authors of [7] do not publish or give us their concrete steps for their claimed no-qRAM algorithm, we can not check which step is possibly wrong or which step leads to the different complexities. Since the herding attack is based on diamond structure, Bao et al's [7] herding attack in no-qRAM setting is also flawed.

B On Bao et al.'s Quantum Herding Attack

In the original estimation by Bao et al. [7, Section 4.3], the overall time complexity of the no-qRAM herding attack is about $2^{((2n+3k)/5)} + 2^{(n/2-k/6)}$, where $2^{((2n+3k)/5)}$ is the time to build a 2^k-diamond, and the time $2^{(n/2-k/6)}$ is to find the linking message M_{link} to the diamond based on Chailloux et al.'s multi-target preimage algorithm [21]. After tradeoff between the two, it achieves optimal when $k = 3n/23$, which results in the overall time complexity $2^{(11n/23)} = 2^{(0.478n)}$, classical memory $2^{(7n/23)} = 2^{(0.304n)}$. Even if we compare our no-qRAM herding attack in Sect. 4 (i.e., time $2^{0.46n}$, classical memory $2^{0.23n}$) with this original complexity estimation of [7], the improvement of our attack is obvious.

However, the algorithm of building diamond structure of [7] is flawed as shown in Appendix A. Their herding attack based on diamond is also wrong. In fact, the time $2^{((2n+3k)/5)}$ will be $2^{((2n+4k)/5)}$ when using our correct diamond building algorithm given in Sect. 3.2. Therefore, the complexity of Bao et al.'s no-qRAM herding attack becomes $2^{((2n+4k)/5)} + 2^{(n/2-k/6)}$ time and $2^{(n+2k)/5}$ classical memory, which achieves optimal when $k = 3n/29$, that results in time $2^{(14n/29)} = 2^{(0.4827n)}$, classical memory $2^{(7n/29)} = 2^{(0.24n)}$. When compared with this corrected Bao et al.'s attack, our attack in Sect. 4 (time=$2^{0.46n}$, classical memory=$2^{0.23n}$) is still better obviously.

References

1. Ambainis, A.: Quantum walk algorithm for element distinctness. SIAM J. Comput. **37**(1), 210–239 (2007)
2. Andreeva, E., et al.: New second-preimage attacks on hash functions. J. Cryptol. **29**(4), 657–696 (2016)
3. Andreeva, E., Bouillaguet, C., Dunkelman, O., Kelsey, J.: Herding, second preimage and trojan message attacks beyond Merkle-Damgård. In: Jacobson, M.J., Rijmen, V., Safavi-Naini, R. (eds.) SAC 2009. LNCS, vol. 5867, pp. 393–414. Springer, Heidelberg (2009). https://doi.org/10.1007/978-3-642-05445-7_25
4. Andreeva, E., et al.: Second preimage attacks on dithered hash functions. In: Smart, N. (ed.) EUROCRYPT 2008. LNCS, vol. 4965, pp. 270–288. Springer, Heidelberg (2008). https://doi.org/10.1007/978-3-540-78967-3_16
5. Banegas, G., Bernstein, D.J.: Low-communication parallel quantum multi-target preimage search. In: Adams, C., Camenisch, J. (eds.) SAC 2017. LNCS, vol. 10719, pp. 325–335. Springer, Cham (2018). https://doi.org/10.1007/978-3-319-72565-9_16
6. Bao, Z., Dinur, I., Guo, J., Leurent, G., Wang, L.: Generic attacks on hash combiners. J. Cryptol. **33**(3), 742–823 (2020)

7. Bao, Z., Guo, J., Li, S., Pham, P.: Evaluating the security of Merkle-Damgård hash functions and combiners in quantum settings. In: Yuan, X., Bai, G., Alcaraz, C., Majumdar, S. (eds.) NSS 2022. LNCS, vol. 13787, pp. 687–711. Springer, Cham (2022). https://doi.org/10.1007/978-3-031-23020-2_39

8. Bao, Z., Wang, L., Guo, J., Gu, D.: Functional graph revisited: updates on (second) preimage attacks on hash combiners. In: Katz, J., Shacham, H. (eds.) CRYPTO 2017. LNCS, vol. 10402, pp. 404–427. Springer, Cham (2017). https://doi.org/10.1007/978-3-319-63715-0_14

9. Benedikt, B.J., Fischlin, M., Huppert, M.: Nostradamus goes quantum. In: Agrawal, S., Lin, D. (eds.) ASIACRYPT 2022. LNCS, vol. 13793, pp. 583–613. Springer, Cham (2022). https://doi.org/10.1007/978-3-031-22969-5_20

10. Bernstein, D.J.: Cost analysis of hash collisions: will quantum computers make SHARCS obsolete. SHARCS **9**, 105 (2009)

11. Biham, E., Dunkelman, O.: A framework for iterative hash functions - HAIFA. IACR Cryptology ePrint Archive, p. 278 (2007)

12. Blackburn, S.R., Stinson, D.R., Upadhyay, J.: On the complexity of the herding attack and some related attacks on hash functions. Des. Codes Cryptogr. **64**(1–2), 171–193 (2012)

13. Bonnetain, X., Hosoyamada, A., Naya-Plasencia, M., Sasaki, Yu., Schrottenloher, A.: Quantum attacks without superposition queries: the offline Simon's algorithm. In: Galbraith, S.D., Moriai, S. (eds.) ASIACRYPT 2019. LNCS, vol. 11921, pp. 552–583. Springer, Cham (2019). https://doi.org/10.1007/978-3-030-34578-5_20

14. Bonnetain, X., Jaques, S.: Quantum period finding against symmetric primitives in practice. IACR Trans. Cryptogr. Hardw. Embed. Syst. **2022**(1), 1–27 (2022)

15. Bonnetain, X., Leurent, G., Naya-Plasencia, M., Schrottenloher, A.: Quantum linearization attacks. In: Tibouchi, M., Wang, H. (eds.) ASIACRYPT 2021, Part I. LNCS, vol. 13090, pp. 422–452. Springer, Cham (2021). https://doi.org/10.1007/978-3-030-92062-3_15

16. Bonnetain, X., Naya-Plasencia, M.: Hidden shift quantum cryptanalysis and implications. In: Peyrin, T., Galbraith, S. (eds.) ASIACRYPT 2018, Part I. LNCS, vol. 11272, pp. 560–592. Springer, Cham (2018). https://doi.org/10.1007/978-3-030-03326-2_19

17. Bonnetain, X., Naya-Plasencia, M., Schrottenloher, A.: On quantum slide attacks. In: Paterson, K.G., Stebila, D. (eds.) SAC 2019. LNCS, vol. 11959, pp. 492–519. Springer, Cham (2020). https://doi.org/10.1007/978-3-030-38471-5_20

18. Bonnetain, X., Schrottenloher, A., Sibleyras, F.: Beyond quadratic speedups in quantum attacks on symmetric schemes. In: Dunkelman, O., Dziembowski, S. (eds.) EUROCRYPT 2022, Part III. LNCS, vol. 13277, pp. 315–344. Springer, Cham (2022). https://doi.org/10.1007/978-3-031-07082-2_12

19. Brassard, G., Hoyer, P., Mosca, M., Tapp, A.: Quantum amplitude amplification and estimation. Contemp. Math. **305**, 53–74 (2002)

20. Brassard, G., HØyer, P., Tapp, A.: Quantum cryptanalysis of hash and claw-free functions. In: Lucchesi, C.L., Moura, A.V. (eds.) LATIN 1998. LNCS, vol. 1380, pp. 163–169. Springer, Heidelberg (1998). https://doi.org/10.1007/BFb0054319

21. Chailloux, A., Naya-Plasencia, M., Schrottenloher, A.: An efficient quantum collision search algorithm and implications on symmetric cryptography. In: Takagi, T., Peyrin, T. (eds.) ASIACRYPT 2017, Part II. LNCS, vol. 10625, pp. 211–240. Springer, Cham (2017). https://doi.org/10.1007/978-3-319-70697-9_8

22. Damgård, I.B.: A design principle for hash functions. In: Brassard, G. (ed.) CRYPTO 1989. LNCS, vol. 435, pp. 416–427. Springer, New York (1990). https://doi.org/10.1007/0-387-34805-0_39

23. Dierks, T., Allen, C.: The TLS protocol version 1.0. Technical report (1999)
24. Dinur, I.: New attacks on the concatenation and XOR hash combiners. In: Fischlin, M., Coron, J.-S. (eds.) EUROCRYPT 2016, Part I. LNCS, vol. 9665, pp. 484–508. Springer, Heidelberg (2016). https://doi.org/10.1007/978-3-662-49890-3_19
25. Dong, X., Dong, B., Wang, X.: Quantum attacks on some feistel block ciphers. Des. Codes Cryptogr. **88**(6), 1179–1203 (2020)
26. Dong, X., Guo, J., Li, S., Pham, P.: Triangulating rebound attack on AES-like hashing. In: Dodis, Y., Shrimpton, T. (eds.) CRYPTO 2022. LNCS, vol. 13507, pp. 94–124. Springer, Cham (2022). https://doi.org/10.1007/978-3-031-15802-5_4
27. Dong, X., Sun, S., Shi, D., Gao, F., Wang, X., Hu, L.: Quantum collision attacks on AES-like hashing with low quantum random access memories. In: Moriai, S., Wang, H. (eds.) ASIACRYPT 2020, Part II. LNCS, vol. 12492, pp. 727–757. Springer, Cham (2020). https://doi.org/10.1007/978-3-030-64834-3_25
28. Dong, X., Zhang, Z., Sun, S., Wei, C., Wang, X., Hu, L.: Automatic classical and quantum rebound attacks on AES-like hashing by exploiting related-key differentials. In: Tibouchi, M., Wang, H. (eds.) ASIACRYPT 2021, Part I. LNCS, vol. 13090, pp. 241–271. Springer, Cham (2021). https://doi.org/10.1007/978-3-030-92062-3_9
29. Flórez Gutiérrez, A., Leurent, G., Naya-Plasencia, M., Perrin, L., Schrottenloher, A., Sibleyras, F.: New results on Gimli: full-permutation distinguishers and improved collisions. In: Moriai, S., Wang, H. (eds.) ASIACRYPT 2020, Part I. LNCS, vol. 12491, pp. 33–63. Springer, Cham (2020). https://doi.org/10.1007/978-3-030-64837-4_2
30. Freier, A., Karlton, P., Kocher, P.: The secure sockets layer (SSL) protocol version 3.0. Technical report (2011)
31. Giovannetti, V., Lloyd, S., Maccone, L.: Architectures for a quantum random access memory. Phys. Rev. A **78**(5), 052310 (2008)
32. Giovannetti, V., Lloyd, S., Maccone, L.: Quantum random access memory. Phys. Rev. Lett. **100**(16), 160501 (2008)
33. Grassi, L., Naya-Plasencia, M., Schrottenloher, A.: Quantum algorithms for the k-xor problem. In: Peyrin, T., Galbraith, S. (eds.) ASIACRYPT 2018, Part I. LNCS, vol. 11272, pp. 527–559. Springer, Cham (2018). https://doi.org/10.1007/978-3-030-03326-2_18
34. Grover, L.K.: A fast quantum mechanical algorithm for database search. In: Proceedings of the Twenty-Eighth Annual ACM Symposium on the Theory of Computing, Philadelphia, Pennsylvania, USA, 22–24 May 1996, pp. 212–219 (1996)
35. Hosoyamada, A., Sasaki, Yu.: Cryptanalysis against symmetric-key schemes with online classical queries and offline quantum computations. In: Smart, N.P. (ed.) CT-RSA 2018. LNCS, vol. 10808, pp. 198–218. Springer, Cham (2018). https://doi.org/10.1007/978-3-319-76953-0_11
36. Hosoyamada, A., Sasaki, Yu.: Finding hash collisions with quantum computers by using differential trails with smaller probability than birthday bound. IACR Cryptology ePrint Archive 2020:213 (2020)
37. Hosoyamada, A., Sasaki, Yu.: Quantum collision attacks on reduced SHA-256 and SHA-512. In: Malkin, T., Peikert, C. (eds.) CRYPTO 2021, Part I. LNCS, vol. 12825, pp. 616–646. Springer, Cham (2021). https://doi.org/10.1007/978-3-030-84242-0_22
38. Ito, G., Hosoyamada, A., Matsumoto, R., Sasaki, Yu., Iwata, T.: Quantum chosen-ciphertext attacks against feistel ciphers. In: Matsui, M. (ed.) CT-RSA 2019. LNCS, vol. 11405, pp. 391–411. Springer, Cham (2019). https://doi.org/10.1007/978-3-030-12612-4_20

39. Jaques, S., Schrottenloher, A.: Low-gate quantum golden collision finding. In: Dunkelman, O., Jacobson, Jr., M.J., O'Flynn, C. (eds.) SAC 2020. LNCS, vol. 12804, pp. 329–359. Springer, Cham (2021). https://doi.org/10.1007/978-3-030-81652-0_13

40. Joux, A.: Multicollisions in iterated hash functions. Application to cascaded constructions. In: Franklin, M. (ed.) CRYPTO 2004. LNCS, vol. 3152, pp. 306–316. Springer, Heidelberg (2004). https://doi.org/10.1007/978-3-540-28628-8_19

41. Kaplan, M., Leurent, G., Leverrier, A., Naya-Plasencia, M.: Breaking symmetric cryptosystems using quantum period finding. In: Robshaw, M., Katz, J. (eds.) CRYPTO 2016. LNCS, vol. 9815, pp. 207–237. Springer, Heidelberg (2016). https://doi.org/10.1007/978-3-662-53008-5_8

42. Kelsey, J., Kohno, T.: Herding hash functions and the nostradamus attack. In: Vaudenay, S. (ed.) EUROCRYPT 2006. LNCS, vol. 4004, pp. 183–200. Springer, Heidelberg (2006). https://doi.org/10.1007/11761679_12

43. Kelsey, J., Schneier, B.: Second preimages on n-bit hash functions for much less than 2^n work. In: Cramer, R. (ed.) EUROCRYPT 2005. LNCS, vol. 3494, pp. 474–490. Springer, Heidelberg (2005). https://doi.org/10.1007/11426639_28

44. Kortelainen, T., Kortelainen, J.: On diamond structures and trojan message attacks. In: Sako, K., Sarkar, P. (eds.) ASIACRYPT 2013, Part II. LNCS, vol. 8270, pp. 524–539. Springer, Heidelberg (2013). https://doi.org/10.1007/978-3-642-42045-0_27

45. Kuperberg, G.: Another subexponential-time quantum algorithm for the dihedral hidden subgroup problem. In: Severini, S., Brandão, F.G.S.L. (eds.) 8th Conference on the Theory of Quantum Computation, Communication and Cryptography, TQC 2013, 21–23 May 2013, Guelph, Canada, volume 22 of LIPIcs, pp. 20–34. Schloss Dagstuhl - Leibniz-Zentrum für Informatik (2013)

46. Kuwakado, H., Morii, M.: Quantum distinguisher between the 3-round feistel cipher and the random permutation. In: IEEE International Symposium on Information Theory, ISIT 2010, 13–18 June 2010, Austin, Texas, USA, Proceedings, pp. 2682–2685 (2010)

47. Kuwakado, H., Morii, M.: Security on the quantum-type even-mansour cipher. In: Proceedings of the International Symposium on Information Theory and its Applications, ISITA 2012, Honolulu, HI, USA, 28–31 October 2012, pp. 312–316 (2012)

48. Leander, G., May, A.: Grover meets Simon – quantumly attacking the FX-construction. In: Takagi, T., Peyrin, T. (eds.) ASIACRYPT 2017, Part II. LNCS, vol. 10625, pp. 161–178. Springer, Cham (2017). https://doi.org/10.1007/978-3-319-70697-9_6

49. Leurent, G., Wang, L.: The sum can be weaker than each part. In: Oswald, E., Fischlin, M. (eds.) EUROCRYPT 2015, Part I. LNCS, vol. 9056, pp. 345–367. Springer, Heidelberg (2015). https://doi.org/10.1007/978-3-662-46800-5_14

50. Liskov, M.: Constructing an ideal hash function from weak ideal compression functions. In: Biham, E., Youssef, A.M. (eds.) SAC 2006. LNCS, vol. 4356, pp. 358–375. Springer, Heidelberg (2007). https://doi.org/10.1007/978-3-540-74462-7_25

51. Mendel, F., Rechberger, C., Schläffer, M.: MD5 is weaker than weak: attacks on concatenated combiners. In: Matsui, M. (ed.) ASIACRYPT 2009. LNCS, vol. 5912, pp. 144–161. Springer, Heidelberg (2009). https://doi.org/10.1007/978-3-642-10366-7_9

52. Merkle, R.C.: A certified digital signature. In: Brassard, G. (ed.) CRYPTO 1989. LNCS, vol. 435, pp. 218–238. Springer, New York (1990). https://doi.org/10.1007/0-387-34805-0_21

53. Naya-Plasencia, M., Schrottenloher, A.: Optimal merging in quantum k-xor and k-sum algorithms. In: Canteaut, A., Ishai, Y. (eds.) EUROCRYPT 2020, Part II. LNCS, vol. 12106, pp. 311–340. Springer, Cham (2020). https://doi.org/10.1007/978-3-030-45724-2_11

54. Nielsen, Chuang, I.L.: Quantum Computation and Quantum Information, 10th Anniversary edn. Cambridge University Press, Cambridge (2016)

55. NIST. The post quantum project. https://csrc.nist.gov/projects/post-quantum-cryptography

56. Preneel, B.: Analysis and design of cryptographic hash functions. Ph.D. thesis, Katholieke Universiteit te Leuven Leuven (1993)

57. Schrottenloher, A.: Quantum linear key-recovery attacks using the QFT. In: Handschuh, H., Lysyanskaya, A. (eds.) CRYPTO 2023. LNCS, vol. 14085, pp. 258–291. Springer, Cham (2023). https://doi.org/10.1007/978-3-031-38554-4_9

58. Schrottenloher, A., Stevens, M.: Simplified MITM modeling for permutations: new (quantum) attacks. In: Dodis, Y., Shrimpton, T. (eds.) CRYPTO 2022, Part III. LNCS, vol. 13509, pp. 717–747. Springer, Cham (2022). https://doi.org/10.1007/978-3-031-15982-4_24

59. Shor, P.W.: Algorithms for quantum computation: discrete logarithms and factoring. In: 35th Annual Symposium on Foundations of Computer Science, Santa Fe, New Mexico, USA, 20–22 November 1994, pp. 124–134 (1994)

60. Simon, D.R.: On the power of quantum computation. SIAM J. Comput. **26**(5), 1474–1483 (1997)

61. Stevens, M., Bursztein, E., Karpman, P., Albertini, A., Markov, Y.: The first collision for full SHA-1. In: Katz, J., Shacham, H. (eds.) CRYPTO 2017, Part I. LNCS, vol. 10401, pp. 570–596. Springer, Cham (2017). https://doi.org/10.1007/978-3-319-63688-7_19

62. Wang, X., Yin, Y.L., Yu, H.: Finding collisions in the full SHA-1. In: Shoup, V. (ed.) CRYPTO 2005. LNCS, vol. 3621, pp. 17–36. Springer, Heidelberg (2005). https://doi.org/10.1007/11535218_2

63. Wang, X., Yu, H.: How to break MD5 and other hash functions. In: Cramer, R. (ed.) EUROCRYPT 2005. LNCS, vol. 3494, pp. 19–35. Springer, Heidelberg (2005). https://doi.org/10.1007/11426639_2

On Quantum Secure Compressing Pseudorandom Functions

Ritam Bhaumik[1] , Benoît Cogliati[2] , Jordan Ethan[3] ,
and Ashwin Jha[3(✉)]

[1] EPFL, Lausanne, Switzerland
ritam.bhaumik@epfl.ch
[2] Thales DIS France SAS, Meudon, France
benoit-michel.cogliati@thalesgroup.com
[3] CISPA Helmholtz Center for Information Security, Saarbrücken, Germany
{jordan.ethan,ashwin.jha}@cispa.de

Abstract. In this paper we characterize all $2n$-bit-to-n-bit Pseudorandom Functions (PRFs) constructed with the minimum number of calls to n-bit-to-n-bit PRFs and arbitrary number of linear functions. First, we show that all two-round constructions are either classically insecure, or vulnerable to quantum period-finding attacks. Second, we categorize three-round constructions depending on their vulnerability to these types of attacks. This allows us to identify classes of constructions that could be proven secure. We then proceed to show the security of the following three candidates against any quantum distinguisher that makes at most $2^{n/4}$ (possibly superposition) queries:

$$\mathsf{TNT}(x_1, x_2) := f_3(x_2 \oplus f_2(x_2 \oplus f_1(x_1)));$$
$$\mathsf{LRQ}(x_1, x_2) := f_2(x_2) \oplus f_3(x_2 \oplus f_1(x_1));$$
$$\mathsf{LRWQ}(x_1, x_2) := f_3(f_1(x_1) \oplus f_2(x_2)).$$

Note that the first construction is a classically secure tweakable block-cipher due to Bao et al., and the third construction was shown to be a quantum-secure tweakable block-cipher by Hosoyamada and Iwata with similar query limits. Of note is our proof framework, an adaptation of Chung et al.'s rigorous formulation of Zhandry's compressed oracle technique in the indistinguishability setup, which could be of independent interest. This framework gives very compact and mostly classical-looking proofs as compared to Hosoyamada-Iwata interpretation of Zhandry's compressed oracle.

Keywords: QPRF · TNT · LRWQ · compressed oracle · Simon's algorithm

The authors would like to thank all the anonymous reviewers who reviewed and provided valuable comments on this paper. This work was carried out under the framework of the French-German-Center for Cybersecurity, a collaboration of CISPA and LORIA. Part of this work was written while Benoît Cogliati and Ritam Bhaumik were respectively employed by the CISPA Helmholtz Center for Information Security, Saarbrücken, Germany, and Inria Paris, where the latter received funding from the European Research Council (ERC) under the European Union's Horizon 2020 research and innovation programme (grant agreement no. 714294 - acronym QUASYModo).

J. Guo and R. Steinfeld (Eds.): ASIACRYPT 2023, LNCS 14440, pp. 34–66, 2023.
https://doi.org/10.1007/978-981-99-8727-6_2

1   Introduction

Quantum Security. In the past two decades, post-quantum security has attracted a lot of attention, especially in public-key security. As for symmetric cryptography, the consensus used to be that the main threat would come from the speedup in exhaustive key-search provided by Grover's algorithm. Hence, a doubling of the key-length would be sufficient to reach security against quantum distinguishers. However, a long line of research work (see e.g. [6–10,13,18,20–23]) has shown that this was not sufficient, as quantum distinguishers were able to be significantly more efficient than Grover's search for some constructions. This has renewed the interest in formally proving [3,5,12,14,16,17,19,26,28] the post-quantum security of symmetric modes of operation or generic constructions.

Pseudorandom Functions. One of the most studied primitive in symmetric-key cryptography is the block cipher. Thanks to the classical PRP-PRF Switching Lemma, block ciphers are known to be secure PRFs in the classical setting as long as the number of adversarial queries is small in front of $2^{n/2}$, where n denotes the block-size. In the quantum setting, this bound degrades to $2^{n/3}$ [27], which can be seen as the quantum equivalent of the so-called birthday bound. Block ciphers can also be used to build other primitives, such as authenticated encryption schemes, or message authentication codes (MACs), that are secure in the classical sense. Among these primitives, $2n$-bit-to-n-bit PRFs are a key component in building higher-level optimally-secure (in the classical sense) schemes. Indeed, combining a universal $2n$-bit hash function with a $2n$-bit-to-n-bit PRF yields an n-bit secure variable-input-length PRF, which can be used as it is as a deterministic MAC, or to construct an optimally secure authenticated encryption scheme using the SIV construction [25]. While these composition results do not yet exist in the quantum world, constructing a (quantum secure) contracting PRF from a block cipher is a key component in building more sophisticated algorithms. A first step in this direction has been taken by Hosoyamada and Iwata — after developing a variant of Zhandry's compressed oracle [28] in [14], they proved that the LRWQ construction, defined by the mapping

$$(x_1, x_2) \longmapsto \mathsf{LRWQ}(x_1, x_2) := f_3(f_1(x_1) \oplus f_2(x_2)),$$

where f_1, f_2, f_3 are random n-bit functions, is a (quantum) secure PRF as long as the number of queries is small in front of $2^{n/4}$ in [17]. Since this construction uses three PRF calls, two natural questions arise from this result:

- can a construction using only two PRF calls be proven secure?
- does there exist any other secure construction using three PRF calls?x

It is worth noting that these questions have conclusively affirmative answers (see fixed-length CBC-MAC [2]) in the classical setting. In this paper, we aim to answer the two questions in the quantum settings.

1.1   Our Contributions

Our first contribution is the systematical study of all possible $2n$-bit-to-n-bit PRFs that are built using two or three PRF calls, and only linear function, as depicted in Fig. 1. In Sect. 2, we start by introducing our notation, and describing the three main attack strategies that we will rely on. Then, in Sect. 3, we prove that all the 2-call constructions are either classically broken, or vulnerable to a quantum period-finding distinguisher. Furthermore, we identify classes of 3-call constructions that are insecure, and categorize candidates that may be secure. Our second contribution is to prove the security of the following constructions:

$$\mathsf{TNT}(x_1, x_2) := f_3(x_2 \oplus f_2(x_2 \oplus f_1(x_1)));$$
$$\mathsf{LRQ}(x_1, x_2) := f_2(x_2) \oplus f_3(x_2 \oplus f_1(x_1));$$
$$\mathsf{LRWQ}(x_1, x_2) := f_3(f_1(x_1) \oplus f_2(x_2)).$$

In Sect. 4 we adapt the rigorous formulation of Zhandry's compressed oracle technique [28] by Chung et al. [11] in the indistinguishability setting. Using this framework, in Sect. 5, we prove that all three constructions are secure PRFs as long as the number of adversarial queries is small in front of $2^{n/4}$. As a byproduct, in Sect. 5.4, by combining our main result with [27, Theorem 7] and [15, Proposition 5], we also prove that the aforementioned three constructions (including TNT [1]) are quantum-secure TBCs against chosen plaintext attacks as long as the number of adversarial queries is small in front of $2^{n/6}$. We note that our combination of Hosoyamada and Iwata's proof strategy and Chung et al. framework leads to compact proofs that look mostly classical in nature. As a comparison, we derive a similar security bound for LRWQ as Hosoyamada and Iwata [17], albeit without the heavy computations from [17].

2   Preliminaries

The set of all binary strings, including the empty string $\perp$, is denoted $\{0,1\}^*$. For some $x, y \in \{0,1\}^*$, $x\|y$ denotes the concatenation of X and Y. For some positive integer m, $[m]$ denotes the set $\{1, \ldots, m\}$, and $\{0,1\}^m$ denotes the set of all m-bit binary strings. Throughout this paper, we fix a positive integer n as the block length. The set $\{0,1\}^n$ can be viewed as the binary field $\mathrm{GF}(2^n)$ by fixing a degree n primitive polynomial. We use $\oplus$ and $\odot$ to denote the field addition (XOR) and field multiplication, respectively, over the finite field $\mathrm{GF}(2^n)$. For $x, y \in \mathrm{GF}(2^n)$, we sometimes also write xy to denote $x \odot y$.

2.1   Security Definitions

In this paper, a *distinguisher* is a quantum algorithm that accesses one or more oracles. The exact model of computation and the nature and modeling of such algorithms and oracles are not strictly necessary for the first part of this paper. So, we postpone a rigorous formalism to a later section (see Sect. 4). For now,

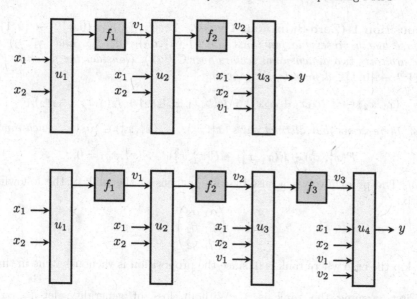

Fig. 1. Graphical representation of the generic $2n$-bit-to-n-bit PRF construction with two (top) and three (bottom) n-bit-to-n-bit PRF calls and linear functions. In this figure f_1, f_2, and f_3 are n-bit-to-n-bit PRFs, u_1, u_2, u_3, and u_4 are $\mathrm{GF}(2^n)$-linear functions, and all wires are n-bit wide.

it suffices to know that we deal with quantum algorithms having access to some oracle(s). We denote the event that a distinguisher $\mathscr{A}$ outputs a bit b after it runs relative to an oracle $\mathcal{O}$ by $\mathscr{A}^{\mathcal{O}} = b$.

For quantum oracles $\mathcal{O}_1$ and $\mathcal{O}_2$, we define the quantum distinguishing advantage of a quantum oracle-algorithm $\mathscr{A}$ by

$$\mathbf{Adv}^{\mathrm{dist}}_{\mathcal{O}_1;\mathcal{O}_2} := \left| \Pr\left(\mathscr{A}^{\mathcal{O}_1} = 1\right) - \Pr\left(\mathcal{O}_2 = 1\right) \right|.$$

Pseudorandom Function. Let $F : \mathcal{K} \times \{0,1\}^m \to \{0,1\}^n$ be a keyed function, indexed with keys from $\mathcal{K}$. The pseudorandom function (or PRF) advantage of some distinguisher $\mathscr{A}$ against F is defined as

$$\mathbf{Adv}^{\mathrm{qprf}}_F(\mathscr{A}) := \mathbf{Adv}^{\mathrm{dist}}_{F_K;f}, \tag{1}$$

where K is drawn uniformly at random from $\mathcal{K}$, and $f : \{0,1\}^m \to \{0,1\}^n$ is a uniform random function.

2.2 Some Useful Attack Strategies

Throughout this paper, we often employ the following attack strategies to construct generic distinguishers against various constructions.

Proposition 1 (Zero-Sum Four-Cycle). *Let $f_1, f_2, f_3 : \{0,1\}^n \to \{0,1\}^n$ be three length preserving functions and let (α_1, α_2), (β_1, β_2), and (γ_1, γ_2) be three arbitrary two dimensional vectors over $\mathrm{GF}(2^n)$. Consider the function $F : \{0,1\}^{2n} \to \{0,1\}^n$ defined by the mapping*

$$(x_1, x_2) \mapsto f_1(\alpha_1 x_1 \oplus \alpha_2 x_2) \oplus f_2(\beta_1 x_1 \oplus \beta_2 x_2) \oplus f_3(\gamma_1 x_1 \oplus \gamma_2 x_2).$$

Then, there exists four distinct pairs $(x_1^1, x_2^1), \ldots, (x_1^4, x_2^4) \in \{0,1\}^{2n}$ such that,

$$F(x_1^1, x_2^1) \oplus F(x_1^2, x_2^2) \oplus F(x_1^3, x_2^3) \oplus F(x_1^4, x_2^4) = 0.$$

Proof. The proof involves a case-by-case analysis of the rank of the following matrix:

$$A = \begin{pmatrix} \alpha_1 & \alpha_2 \\ \beta_1 & \beta_2 \\ \gamma_1 & \gamma_2 \end{pmatrix}$$

We skip the case where rank is 0, since the proposition is vacuously true in that case.

First, assume the rank is 1. Without loss of generality, let (α_1, α_2) be a non-zero vector. Now, one can always find four distinct pairs $(x_1^1, x_2^1), (x_1^2, x_2^2), (x_1^3, x_2^3), (x_1^4, x_2^4) \in \{0,1\}^{2n}$ such that

$$y_1 := \alpha_1 x_1^1 \oplus \alpha_2 x_2^1 = \alpha_1 x_1^2 \oplus \alpha_2 x_2^2, \qquad y_1' := \alpha_1 x_1^3 \oplus \alpha_2 x_2^3 = \alpha_1 x_1^4 \oplus \alpha_2 x_2^4.$$

Since rank of A is 1, for (β_1, β_2) and (γ_1, γ_2) it holds that either they are $(0,0)$ or a non-zero scalar multiple of (α_1, α_2). This straightaway implies that

$$y_2 := \beta_1 x_1^1 \oplus \beta_2 x_2^1 = \beta_1 x_1^2 \oplus \beta_2 x_2^2, \qquad y_2' := \beta_1 x_1^3 \oplus \beta_2 x_2^3 = \beta_1 x_1^4 \oplus \beta_2 x_2^4,$$
$$y_3 := \gamma_1 x_1^1 \oplus \gamma_2 x_2^1 = \gamma_1 x_1^2 \oplus \gamma_2 x_2^2, \qquad y_3' := \gamma_1 x_1^3 \oplus \gamma_2 x_2^3 = \gamma_1 x_1^4 \oplus \gamma_2 x_2^4,$$

whence we get $F(x_1^1, x_2^1) = f_1(y_1) \oplus f_2(y_2) \oplus f_3(y_3) = F(x_1^2, x_2^2)$, and $F(x_1^3, x_2^3) = f_1(y_1') \oplus f_2(y_2') \oplus f_3(y_3') = F(x_1^4, x_2^4)$, which shows the existence of appropriate $(x_1^1, x_2^1), \ldots, (x_1^4, x_2^4) \in \{0,1\}^{2n}$ when the rank of A is 1.

Now, assume the rank is 2. Without loss of generality, let (α_1, α_2) and (β_1, β_2) be two arbitrary independent vectors. Then, since the rank of A is 2, (γ_1, γ_2) is either $(0,0)$ or a non-zero linear combination of (α_1, α_2) and (β_1, β_2). In other words, we have

$$(\gamma_1, \gamma_2) = (a\alpha_1 \oplus b\beta_1, a\alpha_2 \oplus b\beta_2) \tag{2}$$

for some $a, b \in \mathrm{GF}(2^n)$. In particular $a = b = 0$ is also a possibility. In any case, we can always fix some $(y_1, y_2) \neq (y_1', y_2') \in \mathrm{GF}(2^n) \times \mathrm{GF}(2^n)$, such that

$$ay_1 \oplus by_2 = ay_1' \oplus by_2'. \tag{3}$$

Since, (α_1, α_2) is independent of (β_1, β_2), the mapping $(x_1, x_2) \overset{\varphi}{\mapsto} (\alpha_1 x_1 \oplus \alpha_2 x_2, \beta_1 x_1 \oplus \beta_2 x_2)$ is bijective. Let $(x_1^1, x_2^1) = \varphi^{-1}(y_1, y_2)$, $(x_1^2, x_2^2) = \varphi^{-1}(y_1', y_2)$, $(x_1^3, x_2^3) = \varphi^{-1}(y_1', y_2')$, $(x_1^4, x_2^4) = \varphi^{-1}(y_1, y_2')$. From (2) and (3), we have

$$y_3 := \gamma_1 x_1^1 \oplus \gamma_2 x_2^1 = \gamma_1 x_1^3 \oplus \gamma_2 x_2^3, \qquad y_3' := \gamma_1 x_1^2 \oplus \gamma_2 x_2^2 = \gamma_1 x_1^4 \oplus \gamma_2 x_2^4$$

Thus, we have $F(x_1^1, x_2^1) = f_1(y_1) \oplus f_2(y_2) \oplus f_3(y_3)$, $F(x_1^2, x_2^2) = f_1(y_1') \oplus f_2(y_2) \oplus f_3(y_3')$, $F(x_1^3, x_2^3) = f_1(y_1') \oplus f_2(y_2') \oplus f_3(y_3)$, $F(x_1^4, x_2^4) = f_1(y_1) \oplus f_2(y_2') \oplus f_3(y_3')$. This shows the existence of appropriate $(x_1^1, x_2^1), \ldots, (x_1^4, x_2^4) \in \{0,1\}^{2n}$ when the rank of A is 2. $\qquad\qquad\qquad\qquad\qquad\qquad\qquad\qquad\qquad\qquad\qquad\qquad$ $\square$

In our analysis of two call constructions, we often employ the following corollary of Proposition 1.

Corollary 1. *Let* $f_1, f_2 : \{0,1\}^n \to \{0,1\}^n$ *be two length preserving functions and let* (α_1, α_2) *and* (β_1, β_2) *be two arbitrary two dimensional vectors over* $GF(2^n)$. *Consider the function* $F : \{0,1\}^{2n} \to \{0,1\}^n$ *defined by the mapping* $(x_1, x_2) \mapsto f_1(\alpha_1 x_1 \oplus \alpha_2 x_2) \oplus f_2(\beta_1 x_1 \oplus \beta_2 x_2)$. *Then, there exists four distinct pairs* $(x_1^1, x_2^1), \ldots, (x_1^4, x_2^4) \in \{0,1\}^{2n}$ *such that,* $F(x_1^1, x_2^1) \oplus F(x_1^2, x_2^2) \oplus F(x_1^3, x_2^3) \oplus F(x_1^4, x_2^4) = 0$.

A proof of this result follows from the proof of Proposition 1 by setting f_3 to be a constant function evaluating to zero.

Remark 1. Both Proposition 1 and Corollary 1 hold independent of the nature of the underlying functions f_1, f_2, and f_3. Furthermore, the proofs are constructive in nature, which can be utilized by an adversary whose goal is to distinguish F from a uniform random function $\Gamma : \{0,1\}^{2n} \to \{0,1\}^n$. Specifically, finding four distinct inputs $x^1, \ldots, x^4$ such that $\Gamma(x^1) \oplus \Gamma(x^2) \oplus \Gamma(x^3) \oplus \Gamma(x^4) = 0$ is a low probability event. On the other hand, the above results show that such quadruples can be easily derived for a class of functions F, thereby, making them easily distinguishable from a uniform random function.

Proposition 2 (Period Finding). *For any* $f_1, f_2, f_3 : \{0,1\}^n \to \{0,1\}^n$, *suppose* $F : \{0,1\}^{2n} \to \{0,1\}^n$ *is defined by the mapping* $(x_1, x_2) \mapsto f_3(x_2 \oplus f_1(x_1)) \oplus f_2(x_1)$. *Then, for any* $x_1^0 \neq x_1^1 \in \{0,1\}^n$, *the function* $G_{x_1^0, x_1^1} : \{0,1\}^n \to \{0,1\}^n$ *defined by the mapping* $x_2 \mapsto F(x_1^0, x_2) \oplus F(x_1^1, x_2)$ *is periodic and the period* $s(x_1^0, x_1^1) = f_1(x_1^0) \oplus f_1(x_1^1)$.

Proof. For any $x_2 \in \{0,1\}^n$, we have

$$G_{x_1^0, x_1^1}(x_2 \oplus s(x_1^0, x_1^1)) = F(x_1^0, x_2 \oplus s(x_1^0, x_1^1)) \oplus F(x_1^1, x_2 \oplus s(x_1^0, x_1^1))$$
$$= f_3(x_2 \oplus f_1(x_1^0) \oplus f_1(x_1^1) \oplus f_1(x_1^0))$$
$$\oplus f_3(x_2 \oplus f_1(x_1^0) \oplus f_1(x_1^1) \oplus f_1(x_1^1))$$
$$= F(x_1^0, x_2) \oplus F(x_1^1, x_2) = G_{x_1^0, x_1^1}(x_2).$$

While the first two Propositions are interesting even in the classical setting, Proposition 2 is mainly useful in the quantum setting. Specifically, it facilitates the application of Simon's algorithm (see [24] for details). We often employ Proposition 2 in conjunction with the following useful result [20] due to Kaplan et al. which greatly extends the scope of Simon's algorithm.

Let $f : \{0,1\}^n \to \{0,1\}^n$ be a function with some period $s \neq 0$. In [20], Kaplan et al. define

$$\epsilon(f, s) := \max_{t \in \{0,1\}^n \setminus \{0,s\}} \Pr_x (f(x) = f(x \oplus t)) \qquad (4)$$

Theorem 1 ([20], **Theorem 1**). *If $\epsilon(f,s) \le p_0 < 1$, then Simon's algorithm returns s with cn queries, with probability at least $1 - (2\,[(1+p_0)/2]^c)^n$.*

Note that choosing $c > 3/(1-p_0)$ ensures that the error decreases exponentially with n. Thus, it is sufficient to show that $\epsilon(f,s) < 1$. Specifically, it is well-known that $\epsilon(f,s) = \Theta(n2^{-n})$ when f is a random function. Then, Simon's algorithm returns the period with probability close to 1.

Remark 2. Since a uniform random function is aperiodic with very high probability, Proposition 2 can be utilized by an adversary whose goal is to distinguish a periodic random function F from a uniform random function $\Gamma : \{0,1\}^{2n} \to \{0,1\}^n$. Specifically, the adversary can first apply Simon's period finding algorithm in conjunction with Proposition 2 to get a candidate period s in $O(n)$ queries. Followed by this, it can simply make two queries x and $x \oplus s$, and look for a collision at the outputs for these two queries. In a uniform random function this happens with roughly 2^{-n} probability, while for a periodic F, this will happen with probability 1.

Remark 3. In later sections, while declaring a candidate construction insecure, we often refer to Propositions 1 and 2 and Corollary 1 as the source of attack. We skip a formal description of the attacks and their advantage computation, since they involve at most polynomial many queries and achieve almost full advantage. However, we emphasize that such attacks can be easily formalized using the brief strategies proposed in Remarks 1 and 2.

3   Characterizing $2n$-to-n-bit Functions

Our first goal is to identify the minimum number of secret random functions and arbitrary linear functions, required to construct a secure $2n$-to-n-bit PRF. Actually, we go a step further and characterize all the secure (and interesting) PRFs with minimum number of calls. Since LRWQ [17] by Hosoyamada and Iwata can also be considered as a secure PRF, we already have an upper bound of three calls. So, we limit ourselves to at-most-three-calls constructions. The attacks presented here are apparent enough to verify that the query complexity is at most polynomial in n to achieve a constant PRF advantage. So, for the sake of simplicity, we skip computing the exact query complexity and attack advantage for the attacks. Further, to start off, we observe that functions based on just one random function are trivially broken in the classical sense as well. So, we skip them from our discussions, and move on to functions based on two or three random functions.

Let $f_1, f_2, f_3 : \{0,1\}^n \to \{0,1\}^n$ be three independent secret random functions. Let $\alpha = (\alpha_1, \alpha_2) \in \{0,1\}^{2n}$, $\beta = (\beta_1, \beta_2, \beta_3) \in \{0,1\}^{3n}$, $\gamma = (\gamma_1, \gamma_2, \gamma_3, \gamma_4) \in \{0,1\}^{4n}$, $\delta = (\delta_1, \delta_2, \delta_3, \delta_4, \delta_5) \in \{0,1\}^{5n}$ be some public parameters.

3.1   Constructions Based on Two Calls

For a 3×4 matrix

$$A = \begin{pmatrix} \alpha_1 & \alpha_2 & 0 & 0 \\ \beta_1 & \beta_2 & \beta_3 & 0 \\ \gamma_1 & \gamma_2 & \gamma_3 & \gamma_4 \end{pmatrix}$$

our candidate function $F_{A,f_1,f_2} : \{0,1\}^{2n} \to \{0,1\}^n$ indexed by A, f_1, and f_2 is computed as follows on input $(x_1, x_2) \in \{0,1\}^{2n}$:

1. $u_1(x_1, x_2) = \alpha_1 x_1 \oplus \alpha_2 x_2$;
2. $v_1(x_1, x_2) = f_1(u_1(x_1, x_2))$;
3. $u_2(x_1, x_2, v_1) = \beta_1 x_1 \oplus \beta_2 x_2 \oplus \beta_3 v_1$;
4. $v_2(x_1, x_2) = f_2(u_2(x_1, x_2, v_1))$;
5. $u_3(x_1, x_2, v_1, v_2) = \gamma_1 x_1 \oplus \gamma_2 x_2 \oplus \gamma_3 v_1 \oplus \gamma_4 v_2$;
6. $F_{A,f_1,f_2}(x_1, x_2) = y = u_3(x_1, x_2, v_1, v_2)$.

With a slight abuse of notation, we simply write u_i and v_j to denote $u_i(\cdot)$ and $v_j(\cdot)$ for all $i \in [3]$ and $j \in [2]$, whenever the input is known from the context, or the stated fact is independent of the inputs. With this slight simplification, we can represent the entire function using the following system of equations:

$$A \cdot \begin{pmatrix} x_1 \\ x_2 \\ v_1 \\ v_2 \end{pmatrix} = \begin{pmatrix} u_1 \\ u_2 \\ u_3 \end{pmatrix}$$

First, notice that some straightforward simplifications can be done with respect to A:

1. Without loss of generality, we assume that $\gamma_1 = \gamma_2 = 0$, since the adversary can easily create $u_3' = u_3 \oplus \gamma_1 x_1 \oplus \gamma_2 x_2$ for any pair of inputs $(x_1, x_2) \in \{0,1\}^{2n}$.
2. We assume that each row of A is non-zero. Otherwise, there exists $i \in [3]$ such that $u_i = 0$, whence either F is independent of f_1 or f_2, or it is a constant.
3. We assume that each column of A is non-zero as well. Otherwise, for all $i \in [3]$, u_i is independent of one of x_1, x_2, v_1, and v_2, whence F is independent of f_1 or f_2 or it is independent of one of its inputs.
4. We can multiply any row by a non-zero constant. Indeed, for the first two rows, multiplying the input of a uniformly random function by a non-zero constant does not change the distribution of the outputs. For the final row, the adversary can multiply the outputs of the construction by any constant.

Using the above simplifications, from now on we can assume that $\gamma_4 = 1$ by normalizing the final row by γ_4^{-1}. Given these initial simplifications, we do the characterization of F_{A,f_1,f_2} into three cases:

CASE 1: $\beta_1 = \beta_2 = 0$. Then, according to our simplification $\beta_3 = 1$. Therefore,

$$F(x_1, x_2) = (\gamma_3 f_1(u_1)) \oplus (f_2(f_1(u_1))).$$

Using Proposition 1, we can find $(x_1, x_2) \neq (x_1', x_2')$ such that $F(u_1(x_1, x_2)) \oplus F(u_1(x_1', x_2')) = 0$. That gives a classical collision attack.

CASE 2: $(\beta_1 \neq 0$ or $\beta_2 \neq 0)$ and $\alpha_1\beta_2 = \alpha_2\beta_1$. Then, there exists a non-zero $c \in GF(2^n)$, such that $(\beta_1, \beta_2) = (c\alpha_1, c\alpha_2)$. So for every pair of inputs $(x_1, x_2) \neq (x_1', x_2')$, such that $\alpha_1x_1 \oplus \alpha_2x_2 = \alpha_1x_1' \oplus \alpha_2x_2'$, we must have $\beta_1x_1 \oplus \beta_2x_2 = \beta_1x_1' \oplus \beta_2x_2'$. Therefore, $u_1(x_1, x_2) = u_1(x_1', x_2')$ and $u_2(x_1, x_2, v_1) = u_2(x_1', x_2', v_1)$ which implies that $u_3(x_1, x_2, v_1, v_2) = u_3(x_1', x_2', v_1, v_2)$. This clearly gives a collision attack on the construction for inputs (x_1, x_2) and (x_1', x_2').

CASE 3: $(\beta_1 \neq 0$ or $\beta_2 \neq 0)$ and $\alpha_1\beta_2 \neq \alpha_2\beta_1$. Then the construction is reduced to,

$$F(x_1, x_2) = \gamma_3 f_1(\alpha_1x_1 \oplus \alpha_2x_2) \oplus f_2(\beta_1x_1 \oplus \beta_2x_2 \oplus \beta_3 f_1(\alpha_1x_1 \oplus \alpha_2x_2)).$$

Let $f_1' = \gamma_3 f_1$, and $f_1'' = \beta_3 f_1$, and $u_2'(x_1, x_2) = \beta_1x_1 \oplus \beta_2x_2$. Then, the above construction reduces to

$$F(x_1, x_2) = f_1'(u_1(x_1, x_2)) \oplus f_2\left(u_2'(x_1, x_2) \oplus f_1''(u_1(x_1, x_2))\right).$$

Using Proposition 2, we can come up with a periodic function, and hence using Theorem 1, we can find the period in polynomial number of queries.

This concludes the characterization of two-call constructions. Through the above analysis, we have thus established that two calls are not sufficient to construct a $2n$-bit-to-n-bit quantum secure PRF.

3.2   Constructions Based on Three Calls

For a 4×5 matrix

$$A = \begin{pmatrix} \alpha_1 & \alpha_2 & 0 & 0 & 0 \\ \beta_1 & \beta_2 & \beta_3 & 0 & 0 \\ \gamma_1 & \gamma_2 & \gamma_3 & \gamma_4 & 0 \\ \delta_1 & \delta_2 & \delta_3 & \delta_4 & \delta_5 \end{pmatrix}$$

our candidate function $F_{A, f_1, f_2, f_3} : \{0, 1\}^{2n} \to \{0, 1\}^n$ indexed by A, f_1, f_2, and f_3 is computed as follows on input $(x_1, x_2) \in \{0, 1\}^{2n}$:

1. $u_1(x_1, x_2) = \alpha_1x_1 \oplus \alpha_2x_2$;
2. $v_1(x_1, x_2) = f_1(u_1(x_1, x_2))$;
3. $u_2(x_1, x_2, v_1) = \beta_1x_1 \oplus \beta_2x_2 \oplus \beta_3v_1$;
4. $v_2(x_1, x_2) = f_2(u_2(x_1, x_2, v_1))$;
5. $u_3(x_1, x_2, v_1, v_2) = \gamma_1x_1 \oplus \gamma_2x_2 \oplus \gamma_3v_1 \oplus \gamma_4v_2$;
6. $v_3(x_1, x_2) = f_3(u_3(x_1, x_2, v_1, v_2))$;
7. $u_4(x_1, x_2, v_1, v_2, v_3) = \delta_1x_1 \oplus \delta_2x_2 \oplus \delta_3v_1 \oplus \delta_4v_2 \oplus \delta_5v_3$;
8. $F_{A, f_1, f_2, f_3}(x_1, x_2) = y = u_4(x_1, x_2, v_1, v_2, v_3)$.

With similar simplifications as in the case of the two-call analysis, we can represent the entire function using the following system of equations:

$$A \cdot \begin{pmatrix} x_1 \\ x_2 \\ v_1 \\ v_2 \\ v_3 \end{pmatrix} = \begin{pmatrix} u_1 \\ u_2 \\ u_3 \\ u_4 \end{pmatrix} \tag{5}$$

Further, we can make the same initial simplifying assumptions, as made in case of two call constructions, namely

- $\delta_1 = \delta_2 = 0$;
- each row of the matrix is non-zero; and
- each column of the matrix is non-zero.

Further, from now on we assume that $\delta_5 = 1$. Moreover, we claim that the following preconditions are necessary to get a secure construction:

Precondition 1: (α_1, α_2) is independent of (β_1, β_2);
Precondition 2: Either $\gamma_4 \neq 0$, or
(a) (α_1, α_2) is independent of (γ_1, γ_2), and
(b) $(\beta_1, \beta_2, \beta_3)$ should be independent of $(\gamma_1, \gamma_2, \gamma_3)$;
Precondition 3: $\begin{pmatrix} \beta_3 & \gamma_3 \\ \gamma_4 & 0 \end{pmatrix} \neq \begin{pmatrix} 0 & 0 \\ 0 & 0 \end{pmatrix}$.

In Proposition 3, we show that the construction is susceptible to an efficient (quantum) attack if any one of the three preconditions are violated.

Proposition 3. *Preconditions 1, 2, and 3 above are necessary for F_{A,f_1,f_2,f_3} to be a quantum secure PRF.*

Proof. First consider Precondition 1. Our analysis is divided into two cases.

- If $\alpha_1\gamma_2 = \alpha_2\gamma_1$, then we can construct a collision attack on F using a similar argument as used in CASE 2 for two-call constructions.
- Otherwise, the function $(x_1, x_2) \mapsto (\alpha_1 x_1 \oplus \alpha_2 x_2, \gamma_1 x_1 \oplus \gamma_2 x_2)$ is a bijection. Moreover, there exists $c \neq 0$ such that, $(\alpha_1, \alpha_2) = (c\beta_1, c\beta_2)$. Let $u_3'(x_1, x_2) = \gamma_1 x_1 \oplus \gamma_2 x_2$. Then we can rewrite $F(x_1, x_2)$ as $\delta_3 f_1(u_1) \oplus \delta_4 f_2(cu_1 \oplus \beta_3 f_1(u_1)) \oplus f_3(u_3' \oplus \gamma_3 f_1(u_1) \oplus \gamma_4 f_2(cu_1 \oplus \beta_3 f_1(u_1)))$.

We define $F_1, F_2 : \{0,1\}^n \to \{0,1\}^n$ by

$$F_1(u_1) = \delta_3 f_1(u_1) \oplus \delta_4 f_2(cu_1 \oplus \beta_3 f_1(u_1)),$$
$$F_2(u_1) = \gamma_3 f_1(u_1) \oplus \gamma_4 f_2(cu_1 \oplus \beta_3 f_1(u_1)).$$

This reduces $F(x_1, x_2)$ to $F_1(x_1) \oplus f_3(x_2 \oplus F_2(x_1))$, which, as we show in Proposition 2, is susceptible to period finding, and hence distinguishable in polynomial number of queries using Theorem 1.

Next, we take Precondition 2. Without loss of generality, assume that Precondition 1 holds, otherwise a similar attack will work in this case as well (irrespective of whether $\gamma_4 = 0$ or not). First, consider the case when (α_1, α_2) and (γ_1, γ_2) are dependent. Then there exists $c \neq 0$ such that $(c\alpha_1, c\alpha_2) = (\gamma_1, \gamma_2)$. Let $u_2' = \beta_1 x_1 \oplus \beta_2 x_2$, then we can rewrite $F(x_1, x_2)$ as

$$\delta_3 f_1(u_1) \oplus \delta_4 f_2(u_2' \oplus \beta_3 f_1(u_1)) \oplus f_3(cu_1 \oplus \gamma_3 f_1(u_1)).$$

We define $F_1, F_2 : \{0,1\}^n \to \{0,1\}^n$ as

$$F_1(u_1) = \delta_3 f_1(u_1) \oplus f_3(cu_1 \oplus \gamma_3 f_1(u_1)), \qquad F_2(u_1) = \beta_3 f_1(u_1).$$

This reduces $F(x_1, x_2)$ to $F_1(u_1) \oplus \delta_3 f_2(u_2' \oplus F_2(u_1))$, which is susceptible to period finding (using Proposition 2 and Theorem 1). For the case when $(\beta_1, \beta_2, \beta_3)$ and $(\gamma_1, \gamma_2, \gamma_3)$ are dependent, we can argue similarly that the resulting construction is susceptible to period finding.

Finally, we consider Precondition 3. In this case, the adversary can deduce and to some extent manipulate u_1, u_2, u_3 (since he knows the parameters). More precisely, we can rewrite $F(x_1, x_2)$ as $\delta_3 f_1(\alpha_1 x_1 \oplus \alpha_2 x_2) \oplus \delta_4 f_2(\beta_1 x_1 \oplus \beta_2 x_2) \oplus \delta_5 f_3(\gamma_1 x_1 \oplus \gamma_2 x_2)$. Using Proposition 1, we can find four queries whose outputs sum to 0. This gives a simple classical distinguisher. $\qquad\square$

Using our simplifications and preconditions, we can rewrite the three call system given in (5) as

$$\begin{pmatrix} \alpha_1 & \alpha_2 & 0 & 0 & 0 \\ \beta_1 & \beta_2 & \beta_3 & 0 & 0 \\ \gamma_1 & \gamma_2 & \gamma_3 & \gamma_4 & 0 \\ 0 & 0 & \delta_3 & \delta_4 & 1 \end{pmatrix} \begin{pmatrix} x_1 \\ x_2 \\ v_1 \\ v_2 \\ v_3 \end{pmatrix} = \begin{pmatrix} u_1 \\ u_2 \\ u_3 \\ u_4 \end{pmatrix} \tag{6}$$

In the following discussion, we divide our analysis into two cases:

CASE 1: $\gamma_4 = 0$. Without loss of generality assume $\delta_4 = 1$, and consider the three sub cases below:

(a) $\beta_3 = 0$. By Precondition 3, we must have $\gamma_3 \neq 0$. For simplicity assume $\gamma_3 = 1$. Moreover, notice that Precondition 1 implies that without loss of generality,

$$\begin{pmatrix} \alpha_1 & \alpha_2 \\ \beta_1 & \beta_2 \end{pmatrix} = \begin{pmatrix} 1 & 0 \\ 0 & 1 \end{pmatrix}.$$

Next, note that $\gamma_2 \neq 0$, otherwise this violates Precondition 2. Therefore, we are left with the general matrix

$$\begin{pmatrix} 1 & 0 & 0 & 0 & 0 \\ 0 & 1 & 0 & 0 & 0 \\ \gamma_1 & \gamma_2 & 1 & 0 & 0 \\ 0 & 0 & \delta_3 & 1 & 1 \end{pmatrix}, \tag{7}$$

where the blue elements indicate strictly non-zero values. (We stick to this colour code in the rest of this section.) We further simplify the above matrix by setting $\gamma_1 = \delta_3 = 0$, and $\gamma_2 = 1$. (This simplification stems from the point of view of efficiency: a simple XOR is always preferable to a finite field multiplication followed by an XOR.) Finally, we arrive at the following matrix:

$$A_{\mathsf{LRQ}} := \begin{pmatrix} 1 & 0 & 0 & 0 & 0 \\ 0 & 1 & 0 & 0 & 0 \\ 0 & 1 & 1 & 0 & 0 \\ 0 & 0 & 0 & 1 & 1 \end{pmatrix}, \tag{8}$$

and the resulting construction is defined as

$$\mathsf{LRQ}(x_1, x_2) := f_2(x_2) \oplus f_3(x_2 \oplus f_1(x_1)). \tag{9}$$

(b) $\gamma_3 = 0$. By Precondition 3, we must have $\beta_3 \neq 0$. For simplicity, assume $\beta_3 = 1$. Moreover, notice that Precondition 2 implies that without loss of generality,

$$\begin{pmatrix} \alpha_1 & \alpha_2 \\ \gamma_1 & \gamma_2 \end{pmatrix} = \begin{pmatrix} 1 & 0 \\ 0 & 1 \end{pmatrix}.$$

Next , note that we must have $\beta_2 \neq 0$, otherwise this violates Precondition 1. Therefore, we are left with the general matrix

$$\begin{pmatrix} 1 & 0 & 0 & 0 & 0 \\ \beta_1 & \beta_2 & 1 & 0 & 0 \\ 0 & 1 & 0 & 0 & 0 \\ 0 & 0 & \delta_3 & 1 & 1 \end{pmatrix}. \tag{10}$$

On further simplification by setting $\beta_1 = \delta_3 = 0$ and $\beta_2 = 1$, we observe that this corresponds to the same construction as (8) up to a relabelling of functions.

(c) $\beta_3, \gamma_3 \neq 0$. Without loss of generality assume that $\beta_3 = 1$. Then, we are left with the general matrix

$$\begin{pmatrix} \alpha_1 & \alpha_2 & 0 & 0 & 0 \\ \beta_1 & \beta_2 & 1 & 0 & 0 \\ \gamma_1 & \gamma_2 & \gamma_3 & 0 & 0 \\ 0 & 0 & \delta_3 & 1 & 1 \end{pmatrix}, \tag{11}$$

where the red submatrix represents the fact that it satisfies Precondition 1 and 2, i.e., we must have (α_1, α_2) independent of (β_1, β_2) and (γ_1, γ_2), and $(\beta_1, \beta_2, 1)$ independent of $(\gamma_1, \gamma_2, \gamma_3)$. Using similar simplifying arguments as before, and preserving isomorphism up to a relabelling of functions, we arrive at the following interesting matrices:

$$A_{\mathsf{CSUMQ}} := \begin{pmatrix} 1 & 0 & 0 & 0 & 0 \\ 0 & 1 & 1 & 0 & 0 \\ 1 & 1 & 1 & 0 & 0 \\ 0 & 0 & 0 & 1 & 1 \end{pmatrix}, \quad A_{\mathsf{LMQ}} := \begin{pmatrix} 1 & 1 & 0 & 0 & 0 \\ 0 & 1 & 1 & 0 & 0 \\ 1 & 0 & 1 & 0 & 0 \\ 0 & 0 & 0 & 1 & 1 \end{pmatrix}. \tag{12}$$

The resulting constructions are defined as

$$\mathsf{CSUMQ}(x_1, x_2) := f_2(x_2 \oplus f_1(x_1)) \oplus f_3(x_2 \oplus x_1 \oplus f_1(x_1)), \qquad (13)$$
$$\mathsf{LMQ}(x_1, x_2) := f_2(x_2 \oplus f_1(x_1 \oplus x_2)) \oplus f_3(x_1 \oplus f_1(x_1 \oplus x_2)). \quad (14)$$

CASE 2: $\gamma_4 \neq 0$. Without loss of generality, assume that $\gamma_4 = 1$. Consider the following three sub-cases:

(a) $\beta_3 = \gamma_3 = 0$. Then, using Precondition 1, we are left with the general matrix

$$\begin{pmatrix} 1 & 0 & 0 & 0 & 0 \\ 0 & 1 & 0 & 0 & 0 \\ \gamma_1 & \gamma_2 & 0 & 1 & 0 \\ 0 & 0 & \delta_3 & \delta_4 & 1 \end{pmatrix}. \qquad (15)$$

The condition $\gamma_1 \neq 0$ can be easily argued as follows: Suppose, $\gamma_1 = 0$. Then, using Proposition 1, one can find four queries such that the outputs sum to 0, resulting in a classical distinguishing attack. Similarly, $\delta_3 \neq 0$, since each column must have one non-zero entry. Further, by setting $\gamma_2 = \delta_4 = 0$ and $\gamma_1 = \delta_3 = 1$, we arrive at the same construction as in (8) up to a relabelling of functions and input variables.

(b) $\beta_3 = 0$ and $\gamma_3 \neq 0$. Then, using Precondition 1, we are left with the general matrix

$$\begin{pmatrix} 1 & 0 & 0 & 0 & 0 \\ 0 & 1 & 0 & 0 & 0 \\ \gamma_1 & \gamma_2 & \gamma_3 & 1 & 0 \\ 0 & 0 & \delta_3 & \delta_4 & 1 \end{pmatrix}, \qquad (16)$$

By setting $\gamma_1 = \gamma_2 = \delta_3 = \delta_4 = 0$ and $\gamma_3 = 1$, we arrive at the following matrix:

$$A_{\mathsf{LRWQ}} := \begin{pmatrix} 1 & 0 & 0 & 0 & 0 \\ 0 & 1 & 0 & 0 & 0 \\ 0 & 0 & 1 & 1 & 0 \\ 0 & 0 & 0 & 0 & 1 \end{pmatrix}, \qquad (17)$$

which corresponds to the LRWQ construction [17] by Hosoyamada and Iwata, defined as

$$\mathsf{LRWQ}(x_1, x_2) := f_3\left(f_1(x_1) \oplus f_2(x_2)\right). \qquad (18)$$

(c) $\gamma_3 = 0$ and $\beta_3 \neq 0$. Without loss of generality, we assume that $\beta_3 = 1$. Then, using Precondition 1, we are left with the general matrix

$$\begin{pmatrix} 1 & 0 & 0 & 0 & 0 \\ 0 & 1 & 1 & 0 & 0 \\ \gamma_1 & \gamma_2 & 0 & 1 & 0 \\ 0 & 0 & \delta_3 & \delta_4 & 1 \end{pmatrix}, \qquad (19)$$

where red elements indicate that they cannot all be 0. This can be easily argued by looking at the resulting construction. Suppose, $\gamma_1 = \gamma_2 =$

0. Then, the second and third calls can be clubbed together (since the output of the second call is directly fed into the third call), resulting in a reduction to an equivalent two-call construction, which is already shown to be insecure. Now, using the simplification steps, we get the following two matrices:

$$A_{\mathsf{EDMQ}} := \begin{pmatrix} 1 & 0 & 0 & 0 & 0 \\ 0 & 1 & 1 & 0 & 0 \\ 1 & 0 & 0 & 1 & 0 \\ 0 & 0 & 0 & 0 & 1 \end{pmatrix}, \qquad A_{\mathsf{TNT}} := \begin{pmatrix} 1 & 0 & 0 & 0 & 0 \\ 0 & 1 & 1 & 0 & 0 \\ 0 & 1 & 0 & 1 & 0 \\ 0 & 0 & 0 & 0 & 1 \end{pmatrix}, \qquad (20)$$

where the second matrix, i.e., A_{TNT} corresponds to the TNT construction [1] by Bao et al. The corresponding constructions are defined as follows:

$$\mathsf{EDMQ}(x_1, x_2) := f_3(x_1 \oplus f_2(x_2 \oplus f_1(x_1))), \qquad (21)$$

$$\mathsf{TNT}(x_1, x_2) := f_3(x_2 \oplus f_2(x_2 \oplus f_1(x_1))). \qquad (22)$$

(d) $\beta_3, \gamma_3 \neq 0$. In this case, using Precondition 1, we can have the general matrix

$$\begin{pmatrix} 1 & 0 & 0 & 0 & 0 \\ 0 & 1 & \beta_3 & 0 & 0 \\ \gamma_1 & \gamma_2 & \gamma_3 & 1 & 0 \\ 0 & 0 & \delta_3 & \delta_4 & 1 \end{pmatrix}. \qquad (23)$$

Further, by setting $\gamma_1 = \gamma_2 = \delta_3 = \delta_4 = 0$, and $\beta_3 = \gamma_3 = 1$, we get

$$A_{\mathsf{EDMDQ}} := \begin{pmatrix} 1 & 0 & 0 & 0 & 0 \\ 0 & 1 & 1 & 0 & 0 \\ 0 & 0 & 1 & 1 & 0 \\ 0 & 0 & 0 & 0 & 1 \end{pmatrix}, \qquad (24)$$

and the corresponding construction is defined as

$$\mathsf{EDMDQ}(x_1, x_2) := f_3(f_1(x_1) \oplus f_2(x_2 \oplus f_1(x_1))). \qquad (25)$$

A Summary of Interesting Candidates. In Table 1, we summarize the definitions and special features of the seven candidate PRF constructions. Three of the seven candidates—LRQ, LRWQ [17], and TNT [1]—are special as they can act as a tweakable permutation when the underlying primitives are permutations. Furthermore, they are also among the most favorable candidates in terms of desirable implementation features like XOR counts, parallelizability, and state size. So, we concentrate on proving the security of these three candidates. In this paper, we mainly consider the PRF security of these constructions. However, the TPRP[1] security can be easily recovered using a well-known switching result [14,15] due to Hosoyamada and Iwata.[2] See Sect. 5.4 for details.

---

[1] Indistinguishability from a uniform random tweakable permutation.

[2] We remark that the TPRP security would only hold against unidirectional quantum distinguishers.

Table 1. Summary of the possibly secure PRF candidates with minimum number of random function calls.

Candidate	Definition	Memory	XORs	Invertible	Parallel
LRQ	$f_2(x_2) \oplus f_3(x_2 \oplus f_1(x_1))$	$2n$	2	✓	✓
CSUMQ	$f_2(x_2 \oplus f_1(x_1)) \oplus f_3(x_2 \oplus x_1 \oplus f_1(x_1))$	$2n$	3	✗	✓
LMQ	$f_2(x_2 \oplus f_1(x_1 \oplus x_2)) \oplus f_3(x_1 \oplus f_1(x_1 \oplus x_2))$	$2n$	4	✗	✓
LRWQ [17]	$f_3(f_1(x_1) \oplus f_2(x_2))$	$2n$	1	✓	✓
EDMQ	$f_3(x_1 \oplus f_2(x_2 \oplus f_1(x_1)))$	n	2	✗	✗
TNT [1]	$f_3(x_2 \oplus f_2(x_2 \oplus f_1(x_1)))$	n	2	✓	✗
EDMDQ	$f_3(f_1(x_1) \oplus f_2(x_2 \oplus f_1(x_1)))$	n	2	✗	✗

4   Quantum Proof Framework

In this section we develop the rigorous formalism of our quantum proof framework. We begin with a slightly simplified version of the Chung et al. framework [11], extend it to two-domain systems, and establish the Two-Domain Distance Lemma, the core technical tool we use in the proofs of the next section. (For a more detailed description of the underlying linear-algebraic framework, see the full version [4] of this paper.)

Let $\mathcal{Y}$ denote $\{0,1\}^n$. Let $B_C := \{|y\rangle \mid y \in \mathcal{Y}\}$ denote the computational basis of the n-qubit space $\mathbb{C}^{2^n}$. For each $y \in \mathcal{Y}$ let $\widehat{y}$ denote the group homomorphism $z \mapsto (-1)^{y \cdot z}$ from $\mathcal{Y}$ to $\{1, -1\}$ (the latter a group under multiplication). Then $\widehat{\mathcal{Y}} := \{\widehat{y} \mid y \in \mathcal{Y}\}$ forms a group under the group operation $\widehat{y} + \widehat{z} := \widehat{y \oplus z}$ (where $\oplus$ denote bitwise XOR, the group operation in $\mathcal{Y}$); we call $\widehat{\mathcal{Y}}$ the *dual group* of $\mathcal{Y}$. (The definition of the group operation for $\widehat{\mathcal{Y}}$ also implies that $y \mapsto \widehat{y}$ is a group isomorphism from $\mathcal{Y}$ to $\widehat{\mathcal{Y}}$.)

For each $\widehat{y} \in \widehat{\mathcal{Y}}$ define

$$|\widehat{y}\rangle := \frac{1}{2^{n/2}} \sum_{z \in \mathcal{Y}} \widehat{y}(z) |z\rangle = \frac{1}{2^{n/2}} \sum_{z \in \mathcal{Y}} (-1)^{y \cdot z} |z\rangle.$$

Then $B_F := \{|\widehat{y}\rangle \mid \widehat{y} \in \widehat{\mathcal{Y}}\}$ also constitutes a basis of $\mathbb{C}^{2^n}$; we call it the *Fourier basis*. The reverse basis transformation from the Fourier basis to the computational basis is given by

$$|y\rangle := \frac{1}{2^{n/2}} \sum_{\widehat{z} \in \widehat{\mathcal{Y}}} \widehat{z}(y) |\widehat{z}\rangle = \frac{1}{2^{n/2}} \sum_{\widehat{z} \in \widehat{\mathcal{Y}}} (-1)^{z \cdot y} |\widehat{z}\rangle.$$

Next, let $\mathcal{Z}$ denote the set $\mathcal{Y} \cup \{\bot\}$ for a special symbol $\bot$; similarly $\widehat{\mathcal{Z}}$ will denote $\widehat{\mathcal{Y}} \cup \{\bot\}$. We also choose a corresponding norm-1 vector $|\bot\rangle$ orthogonal to $\mathbb{C}^{2^n}$, so that the span of both $\overline{B_C} := \{|y\rangle \mid y \in \mathcal{Z}\}$ and $\overline{B_F} := \{|\widehat{y}\rangle \mid \widehat{y} \in \widehat{\mathcal{Z}}\}$ is $\mathbb{C}^{2^n+1}$; we'll call $\overline{B_C}$ and $\overline{B_F}$ the computational basis and Fourier basis respectively of the extended space $\mathbb{C}^{2^n+1}$.

Functions and Databases. Let $\mathcal{X}$ denote $\{0,1\}^m$ for some arbitrary m, and let $\mathcal{F}$ denote the set of m-bit-to-n-bit classical functions $f : \mathcal{X} \longrightarrow \mathcal{Y}$. The *quantum truth table* of f is defined as

$$|f\rangle := \bigotimes_{x \in \mathcal{X}} |x\rangle \, |f(x)\rangle .$$

Let $\widehat{\mathcal{F}}$ denote the set of *Fourier* functions $\widehat{f} : \mathcal{X} \longrightarrow \widehat{\mathcal{Y}}$. The quantum truth table of $\widehat{f}$ is defined similarly as

$$|\widehat{f}\rangle := \bigotimes_{x \in \mathcal{X}} |x\rangle \, |\widehat{f}(x)\rangle .$$

For a subset $\mathcal{S} \subseteq \mathcal{X}$, a function $f : \mathcal{S} \longrightarrow \mathcal{Y}$ will be called a *partial function* from $\mathcal{X}$ to $\mathcal{Y}$. A partial function f can be extended to a function $d_f : \mathcal{X} \longrightarrow \mathcal{Z}$ by defining $d_f(y) = \bot$ for all $y \in \mathcal{X} \setminus \mathcal{S}$. We call d_f the *database* representing f, with $\bot$ denoting the cells where f is not defined. (When f is a full function, d_f coincides with f.) The database will also be represented as a quantum truth table

$$|d_f\rangle := \bigotimes_{x \in \mathcal{X}} |x\rangle \, |d_f(x)\rangle .$$

Similarly we define partial Fourier functions $\widehat{f} : \mathcal{S} \longrightarrow \widehat{\mathcal{Y}}$, databases $d_{\widehat{f}} : \mathcal{X} \longrightarrow \widehat{\mathcal{Z}}$ representing partial Fourier functions, and their quantum truth tables $|d_{\widehat{f}}\rangle$. When f and $\widehat{f}$ are clear from context, we'll find it convenient to drop the subscripts and write d_f and $d_{\widehat{f}}$ simply as d and $\widehat{d}$ respectively. We'll write $\mathcal{D}$ (resp. $\widehat{\mathcal{D}}$) to denote the set of all databases $d : \mathcal{X} \longrightarrow \mathcal{Z}$ (resp. all Fourier databases $\widehat{d} : \mathcal{X} \longrightarrow \widehat{\mathcal{Z}}$). When convenient we will treat a database d as a relation on $\mathcal{X} \times \mathcal{Y}$ and write $(x,y) \in \mathcal{D}$ to denote $d(x) = y$; $|d|$ will then denote the size of this relation, i.e., the size of $\{x \in \mathcal{X} \mid d(x) \in \mathcal{Y}\}$.

Our notation allows us to define an easy correspondence between classical functions and Fourier functions: for any function $f \in \mathcal{F}$, let $\widehat{f} \in \widehat{\mathcal{F}}$ be defined as the map $x \mapsto \widehat{f(x)}$. Then we have

$$|\widehat{f}\rangle = \frac{1}{2^{n2^m/2}} \sum_{g \in \mathcal{F}} (-1)^{f \cdot g} |g\rangle , \tag{26}$$

where $f \cdot g$ is defined as $\sum_{x \in \mathcal{X}} f(x) \cdot g(x)$. (For a proof of (26) see the full version [4] of this paper.) Thus, $\{|f\rangle \mid f \in \mathcal{F}\}$ and $\{|\widehat{f}\rangle \mid \widehat{f} \in \widehat{\mathcal{F}}\}$ span the same space (isomorphic to $\mathbb{C}^{2^{n2^m}}$). Similarly we can show that $\{|d\rangle \mid d \in \mathcal{D}\}$ and $\{|\widehat{d}\rangle \mid \widehat{d} \in \widehat{\mathcal{D}}\}$ span the same space isomorphic to $\mathbb{C}^{(2^n+1)^{2^m}}$; we call this space the *database space* $\mathbb{D}$. Letting $\mathbf{0}$ denote the constant 0^n function and observing that $\mathbf{0} \cdot g = 0$ for any $g \in \mathcal{F}$, we have

$$|\widehat{\mathbf{0}}\rangle = \frac{1}{2^{n2^m/2}} \sum_{g \in \mathcal{F}} |g\rangle ,$$

the uniform superposition over all functions in $\mathcal{F}$.

The Fourier Oracle. Given a truth-table representation $|f\rangle$ of a function $f \in \mathcal{F}$, the standard oracle acts on the adversary registers $|x\rangle |y\rangle$ and the truth-table registers $|f\rangle$ as

$$\mathsf{stO} |x\rangle |y\rangle \otimes |f\rangle = |x\rangle |y \oplus f(x)\rangle \otimes |f\rangle.$$

If we first put the adversary's response register and the truth-table register in the Fourier basis first, we have

$$\mathsf{stO} |x\rangle |\widehat{y}\rangle \otimes |\widehat{f}\rangle = |x\rangle |\widehat{y}\rangle \otimes |\widehat{f} + \widehat{\delta}_{xy}\rangle, \tag{27}$$

where δ_{xy} is the function in $\mathcal{F}$ defined as

$$\delta_{xy}(z) = y, \qquad \text{when } z = x,$$
$$= 0, \qquad \text{otherwise},$$

and the operations $\oplus$ in $\mathcal{F}$ and $+$ in $\widehat{\mathcal{F}}$ are defined point-wise. (For a proof of (27) see the full version [4] of this paper.) We define the operator $\mathsf{O}_{x\widehat{y}}$ on the truth-table register as

$$\mathsf{O}_{x\widehat{y}} |\widehat{f}\rangle := |\widehat{f} + \widehat{\delta}_{xy}\rangle.$$

Then we can write

$$\mathsf{stO} |x\rangle |\widehat{y}\rangle \otimes |\widehat{f}\rangle = |x\rangle |\widehat{y}\rangle \otimes \mathsf{O}_{x\widehat{y}} |\widehat{f}\rangle.$$

The Compressed Oracle. The *cell compression* unitary comp_0 on $\mathbb{C}^{2^n+1}$ is defined on the basis $\overline{B_F}$ as

$$\mathsf{comp}_0 := |\bot\rangle\langle\widehat{0}| + |\widehat{0}\rangle\langle\bot| + \sum_{\widehat{y} \in \widehat{\mathcal{Y}} \setminus \{\widehat{0}\}} |\widehat{y}\rangle\langle\widehat{y}|.$$

Then, for any $|\widehat{y}\rangle \in \overline{B_F}$, we have

$$\mathsf{comp}_0 |\widehat{y}\rangle = |\bot\rangle, \qquad\qquad \text{when } \widehat{y} = \widehat{0},$$
$$= |\widehat{0}\rangle, \qquad\qquad \text{when } \widehat{y} = \bot,$$
$$= |\widehat{y}\rangle, \qquad\qquad \text{otherwise}.$$

For any r let I_r denote the identity operation over r qubits. Then the *database compression* unitary comp on $\mathbb{D}$ is defined as

$$\mathsf{comp} := \bigotimes_{\mathcal{X}} (I_m \otimes \mathsf{comp}_0).$$

The *compressed oracle* cO is defined jointly on the adversary's registers and the oracle's database registers as

$$\mathsf{cO} := (I_{m+n} \otimes \mathsf{comp}) \circ \mathsf{stO} \circ (I_{m+n} \otimes \mathsf{comp}).$$

For a database $\widehat{d}$ we have

$$\mathsf{cO} |x\rangle |\widehat{y}\rangle \otimes |\widehat{d}\rangle = |x\rangle |\widehat{y}\rangle \otimes \mathsf{cO}_{x\widehat{y}} |\widehat{d}\rangle,$$

where $\mathsf{cO}_{x\widehat{y}} := \mathsf{comp} \circ \mathsf{O}_{x\widehat{y}} \circ \mathsf{comp}$.

Domain-Restricted Databases. For a subset $\tilde{\mathcal{X}}$ of $\mathcal{X}$ we will write $\mathcal{D}|_{\tilde{\mathcal{X}}}$ to denote the set of databases restricted to $\tilde{\mathcal{X}}$, defined equivalently as $\{d|_{\tilde{\mathcal{X}}} \mid d \in \mathcal{D}\}$ or the set of databases $d : \tilde{\mathcal{X}} \longrightarrow \mathcal{Z}$. While this is technically equivalent to a partial function from $\mathcal{X}$ to $\mathcal{Z}$, we emphasise the distinction that in the case of a domain-restricted database, we do not expect it to be queried on any $x \notin \tilde{\mathcal{X}}$.

Since $\mathcal{D}$ is a basis of the database space $\mathbb{D}$, a domain-restricted database space will span a subspace of $\mathbb{D}$ isomorphic to $\mathbb{C}^{(2^n+1)^{|\tilde{\mathcal{X}}|}}$; usually we won't need to refer to this space explicitly. We continue to represent elements of $\tilde{\mathcal{X}}$ as m-bit numbers.

Transition Capacity. For a domain-restricted database-set $\mathcal{D}|_{\tilde{\mathcal{X}}}$, a subset $\mathcal{P} \subseteq \mathcal{D}|_{\tilde{\mathcal{X}}}$ will be called a *database property* on $\mathcal{D}|_{\tilde{\mathcal{X}}}$. We also define the projection

$$\Pi_{\mathcal{P}} := \sum_{d \in \mathcal{P}} |d\rangle\langle d|.$$

For a database $d \in \mathcal{D}|_{\tilde{\mathcal{X}}}$ and an $x \in \tilde{\mathcal{X}}$ define

$$d|^x := \{d' \in \mathcal{D}|_{\tilde{\mathcal{X}}} \mid d'(x') = d(x') \forall x' \in \tilde{\mathcal{X}} \setminus \{x\}\}.$$

In other words, $d|^x$ is the set of databases in $\mathcal{D}|_{\tilde{\mathcal{X}}}$ which are identical to d except (possibly) at x. (Note that since d (resp. x) is also in $\mathcal{D}$ (resp. $\mathcal{X}$), $d|^x$ is only well-defined when we specify $\mathcal{D}|_{\tilde{\mathcal{X}}}$ as well; however, since $\mathcal{D}|_{\tilde{\mathcal{X}}}$ will usually be clear from the context, for notational convenience we leave the dependence of $d|^x$ on $\mathcal{D}|_{\tilde{\mathcal{X}}}$ implicit.)

For two properties $\mathcal{P}$ and $\mathcal{P}'$, the *transition capacity* from $\mathcal{P}$ to $\mathcal{P}'$ is defined as

$$[\![\mathcal{P} \hookrightarrow \mathcal{P}']\!] := \max_{x \in \tilde{\mathcal{X}}, \hat{y} \in \hat{\mathcal{Y}}, d \in \mathcal{D}|_{\tilde{\mathcal{X}}}} \left\| \Pi_{\mathcal{P}' \cap d|^x} \circ \mathrm{cO}_{x\hat{y}} \circ \Pi_{\mathcal{P} \cap d|^x} \right\|.$$

The transition capacity $[\![\mathcal{P} \hookrightarrow \mathcal{P}']\!]$ is roughly a measure of an upper bound for how likely it can be that a database in $\mathcal{P}$ will transition into a database in $\mathcal{P}'$ after a single query to cO.

For any property $\mathcal{P}$ let $\bar{\Pi}_{\mathcal{P}} := I_{m+n} \otimes \Pi_{\mathcal{P}}$. We adapt the following useful proposition from an intermediate result in [11, Proof of Lemma 5.6]. (For a proof see the full version [4] of this paper.)

Proposition 4. *For any pair of properties $\mathcal{P}$ and $\mathcal{P}'$,*

$$[\![\mathcal{P} \hookrightarrow \mathcal{P}']\!] \geq \left\| \bar{\Pi}_{\mathcal{P}'} \circ \mathrm{cO} \circ \bar{\Pi}_{\mathcal{P}} \right\|.$$

For a property $\mathcal{P} \subseteq \mathcal{D}|_{\tilde{\mathcal{X}}}$, let $\mathcal{P}^c$ denote its negation, i.e., $\mathcal{D}|_{\tilde{\mathcal{X}}} \setminus \mathcal{P}$. Then we have the following lemma, adapted from [11, Theorem 5.17]. (For a proof see the full version [4] of this paper.)

Lemma 1 (Transition Capacity Bound). *Let $\mathcal{P}, \mathcal{P}'$ be properties on $\mathcal{D}|_{\widetilde{\mathcal{X}}}$ such that for every $x \in \widetilde{\mathcal{X}}$ and $d \in \mathcal{D}|_{\widetilde{\mathcal{X}}}$, we can find a set $\mathcal{S}_{x,d}^{\mathcal{P}^c \hookrightarrow \mathcal{P}'} \subseteq \mathcal{Y}$ satisfying*

$$\mathcal{P}' \cap d|^{\mathring{x}} \subseteq \{d' \in d|^x \mid d'(x) \in \mathcal{S}_{x,d}^{\mathcal{P}^c \hookrightarrow \mathcal{P}'}\} \subseteq \mathcal{P} \cap d|^x. \tag{28}$$

In other words, for any database $d' \in d|^x$,

$$d' \in \mathcal{P}' \implies d'(x) \in \mathcal{S}_{x,d}^{\mathcal{P}^c \hookrightarrow \mathcal{P}'} \implies d' \in \mathcal{P}.$$

Then we have

$$[\![\mathcal{P}^c \hookrightarrow \mathcal{P}']\!] \leq \max_{x \in \widetilde{\mathcal{X}}, d \in \mathcal{D}|_{\widetilde{\mathcal{X}}}} \sqrt{\frac{10|\mathcal{S}_{x,d}^{\mathcal{P}^c \hookrightarrow \mathcal{P}'}|}{2^n}}.$$

Size-Restricted Properties. For a domain-restricted database-set $\mathcal{D}|_{\widetilde{\mathcal{X}}}$, a property $\mathcal{P} \subseteq \mathcal{D}|_{\widetilde{\mathcal{X}}}$, and some $i \leq |\widetilde{\mathcal{X}}|$, we define

$$\mathcal{P}_{[\leq i]} := \{d \in \mathcal{P} \mid |d| \leq i\}.$$

Then the transition capacity $[\![\mathcal{P}_{[\leq i-1]}^c \hookrightarrow \mathcal{P}_{[\leq i]}]\!]$ is a measure of the maximum probability of a database outside $\mathcal{P}$ with at most $i - 1$ entries changing to a database in $\mathcal{P}$ after a single application $\mathrm{cO}_{x\hat{y}}$. (Note that $\mathcal{P}_{[\leq i-1]}^c$ denotes the size-restriction of $\mathcal{P}^c$, and not the complement of $\mathcal{P}_{[\leq i-1]}$.)

Let $\perp := \{d_\perp\}$ denote the *empty* property (where $d_\perp$ is the empty database, i.e., the constant-$\perp$ function). Then for $\mathcal{P}$ such that $d_\perp \notin \mathcal{P}$, $\perp = \mathcal{P}_{[\leq 0]}^c$. We define

$$\left(\perp \xrightarrow{q} \mathcal{P}\right) := \sum_{i=1}^{q} [\![\mathcal{P}_{[\leq i-1]}^c \hookrightarrow \mathcal{P}_{[\leq i]}]\!],$$

the *q-query transition bound* from $\perp$ to $\mathcal{P}$. In other words, $\left(\perp \xrightarrow{q} \mathcal{P}\right)$ is a measure of the probability that the empty database changes into a database in $\mathcal{P}$ at *any point* during q successive queries. We point out that this is different from the q-query transition capacity defined in [11], which only considers a transition after *exactly* q queries.

Two-Domain Systems. Fix two domains $\widetilde{\mathcal{X}}_0, \widetilde{\mathcal{X}}_1 \subseteq \mathcal{X}$, and define $\mathcal{D}_0 := \mathcal{D}|_{\widetilde{\mathcal{X}}_0}$ and $\mathcal{D}_1 := \mathcal{D}|_{\widetilde{\mathcal{X}}_1}$. Consider properties $\mathcal{B}_0 \subseteq \mathcal{D}_0 \setminus \perp$ and $\mathcal{B}_1 \subseteq \mathcal{D}_1 \setminus \perp$, and define $\mathcal{G}_0 := \mathcal{D}_0 \setminus \mathcal{B}_0$ and $\mathcal{G}_1 := \mathcal{D}_1 \setminus \mathcal{B}_1$. In addition let $\mathcal{I} \subseteq \mathcal{X}$ be an additional domain called the *input domain,* along with two injective input-preparation maps $p_0 : \mathcal{I} \longrightarrow \widetilde{\mathcal{X}}_0$ and $p_1 : \mathcal{I} \longrightarrow \widetilde{\mathcal{X}}_1$ that cast an input from $\mathcal{I}$ into their respective domains. For either bit b let the oracle cO_b be defined as

$$\mathrm{cO}_b |x\rangle |\hat{y}\rangle \otimes |\widehat{d_b}\rangle = |x\rangle |\hat{y}\rangle \otimes \mathrm{cO}_{p_b(x)\hat{y}} |\widehat{d_b}\rangle,$$

for any $x \in \mathcal{I}$, $\hat{y} \in \hat{\mathcal{Y}}$, and $d_b \in \mathcal{D}_b$. Let $I_{\mathbb{D}}$ denote the identity over $\mathbb{D}$ (which is also the identity over the subspaces of $\mathbb{D}$ spanned by $\mathcal{D}_0$ and $\mathcal{D}_1$), and for any unitary U acting over $m + n$ qubits, define the shorthand $\ddot{U} := U \otimes I_{\mathbb{D}}$. Let $\mathbf{U} = (U_1, \ldots, U_q)$ be a sequence of q unitaries, each acting over $m + n$ qubits. Finally, denoting $|\psi_\perp\rangle := |0\rangle\,|\widehat{0}\rangle \otimes |d_\perp\rangle$, define for each bit b

$$\left|\psi_{q,b}(\mathbf{U})\right\rangle := cO_b \circ \ddot{U}_q \circ cO_b \circ \ldots \circ cO_b \circ \ddot{U}_1\,|\psi_\perp\rangle,$$

the state after q applications of cO_b interleaved with the applications of $U_1, \ldots, U_q$ to the adversary's registers. Let $\mathrm{tr}_{\mathbb{D}}$ denote the partial trace over the database registers, and define for each bit b

$$\rho_b(\mathbf{U}) := \mathrm{tr}_{\mathbb{D}}\left(\,|\psi_{q,b}(\mathbf{U})\rangle\langle\psi_{q,b}(\mathbf{U})|\,\right).$$

Let $\|\cdot\|_T$ denote the trace norm. The central tool of our proof technique will be the following result, adapted from [17, Proposition 3].

Lemma 2 (Two-Domain Distance Lemma). *Suppose we can find a map* $h : \mathcal{G}_0 \longrightarrow \mathcal{G}_1$ *such that the following hold:*

- *h is a bijection from $\mathcal{G}_0$ to $\mathcal{G}_1$ (and hence $|\mathcal{G}_0| = |\mathcal{G}_1|$);*
- *For every $i \in [q-1] \cup \{0\}$, $h|_{\mathcal{G}_{0[\leq i]}}$ is a bijection from $\mathcal{G}_{0[\leq i]}$ to $\mathcal{G}_{1[\leq i]}$ (and hence $|\mathcal{G}_{0[\leq i]}| = |\mathcal{G}_{1[\leq i]}|$);*
- *For every $i \in [q]$, $x \in \mathcal{I}$, $\widehat{y} \in \widehat{\mathcal{Y}}$, $d \in \mathcal{G}_{0[\leq i-1]}$, and $d' \in \mathcal{G}_{0[\leq i]}$,*

$$\left\langle d'\,\middle|\,cO_{p_0(x)\widehat{y}}\,\middle|\,d\right\rangle = \left\langle h(d')\,\middle|\,cO_{p_1(x)\widehat{y}}\,\middle|\,h(d)\right\rangle.$$

Then we have

$$\sup_{\mathbf{U}} \|\rho_0(\mathbf{U}) - \rho_1(\mathbf{U})\|_T \leq \left(\perp \xrightarrow{q} \mathcal{B}_0\right)_0 + \left(\perp \xrightarrow{q} \mathcal{B}_1\right)_1,$$

where the transition bounds $\left(\perp \xrightarrow{q} \cdot\right)_0$ and $\left(\perp \xrightarrow{q} \cdot\right)_1$ are defined for queries to cO_0 and cO_1 respectively.

When the oracle in use is clear from the context, we will drop the subscripts for the transition bounds and simply write both as $\left(\perp \xrightarrow{q} \cdot\right)$. We'll also keep the input-preparation maps implicit when there's no scope for ambiguity.

Proof. Fix $\mathbf{U} = (U_1, \ldots, U_q)$, and let $|\psi_{q,b}\rangle := \left|\psi_{q,b}(\mathbf{U})\right\rangle$ for either bit b. For each $i \in [q]$ define $W_{i,b} := cO_b \circ \ddot{U}_i$. Then we can write

$$|\psi_{q,b}\rangle = W_{q,b} \circ W_{q-1,b} \circ \ldots \circ W_{1,b}\,|\psi_\perp\rangle.$$

Let $W_{i,b}^b := \bar{\Pi}_{\mathcal{B}_{b[\leq i]}} \circ W_{i,b}$ and $W_{i,b}^g := \bar{\Pi}_{\mathcal{G}_{b[\leq i]}} \circ W_{i,b}$. Then we have $W_{i,b} = W_{i,b}^b + W_{i,b}^g$. Further, let $|\psi_{i,b}\rangle := W_{i,b} \circ \ldots \circ W_{1,b}\,|\psi_\perp\rangle$, and $|\psi_{i,b}^g\rangle := W_{i,b}^g \circ \ldots \circ W_{1,b}^g\,|\psi_\perp\rangle$.

Claim. For every $i \in [q]$ and each bit b, $\left\|\,|\psi_{i,b}\rangle - |\psi_{i,b}^g\rangle\,\right\| \leq \left(\perp \xrightarrow{i} \mathcal{B}_b\right)_b$.

Proof (of Claim). We will show this by induction. Fix b. For the base case of $i = 1$, we have

$$\Big\| |\psi_{1,b}\rangle - |\psi_{1,b}^g\rangle \Big\| = \Big\| W_{1,b} |\psi_\perp\rangle - W_{1,b}^g |\psi_\perp\rangle \Big\| = \Big\| W_{1,b}^b |\psi_\perp\rangle \Big\|.$$

Since $d_\perp \in \mathcal{G}_b$, and $\ddot{U}_1$ commutes with $\bar{\Pi}_{\mathcal{G}_{b[\leq 0]}}$, we have

$$
\begin{aligned}
\Big\| W_{1,0}^b |\psi_\perp\rangle \Big\| &= \Big\| \bar{\Pi}_{\mathcal{B}_{b[\leq 1]}} \circ W_{1,0} \circ \bar{\Pi}_{\mathcal{G}_{b[\leq 0]}} |\psi_\perp\rangle \Big\| \\
&= \Big\| \bar{\Pi}_{\mathcal{B}_{b[\leq 1]}} \circ c\mathrm{O}_b \circ \ddot{U}_1 \circ \bar{\Pi}_{\mathcal{G}_{b[\leq 0]}} |\psi_\perp\rangle \Big\| \\
&= \Big\| \bar{\Pi}_{\mathcal{B}_{b[\leq 1]}} \circ c\mathrm{O}_b \circ \bar{\Pi}_{\mathcal{G}_{b[\leq 0]}} \circ \ddot{U}_1 |\psi_\perp\rangle \Big\| \\
&\leq \Big\| \bar{\Pi}_{\mathcal{B}_{b[\leq 1]}} \circ c\mathrm{O}_b \circ \bar{\Pi}_{\mathcal{G}_{b[\leq 0]}} \Big\| \leq [\![\mathcal{G}_{b[\leq 0]} \hookrightarrow \mathcal{B}_{b[\leq 1]}]\!]_b = \left(\perp \overset{1}{\rightsquigarrow} \mathcal{B}_b \right)_b,
\end{aligned}
$$

where the last inequality in the last line follows from Proposition 4. This proves the base case. Our induction hypothesis will be that for some $i \geq 2$,

$$\Big\| |\psi_{i-1,b}\rangle - |\psi_{i-1,b}^g\rangle \Big\| \leq \left(\perp \overset{i-1}{\rightsquigarrow} \mathcal{B}_b \right)_b.$$

Then we have

$$
\begin{aligned}
\Big\| |\psi_{i,b}\rangle - |\psi_{i,b}^g\rangle \Big\| &= \Big\| W_{i,b} |\psi_{i-1,b}\rangle - W_{i,b}^g |\psi_{i-1,b}^g\rangle \Big\| \\
&= \Big\| W_{i,b} |\psi_{i-1,b}\rangle - W_{i,b} |\psi_{i-1,b}^g\rangle + W_{i,b} |\psi_{i-1,b}^g\rangle - W_{i,b}^g |\psi_{i-1,b}^g\rangle \Big\| \\
&= \Big\| W_{i,b}(|\psi_{i-1,b}\rangle - |\psi_{i-1,b}^g\rangle) + (W_{i,b} - W_{i,b}^g) |\psi_{i-1,b}^g\rangle \Big\| \\
&\leq \Big\| W_{i,b}(|\psi_{i-1,b}\rangle - |\psi_{i-1,b}^g\rangle) \Big\| + \Big\| W_{i,b}^b |\psi_{i-1,b}^g\rangle \Big\| \\
&\leq \Big\| |\psi_{i-1,b}\rangle - |\psi_{i-1,b}^g\rangle \Big\| + \Big\| \bar{\Pi}_{\mathcal{B}_{b[\leq i]}} \circ W_{i,b} |\psi_{i-1,b}^g\rangle \Big\|.
\end{aligned}
$$

By definition of $|\psi_{i-1,b}^g\rangle$, it is in the column space of $\bar{\Pi}_{\mathcal{G}_{b[\leq i-1]}}$. Thus, by reasoning as in the base case above, we have

$$\Big\| \bar{\Pi}_{\mathcal{B}_{b[\leq i]}} \circ W_{i,b} |\psi_{i-1,b}^g\rangle \Big\| \leq \Big\| \bar{\Pi}_{\mathcal{B}_{b[\leq i]}} \circ c\mathrm{O}_b \circ \bar{\Pi}_{\mathcal{G}_{b[\leq i-1]}} \Big\| \leq [\![\mathcal{G}_{b[\leq i-1]} \hookrightarrow \mathcal{B}_{b[\leq i]}]\!]_b.$$

Using the above inequality and the induction hypothesis we get

$$
\begin{aligned}
\Big\| |\psi_{i,b}\rangle - |\psi_{i,b}^g\rangle \Big\| &\leq \Big\| |\psi_{i-1,b}\rangle - |\psi_{i-1,b}^g\rangle \Big\| + \Big\| \bar{\Pi}_{\mathcal{B}_{b[\leq i]}} \circ W_{i,b} |\psi_{i-1,b}^g\rangle \Big\| \\
&\leq \left(\perp \overset{i-1}{\rightsquigarrow} \mathcal{B}_b \right)_b + [\![\mathcal{G}_{b[\leq i-1]} \hookrightarrow \mathcal{B}_{b[\leq i]}]\!]_b = \left(\perp \overset{i}{\rightsquigarrow} \mathcal{B}_b \right)_b,
\end{aligned}
$$

thus completing the proof of the claim. $\qquad\square$

We next observe that for any $x \in \mathcal{I}, \hat{y} \in \hat{\mathcal{Y}}$, any $i \in [q]$, and any $d \in \mathcal{G}_{0[\leq i]}$,

$$\langle x, \hat{y}, d | \psi_{i,0}^g \rangle = \langle x, \hat{y}, h(d) | \psi_{i,1}^g \rangle. \tag{29}$$

This can be shown inductively by carefully tracking the coefficients on both sides and using the third condition of the lemma statement. (For a detailed proof see the full version [4] of this paper.) Using this observation we can show that for any $i \in [q]$,

$$\text{tr}_{\mathbb{D}} \left(|\psi_{i,0}^g\rangle\langle\psi_{i,0}^g| \right) = \text{tr}_{\mathbb{D}} \left(|\psi_{i,1}^g\rangle\langle\psi_{i,1}^g| \right). \tag{30}$$

Thus we have

$$\begin{aligned}
\|\rho_0(\mathbf{U}) - \rho_1(\mathbf{U})\|_T &= \|\text{tr}_{\mathbb{D}} \left(|\psi_{q,0}\rangle\langle\psi_{q,0}| \right) - \text{tr}_{\mathbb{D}} \left(|\psi_{q,1}\rangle\langle\psi_{q,1}| \right)\|_T \\
&\leq \|\text{tr}_{\mathbb{D}} \left(|\psi_{q,0}^g\rangle\langle\psi_{q,0}^g| \right) - \text{tr}_{\mathbb{D}} \left(|\psi_{q,1}^g\rangle\langle\psi_{q,1}^g| \right)\|_T \\
&\quad + \||\psi_{q,0}\rangle - |\psi_{q,0}^g\rangle\| + \||\psi_{q,1}\rangle - |\psi_{q,1}^g\rangle\| \tag{31} \\
&\leq \left(\perp \overset{q}{\rightsquigarrow} \mathcal{B}_0 \right)_0 + \left(\perp \overset{q}{\rightsquigarrow} \mathcal{B}_1 \right)_1, \tag{32}
\end{aligned}$$

where (32) follows from (30) and the claim. Since the bound above is free of $\mathbf{U}$, taking supremum over $\mathbf{U}$ completes the proof the lemma. □

5 Post-quantum PRF Security of TNT, LRQ and LRWQ

Equipped with the quantum proof machinery developed in Sect. 4, we now delve into the security proofs for the three PRF candidates, namely, TNT, LRQ, and LRWQ.

5.1 Security of TNT

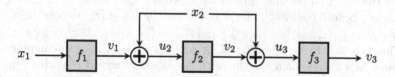

Fig. 2. The TNT construction by Bao et al. [1].

In this section, we analyse the post-quantum security of TNT (see Fig. 2), defined as

$$g_{re}^{TNT}(x_1, x_2) := f_3(f_2(f_1(x_1) \oplus x_2) \oplus x_2)$$

for three n-bit-to-n-bit random functions f_1, f_2, f_3. We want to bound the distinguishing advantage between g_{re}^{TNT} (the *real world*) and a $2n$-bit-to-n-bit random function g_{id} (the *ideal world*).

Theorem 2. *Let $\mathscr{A}$ be a (q, τ)-quantum adversary distinguishing g_{re}^{TNT} from g_{id}. Then there exists $(O(q), \tau_i)$-quantum distinguishers $\mathscr{B}_i$ against f_i, such that*

$$\mathbf{Adv}_{TNT}^{qprf}(\mathscr{A}) \leq \sum_{i=1}^{3} \mathbf{Adv}_{f_i}^{qprf}(\mathscr{B}_i) + 4\sqrt{\frac{10q^4}{2^n}},$$

where $\tau_i \in \tilde{O}(\tau + q^2)$, for all $i \in \{1, 2, 3\}$.

Formulation of the Proof. As a first step, we observe that in order to establish Theorem 2, it is enough to show that when f_1, f_2, f_3 are perfect PRF's,

$$\mathbf{Adv}_{\mathsf{TNT}}^{\mathsf{qprf}}(\mathscr{A}) \leq 4\sqrt{\frac{10q^4}{2^n}}.$$

We will look at a slightly modified representation of the game. Let $\mathcal{X} := \{0,1\}^{3n+2}$, and let $f : \mathcal{X} \longrightarrow \mathcal{Y}$ be a $(3n+2)$-bit-to-n-bit random function, such that for each $x_1, x_2 \in \mathcal{Y}$,

$$f_1(x_1) = f(00\|x_1\|0^{2n}), \qquad\qquad f_2(x_1) = f(01\|x_1\|0^{2n}),$$
$$f_3(x_1) = f(10\|x_1\|0^{2n}), \qquad\qquad g_{\mathsf{id}}(x_1, x_2) = f(11\|x_1\|x_2\|0^n).$$

The distinctness of the first two bits ensures that $f_1, f_2, f_3, g_{\mathsf{id}}$ are all independent. Thus, this game is identical to the one we began with. Next, we replace g_{id} by g_{id}^*, defined as

$$g_{\mathsf{id}}^*(x_1, x_2) := f(11\|x_1\|x_2\|f_2(f_1(x_1) \oplus x_2) \oplus x_2),$$

where we also call f_1 and f_2 in the ideal world. Since $f_2(f_1(x_1) \oplus x_2) \oplus x_2$ is a function of x_1 and x_2, g_{id}^* is still a random function of $x_1\|x_2$, making this game to behave identically with the one we started with.

This setup allows us to use a single database $d_f : \mathcal{X} \longrightarrow \mathcal{Z}$ to keep track of f_1, f_2, f_3, and g_{id}^*; we refer to this database as d_{re} in the real world (tracking f_1, f_2, and f_3) and d_{id} in the ideal world (tracking f_1, f_2, and g_{id}^*). Let $\mathcal{D}_{\mathsf{re}}$ (resp. $\mathcal{D}_{\mathsf{id}}$) be the set of all possible choices for d_{re} (resp. d_{id}).

Let $[x]_1$ denote $00\|x\|0^{2n}$, $[x]_2$ denote $01\|x\|0^{2n}$, and $[x]_3$ denote $10\|x\|0^{2n}$. Define $\widetilde{\mathcal{X}}_{\mathsf{re}} := \{[x]_1, [x]_2, [x]_3 \mid x \in \mathcal{Y}\}$ and $\widetilde{\mathcal{X}}_{\mathsf{id}} := \{[x]_1, [x]_2, 11\|x\|x'\|y \mid x, x', y \in \mathcal{Y}\}$. Then it is easy to see that $\mathcal{D}_{\mathsf{re}} = \mathcal{D}|_{\widetilde{\mathcal{X}}_{\mathsf{re}}}$ and $\mathcal{D}_{\mathsf{id}} = \mathcal{D}|_{\widetilde{\mathcal{X}}_{\mathsf{id}}}$. Thus we can represent our game as a two-domain system, with the labels re and id replacing 0 and 1 from Sect. 4; we extend this convention to the rest of the notation developed in Sect. 4 to avoid defining everything all over again. Then we can say

$$\mathbf{Adv}_{\mathsf{TNT}}^{\mathsf{qprf}}(\mathscr{A}) \leq \sup_{\mathbf{U}} \|\rho_0(\mathbf{U}) - \rho_1(\mathbf{U})\|_T,$$

where there are $3q$ calls to f (and hence to cO) during the game.

Let $\mathcal{B}_{\mathsf{re}}$ be the set of databases d_{re} satisfying the following condition: we can find $x_1, v_1, x_1', v_1', x_2, v_2, x_2', v_2', v_3 \in \mathcal{Y}$ such that

- $([x_1]_1, v_1), ([x_1']_1, v_1'), ([v_1 \oplus x_2]_2, v_2), ([v_1' \oplus x_2']_2, v_2') \in d_{\mathsf{re}};$
- $v_2 \oplus x_2 = v_2' \oplus x_2';$
- $([v_2 \oplus x_2]_3, v_3) \in d_{\mathsf{re}}.$

Next, let $\mathcal{B}_{\mathsf{id}}$ be the set of databases d_{id} satisfying the following condition: we can find $x_1, v_1, x_1', v_1', x_2, v_2, x_2', v_2', v_3 \in \mathcal{Y}$ such that

- $([x_1]_1, v_1), ([x_1']_1, v_1'), ([v_1 \oplus x_2]_2, v_2), ([v_1' \oplus x_2']_2, v_2') \in d_{\mathsf{id}};$
- $v_2 \oplus x_2 = v_2' \oplus x_2';$

– One of $(11\|x_1\|x_2\|(v_2 \oplus x_2), v_3)$ and $(11\|x_1'\|x_2'\|(v_2 \oplus x_2), v_3) \in d_{\mathsf{id}}$.

Let $\mathcal{G}_{\mathsf{re}} := \mathcal{D}_{\mathsf{re}} \setminus \mathcal{B}_{\mathsf{re}}$ and $\mathcal{G}_{\mathsf{id}} := \mathcal{D}_{\mathsf{id}} \setminus \mathcal{B}_{\mathsf{id}}$. Thus the above definitions mean that in both $\mathcal{G}_{\mathsf{re}}$ and $\mathcal{G}_{\mathsf{id}}$, each $u_3 := v_2 \oplus x_2$ is associated with a unique pair (x_1, x_2). Then we can define the bijection $h : \mathcal{G}_{\mathsf{re}} \longrightarrow \mathcal{G}_{\mathsf{id}}$ as follows: for each d_{re} we define $d_{\mathsf{id}} := h(d_{\mathsf{re}})$ such that

– for each $x_1 \in \mathcal{Y}$, $d_{\mathsf{id}}([x_1]_1) = d_{\mathsf{re}}([x_1]_1)$;
– for each $u_2 \in \mathcal{Y}$, $d_{\mathsf{id}}([u_2]_2) = d_{\mathsf{re}}([u_2]_2)$;
– for each $x_1, x_2 \in \mathcal{Y}$ and the associated u_3, $d_{\mathsf{id}}(11\|x_1\|x_2\|u_3) = d_{\mathsf{re}}([u_3]_3)$.

Then h satisfies the conditions of Lemma 2. To complete the proof of Theorem 2, we just need to show that

$$\left(\perp \overset{3q}{\rightsquigarrow} \mathcal{B}_{\mathsf{re}}\right) + \left(\perp \overset{3q}{\rightsquigarrow} \mathcal{B}_{\mathsf{id}}\right) \leq 4\sqrt{\frac{10q^4}{2^n}}.$$

Sequence of Actions. Each query by the adversary to its oracle results in a sequence of three queries to f, one each to f_1, f_2, and one to f_3 in the real world or g_{id}^* in the ideal world, in that order. We view the query response phase as a sequence of $3q$ (possibly duplicate) *actions* and analyze the transition capacity at each action.

ACTION OF f_1: For $i \in \{3k + 1 : 0 \leq k \leq q - 1\}$, we first look at the transition capacity $[\![\mathcal{B}_{\mathsf{re}[\leq i-1]}^c \hookrightarrow \mathcal{B}_{\mathsf{re}[\leq i]}]\!]$. For any d_{re} with $|d_{\mathsf{re}}| \leq i - 1$ and any $x \in \mathcal{Y}$, we have

$$S_{x,d}^{\mathcal{B}_{\mathsf{re}}^c \hookrightarrow \mathcal{B}_{\mathsf{re}}} = \{d_{\mathsf{re}}([u_2]_2) \oplus u_2 \oplus u_3 \mid d_{\mathsf{re}}([u_2]_2) \neq \perp, d_{\mathsf{re}}([u_3]_3) \neq \perp\}.$$

There are at most $\lceil (i - 1)/3 \rceil^2$ choices for the pair (u_2, u_3), so $|S_{x,d}^{\mathcal{B}_{\mathsf{re}}^c \hookrightarrow \mathcal{B}_{\mathsf{re}}}| \leq \lceil (i - 1)/3 \rceil^2 \leq q^2$, and from there using Lemma 1 we have

$$[\![\mathcal{B}_{\mathsf{re}[\leq i-1]}^c \hookrightarrow \mathcal{B}_{\mathsf{re}[\leq i]}]\!] \leq \sqrt{\frac{10q^2}{2^n}}, \qquad \forall i \in \{3k + 1 : 0 \leq k \leq q - 1\}. \tag{33}$$

By the same arguments we can also show that

$$[\![\mathcal{B}_{\mathsf{id}[\leq i-1]}^c \hookrightarrow \mathcal{B}_{\mathsf{id}[\leq i]}]\!] \leq \sqrt{\frac{10q^2}{2^n}}, \qquad \forall i \in \{3k + 1 : 0 \leq k \leq q - 1\}. \tag{34}$$

ACTION OF f_2: Next we look at the transition capacity $[\![\mathcal{B}_{\mathsf{re}[\leq i-1]}^c \hookrightarrow \mathcal{B}_{\mathsf{re}[\leq i]}]\!]$ for $i \in \{3k + 2 : 0 \leq k \leq q - 1\}$. For any d_{re} with $|d_{\mathsf{re}}| \leq i - 1$ and any $x \in \mathcal{Y}$, we have

$$S_{x,d}^{\mathcal{B}_{\mathsf{re}}^c \hookrightarrow \mathcal{B}_{\mathsf{re}}} := \{d_{\mathsf{re}}([x_1]_1) \oplus x \oplus u_3 \mid d_{\mathsf{re}}([x_1]_1) \neq \perp, d_{\mathsf{re}}([u_3]_3) \neq \perp\}.$$

Again, there are at most $\lceil (i-1)/3 \rceil^2$ choices for the pair (x_1, u_3), and arguing as before we have

$$[\mathcal{B}^c_{\mathrm{re}[\leq i-1]} \hookrightarrow \mathcal{B}_{\mathrm{re}[\leq i]}] \leq \sqrt{\frac{10q^2}{2^n}}, \qquad \forall\, i \in \{3k+2 : 0 \leq k \leq q-1\}. \tag{35}$$

By the same arguments we can also show that

$$[\mathcal{B}^c_{\mathrm{id}[\leq i-1]} \hookrightarrow \mathcal{B}_{\mathrm{id}[\leq i]}] \leq \sqrt{\frac{10q^2}{2^n}}, \qquad \forall\, i \in \{3k+2 : 0 \leq k \leq q-1\}. \tag{36}$$

ACTION OF f_3 (RESP. g^*_{id}): Finally, for $i \in \{3k : 1 \leq k \leq q\}$, for any d_{re} with $|d_{\mathrm{re}}| \leq i-1$ (resp. any d_{id} with $|d_{\mathrm{id}}| \leq i-1$) and any $x \in \mathcal{Y}$, since the property $\mathcal{B}_{\mathrm{re}}$ (resp. $\mathcal{B}_{\mathrm{id}}$) does not depend on $d_{\mathrm{re}}([x]_3)$ (resp. $d_{\mathrm{id}}(11\|x_1\|x_2\|x)$), we have $\mathcal{S}^{\mathcal{B}^c_{\mathrm{re}} \hookrightarrow \mathcal{B}_{\mathrm{re}}}_{x,d} = \emptyset$ (resp. $\mathcal{S}^{\mathcal{B}^c_{\mathrm{id}} \hookrightarrow \mathcal{B}_{\mathrm{id}}}_{x,d} = \emptyset$). Thus,

$$[\mathcal{B}^c_{\mathrm{re}[\leq i-1]} \hookrightarrow \mathcal{B}_{\mathrm{re}[\leq i]}] = 0, \qquad \forall\, i \in \{3k : 1 \leq k \leq q\}, \tag{37}$$

and also,

$$[\mathcal{B}^c_{\mathrm{id}[\leq i-1]} \hookrightarrow \mathcal{B}_{\mathrm{id}[\leq i]}] = 0, \qquad \forall\, i \in \{3k : 1 \leq k \leq q\}. \tag{38}$$

Summing over the $3q$ actions using (33)–(38) gives

$$\left(\bot \overset{3q}{\rightsquigarrow} \mathcal{B}_{\mathrm{re}} \right) \leq 2\sqrt{\frac{10q^4}{2^n}}, \qquad \left(\bot \overset{3q}{\rightsquigarrow} \mathcal{B}_{\mathrm{id}} \right) \leq 2\sqrt{\frac{10q^4}{2^n}}. \tag{39}$$

Adding the two inequalities completes the proof of Theorem 2.

5.2 Security of LRQ

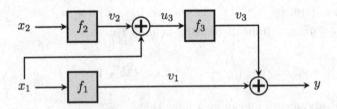

Fig. 3. The LRQ construction.

In this section, we analyze the post-quantum security of LRQ (see Fig. 3), defined as

$$g^{\mathrm{LRQ}}_{\mathrm{re}}(x_1, x_2) := f_1(x_1) \oplus f_3(x_1 \oplus f_2(x_2)).$$

Note that, we have swapped the labels, x_1 with x_2, and f_1 with f_2. This is just an administrative step to aid our proof. The construction remains exactly the same as before up to relabeling.

Theorem 3. *Let $\mathscr{A}$ be a (q, τ)-quantum adversary distinguishing g_{re}^{LRQ} from g_{id}. Then there exists $(O(q), \tau_i)$-quantum distinguishers $\mathscr{B}_i$ against f_i, such that*

$$\mathbf{Adv}_{LRQ}^{qprf}(\mathscr{A}) \leq \sum_{i=1}^{3} \mathbf{Adv}_{f_i}^{qprf}(\mathscr{B}_i) + 2\sqrt{\frac{10q^4}{2^n}},$$

where $\tau_i \in \widetilde{O}(\tau + q^2)$, for all $i \in \{1, 2, 3\}$.

Since the proof follows the same approach of the proof of Theorem 2, we will skip some details of the formulation which are very similar to the earlier proof and can be surmised from the context.

Formulation of the Proof. As before we will simulate all the random functions using a single random function $f : \{0,1\}^{3n+2} \rightarrow \{0,1\}^n$. For each $x_1, x_2 \in \mathcal{Y}$,

$$f_1(x_1) = f(00\|x_1\|0^{2n}), \qquad f_2(x_1) = f(01\|x_1\|0^{2n}),$$
$$f_3(x_1) = f(10\|x_1\|0^{2n}), \qquad g_{id}^*(x_1, x_2) = f(11\|x_1\|x_2\|x_1 \oplus f_2(x_2)).$$

Here we replace g_{id} with the map $(x_1, x_2) \mapsto g_{id}^*(x_1, x_2) \oplus f_1(x_1)$. Since g_{id}^* is a random function of (x_1, x_2) and is independent from f_1, $g_{id}^*(x_1, x_2) \oplus f_1(x_1)$ is identically distributed with $g_{id}(x_1, x_2)$.

Let $\mathcal{D}_{re}, \mathcal{D}_{id}, \widetilde{\mathcal{X}}_{re}, \widetilde{\mathcal{X}}_{id}$ be as before. Let $\mathcal{B}_{re}$ be the set of databases d_{re} satisfying the following condition: we can find $x_1, v_1, x_1', v_1', x_2, v_2, x_2', v_2', v_3 \in \mathcal{Y}$ such that

- $([x_1]_1, v_1), ([x_1']_1, v_1'), ([x_2]_2, v_2), ([x_2']_2, v_2') \in d_{re}$;
- $v_2 \oplus x_1 = v_2' \oplus x_1'$;
- $([v_2 \oplus x_1]_3, v_3) \in d_{re}$.

Next, let $\mathcal{B}_{id}$ be the set of databases d_{id}-satisfying the following condition: we can find $x_1, v_1, x_1', v_1', x_2, v_2, x_2', v_2', v_3, \in \mathcal{Y}$ such that

- $([x_1]_1, v_1), ([x_1']_1, v_1'), ([x_2]_2, v_2), ([x_2']_2, v_2') \in d_{id}$;
- $v_2 \oplus x_1 = v_2' \oplus x_1'$;
- One of $(11\|x_1\|x_2\|(v_2 \oplus x_1), v_3)$ and $(11\|x_1'\|x_2'\|(v_2 \oplus x_1), v_3) \in d_{id}$.

As before et $\mathcal{G}_{re} := \mathcal{D}_{re} \setminus \mathcal{B}_{re}$ and $\mathcal{G}_{id} := \mathcal{D}_{id} \setminus \mathcal{B}_{id}$. Thus the above definitions mean that in both $\mathcal{G}_{re}$ and $\mathcal{G}_{id}$, each $u_3 := v_2 \oplus x_1$ is associated with a unique pair (x_1, x_2). Then we can define the bijection $h : \mathcal{G}_{re} \longrightarrow \mathcal{G}_{id}$ as follows: for each d_{re} we define $d_{id} := h(d_{re})$ such that

- for each $x_1 \in \mathcal{Y}$, $d_{id}([x_1]_1) = d_{re}([x_1]_1)$;
- for each $x_2 \in \mathcal{Y}$, $d_{id}([x_2]_2) = d_{re}([x_2]_2)$;
- for each $x_1, x_2 \in \mathcal{Y}$ and the associated u_3, $d_{id}(11\|x_1\|x_2\|u_3) = d_{re}([u_3]_3)$.

Then h satisfies the conditions of Lemma 2. To complete the proof of Theorem 3, we just need to show that

$$\left(\perp \overset{3q}{\rightsquigarrow} \mathcal{B}_{re}\right) + \left(\perp \overset{3q}{\rightsquigarrow} \mathcal{B}_{id}\right) \leq 2\sqrt{\frac{10q^4}{2^n}}.$$

Sequence of Actions. As before, we deal with three main actions, one each corresponding to f_1, f_2, and f_3 or g_{id}^*.

ACTION OF f_1: For $i \in \{3k + 1 : 0 \le k \le q - 1\}$, for any d_{re} with $|d_{\mathsf{re}}| \le i - 1$ and any $x \in \mathcal{Y}$, since the property $\mathcal{B}_{\mathsf{re}}$ does not depend on $d_{\mathsf{re}}([x]_1)$, we have $S_{x,d}^{\mathcal{B}_{\mathsf{re}}^c \hookrightarrow \mathcal{B}_{\mathsf{re}}} = \emptyset$. Thus,

$$[\![\mathcal{B}_{\mathsf{re}[\le i-1]}^c \hookrightarrow \mathcal{B}_{\mathsf{re}[\le i]}]\!] = 0, \qquad \forall\, i \in \{3k + 1 : 0 \le k \le q - 1\}. \tag{40}$$

By the same arguments

$$[\![\mathcal{B}_{\mathsf{id}[\le i-1]}^c \hookrightarrow \mathcal{B}_{\mathsf{id}[\le i]}]\!] = 0, \qquad \forall\, i \in \{3k + 1 : 0 \le k \le q - 1\}. \tag{41}$$

ACTION OF f_2: Next we look at the transition capacity $[\![\mathcal{B}_{\mathsf{re}[\le i-1]}^c \hookrightarrow \mathcal{B}_{\mathsf{re}[\le i]}]\!]$ for $i \in \{3k + 2 : 0 \le k \le q - 1\}$. For any d_{re} with $|d_{\mathsf{re}}| \le i - 1$ and any $x \in \mathcal{Y}$, we have

$$S_{x,d}^{\mathcal{B}_{\mathsf{re}}^c \hookrightarrow \mathcal{B}_{\mathsf{re}}} := \{x_1 \oplus u_3 \mid d_{\mathsf{re}}([x_1]_1) \ne \bot, d_{\mathsf{re}}([u_3]_3) \ne \bot\}.$$

There are at most $\lceil (i - 1)/3 \rceil^2$ choices for the pair (x_1, u_3), so from Lemma 1 we have

$$[\![\mathcal{B}_{\mathsf{re}[\le i-1]}^c \hookrightarrow \mathcal{B}_{\mathsf{re}[\le i]}]\!] \le \sqrt{\frac{10q^2}{2^n}}, \qquad \forall\, i \in \{3k + 2 : 0 \le k \le q - 1\}. \tag{42}$$

By the same arguments

$$[\![\mathcal{B}_{\mathsf{id}[\le i-1]}^c \hookrightarrow \mathcal{B}_{\mathsf{id}[\le i]}]\!] \le \sqrt{\frac{10q^2}{2^n}}, \qquad \forall\, i \in \{3k + 2 : 0 \le k \le q - 1\}. \tag{43}$$

ACTION OF f_3 (RESP. g_{id}^*): Finally, for $i \in \{3k : 1 \le k \le q\}$, for any d_{re} with $|d_{\mathsf{re}}| \le i - 1$ (resp. any d_{id} with $|d_{\mathsf{id}}| \le i - 1$) and any $x \in \mathcal{Y}$, since the property $\mathcal{B}_{\mathsf{re}}$ (resp. $\mathcal{B}_{\mathsf{id}}$) does not depend on $d_{\mathsf{re}}([x]_3)$ (resp. $d_{\mathsf{id}}(11\|x_1\|x_2\|x)$), we have $S_{x,d}^{\mathcal{B}_{\mathsf{re}}^c \hookrightarrow \mathcal{B}_{\mathsf{re}}} = \emptyset$ (resp. $S_{x,d}^{\mathcal{B}_{\mathsf{id}}^c \hookrightarrow \mathcal{B}_{\mathsf{id}}} = \emptyset$). Thus,

$$[\![\mathcal{B}_{\mathsf{re}[\le i-1]}^c \hookrightarrow \mathcal{B}_{\mathsf{re}[\le i]}]\!] = 0, \qquad \forall\, i \in \{3k : 1 \le k \le q\}, \tag{44}$$

and also,

$$[\![\mathcal{B}_{\mathsf{id}[\le i-1]}^c \hookrightarrow \mathcal{B}_{\mathsf{id}[\le i]}]\!] = 0, \qquad \forall\, i \in \{3k : 1 \le k \le q\}. \tag{45}$$

Summing over the $3q$ actions using (40)–(45) gives

$$\left(\perp \overset{3q}{\leadsto} \mathcal{B}_{\text{re}}\right) \le \sqrt{\frac{10q^4}{2^n}}, \qquad \left(\perp \overset{3q}{\leadsto} \mathcal{B}_{\text{id}}\right) \le \sqrt{\frac{10q^4}{2^n}}. \tag{46}$$

Adding the two inequalities completes the proof of Theorem 3.

5.3 Security of LRWQ

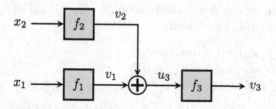

Fig. 4. The LRWQ construction by Hosoyamada et al. [17].

In this section, we analyze the post-quantum security of LRWQ (see Fig. 4), defined as

$$g_{\text{re}}^{\text{LRWQ}}(x_1, x_2) := f_3(f_1(x_1) \oplus f_2(x_2)).$$

Theorem 4. *Let $\mathscr{A}$ be a (q, τ)-quantum adversary distinguishing $g_{\text{re}}^{\text{LRWQ}}$ from g_{id}. Then there exists $(O(q), \tau_i)$-quantum distinguishers $\mathscr{B}_i$ against f_i, such that*

$$\mathbf{Adv}_{\text{LRWQ}}^{\text{qprf}}(\mathscr{A}) \le \sum_{i=1}^{3} \mathbf{Adv}_{f_i}^{\text{qprf}}(\mathscr{B}_i) + 4\sqrt{\frac{10q^4}{2^n}},$$

where $\tau_i \in \widetilde{O}(\tau + q^2)$, for all $i \in \{1, 2, 3\}$.

Formulation of the Proof. As before we will simulate all the random functions using a single random function $f : \{0,1\}^{3n+2} \to \{0,1\}^n$. For each $x_1, x_2 \in \mathcal{Y}$,

$$f_1(x_1) = f(00\|x_1\|0^{2n}), \qquad f_2(x_1) = f(01\|x_1\|0^{2n}),$$
$$f_3(x_1) = f(10\|x_1\|0^{2n}), \qquad g_{\text{id}}^*(x_1, x_2) = f(11\|x_1\|x_2\|f_1(x_1) \oplus f_2(x_2)).$$

Using a similar argument as before we can conclude that this game behaves identical with the standard PRF game.

Let $\mathcal{D}_{\text{re}}, \mathcal{D}_{\text{id}}, \widetilde{\mathcal{X}}_{\text{re}}, \widetilde{\mathcal{X}}_{\text{id}}$ be as before. Let $\mathcal{B}_{\text{re}}$ be the set of databases d_{re} satisfying the following condition: we can find $x_1, v_1, x_1', v_1', x_2, v_2, x_2', v_2', v_3 \in \mathcal{Y}$ such that

- $([x_1]_1, v_1), ([x_1']_1, v_1'), ([x_2]_2, v_2), ([x_2']_2, v_2') \in d_{\text{re}}$;
- $v_1 \oplus v_2 = v_1' \oplus v_2'$;
- $([v_1 \oplus v_2]_3, v_3) \in d_{\text{re}}$.

Next, let $\mathcal{B}_{\text{id}}$ be the set of databases d_{id} satisfying the following condition: we can find $x_1, v_1, x_1', v_1', x_2, v_2, x_2', v_2', y \in \mathcal{Y}$ such that

- $([x_1]_1, v_1), ([x_1']_1, v_1'), ([x_2]_2, v_2), ([x_2']_2, v_2') \in d_{\text{re}}$;
- $v_1 \oplus v_2 = v_1' \oplus v_2'$;
- One of $(11\|x_1\|x_2\|(v_1 \oplus v_2), v_3)$ and $(11\|x_1'\|x_2'\|(v_1 \oplus v_2), v_3) \in d_{\text{id}}$.

As before et $\mathcal{G}_{\text{re}} := \mathcal{D}_{\text{re}} \setminus \mathcal{B}_{\text{re}}$ and $\mathcal{G}_{\text{id}} := \mathcal{D}_{\text{id}} \setminus \mathcal{B}_{\text{id}}$. Thus the above definitions mean that in both $\mathcal{G}_{\text{re}}$ and $\mathcal{G}_{\text{id}}$, each $u_3 := v_1 \oplus v_2$ is associated with a unique pair (x_1, x_2). Then we can define the bijection $h : \mathcal{G}_{\text{re}} \longrightarrow \mathcal{G}_{\text{id}}$ as follows: for each d_{re} we define $d_{\text{id}} := h(d_{\text{re}})$ such that

- for each $x_1 \in \mathcal{Y}$, $d_{\text{id}}([x_1]_1) = d_{\text{re}}([x_1]_1)$;
- for each $x_2 \in \mathcal{Y}$, $d_{\text{id}}([x_2]_2) = d_{\text{re}}([x_2]_2)$;
- for each $x_1, x_2 \in \mathcal{Y}$ and the associated u_3, $d_{\text{id}}(11\|x_1\|x_2\|u_3) = d_{\text{re}}([u_3]_3)$.

Then h satisfies the conditions of Lemma 2. To complete the proof of Theorem 4, we just need to show that

$$\left(\perp \overset{3q}{\rightsquigarrow} \mathcal{B}_{\text{re}}\right) + \left(\perp \overset{3q}{\rightsquigarrow} \mathcal{B}_{\text{id}}\right) \leq 4\sqrt{\frac{10q^4}{2^n}}.$$

Sequence of Actions. As before, we deal with three main actions, one each corresponding to f_1, f_2, and f_3 or g_{id}^*.

ACTION OF f_1: For $i \in \{3k + 1 : 0 \leq k \leq q - 1\}$, we first look at the transition capacity $[\![\mathcal{B}_{\text{re}[\leq i-1]}^c \hookrightarrow \mathcal{B}_{\text{re}[\leq i]}]\!]$. For any d_{re} with $|d_{\text{re}}| \leq i - 1$ and any $x \in \mathcal{Y}$, we have

$$\mathcal{S}_{x,d}^{\mathcal{B}_{\text{re}}^c \hookrightarrow \mathcal{B}_{\text{re}}} = \{d_{\text{re}}([x_2]_2) \oplus u_3 \mid d_{\text{re}}([x_2]_2) \neq \perp, d_{\text{re}}([u_3]_3) \neq \perp\}.$$

There are at most $\lceil (i-1)/3 \rceil^2$ choices for the pair (x_2, u_3), so $|\mathcal{S}_{x,d}^{\mathcal{B}_{\text{re}}^c \hookrightarrow \mathcal{B}_{\text{re}}}| \leq \lceil (i-1)/3 \rceil^2 \leq q^2$, and from there using Lemma 1 we have

$$[\![\mathcal{B}_{\text{re}[\leq i-1]}^c \hookrightarrow \mathcal{B}_{\text{re}[\leq i]}]\!] \leq \sqrt{\frac{10q^2}{2^n}}, \qquad \forall\, i \in \{3k+1 : 0 \leq k \leq q-1\}. \qquad (47)$$

By the same arguments

$$[\![\mathcal{B}_{\text{id}[\leq i-1]}^c \hookrightarrow \mathcal{B}_{\text{id}[\leq i]}]\!] \leq \sqrt{\frac{10q^2}{2^n}}, \qquad \forall\, i \in \{3k+1 : 0 \leq k \leq q-1\}. \qquad (48)$$

ACTION OF f_2: Next we look at the transition capacity $[\![\mathcal{B}_{\text{re}[\leq i-1]}^c \hookrightarrow \mathcal{B}_{\text{re}[\leq i]}]\!]$ for $i \in \{3k + 2 : 0 \leq k \leq q - 1\}$. For any d_{re} with $|d_{\text{re}}| \leq i - 1$ and any $x \in \mathcal{Y}$, we have

$$\mathcal{S}_{x,d}^{\mathcal{B}_{\text{re}}^c \hookrightarrow \mathcal{B}_{\text{re}}} := \{d_{\text{re}}([x_1]_1) \oplus u_3 \mid d_{\text{re}}([x_1]_1) \neq \perp, d_{\text{re}}([u_3]_3) \neq \perp\}.$$

Again, there are at most $\lceil (i-1)/3 \rceil^2$ choices for the pair (x_1, u_3), and arguing as before we have

$$[\![\mathcal{B}^c_{\mathsf{re}[\leq i-1]} \hookrightarrow \mathcal{B}_{\mathsf{re}[\leq i]}]\!] \leq \sqrt{\frac{10q^2}{2^n}}, \qquad \forall\, i \in \{3k+2 : 0 \leq k \leq q-1\}. \qquad (49)$$

By the same arguments

$$[\![\mathcal{B}^c_{\mathsf{id}[\leq i-1]} \hookrightarrow \mathcal{B}_{\mathsf{id}[\leq i]}]\!] \leq \sqrt{\frac{10q^2}{2^n}}, \qquad \forall\, i \in \{3k+2 : 0 \leq k \leq q-1\}. \qquad (50)$$

ACTION OF f_3 (RESP. g^*_{id}): Finally, for $i \in \{3k : 1 \leq k \leq q\}$, for any d_{re} with $|d_{\mathsf{re}}| \leq i-1$ (resp. any d_{id} with $|d_{\mathsf{id}}| \leq i-1$) and any $x \in \mathcal{Y}$, since the property $\mathcal{B}_{\mathsf{re}}$ (resp. $\mathcal{B}_{\mathsf{id}}$) does not depend on $d_{\mathsf{re}}([x]_3)$ (resp. $d_{\mathsf{id}}(11\|x_1\|x_2\|x)$), we have $\mathcal{S}^{\mathcal{B}^c_{\mathsf{re}} \hookrightarrow \mathcal{B}_{\mathsf{re}}}_{x,d} = \emptyset$ (resp. $\mathcal{S}^{\mathcal{B}^c_{\mathsf{id}} \hookrightarrow \mathcal{B}_{\mathsf{id}}}_{x,d} = \emptyset$). Thus,

$$[\![\mathcal{B}^c_{\mathsf{re}[\leq i-1]} \hookrightarrow \mathcal{B}_{\mathsf{re}[\leq i]}]\!] = 0, \qquad \forall\, i \in \{3k : 1 \leq k \leq q\}, \qquad (51)$$

and also,

$$[\![\mathcal{B}^c_{\mathsf{id}[\leq i-1]} \hookrightarrow \mathcal{B}_{\mathsf{id}[\leq i]}]\!] = 0, \qquad \forall\, i \in \{3k : 1 \leq k \leq q\}. \qquad (52)$$

Summing over the $3q$ actions using (47)–(52) gives

$$\left(\perp \overset{3q}{\leadsto} \mathcal{B}_{\mathsf{re}} \right) \leq 2\sqrt{\frac{10q^4}{2^n}}, \qquad \left(\perp \overset{3q}{\leadsto} \mathcal{B}_{\mathsf{id}} \right) \leq 2\sqrt{\frac{10q^4}{2^n}}. \qquad (53)$$

Adding the two inequalities completes the proof of Theorem 4.

5.4   Tweakable Permutation Security of TNT, LRWQ and LRQ

Let $E : \mathcal{K} \times \{0,1\}^n \to \{0,1\}^n$ be a keyed permutation, indexed with keys from $\mathcal{K}$. The pseudorandom permutation (or PRP) advantage of some distinguisher $\mathcal{A}$ against E is defined as

$$\mathbf{Adv}^{\mathsf{qprp}}_E(\mathcal{A}) := \mathbf{Adv}^{\mathsf{dist}}_{E_K;\pi}(\mathcal{A}), \qquad (54)$$

where K is drawn uniformly at random from $\mathcal{K}$, and π is a uniform random permutation of $\{0,1\}^n$. The following result is the well-known quantum analog of the PRP-PRF switching lemma.

Lemma 3 (Theorem 7 in [27]). *Let Γ and Π denote quantum oracles corresponding to a uniform random function and a uniform random permutation from $\{0,1\}^n$ to $\{0,1\}^n$, respectively. Then, for any q-query quantum adversary $\mathcal{A}$, we have $\mathbf{Adv}^{\mathsf{dist}}_{\Gamma;\Pi}(\mathcal{A}) \leq O\left(q^3/2^n\right)$.*

A *tweakable block cipher* $\widetilde{E} : \mathcal{K} \times \{0,1\}^n \times \{0,1\}^n \to \{0,1\}^n$ is a keyed function, indexed with a key and tweak pair from $\mathcal{K} \times \{0,1\}^n$, such that for all $k,t \in \mathcal{K} \times \{0,1\}^n$, $\widetilde{E}(k,t,\cdot)$ is a permutation of $\{0,1\}^n$. The tweakable pseudorandom permutation (or TPRP) advantage of some distinguisher $\mathscr{A}$ against $\widetilde{E}$ is defined as

$$\mathbf{Adv}_{\widetilde{E}}^{\mathsf{qtprp}}(\mathscr{A}) := \mathbf{Adv}_{\widetilde{E}_K;\widetilde{\pi}}^{\mathsf{dist}}(\mathscr{A}), \tag{55}$$

where K is drawn uniformly at random from $\mathcal{K}$, and $\widetilde{\pi}$ is a uniform random tweakable permutation of $\{0,1\}^n$ with n-bit tweaks.

Note that, TNT, LRQ and LRWQ can be viewed as tweakable block ciphers by instantiating f_1, f_2, f_3 with keyed permutations, and utilizing the second input, x_2, as the tweak value. The following result, due to Hosoyamada and Iwata, is the quantum TPRP-PRF switching lemma.

Lemma 4 (Proposition 5 in [15]). *Let Γ denote a uniform random function from $\{0,1\}^{2n}$ to $\{0,1\}^n$, and $\widetilde{\Pi}$ denote a uniform random permutation of $\{0,1\}^n$ with n-bit tweaks. Then, for any q-query quantum adversary $\mathscr{A}$, we have* $\mathbf{Adv}_{\Gamma;\widetilde{\Pi}}^{\mathsf{dist}}(\mathscr{A}) \leq O\left(\sqrt{q^6/2^n}\right).$

Using Lemma 3–4, and Theorem 2–4, we get the following corollary on the TPRP security of TNT, LRQ and LRWQ.

Corollary 2. *For any $\widetilde{E} \in \{\mathsf{TNT}, \mathsf{LRQ}, \mathsf{LRWQ}\}$, let $\mathscr{A}$ be a (q,τ)-quantum adversary distinguishing $\widetilde{E}$ from $\widetilde{\Pi}$, a uniform random tweakable permutation of $\{0,1\}^n$ with n-bit tweaks. Then, there exists $(O(q), \tau_i)$-quantum distinguishers $\mathscr{B}_i$ against f_i, such that*

$$\mathbf{Adv}_{\widetilde{E}}^{\mathsf{qtprp}}(\mathscr{A}) \leq \sum_{i=1}^{3} \mathbf{Adv}_{f_i}^{\mathsf{qprp}}(\mathscr{B}_i) + O\left(\sqrt{\frac{q^4}{2^n}} + \sqrt{\frac{q^6}{2^n}} + \frac{q^3}{2^n}\right),$$

where $\tau_i \in \widetilde{O}(\tau + q^2)$, for all $i \in \{1, 2, 3\}$.

Proof. Suppose $\widetilde{E} = \mathsf{TNT}$. Then, the result follows from one application each of the hybrid step, Lemma 3, Lemma 4, and Theorem 2 in this order. The cases for $\widetilde{E} \in \{\mathsf{LRQ}, \mathsf{LRWQ}\}$ can be argued in a similar fashion. □

6   Conclusion

In this work, we show that 2n-bit-to-n-bit compressing PRFs that are built using two n-bit-to-n-bit PRF calls are insecure in the quantum setting. Furthermore, we identify classes of constructions using three PRF calls that are also broken. Among the constructions that may be secure, we select TNT, LRQ, and LRWQ, as they are the most efficient invertible ones, which allows them to also be used as tweakable block ciphers. We then prove their PRF security against quantum distinguishers that use less than $2^{n/4}$ queries. Our results, also imply that these constructions are quantum secure tweakable block ciphers up to $2^{n/6}$ chosen plaintext queries.

We conjecture that these constructions are secure up to $2^{n/3}$ adversarial queries, and leave the issue of improving the security bound as an interesting open problem.

References

1. Bao, Z., Guo, C., Guo, J., Song, L.: TNT: how to tweak a block cipher. In: Canteaut, A., Ishai, Y. (eds.) EUROCRYPT 2020, Part II. LNCS, vol. 12106, pp. 641–673. Springer, Cham (2020). https://doi.org/10.1007/978-3-030-45724-2_22
2. Bellare, M., Kilian, J., Rogaway, P.: The security of the cipher block chaining message authentication code. J. Comput. Syst. Sci. **61**(3), 362–399 (2000)
3. Bhaumik, R., et al.: QCB: efficient quantum-secure authenticated encryption. In: Tibouchi, M., Wang, H. (eds.) ASIACRYPT 2021, Part I. LNCS, vol. 13090, pp. 668–698. Springer, Cham (2021). https://doi.org/10.1007/978-3-030-92062-3_23
4. Bhaumik, R., Cogliati, B., Ethan, J., Jha, A.: On quantum secure compressing pseudorandom functions. Cryptology ePrint Archive, Report 2023/207 (2023). https://eprint.iacr.org/2023/207
5. Boneh, D., Zhandry, M.: Quantum-secure message authentication codes. In: Johansson, T., Nguyen, P.Q. (eds.) EUROCRYPT 2013. LNCS, vol. 7881, pp. 592–608. Springer, Heidelberg (2013). https://doi.org/10.1007/978-3-642-38348-9_35
6. Bonnetain, X., Naya-Plasencia, M.: Hidden shift quantum cryptanalysis and implications. In: Peyrin, T., Galbraith, S. (eds.) ASIACRYPT 2018, Part I. LNCS, vol. 11272, pp. 560–592. Springer, Cham (2018). https://doi.org/10.1007/978-3-030-03326-2_19
7. Bonnetain, X., Naya-Plasencia, M., Schrottenloher, A.: On quantum slide attacks. In: Paterson, K.G., Stebila, D. (eds.) SAC 2019. LNCS, vol. 11959, pp. 492–519. Springer, Cham (2020). https://doi.org/10.1007/978-3-030-38471-5_20
8. Bonnetain, X., Naya-Plasencia, M., Schrottenloher, A.: Quantum security analysis of AES. IACR Trans. Symm. Cryptol. **2019**(2), 55–93 (2019). https://doi.org/10.13154/tosc.v2019.i2.55-93
9. Bonnetain, X., Schrottenloher, A., Sibleyras, F.: Beyond quadratic speedups in quantum attacks on symmetric schemes. In: Dunkelman, O., Dziembowski, S. (eds.) EUROCRYPT 2022, Part III. LNCS, vol. 13277, pp. 315–344. Springer, Heidelberg (2022). https://doi.org/10.1007/978-3-031-07082-2_12
10. Chailloux, A., Naya-Plasencia, M., Schrottenloher, A.: An efficient quantum collision search algorithm and implications on symmetric cryptography. In: Takagi, T., Peyrin, T. (eds.) ASIACRYPT 2017, Part II. LNCS, vol. 10625, pp. 211–240. Springer, Cham (2017). https://doi.org/10.1007/978-3-319-70697-9_8
11. Chung, K.-M., Fehr, S., Huang, Y.-H., Liao, T.-N.: On the compressed-oracle technique, and post-quantum security of proofs of sequential work. In: Canteaut, A., Standaert, F.-X. (eds.) EUROCRYPT 2021, Part II. LNCS, vol. 12697, pp. 598–629. Springer, Cham (2021). https://doi.org/10.1007/978-3-030-77886-6_21
12. Czajkowski, J., Hülsing, A., Schaffner, C.: Quantum indistinguishability of random sponges. In: Boldyreva, A., Micciancio, D. (eds.) CRYPTO 2019, Part II. LNCS, vol. 11693, pp. 296–325. Springer, Cham (2019). https://doi.org/10.1007/978-3-030-26951-7_11
13. Grassi, L., Naya-Plasencia, M., Schrottenloher, A.: Quantum algorithms for the k-xor problem. In: Peyrin, T., Galbraith, S. (eds.) ASIACRYPT 2018, Part I. LNCS, vol. 11272, pp. 527–559. Springer, Cham (2018). https://doi.org/10.1007/978-3-030-03326-2_18
14. Hosoyamada, A., Iwata, T.: 4-round Luby-Rackoff construction is a qPRP. In: Galbraith, S.D., Moriai, S. (eds.) ASIACRYPT 2019, Part I. LNCS, vol. 11921, pp. 145–174. Springer, Cham (2019). https://doi.org/10.1007/978-3-030-34578-5_6

15. Hosoyamada, A., Iwata, T.: 4-round Luby-Rackoff construction is a qPRP. Cryptology ePrint Archive, Report 2019/243, version 20190913:015401 (2019). https://eprint.iacr.org/archive/2019/243/20190913:015401

16. Hosoyamada, A., Iwata, T.: On tight quantum security of HMAC and NMAC in the quantum random oracle model. In: Malkin, T., Peikert, C. (eds.) CRYPTO 2021, Part I. LNCS, vol. 12825, pp. 585–615. Springer, Cham (2021). https://doi.org/10.1007/978-3-030-84242-0_21

17. Hosoyamada, A., Iwata, T.: Provably quantum-secure tweakable block ciphers. IACR Trans. Symm. Cryptol. **2021**(1), 337–377 (2021). https://doi.org/10.46586/tosc.v2021.i1.337-377

18. Hosoyamada, A., Sasaki, Yu., Xagawa, K.: Quantum multicollision-finding algorithm. In: Takagi, T., Peyrin, T. (eds.) ASIACRYPT 2017, Part II. LNCS, vol. 10625, pp. 179–210. Springer, Cham (2017). https://doi.org/10.1007/978-3-319-70697-9_7

19. Hosoyamada, A., Yasuda, K.: Building quantum-one-way functions from block ciphers: Davies-Meyer and Merkle-Damgård constructions. In: Peyrin, T., Galbraith, S. (eds.) ASIACRYPT 2018, Part I. LNCS, vol. 11272, pp. 275–304. Springer, Cham (2018). https://doi.org/10.1007/978-3-030-03326-2_10

20. Kaplan, M., Leurent, G., Leverrier, A., Naya-Plasencia, M.: Breaking symmetric cryptosystems using quantum period finding. In: Robshaw, M., Katz, J. (eds.) CRYPTO 2016, Part II. LNCS, vol. 9815, pp. 207–237. Springer, Heidelberg (2016). https://doi.org/10.1007/978-3-662-53008-5_8

21. Kaplan, M., Leurent, G., Leverrier, A., Naya-Plasencia, M.: Quantum differential and linear cryptanalysis. IACR Trans. Symm. Cryptol. **2016**(1), 71–94 (2016). https://doi.org/10.13154/tosc.v2016.i1.71-94, https://tosc.iacr.org/index.php/ToSC/article/view/536

22. Kuwakado, H., Morii, M.: Quantum distinguisher between the 3-round Feistel cipher and the random permutation. In: IEEE International Symposium on Information Theory. ISIT 2010, Proceedings, pp. 2682–2685. IEEE (2010). https://doi.org/10.1109/ISIT.2010.5513654

23. Kuwakado, H., Morii, M.: Security on the quantum-type even-mansour cipher. In: International Symposium on Information Theory and Its Applications. ISITA 2012, Proceedings, pp. 312–316. IEEE (2012). https://ieeexplore.ieee.org/document/6400943/

24. Nielsen, M.A., Chuang, I.L.: Quantum Computation and Quantum Information, 10th Anniversary edn. Cambridge University Press, Cambridge (2016). https://www.cambridge.org/de/academic/subjects/physics/quantum-physics-quantum-information-and-quantum-computation/quantum-computation-and-quantum-information-10th-anniversary-edition?format=HB

25. Rogaway, P., Shrimpton, T.: A provable-security treatment of the key-wrap problem. In: Vaudenay, S. (ed.) EUROCRYPT 2006. LNCS, vol. 4004, pp. 373–390. Springer, Heidelberg (2006). https://doi.org/10.1007/11761679_23

26. Song, F., Yun, A.: Quantum security of NMAC and related constructions. In: Katz, J., Shacham, H. (eds.) CRYPTO 2017, Part II. LNCS, vol. 10402, pp. 283–309. Springer, Cham (2017). https://doi.org/10.1007/978-3-319-63715-0_10

27. Zhandry, M.: A note on the quantum collision and set equality problems. Quantum Inf. Comput. **15**(7&8), 557–567 (2015). https://doi.org/10.26421/QIC15.7-8-2

28. Zhandry, M.: How to record quantum queries, and applications to quantum indifferentiability. In: Boldyreva, A., Micciancio, D. (eds.) CRYPTO 2019, Part II. LNCS, vol. 11693, pp. 239–268. Springer, Cham (2019). https://doi.org/10.1007/978-3-030-26951-7_9

Improved Quantum Circuits for AES: Reducing the Depth and the Number of Qubits

Qun Liu[1,3], Bart Preneel[4], Zheng Zhao[1,3], and Meiqin Wang[1,2,3](✉)

[1] School of Cyber Science and Technology, Shandong University,
Qingdao, China
{qunliu,zhaozheng}@mail.sdu.edu.cn, mqwang@sdu.edu.cn
[2] Quan Cheng Laboratory, Jinan, China
[3] Key Laboratory of Cryptologic Technology and Information Security,
Ministry of Education, Shandong University, Jinan, China
[4] imec-COSIC, KU Leuven, Leuven, Belgium
Bart.Preneel@esat.kuleuven.be

Abstract. Quantum computers hold the potential to solve problems that are intractable for classical computers, thereby driving increased interest in the development of new cryptanalytic ciphers. In NIST's post-quantum standardization process, the security categories are defined by the costs of quantum key search against AES. However, the cost estimates provided by Grassl *et al.* for the search are high. NIST has acknowledged that these initial classifications should be approached cautiously, since the costs of the most advanced attacks can be significantly reduced. Therefore, accurate resource estimations are crucial for evaluating the security of ciphers against quantum adversaries.

This paper presents a set of generic techniques for implementing AES quantum oracles, which are essential for quantum attacks such as Grover's algorithms. Firstly, we introduce the mixing-XOR technique to reuse the ancilla qubits. At ASIACRYPT 2022, Huang *et al.* proposed an S-box structure with 120 ancilla qubits. We are able to reduce the number of ancilla qubits to 83 without increasing the T-depth. Secondly, we propose the combined pipeline architecture with the share technique to combine the S-box and its reverse, which achieves it with only 98 ancilla qubits, resulting in a significant reduction of 59% compared to the independent structure. Thirdly, we use a general algorithm to determine the depth of quantum circuits, searching for the in-place circuit of AES MixColumns with depth 16. Applying these improvements, we achieve the lower quantum depth of AES circuits, obtaining more precise resource estimates for Grover's algorithm. For AES-128, -192, and -256, we only require the depth of 730, 876, and 1,018, respectively. Recently, the community has also focused on the trade-off of the time and space cost of quantum circuits for AES. In this regard, we present quantum implementations of AES circuits with a lower DW-cost on the zig-zag architecture. Compared with the circuit proposed by Huang *et al.*, the DW-cost is reduced by 35%.

Keywords: Quantum Circuit · Grover's Algorithm · S-box · AES

© International Association for Cryptologic Research 2023
J. Guo and R. Steinfeld (Eds.): ASIACRYPT 2023, LNCS 14440, pp. 67–98, 2023.
https://doi.org/10.1007/978-981-99-8727-6_3

1 Introduction

With the advancements in quantum computing, it has become crucial to investigate the security of cryptographic primitives against quantum attacks. For symmetric key ciphers such as AES, Grover's search algorithm [9] is the main threat, which provides a quadratic speedup, significantly reducing the time required to perform an exhaustive search for the key. The speedup reflects the asymptotic behavior of Grover's algorithm, providing a rough estimate of the security vulnerabilities introduced by quantum computers when applied to symmetric primitives [14]; moreover, estimating the detailed cost of implementing Grover's algorithm is challenging, hence most authors only use a rough approximation.

In 2016, the National Institute of Standards and Technology (NIST, US) initiated a competition[1] aimed at identifying candidate post-quantum algorithms for standardization. As part of this competition, NIST established various security categories for classifying the algorithms (refer to Table 1). These categories were defined based on the complexity of quantum attacks, which can be quantified in terms of circuit size. Specifically, security categories 1, 3, and 5 correspond to key recovery attacks against AES-128, -192, and -256, respectively.

Table 1. The three security levels for NIST's post-quantum competition defined based on the security of three AES variants.

Category	Cipher	Bound of gate counts
Level-1	AES-128	2^{170}/MAXDEPTH
Level-3	AES-192	2^{233}/MAXDEPTH
Level-5	AES-256	2^{298}/MAXDEPTH

In addition to the gate count, another important parameter known as MAXDEPTH has been introduced. NIST has proposed an approach that limits quantum attacks to a fixed running time or circuit depth. This limitation is motivated by the challenges associated with executing extremely lengthy serial computations. As a result, there is growing interest in improving the estimation of these levels, particularly in terms of optimizing the cost of quantum implementations for AES. This problem is of significant independent interest and has garnered considerable attention.

The introduction of security levels in NIST's post-quantum competition has spurred the search for optimal quantum circuits. With the potential advantages offered by quantum technology, global efforts are currently directed towards the design of practical large-scale quantum computer architectures, aiming to achieve a tangible quantum advantage [7]. At the highest level of abstraction, the first stage generates a quantum circuit from a reduced set of universal quantum gates.

---

[1] https://csrc.nist.gov/CSRC/media/Projects/Post-Quantum-Cryptography/documents/call-for-proposals-final-dec-2016.pdf

The second stage makes the computation robust to errors and thus requires the inclusion of quantum error correction methods. The industrial community has already developed tools for the synthesis and optimization of quantum circuits, including ProjectQ [11,27] and Q# [25], enabling significant advancements in this field.

1.1 Related Work

A quantum circuit can be constructed with the Clifford $+T$ gate set. Similar to [8,16,18,20,21], at ASIACRYPT 2020, Zou *et al.* [29] followed the definitions of the complexity of quantum circuits.

- *Time Complexity.* The time complexity refers to the time required to execute non-parallelizable logical T gates, also known as T-depth.
- *Space Complexity.* The space complexity corresponds to the number of logical qubits needed for the entire quantum computation, often referred to as width.
- *Circuit Complexity.* The circuit complexity is determined by the product of the *time* and *space* complexity, i.e., DW-cost. This metric has been selected as the trade-off metric by Jaques *et al.* at EUROCRYPT 2020 [14] and Huang *et al.* at ASIACRYPT 2022 [12].

Extensive research has been conducted on the design of quantum circuits for AES. The initial circuit proposal by Grassl *et al.* in [8] introduced a zig-zag structure to minimize the number of required qubits. This structure has since been adopted in various works [1,8,18,29]. Langenberg *et al.* [18] presented a new circuit for the AES S-box and key expansion, reducing the qubit count. Building upon this work, Zou *et al.* [29] further optimized the zig-zag structure and introduced new AES S-box circuits.

Early research primarily aimed to reduce qubit counts in quantum circuits. Equally important is minimizing circuit depth, given the challenges of lengthy serial computations required by Grover's algorithm. Additionally, ensuring fault tolerance in quantum circuits is crucial, making the T-depth a significant factor to consider, as emphasized in [12,13].

Nevertheless, the number of qubits can still be a bottleneck. A significant challenge in realizing large-scale quantum computers is the redundancy required for error-correction codes, which demands a large number of physical qubits [10]. Recently, the research community has taken into account both space complexity and time complexity. At EUROCRYPT 2020, Jaques *et al.* [14] proposed several methods to reduce quantum depth and the number of qubits. Building upon this work, Huang *et al.* [12] presented S-boxes of depth 3 and 4, effectively reducing the T-depth and DW-cost. Subsequently, a pipelined architecture was introduced in [13] to further decrease the circuit depth.

1.2 Our Contributions

This paper aligns with the ongoing research direction and prioritizes the depth and the number of qubits as the primary goal. By emphasizing a low-depth metric, we strike a favorable balance between time and space. To further optimize quantum circuits for AES, it becomes crucial to enhance the architecture and building blocks. The contributions put forth by this paper are outlined below.

Improved Structure of S-Box. In a recent study by Huang *et al.* [12] a structure for the AES S-box was proposed utilizing 120 ancilla qubits with a T-depth of 4. In this paper, we introduce the mixing-XOR technique, an algorithm designed to identify idle qubits within linear transformations and repurpose them to store intermediate values. This technique significantly reduces the depth, the number of qubits, and gates required for various quantum circuits. Using this technique, we notably reduce the width of the AES S-box to just 83 ancilla qubits with a T-depth of 4.

Combination of S-Box and S-Box† (Reverse of S-Box). In a study conducted by Jang *et al.* [13], the shallowed pipeline architecture was introduced to evaluate the S-box and its reverse, S-box†, simultaneously for two bytes. The S-box† operation is used to clean up[2] the ancilla qubits used in S-box. During the execution of the S-box, 120 ancilla qubits are utilized to store intermediate values. These ancilla qubits need to be cleaned up by S-box† so that they can be reused in the subsequent round. The approach proposed in [13] requires a total of $120 \times 2 = 240$ ancilla qubits to execute these two operations simultaneously. We propose the combined pipeline architecture with the share technique to combine S-box and S-box† concurrently. This technique significantly reduces the required number of ancilla qubits to just 98, resulting in a 59% reduction.

Improved Quantum Circuit for Reduced Circuit Complexity. We release various quantum circuits for AES-128/192/256 under the combined pipeline architecture, following a similar approach as in [12–14]. Compared with the results in [13], the qubit count and DW-cost are decreased by 42.4%, 41.2%, 36.5% for AES-128, -192, -256, respectively. Notably, the circuits with the AND gate and out-of-place linear layer have a lower depth. For AES-128, -192, and -256, we only require the depth of 730, 876, and 1,018, respectively. When applied to Grover's algorithm, these circuits provide more precise and efficient resource estimates than those proposed in [13,14].

Introducing AND Gates into the Zig-Zag Architecture. We propose modifications to the S-box circuit introduced by Huang *et al.* [12] at ASIACRYPT 2022. Our improved circuit achieves a remarkable reduction in qubit count with the increase of the depth (cf. Sect. 7). By applying the round-in-place zig-zag architecture, the DW-cost for AES-128 is further reduced to 132,800, while the previous best result is 204,800 in [12]. Figure 1 illustrates a comparison of the trade-off between T-depth and width, demonstrating that our circuits exhibit reduced width and DW-cost compared to [12].

---

[2] Cleaning up an ancilla qubit is to assign the value of the qubit to $|0\rangle$ by some reverse operations.

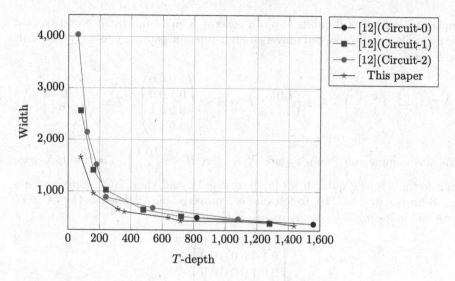

Fig. 1. Width and T-depth for implementing a quantum circuit for AES-128.

1.3   Organization

In Sect. 2, we present our notation and define our metrics. In Sect. 3, we propose an improved structure of the S-box. The combination of S-box and S-box[†] is described in Sect. 4. The quantum circuits for the AES components are presented in Sect. 5. The complete circuits for AES and the resource estimations based on the pipeline and zig-zag architectures are shown in Sect. 6 and Sect. 7. Finally, we conclude and propose future research directions in Sect. 8.

2   Preliminaries

2.1   Notation

Let $\mathbb{F}_2$ be the finite field with two elements 0 and 1 and let $\mathbb{F}_{2^k}$ be the finite field with 2^k elements. Consider $a, b \in \mathbb{F}_2$. Then $\bar{a} = a \oplus 1$ represents the inversion of a, and $a \oplus b$, $a \cdot b$ and $a|b$ denote the XOR, AND and OR operations of a and b. We denote with M a binary $n \times n$ matrix over $\mathbb{F}_2$; $\boldsymbol{x}$ and $\boldsymbol{y}$ are n-bit vectors over $\mathbb{F}_2$ with $\boldsymbol{x} = [x_0 x_1 \ldots x_{n-1}]$ and $\boldsymbol{y} = [y_0 y_1 \ldots y_{n-1}]$. A linear map defined by M is defined as $\boldsymbol{y}^t = M \cdot \boldsymbol{x}^t$. For a linear map M, $M^\dagger$ is defined as the adjoint of M, where $MM^\dagger = I$ and I is the identity map. The linear map is computed by a circuit as the sequential composition of the individual gates.

2.2   Quantum Circuits

A quantum state is typically written as $|u\rangle$ and $|u\rangle_n$ is used to emphasize that the state has n qubits. Quantum gates exploit quantum entanglement and the superposition states of qubits [4,6]. In general, a quantum circuit is constructed by using the widely adopted universal fault-tolerant gate set Clifford phase shift or T gate:

$$H = \frac{1}{\sqrt{2}} \begin{pmatrix} 1 & 1 \\ 1 & -1 \end{pmatrix}, \quad S = \begin{pmatrix} 1 & 0 \\ 0 & i \end{pmatrix}, \quad \text{CNOT} = \begin{pmatrix} 1 & 0 & 0 & 0 \\ 0 & 1 & 0 & 0 \\ 0 & 0 & 0 & 1 \\ 0 & 0 & 1 & 0 \end{pmatrix}, \quad T = \begin{pmatrix} 1 & 0 \\ 0 & e^{i\pi/4} \end{pmatrix}.$$

We also employ the Pauli-X gate $X = HS^2H = \begin{pmatrix} 0 & 1 \\ 1 & 0 \end{pmatrix}$. The Pauli-$X$ gate transforms a single qubit from $|a\rangle$ into $|a \oplus 1\rangle$, and the CNOT gate converts $|a\rangle |b\rangle$ into $|a\rangle |a \oplus b\rangle$. The Toffoli gate is a universal gate defined as the CCNOT gate and maps $|a\rangle |b\rangle |c\rangle$ to $|a\rangle |b\rangle |c \oplus a \cdot b\rangle$:

$$\begin{pmatrix} 1 & 0 & 0 & 0 & 0 & 0 & 0 & 0 \\ 0 & 1 & 0 & 0 & 0 & 0 & 0 & 0 \\ 0 & 0 & 1 & 0 & 0 & 0 & 0 & 0 \\ 0 & 0 & 0 & 1 & 0 & 0 & 0 & 0 \\ 0 & 0 & 0 & 0 & 1 & 0 & 0 & 0 \\ 0 & 0 & 0 & 0 & 0 & 1 & 0 & 0 \\ 0 & 0 & 0 & 0 & 0 & 0 & 0 & 1 \\ 0 & 0 & 0 & 0 & 0 & 0 & 1 & 0 \end{pmatrix}.$$

Optimization Goals. In the evaluation of quantum circuits, considering both time and memory costs is crucial for assessing their efficiency. The metrics of width, T-depth ($\#TD$), and DW-cost are the primary goals of our focus and attention. A forward-looking perspective suggests that each gate has a depth equal to one, with the T gate incurring a cost similar to other gates. This perspective defines the full depth ($\#FD$) as the time cost metric.

Implementing the AND Operation. As is shown in [24], the Clifford gates are much cheaper than the T gate. Thus, the T gate has a higher impact on the running time. In our quantum circuit, the AND operation $a \cdot b$ is the only source of T-depth. Currently, there exist multiple approaches for implementing the AND operations:

- the Toffoli gate with T-depth 1, or 4 (cf. [2,26]), achieving $|a\rangle |b\rangle |c\rangle \rightarrow |a\rangle |b\rangle |c \oplus a \cdot b\rangle$.
- the quantum AND gate using one auxiliary qubit with T-depth 1 (cf. [14]), achieving $|a\rangle |b\rangle |0\rangle \rightarrow |a\rangle |b\rangle |a \cdot b\rangle$.

The main distinction lies in the fact that the target qubit of the AND gate must be in the state $|0\rangle$, whereas the Toffoli gate does not have this requirement on its target qubit. In our paper, we consider the target qubit of the AND operation to be in the state $|0\rangle$, allowing us to convert a Toffoli gate into an AND gate. Consequently, implementing the AND operation becomes a unified process, and whether it is represented as a Toffoli gate or an AND gate depends on specific scenarios.

2.3   Description of AES Family

The Advanced Encryption Standard (AES) [5] is a block cipher with 128-bit state (16 bytes) standardized by NIST. The AES family has three members denoted as AES-128 (10 rounds), AES-192 (12 rounds), and AES-256 (14 rounds) with 128-bit, 192-bit, 256-bit keys, respectively.

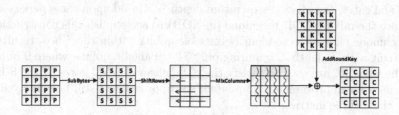

Fig. 2. Structure of an AES round.

The AES round function consists of four operations: AddRoundKey ∘ MixColumns ∘ ShiftRows ∘ SubBytes (see Fig. 2). The 128-bit state is represented in a 4×4 matrix of bytes. Next, we explain each operation.

- AddRoundKey.   The operation exclusive-ors each round key to the state.
- ShiftRows.   It cyclically rotates the cells of the i-th row to the left over i positions, for $i = 0, 1, 2, 3$.
- SubBytes.   The operation applies an 8-bit S-box to each byte of the state in parallel. The 128-bit state is transformed with 16 S-box lookups.
- MixColumns.   The MixColumns operation applies a linear transformation on each column of the state with the matrix

$$M = \begin{pmatrix} 0x02 & 0x03 & 0x01 & 0x01 \\ 0x01 & 0x02 & 0x03 & 0x01 \\ 0x01 & 0x01 & 0x02 & 0x03 \\ 0x03 & 0x01 & 0x01 & 0x02 \end{pmatrix}.$$

For each column in the state, we use MixColumn to represent the operation. Hence, one MixColumns operation consists of four MixColumn operations on the four columns of the state. In SubBytes, 16 S-box operations substitute the individual bytes of the state.

Denote the master key by 32-bit words $W_0, W_1, \ldots, W_{s-1}$, where $s = 4$ for AES-128, $s = 6$ for AES-192, and $s = 8$ for AES-256, respectively. Three operations are used in the algorithm: RotWord cyclically rotates the four bytes to the left by one position; Rcon exclusive-ors a constant to each byte of the word; SubWord applies four S-boxes in parallel to the four bytes of the word.

3   Improved Quantum Circuit Implementations of AES S-Box

In [14], the S-box circuit constructed by Jaques *et al.* for AES requires 120 ancilla qubits with T-depth 6. Subsequently, Huang *et al.* [12] reduced the T-depth to 4 while keeping the number of qubits at 120. In this section, our aim is to construct a new circuit from the classical circuit with a reduced number of qubits and gates, as well as less quantum depth. We build upon these papers and introduce the mixing-XOR technique (m-XOR) to accomplish this construction. The technique enables us to identify reusable qubits within the S-box, resulting in a circuit with T-depth 4, requiring only $74 + 9$ ancilla qubits, where 9 qubits with the value $|0\rangle$ are used to satisfy the parallelism of AND gates. If the S-box circuit used for improvements is updated, our approach can still be employed to reduce these three metrics.

3.1   M-XOR Technique

Two operations are used in quantum linear circuits:

- The *updating* operation is *in-place* and can be implemented by a CNOT gate $|a\rangle |b\rangle \rightarrow |a\rangle |a \oplus b\rangle$, defined as $\text{CNOT}(a, b)$.
- The *creating* operation is *out-of-place*, requiring two CNOT gates $|a\rangle |b\rangle |c\rangle \rightarrow |a\rangle |b\rangle |c \oplus a\rangle$ and $|a\rangle |b\rangle |c \oplus a\rangle \rightarrow |a\rangle |b\rangle |c \oplus a \oplus b\rangle$, defined as $\text{CNOT2}(a, b, c)$.

which correspond to s-XOR and g-XOR in classical circuits (cf. [15,28]). We observe that it is beneficial to transform a *creating* operation into an *updating* operation. Based on Observation 1, we propose the m-XOR technique to construct the quantum circuit from the classical circuit with a reduced number of qubits and gates, as well as less quantum depth.

Observation 1. *Given a quantum circuit with creating operations, some qubits can be reused by transforming creating operations into updating operations.*

Definition 1 (m-XOR technique). *The m-XOR technique mixes updating operations and creating operations to implement a linear transformation with the lowest number of qubits.*

Example 1. Given that we assign two qubits to q_a and q_b, the subsequent operation is a *creating* operation: $q_c = q_c \oplus (q_a \oplus q_b)$. If q_a is not further utilized in the subsequent circuit, this operation can be converted to an *updating* operation: $q_a = q_a \oplus q_b$. When utilizing q_c, we simply select the qubit q_a.

The detection of idle qubits forms the essence of this technique. Proposition 1 outlines the qubits that can be eliminated from the circuit.

Proposition 1. *In a sequentially written quantum circuit, the conversion from a creating operation $t_c = t_c \oplus (t_a \oplus t_b)$ to an updating operation $t_a = t_a \oplus t_b$ requires the fulfillment of the following conditions:*

– t_a *should not be utilized in the subsequent circuit.*
– t_c *does not appear in the previous circuit.*

To successfully perform the conversion, both conditions must be satisfied. Failing to meet either condition can compromise the correctness of the circuit.

Proof. For the operation $t_c = t_c \oplus (t_a \oplus t_b)$, the question is how to save the value of t_c. If t_a is involved in subsequent computations, it cannot be safely updated. If t_a is not used in the subsequent circuit, we can use $t_a = t_a \oplus t_b$ to replace t_c, which requires that t_c does not appear in the previous circuit. Otherwise, t_c is not initialized to $|0\rangle$ and the transformation ignores the original value of t_c.   □

Proposition 1 implies Algorithm 1 to optimize a quantum circuit using the m-XOR technique.

Algorithm 1. Transformation from *creating* operations into *updating* operations

Input: A sequentially written quantum circuit $\mathcal{C}$ in sequence
Output: The optimized quantum circuit with a reduced number of qubits and gates, as well as less quantum depth

```
 1: for each gate g ∈ C do
 2:     if g is creating operation t_c = t_c ⊕ (t_a ⊕ t_b) then
 3:         if t_c appears in the previous circuit then
 4:             Continue
 5:         end if
 6:         Check the subsequent circuit and count the number n_a that t_a is used
 7:         Check the subsequent circuit and count the number n_b that t_b is used
 8:         if n_i = 0 (i = a or b) then
 9:             Replace t_c with t_i in g and in the subsequent circuit
10:         end if
11:     end if
12: end for
13: return C
```

3.2 Applying the m-XOR Technique to AES S-Box

We apply Algorithm 1 to optimize the AES S-box from [12]. The circuit contains 34 AND operations, 120 *creating* operations, and 4 X gates. Apart from the 8-bit inputs $u_0, u_1, \ldots, u_7$ and the 8-bit outputs $s_0, s_1, \ldots, s_7$, the circuit of the S-box requires 120 ancilla qubits: $t_0, \ldots, t_{26}, m_0, \ldots, m_{62}$, and $l_0, \ldots, l_{29}$.

We find that 46 qubits are unnecessary. Our optimized S-box circuit requires only 74 ancilla qubits, denoted as $q_0, q_1, \ldots, q_{73}$. A detailed list of all allocated qubits is provided in Table 2. To facilitate the description, we introduce the AND operation and the X gate, which are defined as follows:

$$\text{AND}(a, b, c) \rightarrow c = a \cdot b,$$
$$\text{X}(a) \rightarrow a = a \oplus 1.$$

Table 2. New structure of S-box of AES with 74 ancilla qubits.

No.	Gate	No.	Gate	No.	Gate
0	CNOT2(u_7, u_4, q_0)	53	AND(q_{15}, q_9, q_{26})	106	CNOT(q_{25}, q_{63})
1	CNOT2(u_7, u_2, q_1)	54	AND(q_{61}, q_{21}, q_{32})	107	CNOT(q_{40}, q_{64})
2	CNOT(u_1, u_7)	55	AND(q_{16}, q_{60}, q_{35})	108	CNOT(q_{36}, q_{65})
3	CNOT2(u_4, u_2, q_2)	56	CNOT(q_{25}, q_{63})	109	CNOT(q_{21}, q_{66})
4	CNOT(u_1, u_3)	57	CNOT2(q_{16}, q_{26}, q_{27})	110	CNOT(q_{39}, q_{67})
5	CNOT2(q_0, u_3, q_3)	58	CNOT2(q_9, q_{16}, q_{28})	111	CNOT(q_{33}, q_{68})
6	CNOT2(u_6, u_5, q_4)	59	CNOT(q_{28}, q_{62})	112	CNOT(q_{16}, q_{69})
7	CNOT2(u_0, q_3, q_5)	60	CNOT2(q_{21}, q_{26}, q_{29})	113	CNOT(q_{38}, q_{70})
8	CNOT2(u_0, q_4, q_6)	61	CNOT2(q_{28}, q_{26}, q_{34})	114	CNOT(q_{41}, q_{71})
9	CNOT2(q_3, q_4, q_7)	62	AND(q_{29}, q_{28}, q_{30})	115	CNOT(q_{37}, q_{72})
10	CNOT(u_2, u_6)	63	AND(q_{27}, q_{25}, q_{31})	116	CNOT2(q_{57}, q_{58}, q_{60})
11	CNOT(u_2, u_5)	64	AND(q_{62}, q_{32}, q_{33})	117	CNOT2(q_{46}, q_{52}, q_{61})
12	CNOT2(u_7, q_2, q_8)	65	AND(q_{63}, q_{35}, q_{36})	118	CNOT2(q_{42}, q_{44}, q_{62})
13	CNOT2(q_3, u_6, q_9)	66	CNOT(q_{25}, q_{26})	119	CNOT2(q_{43}, q_{51}, q_{63})
14	CNOT(u_3, u_6)	67	CNOT(q_{30}, q_{16})	120	CNOT2(q_{50}, q_{54}, q_{64})
15	CNOT(u_5, u_3)	68	CNOT(q_{34}, q_{33})	121	CNOT2(q_{45}, q_{57}, q_{65})
16	CNOT2(q_6, u_3, q_{10})	69	CNOT(q_{31}, q_{21})	122	CNOT2(q_{58}, q_{65}, q_{66})
17	CNOT(u_0, u_4)	70	CNOT(q_{26}, q_{36})	123	CNOT2(q_{42}, q_{63}, q_{67})
18	CNOT(q_4, u_4)	71	CNOT2(q_{33}, q_{36}, q_{37})	124	CNOT2(q_{47}, q_{55}, q_{68})
19	CNOT2(q_0, u_4, q_{11})	72	CNOT2(q_{16}, q_{21}, q_{38})	125	CNOT2(q_{48}, q_{49}, q_{69})
20	CNOT(u_0, u_1)	73	CNOT2(q_{16}, q_{33}, q_{39})	126	CNOT2(q_{49}, q_{64}, q_{70})
21	CNOT(u_1, q_4)	74	CNOT2(q_{21}, q_{36}, q_{40})	127	CNOT2(q_{56}, q_{62}, q_{71})
22	CNOT2(q_1, q_4, q_{12})	75	CNOT2(q_{38}, q_{37}, q_{41})	128	CNOT2(q_{44}, q_{47}, q_{72})
23	CNOT2(q_1, q_7, q_{13})	76	CNOT(q_{40}, q_{64})	129	CNOT2(q_{66}, q_{70}, q_{73})
24	CNOT2(q_{11}, q_{10}, q_{14})	77	CNOT(q_{36}, q_{65})	130	CNOT(q_{60}, q_{46})
25	CNOT2(u_7, u_3, q_{15})	78	CNOT(q_{21}, q_{66})	131	CNOT(q_{57}, q_{48})
26	CNOT(q_0, u_5)	79	CNOT(q_{39}, q_{67})	132	CNOT(q_{61}, q_{51})
27	AND(q_8, q_3, q_{16})	80	CNOT(q_{33}, q_{68})	133	CNOT(q_{60}, q_{52})
28	AND(q_{12}, q_5, q_{17})	81	CNOT(q_{16}, q_{69})	134	CNOT(q_{61}, q_{53})
29	AND(u_4, u_0, q_{18})	82	CNOT(q_{38}, q_{70})	135	CNOT(q_{68}, q_{54})
30	AND(u_7, u_3, q_{19})	83	CNOT(q_{41}, q_{71})	136	CNOT(q_{64}, q_{59})
31	AND(q_4, q_6, q_{20})	84	CNOT(q_{37}, q_{72})	137	CNOT(q_{61}, q_{60})
32	AND(q_{11}, q_{10}, q_{21})	85	AND(q_{40}, q_3, q_{42})	138	CNOT2(q_{61}, q_{67}, s_4)
33	AND(q_0, u_6, q_{22})	86	AND(q_{36}, q_5, q_{43})	139	CNOT2(q_{63}, q_{72}, s_3)
34	AND(q_2, u_5, q_{23})	87	AND(q_{21}, u_0, q_{44})	140	CNOT2(q_{54}, q_{62}, s_0)
35	AND(q_1, q_7, q_{24})	88	AND(q_{39}, u_3, q_{45})	141	CNOT2(q_{51}, q_{69}, s_7)
36	CNOT(q_{16}, q_9)	89	AND(q_{33}, q_6, q_{46})	142	CNOT2(q_{67}, q_{69}, s_6)
37	CNOT(q_{18}, q_{16})	90	AND(q_{16}, q_{10}, q_{47})	143	CNOT2(q_{68}, q_{70}, s_1)
38	CNOT(q_{19}, q_{15})	91	AND(q_{38}, u_6, q_{48})	144	CNOT2(q_{71}, q_{48}, s_5)
39	CNOT(q_{19}, q_{21})	92	AND(q_{41}, u_5, q_{49})	145	CNOT2(q_{71}, q_{53}, s_2)
40	CNOT(q_{22}, q_{23})	93	AND(q_{37}, q_7, q_{50})	146	CNOT(q_{66}, s_7)
41	CNOT(q_{22}, q_{24})	94	AND(q_{64}, q_8, q_{51})	147	CNOT(q_{52}, s_6)
42	CNOT(q_{17}, q_9)	95	AND(q_{65}, q_{12}, q_{52})	148	CNOT(q_{59}, s_5)
43	CNOT(q_{13}, q_{16})	96	AND(q_{66}, u_4, q_{53})	149	X(s_6)
44	CNOT(q_{20}, q_{15})	97	AND(q_{67}, u_7, q_{54})	150	X(s_5)
45	CNOT(q_{24}, q_{21})	98	AND(q_{68}, q_4, q_{55})	151	CNOT(q_{66}, s_4)
46	CNOT(q_{23}, q_9)	99	AND(q_{69}, q_{11}, q_{56})	152	CNOT(q_{60}, s_3)
47	CNOT(q_{24}, q_{16})	100	AND(q_{70}, q_0, q_{57})	153	CNOT(q_{73}, s_2)
48	CNOT(q_{23}, q_{15})	101	AND(q_{71}, q_2, q_{58})	154	CNOT(q_{46}, s_1)
49	CNOT(q_{14}, q_{21})	102	AND(q_{72}, q_1, q_{59})	155	CNOT(q_{66}, s_0)
50	CNOT2(q_{15}, q_{21}, q_{25})	103	CNOT(q_{15}, q_{60})	156	X(s_1)
51	CNOT(q_{15}, q_{60})	104	CNOT(q_9, q_{61})	157	X(s_0)
52	CNOT(q_9, q_{61})	105	CNOT(q_{28}, q_{62})		

We take an example to show the process. In No. 2 of the previous circuit, the operation $CNOT2(u_7, u_1, t_2)$ statistics Proposition 1. Therefore, we can use u_7 to save the value of t_2, reducing one ancilla qubit and one CNOT gate. The gate substitution is

$$CNOT2(u_7, u_1, t_2) \rightarrow CNOT(u_1, u_7).$$

3.3 Comparisons of Resource Estimations of the AES S-Box

There are various implementations of S-box quantum circuits. Some circuits use Toffoli gates, while others use AND gates. We show the comparison of different Toffoli-based circuits in Table 3.

Table 3. Comparison of implementations of S-box using Toffoli gates. "6 + 16" represents 6 ancilla qubits and 16 input and output qubits of the AES S-box.

Source	Width	#Toffoli	#CNOT	#1qCliff	Toffoli depth
[18]	16+16	55	314	4	40
[29]	6 + 16	52	326	4	41
[29]	7 + 16	48	330	4	39
[29]	8 + 16	46	332	4	37
[21]	5 + 16	57	193	4	24
[21]	6 + 16	57	195	4	22
[14]	120 + 16	34	186	4	6
[12]	120 + 16	34	214	4	4
This paper	**74 + 16**	34	**168**	4	4

Next, we compare the S-box circuits utilizing AND gates with [12,14]. The authors estimated both the S-box and S-box† using Q#. To ensure a fair comparison, we adopt the same approach (cf. Table 4). As mentioned in [12], for the 4-th AND layer, the execution of 18 parallel AND gates is required, with each gate necessitating an ancilla qubit, resulting in a total of 18 qubits. We find that $q_{73}, s_0, s_1, \ldots, s_7$ remain $|0\rangle$ after the 4-th AND layer. Thus, the remaining 9 qubits need to be allocated. Thus, the width of the S-box circuit is $74 + 16 + 9 = 99$. We find that the optimized quantum circuit has a reduced number of qubits and gates, as well as less quantum depth.

4 Improved Combination of S-Box and S-Box†

In [14], Jaques *et al.* used the pipeline architecture for AES. Subsequently, Jang *et al.* [13] proposed the shallowed pipeline architecture, which necessitates $120 + 120 = 240$ ancilla qubits for executing S-box and S-box†. In this section, we

Table 4. Comparison of several implementations of S-box and S-box† based on the AND gates. Here #M counts the number of Measurements.

Source	Width	#CNOT	#1qCliff	#T	#M	#TD	#FD
[14]	136	664	205	136	34	6	117
[12]	136	718	208	136	34	4	109
This paper	**99**	**624**	**204**	136	34	4	**101**

present the combined pipeline architecture with the share technique to combine the S-box and S-box†. The combined architecture demonstrates a significant efficiency improvement by utilizing only $74 + 24 = 98$ ancilla qubits. Note that we do not use the inverse S-box in the pipeline architecture.

4.1 Pipeline Architecture for AES

A pipeline architecture is employed to reduce the reuse of qubits and achieve lower T-depth in circuit execution. As is shown in [13], the resource estimation based on AND gates and the pipeline architecture in [14] may underestimate the depth/width cost of the circuits, partly due to the bugs in Q#^{3}. Then, Jang *et al.* [13] proposed a shallowed pipeline architecture as depicted in Fig. 3. In the following, we provide a detailed description of each component.

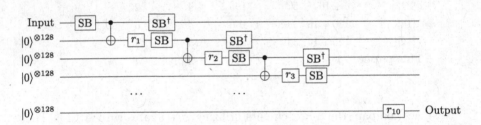

Fig. 3. The shallowed pipeline architecture.

The SubBytes operation comprises 16 distinct S-boxes applied to 16 bytes, denoted as SB in Fig. 3. For the i-th round function R_i, we represent R_i as the sum of SB and r_i. Each S-box takes an 8-qubit input, utilizes a set of ancilla qubits Q_i^1 for each byte B_i ($0 \leq i \leq 15$), and produces an 8-qubit output on the subsequent line. In [13], $|Q_i^1| = 120$. If we do not clean up the ancilla qubits in each Q_i^1, we would need to allocate an ancilla qubit set for the subsequent S-box operations, resulting in a total of 10 rounds $\times$ 16 bytes $\times$ 120 qubits $=$ 19, 200 qubits.

Hence, the use of SB†, which represents the adjoint of SB, becomes necessary to clear the ancilla qubits. During the execution of SB, 16 sets of ancilla qubits

---

^{3} https://github.com/microsoft/qsharp-runtime/issues/1037.

Q_i^1 $(0 \leq i \leq 15)$ are utilized. Subsequently, SB† is employed to clean up the qubits in each Q_i^1. To ensure that the T-depth does not increase, the execution of SB† in R_j and SB in R_{j+1} is performed simultaneously. To achieve this, 16 sets of ancilla qubits Q_k^2 $(0 \leq k \leq 15)$ are required. We illustrate this relationship using an example.

Example 2. We begin with an initial set of 16 Q_i^1 $(0 \leq i \leq 15)$ and 16 Q_k^2 $(0 \leq k \leq 15)$.

- In R_1, SB uses 16 Q_i^1 $(0 \leq i \leq 15)$.
- In R_2, SB uses 16 Q_k^2 $(0 \leq k \leq 15)$ and SB† cleans up the qubits in 16 Q_i^1 $(0 \leq i \leq 15)$.
- Then, in round R_3, SB uses the 16 Q_i^1 $(0 \leq i \leq 15)$ sets, and SB† clears the qubits in the 16 Q_k^2 $(0 \leq k \leq 15)$ sets.
- These two sets of ancilla qubits are alternated in the remaining rounds.
- The total count of ancilla qubits is $2 \times 16 \times 120 = 3840$.

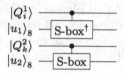

Fig. 4. Independent structure to execute S-box and S-box† simultaneously.

4.2   Combined Pipeline Architecture

For each byte B_i of the state, there are two ancilla qubit sets Q_i^1 and Q_i^2 used in S-box and S-box† (see Fig. 4). With the S-box circuit from [12], the independent structure in [13] requires $|Q_i^1| + |Q_i^2| = 120 + 120 = 240$ ancilla qubits. For 16 bytes of AES, the total ancilla qubit count is $240 \times 16 = 3840$.

We point out that there are unnecessary qubits for this operation, which is based on Observation 2.

Observation 2. *In the independent structure of S-box and S-box†, during the execution of S-box†, the qubits are consistently cleaned up, and these qubits are not utilized in the S-box operation. Conversely, S-box employs a fresh qubit set to select the available qubits.*

Thus, it should be explored to reuse the qubits cleaned up by S-box† immediately. We propose the *share technique* that combines the qubit sets of S-box and S-box† (see Fig. 5). The combination only uses one set, the share set SQ_i. After the analysis in Sect. 4.3, we have $|SQ_i| = 74 + 24 = 98$, which is much smaller than $|Q_i^1| + |Q_i^2| = 240$. Using the combined S-box and S-box†, we can propose the combined pipeline architecture for AES (cf. Fig. 6).

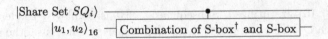

Fig. 5. Combined structure to execute S-box and S-box† simultaneously.

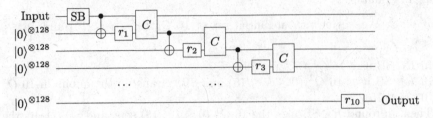

Fig. 6. The combined pipeline architecture, where C is the combined S-box and S-box†.

Discussion on Different Pipeline Architectures. We employ a simple structure to discuss this distinction. Assume that an r-round cipher ($r \geq 1$) consists of only two components, SB and MixColumns, with corresponding depths of d_s ($d_s \geq 1$) and d_m ($d_m \geq 1$). Additionally, SB requires q_s ($q_s \geq 0$) ancilla qubits, MixColumns requires q_m ($q_m \geq 0$) ancilla qubits, and each round requires q_r ($q_r \geq 1$) qubits. Table 5 shows the comparison.

Table 5. Comparison of different pipeline architectures.

Architecture	Width	#FD
Original architecture [14]	$(r+1) \cdot q_r + q_s + q_m$	$d_s + \max(d_s, d_m)$
Shallowed architecture [13]	$(r+1) \cdot q_r + \max(2q_s, q_m)$	$d_s + d_m$
Combined architecture	$(r+1) \cdot q_r + \max((1+\epsilon) \cdot q_s, q_m)$	$d_s + d_m$

In the original pipeline architecture, we first execute SB, and then run SB† and MixColumns simultaneously. Then, we use $((r+1) \cdot q_r + q_s + q_m)$ qubits with depth $(d_s + \max(d_s, d_m))$. For the shallowed pipeline architecture, we use the independent structure to execute SB and SB† simultaneously and then execute MixColumns. The circuit requires $((r+1) \cdot q_r + \max(2q_s, q_m))$ qubits with depth $(d_s + d_m)$. In the combined pipeline architecture, we use the combined structure to execute SB and SB† simultaneously and then execute MixColumns. For the share set, we use $(1 + \epsilon)q_s$ qubits, where ϵ depends on the size of the share set and we have $0 \leq \epsilon \leq 1$. Then, we can obtain the following observation.

Observation 3. *If $d_s > d_m$, the shallowed and combined pipeline architectures have the lowest circuit depth. If $q_m > \epsilon \cdot q_s$, the combined pipeline architecture has the lowest width.*

4.3   Share Technique

The share technique is based on Observation 4, where we determine which qubits can be reused and preassign them accordingly.

Observation 4. *Suppose that S-box and S-box† are executed simultaneously. When S-box† clears up a qubit, the qubit can be immediately reused by S-box.*

Next, we introduce the general share technique in Definition 2. This technique utilizes five sets that satisfy Property 1, defined as follows.

Definition 2. *The share technique utilizes a set SQ_i to execute S-box and S-box† simultaneously for a single byte B_i. Four sets are employed to split SQ_i, where the set with subscript public stores the qubits in the state $|0\rangle$, and the set with subscript private stores the qubits that are being used.*

- *$q_{private}^{old}$ is the set of qubits that will be cleaned up by S-box†.*
- *q_{public}^{old} is the set of unallocated qubits for S-box†.*
- *$q_{private}^{new}$ is the set of qubits used by S-box.*
- *q_{public}^{new} is the set of qubits that are not used by S-box.*

Property 1. The five qubit sets in the public qubit technique satisfy the following equations:

$$SQ_i = q_{private}^{old} \cup q_{public}^{old} = q_{private}^{new} \cup q_{public}^{new},$$
$$q_{private}^{old} \cap q_{public}^{old} = \phi, \ q_{private}^{new} \cap q_{public}^{new} = \phi. \tag{1}$$

These equations can be explained as follows: S-box and S-box† utilize the share set SQ_i in our optimization, where we set $|SQ_i| = 74 + 24 = 98$. For each S-box operation, an ancilla qubit set stores 74 qubits, resulting in $|q_{private}^{old}| = 74$, and $|q_{public}^{old}| = |SQ_i/q_{private}^{old}| = 24$. When S-box† cleans up one qubit q, we have

$$q_{private}^{old} = q_{private}^{old}/\{q\}, \qquad q_{public}^{old} = q_{public}^{old} \cup \{q\}. \tag{2}$$

At the same time, S-box requires qubits to store intermediate values. S-box chooses these qubits from q_{public}^{old}. Assuming that q is chosen by S-box, we have

$$q_{public}^{old} = q_{public}^{old}/\{q\}, \qquad q_{private}^{new} = q_{private}^{new} \cup \{q\}. \tag{3}$$

Finally, after completing the combination, we assign the qubits not used in S-box to q_{public}^{new}, i.e., $q_{public}^{new} = SQ/q_{private}^{new}$. Since this S-box also uses 74 ancilla qubits, we have

$$|q_{private}^{new}| = |q_{private}^{old}| = 74, \qquad |q_{public}^{new}| = |q_{public}^{old}| = 24. \tag{4}$$

Proposition 2 demonstrates that the sizes of the five qubit sets remain unchanged after executing the combination in the share technique.

Proposition 2. *In the share technique, after completing the combination of S-box and S-box†, the sizes of the five qubit sets remain constant.*

Proof. During the combination process, we set $|SQ_i| = a$ and $|q_{private}^{old}| = u$. By Property 1, $|q_{public}^{old}|$ is $z = a - u$.

Next, we examine the combination process in detail. S-box† cleans up all the qubits in $q_{private}^{old}$ and adds them to q_{public}^{old}. This results in a total of $u + z = a$ qubits in q_{public}^{old}. When executing S-box, u qubits are selected from q_{public}^{old}. Therefore, $|q_{public}^{old}|$ remains $a - u = z$. Additionally, the unselected qubits from $|q_{public}^{old}|$, which amount to z, are stored in $|q_{public}^{new}|$.

In conclusion, as long as q_{public}^{old} contains a sufficient number of qubits, the sizes of the qubit sets remain unchanged. This completes the proof. □

Example 3. Suppose we visualize the unallocated qubits in q_{public}^{old} as a pool of water, as shown in Fig. 7. The water in the pool represents the available qubits for allocation. The process in which S-box† cleans up the qubits can be likened to adding water to the pool, replenishing the available qubits. When S-box requires an ancilla qubit, it can be seen as drawing water (qubits) from the pool.

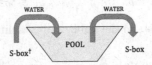

Fig. 7. The water pool in the public qubit technique.

We provide Algorithm 2 to decide the size of SQ_i. In the aforementioned process, the ability to execute the S-box depends on the availability of qubits in the pool. If the pool is empty, the S-box cannot be executed. Specifically, if we find $|q_{public}^{old}| = 0$, it means that no qubits can be selected from q_{public}^{old}, indicating that $|SQ_i|$ is too small to accommodate the S-box operation. Here, $|SQ_i|$ represents the maximum capacity of the "pool" to hold qubits. Therefore, we gradually increase the size until Algorithm 2 no longer returns "Error".

As a result, SQ_i is composed of two parts: the initially set qubits, which are assigned the value $|0\rangle$ and stored in q_{public}^{old}, and the qubits that require cleaning by S-box†, which are stored in $q_{private}^{new}$.

4.4   Applying the Share Technique to the AES S-Box

In this section, we present the complete combination of AES S-box and S-box† using the share technique. We illustrate the implementation of the S-box based on the structure provided in Table 2. To facilitate the combination, we propose a method to split the S-box circuit based on its T-depth. The S-box circuit is divided into several layers, taking into account the T-depth of each gate. The layering scheme is as follows:

Algorithm 2. Combination of S-box and S-box†

Input: Public qubit set SQ_i, used qubit set $q_{private}^{old}$, and unallocated qubit set q_{public}^{old}
Output: New used qubit set $q_{private}^{new}$, and new unallocated qubit set q_{public}^{new}
1: The depth d_{max} is the maximum of depth of S-box and S-box†
2: **for** the current depth d from 1 to d_{max} **do**
3:     **if** $|q_{public}^{old}| = 0$ **then**
4:         **return Error**
5:     **end if**
6:     Choose $q \in q_{public}^{old}$, execute S-box under depth d, and put q into $q_{private}^{new}$
7:     Execute S-box† under depth d. If one qubit q' is cleaned up, put q' into q_{public}^{old}
8: **end for**
9: $q_{public}^{new} = SQ_i / q_{private}^{new}$
10: **return** q_{public}^{new} and $q_{private}^{new}$

- The first layer consists of the gates that precede the execution of T gates (No. 0–26).
- The second layer includes gates with T-depth 1 (No. 27–35).
- The third layer encompasses gates between T-depth 1 and 2 (No. 36–52).
- The fourth layer comprises gates with T-depth 2 (No. 53–55).
- The remaining layers are split according to the proposed method: No. 56–61, No. 62–65, No. 66–84, No. 85–102, No. 103–157.

The circuit is executed in order, with a total of nine layers. We denote each layer as L_i. For S-box†, the order of execution is reversed. The ancilla qubits involved in each layer are specified in Table 6.

Table 6. The layers and the corresponding ancilla qubits in S-box and S-box†.

S-box	Ancilla qubits	S-box†
L_1	$q_0, q_1, q_2, q_3, q_4, q_5, q_6, q_7, q_8, q_9, q_{10}, q_{11}, q_{12}, q_{13}, q_{14}, q_{15}$	L_9
L_2	$q_{16}, q_{17}, q_{18}, q_{19}, q_{20}, q_{21}, q_{22}, q_{23}, q_{24}$	L_8
L_3	q_{25}, q_{60}, q_{61}	L_7
L_4	q_{26}, q_{32}, q_{35}	L_6
L_5	$q_{27}, q_{28}, q_{29}, q_{34}, q_{62}, q_{63}$	L_5
L_6	$q_{30}, q_{31}, q_{33}, q_{36}$	L_4
L_7	$q_{37}, q_{38}, q_{39}, q_{40}, q_{41}, q_{64}, q_{65}, q_{66}, q_{67}, q_{68}, q_{69}, q_{70}, q_{71}, q_{72}$	L_3
L_8	$q_{42}, q_{43}, q_{44}, q_{45}, q_{46}, q_{47}, q_{48}, q_{49}, q_{50}, q_{51}, q_{52}, q_{53}, q_{54}, q_{55}, q_{56}, q_{57}, q_{58}, q_{59}$	L_2
L_9	q_{73}	L_1

In the case of S-box, in each layer L_i, every qubit q represents the qubit that is initially used by the S-box. Prior to L_i, the qubit q is initialized to $|0\rangle$. Conversely, for S-box†, in each layer L_i, each qubit q indicates the qubit that is cleaned up by S-box†. After the completion of L_i, the qubit q is reset to $|0\rangle$.

Table 7. Qubit allocation for the combination of S-box and S-box†. "Previous Pool" is the qubit count of the previous pool in L_i. "Need" is the qubit count that S-box requires in L_i. "Preset Qubits" is the number of qubits that we preset. "Cleaning" is the qubit count that S-box† cleans up. "New Pool" is the qubit count of the new pool.

Layer	Previous pool	Need	Preset qubits	Cleaning	New pool
L_1	0	16	16	1	1
L_2	1	9	8	18	18
L_3	18	3	0	14	29
L_4	29	3	0	4	30
L_5	30	6	0	6	30
L_6	30	4	0	3	29
L_7	29	14	0	3	18
L_8	18	18	0	9	9
L_9	9	1	0	16	24

To ensure that the T-depth remains unchanged, we align each layer in S-box and S-box†. In each layer L_i, when S-box requires a qubit in the $|0\rangle$ state, we check if the water pool is empty. If the pool is empty, we preset a qubit in the pool, thereby increasing the size of SQ_i. After the completion of L_i, the qubits that are cleaned up by S-box† are placed back into the pool for the next layer L_{i+1}. The size of SQ_i is the sum of $q_{private}^{old}$ and the number of preset qubits. The complete qubit allocation is illustrated in Table 7, and we provide a detailed explanation below.

- Prior to L_1, there are no qubits in the pool.
- During the execution of L_1, we preset 16 qubits in S-box. Then, one qubit is cleaned up by S-box† and added to the pool.
- In L_2, we need to preset an additional 8 qubits in the pool. A total of 18 qubits are cleaned up by S-box†, resulting in a pool size of 18 qubits.
- The subsequent steps follow a similar pattern.

Table 8. Cost comparison of the cost of the combination of S-box and S-box†. Here 32 qubits represent 16-bit inputs and 16-bit outputs of two bytes.

Source	Method	Width	#CNOT	#Toffoli(AND)	Toffoli(AND) depth
[13]	Independence	$120 + 120 + 32 = 240 + 32$	428	68	4
This paper	**Combination**	$74 + 24 + 32 = 98 + 32$	**312**	68	4

In total, we preset 24 qubits in the pool. Consequently, $|SQ_i| = 74 + 24 = 98$. Prior to executing the combination, 74 ancilla qubits are utilized, and then we allocate 24 qubits with an initial state of $|0\rangle$ in q_{public}^{old}. After the combination, there are still 24 qubits remaining in the pool for subsequent combinations (see Proposition 2). Therefore, we have $|SQ| = 98$, $|q^{old}_{public}| = 24$, $|q^{old}_{private}| = 74$, $|q^{new}_{public}| = 24$, and $|q^{new}_{private}| = 74$. We give the complete comparison in Table 8. The number of ancilla qubits is reduced from 240 to 98.

5 The Components of Quantum Circuits for AES

This section describes the quantum circuits for the AES components Mix-Columns, Key Schedule, AddRoundKey, and ShiftRows. We mainly introduce the improvement of the depth of MixColumns. Other components are similar to the previous work.

5.1 Implementation of MixColumns

The implementation of MixColumns has been widely studied [12,13,29]. Usually, we can use optimized classical circuits to reduce the cost (see for example [17, 19,22,23,28]).

Table 9. New circuit of MixColumns with quantum depth 16. Here every number represents a qubit. Update(b, a) represents the CNOT operation $|a\rangle |b\rangle \rightarrow |a\rangle |a \oplus b\rangle$. $|y_0\rangle, |y_1\rangle, \ldots, |y_{31}\rangle$ are represented by 24, 1, 10, 11, 12, 13, 30, 15, 8, 25, 2, 3, 4, 5, 14, 7, 0, 17, 26, 19, 20, 29, 22, 31, 16, 9, 18, 27, 28, 21, 6, 23, respectively.

Operation	Operation	Operation	Operation	Operation	Operation
Depth 1	Update(12, 28)	Update(11, 27)	Update(5, 4)	Update(7, 31)	Update(11, 3)
Update(31, 23)	**Depth 3**	Update(13, 21)	**Depth 8**	Update(4, 28)	Update(9, 1)
Update(24, 8)	Update(7, 15)	Update(30, 14)	Update(18, 23)	**Depth 11**	**Depth 14**
Update(21, 29)	Update(8, 23)	Update(18, 17)	Update(20, 11)	Update(23, 6)	Update(22, 30)
Update(26, 18)	Update(9, 25)	Update(28, 23)	Update(19, 26)	Update(1, 25)	Update(13, 5)
Update(1, 17)	Update(4, 12)	**Depth 6**	Update(3, 10)	Update(19, 31)	Update(7, 15)
Update(11, 3)	Update(6, 13)	Update(0, 31)	Update(12, 7)	Update(17, 7)	Update(16, 8)
Update(10, 2)	Update(2, 17)	Update(14, 5)	Update(24, 16)	Update(10, 2)	Update(3, 27)
Update(28, 20)	Update(5, 28)	Update(27, 2)	**Depth 9**	Update(28, 20)	Update(1, 17)
Update(14, 22)	**Depth 4**	Update(21, 20)	Update(23, 30)	Update(26, 18)	**Depth 15**
Update(27, 19)	Update(25, 8)	Update(28, 19)	Update(26, 1)	**Depth 12**	Update(14, 22)
Update(13, 5)	Update(16, 7)	Update(17, 24)	Update(18, 10)	Update(31, 22)	Update(5, 21)
Depth 2	Update(12, 11)	**Depth 7**	Update(3, 7)	Update(25, 16)	Update(15, 31)
Update(23, 7)	Update(30, 13)	Update(0, 24)	Update(20, 31)	Update(6, 14)	Update(27, 19)
Update(25, 1)	Update(15, 14)	Update(14, 29)	Update(4, 12)	Update(19, 11)	Update(8, 24)
Update(22, 6)	Update(29, 28)	Update(27, 18)	**Depth 10**	Update(1, 0)	Update(17, 25)
Update(20, 4)	Update(17, 23)	Update(20, 12)	Update(23, 15)	**Depth 13**	**Depth 16**
Update(17, 9)	**Depth 5**	Update(2, 26)	Update(18, 9)	Update(22, 13)	Update(31, 23)
Update(29, 13)	Update(8, 0)	Update(28, 3)	Update(10, 1)	Update(16, 7)	Update(21, 29)

In quantum key search, the full depth of the circuit influences the time cost for Grover's search. However, the depth in classical circuits and quantum circuits is different. The main reason is that one qubit cannot be used in two gates simultaneously. The previous work merely translated the optimal classical circuits into quantum circuits. However, we believe that relaxing the gate count constraint could lead to better depth performance. Therefore, we relaxed the gate count constraint in Xiang *et al.*'s approach in [28] and generated a series of candidate circuits. Then, we can calculate their quantum depth quickly. As a result, we obtained an in-place circuit with a depth of 16 (cf. Table 9) for comparison (cf. Table 10).

Table 10. Comparison of MixColumns implementations for each column.

Source	#CNOT	Width	#FD
[3, 23]	206	135	13
[19]	210	137	**11**
[14]	277	32	111
[8, 29]	277	32	39
[28]	92	32	30
This Paper	98	32	**16**

5.2   Implementation of the Key Schedule

In the key schedule of AES, we use several 32-bit words to save the key. For AES-128, we use 128 qubits to represent the 128-bit master key (called W_0, W_1, W_2, W_3). After executing XOR operations for these qubits and the 128-bit state, we update 128 qubits for the next AddRoundKey operation.

The schedule is similar to [12–14]. Firstly, we use four ancilla qubit set SQ_i ($0 \leq I \leq 3$) to run SubWord, which requires $4 \times 98 = 392$ ancilla qubits. All the S-boxes in the key schedule and round function are designed to operate in parallel. SubWord† is executed in the next round to clean up the ancilla qubits, which is introduced in Sect. 4. The 32-bit output values of SubWord are XORed to $|W_{4i+0}\rangle$. The Rcon operation is implemented with X gates for the corresponding qubits to generate W_{4i+4}. Finally, $W_{4i+5}, W_{4i+6}, W_{4i+7}$ are updated by CNOT gates. Rcon is executed by adding X gates. The schedule in our pipeline architecture is similar to [12–14].

5.3   Implementation of AddRoundKey and ShiftRows

In AddRoundKey, 128 CNOT gates are required and no ancilla qubits are set. For the ShiftRows operation, the swap for qubits is a logical operation that only changes the index of qubits. Therefore, the operation does not require any gates.

6   Quantum Circuit of AES Based on the Pipelined Architecture

As mentioned in Sect. 4, the pipelined architecture is suitable for implementing low-depth AES circuits. In this section, we have made improvements with different quantum circuits based on the combined pipeline architecture using ProjectQ. The code is available at https://github.com/QunLiu-sdu/Improved-Quantum-Circuits-for-AES. Then, we provide a more precise analysis of the Grover algorithm's complexity.

6.1   Resource Estimations Based on the Toffoli Gate and and Gate

In [12,13,18,20,21,29], the authors present the quantum resources needed for the circuits without decomposing the Toffoli gates. We adhere to the same circuit metrics to facilitate a fair comparison.

Grover's algorithm requires us to estimate the complexity resulting from decomposing Toffoli gates. According to [26], the Toffoli gate can be decomposed:

- the circuit with T-depth 1 and 4 ancilla qubits;
- the circuit with T-depth 4 and 0 ancilla qubits.

On the other hand, in [13,14], the authors recommend using AND gates to achieve a lower complexity for Grover's algorithm. We also utilize AND-based decomposition to construct AES quantum circuits. In fact, the circuits constructed using this method have the lowest circuit depth. We applied these circuits to Grover's algorithm, obtaining more precise resource estimates.

The structure of each AES round is shown in Fig. 6. For each round, 20 S-boxes are executed in parallel (16 S-boxes for SubBytes and 4 S-boxes for Sub-Word). In R_1, we execute 20 S-boxes with 20 shared qubit sets because no S-boxes[†] are required. In other rounds, we execute 20 combinations of S-box and S-box[†]. After S-box operations, the output is saved in 128 new qubits for the ShiftRows, MixColumns, and AddRoundKey operations.

Moreover, for each AES quantum circuit, we considered two implementations for the linear layer:

- in-place circuit, which utilizes the circuit found by us with depth 16.
- out-of-place circuit, which is from [19] with depth 11.

In Table 11, the results use the Toffoli gate and do not decompose it. Our circuit achieves the optimal trade-off between Toffoli depth and width. In conclusion, compared with the previous lowest results in [21], the product of our implementations achieved a reduction of 35%, 38%, 36% for AES-128, -192, and -256, respectively. Compared with the shallowed architecture in [13], the number of qubits achieves a reduction of 42%, 41%, and 36%, respectively.

In Table 12, we show the results of decomposing Toffoli gates into circuits with T-depth 4. Compared with the shallowed architecture in [13], the number of qubits, full depth, and DW-cost achieve a reduction. The minimum depth of circuits is 770, 924, and 1074 for AES-128, -192, and -256 respectively. Table 13 also shows the results of decomposing Toffoli gates into circuits with T-depth 1. To reduce the T-depth, we employed additional qubits to implement the quantum circuit.

The circuits using the AND gates are shown in Table 14, which achieves the lower circuit depth. For the in-place version, the circuit depth achieves a reduction of 13.8%, 13.6%, and 14.3%, respectively. It is worth noting that the circuits with the AND gate and out-of-place linear layer have a lower depth. For AES-128, -192, and -256, we only require the depth of 730, 876, and 1,018, respectively.

In conclusion, for the different types of AND operations, we find that the circuits decomposed using AND gates have the lowest complexity for Grover's algorithm, which we show in Sect. 6.2. We also used the AES S-box with T-depth 3 proposed in [12]. Since the number of gates was almost doubled, we were not able to obtain high-quality Grover algorithm attack complexity.

Table 11. Comparisons of quantum resources of AES without decomposing the Toffoli gates.

Cipher	Source	#CNOT	#NOT	#Toffoli	Toffoli depth	Width	Toffoli depth × Width
AES-128	[8]	166,548	1,456	151,552	12,672	984	12,469,248
	[1]	192,832	1,370	150,528	–	976	–.
	[20]	53,360	1,072	16,688	12,168	264	3,212,352
	[18]	107,960	1,570	16,940	1,880	864	1,624,320
	[29]	128,517	4,528	19,788	2,016	512	1,032,192
	[12]$(p = 9)$	126,016	2,528	17,888	1,558	374	582,692
	[20]	53,496	1,072	16,664	1,472	328	482,816
	[12]$(p = 18)$	126,016	2,528	17,888	820	492	403,440
	[13]	81,312	800	12,240	40	6,368	254,720
	[21]$(m = 16)$	77,984	2,224	19,608	476	474	225,624
	This paper(out-of-place)	75,024	800	12,920	40	**4,823**	192,920
	This paper(in-place)	65,736	800	12,920	40	**3,667**	146,680
AES-192	[8]	189,432	1,608	172,032	11,088	1,112	12,329,856
	[20]	70,736	1,160	19,328	14,496	328	4,754,688
	[18]	125,580	1,692	19,580	1,640	896	1,469,440
	[29]	152,378	5,128	22,380	2,022	640	1,294,080
	[13]	92,856	896	14,008	48	6,688	321,024
	[21]$(m = 16)$	90,832	2,568	22,800	572	538	307,736
	This paper(out-of-place)	85,808	896	14,552	48	**5,356**	257,088
	This paper(in-place)	74,456	896	14,552	48	**3,935**	188,880
AES-256	[8]	233,836	1,943	215,040	14,976	1,336	20,007,936
	[20]	74,472	1,367	23,480	17,412	392	6,825,504
	[18]	151,011	1,992	23,760	2,160	1,232	2,661,120
	[29]	177,645	6,103	26,774	2,292	768	1,760,256
	[13]	113,744	1,103	17,408	56	6,976	390,656
	[21]$(m = 16)$	110,688	3,069	27,816	646	502	388,892
	This paper(out-of-place)	106,704	1,119	18,360	56	**6,097**	341,432
	This paper(in-place)	93,288	1,119	18,360	56	**4,429**	248,024

Table 12. Comparisons of quantum resources of AES decomposing Toffoli gates with T-depth 4.

Cipher	Source	#CNOT	#1qCliff	#T	T-depth	Width	DW-cost	#FD
AES-128	[13](out-of-place)	164,256	16,832	85,680	160	7,520	1,203,200	799
	This paper(out-of-place)	152,544	19,080	90,440	160	4,844	775,040	**770**
	[13](in-place)	154,752	14,400	85,680	160	6,368	1,018,880	978
	This paper(in-place)	143,256	19,080	90,440	160	**3,688**	590,080	840
AES-192	[13](out-of-place)	188,520	19,440	98,056	192	8,096	1,554,432	955
	This paper(out-of-place)	173,120	21,384	101,864	192	5,356	1,028,352	**924**
	[13](in-place)	176,904	16,400	98,056	192	6,688	1,284,096	1,174
	This paper(in-place)	161,768	21,384	101,864	192	**3,944**	755,136	1,010
AES-256	[13](out-of-place)	231,920	23,519	121,856	224	8,640	1,935,360	1,118
	This paper(out-of-place)	216,864	26,759	128,520	224	6,124	1,371,776	**1,074**
	[13](in-place)	218,192	19,871	121,856	224	6,976	1,562,624	1,377
	This paper(in-place)	203,448	26,759	128,520	224	**4,456**	998,144	1,176

Table 13. Comparisons of quantum resources of AES decomposing Toffoli gates with T-depth 1.

Cipher	Source	#CNOT	#1qCliff	#T	T-depth	Width	DW-cost	#FD
AES-128	**This paper**(out-of-place)	281,744	19,080	90,440	40	4,844	193,760	**750**
	This paper(in-place)	272,456	19,080	90,440	40	**3,691**	147,640	820
AES-192	**This paper**(out-of-place)	318,640	21,384	101,864	48	5,356	257,088	**900**
	This paper(in-place)	307,288	21,384	101,864	48	**3,947**	189,456	986
AES-256	**This paper**(out-of-place)	400,464	26,759	128,520	56	6,124	342,944	**1,046**
	This paper(in-place)	387,048	26,759	128,520	56	**4,459**	249,704	1,148

Table 14. Comparisons of quantum resources with the AND gates.

Cipher	Source	#CNOT	#1qCliff	#T	#M	T-depth	Width	DW-cost	#FD
AES-128	[13](out-of-place)	152,496	39,952	27,200	5,440	40	7,524	300,960	749
	This paper(out-of-place)	141,664	51,800	27,200	6,120	40	**4,844**	193,760	730
	[13](in-place)	142,992	37,520	27,200	5,440	40	6,372	254,880	928
	This paper(in-place)	132,376	51,800	27,200	6,120	40	**3,689**	147,560	800
AES-192	[13](out-of-place)	174,152	46,232	30,464	6,392	48	8,100	388,800	895
	This paper(out-of-place)	160,608	58,424	30,464	6,936	48	**5,356**	257,088	876
	[13](in-place)	162,536	43,192	30,464	6,392	48	6,692	321,216	1,114
	This paper(in-place)	149,256	58,424	30,464	6,936	48	**3,945**	189,360	962
AES-256	[13](out-of-place)	213,624	56,975	37,536	8,024	56	8,644	484,064	1,048
	This paper(out-of-place)	200,544	73,879	38,080	8,840	56	**6,124**	342,944	1,018
	[13](in-place)	199,896	53,327	37,536	8,024	56	6,980	390,880	1,307
	This paper(in-place)	187,128	73,879	38,080	8,840	56	**4,457**	249,592	1,120

6.2 Performance of Grover's Algorithm

In this part, based on the circuits implemented using AND gates and the out-of-place linear layer, we applied these AES circuits to Grover's algorithm, obtaining more precise and efficient resource estimates (cf. Table 15). "$r = \lceil k/n \rceil$" (plaintext, ciphertext) is the number of pairs that are required to recover a unique key. For AES-128, we just choose $r = 1$. For AES-192/-256, we choose $r = 2$. It implies that we need to use two plaintext-ciphertext pairs to determine the key. In terms of resources corresponding to Grover's algorithm, one key expansion algorithm corresponds to two round functions. We primarily focus on four metrics, $FD \times G$, $FD \times W$, $FD^2 \times G$, and $FD^2 \times W$.

Table 15. Quantum resources required for Grover's search on AES.

Cipher	r	Source	Width (W)	Gates (G)	#FD	$FD \times G$	$FD \times W$	$FD^2 \times G$	$FD^2 \times W$
AES-128	1	[14]	1.92×2^{11}	1.33×2^{82}	1.08×2^{75}	1.436×2^{157}	1.038×2^{87}	1.551×2^{232}	1.120×2^{162}
		[13]	1.84×2^{12}	1.36×2^{82}	1.15×2^{74}	1.564×2^{156}	1.055×2^{87}	1.797×2^{230}	1.212×2^{161}
		This paper	1.18×2^{12}	1.37×2^{82}	1.12×2^{74}	$\mathbf{1.535 \times 2^{156}}$	$\mathbf{1.325 \times 2^{86}}$	$\mathbf{1.719 \times 2^{230}}$	$\mathbf{1.480 \times 2^{160}}$
AES-192	2	[14]	1.02×2^{13}	1.50×2^{115}	1.14×2^{107}	1.710×2^{222}	1.163×2^{120}	1.949×2^{239}	1.326×2^{227}
		[13]	1.84×2^{13}	1.45×2^{115}	1.37×2^{106}	1.988×2^{221}	1.261×2^{120}	1.365×2^{328}	1.731×2^{226}
		This paper	1.24×2^{13}	1.44×2^{115}	1.35×2^{106}	$\mathbf{1.944 \times 2^{221}}$	$\mathbf{1.679 \times 2^{119}}$	$\mathbf{1.312 \times 2^{328}}$	$\mathbf{1.130 \times 2^{226}}$
AES-256	2	[14]	1.09×2^{13}	1.84×2^{147}	1.29×2^{139}	1.187×2^{287}	1.401×2^{152}	1.531×2^{426}	1.814×2^{291}
		[13]	1.96×2^{13}	1.74×2^{147}	1.61×2^{138}	1.398×2^{286}	1.576×2^{152}	1.123×2^{425}	1.266×2^{291}
		This paper	1.43×2^{13}	1.76×2^{147}	1.56×2^{138}	$\mathbf{1.373 \times 2^{286}}$	$\mathbf{1.117 \times 2^{152}}$	$\mathbf{1.071 \times 2^{425}}$	$\mathbf{1.740 \times 2^{290}}$

7 Quantum Circuit of AES Based on the Zig-Zag Architecture

In this section, we propose AES circuits based on the zig-zag architecture utilizing AND gates. The zig-zag architecture is typically employed for low-width implementations.

At ASIACRYPT 2022, Huang *et al.* [12] aimed to reduce the DW-cost in the zig-zag architecture by introducing low-depth S-boxes based on AND gates. They proposed an improved zig-zag architecture based on the round-in-place technique. The S-box requires 120 ancilla qubits with T-depth 4, resulting in a minimum DW-cost of 204,800 (width $\times$ T-depth $= 2,560 \times 80$) for AES-128. We notice that several papers have adopted similar circuits based on the round-in-place technique to optimize the quantum circuit for AES (cf. [21]).

Our approach begins by introducing the zig-zag architecture and round-in-place technique. We then highlight the advantages of utilizing the *round-in-place zig-zag* architecture iteratively, offering an improved trade-off between width and T-depth. Subsequently, we propose a new circuit for the AES S-box that significantly reduces the required ancilla qubits to just $60 + 10$. By employing this optimized S-box in the circuits in [12], we achieve a substantial reduction in DW-cost, resulting in a final value of 132,800 (width $\times$ T-depth $= 1,660 \times 80$).

7.1 Zig-Zag Architecture and Round-in-Place Technique in [12]

The zig-zag architecture is proposed in [8], which reduces the number of qubits by performing reverse operations in each round (cf. Fig. 8). R_1, R_2, R_3, and R_4 are performed in order. Then, $R_3^\dagger$, $R_2^\dagger$, and $R_1^\dagger$ are utilized to clean up the 4-*th*, 3-*rd*, and 2-*nd* lines, which can be reused to store the outputs of R_7, R_6, and R_5, respectively. Other rounds proceed similarly. This method requires a larger T-depth. Subsequently, at ASIACRYPT 2020, Zou *et al.* [29] improved the zig-zag architecture and implemented AES-128 with 512 qubits and Toffoli depth 2016.

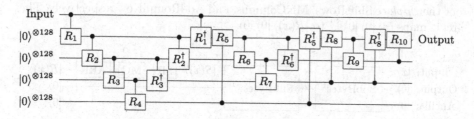

Fig. 8. Zig-zag architecture.

Huang *et al.* [12] improved the zig-zag architecture based on a round-in-place technique. We simply introduce the technique. Suppose U_f is a circuit that map $|x\rangle\,|0\rangle\,|0\rangle^{\otimes a}$ to $|x\rangle\,|S(x)\rangle\,|0\rangle^{\otimes a}$, where $|0\rangle^{\otimes a}$ denotes the ancilla qubits, then, U_f is not *in-place*. If we also have the inverse circuit $U_{f^{-1}}$ that maps $|S(x)\rangle\,|x\rangle\,|0\rangle^{\otimes a}$ to $|S(x)\rangle\,|0\rangle\,|0\rangle^{\otimes a}$, we can achieve the *in-place* circuit by swapping $|x\rangle$ and $|S(x)\rangle$. Figure 9 shows a round-in-place S-box circuit, which maps $|x\rangle\,|0\rangle\,|0\rangle^{\otimes a}$ to $|S(x)\rangle\,|0\rangle\,|0\rangle^{\otimes a}$.

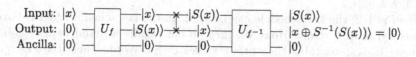

Fig. 9. Round-in-place S-box circuit.

Usually, U_f is easy to construct. Huang *et al.* [12] provide a method to convert U_f into $U_{f^{-1}}$. Suppose $x, y \in \mathbb{F}_2^8$ are the input and output of U_f. we have $y = LS_0(x) + c$, where L is a linear function and $S_0(x)$ is the inverse of x in $\mathbb{F}_2^8$. Then, $x = S_0^{-1}L^{-1}(y + c) = S_0L^{-1}(y + c) = L^{-1}(LS_0)L^{-1}(y + c)$. Let the last 4 X gates of AES S-box be U_c. $U_f = U_0 + U_c$, where U_0 implements $|x\rangle\,|0\rangle\,|0\rangle \rightarrow |x\rangle\,|LS_0(x)\rangle\,|0\rangle$. Then, the circuit in Fig. 10 is $U_{f^{-1}}$, where U_L and $U_{L^{-1}}$ are the circuits of L and L^{-1}, respectively. Huang *et al.* provide an SAT-based method and implement U_L or $U_{L^{-1}}$ by 14 CNOT gates. Finally, adding $14 \times 3 = 42$ CNOT gates and 4 X gates, U_f can be converted into $U_{f^{-1}}$.

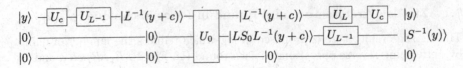

Fig. 10. The circuit of U_{f-1} based on U_f.

Based on the *round-in-place* S-box circuit, one can construct the *round-in-place* round function R_i easily. Figure 11 shows the round function. SubByte[1] uses S-box circuits. SubByte^{-1} uses S-box^{-1} circuits. SB, MC, and ARK represent the *in-place* ShiftRows, MixColumns, and AddRoundKey, respectively. The circuit maps $|x\rangle\,|0\rangle\,|0\rangle^{\otimes a}$ to $|R(x)\rangle\,|0\rangle\,|0\rangle^{\otimes a}$.

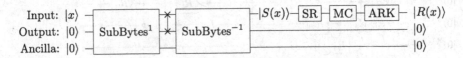

Fig. 11. Round-in-place round function of AES.

7.2 Executing the Round-in-Place Round Function Iteratively

In [12,21], the authors provide a method for executing the round-in-place round function iteratively. We simply introduce the technique. For AES, there are 16 bytes for the state. Each byte requires an ancilla qubit set to run round-in-place S-box circuits. If only m S-boxes of SubBytes are executed in parallel, then $16/m$ ancilla qubit sets are needed. We define the number of iterations as $i = 16/m$ ($i = 1, 2, 4, 8, 16$).

For $i = 1, 2$, the key schedule can be split. In the key schedule, four S-boxes are needed in each round. However, they do not require a round-in-place S-box because $|W_{4i+0}\rangle$ contains the output values of SubWord. Thus, the schedule only uses the U_f mapping $|x\rangle\,|y\rangle\,|0\rangle^{\otimes a}$ to $|x\rangle\,|y \oplus S(x)\rangle\,|0\rangle^{\otimes a}$. The S-box used in the schedule is single-depth, while the round-in-place S-box in the round function is double-depth. We can split the SubWord in the key schedule into two parts (cf. Fig. 12). SubWord$_{\frac{1}{2}}$ indicates that only half of SubWord is used in the operations. The first part and SubByte[1] are executed in parallel. The second part and SubByte^{-1} are executed in parallel. For more detailed information, refer to [12,21].

For $i = 4, 8, 16$, we execute two operations in parallel (cf. Fig. 13). We take $i = 4$ as an example. SB$_{\frac{1}{4}}$ represents a quarter of SubBytes and SW$_{\frac{1}{4}}$ represents a quarter of SubWord. It requires five ancilla qubit sets and the T-depth is four double-depth S-boxes.

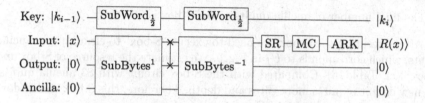

Fig. 12. Two parts in round function for $i = 1$.

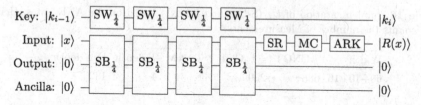

Fig. 13. Round-in-place round function executing SubBytes and SubWord in parallel for $i = 4$.

7.3   Constructing a Low-Width S-Box Circuit

To improve the circuit, we constructed a new AES S-box circuit with only $60 + 10$ ancilla qubits. The circuit is suitable for the *round-in-place* zig-zag architecture with AND gates.

Next, we present this construction method, which always allows the use of the minimum number of qubits without increasing the T-depth. Our approach first satisfies the maximum parallel count of AND gates in different layers.

- For the structure of AES S-box with T-depth 4 in [12], 8 input qubits $u_0, \ldots, u_7$, and 8 output qubits $s_0, \ldots, s_7$.
- We consider that the target qubit of each AND gate is allocated as $|0\rangle$. $q_0, q_1, \ldots, q_{33}$ are allocated for each target qubit. There are 9, 3, 4, and 18 target qubits in T-depth 1, 2, 3, and 4, respectively.
- Because the layer in T-depth 4 contains the most AND gates, we must satisfy its parallelism first. Thus, $q_{34}, q_{35}, \ldots, q_{50}$ are allocated as the inputs of these AND gates.
- However, the AND gates in T-depth 4 still cannot be implemented in parallel. The main reason is that nine qubits are included in two AND gates at the same time.
- We have to allocate nine qubits $q_{51}, q_{52}, \ldots, q_{59}$ to restore these qubits. Thus, there are 60 ancilla qubits $q_0, q_1, \ldots, q_{59}$ in T-depth 4. Note that $q_{51}, q_{52}, \ldots, q_{59}$ can be reset as $|0\rangle$ after these AND gates and be used in other AND gates.
- In other layers, AND gates do not require any more ancilla qubits. The lower bound on the number of ancilla qubits is 60.
- For the 4-*th* AND layer, 18 ancilla qubits are required for the AND gates. Apart from 8 qubits from $s_0, s_1, \ldots, s_7$, we need to allocate 10 ancilla qubits.

– The final number of ancilla qubits of the S-box is 70.

After executing the S-box, we need to execute S-box† to clean up the ancilla qubits, which corresponds to U_f in Fig. 9. We estimate the resource of S-box and S-box† (cf. Table 16). Compared with the S-box circuit with 83 ancilla qubits, the new circuit requires more gates and depth. Therefore, this S-box circuit does not optimize the complexity of Grover's algorithm.

Table 16. Implementation of U_f (S-box and S-box†) based on the AND gates. Here #M counts the number of Measurements.

Width	#CNOT	#1qCliff	#T	#M	T-depth	Full depth
60+10+16	688	220	136	34	4	132

Figure 10 shows how to transform U_f into $U_{f^{-1}}$, which requires 42 additional CNOT gates and 4 X gates based on U_f. Thus, $U_{f^{-1}}$ requires $688 + 42 = 730$ CNOT gates and $220 + 4 = 224$ 1qClifford gates.

In the previous work [12,29], there are two types of S-boxes. The first type is used in SubBytes, called the $\mathcal{C}^0$-circuit, which maps $|x\rangle |0\rangle |0\rangle^{\otimes a}$ to $|x\rangle |S(x)\rangle |0\rangle^{\otimes a}$. The second type is used in SubWord, called the $\mathcal{C}^*$-circuit, which maps $|x\rangle |y\rangle |0\rangle^{\otimes a}$ to $|x\rangle |y \oplus S(x)\rangle |0\rangle^{\otimes a}$. We follow a unified principle to design the circuit of the AES S-box. If the output qubits $s_0, s_1, \ldots, s_7$ are only used to save the output, the S-box is suitable for both $\mathcal{C}^0$- and $\mathcal{C}^*$-circuits. Note that for the $\mathcal{C}^*$-circuit, 18 ancilla qubits are also required for the AND gates. As 8 qubits from $s_0, s_1, \ldots, s_7$ can not be used. we need to allocate 18 ancilla qubits.

7.4   Applying New S-Box Circuit into the Architecture in [12]

With reference to Fig. 12, we can calculate the resources for each round of AES. We take AES-128 as an example. Note that there is no MixColumns operation in the last round of AES. In SubBytes[1], there are 16 U_f. In SubBytes^{-1}, there are 16 $U_{f^{-1}}$. In MixColumns, there are $92 \times 4 = 368$ CNOT gates. In AddRoundKey, there are 128 CNOT gates. In the Key Schedule, there are 4 U_f, and at most 4 X gates for Rcon. Therefore, one round of AES requires 20 U_f, 16 $U_{f^{-1}}$, $368 + 128 = 496$ CNOT gates, and at most 4 X gates for Rcon. AES-128 requires $10 \times 20 = 200$ U_f, $10 \times 16 = 160$ $U_{f^{-1}}$, $10 \times 496 - 368 = 4592$ CNOT gates, and $8 \times 1 + 2 \times 4 = 16$ X gates.

Next, based on the number of iterations i ($i = 1, 2, 4, 8, 16$), different trade-offs of width/T-depth are provided in Table 17. We describe how to calculate the number of ancilla qubits and T-depth.

For the case of $i = 1, 2$, we execute the two-part round function (cf. Fig. 12), which allows the key schedule to require only $\frac{2}{i} \times (60 + 18)$ ancilla qubits. In round function, SubBytes[1] and SubBytes^{-1} require $\frac{16}{i} \times (60 + 10)$ ancilla qubits. The number of ancilla qubits is $\frac{2}{i} \times 78 + \frac{16}{i} \times 70$. Then, 256 input qubits and

Table 17. Different trade-offs of width/T-depth for quantum circuit of AES-128.

AES-128	Width	T-depth	DW-cost
$i = 1$	$256 + 128 + 156 + 1120 = 1660$	$80 \times 1 = 80$	**132,800**
$i = 2$	$256 + 64 + 78 + 560 = 958$	$80 \times 2 = 160$	153,280
$i = 4$	$256 + 32 + 78 + 280 = 646$	$80 \times 4 = 320$	206,720
$i = 8$	$256 + 16 + 78 + 140 = 490$	$80 \times 8 = 640$	313,600
$i = 16$	$256 + 8 + 78 + 70 = 412$	$80 \times 16 = 1280$	527,360

$\frac{128}{i}$ output qubits are needed. For each round, the T-depth is $4 \times 2 \times i = 8i$. Therefore, T-depth of AES-128 is $10 \times 8i = 80i$.

For the case of $i = 4, 8, 16$, we execute the round function like Fig. 13. The key schedule requires 78 ancilla qubits. In round function, SubBytes^1 and SubBytes^{-1} require $\frac{16}{i} \times 70$ ancilla qubits. The number of ancilla qubits is $78 + \frac{16}{i} \times 70$. Then, 256 input qubits and $\frac{128}{i}$ output qubits are needed. The T-depth is $10 \times i \times 2 \times 4 = 80i$.

Furthermore, we can also make an interleaved execution of the S-boxes between key schedule and round functions, reducing the number of additional qubits by increasing the T-depth (cf. Fig. 14). However, this method does not affect the lowest DW-cost. Therefore, we compared this approach with the circuits used in [12] in Fig. 1.

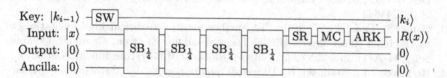

Fig. 14. Round-in-place round function executing SubBytes and SubWord serially for $i = 4$.

Finally, AES-128 can be implemented by the *round-in-place* round function with the lower DW-cost 132,800, while the previous best result is 204,800 in [12]. For AES-192, we achieve a circuit with DW-cost (width $\times$ T-depth) $1,724 \times 96 = 165,504$. For AES-256, we achieve a circuit with DW-cost (width $\times$ T-depth) $1,788 \times 112 = 200,256$.

8   Conclusion

In this paper, we investigated the optimization of quantum circuits for AES variants (-128, -192, -256). We provided an improved structure of the S-box based on the m-XOR technique and combined the S-box and S-box† based on the share technique. Then, we introduce the implementations of the AES components. Next, we estimated the required resources based on the pipelined and zig-zag architectures with Toffoli gates and AND gates. The combined pipeline architecture reduces the depth and the number of qubits required for various quantum circuits. Although our circuits perform well in the quantum case, we believe that further improvements are possible by exploiting the structure of the S-box. If a superior S-box circuit is proposed, our method can be immediately applied to reduce the complexity of the AES quantum circuit.

Acknowledgements. The authors would like to thank the anonymous reviewers for their valuable comments and suggestions to improve the quality of the paper. This work is supported by the National Key Research and Development Program of China (Grant No. 2018YFA0704702), the National Natural Science Foundation of China (Grant No. 62032014), the Major Basic Research Project of Natural Science Foundation of Shandong Province, China (Grant No. ZR202010220025), Quan Cheng Laboratory (Grant No. QCLZD202306).

References

1. Almazrooie, M., Samsudin, A., Abdullah, R., Mutter, K.N.: Quantum reversible circuit of AES-128. Quantum Inf. Process. **17**(5), 1–30 (2018)
2. Amy, M., Maslov, D., Mosca, M., Roetteler, M.: A meet-in-the-middle algorithm for fast synthesis of depth-optimal quantum circuits. IEEE Trans. Comput. Aided Des. Integr. Circuits Syst. **32**(6), 818–830 (2013). https://doi.org/10.1109/TCAD. 2013.2244643
3. Banik, S., Funabiki, Y., Isobe, T.: Further results on efficient implementations of block cipher linear layers. IEICE Trans. Fundam. Electron. Commun. Comput. Sci. **104-A**(1), 213–225 (2021). https://doi.org/10.1587/transfun.2020CIP0013
4. Brylinski, J.L., Brylinski, R.: Universal quantum gates. In: Mathematics of Quantum Computation, pp. 117–134. Chapman and Hall/CRC, Boca Raton (2002)
5. Daemen, J., Rijmen, V.: The Design of Rijndael - The Advanced Encryption Standard (AES), 2nd edn. Information Security and Cryptography, Springer, Cham (2020). https://doi.org/10.1007/978-3-662-60769-5
6. DiVincenzo, D.P.: Quantum gates and circuits. Proc. Roy. Soc. Lond. Ser. A Math. Phys. Eng. Sci. **454**, 261–276 (1998)
7. Fowler, A.G., Mariantoni, M., Martinis, J.M., Cleland, A.N.: Surface codes: towards practical large-scale quantum computation. Phys. Rev. A **86**, 032324 (2012). https://doi.org/10.1103/PhysRevA.86.032324
8. Grassl, M., Langenberg, B., Roetteler, M., Steinwandt, R.: Applying Grover's algorithm to AES: quantum resource estimates. In: Takagi, T. (ed.) PQCrypto 2016. LNCS, vol. 9606, pp. 29–43. Springer, Cham (2016). https://doi.org/10.1007/978-3-319-29360-8_3

9. Grover, L.K.: A fast quantum mechanical algorithm for database search. In: Miller, G.L. (ed.) Proceedings of the Twenty-Eighth Annual ACM Symposium on the Theory of Computing, Philadelphia, Pennsylvania, USA, 22–24 May 1996, pp. 212–219. ACM (1996). https://doi.org/10.1145/237814.237866

10. Hanks, M., Estarellas, M.P., Munro, W.J., Nemoto, K.: Effective compression of quantum braided circuits aided by ZX-calculus. Phys. Rev. X **10**(4), 041030 (2020)

11. Häner, T., Steiger, D.S., Svore, K., Troyer, M.: A software methodology for compiling quantum programs. Quantum Sci. Technol. **3**(2), 020501 (2018). https://doi.org/10.1088/2058-9565/aaa5cc

12. Huang, Z., Sun, S.: Synthesizing quantum circuits of AES with lower T-depth and less qubits. In: Agrawal, S., Lin, D. (eds.) ASIACRYPT 2022, Part III. LNCS, vol. 13793, pp. 614–644. Springer, Cham (2022). https://doi.org/10.1007/978-3-031-22969-5_21

13. Jang, K., Baksi, A., Song, G., Kim, H., Seo, H., Chattopadhyay, A.: Quantum analysis of AES. IACR Cryptololgy ePrint Archive, p. 683 (2022)

14. Jaques, S., Naehrig, M., Roetteler, M., Virdia, F.: Implementing Grover oracles for quantum key search on AES and LowMC. In: Canteaut, A., Ishai, Y. (eds.) EUROCRYPT 2020. LNCS, vol. 12106, pp. 280–310. Springer, Cham (2020). https://doi.org/10.1007/978-3-030-45724-2_10

15. Jean, J., Peyrin, T., Sim, S.M., Tourteaux, J.: Optimizing implementations of lightweight building blocks. IACR Trans. Symm. Cryptol. **2017**(4), 130–168 (2017). https://doi.org/10.13154/tosc.v2017.i4.130-168

16. Kim, P., Han, D., Jeong, K.C.: Time-space complexity of quantum search algorithms in symmetric cryptanalysis: applying to AES and SHA-2. Quantum Inf. Process. **17**(12), 339 (2018). https://doi.org/10.1007/s11128-018-2107-3

17. Kranz, T., Leander, G., Stoffelen, K., Wiemer, F.: Shorter linear straight-line programs for MDS matrices. IACR Trans. Symm. Cryptol. **2017**(4), 188–211 (2017). https://doi.org/10.13154/tosc.v2017.i4.188-211

18. Langenberg, B., Pham, H., Steinwandt, R.: Reducing the cost of implementing the Advanced Encryption Standard as a quantum circuit. IEEE Trans. Quantum Eng. **1**, 1–12 (2020). https://doi.org/10.1109/TQE.2020.2965697

19. Li, S., Sun, S., Li, C., Wei, Z., Hu, L.: Constructing low-latency involutory MDS matrices with lightweight circuits. IACR Trans. Symm. Cryptol. **2019**(1), 84–117 (2019). https://doi.org/10.13154/tosc.v2019.i1.84-117

20. Li, Z., Gao, F., Qin, S., Wen, Q.: New record in the number of qubits for a quantum implementation of AES. Front. Phys. **11**, 1171753 (2023)

21. Lin, D., Xiang, Z., Xu, R., Zhang, S., Zeng, X.: Optimized quantum implementation of AES. Cryptology ePrint Archive (2023)

22. Lin, D., Xiang, Z., Zeng, X., Zhang, S.: A framework to optimize implementations of matrices. In: Paterson, K.G. (ed.) CT-RSA 2021. LNCS, vol. 12704, pp. 609–632. Springer, Cham (2021). https://doi.org/10.1007/978-3-030-75539-3_25

23. Liu, Q., Wang, W., Fan, Y., Wu, L., Sun, L., Wang, M.: Towards low-latency implementation of linear layers. IACR Trans. Symm. Cryptol. **2022**(1), 158–182 (2022). https://doi.org/10.46586/tosc.v2022.i1.158-182

24. Nielsen, M.A., Chuang, I.L.: Quantum Computation and Quantum Information, 10th Anniversary edn. Cambridge University Press, Cambridge (2016)

25. Q#, M.: Quantum development. https://devblogs.microsoft.com/qsharp/

26. Selinger, P.: Quantum circuits of t-depth one. CoRR abs/1210.0974 (2012). arxiv.org/abs/1210.0974

27. Steiger, D.S., Häner, T., Troyer, M.: ProjectQ: an open source software framework for quantum computing. Quantum **2**, 49 (2018). https://doi.org/10.22331/q-2018-01-31-49

28. Xiang, Z., Zeng, X., Lin, D., Bao, Z., Zhang, S.: Optimizing implementations of linear layers. IACR Trans. Symm. Cryptol. **2020**(2), 120–145 (2020). https://doi.org/10.13154/tosc.v2020.i2.120-145

29. Zou, J., Wei, Z., Sun, S., Liu, X., Wu, W.: Quantum circuit implementations of AES with fewer qubits. In: Moriai, S., Wang, H. (eds.) ASIACRYPT 2020. LNCS, vol. 12492, pp. 697–726. Springer, Cham (2020). https://doi.org/10.1007/978-3-030-64834-3_24

Hidden Stabilizers, the Isogeny to Endomorphism Ring Problem and the Cryptanalysis of pSIDH

Mingjie Chen[1], Muhammad Imran[2], Gábor Ivanyos[3],
Péter Kutas[1,6(✉)], Antonin Leroux[4,5], and Christophe Petit[1,7]

[1] University of Birmingham, Birmingham, UK
kutasp@gmail.com
[2] Budapest University of Technology and Economics, Budapest, Hungary
[3] Institute for Computer Science and Control, Hungarian Research Network,
Budapest, Hungary
[4] DGA-MI, Bruz, France
[5] IRMAR, UMR 6625, Université de Rennes, Rennes, France
[6] Eötvös Loránd University, Budapest, Hungary
[7] Université libre de Bruxelles, Bruxelles, Belgium

Abstract. The *Isogeny to Endomorphism Ring Problem* (IsERP) asks to compute the endomorphism ring of the codomain of an isogeny between supersingular curves in characteristic p given only a *representation* for this isogeny, i.e. some data and an algorithm to evaluate this isogeny on any torsion point. This problem plays a central role in isogeny-based cryptography; it underlies the security of pSIDH protocol (ASIACRYPT 2022) and it is at the heart of the recent attacks that broke the SIDH key exchange. Prior to this work, no efficient algorithm was known to solve IsERP for a generic isogeny degree, the hardest case seemingly when the degree is prime.

In this paper, we introduce a new quantum polynomial-time algorithm to solve IsERP for isogenies whose degrees are odd and have $O(\log \log p)$ many prime factors. As main technical tools, our algorithm uses a quantum algorithm for computing hidden Borel subgroups, a group action on supersingular isogenies from EUROCRYPT 2021, various algorithms for the Deuring correspondence and a new algorithm to lift arbitrary quaternion order elements modulo an odd integer N with $O(\log \log p)$ many prime factors to powersmooth elements.

As a main consequence for cryptography, we obtain a quantum polynomial-time key recovery attack on pSIDH. The technical tools we use may also be of independent interest.

1 Introduction

The problem of computing an isogeny between two supersingular elliptic curves is believed to be hard, even for a quantum computer. The assumption that this statement is true led to the idea of using isogenies to build post-quantum cryptography.

J. Guo and R. Steinfeld (Eds.): ASIACRYPT 2023, LNCS 14440, pp. 99–130, 2023.
https://doi.org/10.1007/978-981-99-8727-6_4

However, building actual cryptography from this principle is not easy and the security of concrete isogeny-based protocols is based on weaker versions of the isogeny problem, where the attacker is given more information. The nature of this additional information differs from one proposal to another but the heart of the problem remains the same.

At the core of the cryptanalytic efforts to attack the isogeny problems lies another problem: the endomorphism ring problem, which requires to compute the endomorphism ring of a curve given in input. In fact, computing isogenies and computing endomorphism rings are computationally equivalent problem for supersingular curves [EHL+18, Wes21]. However, this equivalence result does not fully answer the following question : given a "reasonable" representation of an isogeny $\phi : E \to E'$ and the knowledge of the endomorphism ring of the starting curve E, can we always efficiently compute the endomorphism ring of the codomain E'? This question leads to the following problem, where the exact definition of *weak isogeny representation* will be given in Sect. 2.4.

Problem 1.1 (Isogeny to Endomorphism Ring Problem (IsERP)). Let E be a supersingular elliptic curve over $\mathbb{F}_{p^2}$ and let $\phi : E \to E_1$ be an isogeny of degree N for some integer N. Given $\text{End}(E)$ and a weak isogeny representation for ϕ, compute $\text{End}(E_1)$.

The answer to this question is known to be yes when the degree of ϕ is powersmooth (and this is what is used in the equivalence results mentioned above), but the question remains open for an arbitrary degree. For a prime degree, this problem can be seen as the generalization of the key recovery problem for the pSIDH scheme recently introduced by Leroux [Ler22a]. The best known algorithm has subexponential quantum complexity in N, and the generic endomorphism ring attack has complexity exponential in $\log p$.

Isogeny-Based Cryptography. Isogeny-based cryptography originates in Couveignes' seminal work [Cou99] where he proposed to use the natural class group action on ordinary elliptic curves to instantiate a potentially quantum-resistant version of the Diffie-Hellman key exchange. The reasoning for that is that the discrete logarithm problem has more structure than needed to instantiate a key exchange, and this structure is exploited in Shor's algorithm [Sho97]. Couveignes' ideas were rediscovered by Rostovtsev and Stolbunov [RS06] and thus the resulting scheme is referred to as the CRS key exchange. These ideas were far from practical and a major breakthrough came with the invention of CSIDH [CLM+18]. The idea is quite similar but one uses supersingular elliptic curves defined over $\mathbb{F}_p$ and the acting group is the class group of $\mathbb{Z}[\sqrt{-p}]$. In other words one considers supersingular curves defined over $\mathbb{F}_p$ together with isogenies defined over $\mathbb{F}_p$ as well.

The same idea does not apply to supersingular curves defined over $\mathbb{F}_{p^2}$ because the endomorphism rings are non-commutative (hence the natural class group action of left ideals modulo principal left ideals is a non-commutative group action). This means that providing codomains of secret isogenies (i.e., curves E_A, E_B) is not enough to arrive at a shared secret that both parties can compute. Thus in order to instantiate a Diffie-Hellman-like key exchange on the full set of supersingular curves parties must provide additional information. In 2011 De Feo and Jao proposed SIDH [JDF11] where both parties share the images of other person's torsion basis under their secret isogeny. This motivated the following problem:

Problem 1.2. Let E be a supersingular elliptic curve and let A, B be coprime smooth numbers. Let $\phi : E \rightarrow E_A$ be a secret isogeny of degree A. One is provided with the action of ϕ on $E[B]$. Compute ϕ.

In [Pet17] it was shown that this problem can be solved in polynomial time for certain parameter sets (where $B > p^2 A^2$). In order to instantiate SIDH efficiently one usually uses parameters A, B, p such that AB divides $p + 1$ as then all computations can be carried out over $\mathbb{F}_{p^2}$ so in some sense these initial results seemed theoretical. Then the initial idea of Petit [Pet17] was improved in [QKL+21] to $B > \sqrt{p}A^2$ which already included parameter sets which could have been used in SIDH variants. Nevertheless none of these attacks directly impacted SIDH where A and B are roughly the same size. Then in 2022 Castryck and Decru [CD22] (and independently Maino and Martindale [MM22]) vastly improved these using ingenious techniques (utilizing superspecial abelian surfaces) which break SIDH with known endomorphism ring in polynomial time even if A and B are balanced. Finally, Robert proposed a polynomial-time attack on SIDH with unknown endomorphism ring (furthermore, he only needs $B^2 > A$ as opposed to $B > A$ in other attacks).

These attacks have shown that using smooth degree isogenies and providing torsion point information will potentially not lead to secure and efficient cryptographic constructions (in [FMP23] some countermeasures are proposed, but the ones that are not broken are much less efficient than the original SIDH construction). Thus, in order to navigate in the supersingular isogeny graph parties have to share some other kind of extra information.

Alternative Isogeny Representations. In the pSIDH protocol introduced by Leroux [Ler22a], one reveals *suborder representations* for isogenies of large prime degrees to build a key exchange. Suborder representations are a particular kind of weak isogeny representations, i.e. some data to represent isogenies together with an algorithm to efficiently evaluate these isogenies on any point up to a scalar. Prime degree isogenies were not really used before as one cannot write down the isogeny itself (but one can compute its codomain with non-trivial techniques). More recently, a similar type of secret isogeny was used in the SCALLOP scheme [DFFK+23]. In SCALLOP, a partial isogeny representation is revealed to the attacker.

From a cryptanalytic point of view, the unlimited amount of torsion information provided by the isogeny representation revealed in pSIDH (and more generally, any isogeny representation) is very interesting. However, when the kernel points are not defined over a small extension, the known algorithms do not apply and it is still unclear how to exploit the isogeny representation to recover the secret isogeny.

Leroux studied the case where a specific isogeny representation (the suborder representation) is revealed, but we can generalize this setting to any isogeny representation. He showed that computing the endomorphism ring of the codomain would make pSIDH insecure, therefore motivating Problem 1.1 in the prime case.

More recently, Robert introduced yet another isogeny representation based on torsion point images and the recent SIDH attacks [Rob22]. This representation could be used (for isogenies with large prime degrees) instead of the suborder representation to derive a key exchange protocol similar to pSIDH, and this protocol would be similarly affected by our new results.

A Group Action for SIDH and pSIDH. In [KMPW21] the authors introduce a group action on a particular set of supersingular elliptic curves. Let E be a supersingular elliptic curve with endomorphism ring isomorphic to O. Then $(O/NO)^*$ acts naturally on the set of cyclic subgroups of E of order N. If there is a one-to-one correspondence between cyclic subgroups and N-isogenous curves, then one can look at this action as acting on a set of curves. This action was used to provide a subexponential quantum key recovery attack on overstretched SIDH parameters.

The reason the attack only works for overstretched parameter sets is that in general this group action is not easy to evaluate (thus substantial amount of extra information on the secret isogeny is needed). This motivates the following problem where the name Malleability Oracle Problem comes from the term introduced in [KMPW21].

Problem 1.3 (Malleability Oracle Problem). Let E be a supersingular elliptic curve and let $\phi : E \to E'$ be a secret isogeny with kernel generated by A. Let $\sigma \in \text{End}(E)$. Find the j-invariant of $E/\langle \sigma(A) \rangle$.

Contributions. Our main result is the following theorem on the resolution of IsERP.

Theorem 1.4. *Let $N = \prod \ell_i^{e_i} \neq p$ be an odd integer that is of size polynomial in p and has $O(\log(\log p))$ divisors. Then there exists a quantum polynomial-time algorithm that solves the IsERP.*

We first provide a reduction from the IsERP to the Powersmooth Quaternion Lifting Problem (PQLP). The PQLP is the problem of finding a powersmooth representative for a given class in $\mathcal{O}/N\mathcal{O}$ for some integer N and maximal order $\mathcal{O}$ in the quaternion algebra $\mathcal{B}_{p,\infty}$.

Our reduction from the IsERP to PQLP is obtained through a quantum equivalence between the IsERP and a problem similar to Problem 1.3, which we call the Group Action Evaluation Problem. The most difficult direction of this equivalence (reducing the IsERP to the Group Action Evaluation Problem) is obtained with a quantum polynomial-time algorithm. The other reduction is classical and uses standard tools for the Deuring correspondence.

The quantum polynomial reduction relies on a special case of the well-known hidden subgroup problem (HSP), namely when the acting group is $\mathrm{GL}_2(\mathbb{Z}/N\mathbb{Z})$ and the hidden subgroup is a conjugate of the subgroup of upper triangular matrices. This problem was previously studied only for prime N [DMR10] and in this paper we provide a polynomial-time quantum algorithm for any N. Furthermore, whenever N is smooth we propose a classical polynomial-time algorithm which might be of independent interest.

We then propose a classical polynomial-time algorithm for the PQLP. The algorithm relies on several tools developed in KLPT [KLPT14]. Namely we decompose elements $\sigma \in \mathcal{O}$ as $\alpha_1 \gamma \alpha_2 \gamma \alpha_3$ where the α_i lie in a special subset of $\mathcal{O}$ (linear combinations of j, ij) that can be lifted efficiently to powersmooth elements, and γ is a fixed element of $\mathcal{O}$ of powersmooth norm. Finding γ and lifting the α_i are accomplished with slightly modified subroutines of KLPT, whereas the decomposition itself is inspired by similar decompositions in other contexts [PLQ08]. The lifting algorithm requires that N is odd and has $O(\log\log p)$ prime factors. We look at approaches to generalize this algorithm to arbitrary N (thus solve IsERP for arbitrary degrees) in [CII+23, Appendix D]. We have also implemented this algorithm for prime N in Sagemath [The22], available on GitHub [git23].

The rest of the paper is organized as follows: in Sect. 2, we introduce some necessary background. Then, in Sect. 3, we introduce a quantum algorithm to solve the Borel Hidden Subgroup Problem. In Sect. 4 we define the Group Action Evaluation Problem and the Powersmooth Quaternion Lift Problem (PQLP). We show various reductions between the two problems and the IsERP, most importantly reducing IsERP to the PQLP. In Sect. 5 we describe our polynomial-time algorithm for PQLP, which leads to a resolution of the IsERP through the reductions. Finally in Sect. 6, we discuss the impacts of our results on isogeny-based cryptography.

2   Preliminaries

Below, we give a brief introduction to some necessary mathematical background. More details on elliptic curves and isogenies can be found in [Sil09]. The book of John Voight [Voi18] is a good reference regarding quaternion algebras and the Deuring correspondence. In the remaining of this paper, we fix a prime $p > 2$.

2.1   Supersingular Elliptic Curves and Isogenies

Let E_1, E_2 be elliptic curves defined over a finite field $\mathbb{F}_q$. An isogeny is a non-constant rational map from E_1 to E_2 that is simultaneously a group homomorphism. Equivalently, it is a non-constant rational map that sends the point of infinity of E_1 to the point of infinity of E_2. An isogeny induces a field extension $K(E_1)/K(E_2)$ of function fields. An isogeny is called separable, inseparable or purely inseparable if the extension of function field is of the respective type. The degree of the isogeny is the degree of the field extension $K(E_1)/K(E_2)$. The kernel of an isogeny $\phi : E_1 \to E_2$ is a finite subgroup of E_1. If the isogeny is separable, then the size of the kernel is equal to the degree of the isogeny (more generally, the size of the kernel equals the separable degree of the field extension $K(E_1)/K(E_2)$). For every isogeny $\phi : E_1 \to E_2$ there exists a dual isogeny $\hat{\phi} : E_2 \to E_1$ such that $\deg(\phi) = \deg(\hat{\phi}) = d$ and $\phi \circ \hat{\phi} = [d]_{E_2}$ (and $\hat{\phi} \circ \phi = [d]_{E_1}$). Isogenies (together with the zero map) from E to itself are called endomorphisms. Endomorphisms of an elliptic curve form a ring under addition and composition. An elliptic curve over a finite field is called ordinary if its endomorphism ring is commutative, and supersingular otherwise.

2.2   Quaternion Algebras

The endomorphism rings of supersingular elliptic curves over $\mathbb{F}_{p^2}$ are isomorphic to maximal orders of $B_{p,\infty}$, the quaternion algebra ramified at p and ∞. We fix a basis $1, i, j, k$ of $B_{p,\infty}$, satisfying $i^2 = -q$, $j^2 = -p$ and $k = ij = -ji$ for some integer q. The canonical involution of conjugation sends an element $\alpha = a + ib + jc + kd$ to $\overline{\alpha} = a - (ib + jc + kd)$. A *fractional ideal* I in $B_{p,\infty}$ is a $\mathbb{Z}$-lattice of rank four. We denote by $n(I)$ the *norm* of I as the largest rational number such that $n(\alpha) \in n(I)\mathbb{Z}$ for any $\alpha \in I$. An order $\mathcal{O}$ is a subring of $B_{p,\infty}$ that is also a fractional ideal. An order is called *maximal* when it is not contained in any other larger order. The left order of a fractional ideal is defined as $\mathcal{O}_L(I) = \{\alpha \in B_{p,\infty} \mid \alpha I \subset I\}$ and similarly for the right order $\mathcal{O}_R(I)$. Then I is said to be a right $\mathcal{O}_R(I)$-ideal or a left $\mathcal{O}_L(I)$-ideal. A fractional ideal is *integral* if it is contained in its left order, or equivalently in its right order; we refer to integral ideals hereafter as ideals. Eichler orders are the intersection of two maximal orders. If I is an ideal, we can define the Eichler order associated to I as $\mathcal{O}_L(I) \cap \mathcal{O}_R(I)$. In that case, it can be shown that $\mathcal{O}_L(I) \cap \mathcal{O}_R(I) = \mathbb{Z} + I$ (see [DFKL+20]).

2.3   The Deuring Correspondence

Fix a supersingular elliptic curve E_0, and an order $\mathcal{O}_0 \simeq \mathrm{End}(E_0)$. The curve/order correspondence allows one to associate to each outgoing isogeny $\varphi : E_0 \to E_1$ an integral left $\mathcal{O}_0$-ideal, and every such ideal arises in this way (see [Koh96] for instance). Through this correspondence, the ring $\mathrm{End}(E_1)$ is isomorphic to the right order of this ideal. This isogeny/ideal correspondence is defined in [Wat69], and in the separable case, it is explicitly given as follows.

Definition 2.1. *Given I an integral left $\mathcal{O}_0$-ideal coprime to p, we define the I-torsion $E_0[I] = \{P \in E_0(\overline{\mathbb{F}}_{p^2}) : \alpha(P) = 0 \text{ for all } \alpha \in I\}$. To I, we associate the separable isogeny φ_I of kernel $E_0[I]$. Conversely given a separable isogeny φ, the corresponding ideal is defined as $I_\varphi = \{\alpha \in \mathcal{O}_0 : \alpha(P) = 0 \text{ for all } P \in \ker(\varphi)\}$.*

We summarize properties of the Deuring correspondence in Table 1, borrowed from [DFKL+20].

Table 1. The Deuring correspondence, a summary [DFKL+20].

Supersingular j-invariants over $\mathbb{F}_{p^2}$	Maximal orders in $\mathcal{B}_{p,\infty}$
$j(E)$ (up to Galois conjugacy)	$\mathcal{O} \cong \text{End}(E)$ (up to isomorphism)
(E_1, φ) with $\varphi : E \to E_1$	I_φ integral left $\mathcal{O}$-ideal and right $\mathcal{O}_1$-ideal
$\theta \in \text{End}(E_0)$	Principal ideal $\mathcal{O}\theta$
$\deg(\varphi)$	$n(I_\varphi)$

2.4   Isogeny Representation

In this subsection, we look at isogenies through a more algorithmic prism. Specifically, we consider the following question: what does it mean to "compute" an isogeny? A natural answer is a rational map representation of the isogeny. Other representations are however possible, and in [PL17, Sect. 2.4] and [Ler22a] it is argued that any such representation should allow efficient evaluation at arbitrary points (for a more complete study, look at [Ler22b, chapter 4]). More formally, Leroux defines an isogeny representation as some data s_ϕ associated to an isogeny $\phi : E \to E'$ of degree N such that there are two algorithms: one to "verify" and one to "evaluate" ϕ.

The motivation to have a verification algorithm is found in a cryptographic context where an adversary might try to cheat by revealing something that is not a valid isogeny representation. But, in the more cryptanalatic point of view of this paper, we can assume that we work with a valid isogeny representation. This is why we take a relaxed definition of isogeny representation where we only require an evaluation algorithm (a verification algorithm can probably be derived from the evaluation algorithm anyway). Moreover, we assume that the representation is "efficient" meaning that is has polynomial size and the evaluation algorithm is polynomial-time in the log of the degree and the prime. We give a detailed version below. In our context, it is sufficient that the evaluation algorithm gives evaluation of points up to a (common) scalar which is why we qualify our isogeny representation as *weak*.

Definition 2.2. *A weak isogeny representation for the isogeny $\phi : E \to E'$ of degree N, is a data s_ϕ of size $O(polylog(p + N))$ (associated to a unique isogeny ϕ), such that there exists an algorithm $\mathcal{E}$ that takes s_ϕ and a point P of the curve E of order d in input and computes $\lambda(d)\phi(P)$ in $O(polylog(d + N + |P|))$ for any point P of E, where $|P|$ is the bitsize of the representation of P.*

The notion of isogeny representation is particularly relevant when the degree N is a big prime and the kernel points are defined over an $\mathbb{F}_p$-extension of big degree (this is exactly the setting of pSIDH [Ler22a]). Indeed, in that case, the standard ways to represent isogenies (with polynomials, or kernel points) are not compact or efficient enough to match our definition.

The Deuring correspondence gave us the tools to obtain efficient representations with a natural isogeny representation obtained by taking s_ϕ as the ideal I_ϕ

corresponding to ϕ. This ideal representation matches Definition 2.2, however it also reveals the endomorphism ring of E'. One of the motivations of Leroux in [Ler22a] to introduce another isogeny representation (called the suborder representation) is to have an isogeny representation that does not directly reveal the endomorphism ring of the codomain. This suborder representation matches our notion of weak isogeny representation as defined in Definition 2.2. The main contribution of this paper implies that the suborder representation does not hide the endomorphism ring of the codomain to a quantum computer, even when the degree is prime.

Since then, Robert [Rob22] suggested to use the techniques introduced to attack SIDH in order to obtain another isogeny representation (this one not even requiring to reveal the endomorphism ring of the domain). Our analysis holds for any suborder representation, hence it also applies to Robert's one.

2.5 The pSIDH Key Exchange

As an application of the hardness of computing the endomorphism ring from the suborder representation, Leroux introduced a key exchange called pSIDH. The principle can be summarized as follows: use the evaluation algorithm for the suborder representation to perform an SIDH-like key exchange, but for isogenies of big prime degree. The SIDH and pSIDH key exchange both use the following commutative isogeny diagram:

$$
\begin{array}{ccc}
E_B & \xrightarrow{\psi_A} & E_{AB} \\
\phi_B \uparrow & & \uparrow \psi_B \\
E_0 & \xrightarrow{\phi_A} & E_A
\end{array}
$$

In pSIDH, Alice and Bob's secret keys are ideal representations for the isogenies ϕ_A and ϕ_B (or equivalently the endomorphism ring of the two curves E_A and E_B), and their associated public keys are the suborder representations for ϕ_A and ϕ_B.

Leroux showed that the knowledge of $\text{End}(E_A)$ (resp. $\text{End}(E_B)$) and the suborder representation of ϕ_B (resp. ϕ_A) was enough to compute the end curve E_{AB} from which the common secret can be derived efficiently. The mechanism behind this computation is quite complicated and is not relevant for us since we target the key recovery problem. We refer to [Ler22a] for more details.

2.6 The Hidden Subgroup Problem

The hidden subgroup problem (HSP for short) in a group G is defined as the problem of finding a subgroup $H \leq G$ given a function f on G satisfying that f is constant on the left cosets of H and takes different values on different cosets, i.e., $f(x) = f(y)$ if and only if $x^{-1}y \in H$. There is also a right version of the hidden subgroup problem where the level sets of the hiding function f are the right cosets of H. As taking inverses in G maps left cosets to right cosets and vice versa, the two versions of HSP are equivalent. (One just needs to replace the hiding function with its composition with taking inverses.) Although the equivalence is straightforward, it is useful as in certain cases it is easier to understand right cosets than left ones (or conversely).

The framework of HSP captures many computational problems including some problems which most cryptographic protocols used today rely on, e.g., factoring and the discrete logarithm problem. Shor's quantum algorithms [Sho97] can solve factoring and the discrete logarithm problem efficiently. Furthermore, quantum polynomial time algorithms for the finite abelian HSP generalizing Shor's algorithm are available, see [Kit95, BL95].

It is well known that the graph isomorphism problem can be cast as HSP in symmetric. Also, a method solving the HSP in dihedral groups via the standard approach would also solve a special, though still presumably hard special case of the shortest vector problem. However, in contrast to the abelian case, there are only a few positive results known for HSP in finite non-commutative groups. As shown in [EH00], HSP in dihedral groups is related to another problem called the hidden shift problem. The hidden shift problem in a group G is the problem of finding an element $s \in G$ given two functions f_1 and f_2 on G satisfying that $f_1(g) = f_2(gs)$ for every $g \in G$. If f_1 and f_2 are injective then the hidden shift problem in an abelian group G is equivalent to a hidden subgroup problem in the semidirect product $G \rtimes \mathbb{Z}/2\mathbb{Z}$. This is of particular interest in isogeny contexts, as the key recovery problem in CSIDH can be reduced to the injective hidden shift problem in abelian groups in order to produce quantum subexponential-time attacks based on Kuperberg's algorithm [Kup05].

In this paper, we consider a restricted HSP in the general linear group. We use the term Borel hidden subgroup problem for it.

Problem 2.3. Let $N \in \mathbb{Z}_{\geq 1}$ and let $\mathbb{Z}/N\mathbb{Z}$ be the group of integers modulo N. The Borel HSP is the hidden subgroup problem in the general linear group $\mathrm{GL}_n(\mathbb{Z}/N\mathbb{Z})$ for $N \in \mathbb{Z}_{\geq 1}$, i.e., the group of invertible n by n matrices with entries from $\mathbb{Z}/N\mathbb{Z}$, where the hidden subgroup H is promised to be a conjugate of the subgroup consisting of the upper triangular matrices.

Restricting the possible hidden subgroups in non-abelian groups may lead to efficient algorithms to find them. Denney et al. in [DMR10] proposed a polynomial-time algorithm for the Borel HSP in $\mathrm{GL}_2(\mathbb{F}_p)$ for prime numbers p. A quantum algorithm for the more general case of $\mathrm{GL}_n(\mathbb{F}_q)$ over fields of size $q = p^k$, is provided by Ivanyos in [Iva12]. That algorithm runs in polynomial time if q is not much smaller than n.

In this paper, we consider the Borel HSP for $\mathrm{GL}_2(\mathbb{Z}_N)$ for any integer N greater than one, and we present both classical and quantum algorithms for different parameters N. Note that $\mathrm{GL}_2(\mathbb{Z}/N\mathbb{Z})$ acts as a permutation group on the set of the free cyclic $\mathbb{Z}/N\mathbb{Z}$-submodules of $(\mathbb{Z}/N\mathbb{Z})^2$ and each Borel subgroup H in $\mathrm{GL}_2(\mathbb{Z}/N\mathbb{Z})$ is the stabilizer of a free cyclic $\mathbb{Z}/N\mathbb{Z}$-submodule S

of $(\mathbb{Z}/N\mathbb{Z})^2$, thus finding the Borel subgroup is equivalent to finding the corresponding cyclic submodule. The main tool of the classical algorithm is a testing procedure to determine whether elements of $(\mathbb{Z}/N\mathbb{Z})^2$ are in S. The classical algorithm solves the Borel HSP efficiently for any smooth number N, while the quantum algorithm efficiently solves the Borel HSP for arbitrary N. The main idea of the quantum algorithm is based on the observation that the problem can be reduced to another restricted hidden subgroup problem in the group $G = (\mathbb{Z}/N\mathbb{Z})^2 \rtimes (\mathbb{Z}/N\mathbb{Z})^*$ where the hidden subgroup is promised to be a complement of the normal subgroup $(\mathbb{Z}/N\mathbb{Z})^2$. The latter restricted HSP can be cast as an instance of the multiple shift problem considered in [IPS18], which can itself be seen as a generalization of the hidden shift problem.

Problem 2.4. The hidden multiple shift problem HMS(N, n, r) is parameterized by three positive integers N, n and r, where $N > 1$ and $2 \leq r \leq N - 1$. Assume that we have a set $H \subseteq \mathbb{Z}/N\mathbb{Z}$ of cardinality r and a function $f_s : (\mathbb{Z}/N\mathbb{Z})^n \times H \to \{0,1\}^l$, defined as $f_s(x, h) = f(x - hs)$ where $s \in (\mathbb{Z}/N\mathbb{Z})^n$ and $f : (\mathbb{Z}/N\mathbb{Z})^n \to \{0,1\}^l$ is an injective function. Given f_s by an oracle, the task is to find $s \bmod \frac{N}{\delta(H,N)}$, where $\delta(H, N)$ is defined as the largest divisor of N such that $h - h'$ is divisible by $\delta(H, N)$ for every $h, h' \in H$.

A special case of the HMS problem was first considered by Childs and van Dam [CVD05]. They presented a quantum polynomial time algorithm for the case when $n = 1$ and H is a contiguous interval of size $N^{\Omega(1)}$. For general n, an algorithm in [IPS18] solves HMS(N, n, r) in $O(\text{poly}(n)(\frac{N}{r})^{n+O(1)})$. For a set H of small size, HMS is close to the hidden shift problem. Specifically, HMS$(N, n, 2)$ is the standard hidden shift problem, though modulo a divisor of N depending on the difference of the two elements of H. On the other extreme, for $r = N$, HMS is an abelian hidden subgroup problem in the group $(\mathbb{Z}/N\mathbb{Z})^{n+1}$. Intuitively, the larger r is, the easier HMS(N, n, r) becomes. Below we restate the above mentioned result from [IPS18] for the special case $n = 1$.

Theorem 2.5. *There is a quantum algorithm that solves the HMS(N, 1, r) in time* $\left(\frac{N}{r}\right)^{O(1)}$ *with high probability.*

2.7   The Malleability Oracle

In [KMPW21] the authors introduce a general framework dubbed the malleability oracle. Let G be a group acting on a set X and let $f : X \to I$ be an injective function where I is some set. The input of the malleability oracle is an element $g \in G$ and a value $f(x)$ (x is not provided) and the output is $f(g * x)$. It is shown in [KMPW21, Theorem 3.3] that if G is abelian and the action of G on X is free and transitive then inverting $f(x)$ can be reduced to an abelian hidden shift problem. The idea of the proof is as follows. One takes an arbitrary known x_0 and the corresponding $f(x_0)$. Then one can define two functions f_0, f_1 from G to I where $f_0(g) = f(g * x_0)$ and $f_1(g) = f(g * x)$. These functions are well-defined as f was injective. Now since the action of G is transitive there is an element

s that takes x_0 to x. One can easily see that f and f_0 are shifts of each other and the shift is realized by that element s. Since the action is free, f and f_0 will be injective functions themselves hence one can apply Kuperberg's algorithm to find s and finally that is enough to compute x.

Remark 2.6. It follows from the proof that it is not strictly necessary for the action to be transitive. It is enough if we know any element in the orbit of the secret x. For instance it suffices if there are only a few orbits and we have a representative of each of them (as we can run Kuperberg's algorithm multiple times with different x_0s).

The way to interpret this result is as follows. If one has a way instantiating the malleability oracle, then one can utilize that to invert the function in subexponential time. For isogeny-based cryptography the natural function to be considered here is the one-way function sending a subgroup H to the elliptic curve E/H. In [KMPW21] it is shown that [KMPW21, Theorem 3.3] applies to two scenarios:

- In CSIDH when curves and isogenies are defined over $\mathbb{F}_p$. This result was not novel as it is the same as the original hidden shift attack
- In SIDH when one knows the image of the secret isogeny on a sufficiently large torsion group

We explain the second application a bit further. Let E be a supersingular elliptic curve with known endomorphism ring O. Here we assume that one can evaluate every element of O efficiently on points of E. Let N be any integer. Then O/NO is isomorphic to $M_2(\mathbb{Z}/N\mathbb{Z})$ [Voi18, Theorem 42.1.9]. This implies that $(O/NO)^*$ is isomorphic to $G = \mathrm{GL}_2(\mathbb{Z}/N\mathbb{Z})$. Now it is clear that G acts on cyclic subgroups of order N of E by evaluation. When there is a one-to-one correspondence between cyclic subgroups of order N and N-isogenous curves to E, then this implies an action on N-isogenous curves to E. What would a malleability oracle look like in this framework? One is given a curve E' that is N-isogenous to E. Let A be the corresponding secret kernel. Now the input of the oracle is an endomorphism σ (whose degree is coprime to N) and then it returns $E/\sigma(A)$. [KMPW21, Theorem 3.3.] "almost" states that if one has access to such an oracle, then one can compute A via a hidden shift algorithm. The "almost" part comes from the fact that G here is not abelian and the group action is not free. In [KMPW21] it is shown that one can get around this issue by essentially just utilizing a subgroup of G that is abelian (and evoking some small technical conditions).

One can look at this result as a subexponential quantum reduction from finding a certain N-isogeny to being able to instantiate the malleability oracle, which is formulated as Problem 1.3. The results of Sect. 4 will be related to a generalization of 1.3.

In [KMPW21] the authors were able to solve Problem 1.3 when $\deg(\phi) = 2^k$ and the action of ϕ is known on a sufficiently large subgroup of E. In order to achieve this result one had to throw away most of the available information (by restricting G to a small abelian subgroup) in order to fit the malleability oracle framework. In this paper we show that utilizing the entire G-action improves on [KMPW21] significantly.

The second claim can be reinterpreted in the context of the IsERP problem. Namely when the isogeny degree is a power of 2 and the isogeny is provided with some isogeny representation, then one can compute the endomorphism ring of the codomain in quantum subexponential time (assuming the endomorphism ring of the domain curve was known).

3   The Borel Hidden Subgroup Problem

In this section, we present both classical and quantum algorithms for the "two-dimensional" Borel hidden subgroup problem. The classical algorithm solves the Borel HSP efficiently in the group $GL_2(\mathbb{Z}/N\mathbb{Z})$ for smooth number N, while the quantum algorithm solves it efficiently for any positive odd number N. For an even number N we can use a classical procedure applied to the 2-part of N with the quantum one for the odd part of N to obtain a quantum method for every N.

Let N be an integer greater than one. By fixing a basis, we have an explicit isomorphism $End((\mathbb{Z}/N\mathbb{Z})^2) \cong M_2(\mathbb{Z}/N\mathbb{Z})$ and $Aut((\mathbb{Z}/N\mathbb{Z})^2) \cong GL_2(\mathbb{Z}/N\mathbb{Z})$. Note that $GL_2(\mathbb{Z}/N\mathbb{Z})$ acts as a permutation group on the set of the free cyclic $\mathbb{Z}/N\mathbb{Z}$-submodules of $(\mathbb{Z}/N\mathbb{Z})^2$. Let H be the stabilizer of a secret free cyclic submodule S. In the matrix notation, H is a conjugate of the subgroup consisting of the upper triangular matrices in $GL_2(\mathbb{Z}/N\mathbb{Z})$. That is, in an appropriate basis for $(\mathbb{Z}/N\mathbb{Z})^2$, the elements of H are of the form

$$\begin{pmatrix} * & * \\ 0 & * \end{pmatrix},$$

where the diagonal entries are units in $\mathbb{Z}/N\mathbb{Z}$. (Here the first basis element is a generator for S.) The Borel HSP in $GL_2(\mathbb{Z}/N\mathbb{Z})$ is the following: we are given a function on $GL_2(\mathbb{Z}/N\mathbb{Z})$ (given by an oracle) that is constant on the left cosets of H and takes different values on distinct cosets, the task is to find H, or equivalently the submodule S.

Using Chinese remaindering, one can reduce the case when N is any number of known factorization to instances of the prime power case.

Lemma 3.1. *Let $N = N_1 N_2$ be a known decomposition of N where $\gcd(N_1, N_2) = 1$. Then we have*

$$GL_2(\mathbb{Z}/N\mathbb{Z}) \cong GL_2(\mathbb{Z}/N_1\mathbb{Z}) \times GL_2(\mathbb{Z}/N_2\mathbb{Z}).$$

Moreover, one can reduce the Borel HSP in $GL_2(\mathbb{Z}/N\mathbb{Z})$ to the Borel HSP in $GL_2(\mathbb{Z}/N_i\mathbb{Z})$ for $i = 1, 2$.

Proof. By the Chinese Remainder Theorem, $\mathbb{Z}/N\mathbb{Z} \cong \mathbb{Z}/N_1\mathbb{Z} \oplus \mathbb{Z}/N_2\mathbb{Z}$, $(\mathbb{Z}/N\mathbb{Z})^2 \cong (\mathbb{Z}/N_1\mathbb{Z})^2 \oplus (\mathbb{Z}/N_2\mathbb{Z})^2$, $End((\mathbb{Z}/N\mathbb{Z})^2) \cong End((\mathbb{Z}/N_1\mathbb{Z})^2) \oplus End((\mathbb{Z}/$

$N_2\mathbb{Z})^2$). Furthermore, these isomorphisms can be efficiently computed using the extended Euclidean algorithm. The restriction of the third isomorphism also gives $\mathrm{Aut}((\mathbb{Z}/N\mathbb{Z})^2) \cong \mathrm{Aut}((\mathbb{Z}/N_1\mathbb{Z})^2) \times \mathrm{Aut}((\mathbb{Z}/N_2\mathbb{Z})^2)$. The stabilizer H of the free cyclic submodule S generated by $(A_1, A_2) \in (\mathbb{Z}/N_1\mathbb{Z})^2 \oplus (\mathbb{Z}/N_2\mathbb{Z})^2$ is the direct product of the stabilizers H_i of S_i, where S_i are the free cyclic submodules over $\mathbb{Z}/N_i\mathbb{Z}$ generated by A_i. Hiding functions for H_i can be obtained by restricting the hiding function for H to the component $\mathrm{Aut}((\mathbb{Z}/N_i\mathbb{Z})^2)$. $\square$

3.1   A Classical Borel HSP Algorithm

Based on iterated applications of Lemma 3.1, we can focus on the prime power case. (Note that the factorization of N can be computed in deterministic time polynomial in $B \log N$ where B is an upper bound on the prime divisors of N.) Therefore, we assume $N = q^k$ for a prime number q.

An important subroutine in our algorithm is a procedure for testing whether an element $u \in (\mathbb{Z}/N\mathbb{Z})^2$ is in S based on the following observations. If $u \in S$ then for any $\varphi \in \mathrm{End}((\mathbb{Z}/N\mathbb{Z})^2)$ such that $\varphi + \mathrm{Id} \in \mathrm{GL}_2(\mathbb{Z}/N\mathbb{Z})$ and $\varphi((\mathbb{Z}/N\mathbb{Z})^2) \leq \mathbb{Z}/N\mathbb{Z}u$ we have $\varphi + \mathrm{Id} \in H$. This is because for $u \in S$ we have $\varphi(u) \in \mathbb{Z}/N\mathbb{Z}u \leq S$ and $\mathrm{Id}(u) = u \in S$. On the other hand, if $u \notin S$ then there exists an element $\varphi \in \mathrm{End}((\mathbb{Z}/N\mathbb{Z})^2)$ with $\varphi(V) \leq \mathbb{Z}/N\mathbb{Z}u$ and $\varphi(S) \nleq S$. Indeed, if $\{v, w\}$ is an $\mathbb{Z}/N\mathbb{Z}$-basis of $(\mathbb{Z}/N\mathbb{Z})^2$ such that v is a generator of S, then the map sending v to u and w to zero satisfies these properties.

Another ingredient of the testing procedure is the following.

Lemma 3.2. *If $\varphi + \mathrm{Id} \in \mathrm{GL}_2(\mathbb{Z}/N\mathbb{Z})$ then $\varphi(S) \leq S$ if and only if $\varphi + \mathrm{Id} \in H$.*

Proof. If $\varphi(S) \leq S$ then $(\varphi + \mathrm{Id})S \leq \varphi(S) + S = S$. To see the reverse implication, assume that $\varphi(v) \notin S$ for some $v \in S$. Then $\varphi(v) + v$ is in the coset $\varphi(v) + S$ disjoint from S. $\square$

Thus for φ with $\varphi + \mathrm{Id} \in \mathrm{GL}_2(\mathbb{Z}/N\mathbb{Z})$ we can test whether $\varphi(S) \leq S$ by comparing the value of the hiding function taken on $\varphi + \mathrm{Id}$ with that on Id.

Testing Procedure: Let w_1, w_2 be a fixed basis of $(\mathbb{Z}/N\mathbb{Z})^2$. Given $u \in (\mathbb{Z}/N\mathbb{Z})^2$ we define two maps φ_1, φ_2 by $\varphi_i(w_i) = u$ and $\varphi_i(w_{3-i}) = 0$. Note that φ_1 and φ_2 generate $E_u := \{\varphi \in \mathrm{End}((\mathbb{Z}/N\mathbb{Z})^2) : \varphi((\mathbb{Z}/N\mathbb{Z})^2) \leq \mathbb{Z}/N\mathbb{Z}u\}$ as an $\mathbb{Z}/N\mathbb{Z}$-submodule of $\mathrm{End}((\mathbb{Z}/N\mathbb{Z})^2)$. Therefore if $\varphi_i(S) \leq S$ $(i = 1, 2)$ then for every element $\varphi \in E_u$ we have $\varphi(S) \leq S$. If $u \in q(\mathbb{Z}/N\mathbb{Z})$ then $\varphi_i - \mathrm{Id} \in q\,\mathrm{End}((\mathbb{Z}/N\mathbb{Z})^2) - \mathrm{Id} \subseteq \mathrm{GL}_2(\mathbb{Z}/N\mathbb{Z})$ $(i = 1, 2)$, so we can test whether $u \in S$ by testing $\varphi_i(S) \leq S$ $(i = 1, 2)$ by comparing the value of the hiding function taken on $\varphi_i + \mathrm{Id}$ with that on Id. If $q \neq 2$ then either $\varphi_i - \mathrm{Id}$ or $-\varphi_i - \mathrm{Id}$ (or both) fall in $\mathrm{GL}_2(\mathbb{Z}/N\mathbb{Z})$ (depending on the nonzero eigenvalue of φ_i modulo q), so the test above works with a minor modification for $u \notin q(\mathbb{Z}/N\mathbb{Z})$ as well. Finally, to cover the case $q = 2$ and $u \notin q(\mathbb{Z}/N\mathbb{Z})$ observe that $u \in S$ if and only if $S = \mathbb{Z}/N\mathbb{Z}u$. To test whether this is the case we compute generators for the subgroup $H_{\mathbb{Z}/N\mathbb{Z}u} = \{\varphi \in \mathrm{GL}_2(\mathbb{Z}/N\mathbb{Z}) : \varphi(u) \in \mathbb{Z}/N\mathbb{Z}u\}$ and test membership of these generators for membership in H again by comparing values of the hiding function.

Equipped with the testing procedure, we compute S from "bottom up" as follows. First we compute $S \cap q^{k-1}(\mathbb{Z}/N\mathbb{Z})^2$. Note that $q^{k-1}(\mathbb{Z}/N\mathbb{Z})^2 \cong (\mathbb{Z}/q\mathbb{Z})^2$ and there are $q + 1$ possibilities for $S_{k-1} = S \cap q^{k-1}(\mathbb{Z}/N\mathbb{Z})^2$. We can find $S \cap q^{k-1}(\mathbb{Z}/N\mathbb{Z})^2$ by brute force based on the testing procedure on all $q + 1$ submodules corresponding to each possibility in time $q$poly log $|N|$. Assume that we have computed $S_l = S \cap q^l(\mathbb{Z}/N\mathbb{Z})^2$ for some $l > 0$. Then we compute $V_l = \{v \in q^{l-1}(\mathbb{Z}/N\mathbb{Z})^2 : qv \in S_l\}$ and by an exhaustive search in the factor V_l/S_l we find $S_{l-1} = S \cap q^{l-1}(\mathbb{Z}/N\mathbb{Z})^2$ using again the test in time $q$poly log $|N|$. Note that V_l/S_l is an elementary abelian group of rank at most two. (A factor of a subgroup of an abelian q-group generated by 2 elements is also 2-generated.) The total cost is kqpoly log $|N|$.

We deduce the following result.

Theorem 3.3. *There is a classical algorithm that solves the Borel hidden subgroup problem in $\mathrm{GL}_2(\mathbb{Z}/N\mathbb{Z})$ in time* poly$(B \log N)$ *where B is an upper bound for the largest prime factor of N.*

3.2 A Quantum Algorithm

Denney, Moore and Russell [DMR10] proposed a quantum polynomial time algorithm that solves the problem in the case when N is a prime. In this subsection we extend their method to arbitrary N as follows. Based on Lemma 3.1 and Theorem 3.3, it is sufficient to give a procedure that works modulo the odd part of N. Thus, in the rest of the discussion we can and do assume that N is odd.

We use the notation introduced at the beginning of the section. In particular, H is the stabilizer of a secret free cyclic $\mathbb{Z}/N\mathbb{Z}$-submodule S of $(\mathbb{Z}/N\mathbb{Z})^2$. Note that $(\mathbb{Z}/N\mathbb{Z})^2/S$ is again a free cyclic $\mathbb{Z}/N\mathbb{Z}$-module whence for $w = (1,0)^T$ or $w = (0,1)^T$ we have that S and w generate $(\mathbb{Z}/N\mathbb{Z})^2$. We describe an algorithm that works under the assumption that S and $w = (1,0)^T$ generate V. If that fails, we repeat it after an appropriate basis change.

From the assumption, it follows that there is a unique element $s \in \mathbb{Z}/N\mathbb{Z}$ such that S is generated by $v = (s,1)^T$. We restrict the hidden subgroup problem to the stabilizer K of the vector w. Note that K is the group consisting of invertible matrices of the form

$$\begin{pmatrix} 1 & * \\ 0 & * \end{pmatrix}.$$

Observe that K is isomorphic to the semidirect $\mathbb{Z}/N\mathbb{Z} \rtimes (\mathbb{Z}/N\mathbb{Z})^*$ where the action of $(\mathbb{Z}/N\mathbb{Z})^*$ on $\mathbb{Z}/N\mathbb{Z}$ is the multiplication by its elements and the hidden subgroup $H \cap K$ is the stabilizer of the free cyclic submodule S in K. Note that the stabilizer of the submodule $(\mathbb{Z}/N\mathbb{Z})v$ in K is the conjugate of the stabilizer of the submodule of $(\mathbb{Z}/N\mathbb{Z})^2$ generated by $(0,1)^T$ in K by the unitriangular matrix

$$\begin{pmatrix} 1 & s \\ 0 & 1 \end{pmatrix}$$

transporting $(0,1)^T$ to $v = (s,1)^T$. Hence, by a straightforward calculation, the stabilizer $H \cap K$ of the submodule $\mathbb{Z}/N\mathbb{Z}v$ in K is the subgroup

$$K_s = \left\{ \begin{pmatrix} 1 & hs - s \\ 0 & h \end{pmatrix} : h \in (\mathbb{Z}/N\mathbb{Z})^* \right\}. \tag{1}$$

As N is odd, the images of the matrices of the form $M - \mathrm{Id}$ where $M \in H \cap K$:

$$\left\{ \begin{pmatrix} 0 & (h-1)s \\ 0 & h-1 \end{pmatrix} : h \in (\mathbb{Z}/N\mathbb{Z})^* \right\}$$

generate the submodule $\mathbb{Z}/N\mathbb{Z}v$. Indeed, $2 \in (\mathbb{Z}/N\mathbb{Z})^*$ and hence we have $M = \begin{pmatrix} 1 & s \\ 0 & 2 \end{pmatrix} \in H \cap K$ and so the image of $M - \mathrm{Id}$ is $\mathbb{Z}/N\mathbb{Z}v$.

As shown in the *preprint version* of [IPS18], the HSP in $K \cong \mathbb{Z}/N\mathbb{Z} \rtimes (\mathbb{Z}/N\mathbb{Z})^*$ where the hidden subgroup H is a conjugate of the complement $(\mathbb{Z}/N\mathbb{Z})^*$ can be cast as an instance of the hidden multiple shift problem $HMS(N, 1, r)$ with $r = \phi(N)$, the Euler's totient function of N. To see this, note that from (1) it follows that the *right* cosets of K_s are of the form

$$K_s \cdot \left\{ \begin{pmatrix} 1 & a \\ 0 & 1 \end{pmatrix} : h \in (\mathbb{Z}/N\mathbb{Z})^* \right\} = \left\{ \begin{pmatrix} 1 & hs - s + a \\ a & h \end{pmatrix} : h \in (\mathbb{Z}/N\mathbb{Z})^* \right\}.$$

Therefore, when we encode the elements g of K by the second column of $g - \mathrm{Id}$, the right version of the HSP gives an instance of the hidden multiple shift problem on $H \times \{h - 1 : h \in (\mathbb{Z}/N\mathbb{Z})^*\}$. As already noted in Sect. 2.6, the left version of the HSP is equivalent to the right one. Therefore, since $HMS(N, 1, \phi(N))$ can be solved efficiently by Theorem 2.5, we obtain the following result.

Theorem 3.4. *There is a quantum algorithm that efficiently finds the associated free cyclic submodule S for the hidden Borel subgroup H in $\mathrm{GL}_2(\mathbb{Z}/N\mathbb{Z})$ in time $(\log N)^{O(1)}$.*

4   On the Isogeny to Endomorphism Ring Problem

In this section, we study the IsERP and its connection to other algorithmic problems. Our final result provides a reduction from the IsERP to a pure quaternion problem, the PQLP (Problem 4.10), but we obtain this reduction through a quantum equivalence between the IsERP and the Group Action Evaluation Problem, that can be seen as a generalization of Problem 1.3. Most of the work in this section is dedicated to this equivalence.

In Sect. 4.1, we formally introduce the group action we consider. Then, in Sect. 4.2, we prove the result. Finally, in Sect. 4.3 we give the link with the PQLP and study the hardness of this problem.

4.1   The Group Action of $GL_2(\mathbb{Z}/N\mathbb{Z})$ on N-Isogenies.

In this section, we cover all necessary results on the group action we will consider. For that, it is important to understand how 2×2 matrices $\mod N$ appear naturally when you consider the action of endomorphisms on the N-torsion. This comes from the isomorphism $\operatorname{End}(E)/N \operatorname{End}(E) \cong M_2(\mathbb{Z}/N\mathbb{Z})$ which is a natural extension of the isomorphism $E[N] \cong \mathbb{Z}/N\mathbb{Z}^2$. We elaborate on that in the next paragraph.

The Isomorphism. Let P, Q be a basis of $E[N]$. We identify any point $R = [x]P + [y]Q$ as the vector $v_R = (x, y)^T$. Then, an endomorphism $\sigma \in \operatorname{End}(E)$ can be seen as a matrix in $M_\sigma \in M_2(\mathbb{Z}/N\mathbb{Z})$ through its action on the basis P, Q. If we have $\sigma(P) = [a]P + [b]Q$ and $\sigma(Q) = [c]P + [d]Q$, then we can define M_σ as $\begin{pmatrix} a & c \\ b & d \end{pmatrix}$ and the representation of $\sigma(R)$ is given by $M_\sigma v_R$. In that case, it can be easily shown that $\det M_\sigma = \deg \sigma \mod N$.

If one wants to compute an explicit isomorphism between $\operatorname{End}(E)/N \operatorname{End}(E)$ and $M_2(\mathbb{Z}/N\mathbb{Z})$ one can use the above method of evaluating a basis of $\operatorname{End}(E)$ on a basis of $E[N]$. However, when $E[N]$ is defined over a large extension field (e.g., N is large random prime), then this method is not efficient.

The issue can be circumvented by looking at the problem from a slightly different angle. Namely we have basis of $\operatorname{End}(E)/N \operatorname{End}(E)$ and we also have a multiplication table of the basis elements. Such a representation is called a structure constant representation. Rónyai [Rón90] proposed a polynomial-time algorithm for this problem when N is prime. The next lemma generalizes the algorithm to arbitrary N whose factorization is known.

Proposition 4.1. *Let A be a ring isomorphic to $M_2(\mathbb{Z}/N\mathbb{Z})$ given by a structure constant representation. Suppose that factorization of N is known. Then there exists a polynomial-time algorithm that computes an explicit isomorphism between A and $M_2(\mathbb{Z}/N\mathbb{Z})$.*

Proof. First we reduce the problem to the case where N is prime power. Let $N = ab$ where a and b are coprime. Then A/aA is isomorphic $M_2^?(\mathbb{Z}/a\mathbb{Z})$ and A/bA is isomorphic to $M_2(\mathbb{Z}/b\mathbb{Z})$. Since $M_2(\mathbb{Z}/a\mathbb{Z}) \times M_2(\mathbb{Z}/b\mathbb{Z})$ is isomorphic to $M_2(\mathbb{Z}/N\mathbb{Z})$, knowing an explicit isomorphism between A/aA and $M_2(\mathbb{Z}/a\mathbb{Z})$ and an explicit isomorphism between A/bA and $M_2(\mathbb{Z}/b\mathbb{Z})$ is enough to recover the isomorphism between A and $M_2(\mathbb{Z}/N\mathbb{Z})$. Using this procedure iteratively (using the fact that the factorization of N is known) one can reduce to the case where $N = q^k$ where q is some prime number.

Now suppose that A is isomorphic to $M_2(\mathbb{Z}/q^k\mathbb{Z})$. Observe that A/qA is isomorphic to $M_2(\mathbb{Z}/q\mathbb{Z})$. One can compute a non-trivial idempotent in A/qA using Rónyai's algorithm [Rón90], let that be e_0. Now observe that qA is the Jacobson radical of A. Indeed, since qA is clearly contained in the radical and A/qA is semisimple. Then [DK12, Corollary 3.1.2] says that e_0 can be lifted modulo qA to an idempotent of A. Now we know the existence, we show how one can do that algorithmically.

One has that $e_0^2 - e_0 \in qA$ and e_0 and $e_0 - 1$ are not in qA. Our goal is to find an element e which is an idempotent of A. We will perform an iteration which starts with e_0 and in the ith step we return an element e_i for which $e_i^2 - e_i \in q^{i+1}A$. Suppose we have an element e_{i-1} for which $e_{i-1}^2 - e_{i-1} \in q^i A$. Now we are looking for an $f \in A$ such that $(e_{i-1} + fq^i)^2 - (e_{i-1} + fq^i) \in q^{i+1}A$. Let $(e_{i-1}^2 - e_{i-1})/q = E_{i-1}$. Then this is equivalent to $e_{i-1}f + fe_{i-1} \equiv 1 - E_{i-1} \pmod{()q}$. This is a system of linear equations that has a solution by [DK12, Corollary 3.1.2] thus can be found efficiently. Now we have thus found an idempotent e of A.

Since A is a 2×2 matrix ring, $I = Ae$ is an irreducible A-module. Then the left action of A on I provides an explicit isomorphism between A and $M_2(\mathbb{Z}/q\mathbb{Z})$. We could not find a reference for this fact, so we present a quick simple proof. Let $\begin{pmatrix} a & b \\ c & (1-a) \end{pmatrix}$ be an idempotent matrix. We can assume that it has the above form as e is not congruent to 0 or the identity matrix modulo qA. We also have that $a(1-a) = bc$. Now the following is a generating set (as an abelian group) of Ae:

$$\begin{pmatrix} a & b \\ 0 & 0 \end{pmatrix}, \begin{pmatrix} 0 & 0 \\ a & b \end{pmatrix}, \begin{pmatrix} c & (1-a) \\ 0 & 0 \end{pmatrix}, \begin{pmatrix} 0 & 0 \\ c & (1-a) \end{pmatrix}.$$

One has that either a or $1 - a$ is invertible in $\mathbb{Z}/q^k\mathbb{Z}$, one may suppose that a is invertible (the calculation is the same in the other case). Then it is clear that every element of the form

$$\begin{pmatrix} \alpha & \alpha(b/a) \\ \beta & \beta(b/a) \end{pmatrix}$$

is in the left ideal for any $\alpha, \beta \in \mathbb{Z}/q^k\mathbb{Z}$. We show that every element of Ae is of this form. This follows from the fact that every element of the form

$$\begin{pmatrix} \gamma c & \gamma(1-a) \\ \delta c & \delta(1-a) \end{pmatrix}$$

can be written in this form (a linear combination of the second two basis elements) because if $\gamma c = \alpha$ and $\delta c = \beta$, then $\alpha(b/a) = \gamma(1-a)$ and $\beta(b/a) = \delta(1-a)$ (because $cb/a = (1-a)$). Finally, it is clear that the map $\begin{pmatrix} \alpha & \alpha(b/a) \\ \beta & \beta(b/a) \end{pmatrix} \mapsto (\alpha, \beta)$ is an isomorphism of A-modules. $\quad\square$

Remark 4.2. Once an idempotent e is found, one can finish the proof in an alternate way as well. Namely one can show that $\mathrm{Im}(e) = \ker(e)$ is a cyclic subgroup of $(\mathbb{Z}/q^k\mathbb{Z})^2$ of cardinality q^k. Then a generator of $\ker(e)$ and $\ker(1 - e)$ will be a basis in which e is $\begin{pmatrix} 1 & 0 \\ 0 & 0 \end{pmatrix}$ which shows indeed that the left ideal generated by e is minimal.

The Group Action of Invertible Matrices on Isogenies. Now, let us take a cyclic subgroup $G \subset E[N]$ of order N (this is a submodule of rank 1 inside $(\mathbb{Z}/N\mathbb{Z})^2$ with our isomorphism). If $\sigma \in \mathrm{GL}_2(\mathbb{Z}/N\mathbb{Z})$, then it is clear that $\sigma(G)$ is also a cyclic subgroup of order N. Thus, we have a natural action of $\mathrm{GL}_2(\mathbb{Z}/N\mathbb{Z})$ on the cyclic subgroups of order N.

This group action on subgroups of order N can naturally be extended to a group action of $\mathrm{GL}_2(\mathbb{Z}/N\mathbb{Z})$ on the set of N-isogenies from E through the bijection between cyclic subgroups of order N and N-isogenies given by $G \mapsto (\phi_G : E \to E/G)$ (and whose inverse is simply $\phi \mapsto \ker \phi$).

Composing this bijection with the group action we already have, we get the following group action

$$M_\sigma \star \phi_G \mapsto \phi_{\sigma(G)}. \tag{2}$$

This action is always well-defined. However, for computational purposes, we want ways to efficiently represent its elements and compute the action $\star$. These considerations motivate the remaining of this paper.

The problem we consider is the following:

Problem 4.3 (Group Action Evaluation Problem). Let E be a supersingular elliptic curve over $\mathbb{F}_{p^2}$ and let $\phi : E \to E_1$ be an isogeny of degree N for some integer N. Given $\mathrm{End}(E)$, an isogeny representation for ϕ, M in $\mathrm{GL}_2(\mathbb{Z}/N\mathbb{Z})$, find an isogeny representation of $M \star \phi$.

The Stabilizer Subgroups. One last thing that will be important to apply our results to this group action is to identify the stabilizer subgroup associated to a given isogeny ϕ. In fact, those are pretty easy to identify and are well-known objects. The answer is given by the following proposition.

Proposition 4.4. *Let* $\phi : E \to E'$ *be an isogeny of degree* N*. The stabilizer subgroup associated to* ϕ *through the group action defined in Eq. (2) is made of the matrices* M_σ *such that* σ *is in the Eichler order* $\mathbb{Z} + I_\phi$ *where* I_ϕ *is the ideal associated to* ϕ *under the Deuring correspondence.*

Proof. By definition of the group action, the stabilizer subgroup is obtained with the matrices M_σ such that $\sigma(\ker \phi) = \ker \phi$. This means that σ acts as a scalar λ_σ on $\ker \phi$. Thus, $\ker \phi \subset \ker(\sigma - \lambda_\sigma)$ and by definition of I_ϕ, we have that $\sigma - \lambda_\sigma \in I_\phi$, hence $\sigma \in \mathbb{Z} + I_\phi$. Conversely, it is clear that any element in $\mathbb{Z} + I_\phi$ acts as a scalar on $\ker \phi$ and so is part of the stabilizer. For the proof that $\mathbb{Z} + I_\phi$ is an Eichler order, see [DFKL+20]. □

Remark 4.5. Writing the stabilizer subgroups as Eichler orders of the form $\mathbb{Z} + I_\phi$ will help us prove that computing the stabilizer subgroup is essentially equivalent to finding the endomorphism ring of the codomain of ϕ (which is isomorphic to the right order of I_ϕ).

Proposition 4.6. *The stabilizer subgroups are conjugates of the subgroup of upper triangular matrices (i.e., a Borel subgroup).*

Proof. Follows from [Voi18, 23.1.3]. For an elementary proof see [CII+23, Appendix B].   □

4.2   The Main Reductions

In this section, we prove a quantum polynomial-time equivalence between the Group Action Evaluation Problem and the IsERP.

Theorem 4.7. *The Group Action Evaluation Problem reduces to the IsERP in classical polynomial-time.*

Proof. Assume we have an efficient algorithm to solve the IsERP. Let us take an instance of the Group Action Evaluation Problem. So we have $N, E, \text{End}(E)$, a representation for ϕ and a matrix M, and we want to compute a representation for $M * \phi$.

The first step of the reduction is to compute the ideal I_ϕ associated to ϕ. There are several ways to do that, but to keep this proof short, we will use some of the results proven in [Ler22a]. Thus, our first step is to build a suborder representation for the isogeny ϕ as in [Ler22a]. The suborder representation is made of endomorphisms of $\mathbb{Z} + N \text{End}(E) \hookrightarrow \text{End}(E')$ of powersmooth norm. Since we know $\text{End}(E)$ and $\text{End}(E')$, the algorithms of the Deuring correspondence can be used to compute their kernels in polynomial time (their norm being powersmooth implies that their kernels are defined over a small extension). Then, we can compute the suborder representation using Vélu's formulas. Once we have the suborder representation, we can apply the equivalence between the SOIP and the SOERP [Ler22a, Proposition 13] to find the ideal I_ϕ. Once I_ϕ has been computed, we need to compute the ideal $I_{M\star\phi}$. For that we are going to use a σ such that $M_\sigma = M$. We can build such a σ in polynomial time from $\text{End}(E)$ using Proposition 4.1.

Once a good σ is known, we get the ideal $I_{M\star\phi}$ as $\sigma(I_\phi \cap \mathcal{O}\sigma)\sigma^{-1} + N\mathcal{O}$ (where we take $\mathcal{O} \cong \text{End}(E)$). Since the ideal $I_{M_\sigma\star\phi}$ is a valid isogeny representation, this proves the result.   □

Theorem 4.8. *The IsERP reduces to the Group Action Evaluation Problem in quantum polynomial time.*

Proof. Assume we can solve the Group Action Evaluation Problem.

Let us take an input of the IsERP, we have a curve E, its endomorphism ring $\text{End}(E)$, an integer N and the isogeny representation associated to an isogeny ϕ of degree N.

The algorithm to solve the Group Action Evaluation Problem allows us to compute efficiently the group action introduced in Sect. 4.1. Using Proposition 4.6 and Theorem 3.4 one can compute the stabilizer subgroup associated to ϕ. As the stabilizer subgroups of ϕ give us matrices corresponding to some σ in the Eichler order $\mathbb{Z} + I_\phi$, we can compute the embedding of this order in $\mathcal{O} \cong \text{End}(E)$ in polynomial time using the algorithm of Proposition 4.1. Then, we can extract the ideal I_ϕ and compute $O_R(I_\phi)$ which is isomorphic to $\text{End}(E')$ and this gives the result.

□

When the degree N is smooth, we can modify the proof of Theorem 4.8 to get a classical reduction by using Theorem 3.3 instead of Theorem 3.4.

Theorem 4.9. *Suppose that degree of the secret isogeny is smooth. Then IsERP reduces to the Group Action Evaluation Problem in classical polynomial time.*

4.3 Reduction of the Group Action Evaluation Problem to the PQLP

In this section, we reduce the Group Action Evaluation Problem to another problem that we call the Powersmooth Quaternion Lift Problem (PQLP). The PQLP can be stated as follows:

Problem 4.10. Let $\mathcal{O}$ be a maximal order in $\mathcal{B}_{p,\infty}$. Given an integer N and an element $\sigma_0 \in \mathcal{O}$ such that $(n(\sigma_0), N) = 1$, find $\sigma = \lambda\sigma_0 \bmod N\mathcal{O}$ of powersmooth norm with some λ coprime to N.

We use $\text{PQLP}_{\mathcal{O}}(\sigma_0)$ to denote the set of $\sigma \in \mathcal{O}$ that satisfy the conditions in Problem 4.10 with respect to $\sigma_0 \in \mathcal{O}$. The high level idea of the reduction from the PQLP to the Group Action Evaluation Problem is close to the approach introduced in [KMPW21]. Given a matrix M, the goal is to find a good representative of the class of M, i.e. a $\sigma \in \text{End}(E)$ of powersmooth norm, such that $M = M_\sigma$. Then, we can use Vélu's formulae to solve the Group Action Evaluation Problem.

Proposition 4.11. *The Group Action Evaluation Problem reduces to PQLP in classical polynomial time.*

Proof. Let us take an instance of our problem. We have $N, E, \text{End}(E)$, an isogeny representation for $\phi : E \to E'$ of degree N and a matrix M.

We need to show that if we know a $\sigma \in \text{End}(E)$ (represented as a quaternion element in a maximal order $\mathcal{O} \cong \text{End}(E)$) of powersmooth norm such that $M_\sigma = M$, then we can compute a representation for $M \star \phi$ in polynomial time. For that, we will use the following commutative isogeny diagram

$$
\begin{array}{ccc}
E' & \xrightarrow{\ \sigma'\ } & E'/\sigma(\ker \phi) \\
{\scriptstyle \phi}\uparrow & & \uparrow{\scriptstyle M\star\phi} \\
E & \xrightarrow{\ \ \sigma\ \ } & E
\end{array}
$$

where σ' has the same degree as σ and is defined by $\ker \sigma' = \phi(\ker \sigma)$. Since the isogeny σ' has powersmooth degree, it can be computed in polynomial time once $\ker \sigma'$ has been computed. Since, we can evaluate ϕ, it suffices to compute $\ker \sigma$ and this can be done in polynomial-time since we known $\text{End}(E)$.

Since the diagram is commutative, we have that $\sigma' \circ \phi = M \star \phi \circ \sigma$ and this gives us the way to evaluate efficiently $M \star \phi$ on almost all torsion (as soon as the order is coprime to $\deg \sigma$) as $M \star \phi = \hat{\sigma}' \circ \phi \circ \sigma / \deg \sigma$. This is sufficient to build a suborder representation of $M \star \phi$ (see the algorithm outlined in the proof of Theorem 4.8).

This proves that the main computational task is to find this σ of powersmooth norm. Thus, it suffices to apply an algorithm to solve the PQLP on input N, $\mathrm{End}(E)$ and a σ_0 such that $M_{\sigma_0} = M$ (that we can find using Proposition 4.1). $\qquad\square$

5   Resolution of the PQLP

In this section, we solve the PQLP (Problem 4.10) with conditions imposed on the factors of N, as detailed in the following theorem.

Theorem 5.1. *Let $N = \prod \ell_i^{e_i} \neq p$ be an odd integer that is of size polynomial in p and has $O(\log(\log p))$ factors, then there exists a randomized classical polynomial time algorithm that solves the PQLP.*

This theorem follows from the correctness of Algorithm 3 which is introduced and discussed in Sect. 5.2. The successive reductions from the IsERP to the Group Action Evaluation Problem, and subsequently to the PQLP, demonstrate the existence of a polynomial time algorithm that solves the IsERP, given N satisfies the conditions in Theorem 5.1. As a direct consequence, this breaks pSIDH quantumly since N is a large prime in pSIDH. As mentioned previously, the IsERP is easy when N is powersmooth. We briefly discuss some approaches to solve the general case in [CII+23, Appendix D].

In Sect. 5.1, we give a summary of useful known algorithms and provide variants for RepresentInteger, StrongApproximation and KLPT to better accommodate our specific application. Following this, we introduce our primary strategy for resolving the PQLP in Sect. 5.2. In Sect. 5.3, we deal with a critical technical point which we introduce as the Quaternion Decomposition problem. The crux of this problem, and indeed our main conceptual contribution, is the decomposition of σ_0 into elements that are easy to lift, and elements already possessing a powersmooth norm. Finally in Sect. 5.4, we provide a quantum algorithm that solves the PQLP.

5.1   Algorithmic Building Blocks

Our algorithm for the PQLP is founded on algorithmic building blocks initially introduced in [KLPT14] and later extended in other work, such as [DFKL+20]. We provide a brief recap of these algorithms here, along with several new variants tailored to suit our requirements. We fix $\log^c p$ to be our powersmooth bound for some constant c, and this bound is inherently implied whenever we reference the term 'powersmooth'.

As in [KLPT14], for each p, we fix a special p-extremal maximal order $\mathcal{O}_0$.

$$\mathcal{O}_0 = \begin{cases} \mathbb{Z}\langle i, \frac{1+j}{2}\rangle \text{ where } i^2 = -1, j^2 = -p, & \text{for } p \equiv 3 \bmod 4, \\ \mathbb{Z}\langle \frac{1+i}{2}, j, \frac{ci+k}{q}\rangle \text{ where } i^2 = -q, j^2 = -p, & \text{for } p \equiv 1 \bmod 4, \end{cases} \quad (3)$$

where c is any root of $x^2 + p \bmod q$. In the second case, q is required to satisfy that $q \equiv 3 \bmod 4$ is a prime and $\left(\frac{-p}{q}\right) = 1$. We add one extra condition that $(q, N) = 1$. Under the generalized Riemann hypothesis (GRH), the smallest q is of size $O(\log^2 p)$. For the ease of exposition, we define q to be 1 when we are in the first case (i.e., when $p \equiv 3 \bmod 4$).

For each $\mathcal{O}_0$, we identify a suborder of the form $R + Rj$ for $R = \mathbb{Z}[i]$ (note that we are making a slightly different choice here than the R in [KLPT14] where they always take R to the maximal order in $\mathbb{Q}(i)$). For an element $\alpha = a + bi \in R$, we use $\mathsf{Re}_R(\alpha)$ to denote a and $\mathsf{Im}_R(\alpha)$ to denote b. Let D denote the index $[\mathcal{O}_0 : R + Rj]$, then

$$D = \begin{cases} 4, & \text{for } p \equiv 3 \bmod 4, \\ 4q, & \text{for } p \equiv 1 \bmod 4. \end{cases} \quad (4)$$

We will now detail the algorithmic building blocks, sourced from [KLPT14] or [DFKL+20].

- $\mathsf{Cornacchia}(M)$: on an input M that is a prime integer not equal to q, outputs either $\perp$ if M cannot be represented by $x^2 + qy^2$, or a solution x, y to the equation $M = x^2 + qy^2$.
- $\mathsf{RepresentInteger}_{\mathcal{O}_0}(M)$: on an input $M > p$, outputs $\gamma \in \mathcal{O}_0$ such that $n(\gamma) = M$.
- $\mathsf{StrongApproximation}_F(N, \mu_0)$: on inputs an integer $F > pN^4$, a prime N and $\mu_0 \in Rj$, outputs $\lambda \notin N\mathbb{Z}$ and $\mu \in \mathcal{O}_0$ of norm dividing F such that $\mu = \lambda\mu_0 \bmod N\mathcal{O}_0$.
- $\mathsf{KLTP}_M(I)$: on inputs an integer $M > p^3$ and an ideal I, outputs an equivalent ideal J such that $n(J) = M$.

Let us denote the output γ of $\mathsf{RepresentInteger}_{\mathcal{O}_0}(M)$ as $C + Dj$ with $C, D \in R$. To fit our algorithm's specific use case, we require not only that $n(\gamma)$ is powersmooth, but also that C, D satisfy additional conditions relative to some inputs $A, B \in R$, which are determined by σ_0 from the PQLP. As a result, we introduce the following variant named $\mathsf{RepresentInteger'}_{R+Rj}(N, A, B)$. This variant necessitates more randomized steps to find the desired outputs $C, D \in R$.

Heuristic 5.2. *We assume that M', $z^2 + qt^2$, $\mathsf{Im}_R(A\bar{B}C\bar{D})$ and $q(4p^2 n(AB CD) - (n(AC) - pn(AD))^2)$ appearing in Algorithm 1 behave like random integers of the same size.*

Lemma 5.3. *Let N be as in Theorem 5.1, assuming Heuristic 5.2, Algorithm 1 returns a solution in polynomial time.*

Algorithm 1: RepresentInteger$'_{R+Rj}(N, A, B)$

Input: An integer N and $A, B \in R$

Output: $C, D \in R$ such that: i) $(n(C + Dj), N) = 1$ and $n(C + Dj)$ is powersmooth; ii) $(n(C), N) = 1$; iii) $(n(D), N) = 1$; iv) $(N, \text{Im}_R(A\bar{B}C\bar{D})) = 1$ and v) $q(4p^2 n(ABCD) - (n(AC) - pn(AD))^2)$ is a square modulo N.

1 Let k be the smallest integer such that the number of prime factors of N is less than $k \log \log p$, randomly generate M of size $\lfloor p \log^{3k+4} p \log \log p \rfloor$ that is powersmooth and coprime to N.

2 Set $m = \lfloor \sqrt{\frac{M}{p(q+1)}} \rfloor$ and sample random integers $z, t \in [-m, m]^2$.

3 Set $M' = M - p(z^2 + qt^2)$.

4 **If** $(z^2 + qt^2, N) \neq 1$ *or* $(M', N) \neq 1$ *or* M' *is not a prime* **then**

5 $\quad$ Go back to Step 2.

6 **If** Cornacchia$(M') = \perp$ **then**

7 $\quad$ Go back to Step 2.

8 $x, y =$ Cornacchia(M').

9 $C \leftarrow x + yi, D \leftarrow z + ti$.

10 **If** $(N, \text{Im}_R(A\bar{B}C\bar{D})) \neq 1$ **then**

11 $\quad$ Go back to Step 2.

12 **If** $q(4p^2 n(ABCD) - (n(AC) - pn(AD))^2)$ *is not a square modulo* N **then**

13 $\quad$ Go back to Step 2.

14 **Return** C, D.

Proof. For Step 4, by assumption, M' is a prime with probability $1/O(\log p)$, and once we ensure that M' is a prime, $(M', N) = 1$ holds with a negligible failure rate. On the other hand, since the number of prime factors of N is less than $k \log \log p$, the probability that $(z^2 + qt^2, N) = 1$ holds is at least $1/O(\log^k p)$. Therefore, Step 4 succeeds with probability greater than $1/O(\log^{k+1} p)$. For Step 10, similarly it succeeds with probability at least $1/O(\log^k p)$. For Step 6, $x^2 + qy^2 = M'$ has a solution if and only if (M') is a product of two principal ideals in $\mathbb{Z}[i]$. M' is split or ramifies in $\mathbb{Z}[i]$ with probability $1/2$, and a random invertible ideal in $\mathbb{Z}[i]$ is principal with probability $1/\#\mathcal{Cl}(\mathbb{Z}[i]) > 1/O(\sqrt{q} \log q)$ [Coh95, Sect. 5.10.1]. Since q is at most $O(\log^2 p)$, this step succeeds with probability greater than $1/O(\log p \log \log p)$. Finally, for an integer to be a square modulo N, it's equivalent to this integer being a square modulo each prime factor of N. Therefore, Step 12 succeeds with probability at least $1/O(\log^k p)$. In total, the success probability is greater than $1/O(\log^{2+3k} p \log \log p)$. In Step 2, there will be $O(\log^{3k+2} p \log \log p)$ pairs of (z, t), therefore Algorithm 1 will return a solution in polynomial time. $\qed$

We also provide a generalization of the StrongApproximation algorithm to allow for composite N (note that in this algorithm we don't have restriction on the number of factors of N). The subscript $_{ps}$ refers to powersmooth.

Algorithm 2: StrongApproximation$_{ps}(N, \mu_0)$

Input: An odd integer N and $\mu_0 \in Rj$ such that $(n(\mu_0), N) = 1$.
Output: $\lambda \in \mathbb{Z}$ such that $(\lambda, N) = 1$ and $\mu \in R$ with powersmooth norm such that $\mu = \lambda\mu_0 \bmod N\mathcal{O}_0$.

1 Write μ_0 as $(t + si)j$ with $t, s \in \mathbb{Z}$.
2 · Let $S = \{\ell \text{ such that } \ell \mid N \text{ and } \left(\frac{n(\mu_0)}{\ell}\right) = -1\}$.
3 Randomly generate $\#S$ many prime p_i's such that $p_i < \log^c p$ and let $\epsilon_{ij} \in \{0, 1\}$ be the exponent such that $\left(\frac{p_i}{\ell_j}\right) = (-1)^{\epsilon_{ij}}$.
4 Solve the system of $\#S \times \#S$ equations $\Sigma_{i=1}^{\#S} \epsilon_{ij} x_i = 1$ for $j = 1, \cdots, \#S$ in $\mathbf{F}_2$.
5 **If** *There is no solution found in Step 4* **then**
6 | Go back to Step 3

7 $F = \prod_{i=1}^{\#S} p_i^{x_i}$.
8 Multiply a $\log^c p$-powersmooth square factor that is coprime to $n(\mu_0)$ to F to ensure $F > pN^4$.
9 Denote one of the square root of $\frac{F}{n(\mu_0)}$ modulo N by λ.
10 Randomly generate c, d such that $\lambda p(2tc + 2qsd) \equiv (F - \lambda^2 p(t^2 + qs^2))/N \bmod N$.
11 Set $M = (F - p((\lambda t + cN)^2 + q(\lambda s + dN)^2))/N^2$.
12 **If** M *is not a prime or* Cornacchia$(M) = \bot$ **then**
13 | Go back to Step 10

14 $a, b = $ Cornacchia(M).
15 **Return** $\lambda\mu_0 + N(a + bi + (c + di)j), \lambda$.

Heuristic 5.4. *We assume that M appearing in Algorithm 2 behaves like a random integer of the same size.*

Lemma 5.5. *Consider a linear equation $N_1 x + N_2 y = N_3 \bmod N$ where $\gcd(N, N_1) = d_1, \gcd(N, N_2) = d_2$ and $(d_1, d_2) = 1$. Then this equation has N solutions in $(\mathbb{Z}/N\mathbb{Z})^2$.*

Proof. This can be seen by checking how many solutions there are for equation $N_1 x + N_2 y = N_3 \bmod \ell_i^{e_i}$ with $\ell_i^{e_i}$ being a prime power divisor of N and then using Chinese Reminder Theorem. □

Lemma 5.6. *Let N be an odd integer, assuming Heuristic 5.4, Algorithm 2 returns a solution in polynomial time.*

Proof. The $\#S \times \#S$ linear equations behave like a random system of linear equations of the same dimension, therefore, repeating Step 3 constant number of times will give rise to a linear system over $\mathbf{F}_2$ that is solvable. We have ensured that F generated in Step 8 is such that $\frac{F}{n(\mu_0)}$ is a square modulo N, hence Step 9 makes sense. Similar to what is discussed in the proof of Lemma 5.3, Step 12 succeeds with probability at least $1/O(\log^2 p \log \log p)$. To make sure this algorithm gets passed to Step 14, we need $O(\log^2 p \log \log p)$ many solutions from Step 10. According to Lemma 5.5, this happens if $O(\log^2 p \log \log p) < N$, and this holds since N is assumed to be of size polynomial in p. □

Finally, another variant we introduce here is $\mathsf{KLTP}'_M(\mathcal{O}_0, \mathcal{O})$. Here M is an integer such that $M > p^3$. This algorithm first computes a connecting ideal I' from $\mathcal{O}_0$ to $\mathcal{O}$, then computes an equivalent left $\mathcal{O}_0$-ideal I of norm M whose right order is $\alpha^{-1}\mathcal{O}\alpha$ for some nonzero $\alpha \in \mathcal{B}_{p,\infty}$ using $\mathsf{KLPT}_M(I')$. This KLPT' algorithm outputs I and α.

5.2   The Main Algorithm

In this section, we first present a strategy that solves Problem 4.10 for special orders $\mathcal{O}_0$. Then, we expand this strategy to address more general orders $\mathcal{O}$. Let $\sigma_0 \in \mathcal{O}_0$ be as in Problem 4.10, the method proceeds as follows.

1. Find $\sigma_0' \in R + Rj$ such that $\sigma_0' = \sigma_0 \bmod N\mathcal{O}_0$. Since $[\mathcal{O}_0 : R + Rj] = D$, $D\sigma_0 \in R + Rj$. Let $D' \in \mathbb{Z}$ be such that $D'D \equiv 1 \bmod N$, such D' exists since $(D, N) = 1$, then $\sigma_0' = D'D\sigma_0 \in R + Rj$ and $\sigma_0' = \sigma_0 \bmod N\mathcal{O}_0$. By an abuse of notation, we will use σ_0 to denote σ_0' in what follows.
2. Write $\sigma_0 = A + Bj$ with $A, B \in R$, let γ be the output of Represent Integer$'_{R+Rj}(N, A, B)$. Intuitively, γ is an element in $R + Rj$ that has powermooth norm and satisfies extra properties to ensure the next step has a solution.
3. Find $\alpha_1, \alpha_2, \alpha_3 \in Rj$ such that $\sigma_0 = \alpha_1 \gamma \alpha_2 \gamma \alpha_3 \bmod N\mathcal{O}_0$. This is the main technical point in this method, we introduce it as Problem 5.7 and discuss it in detail in Sect. 5.3.
4. Find $\gamma_i \in \mathcal{O}_0$ such that $\gamma_i = \lambda_i \alpha_i \bmod N\mathcal{O}_0$, $n(\gamma_i)$ is powersmooth and $(\lambda_i, N) = 1$ for $i = 1, 2, 3$. These are exactly the outputs of StrongApproximation$_{ps}(N, \alpha_i)$.
5. The element $\gamma_1 \gamma \gamma_2 \gamma \gamma_3 \in \mathcal{O}_0$ satisfies that $\sigma_0 = \lambda \gamma_1 \gamma \gamma_2 \gamma \gamma_3 \bmod N\mathcal{O}_0$ with $n(\gamma_1 \gamma \gamma_2 \gamma \gamma_3)$ powersmooth and λ coprime to N.

In general, let $\mathcal{O}$ be a maximal order in $\mathcal{B}_{p,\infty}$, and let $n_I > p^3$ be a random integer that is coprime to N. Let $n_I' \in \mathbb{Z}$ such that $n_I' n_I \equiv 1 \bmod N$. Let I, α be the outputs of $\mathsf{KLPT}_{n_I}(\mathcal{O}_0, \mathcal{O})$ such that I is a connecting ideal from $\mathcal{O}_0$ to $\mathcal{O}' := \alpha^{-1}\mathcal{O}\alpha$ and $n(I) = n_I$. We then have inclusions $n_I\mathcal{O}' \subseteq \mathcal{O}_0$ and $n_I\mathcal{O}_0 \subseteq \mathcal{O}'$, therefore $n_I\alpha^{-1}\sigma_0\alpha \in \mathcal{O}_0$. Let $\sigma \in \mathsf{PQLP}_{\mathcal{O}_0}(n_I\alpha^{-1}\sigma_0\alpha)$, then $\sigma = n_I\alpha^{-1}\sigma_0\alpha \bmod N\mathcal{O}_0$. Multiplying n_I with both sides of the equation yields that $n_I\sigma = n_I^2\alpha^{-1}\sigma_0\alpha \bmod N\mathcal{O}'$. Multiplying $n_I'^2$ on both sides gives that $n_I'\sigma = \alpha^{-1}\sigma_0\alpha \bmod N\mathcal{O}'$. Since n_I' is coprime to N, $\sigma \in \mathsf{PQLP}_{\mathcal{O}'}(\alpha^{-1}\sigma_0\alpha)$, therefore $\alpha\sigma\alpha^{-1} \in \mathsf{PQLP}_{\mathcal{O}}(\sigma_0)$.

We summarize the discussions above and present Algorithm 3.

5.3   Quaternion Decomposition

In this section, we discuss how to perform Step 3 from the strategy outline. We start with introducing a new problem.

Algorithm 3: $\text{PQLP}_{\mathcal{O}}(N, \sigma_0)$

Input: An odd integer N that is of size polynomial in p and has $O(\log \log p)$ distinct prime factors, a maximal order $\mathcal{O}$, and an element $\sigma_0 \in \mathcal{O}$ such that $(n(\sigma_0), N) = 1$.

Output: $\sigma \in \text{PQLP}_{\mathcal{O}}(\sigma_0)$.

1 Compute D' such that $D'D \equiv 1 \bmod N$.
2 $\sigma_0 \leftarrow D'D\sigma_0$
3 Write σ_0 as $A + Bj$ with $A, B \in R$
4 $\gamma \leftarrow \text{RepresentInteger}'_{R+Rj}(N, A, B)$
5 $\alpha_1, \alpha_2, \alpha_3 \leftarrow \text{QuaternionDecomposition}(\sigma_0, \gamma, N)(\text{Algorithm } 4)$
6 $\lambda_i, \gamma_i \leftarrow \text{StrongApproximation}_{ps}(N, \alpha_i)$ for $i = 1, 2, 3$
7 $\sigma \leftarrow \gamma_1 \gamma \gamma_2 \gamma \gamma_3$
8 Randomly generate $n_I > p^3$ that is coprime to N.
9 $I, \alpha \leftarrow \text{KLPT}_{n_I}(\mathcal{O}_0, \mathcal{O})$
10 **Return** $\alpha \gamma_1 \gamma \gamma_2 \gamma \gamma_3 \alpha^{-1}$.

Problem 5.7 (Quaternion Decomposition). Let N be an odd integer, and $\mathcal{O}_0, R$ be as defined in Sect. 5.1. Let $\sigma_0 = A + Bj, \gamma = C + Dj \in R + Rj$ be such that:
i) $(n(\gamma), N) = 1$ and $n(\gamma)$ is powersmooth; ii) $(n(C), N) = 1$; iii) $(n(D), N) = 1$;
iv) $(N, \text{Im}_R(A\bar{B}C\bar{D}))$ and v) $q(4p^2 n(ABCD) - (n(AC) - pn(AD))^2)$ is a square modulo N. Find $\alpha_1, \alpha_2, \alpha_3 \in Rj$ such that $\sigma_0 = \alpha_1 \gamma \alpha_2 \gamma \alpha_3 \bmod N\mathcal{O}_0$.

Suppose one could find $\alpha_1, \alpha_2, \alpha_3 \in Rj$ such that

$$\sigma_0 \bar{\alpha}_3 \bar{\gamma} = \alpha_1 \gamma \alpha_2 \bmod N\mathcal{O}_0, \tag{5}$$

and $(n(\alpha_3), N) = 1$, then

$$\sigma_0 = n'_{\alpha_3} n'_\gamma \alpha_1 \gamma \alpha_2 \gamma \alpha_3.$$

Here n'_{α_3} and n'_γ are integers such that $n'_{\alpha_3} n(\alpha_3) \equiv 1 \bmod N$ and $n'_\gamma n(\gamma) \equiv 1 \bmod N$ respectively. We then search for solutions $\alpha_1, \alpha_2, \alpha_3 \in Rj$ for Eq. (5) with $(n(\alpha_3), 1) = 1$ instead.

Let us write α_i's as $x_i j$ with x_i's being unknowns that we wish to find in R, writing Eq. (5) in terms of A, B, C, D, x_1, x_2 and x_3 gives rise to the following:

$$\text{Equation (5)} \iff (A + Bj)(-j)\bar{x}_3(\bar{C} - j\bar{D}) = x_1 j(C + Dj)x_2 j \bmod N\mathcal{O}_0$$
$$\iff (-Ax_3 j + pB\bar{x}_3)(\bar{C} - j\bar{D}) = (x_1 \bar{C}j - px_1 \bar{D})x_2 j \bmod N\mathcal{O}_0$$
$$\iff (-pA\bar{D}x_3 + pB\bar{C}\bar{x}_3) + (-ACx_3 - pBD\bar{x}_3)j = -p\bar{C}x_1\bar{x}_2 - p\bar{D}x_1 x_2 j \bmod N\mathcal{O}_0$$

Therefore, in order to solve the original equation, it suffices to find $x_1, x_2, x_3 \in R$ with $(n(x_3), N) = 1$ such that

$$\begin{cases} pA\bar{D}x_3 - pB\bar{C}\bar{x}_3 = p\bar{C}x_1\bar{x}_2 \bmod NR, \\ ACx_3 + pBD\bar{x}_3 = p\bar{D}x_1 x_2 \bmod NR. \end{cases} \tag{6}$$

Note that the modulo condition in Eq. (6) holds not just in $N\mathcal{O}_0$ but in NR since $[\mathcal{O}_K : R] = 1$ or 2 is coprime to N. By assumption, $n(C)$ and $n(D)$ are both coprime to N, let $n'_C, n'_D \in \mathbb{Z}$ be integers such that $n'_C n(C) \equiv 1 \bmod N$ and $n'_D n(D) \equiv 1 \bmod N$ respectively, and let $p' \in \mathbb{Z}$ be such that $p'p \equiv 1 \bmod N$, then Eq. (6) is equivalent to

$$\begin{cases} (n'_C p')(pA\bar{D}x_3 - pB\bar{C}\bar{x}_3) = x_1\bar{x}_2 \bmod NR, \\ (n'_D p')(ACx_3 + pBD\bar{x}_3) = x_1 x_2 \bmod NR. \end{cases} \tag{7}$$

Lemma 5.8 *Equation (7) has a solution* $(x_1, x_2, x_3) \in R^3$ *if and only if there exists* $x_3 \in R$ *such that* $x := (n'_C p')(pA\bar{D}x_3 - pB\bar{C}\bar{x}_3)$ *and* $y := (n'_D p')(ACx_3 + pBD\bar{x}_3)$ *have same norm modulo* N.

Proof One solution to Eq. (7) clearly implies $n(x) = n(y) = n(x_1)n(x_2)$. For the other direction, we provide a simple proof here for the case when N is a prime that is inert in R, and refer to [CII+23, Appendix C] for the general case when N is an arbitrary odd integer. Since N is a prime that is inert in R, $R/(N) \cong \mathbb{F}_{N^2}$. Hilbert's Theorem 90 implies that if $a \in R/(N)$ has norm 1, then $a = b/\bar{b}$ for $b \in R/(N)$. Since $n(x) = n(y)$ and both $x, y \notin NR$, we have that $n(x/y) = 1$, therefore $x/y = z/\bar{z}$ for some nonzero $z \in R/(N)$. Consequently, x_1, x_2 can be chosen to be lifts of yz and $1/z$ to R respectively.   □

Remark 5.9 The method we present for odd integers N is constructive, therefore leads to an algorithm that finds x_1, x_2 given x_3 such that $n(x) = n(y)$. We call this algoithm EquivNormConjugationProduct(x_3).

The condition $n(x) = n(y)$ is equivalent to $n(CDpx) = n(CDpy)$. And one could calculate explicitly that

$$n(CDpx) = p^2 n(A)n^2(D)n(x_3) + p^2 n(B)n(C)n(D)n(x_3) - 2p^2 n(D)\mathrm{Re}_R(A\bar{B}C\bar{D}x_3^2),$$
$$n(CDpy) = n(A)n^2(C)n(x_3) + p^2 n(B)n(C)n(D)n(x_3) + 2pn(C)\mathrm{Re}_R(A\bar{B}C\bar{D}x_3^2).$$

We now aim to find $x_3 = s + ti \in R$ with $(n(x_3), N) = 1$ such that $n(CDpx) - n(CDpy) = n(\gamma)\big(n(A)(n(C) - pn(D)) + 2p\mathrm{Re}_R(A\bar{B}C\bar{D}x_3^2)\big) = 0 \bmod N$. Plugging in $x_3 = s + ti$, finding x_3 is equivalent to finding $(s, t) \in \mathbb{Z}^2$ such that

$$f(s,t) := C_1 s^2 + C_2 st + C_3 t^2 = 0 \bmod N, \tag{8}$$

where $C_1 = \big(n(A)(n(C) - pn(D)) + 2p\mathrm{Re}_R(A\bar{B}C\bar{D})\big), C_2 = -4qp(\mathrm{Im}_R A\bar{B}C\bar{D})$ and $C_3 = \big(qn(A)(n(C) - pn(D)) - 2qp\mathrm{Re}_R(A\bar{B}C\bar{D})\big)$. Clearly, a solution (s, t) exists if and only if the discriminant

$$4q(4p^2 n(ABCD) - (n(AC) - pn(AD))^2) \tag{9}$$

of the quadratic equation is a square modulo N. By our assumption this is the case. Then (s, t) viewed in $(\mathbb{Z}/N\mathbb{Z})^2$ is defined up to a scalar, and we could simply choose $s = 1$ and let t_0 be one of the root of $f(1, t) \equiv 0 \bmod N$.

Finally, suppose $(n(x_3), N) = 1$ does not hold, this implies $(N, \mathsf{Im}_R(A\bar{B}C\bar{D}))$ which contradicts our assumption. Therefore, we have shown that we could find a solution $x_3 = s + ti$ where s, t satisfies Eq. (8) and $(n(x_3), 1) = 1$.

We now summarize our algorithm for solving Problem 5.7 in Algorithm 4.

Algorithm 4: QuaternionDecomposition(N,A,B,C,D)

Input: N, A, B, C, D as in Problem 5.7.
Output: $x_1, x_2, x_3 \in R$ such that
$\quad\quad A + Bj = \lambda x_1 j(C + Dj)x_2 j(C + Dj)x_3 j$ mod $N\mathcal{O}_0$ where λ is some
$\quad\quad$ integer that is coprime to N.

1 $t_0 \leftarrow$ root of $\Big(n(A)\big(n(C) - pn(D)\big) + 2p\mathsf{Re}_R(A\bar{B}C\bar{D})\Big) - 4qp\mathsf{Im}_R(A\bar{B}C\bar{D})t +$
$\quad\Big(qn(A)\big(n(C) - pn(D)\big) - 2qp\mathsf{Re}_R(A\bar{B}C\bar{D})\Big)t^2 = 0$ mod N.

2 $x_3 \leftarrow 1 + t_0 i$

3 $x_1, x_2 \leftarrow$ EquivNormConjugationProduct(x_3)

4 **Return** x_1, x_2, x_3.

5.4 Quantum Algorithm for the PQLP

As discussed earlier, Theorem 5.1 implies that we can solve the IsERP in quantum polynomial time. However, Theorem 5.1 only guarantees a randomized polynomial-time algorithm, and it might be advantageous to avoid that inside a quantum algorithm. So instead of lifting elements inside the quantum algorithm we lift $O(\log N)$ elements first and then utilize them to make the lifting procedure inside the quantum algorithm deterministic (and free of any heuristic after the precomputation has succeeded).

Theorem 5.10 *There is an algorithm that solves the PQLP in quantum polynomial time.*

Proof We provide a proof for the case where N is a prime number. The proof for general N is in [CII+23, Appendix A]. For any matrix M in $\mathrm{GL}_2(\mathbb{Z}/N\mathbb{Z})$, M can be written as $PL \cdot D \cdot U$ where P is a permutation matrix, L is a lower unitriangular (it is lower triangular with 1-s in the diagonal), D is diagonal, and U is upper unitriangular (it is upper triangular with 1-s in the diagonal). This decomposition can be found in polynomial time using Gaussian elimination. Now one has to decompose L, D and U separately. Any lower unitriangular matrix can be written as a power of $A = \begin{pmatrix} 1 & 0 \\ g & 1 \end{pmatrix}$ where g is a generator of $(\mathbb{Z}/N\mathbb{Z})^*$. Similarly, every upper unitriangular matrix can be written as a power of $B = \begin{pmatrix} 1 & g \\ 0 & 1 \end{pmatrix}$. Any diagonal matrix can be written as $C^k D^l$ where

$$C = \begin{pmatrix} g & 0 \\ 0 & 1 \end{pmatrix}, D = \begin{pmatrix} 1 & 0 \\ 0 & g \end{pmatrix}.$$

This shows that every element in $GL_2(\mathbb{Z}/N\mathbb{Z})$ can be written as $PA^aB^bC^cD^d$. Thus instead of lifting elements inside the main quantum algorithm using Theorem 5.1 one can precompute lifts of P, A, B, C, D and then decompose a matrix $M \in GL_2(\mathbb{Z}/N\mathbb{Z})$ as $A^aB^bC^cD^d$ to obtain a lift of M.

This decomposition requires several instances of the discrete logarithm problem in $\mathbb{Z}/N\mathbb{Z}$ which can be computed in quantum polynomial time. The only issue is that if one computes a powersmooth lift of A (or B, C or D) then A^a is not going to be powersmooth if a is large. To circumvent this issue one also computes lifts of $A^{2^k}, B^{2^k}, C^{2^k}$ and D^{2^k} for every k between 1 and $\log_2(N)$. Furthermore, one computes lifts which are coprime (this can be ensured easily as StrongApproximation can lift an element in $\mathbb{Z}[i]j$ to any number that is bigger than $p^{O(1)}$).

This way $PA^aB^bC^cD^d$ will also be powersmooth as it is the product of $4\log N + 1$ powersmooth numbers. Lifting $4\log N + 1$ numbers can be done in classical polynomial time using Theorem 5.1.

$\square$

6 Impact on Isogeny-Based Cryptography

The most important application of Theorem 1.4 is that it breaks pSIDH in quantum polynomial time as N is a prime number in pSIDH. Another application is on SCALLOP [DFFK+23]. Even though Theorem 1.4 does not break SCALLOP, it shows that its security reduces to the problem of evaluating the secret prime degree isogeny (up to a scalar). In [DFFK+23] it is already discussed that one can deduce some information on the secret isogeny ϕ by utilizing the fact that one can evaluate $\phi \circ \theta \circ \hat{\phi}$ efficiently on any point where θ is some fixed endomorphism on a curve which has an endomorphism of low degree (typically that curve is j-1728 and θ is the non-trivial automorphism).

Our results mildly generalize to the following setting. Let E be a supersingular elliptic curve that does not possess a non-scalar endomorphism of degree N^2. In other words there is a one-to-one correspondence between cyclic subgroups of order N and N-isogenous curves. Our results imply that if given some curve E/A and an endomorphism σ one can compute $E/\sigma(A)$, then one can also compute the endomorphism ring of E/A in quantum polynomial time (and actually the corresponding isogeny itself its degree is smooth). The difference between our previous results here is that we do not need an isogeny representation for the isogeny corresponding to the subgroup generated by A as long as we can evaluate the above group action. At the moment we do not see any particular application for this observation but it might prove to be a useful cryptanalysis tool in the future.

Acknowledgements. Gábor Ivanyos is supported in part by the Hungarian Ministry of Innovation and Technology NRDI Office within the framework of the Artificial Intelligence National Laboratory Program. Péter Kutas is supported by the Hungarian Ministry of Innovation and Technology NRDI Office within the framework of the Quantum

Information National Laboratory Program, the J'anos Bolyai Research Scholarship of the Hungarian Academy of Sciences and by the UNKP-22-5 New National Excellence Program. Mingjie Chen, Péter Kutas and Christophe Petit are partly supported by EPSRC through grant number EP/V011324/1.

References

[BL95] Boneh, D., Lipton, R.J.: Quantum cryptanalysis of hidden linear functions. In: Coppersmith, D. (ed.) CRYPTO 1995. LNCS, vol. 963, pp. 424–437. Springer, Heidelberg (1995). https://doi.org/10.1007/3-540-44750-4_34

[CD22] Castryck, W., Decru, T.: An efficient key recovery attack on SIDH. In: Hazay, C., Stam, M. (eds.) Advances in Cryptology – EUROCRYPT 2023: 42nd Annual International Conference on the Theory and Applications of Cryptographic Techniques, Lyon, 23–27 April 2023, Proceedings, Part V, pp. 423–447. Springer, Cham (2023). https://doi.org/10.1007/978-3-031-30589-4_15

[CII+23] Chen, M., Imran, M., Ivanyos, G., Kutas, P., Leroux, A., Petit, C.: Hidden stabilizers, the isogeny to endomorphism ring problem and the cryptanalysis of Psidh. Cryptology ePrint Archive, Paper 2023/779 (2023). https://eprint.iacr.org/2023/779

[CLM+18] Castryck, W., Lange, T., Martindale, C., Panny, L., Renes, J.: CSIDH: an efficient post-quantum commutative group action. In: Peyrin, T., Galbraith, S. (eds.) ASIACRYPT 2018. LNCS, vol. 11274, pp. 395–427. Springer, Cham (2018). https://doi.org/10.1007/978-3-030-03332-3_15

[Coh95] Cohen, H.: A Course in Computational Algebraic Number Theory. Springer, Heidelberg (1995)

[Cou99] Couveignes, J.-M.: Hard Homogeneous Spaces (1999). https://eprint.iacr.org/2006/291

[CVD05] Childs, A.M., Dam, W.V.: Quantum algorithm for a generalized hidden shift problem. arXiv preprint arXiv:quant-ph/0507190 (2005)

[DFFK+23] Feo, L.D., et al.: Scallop: Scaling the CSI-Fish. PKC (2023)

[DFKL+20] De Feo, L., Kohel, D., Leroux, A., Petit, C., Wesolowski, B.: SQISign: compact post-quantum signatures from quaternions and isogenies. In: Moriai, S., Wang, H. (eds.) ASIACRYPT 2020. LNCS, vol. 12491, pp. 64–93. Springer, Cham (2020). https://doi.org/10.1007/978-3-030-64837-4_3

[DK12] Drozd, Y.A., Kirichenko, V.V.: Finite Dimensional Algebras. Springer (2012)

[DMR10] Denney, A., Moore, C., Russell, A.: Finding conjugate stabilizer subgroups in PSL and related groups. Quantum Inf. Comput. 10, 282–291 (2010)

[EH00] Ettinger, M., Høyer, P.: On quantum algorithms for noncommutative hidden subgroups. Adv. Appl. Math. 25(3), 239–251 (2000)

[EHL+18] Eisenträger, K., Hallgren, S., Lauter, K., Morrison, T., Petit, C.: Supersingular isogeny graphs and endomorphism rings: reductions and solutions. In: Nielsen, J.B., Rijmen, V. (eds.) EUROCRYPT 2018. LNCS, vol. 10822, pp. 329–368. Springer, Cham (2018). https://doi.org/10.1007/978-3-319-78372-7_11

[FMP23] Fouotsa, T.B., Moriya, T., Petit, C.: M-SIDH and MD-SIDH: countering SIDH attacks by masking information. In: Hazay, C., Stam, M. (eds.) Advances in Cryptology – EUROCRYPT 2023: 42nd Annual International Conference on the Theory and Applications of Cryptographic Techniques, Lyon, 23–27 April 2023, Proceedings, Part V, pp. 282–309. Springer, Cham (2023). https://doi.org/10.1007/978-3-031-30589-4_10

[git23] Pqlp-prime github repository (2023). https://github.com/pqcisogeny/PQLP_prime.git

[IPS18] Ivanyos, G., Prakash, A., Santha, M.: On learning linear functions from subset and its applications in quantum computing. In: Azar, Y., Bast, H., Herman, G. (eds.) 26th Annual European Symposium on Algorithms (ESA 2018), volume 112 of Leibniz International Proceedings in Informatics (LIPIcs), Dagstuhl, pp. 66:1–66:14. Schloss Dagstuhl-Leibniz-Zentrum fuer Informatik (2018)

[Iva12] Ivanyos, G.: Finding hidden Borel subgroups of the general linear group. Quantum Inf. Comput. **12**(7–8), 661–669 (2012)

[JDF11] Jao, D., De Feo, L.: Towards quantum-resistant cryptosystems from supersingular elliptic curve isogenies. In: Yang, B.-Y. (ed.) PQCrypto 2011. LNCS, vol. 7071, pp. 19–34. Springer, Heidelberg (2011). https://doi.org/10.1007/978-3-642-25405-5_2

[Kit95] Yu Kitaev, A.: Quantum measurements and the abelian stabilizer problem. arXiv preprint arXiv:quant-ph/9511026 (1995)

[KLPT14] Kohel, D., Lauter, K., Petit, C., Tignol, J.-P.: On the quaternion ℓ-isogeny path problem. LMS J. Comput. Math. **17**(A), 418–432 (2014)

[KMPW21] Kutas, P., Merz, S.-P., Petit, C., Weitkämper, C.: One-way functions and malleability oracles: hidden shift attacks on isogeny-based protocols. In: Canteaut, A., Standaert, F.-X. (eds.) EUROCRYPT 2021. LNCS, vol. 12696, pp. 242–271. Springer, Cham (2021). https://doi.org/10.1007/978-3-030-77870-5_9

[Koh96] Kohel, D.R.: Endomorphism rings of elliptic curves over finite fields. Ph.D. thesis, University of California, Berkeley (1996)

[Kup05] Kuperberg, G.: A subexponential-time quantum algorithm for the dihedral hidden subgroup problem. SIAM J. Comput. **35**(1), 170–188 (2005)

[Ler22a] Leroux, A.: A new isogeny representation and applications to cryptography. In: Agrawal, S., Lin, D. (eds.) Advances in Cryptology – ASIACRYPT 2022: 28th International Conference on the Theory and Application of Cryptology and Information Security, Taipei, 5–9 December 2022, Proceedings, Part II, pp. 3–35. Springer, Cham (2022). https://doi.org/10.1007/978-3-031-22966-4_1

[Ler22b] Leroux, A.: Quaternion Algebra and isogeny-based cryptography. Ph.D. thesis, Ecole doctorale de l'Institut Polytechnique de Paris (2022)

[MM22] Maino, L., Martindale, C.: An attack on Sidh with arbitrary starting curve. Cryptology ePrint Archive (2022)

[Pet17] Petit, C.: Faster algorithms for isogeny problems using torsion point images. In: Takagi, T., Peyrin, T. (eds.) ASIACRYPT 2017. LNCS, vol. 10625, pp. 330–353. Springer, Cham (2017). https://doi.org/10.1007/978-3-319-70697-9_12

[PL17] Petit, C., Lauter, K.: Hard and easy problems for supersingular isogeny graphs. Cryptology ePrint Archive, Report 2017/962 (2017). https://eprint.iacr.org/2017/962

[PLQ08] Petit, C., Lauter, K., Quisquater, J.-J.: Full cryptanalysis of LPS and morgenstern hash functions. In: Ostrovsky, R., De Prisco, R., Visconti, I. (eds.) SCN 2008. LNCS, vol. 5229, pp. 263–277. Springer, Heidelberg (2008). https://doi.org/10.1007/978-3-540-85855-3_18

[QKL+21] de Quehen, V., et al.: Improved Torsion-point attacks on SIDH variants. In: Malkin, T., Peikert, C. (eds.) CRYPTO 2021. LNCS, vol. 12827, pp. 432–470. Springer, Cham (2021). https://doi.org/10.1007/978-3-030-84252-9_15

[Rob22] Robert, D.: Evaluating isogenies in polylogarithmic time. Cryptology ePrint Archive (2022)

[Rón90] Rónyai, L.: Computing the structure of finite algebras. J. Symb. Comput. **9**(3), 355–373 (1990)

[RS06] Rostovtsev, A., Stolbunov, A.: Public-key cryptosystem based on isogenies. IACR Cryptol. ePrint Arch. **2006**, 145 (2006)

[Sho97] Shor, P.W.: Polynomial-time algorithms for prime factorization and discrete logarithms on a quantum computer. SIAM J. Comput. **26**(5), 1484–1509 (1997)

[Sil09] Silverman, J.H.: The arithmetic of elliptic curves, vol. 106. Springer (2009)

[The22] The Sage Developers. SageMath, the Sage Mathematics Software System (Version 9.4) (2022). https://www.sagemath.org

[Voi18] Voight, J.: Quaternion algebras. Preprint **13**, 23–24 (2018)

[Wat69] Waterhouse, W.C.: Abelian varieties over finite fields. In: Annales scientifiques de l'École Normale Supérieure, vol. 2, pp. 521–560 (1969)

[Wes21] Wesolowski, B.: The supersingular isogeny path and endomorphism ring problems are equivalent. Cryptology ePrint Archive, Report 2021/919 (2021). https://ia.cr/2021/919

Concrete Analysis of Quantum Lattice Enumeration

Shi Bai[1]([⊠])(iD), Maya-Iggy van Hoof[2], Floyd B. Johnson[1], Tanja Lange[3], and Tran Ngo[1](iD)

[1] Florida Atlantic University, Boca Raton, USA
shih.bai@gmail.com, johnsonf2017@fau.edu
[2] Horst Görtz Institute for IT-Security, Ruhr University Bochum, Bochum, Germany
iggy.hoof@rub.de
[3] Eindhoven University of Technology, Eindhoven, The Netherlands
tanja@hyperelliptic.org

Abstract. Lattice reduction algorithms such as BKZ (Block-Korkine-Zolotarev) play a central role in estimating the security of lattice-based cryptography. The subroutine in BKZ which finds the shortest vector in a projected sublattice can be instantiated with enumeration algorithms. The enumeration procedure can be seen as a depth-first search on some "enumeration tree" whose nodes denote a partial assignment of the coefficients, corresponding to lattice points as a linear combination of the lattice basis with the coefficients. This work provides a concrete analysis for the cost of quantum lattice enumeration based on Montanaro's quantum tree backtracking algorithm. More precisely, we give a concrete implementation in the quantum circuit model. We also show how to optimize the circuit depth by parallelizing the components. Based on the circuit designed, we discuss the concrete quantum resource estimates required for lattice enumeration.

Keywords: Lattices · Quantum algorithms · Enumeration · Quantum backtracking

1 Introduction

A Euclidean lattice is the set of all integral linear combinations of n linearly independent basis vectors $\mathbf{b}_1, \cdots, \mathbf{b}_n \in \mathbb{Q}^m$. Lattices have attracted considerable interest in recent years as they can be used to construct cryptographic

Author list in alphabetical order; see https://ams.org/profession/leaders/CultureStatement04.pdf. This research was funded in part by the U.S. National Science Foundation under Grant No. 2044855 & 2122229, the Deutsche Forschungsgemeinschaft (DFG, German Research Foundation) under Germany's Excellence Strategy–EXC 2092 CASA–390781972 "Cyber Security in the Age of Large-Scale Adversaries", and the Taiwan's Executive Yuan Data Safety and Talent Cultivation Project (AS-KPQ-109-DSTCP). This work was done in part while Tanja Lange was visiting the Simons Institute for the Theory of Computing and in part when she was with Academia Sinica, Taiwan.

J. Guo and R. Steinfeld (Eds.): ASIACRYPT 2023, LNCS 14440, pp. 131–166, 2023.
https://doi.org/10.1007/978-981-99-8727-6_5

schemes which are conjectured to be quantum-resistant. The benefits of using lattices are reflected by three out of the four selected schemes (Kyber [ABD+21], Dilithium [BDK+21] and Falcon [FHK+20]) in NIST's Post-Quantum Cryptography Standardization process [NIS16] having their security rely on the presumed intractability of lattice problems.

A fundamental computational problem in lattice-based cryptography is the approximated shortest vector problem, denoted SVP_γ where $\gamma \geq 1$ is called the approximation factor. In SVP_γ, one is given a lattice basis as input, and asked to find a nonzero lattice point of length within a factor γ of the length of the shortest nonzero vector. Lattice reduction algorithms such as Block-Korkine-Zolotarev (BKZ) [SE94] and its variants [GNR10, CN11, MW16, AWHT16] are considered as the most practical algorithms for solving the approximated shortest vector problem, balancing the quality (e.g., approximation factor) and run-time. Thus they play a central role in estimating the security of lattice-based cryptography. A lattice reduction algorithm relies on subroutines to find shortest vectors in smaller dimensional projected sublattices. This smaller dimension is a parameter of the algorithm called the "block size". There are two main families of algorithms for instantiating this subroutine: algorithms based on sieving [AKS01, NV08, MV10b, BDGL16] and algorithms based on enumeration [Kan83, FP85, SE94]. Sieving algorithms have better asymptotic performance but require much more memory. This paper focuses on enumeration algorithms.

The enumeration procedure can be seen as a depth-first search on some "enumeration tree", where a tree path encodes a partial assignment of the coefficients. Classically, the enumeration algorithm explores the tree nodes in a depth-first way as far as possible along a branch before backtracking. During the search, the algorithm only needs to hold the information for the nodes in the current path (e.g., from the root to the node being searched), thus requiring polynomial memory w.r.t the lattice dimension. This is one of the main benefits of using enumeration for lattice reduction. On the other hand, such a tree backtracking algorithm requires local knowledge before each iteration and thus cannot be instantiated straightforwardly by a quantum search algorithm such as Grover [Gro96]. Recall that Grover's algorithm assumes black-box access to every point in the input domain. In a tree backtracking scenario, these points are the coefficients of the linear combinations, which need not to be known in advance. This motivates the study of quantum algorithms for lattice enumeration.

Prior and related work. Montanaro presented an interesting quantum algorithm [Mon18] to solve the tree backtracking problem. The approach is based on the use of a quantum walk algorithm of Belovs [Bel13]. Montanaro's algorithm was originally presented in the context of solving the constraint satisfaction problem (CSP). A standard approach to solve CSP is via tree backtracking. Let T_u be an upper bound on the number of nodes in the tree and n be the tree depth. Montanaro's first algorithm detects the existence of a solution in the tree in $O(\sqrt{T_u}n)$ steps using quantum phase estimation. This provides a quadratic speed-up to the classical tree backtracking algorithm. A second algorithm of Montanaro uses the aforementioned detection algorithm to locate the solution, by applying the first algorithm iteratively, on each child of a node, which contains the solution. This leads to, at most, a polynomial increase in the running-time, e.g., it finds a solution in time $O(\sqrt{\mathcal{T}} n^{1.5} \log n)$, where $\mathcal{T}$ is the number of nodes in the tree. In lattice enumeration, the bound $\mathcal{T}$ (or $\mathcal{T}_u$) is usually super-exponential in terms of the input dimension n. Both algorithms use poly(n) space.

In a classical tree backtracking algorithm, it often happens that the actual number of nodes visited $\mathcal{T}'$ is much smaller than the tree size $\mathcal{T}$, for example, if the classical algorithms are optimized to search the most promising branches first. Ambainis and Kokainis [AK17] described a quantum algorithm which is better for such cases. More precisely, their quantum algorithm solves the search tree backtracking problem in $\tilde{O}(\sqrt{\mathcal{T}'} n^{1.5})$ steps, i.e., achieving the same complexity (up to logarithmic factors) as before but now in $\mathcal{T}'$, the number of nodes *examined* in the classical algorithm, instead of in $\mathcal{T}$, the total number of nodes.

As lattice point enumeration can be phrased as a tree backtracking procedure, a natural question is whether one can apply Montanaro's algorithm to the problem of lattice point enumeration. It has been briefly mentioned in previous work [ADPS16, ABB+17, PLP16] that Montanaro's algorithm can be used to speed up enumeration. Applicability was later confirmed in the work by Aono, Nguyen and Shen [ANS18], with more details given. They also proposed methods to apply the quantum algorithm to the extreme pruned enumeration, including both cylinder pruning and discrete pruning. Their work targeted a higher level, focusing on asymptotic strategies for optimizing the extreme pruning in the quantum backtracking algorithm, without going into detail about the quantum circuit and resource estimates. Indeed, they left as an open question in [ANS18]: *"We stress that this is just a first assessment of quantum enumeration. If one is interested in more precise estimates, such as the number of quantum gates, one would need to assess the quantum cost of the algorithm of Montanaro and that of Ambainis and Kokainis"*. This is the research question that we are focusing on in this paper.

In terms of concrete estimates, Campbell, Khurana and Montanaro [CKM19] and Martiel and Remaud [MR20] have both considered the implementation of Montanaro's backtracking algorithm in the context of graph coloring and SAT (satisfiability) problems, where the first work focuses on optimizing the circuit depth and the second work focuses on optimizing memory.

Recently, Albrecht, Prokop, Shen and Wallden [APSW22] considered how Noisy Intermediate Scale Quantum (NISQ) devices can be used to solve lattice enumeration. More precisely, they describe a mapping that encodes the SVP problem into the ground state of a Hamiltonian operator and use variational quantum algorithms such as the Variational Quantum Eigensolver [PMS+14, MRBAG16] to solve the encoded optimization problem. Their simulated experiments show that between 1000 and 1600 qubits are sufficient to encode the SVP for a 180-dimensional lattice, which matches the current record dimension [DSvW21a] in the "Darmstadt SVP Challenge". Compared to [APSW22], our implementation is based on the quantum circuit model, which assumes fault-tolerant components.

Finally, there is no doubt that estimating the quantum resources required plays an important role in the cryptanalysis for post-quantum era. Substantial progress has been made for various problems, including Grover's algorithm for AES [GLRS16, BNS19, JNRV20], Shor's algorithm for ECDLP [RNSL17, BBVL21], algorithms by Kuperberg, Regev and Childs-Jao-Soukharev for CSIDH [BLMP19, BS20], and quantum lattice sieving for SVP [AGPS20]. This work aims to fill the gap for resource estimates of quantum lattice enumeration.

Contribution. To the best of our knowledge, no prior work has considered the concrete design and resource estimates for lattice enumeration in the quantum circuit model. In this work, we provide a concrete implementation of Montanaro's algorithm for lattice enumeration, together with resource estimates, in the quantum circuit model.

Overall, Montanaro's algorithm conducts phase estimation for an operator $U := R_B R_A$ on the root of the enumeration tree. We will describe the implementation in a modular approach: starting with the general phase estimation circuit, and the implementation of operators R_A and R_B and their components, and then covering the implementation of some predicate function P, which is used as an oracle inside the implementation of the operators R_A and R_B.

Our implementation is based on the so-called "Clifford+T" approach, which forms a universal gate set. This choice of gate set is motivated by fault-tolerant computation. The non-Clifford gates in our implementation consist of Toffoli and T gates, where Toffoli gates can be constructed using T gates. Their fault-tolerant implementation is often more expensive compared to Clifford gates. Thus we will optimize the circuit by optimizing the T depth. We will also show how to parallelize the circuit components to optimize the T depth of the circuit. Such optimization is motivated by NIST's Post-Quantum Cryptography Standardization process [NIS16]. NIST suggests that quantum attacks are restricted to a fixed circuit depth, namely the "maxdepth" parameter. This parameter is derived from the difficulty of running extremely long serial computations on quantum computers. Example values for "maxdepth" range from 2^{40} logical gates to 2^{96} logical gates, making the circuit depth the crucial parameter.

For simplicity of discussion, our implementation is designed for Montanaro's detection algorithm (e.g., see Theorem 1). The solution finding algorithm (e.g., see Theorem 2) and the improved method by Ambainis and Kokainis [AK17] use the detection algorithm as a main computational component.

Based on the proposed circuit, we will also discuss the quantum resource estimates required for lattice enumeration. The complexity of quantum attacks can be measured in terms of circuit depth and size. Overall, our circuit has T depth and size bounded respectively by

$$32\sqrt{Tn} \cdot \left[16np(\log B + 2\log n + p^{0.158}) + O(n\log B) + 8d^2 \log(d\sqrt{Tn}) + 4d^2 \log d + O(d^2) \right];$$

$$32\sqrt{Tn} \cdot \left[8(d+1)(14pn^2(B+1) + O(n^2 B)) + 8d^2 \log(d\sqrt{Tn}) + 16d^2 \log d + O(d^2) \right],$$

where n is the lattice dimension, d is the degree of the enumeration tree (maximum number of children for any node), p is the precision required in the arithmetic and B bounds the coefficients size. This is presented in parameterized form since one can adapt these parameters given a concrete input. We also keep some of the lower-order terms coming from different components of the estimate.

For cryptographic size lattices, it is reasonable to expect $d \approx n, B \approx n^2, p \approx 3n$ under common heuristics (e.g., see discussions in Subsects. 4.4 & 4.5). Let $\log(\mathcal{T}) \approx c \cdot n \log n$ where c denotes the dominating constant and $c \leq \frac{1}{2e}$ [ABF+20, ABLR21]. The T-depth and size is about

$$(128cn^3 \log n + O(n^{2.158}))\sqrt{\mathcal{T}}n \text{ and } (10752n^6 + O(n^5))\sqrt{\mathcal{T}}n.$$

It is tempting to plug-in the best tree size estimate $\log(\mathcal{T}) \approx 0.125n \log n - 0.654n + 25.84$ from [ABLR21] so $c \approx 0.125$. However, we stress that this is not accurate, as the classical simulation [ABLR21] involves extensive extreme pruning steps and preprocessing, whose implementation and impacts are left as future work (see discussions in the next subsection).

Comparison and discussion. The security of lattice-based schemes is often estimated by a lattice reduction algorithm like BKZ, instantiated with sieving as the SVP solver. Sieving algorithms have been shown to be faster than enumeration in the classical setting, both asymptotically and in practice [ADH+19]. Concrete experiments were also demonstrated in [ADH+19, DSvW21b]. However, the comparison of concrete resources in the quantum world is considerably more complicated and has not been thoroughly studied, to the best of our knowledge.

Let d be the lattice dimension. The best lattice sieving algorithm [BDGL16] has a running-time of $2^{0.292d+o(d)}$ and memory requirement of $2^{0.210d+o(d)}$, using locality sensitive hashing. This has been adapted to a quantum sieving algorithm [Laa15], which runs asymptotically in $2^{0.265d+o(d)}$ and also requires a quantum memory of $2^{0.210d+o(d)}$. This was improved in [CL21] and further in [BCSS23], by replacing the Grover oracle with quantum random walks. This results in the fastest quantum sieving algorithm known to date with a complexity of $2^{0.2563d+o(d)}$ [BCSS23]. All of these works focus on resource estimates in an asymptotic sense, i.e., without detailing the circuit design or concrete resources. One exception is [AGPS20], which provides concrete quantum resource estimates (with Grover-based search) for several dominant parts of lattice sieving algorithms: a primary optimization target of [AGPS20] is the implementation of the "popcount" operation in sieving. Quantum enumeration via backtracking algorithm has been studied in [ANS18] in the query model, where the concrete cost for each query is not detailed. As a result, the actual cost may be significantly higher than the asymptotic estimate. This has also been stressed in [ABLR21] as an open question, e.g., *"This suggests an analogous investigation to [AGPS20] for quantum enumeration as a pressing research question"*. Our paper aims to take a step forward in understanding this question for quantum enumeration. Our work is similar to [AGPS20] in philosophy, providing a concrete implementation of the dominant arithmetic for lattice enumeration. Therefore, similar to [AGPS20], our estimates are neither upper bounds nor lower bounds.

Given the (limited) research results in quantum enumeration and sieving, it is premature to conclude the crossover point between quantum enumeration and quantum sieving at this stage. This work does not fully settle this question, but takes a step forward in better understanding of where the crossover points will be based on gate design and qubit resources for quantum enumeration. We highlight several open questions that will be most critical in answering this question.

First, the dominating term in our estimates is the $O(\sqrt{T}n)$ term due to the phase estimation. It would be interesting to investigate quantum algorithms for parallelizing the phase estimation step in order to reduce the depth even further. Second, the concrete cost of extreme pruning in quantum enumeration requires further study. It has been proposed [ANS18] that one can run Montanaro's algorithm on a combined tree with all re-randomized bases. This has the advantage of enclosing the number of trees within the square root in the complexity. In an intuitive manner, all re-randomized bases can be fed in, inevitably increasing the memory. By comparison, in the classical setting, each enumeration can occur sequentially after another, so memory is not increased. Alternatively, Montanaro's algorithm can be run on each basis separately to control the memory while sacrificing the running time. Third, a binary tree conversion oracle is used in [ANS18] with some overheads, whose concrete cost is unknown. Investigating the overhead introduced by the transformation will provide a more precise picture for quantum enumeration. This paper focuses on the 'backbone' implementation so we will leave these questions for future research.

2   Preliminaries

Notations. We let lower-case bold letters denote column vectors and upper-case bold letters denote matrices. A matrix $\mathbf{B} = (\mathbf{b}_1, \mathbf{b}_2, \cdots, \mathbf{b}_n)$ is presented in a column-wise way. We let matrix indices start with index 1. For a vector $\mathbf{x}$, we use $\|\mathbf{x}\|$ to denote its ℓ_2-norm. For $n \geq 1$ and $r > 0$, we let $V_n(r)$ denote the volume of the n-dimensional ball of radius r. We also let v_n denote the volume of an n-dimensional unit ball where $v_n = \pi^{n/2}/\Gamma(1 + n/2) \approx \left(\frac{2\pi e}{n}\right)^{n/2}/\sqrt{n\pi}$. We denote by log the logarithm to base 2 and by ln the natural logarithm.

Euclidean lattices. A lattice $\mathcal{L}$ is an additive discrete subgroup of $\mathbb{Q}^m$. Equivalently, it can be described as the set of all integral linear combinations of n linearly independent basis vectors: Let $\mathbf{B} = (\mathbf{b}_1, \cdots, \mathbf{b}_n) \in \mathbb{Q}^{m \times n}$ be a full rank matrix. The lattice $\mathcal{L}$ generated by $\mathbf{B}$ is defined as $\mathcal{L}(\mathbf{B}) = \{\mathbf{B}\mathbf{x} \mid \forall \mathbf{x} \in \mathbb{Z}^n\}$. Let n be the rank (or dimension) of the lattice $\mathcal{L}$. It is called a full rank lattice when $m = n$. The matrix $\mathbf{B}$ is called a basis of $\mathcal{L}(\mathbf{B})$. Given a matrix $\mathbf{B}$ and a vector $\mathbf{v}$, we let $\pi_i(\mathbf{v})$ denote the orthogonal projection of $\mathbf{v}$ onto the linear subspace $(\mathbf{b}_1, \cdots, \mathbf{b}_{i-1})^\perp$. Further, we let $\pi_i(\mathbf{B}_{[i:j]})$ denote the block $(\pi_i(\mathbf{b}_i), \ldots, \pi_i(\mathbf{b}_{j-1}))$, let $\pi_i(\mathcal{L}_{[i:j]})$ denote the corresponding lattice generated by $\pi_i(\mathbf{B}_{[i:j]})$, and let $\mathbf{B}^* = [\mathbf{b}_1^*, \cdots, \mathbf{b}_n^*]$ denote the Gram–Schmidt orthogonalization of $\mathbf{B}$, thus $\mathbf{b}_i^* = \pi_i(\mathbf{b}_i)$. The volume (or determinant) of $\mathcal{L}(\mathbf{B})$ is defined as $\mathrm{vol}(\mathcal{L}(\mathbf{B})) = \prod_{i \leq n} \|\mathbf{b}_i^*\|$, which does not depend on the choice of basis of $\mathcal{L}$.

The norm of a shortest non-zero vector in $\mathcal{L}$ is denoted by $\lambda_1(\mathcal{L})$ which is called the minimum of the lattice $\mathcal{L}$. Let $\mathcal{L}$ be a rank-n lattice. Minkowski's convex body theorem states that $\lambda_1(\mathcal{L}) \leq 2 \cdot v_n^{-1/n} \cdot \mathrm{vol}(\mathcal{L})^{1/n}$. The analysis of lattice algorithms often relies on heuristic assumptions such as the so-called Gaussian Heuristic (GH). Let $\mathcal{S}$ be a measurable set in the span of $\mathcal{L}$. The Gaussian Heuristic states that the number of lattice points in $\mathcal{S}$ is $|\mathcal{L} \cap \mathcal{S}| \approx$ $\mathrm{vol}(\mathcal{S})/\mathrm{vol}(\mathcal{L})$. When $\mathcal{S}$ is an n-dimensional ball of radius r, the latter quantity is about $(v_n \cdot r^n)/\mathrm{vol}(\mathcal{L})$. Taking $v_n \cdot r^n \approx \mathrm{vol}(\mathcal{L})$, we see that $\lambda_1(\mathcal{L})$ is about $\mathrm{GH}(\mathcal{L}) := v_n^{-1/n} \cdot \mathrm{vol}(\mathcal{L})^{1/n} \approx \sqrt{n/(2\pi e)} \cdot \mathrm{vol}(\mathcal{L})^{1/n}$. The Gaussian heuristic holds for random lattices, see [BL21] for definitions of distributions. Let $\mathbf{B}$ be a lattice basis for $\mathcal{L}$. We define the Root Hermite Factor of the basis $\mathbf{B}$ as $\delta(\mathbf{B}) = (\|\mathbf{b}_1\|/\mathrm{vol}(\mathcal{L})^{1/n})^{1/(n-1)}$. Here, we use the normalization by the $(n-1)$-th root (sometimes it is defined by normalization with the n-th root).

Two fundamental average-case problems used in lattice-based cryptography are the short integer solution problem (SIS) [Ajt96,MR04] and the learning with errors problem (LWE) [Reg05]. Algorithms for solving the LWE and SIS problems often involve algorithms for solving worst-case problems such as the approximated shortest vector problem (SVP_γ). On input a lattice basis $\mathbf{B}$, SVP_γ asks to find a non-zero lattice vector $\mathbf{v} \in \mathcal{L}(\mathbf{B})$ such that $\|\mathbf{v}\| \leq \gamma \cdot \lambda_1(\mathcal{L}(\mathbf{B}))$. When $\gamma = 1$, it is exact SVP.

Lattice algorithms. The difficulty of solving SVP_γ varies with respect to its approximation factor γ, which is usually a function of the rank n of the lattice. When $\gamma = 2^{\Omega(n)}$, the LLL algorithm [LLJL82] finds a SVP_γ solution in polynomial time. The time complexities of the best known algorithms that find the exact solutions (e.g. $\gamma = 1$) are at least exponential in the dimension of the lattice: representative exact algorithms include enumeration algorithms [Kan83,FP85,SE94], sieving algorithms [AKS01] and Voronoi cell algorithms [MV10a]. Most cryptographic constructions rely on lattice problems with approximation factors that are polynomial or slightly sub-exponential in n. In such a regime, the best practical algorithms are lattice reduction algorithms such as Block-Korkine-Zolotarev (BKZ) [Sch87,CN11,HPS11]. Given a input basis, these output a basis made of relatively short vectors.

For a lattice basis $\mathbf{B}$, let $\mu_{i,j} := \langle \mathbf{b}_i, \mathbf{b}_j^* \rangle / \langle \mathbf{b}_j^*, \mathbf{b}_j^* \rangle$. It is size-reduced if $\forall i \geq j$, $|\mu_{i,j}| \leq 1/2$, HKZ-reduced (Hermite-Korkine-Zolotarev) if it is size-reduced and satisfies: $\|\mathbf{b}_i^*\| = \lambda_1(\pi_i(\mathcal{L}_{[i:n]}))$, $\forall i \leq n$, and BKZ-β reduced with blocksize β if it is size-reduced and satisfies $\|\mathbf{b}_i^*\| = \lambda_1(\pi_i(\mathcal{L}_{[i,\min(i+\beta-1,n)]}))$, $\forall i \leq n$. BKZ algorithms, such as [SE94], take as inputs a block-size β and a basis $\mathbf{B}$ of a lattice $\mathcal{L}$, and output a basis which is close to being BKZ-β reduced. A typical BKZ algorithm invokes SVP solvers on consecutive local blocks $\pi_k(\mathbf{B}_{[k,\min(k+\beta-1,n)]})$ for all $k < n$ (this is called a *BKZ tour*). After each run of the SVP-solver, if we find $\lambda_1(\pi_k(\mathbf{B}_{[k,\min(k+\beta-1,n)]})) < \alpha \cdot \|\mathbf{b}_k^*\|$ for some relax factor $\alpha \geq 1$, then BKZ updates this block by inserting the shorter vector found by the SVP-solver at index k. LLL reductions are used whenever there is an update on the basis. The BKZ tours are repeated and the whole algorithm terminates when no change occurs at all during a tour or some termination condition is met. A useful heuristic is the *Geometric Series Assumption* (GSA) introduced in [Sch03], which states that the Gram-Schmidt norms $\{\|\mathbf{b}_i^*\|\}_{i \leq n}$ of a BKZ-β

reduced basis behave as a geometric series, i.e., there exists a constant $r > 1$ such that $\|\mathbf{b}_i^*\|/\|\mathbf{b}_{i+1}^*\| \approx r$ for all $i < n$, where $r \approx \beta^{1/\beta}$ asymptotically.

Lattice enumeration. Lattice reduction algorithms such as BKZ make calls to exact (or approximate) SVP oracles of smaller dimensions. These SVP solvers can be instantiated by the aforementioned exact SVP algorithms. In this work, we focus on exact SVP solvers instantiated by enumeration. In short, such algorithms proceed with an exhaustive search for all (or partial) lattice vectors within a certain region. We review the algorithms of [Kan83, FP85, SE94].

Given a basis $\mathbf{B}$ of $\mathcal{L}$ and a good upper bound R for the length of a shortest vector in $\mathcal{L}$, an enumeration algorithm outputs a shortest vector $\mathbf{v}$ with $\|\mathbf{v}\| \leq R$ if such a vector exists. To find $\mathbf{v}$, the enumeration algorithm searches over a tree formed by all vectors of norm bounded by R. This can be achieved by writing $\mathbf{v} = \sum_{j=1}^n v_j \mathbf{b}_j = \sum_{j=1}^n (v_j + \sum_{i=j+1}^n \mu_{i,j} v_i) \mathbf{b}_j^*$ and bounding each of the projections:

$$\|\pi_{n+1-l}(\mathbf{v})\|^2 = \sum_{j=n+1-l}^n \left(v_j + \sum_{i=j+1}^n \mu_{i,j} v_i \right)^2 \|\mathbf{b}_j^*\|^2 \leq R^2, \ \forall \, 1 \leq l \leq n. \qquad (1)$$

The Schnorr-Euchner algorithm [SE94] conducts a depth first search of the enumeration tree. More precisely, the algorithm starts with $l = 1$ and fixes some v_n in a bounded range as determined by $\|\pi_n(\mathbf{v})\|^2 \leq R^2$. Inductively, assume the algorithm has proceeded to level $l \geq 2$ and hence all v_{n+2-i} for $2 \leq i \leq l$ are fixed. Using $\|\pi_{n+1-l}(\mathbf{v})\|^2 \leq R^2$, a permissible range for the coefficient v_{n+1-l} can be derived. The algorithm backtracks when the range becomes invalid and succeeds when it reaches a leaf. This procedure thus creates an enumeration tree of depth n and only requires $\text{poly}(n)$ memory. The running time of an enumeration-based algorithm depends heavily on the quality of the input lattice basis $\mathbf{B}$. In Kannan's enumeration algorithm [Kan83], a strong preprocessing is performed before enumeration, to achieve a quasi-HKZ shape. Subsequent analysis [HS07] shows the Kannan's enumeration achieves a worst-case running-time of $n^{n/2e+o(n)}$. Heuristically the number of enumerated lattice vectors can be estimated using the Gaussian heuristic. To speed up the enumeration, Schnorr and Hörner [SH95] proposed a technique known as tree pruning. The idea is to reduce the search space by performing the search on a subset of all possible solutions, which are more likely to be short. An improved algorithm, namely extreme pruning, was proposed by Gama, Nguyen and Regev [GNR10]. The main idea is to heavily prune the enumeration tree and repeat the procedure by rerandomizing the basis. They also proposed methods for choosing the pruning parameters to optimize the running-time versus success probability. This leads to the current-state-of-the-art of enumeration-based lattice reduction algorithms, which has been adopted in BKZ 2.0 [CN11] and implemented in the FPLLL library [dt22] and the progressive preprocessing lattice reduction library [AWHT16]. In this work, for convenience, it is sufficient to assume the bound R in inequality (1) can be replaced by some number $R_l := f(R, l, \mathbf{B})$ where f can be pre-computed.

Quantum circuits. In this work, we will formulate the quantum architecture based on the quantum circuit model. As stated before, the gate count uses the

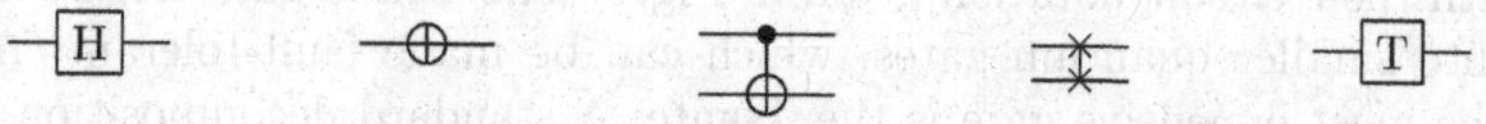

(a) H-gate   **(b)** NOT   **(c)** CNOT   **(d)** SWAP   **(e)** T-gate

Fig. 1. Basic quantum gates.

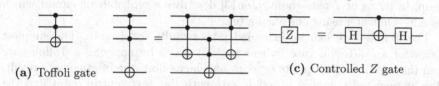

(a) Toffoli gate

(b) 3-Toffoli gate, using 3 Toffoli gates and 1 ancillary qubit

(c) Controlled Z gate

Fig. 2. Synthesized quantum gates.

"Clifford+T" gate set. Such choice of gate set is motivated by fault-tolerant computation, as many quantum error correcting codes can naturally implement Clifford gates. The T-gate is non-Clifford and used to implement the useful Toffoli gate. As fault-tolerant implementation of T-gates is more involved than for Clifford gates, our resource estimates minimize T-depth and T-gate count

We assume the implementations of the following gates are the primitive building blocks and give their circuit notation in Fig. 1.

The Hadamard-gate (denoted H) acts on a single qubit. In outer product notation, $H = \frac{1}{\sqrt{2}}(|0\rangle\langle 0| + |1\rangle\langle 0| + |0\rangle\langle 1| - |1\rangle\langle 1|)$. We denote $|+\rangle := H|1\rangle$ and $|-\rangle := H|0\rangle$. The multi-bit H gate is defined as $H^{\otimes n} := H \otimes \cdots \otimes H$ with n such H gates. The NOT-gate (sometimes called the X-gate) is a single-qubit gate, which flips the bit when the inputs are from the standard basis. As outer product, $NOT = |1\rangle\langle 0| + |0\rangle\langle 1|$. The CNOT-gate is a two-qubit operation, where the first qubit is usually referred to as the control qubit and the second qubit as the target qubit. As outer product, $CNOT = |00\rangle\langle 00| + |01\rangle\langle 01| + |10\rangle\langle 11| + |11\rangle\langle 10|$. The SWAP-gate is a two-qubit operation that swaps the state of the two input qubits. As outer product, $SWAP = |00\rangle\langle 00| + |11\rangle\langle 11| + |01\rangle\langle 10| + |10\rangle\langle 01|$. The SWAP gate can be implemented for free by reassigning the labels, assuming distance between qubits does not matter. The T-gate is a single-qubit gate, which rotates the Z-axis of the Bloch sphere by 45' degree. As outer product, $T = |0\rangle\langle 0| + e^{i\pi/4}|1\rangle\langle 1|$. The Eastin-Knill theorem [EK09] shows that not all the unitary operators in a universal operator set can be implemented transversally. Implementations often choose the T-gate as the non-transversal gate.

We will also use several controlled gates that can be implemented from the above primitive quantum gates. This includes the Toffoli gate and controlled-Z gate, with their circuit notation given in Fig. 2. The Toffoli gate can be decomposed into smaller quantum gates, which can be made fault-tolerant. Among them, the most expensive gate is the T-gate. A standard decomposition of the Toffoli gate into the Clifford+T set can be found in [NC11], which has a T-count of 7 with a T-depth of 6. This has been improved in the design of [AMMR13] which has a T-count of 7 and a T-depth of 3. This appears to be the best T-depth without ancillas. With ancillas, the T-depth can be reduced to 1, as described in [Sel13]. This is mostly useful when the T-gate is expensive and ancillas are cheap. In terms of T-gate count, [Jon13] describes a probabilistic circuit which has a T-count of 4 using one ancilla bit.

The Toffoli gate can be extended into a multi-Toffoli gate. The simplest design for an n-Toffoli gate (where $n > 2$) starts by applying a Toffoli gate from the first 2 control qubits onto an ancillary qubit, the intermediate result. Then it repeatedly applies a Toffoli gate with the next control qubit and the current intermediate result onto a new ancillary qubit to get a new intermediate result. Finally, it copies the result onto the target qubit with a CNOT-gate, or replaces the last ancillary qubit with the target qubit. It also needs to clean up the intermediate results with Toffoli gates, using in total $2n - 2$ Toffoli gates, $n - 1$ ancillary qubits and a CNOT gate. If the last ancillary qubit is replaced with the target, $2n - 3$ Toffoli gates and $n - 2$ ancillary qubits suffice.

The Z gate is a gate to flip the phase of the $|1\rangle$ state. In outer product form, $Z = |0\rangle\langle 0| - |1\rangle\langle 1|$. The Z gate can be implemented by putting a NOT gate between 2 Hadamard gates. It can be controlled by replacing the NOT gate with a CNOT, Toffoli or multi-Toffoli gate.

The $R_y(\theta)$ gate rotates by $\theta/2$ degrees around the y-axis of the Bloch sphere. In outer product form, $R_y(\theta) = \cos(\theta/2)|0\rangle\langle 0| - \sin(\theta/2)|0\rangle\langle 1| + \sin(\theta/2)|1\rangle\langle 0| + \cos(\theta/2)|1\rangle\langle 1|$. To get it, we first need to introduce the $R_x(\theta)$ and $R_z(\theta)$ gates, rotating around the x- and z-axes respectively. The $R_z(\theta)$ gate can be made from the base set using $4\log(\frac{1}{\epsilon}) + O(\log(\log(\frac{1}{\epsilon})))$ T-gates for ϵ accuracy [RS16]. The $R_x(\theta)$ gate can be made using $R_x(\theta) = H R_z(\theta) H$, which then can be turned into the $R_y(\theta)$ gate using $R_y(\theta) = T^2 R_x(\theta) T^6$. So to get $R_y(\theta)$ we need 8 T gates, 2 Hadamard gates, and a $R_z(\theta)$-gate. The $R_y(\theta)$ gate can be decomposed into $\text{NOT}R_y(-\theta/2)\text{NOT}R_y(\theta/2)$, meaning it can be made controllable by replacing the NOT gates with CNOT, Toffoli or multi-Toffoli gates. Finally, the Hadamard gate can be decomposed into $R_y(\frac{\pi}{4})ZR_y(-\frac{\pi}{4})$. By making the Z gate controllable, we can make a controllable Hadamard gate.

Cost model. We make a number of assumptions for our quantum resource cost model. We assume a full capacity of parallelism, e.g., the circuit can run any number of gates simultaneously as long as these gates act independently on different qubits. The time complexity of the circuit depends on its depth, which is why we mainly focus on Toffoli and T gates. We use Toffoli and T gates simultaneously, and as noted above, the Toffoli gate can be implemented using a circuit of T gates with T-depth 1. Some component may involve a polynomial number of ancillas, which we sometimes trade off in favor of a smaller circuit depth. Overall we aim to optimize the circuit depth and then the circuit size.

3   Quantum Tree Backtracking

Our implementation focuses on the quantum tree backtracking algorithm of Montanaro [Mon18], based on the electric network framework [Bel13], for detecting a solution. Montanaro's algorithm was presented for solving the so-called constraint satisfaction problem (CSP). Some further background on tree backtracking for solving the CSP is given in Appendix B. In this section, we provide some details about Montanaro's algorithm, to facilitate our concrete implementation and circuit presented in Sect. 4.

It can be seen that lattice enumeration allows for tree backtracking, which we will denote as "enumeration trees". Indeed, inequality (1) suggests that, at the l-th ($l \geq 2$) level of the tree, $v_{n+2-l}, \ldots, v_n$ are already determined. To go down the tree, it remains to bound and select a value, if it exists, for v_{n+1-l} according to Inequality (1). We let d denote the maximal number of choices of v_i. Thus this can be represented by a tree with up to n layers and degree d.

3.1   Montanaro's Algorithms

A first algorithm of Montanaro detects whether the tree contains a solution for some predicate P in $O(\sqrt{T}n)$ steps where T is an upper bound on the tree size and n is the height of the tree. This is given in Theorem 1.

Theorem 1 ([Mon18, Theorem 1.1]). *Let T be an upper bound on the number of vertices in a tree formed by some constraint. Then for any $0 < \delta < 1$ there is a quantum algorithm which, given T, evaluates a predicate P and a function h (which determines how to extend a given partial assignment) for $O(\sqrt{T}n \log(1/\delta))$ times each, outputs true if there exists x such that $P(x)$ is true, and outputs false otherwise. The algorithm uses $\mathrm{poly}(n)$ qubits, $O(1)$ auxiliary operations per use of P and h, and fails with probability at most δ.*

In the lattice enumeration context, an upper bound T is often superexponential in n and the tree height n can be the lattice dimension. An upper bound T on the tree size is an input in the above theorem. This detection algorithm can be modified to actually locate the solution, via repeated applications on the subtrees. This leads to Montanaro's second algorithm:

Theorem 2 ([Mon18, Theorem 1.2]). *Let T be the number of vertices in a tree formed by some constraint. Then for any $0 < \delta < 1$ there is a quantum algorithm which makes $O(\sqrt{T}n^{1.5} \log n \log(1/\delta))$ evaluations of each of P and h, and outputs x such that $P(x)$ is true, or "not found" if no such x exists. If we are promised that there exists a unique x_0 such that $P(x_0)$ is true, there is a quantum algorithm which outputs x_0 making $O(\sqrt{T}n \log^3 n \log(1/\delta))$ evaluations of each of P and h. In both cases the algorithm uses $\mathrm{poly}(n)$ space, $O(1)$ auxiliary operations per use of P and h, and fails with probability at most δ.*

In the second algorithm in Theorem 2, T denotes the actual number of vertices in the tree, which needs not to be given as an input to the algorithm. In both algorithms, the tree degree d is assumed to be $O(1)$ in the analysis.

The main essence of Theorem 1 is an algorithm to determine the presence of a solution given a tree root. This detection algorithm also serves as the main computational component in Theorem 2. We will thus focus on the algorithm in Theorem 1 for detecting a solution. During the algorithm, the state is a superposition of all the possible paths in the tree, and the primary tool we need from quantum computing is phase estimation, as described in Theorem 3.

Theorem 3 ([Kit96, CEMM98]). *Assume a unitary U is given as a black box. There exists a quantum algorithm that, given an eigenvector ψ of U with eigenvalue $e^{i\phi}$, outputs a real number w such that $|w - \phi| \leq \delta$ with probability at least $9/10$. Moreover, the algorithm uses $O(1/\delta)$ controlled applications of U and $\frac{1}{\delta} \text{poly}(\log(1/\delta))$ other elementary operations.*

To get a precision of $\delta = 2^{-s}$ for some positive integer s, we need to apply controlled-U 2^s times and use $O(s^2)$ more gates to perform a quantum Fourier transform on s qubits. Also in practice, we end up only caring about being able to distinguish the eigenvalue $1 = e^{i0}$ from other eigenvalues, so we only need to check if the output w is close to 0 or not. We then construct a single 'walk step' U, that reflects over superpositions of nodes and their children, except for marked leaves. We construct this walk step such that it keeps the sign of the uniform superposition over the vertices and the path from the root to a leaf that contains a solution. If we had a path, we could use phase estimation to detect if the eigenvalue of this path was one. However, if we had a path, we could just test if the leaf contains a solution. Instead, we use that the root is 'close enough' to a path and test the eigenvalue of the root. If a marked vertex (one that contains a solution) exists, it is likely that phase estimation would output eigenvalue 1. On the other hand, if the tree does not contain a solution, it is less likely that phase estimation would output eigenvalue 1, since 1 is 'not very close' to the uniform superposition of vertices. Thus, by repeating the phase estimation with high precision, we can eventually get the desired confidence.

The walk steps Montanaro introduced use a diffusion operator D_x which acts on the Hilbert space spanned by a node $|x\rangle$ and its children. Let d_x denote the degree of the node $|x\rangle$ and $x \to y$ mean y is a child of x. D_x is defined as:

- If x is marked, D_x is the identity.
- If x is not marked and not the root, it changes the sign of the uniform superposition of x and its children y and leaves any orthogonal superpositions alone. This can be described by a Householder transformation, e.g.:

$$D_x := I - 2|\psi_x\rangle\langle\psi_x|, \text{ with } |\psi_x\rangle := (1/\sqrt{d_x})(|x\rangle + \sum_{y, x \to y} |y\rangle).$$

- At the root, $D_r := I - 2|\psi_r\rangle\langle\psi_r|$ where

$$|\psi_r\rangle = (1/\sqrt{1 + d_r n})(|r\rangle + \sqrt{n} \sum_{y, r \to y} |y\rangle).$$

It is worthwhile to note the D_x operator affects the node x and its children simultaneously. Montanaro's algorithm splits the tree into vertices of even and odd distance from the root, called set A for even and set B for odd, using that trees are bipartite. Each step of the 'walk' consists of applying $R_B R_A$ where $R_A = \bigoplus_{x \in A} D_x$ and $R_B = |r\rangle\langle r| + \bigoplus_{x \in B} D_x$. The operator R_A applies the diffusion operator to all vertices of even distance from the root (including the root) and their children, changing the sign of any ψ_x (or ψ_r), but leaving orthogonal states untouched. The operator R_B acts similarly on vertices of odd distance together with the root, and the $|r\rangle\langle r|$ in R_B actually leaves the root untouched. Now this operator has been constructed such that we have two possible eigenvectors $|\phi\rangle, |\eta\rangle$ not orthogonal to $|r\rangle$ with eigenvalue 1, where

$$|\phi\rangle = \sqrt{n}|r\rangle + \sum_{x \neq r, x \rightsquigarrow x_0} (-1)^{l(x)}|x\rangle \text{ and } |\eta\rangle = |r\rangle + \sqrt{n}\sum_{x \neq r}|x\rangle,$$

where $l(x)$ is the distance of x to the root and $x \rightsquigarrow x_0$ means every x on the path to a marked vertex x_0 (including x_0). If no marked vertex exists $|\eta\rangle$ has eigenvalue 1 else $|\phi\rangle$ has eigenvalue 1. Finally we apply quantum phase estimation of $R_B R_A$ to $|r\rangle$, and check if it has eigenvalue 1. This returns 1 with probability greater than $1/2$ if a marked vertex exists and smaller than $1/4$ if it does not [Mon18, Lemma 2.4]. To conclude, Montanaro's tree backtracking algorithm for detecting a solution is described in Algorithm 1. Montanaro showed that this detection algorithm fails with probability at most δ when the phase estimation is invoked for $K = \lceil \gamma \log(1/\delta) \rceil$ times for some universal constant γ.

Algorithm 1. Detecting a solution (Alg. 2 of [Mon18]), universal constants β, γ.

Input: Operators R_A, R_B, a failure probability δ, upper bounds on the depth n and the number of vertices T.
Output: Solution exists or not.

Repeat the following subroutine $K = \lceil \gamma \log(1/\delta) \rceil$ times:
   (a) Apply phase estimation to the operator $R_B R_A$ on $|r\rangle$ with precision $\beta/\sqrt{Tn}$.
   (b) If the eigenvalue is 1, accept; otherwise, reject.
If the number of acceptances is at least $3K/8$, return "solution exists"; otherwise, return "no solution".

3.2 Quantum Lattice Enumeration

Aono, Nguyen and Shen [ANS18] adapted the algorithms by Montanaro [Mon18] and Ambainis and Kokainis's [AK17] to the context of lattice point enumeration. They obtain the following theorems:

Theorem 4 ([ANS18, Theorem 7 & 8]). *For any $\delta > 0$, given an LLL-reduced basis B and a radius R together with a pruning function f, there is a quantum algorithm that outputs a shortest non-zero vector v in $\mathcal{L}(B) \cap P_f(B, R)$, with correctness probability $\geq 1 - \delta$, in time $O(\sqrt{T}n^3\beta \operatorname{poly}(\log(n), \log(1/\epsilon), \log(\beta)))$, where β is the bit-size of input vectors. Applying this to Kannan's algorithm leads to a quantum enumeration algorithm of $n^{n/4e+o(n)} \cdot \operatorname{poly}(\log(n), \log(1/\epsilon), \beta)$.*

There are two interesting modifications in [ANS18]. First, one can transform a tree of depth n and degree d to a binary tree of depth $n \log d$. The access to the predicate of the original tree can be modified efficiently to a predicate access to the transformed tree. For an LLL-reduced basis, the enumeration tree has $d \leq 2^n$ and thus leads to a binary tree of depth $O(n^2)$. The main idea in the proof of Theorem 4 is to apply Montanaro's [Mon18] second algorithm iteratively on the transformed binary tree. Second, [ANS18] proposes to run the quantum algorithm on a combined tree, consisting of m rerandomized bases, in the extreme pruning setup. This leads to a factor of $O(\sqrt{m})$ savings on the quantum enumeration, compared to calling the procedure m times sequentially. Our work focuses on the implementation aspects. Thus we do not repeat the details on extreme pruning and the binary tree transform, as already given in [ANS18].

4   Using Backtracking for Enumeration

In this section, we describe the circuit for the quantum lattice enumeration, based on Montanaro's tree backtracking [Mon18]. We also give the resource estimate, which is based on a design optimized w.r.t the T-depth. Overall, the algorithm conducts phase estimation of some operator $R_B R_A$ on the root of subtrees. We make the implementation modular, starting with the phase estimation, and the implementation of R_A or R_B, and then the implementation of the predicate which is used as an oracle inside the implementation of R_A and R_B.

4.1   Phase Estimation

To start with, the main algorithm of Montanaro [Mon18] (see Algorithm 1) detects if there exists a solution in a given subtree. Note that Step (a) in Algorithm 1 can run in parallel, thus the main computation is the phase estimation step of the operator $R_B R_A$ on the input $|r\rangle$ where $|r\rangle$ denotes the root of the tree. For completeness, Fig. 3 shows a general phase estimation circuit. Step (a) in Algorithm 1 implies that, for the correctness of phase estimation, one requires the precision to be $\approx \beta/\sqrt{\mathcal{T}n}$ (note β is some universal constant independent of the input size). This means that controlled-U operators show up $O(\sqrt{\mathcal{T}n})$ times.

In [CKM19], Campbell, Khurana and Montanaro have given a more precise estimate on the hidden constant. For example, to achieve a failure probability $\delta \leq 0.1$ (see Algorithm 1 for δ), one can take the number of repetitions $K = 79$ and then the number of controlled-U operators can be bounded by $32\sqrt{\mathcal{T}n}$. Note that the input $|0\rangle^{\otimes m}$ takes $m = O(\log(\mathcal{T}n))$ qubits. Asymptotically, $\mathcal{T}$ upperbounds the tree size which is about $n^{cn+o(n)}$ where $c \leq \frac{1}{2e}$ [ABF+20, ABLR21]. Thus m is about $O(n \log n)$. The quantum Fourier transform (QFT) step can be constructed in $O(\log^2(\mathcal{T}n))$ primitive gates. We will see in Subsect. 4.2 that the input to the U operators requires about $\Theta(n \log d)$ qubits.

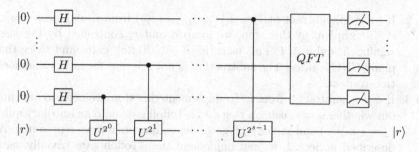

Fig. 3. Circuit for phase estimation where $U := R_B R_A$.

4.2 Implementation of R_A and R_B

In the phase estimation algorithm, e.g., Fig. 3, a key step is the controlled-U operator. We consider implementing a single step of the operator $U = R_B R_A$. Montanaro provides a high level description to implement $R_A = \bigoplus_{x \in A} D_x$, with R_B being analogous, in Algorithm 3 of [Mon18]. We implement this algorithm for lattice enumeration step by step and give the number of gates and ancillary qubits required.

Implementation of R_A (and R_B). The input of the algorithm is:

- An integer $|l\rangle$ which is the depth we are at, ranging from 0 (indicating we are at the root) to n (indicating we are at a leaf). This corresponds to the value l as in Inequality (1) for lattice enumeration.
- An array $|v\rangle = |v_1\rangle \ldots |v_n\rangle$ which is the path in the tree, and each $v_i \in [d] \cup \{*\}$, where $[d] = \{1, \ldots, d\}$, and $*$ denotes unassigned. Each element of $[d]$ corresponds to one child of the node. The indices i correspond to the values i in Inequality (1).
- Access to an oracle P, which given a path in the tree $|l\rangle |v\rangle$ returns true, false or indeterminate.
- Access to a heuristic h to determine the next index to branch on. In the lattice enumeration context, this simply decreases from n to 1.

The input thus requires $\lceil \log n \rceil + n \lceil \log d + 1 \rceil$ qubits where the coefficients v_i are the dominating terms. The algorithm also needs some ancillary qubits: (1) $\mathcal{H}_{\text{anc}}$ which stores $a \in [d] \cup \{*\}$ and starts in $|*\rangle$. (2) $\mathcal{H}_{\text{children}}$ which stores an array $S \subseteq [d]$ and starts empty. Note $\mathcal{H}_{\text{anc}}, \mathcal{H}_{\text{children}}$ take up $\lceil \log d + 1 \rceil$ and d qubits respectively. The algorithm also uses some extra qubits to do intermediate computations that we will describe later.

We now describe the algorithm (Algorithm 3 of Montanaro [Mon18]) and its implementation. Note, to be consistent with the description of Algorithm 3 of Montanaro [Mon18], the indices are from 1 to n. This should be reversed outside this subsection when considering our application as in Inequality (1).

Step 1. If $P(|l\rangle |v\rangle)$ is true, return. To implement this step, we call P and save the output of $P(|l\rangle |v\rangle)$ in an ancillary qubit $|c_1\rangle$ where $c_1 = 1$ when P returned NOT true and 0 otherwise, which we will use later.

Step 2. If l is odd, subtract $h((i_1, v_1), \ldots, (i_{l-1}, v_{l-1}))$ from i_l and swap a with v_l. To implement this step, we swap a and v_l controlled by the least significant qubit of l. This uses $\lceil \log d + 1 \rceil$ Toffoli gates and twice that many CNOT gates. The subtraction is not relevant for lattice enumeration context.

Step 3. If $a \neq *$, subtract 1 from l. To implement this step, we need to first find out whether $a = *$, using a $\lceil \log d + 1 \rceil$-Toffoli gate onto an ancillary qubit $c_3 = 1(a \neq *)$ and some NOT gates depending on how we represent $*$. As described in Sect. 2, we can implement the i-Toffoli gate trivially using $2i - 3$ Toffoli gates and $i - 2$ ancillary qubits, starting and ending in $|0\rangle$. Then we do a controlled reverse incrementer circuit on l controlled by c_3, using Gidney's design [Gid15]. The incrementer circuit (using the $n - 2$ zeroed bit design) uses $2\lceil \log n \rceil - 4$ Toffoli gates, $\lceil \log n \rceil - 1$ CNOT gates and 1 NOT gate using $\lceil \log n \rceil - 2$ ancillary qubits. To make it controllable, we convert the CNOT gates into Toffoli gates, additionally controlled by c_3, and the NOT gate into a CNOT gate also controlled by c_3.

Step 4. This is skipped.

Step 5. For each $w \in [d]$: If $P(|l+1\rangle|v_1\rangle \ldots |v_l\rangle|w\rangle)$ is not false, set $S = S \cup \{w\}$. $|S\rangle$ is implemented as a string of d qubits, each representing one entry of $[d]$. For each $w \in [d]$ we access P, check whether the result is false or not, and change the appropriate qubit of $|S\rangle$, which starts as the $|0\rangle^d$ state. We repeat this step d times for a total of d uses of the oracle P and CNOT gates. We leave d ancillary qubits with the intermediate results to decrease calls to P.

Step 6. If $l = 0$, perform the operation $I - 2|\phi_{n,S}\rangle\langle\phi_{n,S}|$ on a. Otherwise, perform the operation $I - 2|\phi_{1,S}\rangle\langle\phi_{1,S}|$ on a. This is the step where we perform D_x. To do this, we need the function $U_{\alpha,S}$:

$$|*\rangle \mapsto \frac{1}{\sqrt{\alpha|S|+1}} \left(|*\rangle + \sqrt{\alpha} \sum_{i \in S} |i\rangle \right).$$

$U_{\alpha,S}$ maps $|*\rangle$ into $|\phi_{\alpha,S}\rangle$. We can then do

$$U_{\alpha,S} \left(I - 2|*\rangle\langle*| \right) U_{\alpha,S}^{-1} = I - 2|\phi_{\alpha,S}\rangle\langle\phi_{\alpha,S}|.$$

The operator $I - 2|*\rangle\langle*|$ requires a check whether $|a\rangle = |*\rangle$ and applies a conditional Z gate if $|a\rangle = |*\rangle$, using a $\lceil \log d + 1 \rceil + 1$-Toffoli gate. Additionally condition the Z gate on c_1 as well as the relevant qubit used in the Fourier transform. No other step has to be controlled to make $R_B R_A$ controllable.

Step 7. Uncompute S and j by reversing Steps 5 and 4, making d more uses of P.

Step 8. If $a \neq *$, add 1 to l. If l is now odd, add $h((i_1, v_1), \ldots, (i_{l-1}, v_{l-1}))$ to i_l and swap v_l with a. (Now $a = *$ again.) Another uncomputation step, reverse Steps 3, 2 & 1 with the same cost.

Table 1. Summary of circuit and gates required. Ancillary qubits are required until they are subtracted, zeroed qubits are required only for one step and are returned to zero in that step.

Step	TOF	CNOT	P calls	Ancillas	Zeroed qubits
1	0	0	1	1	0
2	$\lceil \log d + 1 \rceil$	$2\lceil \log d + 1 \rceil$	0	0	0
3	$5\lceil \log d + 1 \rceil - 8$	2	0	1	$\lceil \log d + 1 \rceil - 2$
5	0	d	d	d	0
6	$2U_{\alpha,S}^{-1} + 2\lceil \log d + 1 \rceil - 1$	$2U_{\alpha,S}^{-1}$	0	0	$U_{\alpha,S}^{-1}$
7,8	$6\lceil \log d + 1 \rceil - 8$	$d + 2\lceil \log d + 1 \rceil + 2$	$d + 1$	$-(d+2)$	$\lceil \log d + 1 \rceil - 2$

The number of gates required and the number of additional qubits needed is summarized in Table 1.

As described in Subsect. 4.3, the cost of $U_{\alpha,S}^{-1}$ is:

$$2\lceil \log n \rceil + \lceil \log d \rceil (2d^2 + 8d + 2) + \frac{5}{2}d^2 + \frac{11}{2}d + 1$$

TOF gates, $\frac{d}{2}\lceil \log d + 1 \rceil + d^2 + 3d$ CNOT gates, $2d + 1 + \lceil \log d \rceil$ zeroed qubits taking into account the cost saving of doing $U_{\alpha,S}^{-1}(I - 2|\phi_{1,S}\rangle\langle\phi_{1,S}|)U_{\alpha,S}$ and an additional T-depth of

$$4d^2(\log(d/\epsilon) + 5/2) - 12d(\log(d/\epsilon) + 5/2) + 8\log(d/\epsilon) + 20$$

due to error correction for maximum error ϵ.

Parallelizing Steps 5 & 7. In the case where calls to P dominate the cost, which we will see is our case, Step 5 and its inverse Step 7 can easily be parallelized by making d copies of $|l\rangle|v\rangle$ and then calling P to $|l+1\rangle|v_1\rangle \ldots |v_l\rangle|w\rangle$ for each $w \in [d]$ in parallel. This reduces the depth of R_A from $2d + 2$ calls to P to 4 calls to P. The additional cost is $2d(\lceil \log n \rceil + n\lceil \log d + 1 \rceil)$ CNOT gates.

4.3   The Function $U_{\alpha,S}$

Performing the map $U_{\alpha,S}$ for variable degree requires us to implement the map

$$|S\rangle|0\rangle \mapsto |S\rangle \frac{1}{\sqrt{|S|}} \sum_{S_i \in S} |i\rangle.$$

For this we will need $d+1$ ancillary qubits for the transformation starting in $|1\rangle$, which we will call $|\sigma\rangle$, and $|s\rangle$ of size $\lceil \log d \rceil$ to store the size of S. To calculate the size of S we calculate the Hamming weight of the string $|S\rangle$, which we will put into ancillary qubit array $|s\rangle$. To implement the Hamming weight function, we need at most $2d - 2$ Toffoli gates, using the design from [BP05] (lower bounding the Hamming weight of d to 1). The classical design can be turned into a quantum circuit by replacing the conjunction gates with Toffoli gates and XOR gates with CNOT gates, with an additional $d - 1$ Toffoli gates to clean up zeroed ancillary space. The CNOT complexity of this is bounded by $4d - 2$, modifying adder design which is described in [BP05]. We also need to distinguish the cases: use a $\lceil \log n \rceil$-Toffoli gate to get ancillary qubits $|\beta\rangle = 1(l = 0)$. Next we fix the state of $|*\rangle$ by applying a rotation. To do this, we have to repeat for $i = 0, \ldots, d$:

1. Check if $s = i$ using some NOT gates and one $\lceil \log d \rceil$-Toffoli gate to add everything together, putting the result in ancillary qubit $|c_6\rangle$.
2. Controlled by $|c_6\rangle$ and $|\beta\rangle$ perform the rotation $|1\rangle \rightarrow \frac{1}{\sqrt{ni+1}}|0\rangle + \sqrt{\frac{ni}{ni+1}}|1\rangle$ on the last qubit of $|\sigma\rangle$ using $R_{\sin^{-1}(\frac{1}{\sqrt{ni+1}})}$, $R_{-\sin^{-1}(\frac{1}{\sqrt{ni+1}})}$ and 2 TOF gates.
3. Controlled by $|c_6\rangle$ and $\text{NOT}|\beta\rangle$ perform the rotation $|1\rangle \rightarrow \frac{1}{\sqrt{i+1}}|0\rangle + \sqrt{\frac{i}{i+1}}|1\rangle$ on the last qubit of $|\sigma\rangle$ using $R_{\sin^{-1}(\frac{1}{\sqrt{i+1}})}$, $R_{-\sin^{-1}(\frac{1}{\sqrt{i+1}})}$ and 2 TOF gates.
4. Uncompute $|c_6\rangle$. This can be done with only 1 Toffoli gate by ignoring the cleanup of the $\lceil \log d \rceil$-Toffoli gate in Step 1 and keeping the ancillary qubits around, cleaning them up now.

This also provides a sketch for creating the rest of the desired superposition. Figure 4 shows an example of how to create a uniform superposition over 3 qubits. We will do the same over a variable number of qubits.

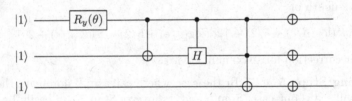

Fig. 4. Circuit to turn $|111\rangle$ into $(|100\rangle + |010\rangle + |001\rangle)/\sqrt{3}$. $\theta = 2\cos^{-1}(1/\sqrt{3})$.

The remaining d qubits of $|\sigma\rangle$ will function as the d elements of S. We will also need d more ancillary qubits to save some multi-Toffoli gates, $|t_1\rangle, \ldots, |t_d\rangle$ starting in $|0\rangle$. For $i = 1, \ldots, d$:

1. Apply a Toffoli gate to $|t_i\rangle$ controlled by $|t_{i-1}\rangle$ and $|\sigma_{i-1}\rangle$ to make sure $|\sigma\rangle$ is 1 up to this point. At $i = 1$ use a CNOT gate controlled by $|\sigma_{d+1}\rangle$ instead.
2. Now, for $j = 1, \ldots, d + 1 - i$:
   (a) Check if $|s\rangle = j$ using some NOT gates and one $\lceil \log d \rceil$-Toffoli gate, putting the result in $|T_{i,j}\rangle$.
   (b) If $j > 2$: controlled by $|T_{i,j}\rangle$, $|t_i\rangle$ and $|S_i\rangle$ perform the rotation $|1\rangle \rightarrow \frac{1}{\sqrt{j}}|0\rangle + \sqrt{\frac{j-1}{j}}|1\rangle$ on $|\sigma_i\rangle$ using $R_{\sin^{-1}(\frac{1}{\sqrt{j}})}$, $R_{-\sin^{-1}(\frac{j-1}{\sqrt{j}})}$, 4 TOF gates and 2 CNOT gates.
   (c) If $j = 2$: controlled by $|T_{i,j}\rangle$, $|t_i\rangle$ and $|S_i\rangle$ perform a NOT gate and a conditional Hadamard gate on $|\sigma\rangle_i$ to perform the rotation $|1\rangle \rightarrow |+\rangle$, using 4 TOF gates and 3 CNOT gates.

    (d) If $j = 1$: controlled by $|T_{i,j}\rangle$, $|t_i\rangle$ and $|S_i\rangle$ perform a 3-Toffoli gate on $|\sigma_i\rangle$ to perform $|1\rangle \to |0\rangle$.

    (e) Uncompute $|T_{i,j}\rangle$, using the same strategy as for c_6.

3. Perform a conditional decrementer gate on $|s\rangle$ conditioned by S_i so it is equal to the number of remaining entries of $|S\rangle$.

We can optionally uncompute $|t_1\rangle, \ldots, |t_d\rangle$ at the end using half of a d-Toffoli gate (Step 1 is the first half of this d-Toffoli gate). $|s\rangle$ is always $|0\rangle$ at the final step of the algorithm. Apply a NOT gate to every qubit of $|\sigma\rangle$ to see that we are close to the desired superposition:

$$
\begin{aligned}
|\beta\rangle|\sigma\rangle = \quad &|0\rangle \left(\tfrac{1}{\sqrt{|S|+1}} \left(|0^d 1\rangle + \textstyle\sum_{S_i \in S} |0^{i-1} 1 0^{d-i} 0\rangle \right) \right) \\
+ &|1\rangle \left(\tfrac{1}{\sqrt{n|S|+1}} \left(|0^d 1\rangle + \sqrt{n} \textstyle\sum_{S_i \in S} |0^{i-1} 1 0^{d-i} 0\rangle \right) \right).
\end{aligned}
$$

Next, apply NOT to qubits of $|a\rangle$ so $|*\rangle \to |0\rangle$. Then, for each $i = 1, \ldots, d+1$, apply CNOTs controlled by $|\sigma_i\rangle$ to $|a\rangle$ to set it to $|S_i\rangle$ for $i = 1, \ldots, d$ and $|*\rangle$ for $i = d + 1$. Finally, uncompute $|\sigma\rangle$ with $d + 1$ $\lceil \log d + 1 \rceil$-Toffoli gates and $|\beta\rangle$ with a $\lceil \log n \rceil$-Toffoli gate. The number of Toffoli gates in $U_{\alpha,S}$ is

$$
2\lceil \log n \rceil + \lceil \log d \rceil (2d^2 + 8d + 2) + \frac{5}{2}d^2 + \frac{15}{2}d - 1,
$$

the number of CNOT gates is $\frac{d}{2}\lceil \log d + 1 \rceil + d^2 + 7d - 2$ and the number of ancillary qubits is $2d + 1 + \lceil \log d \rceil$, skipping uncomputation of $|\beta\rangle$ and $|t_1\rangle, \ldots, |t_d\rangle$. However, since we do $U_{\alpha,S}^{-1}$ first, some operation on $|a\rangle$ and then $U_{\alpha,S}$, we can skip the computation of $|s\rangle$ as well, saving $2d - 2$ Toffoli gates and $4d - 2$ CNOT gates, and only uncompute $|\beta\rangle, |t_1\rangle, \ldots, |t_d\rangle$ instead of computing them.

Dealing with errors from the rotations. When applying the rotation gates, we introduce an error [RS16]. Because the final superposition will have up to d rotations[1] applied, the total maximum error is $\max(\epsilon_i, 1 - \Pi_{i=1,\ldots,d}(1 - \epsilon_i))$ where ϵ_i is the error at layer i. If we want to bound the error by some target ϵ, we can set ϵ_i to $1 - \sqrt[d]{1 - \epsilon} \approx \epsilon/d$. Since each rotation gate has worst case T-depth $4\log(1/\epsilon_i) + 10$ [Sel15, RS16, Section 8.3] and we do a total of $d(d + 1) - 4d + 2$ rotations, we get a total T-depth of $4d^2(\log(d/\epsilon) + 5/2) - 12d(\log(d/\epsilon) + 5/2) + 8\log(d/\epsilon) + 20$, which is dominated by $4d^2 \log(d/\epsilon)$ and cannot be parallelized.

4.4 Bounds and Arithmetic in the Predicate

A predicate function P is used in Step 1, 5, 7 & 8 for the implementation of R_A (and R_B) in Subsect. 4.2. In this subsection, we will discuss some bounds and the main arithmetic used in the predicate. The implementation of the predicate and resources are presented in Subsect. 4.5.

---

[1] At each $i = 1, \ldots, d$, only 0 or 1 rotation gates actually introduce this error. Conditional rotation gates where the condition is not met cancel the error introduced, since $\mathrm{NOT} R_k(-\theta) \mathrm{NOT} = R_z(\theta)$, meaning they have the same error.

The predicate takes inputs of the form $|l\rangle|v_n\rangle \cdots |v_{n-l+1}\rangle|*\rangle$ for $1 \le l \le n$ and checks whether it satisfies Inequality (1). It returns one of false, satisfied or true. Note that the true is triggered when the inequality is satisfied and the level is $l = n$. Thus we may simply assume $P(\bullet)$ returns either false or satisfied. Observe that here we denote the index i in reverse order to be consistent with the notation in Inequality (1). Thus the main computational step at the l-th level (e.g., with input $|l\rangle$) in the predicate is to check if v_j satisfies:

$$\underbrace{\sum_{j \ge n+1-l}}_{(III)} \underbrace{(\underbrace{\sum_{i \ge j} \mu_{i,j} \cdot v_i}_{(I)})^2}_{(II)} \cdot \underbrace{\|\mathbf{b}_j^*\|^2}_{(IV)} \le R^2, \tag{2}$$

where R is the enumeration radius (e.g., $R = \|\mathbf{b}_1\|$ or $R = \mathrm{GH}(\mathcal{L})$). In the case of pruning, R can be replaced by a pruning function R_l that can be pre-computed classically. For convenience, we mark the steps of the computation by $(I)-(IV)$ that we will refer to later.

Simplified model. We make a few simplifications to the description, to avoid the implementation becoming overly complicated and unreadable. First, Step 5 of Algorithm 3 of Montanaro [Mon18] (see Subsect. 4.2) asks to check $\forall w \in [d]$, if $P(|l + 1\rangle|v_n\rangle...|v_{n-l+1}\rangle|w\rangle)$ is not false. These superpositions $|v_i\rangle$ and $|w\rangle$ stand for indices of the nodes (say, as the children). However, to compute the predicate, one requires the superpositions corresponding to the actual values of the v_i. It is not efficient to store these superpositions, but one can compute them on-demand given the inputs $|l + 1\rangle|v_n\rangle...|v_{n-l+1}\rangle$. We denote such a procedure as a *"translator"* which translates the input indices into the concrete values. The algorithm will start with the first index $|v_n\rangle$ (indexing to children) and then compute the concrete value corresponding to the index. One does this iteratively, and similarly for the new input $|w\rangle$, it determines which (indices of) children $|w\rangle$ to keep in the walk (e.g., set $S = S \cup \{w\}$ in Step 5). This procedure invokes at most n executions of the predicate P in serial with inputs $\{|v_n\rangle \cdots |v_{n-i+1}\rangle\}$ for $i = 1$ to l. We will factor such depth/size increment into the final estimate. Note that Step 5 for different inputs $|w\rangle$ can be parallelized. Thus, we may abuse the notation for v_i, which denotes both the index of the node and the actual value.

In the predicate, we will need to use the elements $\mu_{i,j}$ and $\|\mathbf{b}_i^*\|^2$, which are classic data. The address indices (e.g., i, j) are also classic, so this can be done in a quantum circuit model using a universal quantum gate set. The Gram-Schmidt coefficients μ_{ij} for $i > j$ take about $n^2/2$ registers, each of p bits. We will need the squared vector norm $\|\mathbf{b}_i^*\|^2$ for all i, which takes $n \cdot p$ bits. We will omit this circuit for simplicity. There might be a need to use the qRAM for the case of extreme pruning, but in this work, we only need to store/access the classical information so a plain quantum circuit would work.

Let d denote the maximum degree of the enumeration tree, B be a bound for $\max_i |v_i|$ and n denote the tree depth (e.g., the lattice dimension or the transformed binary tree height as in [ANS18]). In enumeration, floating-point arithmetic is also needed, thus we denote p as the precision required. We will discuss p, d, B as functions of n.

Precision requirement. In a standard implementation of lattice enumeration and lattice reduction, one uses floating-point numbers to speed up the computation (instead of working in $\mathbb{Q}$). For example, this is the approach used in the FPLLL library [dt22] and the progressive lattice reduction library [AWHT16].

To guarantee the correctness of lattice enumeration, one would require sufficient precision working over floating point numbers. Equivalently, this is the required precision for the enumeration tree to contain the solution node. The precision required in lattice enumeration over floating point numbers has been studied in [PS08]. Theorem 3 of [PS08] shows that to solve SVP-γ where $\gamma = 1.01$ the precision of the floating point numbers used needs to be $\Theta(n)$ for an n-dimensional lattice to guarantee correctness. Similarly, the precision required in an LLL reduction over floating point numbers (one can think of this as the starting step of a lattice reduction algorithm) cannot be too small. This has been studied in Theorem 1 of [NS05]. Asymptotically, a floating-point precision $\log_2(3)n \approx 1.6n + o(n)$ suffices. In practice, however, the constant 1.6 can be reduced to about 0.3 in folklore. Heuristically, the enumeration works on a more reduced basis than LLL-reduced and it requires smaller precision than that of LLL. Thus we will use the folklore value and assume the precision p' required for a correct enumeration is $p' \approx 0.3n$.

Our targeted dimension n for lattice enumeration would be about 400. For example, Kyber-512 [ABD+21] requires BKZ blocksize 406, Dilithium (security level 2) [BDK+21] requires blocksize 423 and Falcon-512 requires [FHK+20] blocksize 411. This heuristically requires a precision of $p' \approx 120$ bits. For larger dimension, the precision can be increased as needed.

Bounds on tree degree. The enumeration tree size $\mathcal{T}$ can be bounded by $n^{n/2e+o(n)}$, by the analysis in [HS07]. In practice, the tree size can be estimated using the Gaussian heuristic, given the lengths of Gram-Schmidt vectors. In an ideal case, $d = O(n)$ by taking $d^n \approx n^{n/2e+o(n)}$ if one assumes the nodes are uniformly distributed over a perfect d-ary tree. This argument is not true. For example, in a LLL-reduced basis, $\mathbf{b}_n^*$ could already be about 2^{n-1} times smaller than the enumeration radius R (say, $\|\mathbf{b_1}\|$). Thus the number of v_n can be already huge. The situation is much better if the input basis is preprocessed. It is conceptually simpler to assume the basis is already well-preprocessed: e.g., we assume the input basis is already HKZ reduced and revisit the enumeration. Alternatively, one can preprocess the basis with blocksize $n - o(n)$ which amortizes the running-time and leads to a similar quality (e.g., see Theorem 5 of [ABF+20] for a similar approach). We discuss several methods to bound d. For convenience, we let d_i denote the maximum degree for nodes at the i-th level in the tree. This corresponds to the maximum number of choices for v_i over fixed $\{v_{i+1}, \ldots, v_n\}$'s.

To begin, we bound the number of choices for v_n. One can model the geometry of an HKZ-reduced basis with the following (logarithmic) Gram–Schmidt length profile, following the same approach as in [HPS11, ABF+20].

$$u_k = (\ln k)/2 + (u_1 + u_2 + \cdots + u_k)/k, \ \forall k \le n, \text{ and } u_1 = 0. \tag{3}$$

In this equation, we let $u_1, \ldots, u_n$ be the Gram–Schmidt log-norms in reversed order of an HKZ-reduced basis. The low-order terms are omitted. Lemma 2 of in [ABF+20] bounds the u_i by

$$(\ln^2 k)/4 + (\ln k)/2 \le u_k < (\ln^2 k)/4 + (\ln k)/2 + 1.$$

Thus the number of choices for v_n can be bounded by $2\|\mathbf{b}_1\|/\|\mathbf{b}_n^*\| + 1 \approx 2e^{u_n - u_1} + 1 \approx n^{(\ln n)/4}$. We have assumed the HKZ Gram–Schmidt profile fitting the exact form in Eq. (3). Alternatively, if one can bear with the Geometric Series Assumption (though it seems not plausible for the HKZ case) of ratio $r \approx n^{1/n}$, one can obtain a much better bound for v_n which is about n. We can then bound degrees for the remaining v_i. Observe that, when the Gram-Schmidt vectors have a non-increasing length profile (e.g., $\forall i, \|\mathbf{b}_i\|^* \ge \|\mathbf{b}_{i+1}\|^*$), the number of choices for v_i is no larger than the number of choices for v_{i+1}.

A better method, in practice, is to use the concrete values of each $R/\|\mathbf{b}_i^*\|$ to bound the degree d_i. This also works when the Gram-Schmidt vectors' lengths are not monotonic. Note the maximum number of choices d_i for v_i can be solely bounded by R and $\|\mathbf{b}_i^*\|$. To facilitate a running example discussion, we take $d \approx n^2$ (the exponent 2 is motivated by plugging $n \approx 400$ into the asymptotic $n^{(\ln n)/4}$). The final estimates will be given in a parameterized form and can be adapted to other parameters.

Bounds on coefficients. We will also need to bound $B = \max_i |v_i|$. This will be used to determine the arithmetic discussed in the next paragraph. If a basis satisfies the so-called dual Korkine-Zolotarev condition, then B can be bounded by $n^{1.5}$ [HR14]. However, a dual Korkine-Zolotarev reduction requires to solve the SVP problem. Albrecht, Prokop, Shen and Wallden [APSW22] have bounded each $|v_i| \le R \cdot \|\mathbf{b}_i^\dagger\|$, where $\mathbf{b}_i^\dagger$ denotes the i-th vector in the dual basis of $\mathbf{B}$ (see Lemma 1 of [APSW22]). This gives a useful method to compute the bound in practice, e.g., one can set some radius R and then take the largest $\|\mathbf{b}_i^\dagger\|$ to bound B. This can be done classically before the start of quantum tree backtracking. We can also bound B by Inequality (2). Following our running example, v_n can be bounded by n^2. Working backwards on Inequality (2) and using that $\|\mu_{i,j}\| \le 1/2$, the largest v_i can be bounded by $O(n^4)$ in our example.

Fixed-point arithmetic. To compute the predicate, Inequality (2) involves floating point addition and multiplications of p'-bits. To the best of our knowledge, the quantum circuits for floating point arithmetic are much more expensive than those for integer arithmetic. To deal with the lack of efficient circuits, we will normalize the numbers to fixed-point numbers, with adequate precision.

For example, Haener, Soeken, Roetteler and Svore [HSRS18] have studied floating-point addition and multiplication circuits based on reversible networks that are obtained from a LUT-Based hierarchical reversible logic synthesis approach [SRWDM17]. A hand-optimized circuit is also proposed in the same work, that improves the automatically generated circuits. In general, floating-point circuits require shifting and re-normalization gates, which are expensive to construct in general. For example, the floating-point circuit described in [SRWDM17] for a 64-bit adder has T-count 26348 and T-depth 7224.

The method of [HSRS18] works for general floating-point arithmetic. We observe that the computation in Inequality (2) is often simpler than generic floating-point arithmetic. For example, Step (I) in Inequality (2) involves integer-floating point multiplication $\mu_{i,j} \cdot v_i$. One can use repeated additions $\sum_{\#v_i} \mu_{i,j}$ and thus this boils down to an addition of two floating points. This floating point arithmetic can be emulated by integer arithmetic with the same precision/mantissa, as long as no overflow happens. We can use the quantum circuit for integer addition by Takahashi, Tani and Kunihiro [TTK10]. Their construction has size $7p + O(1)$, with circuit depth $5p + O(1)$ and Toffoli depth $2p + O(1)$.

We will need to set the precision to accommodate sufficient mantissa and to avoid overflow. Starting with the precision p' (say, ≈ 120 in our running-example) for the floating-point mantissa. Step (I) of Inequality (2) increases the bit size by at most $\log B$. Step (II) of Inequality (2) increases the bit size by at most $\log n$. The squaring and multiplication after Step (II) increase the bit size by at most 4 times. In the end, Step (III) has a summation of at most n items. Therefore, one can set the precision $p = 4(p' + \log(B) + \log(n)) + \log(n)$. This is $\approx 4p' + 21 \log n$ for our running example. Thus one can use fixed-point arithmetic such as the integer arithmetic with precision p.

To do this, we can normalize the $\mu_{i,j}$ and $\|\mathbf{b}_i^*\|^2$ before starting the quantum step (e.g., similar normalization on the exponent has been used in the FPLLL library [dt22] for a different context). When the $\mu_{i,j}$'s (and $\|\mathbf{b}_i^*\|^2$) have similar magnitudes among themselves (e.g., similar exponents in the floating-point representation), the normalization will not cancel out any values. We have assumed the $\mu_{i,j}$ and $\|\mathbf{b}_i^*\|^2$ have similar magnitudes (e.g., see Appendix A for experiments on this). If this is not the case, one can use more precision to take care of this. For values $\|\mathbf{b}_i^*\|^2$, the maximal difference on the magnitude heuristically happens on $\|\mathbf{b}_1\|^2/\|\mathbf{b}_n^*\|^2$. This is asymptotically $n^{\ln n/2}$ for an HKZ reduced basis and thus adds $\approx \ln^2 n$ to the precision. The distribution of $\mu_{i,j}$ has been studied in the context of random sampling methods in [Sch03], and assumed to be uniform in $[-1/2, 1/2]$ in those scenarios. If we assume so, an additional precision of $O(\log n)$ with some small hidden constant is sufficient. In experiments, they seem to concentrate towards the boundary for those $i \approx j$ for LLL-reduced bases (see [NS06] for the distribution of $\mu_{i,j}$ in experiments). In Appendix A, we demonstrate further experiments on this. To summarize, one can take $p \approx 4p' + 4 \log B + \log^2 n + 7 \log n \in \Theta(n)$.

For our running example, e.g., $p \approx 10p'$ is sufficient for our targeted dimension. The value 10 here is chosen for convenience and can be substituted by a practical value given the input, which is likely to be much smaller.

4.5   Implementation of the Predicate

The circuit of predicate P is given in Fig. 5a which consists of several components as plotted in Fig. 5b. We start with the description of the registers. First, the inputs of the predicate are superpositions $|l\rangle$ and $|v_i\rangle$. We need two input registers: for $|l\rangle$ this is $\log n$ bits, and for $|v_i\rangle$ this is $n \log d$ bits. We also need to access classic data $\mu_{i,j}$ and $\|\mathbf{b}_i^*\|^2$, and this can be done by using universal quantum gate set. We need an addressing register of $\log n$ bits and an output register of $(n^2/2+n) \cdot p$ bits. In total, the input size is $\log n + n \log d + (n^2/2+n) \cdot p$

bits. We also need $\text{poly}(n)$ ancillary qubits for intermediate results that we will omit in the discussion. The circuit starts by looking at the input $|l\rangle$ and decides the routing to the arithmetic components. We will thus focus on the arithmetic gates which are the dominating components.

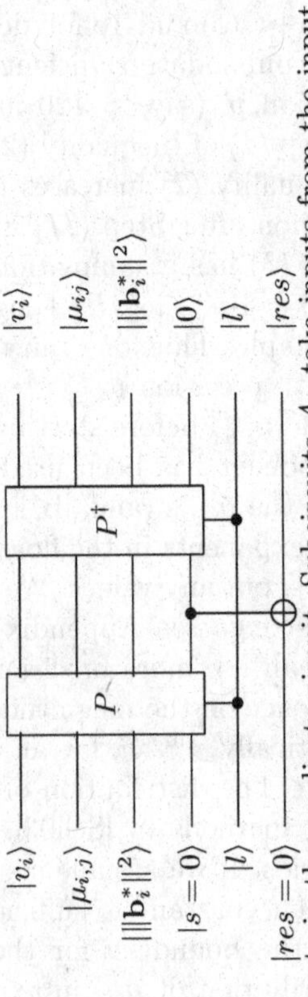

(a) Overall predicate circuit. Predicate P returns $|s\rangle$ that controls return value $|res\rangle$. Input $|l\rangle$ controls the routing to the predicate components given in Figure 5b. We uncompute P and reset the registers.

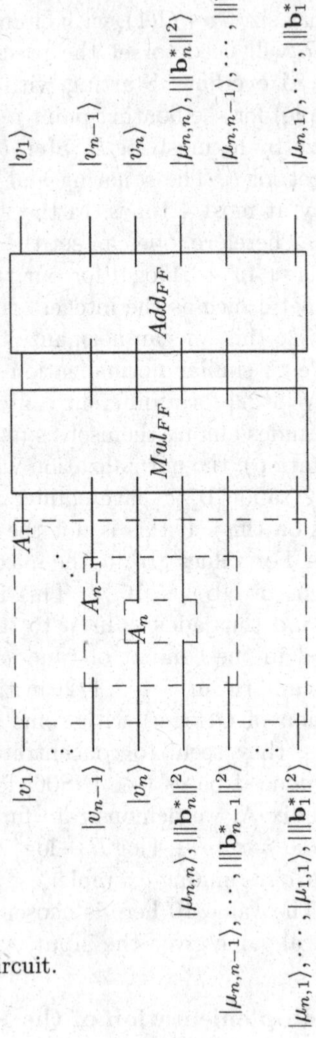

(b) Components in the predicate circuit. Subcircuits A_k take inputs from the input wires which computes all terms $\sum_{i\geq j}\mu_{i,j}v_i$ for $j \geq k$. The Mul_{FF} gate computes the squaring and multiplication in $(\sum_{i\geq j}\mu_{i,j}v_i)^2 \cdot \|\mathbf{b}_j^*\|^2$. The Add_{FF} gate computes the final summation in Step (III) of Inequality (2) using a binary tree of adders.

Fig. 5. Predicate circuit.

For fixed l and v_i, the main task is to compute the left-hand side of Inequality (2). We describe the implementation and resource estimate. In Fig. 5b, each of the boxes A_{n-l+1} denotes a subcircuit, which computes the terms $s_j := \left(\sum_{i \geq j} \mu_{i,j} v_i \right)$ for $j \geq n - l + 1$. For a fixed input l, there are l such terms s_j to compute in the circuit A_{n-l+1}. The computation of s_j, for different indices j, can be parallelized by making at most n copies of each $|v_i\rangle$ (observe that the same v_i's are used at most n times in different indices j). One can also note that $A_k \subset A_{k-1}$ for $k \in (1,n]$ as A_k computes all the terms required by A_{k-1} except s_{k-1}. Thus A_l can be regarded as a subcircuit of A_{l-1}. The predicate circuit starts by looking at the input $|l\rangle$ and deciding the routing to the required A_{n-l+1}. We discuss the computation in A_{n-l+1}.

Step 1. First, the circuit computes each of the terms $\mu_{i,j} \cdot v_i$ (for fixed i, j), one can use repeated addition of at most B numbers at precision p. A serial implementation requires a depth $O(B)$ of adders. One can parallelize this using a binary tree of adders. This has a depth of $\lceil \log B \rceil$ in terms of adders. Using [TTK10], each circuit (for computing a single $\mu_{i,j} v_i$) has a Toffoli depth of $\approx (2p + O(1)) \log(B)$ and circuit size bounded by about $(7p + O(1))B$.

Step 2. Within the computation of s_j for a fixed j, the computation of at most n terms $\mu_{i,j} v_i$ for different i can be parallelized. Thus the circuit has about the same depth as in Step 1, but with an increment of n times on the size.

Step 3. To compute $s_j = \left(\sum_{i \geq j} \mu_{i,j} v_i \right)$ for a single j, one can again use a binary tree of adders. This adds the Toffoli depth by $(2p + O(1)) \log(n)$ and circuit size by $(7p + O(1))n$.

Step 4. As discussed above, the computation of s_j for different indices j can be made in parallel by making at most n copies of the input. This process requires a poly number of the CNOT gates which we will omit. Therefore the circuit depth remains similar and size increases by at most n times. The circuit discussed so far has Toffoli depth of $2p(\log B + \log n) + O(\log B) + O(\log n)$ and size about $n^2(7p(B+1) + O(B) + O(1))$. This completes all the computation in A_{n-l+1} for the input l.

Step 5. Given all s_j's for $j \geq n - l + 1$, we need to compute $\sum_{j \geq n-l+1} s_j^2 \|\mathbf{b}_j^*\|^2$. This involves squaring, multiplication and a final summation.

– The squaring and multiplication are done by the subcircuit Mul_{FF} in Fig. 5a. Computing $s_j^2 \|\mathbf{b}_j^*\|^2$ for different j can be done in parallel. For integer squaring/multiplication, we use the quantum circuit designed by Parent, Roetteler and Mosca [PRM17]. This is a Karatsuba based circuit which fits our input size. Their construction has (Toffoli) size and depth bounded by $98p^{1.585}$ and $p^{1.158}$ respectively.

– The final summation, over $s_j^2 \|\mathbf{b}_j^*\|^2$ for all $j \geq n-l+1$, can be implemented by a binary tree of adders, which has a Toffoli depth $(2p+O(1)) \log n$ and circuit size $(7p + O(1))n$.

Step 6. There is a final comparison to decide the returned value, which we ignore.

Taking into account the $P^\dagger$, the predicate circuit has Toffoli depth about $4p(\log B + 2\log n + p^{0.158}) + O(\log B) + O(\log n)$. For usual parameters, $O(\log n)$ subsumes in $O(\log B)$ where the hidden constants are small integers. Thus it becomes $4p(\log B + 2\log n + p^{0.158}) + O(\log B)$. The precision $p \approx 1.2n + 4\log B + \log^2 n + 7\log n \in \Theta(n)$ for most inputs of interest. If the bound B is large, the term $(4p\log B)$ (e.g., this term corresponds to the repeated addition of $O(B)$ terms) dominates the running-time. If the bound $B = \mathrm{poly}(n)$, the multiplication $4p^{1.158}$ could dominate the running-time. The Toffoli size is bounded by $14pn^2 B + n^2 O(B) + 14n^2 p + O(n^2)$. Note the constant in $O(B)$ is small, but the constant in $O(n^2)$ subsumes terms like $196p^{1.585}$.

We discuss several usual cases that are relevant in either theory or practice, depending on the relation of B with respect to dimension.

(i) In an LLL-reduced basis, $B \approx 2^n$ which will dominate the size. The Toffoli depth is about $4p(n + O(n^{0.158}))$ and size is about $(14p + O(1))n^2 2^n$.

(ii) For an HKZ-reduced basis, $B \approx n^{\ln n}$. The Toffoli depth is bounded by $4p(p^{0.158} + O(\log^2 n))$ and size is about $(14p + O(1))n^2 n^{\ln n}$.

(iii) In our running-example, we took $B \approx n^4$ and $p = 3n$, the Toffoli depth and size have order $12n(6\log n + (3n)^{0.158}) + O(\log n)$ and $42n^7 + O(n^6))$.

(iv) In practice, for cryptographic size lattices, it is reasonable to have $B \approx n^2$. The Toffoli depth and size have order $4p(4\log n + p^{0.158}) + O(\log n)$ and $14pn^4 + O(n^4)$.

Finally, we note this is a single evaluation of the predicate. As discussed in the "Simplified Model" paragraph of Subsect. 4.4, one needs to iteratively compute the values, which scales the depth/size by a factor of at most n.

4.6   Summary of Resource Estimates

We summarize the resource estimates developed from the previous subsections. In a single controlled-$R_B R_A$ operator, there are two expensive operations. First, the predicate is called in Steps 1 and 5, where the latter can be parallelized. One can scale the depth by 2 and size by $d + 1$. In addition, the uncomputation in Steps 7 and 8 scale the depth by another factor of 2 and size by $d + 1$. Second, the operation $I - 2|\phi_{1,S}\rangle\langle\phi_{1,S}|$ is performed on $|a\rangle$ in Step 6. We factor out the Toffoli gates and give the resource estimates in terms of T size and depth. We use the Toffoli gate as implemented in [Sel13] where Toffoli uses four T-gates and has a T-depth of one. Overall, the circuit has T-depth bounded by

$$16np(\log B + 2\log n + p^{0.158}) + O(n\log B) + 8d^2\log(d/\epsilon) + 4d^2\log d + O(d^2)$$

and T-size bounded by

$$8(d+1)(14pn^2(B+1) + O(n^2 B)) + 8d^2\log(d/\epsilon) + 16d^2\log d + O(d^2)$$

In practice, for cryptographic size lattices where $n \gtrsim 400$, it is reasonable to expect $d \approx n, B \approx n^2$ and $p \le 3n$ (see Appendix A for experiments on this), where the T-depth and size have order $48n^{2.158} + 8n^2 \log(n/\epsilon) + O(n^2 \log n)$ and $336n^6 + 8n^2 \log(n/\epsilon) + O(n^5)$.

Overall, we aim for a constant failure probability of $\delta \approx 0.1$. The number of controlled-U operators applied can be bounded by about $32\sqrt{\mathcal{T}n}$ (see [CKM19]). We factor out the total error into ϵ by a scalar of $\sqrt{\mathcal{T}n}$ and the T-depth and size have order $O(\sqrt{\mathcal{T}n}\,(n^{2.158} + n^2 \log \mathcal{T}))$ and $O(\sqrt{\mathcal{T}n}\,(n^6 + n^2 \log(\mathcal{T})))$.

One can also apply the resource estimates on the transformed binary tree, following the method proposed in [ANS18]. In such a case, one should also modify the tree height from n to $n \log d$ in the analysis, as well as investigate the overheads brought in due to the transformation. We leave this as future work.

A   Experiments Supporting the Heuristics

In this section, we provide some additional experiments to verify some heuristics we have made in the previous section for the resource estimates. These heuristic arguments are not strictly required for the quantum resource estimates as the estimates were presented in parameterized form (in terms of tree depth, degree, bound for v_i and precision). However, readers may find them useful for a more precise estimate given practical parameters of cryptographic relevance.

A.1   Experiments on the Bounds for d and B

First, Subsect. 4.4 uses a running example where $d \approx n^2, B \approx n^4$. It was also used that: "in practice, for cryptographic size lattices, it is reasonable to expect $d \approx n, B \approx n^2, p \approx 3n$" for a well-preprocessed basis. Notice that such heuristics are not asymptotically correct, even on a HKZ reduced basis. However, we are mostly interested in practical parameters for cryptographic size lattices. We conduct some experiments to verify that it is reasonable to bound $d \approx n$ and $B \approx n^2$.

In the first experiment (Fig. 6), we took the top-25 solved SVP problems from the SVP Challenge project[2], and checked the bound for B with respect to the actually found short vector $\mathbf{v}$ as well as the bound for d (given a preprocessed basis). The dimensions of these solved SVP problems are $\{140 - 158, 160, 162, 170, 176, 178, 180\}$. In case there are multiple solutions, we take the solution $\mathbf{v}$ of the smallest norm. For each input basis of dimension n, we preprocess the basis by BKZ$-(\lceil \frac{n}{3} \rceil)$ and then compute the coefficients of $\mathbf{v}$ with respect to the reduced basis $\{\mathbf{b}_i\}_i$. The BKZ preprocessing is conducted using FPYLLL[3] with early abort and the default extreme pruning profile.

In the end, we compute two values: the maximum size of v_i's as in $\mathbf{v} = \sum_i v_i \mathbf{b}_i$ and $\|\mathbf{v}\|/\|b_n^*\|$. The first value can be used as B and the second value can be used to bound d (assuming a non-decreasing Gram–Schmidt length profile). We also scale the first value by $1/n^2$ and the second value by $1/n$ to give an idea

---

[2] https://www.latticechallenge.org/svp-challenge/.
[3] https://github.com/fplll/fpylll.

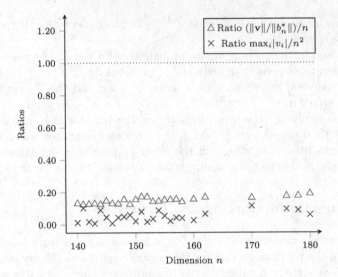

Fig. 6. Bounds d and B, based on solved SVP Challenges.

about B/n^2 and d/n (other scaling factors could be chosen). The results are plotted in Fig. 6, where the x-axis denotes the input dimension and the y-axis denotes the two ratios (red/blue). One can observe that, in these experiments, the ratios $\max_i |v_i|/n^2$ and $(\|\mathbf{v}\|/\|b_n^*\|)/n$ are always smaller than 0.2. Thus it seems reasonable to assume the bounds $d \approx n, B \approx n^2$.

In the second experiment (Fig. 7), we further check the bound for B in both experiments and simulations, using the Gaussian heuristic. In the simulation, we generate lattices of rank $n = \{60, 68, 76, \cdots, 500\}$ using the SVP Challenge generator. Each lattice is preprocessed by $\mathrm{BKZ}-(\lceil \frac{n}{3} \rceil)$ in simulation. In the end of simulation, the ratio $(GH/\|b_n^*\|)/n$ is recorded, where GH denotes the expected length of shortest vectors indicated by the Gaussian heuristic. It seems that the ratio follows a slightly quadratic function. Fitting using NumPy[4] gives a curve of $1.8886 \times 10^{-6} \cdot n^2 + 0.0003 \cdot n + 0.0454$ which is plotted in Fig. 7. One can see this grows very slowly with n. Furthermore, we also conduct BKZ experiments: we generate lattices of rank $n = \{60, 64, 68, \cdots, 192\}$ using the SVP Challenge generator. For each rank, we generate 32 random instances with different seeds. The lattices are then preprocessed by $\mathrm{BKZ}-(\lceil \frac{n}{3} \rceil)$. The BKZ preprocessing is conducted using FPYLLL with early abort and the default extreme pruning profile. In the end, the average ratio $(GH/\|b_n^*\|)/n$ is recorded. One can see the experimental results follow very closely with the simulated results (but slightly larger, possibly due to the use of early abort in experiments). One can also notice these bases are weakly reduced, e.g., compared to a HKZ reduced basis. Using heavier preprocessing will lead to even smaller values on bounds B and d. We leave it for future work to develop better practical bounds.

---

[4] https://numpy.org/.

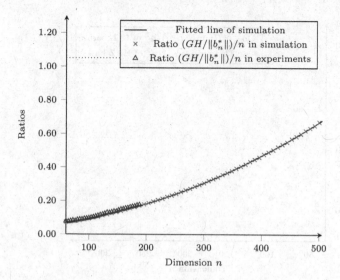

Fig. 7. Bound B, based on BKZ experiments and simulations.

A.2 Experiments on the Bounds for $\mu_{i,j}$

Subsection 4.4 also assumed that the $\mu_{i,j}$'s have similar magnitude (see the "Precision requirement" paragraph) in a somewhat reduced basis, so one does not need to increase the precision too much to take care of this.

The distribution of $\mu_{i,j}$ has been studied in [Sch03] in the context of random sampling methods, which is assumed to be uniform in $[-1/2, 1/2]$. By such assumption, the maximal ratio on the magnitude of various $\mu_{i,j}$ is roughly $O(n^2)$. Thus an additional precision of $O(\log n)$ with some small hidden constant is sufficient. In experiments, they seem to concentrated towards the boundary for those $i \approx j$ for LLL-reduced bases, e.g., see [NS06] for the distribution of $\mu_{i,j}$ in experiments. We conduct further experiments: we generate random q-ary lattices using the "IntegerMatrix.random" function in FPYLLL whose dimensions range from $n = 140$ to 320 with a stepping of 2. We process the basis with LLL. In the end, we compute the ratio $(1/ \min_{i,j} \mu_{i,j})/n^2$ for $i > j$. For each dimension n, we generated and ran 32 random instances, and calculated the average ratios. We also verified the values of $\mu_{i,j}$ using SageMath's "Matrix" object[5] with rational entries to calculate the Gram-Schmidt coefficient for very high precision (e.g., to avoid potential overflow in floating-point numbers). The results are plotted in Fig. 8, where the x-axis denotes the input dimension and the y-axis records the logarithm (base 2) of the averaged ratios. One can observe that the logarithm of the averaged ratios $\log_2((1/ \min_{i,j} \mu_{i,j})/n^2)$ is bounded from above by some small constant (≈ 6.1 in this experiment).

Heuristically, the variance in the size of $\mu_{i,j}$ can grow for more reduced bases. Thus we conduct further experiments to check the magnitude of the $\mu_{i,j}$'s for

---

[5] https://www.sagemath.org/.

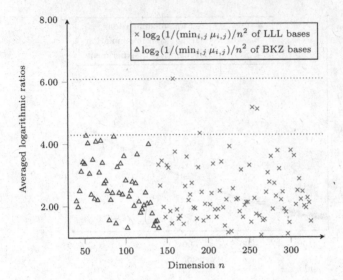

Fig. 8. Experiments on the bound for $\mu_{i,j}$ in LLL/BKZ reduced basis.

reduced bases preprocessed by larger blocksizes. We generate random q-ary lattices ranging from $n = 40$ to 140 and preprocess the basis with BKZ-$\frac{n}{2}$. In the end, we compute the same ratio $(1/\min_{i,j} \mu_{i,j})/n^2$. For each dimension n, we generated and ran 128 random instances, and calculated the average ratios. The results are also given in Fig. 8. One can observe that the logarithm of the averaged ratios is also bounded from above by some small constant (≈ 4.3 in this experiment). Thus it seems reasonable to assume an additional precision of $O(\log n)$ with some small hidden constant in the fixed precision arithmetic.

B   Constraint Satisfaction Problem and Tree Backtracking

A common use of tree backtracking is for solving the so-called constraint satisfaction problem (CSP). This is also the context for which the original algorithm of Montanaro [Mon18] focused on. We give some background on this.

In CSP, we assign values from a fixed list to a fixed number of variables, thus using a tree structure is a natural way to go through every possible answer. For example the boolean satisfiability problem, or SAT, gives us n variables we can assign as either true or false. The question is, given a series of logic statements, can we make the final result true? As a concrete example for $n = 3$, we consider statement $(x_1 \vee x_2) \wedge (\neg x_2 \vee x_3)$. To solve this, one can construct a full tree with $n + 1$ layers, each node having 2 children (denoting, true or false), which would allow us to see all possible answers and see if we have a solution. The root corresponds to having no assigned values, with layer i in the full tree assigning true or false to variable x_i, as seen in Fig. 9.

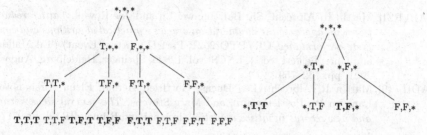

Fig. 9. Full tree (left) and backtracking tree (right) to solve $(x_1 \vee x_2) \wedge (\neg x_2 \vee x_3)$.

Continuing to explore the tree, we can see that if we assign false to both x_1 and x_2, it is not sensible to continue down this path in the tree. We would prefer to cut our losses, go back a bit and continue to the next possibility. This strategy is called backtracking, see also Fig. 9. Instead of only checking at the leaves whether our assignment is correct, at each node we check some predicate function, that checks the partial assignment and returns true, false or indeterminate to see how our current assignment is doing. If this predicate returns false, we stop the path there and try to make different choices, if it returns indeterminate or true we continue. Furthermore, assigning a value to x_2 first will solve either $(x_1 \vee x_2)$ or $(\neg x_2 \vee x_3)$. To decide what to assign, we need some heuristic to decide what is the best variable to look at next, in this case looking at the variable that appears in the most parts that are not true yet.

Lattice enumeration constructs such trees as well, which we will denote as "enumeration trees". Inequality (1) suggests that, at the l-th ($l \geq 2$) level of the tree, $v_{n+2-l}, \ldots, v_n$ are already determined. To go down the tree, it remains to bound and select a value (if it exists) for v_{n+1-l} according to Inequality (1). We let d denote the maximal number of choices of v_i. Thus this can be represented by a tree with up to n layers and degree d.

References

[ABB+17] Erdem Alkim, Nina Bindel, Johannes A. Buchmann, Özgür Dagdelen, Edward Eaton, Gus Gutoski, Juliane Krämer, and Filip Pawlega, *Revisiting TESLA in the quantum random oracle model*, Post-Quantum Cryptography - 8th International Workshop, PQCrypto 2017 (Tanja Lange and Tsuyoshi Takagi, eds.), Springer, Heidelberg, 2017, pp. 143–162

[ABD+21] Roberto Avanzi, Joppe Bos, Léo Ducas, Eike Kiltz, Tancrède Lepoint, Vadim Lyubashevsky, John M. Schanck, Peter Schwabe, Gregor Seiler, and Damien Stehlé, *CRYSTALS-KYBER: algorithm specifications and supporting documentation*, 2021, Submission to the NIST's post-quantum cryptography standardization process

[ABF+20] Martin R. Albrecht, Shi Bai, Pierre-Alain Fouque, Paul Kirchner, Damien Stehlé, and Weiqiang Wen, *Faster enumeration-based lattice reduction: Root hermite factor $k^{1/(2k)}$ time $k^{k/8+o(k)}$*, CRYPTO 2020, Part II (Daniele Micciancio and Thomas Ristenpart, eds.), LNCS, vol. 12171, Springer, Heidelberg, August 2020, pp. 186–212

[ABLR21] Martin R. Albrecht, Shi Bai, Jianwei Li, and Joe Rowell, *Lattice reduction with approximate enumeration oracles - practical algorithms and concrete performance*, CRYPTO 2021, Part II (Virtual Event) (Tal Malkin and Chris Peikert, eds.), LNCS, vol. 12826, Springer, Heidelberg, August 2021, pp. 732–759

[ADH+19] Martin R. Albrecht, Léo Ducas, Gottfried Herold, Elena Kirshanova, Eamonn W. Postlethwaite, and Marc Stevens, *The general sieve kernel and new records in lattice reduction*, in Ishai and Rijmen [IR19], pp. 717–746

[ADPS16] Erdem Alkim, Léo Ducas, Thomas Pöppelmann, and Peter Schwabe, *Post-quantum key exchange: A New Hope*, Proceedings of the 25th USENIX Conference on Security Symposium (USA), SEC'16, USENIX Association, 2016, p. 327–343

[AGPS20] Martin R. Albrecht, Vlad Gheorghiu, Eamonn W. Postlethwaite, and John M. Schanck, *Estimating quantum speedups for lattice sieves*, ASIACRYPT 2020, Part II (Shiho Moriai and Huaxiong Wang, eds.), LNCS, vol. 12492, Springer, Heidelberg, December 2020, pp. 583–613

[Ajt96] Miklós Ajtai, *Generating hard instances of lattice problems (extended abstract)*, in STOC 1996 [STO96], pp. 99–108

[AK17] Andris Ambainis and Martins Kokainis, *Quantum algorithm for tree size estimation, with applications to backtracking and 2-player games*, Proceedings of the 49th Annual ACM SIGACT Symposium on Theory of Computing (New York, NY, USA), STOC 2017, Association for Computing Machinery, 2017, p. 989–1002

[AKS01] Miklós Ajtai, Ravi Kumar, and D. Sivakumar, *A sieve algorithm for the shortest lattice vector problem*, 33rd ACM STOC, ACM Press, July 2001, pp. 601–610

[AMMR13] Matthew Amy, Dmitri Maslov, Michele Mosca, and Martin Roetteler, *A meet-in-the-middle algorithm for fast synthesis of depth-optimal quantum circuits*, Trans. Comp.-Aided Des. Integ. Cir. Sys. **32** (2013), no. 6, 818–830

[ANS18] Yoshinori Aono, Phong Q. Nguyen, and Yixin Shen, *Quantum lattice enumeration and tweaking discrete pruning*, ASIACRYPT 2018, Part I (Thomas Peyrin and Steven Galbraith, eds.), LNCS, vol. 11272, Springer, Heidelberg, December 2018, pp. 405–434

[APSW22] Martin R. Albrecht, Miloš Prokop, Yixin Shen, and Petros Wallden, *Variational quantum solutions to the shortest vector problem*, Cryptology ePrint Archive, Paper 2022/233, 2022, https://eprint.iacr.org/2022/233

[AWHT16] Yoshinori Aono, Yuntao Wang, Takuya Hayashi, and Tsuyoshi Takagi, *Improved progressive BKZ algorithms and their precise cost estimation by sharp simulator*, in Fischlin and Coron [FC16], pp. 789–819

[BBVL21] Gustavo Banegas, Daniel J. Bernstein, Iggy Van Hoof, and Tanja Lange, *Concrete quantum cryptanalysis of binary elliptic curves*, IACR TCHES **2021** (2021), no. 1, 451–472, https://tches.iacr.org/index.php/TCHES/article/view/8741

[BCSS23] Xavier Bonnetain, André Chailloux, André Schrottenloher, and Yixin Shen, *Finding many collisions via reusable quantum walks: Application to lattice sieving*, EUROCRYPT 2023, Part V (Carmit Hazay and Martijn Stam, eds.), LNCS, vol. 14008, Springer, Heidelberg, April 2023, pp. 221–251

[BDGL16] Anja Becker, Léo Ducas, Nicolas Gama, and Thijs Laarhoven, *New directions in nearest neighbor searching with applications to lattice sieving*, 27th SODA (Robert Krauthgamer, ed.), ACM-SIAM, January 2016, pp. 10–24

[BDK+21] Shi Bai, Léo Ducas, Eike Kiltz, Tancrède Lepoint, Vadim Lyubashevsky, Peter Schwabe, Gregor Seiler, and Damien Stehlé, *CRYSTALS-Dilithium: algorithm specifications and supporting documentation*, 2021, Submission to the NIST's post-quantum cryptography standardization process

[Bel13] Aleksandrs Belovs, *Quantum walks and electric networks*, arXiv e-prints (2013), arXiv:1302.3143

[BL21] Daniel J. Bernstein and Tanja Lange, *Non-randomness of S-unit lattices*, Cryptology ePrint Archive, Report 2021/1428, 2021, https://eprint.iacr.org/2021/1428

[BLMP19] Daniel J. Bernstein, Tanja Lange, Chloe Martindale, and Lorenz Panny, *Quantum circuits for the CSIDH: Optimizing quantum evaluation of isogenies*, in Ishai and Rijmen [IR19], pp. 409–441

[BNS19] Xavier Bonnetain, María Naya-Plasencia, and André Schrottenloher, *Quantum security analysis of AES*, IACR Trans. Symm. Cryptol. **2019** (2019), no. 2, 55–93

[BP05] Joan Boyar and René Peralta, *The exact multiplicative complexity of the hamming weight function*, Electron. Colloquium Comput. Complex. **TR05-049** (2005)

[BS20] Xavier Bonnetain and André Schrottenloher, *Quantum security analysis of CSIDH*, in Canteaut and Ishai [CI20], pp. 493–522

[CEMM98] Richard Cleve, Artur Ekert, Chiara Macchiavello, and Michele Mosca, *Quantum algorithms revisited*, Proceedings of the Royal Society of London. Series A: Mathematical, Physical and Engineering Sciences **454** (1998), no. 1969, 339–354

[CI20] Anne Canteaut and Yuval Ishai (eds.), *Eurocrypt 2020, part ii*, LNCS, vol. 12106, Springer, Heidelberg, May 2020

[CKM19] Earl Campbell, Ankur Khurana, and Ashley Montanaro, *Applying quantum algorithms to constraint satisfaction problems*, Quantum **3** (2019), 167

[CL21] André Chailloux and Johanna Loyer, *Lattice sieving via quantum random walks*, ASIACRYPT 2021, Part IV (Mehdi Tibouchi and Huaxiong Wang, eds.), LNCS, vol. 13093, Springer, Heidelberg, December 2021, pp. 63–91

[CN11] Yuanmi Chen and Phong Q. Nguyen, *BKZ 2.0: Better lattice security estimates*, ASIACRYPT 2011 (Dong Hoon Lee and Xiaoyun Wang, eds.), LNCS, vol. 7073, Springer, Heidelberg, December 2011, pp. 1–20

[DSvW21a] Léo Ducas, Marc Stevens, and Wessel van Woerden, *Advanced lattice sieving on gpus, with tensor cores*, Advances in Cryptology – EUROCRYPT 2021: 40th Annual International Conference on the Theory and Applications of Cryptographic Techniques, Zagreb, Croatia, October 17–21, 2021, Proceedings, Part II (Berlin, Heidelberg), Springer-Verlag, 2021, p. 249–279

[DSvW21b] Léo Ducas, Marc Stevens, and Wessel P. J. van Woerden, *Advanced lattice sieving on GPUs, with tensor cores*, EUROCRYPT 2021, Part II (Anne Canteaut and François-Xavier Standaert, eds.), LNCS, vol. 12697, Springer, Heidelberg, October 2021, pp. 249–279

[dt22] The FPLLL development team, *fplll, a lattice reduction library, Version: 5.4.2*, Available at https://github.com/fplll/fplll, 2022

[EK09] Bryan Eastin and Emanuel Knill, *Restrictions on transversal encoded quantum gate sets*, Phys. Rev. Lett. **102** (2009), 110502

[FC16] Marc Fischlin and Jean-Sébastien Coron (eds.), *Eurocrypt 2016, part i*, LNCS, vol. 9665, Springer, Heidelberg, May 2016

[FHK+20] Pierre-Alain Fouque, Jeffrey Hoffstein, Paul Kirchner, Vadim Lyubashevsky, Thomas Pornin, Thomas Prest, Thomas Ricosset, Gregor Seiler, William Whyte, and Zhenfei Zhang, *Falcon: Fast-Fourier Lattice-based Compact Signatures over NTRU. specification v1.2*, 2020, Submission to the NIST's post-quantum cryptography standardization process

[FP85] Ulrich Fincke and Michael Pohst, *Improved methods for calculating vectors of short length in a lattice, including a complexity analysis*, Mathematics of Computation **44** (1985), no. 170, 463–463

[Gid15] Craig Gidney, *Constructing large increment gates*, 2015, Last retrieved 18 Oct 2022 at https://algassert.com/circuits/2015/06/12/Constructing-Large-Increment-Gates.html

[GLRS16] Markus Grassl, Brandon Langenberg, Martin Roetteler, and Rainer Steinwandt, *Applying grover's algorithm to AES: Quantum resource estimates*, Post-Quantum Cryptography - 7th International Workshop, PQCrypto 2016 (Tsuyoshi Takagi, ed.), Springer, Heidelberg, 2016, pp. 29–43

[GNR10] Nicolas Gama, Phong Q. Nguyen, and Oded Regev, *Lattice enumeration using extreme pruning*, EUROCRYPT 2010 (Henri Gilbert, ed.), LNCS, vol. 6110, Springer, Heidelberg, May / June 2010, pp. 257–278

[Gro96] Lov K. Grover, *A fast quantum mechanical algorithm for database search*, in STOC 1996 [STO96], pp. 212–219

[HPS11] Guillaume Hanrot, Xavier Pujol, and Damien Stehlé, *Analyzing blockwise lattice algorithms using dynamical systems*, CRYPTO 2011 (Phillip Rogaway, ed.), LNCS, vol. 6841, Springer, Heidelberg, August 2011, pp. 447–464

[HR14] Ishay Haviv and Oded Regev, *On the lattice isomorphism problem*, 25th SODA (Chandra Chekuri, ed.), ACM-SIAM, January 2014, pp. 391–404

[HS07] Guillaume Hanrot and Damien Stehlé, *Improved analysis of kannan's shortest lattice vector algorithm*, CRYPTO 2007 (Alfred Menezes, ed.), LNCS, vol. 4622, Springer, Heidelberg, August 2007, pp. 170–186

[HSRS18] Thomas Haener, Mathias Soeken, Martin Roetteler, and Krysta M. Svore, *Quantum circuits for floating-point arithmetic*, Reversible Computation (Cham) (Jarkko Kari and Irek Ulidowski, eds.), Springer International Publishing, 2018, pp. 162–174

[IR19] Yuval Ishai and Vincent Rijmen (eds.), *Eurocrypt 2019, part ii*, LNCS, vol. 11477, Springer, Heidelberg, May 2019

[JNRV20] Samuel Jaques, Michael Naehrig, Martin Roetteler, and Fernando Virdia, *Implementing grover oracles for quantum key search on AES and LowMC*, in Canteaut and Ishai [CI20], pp. 280–310

[Jon13] Cody Jones, *Low-overhead constructions for the fault-tolerant toffoli gate*, Phys. Rev. A **87** (2013), 022328

[Kan83] Ravi Kannan, *Improved algorithms for integer programming and related lattice problems*, 15th ACM STOC, ACM Press, April 1983, pp. 193–206

[Kit96] Alexei Y. Kitaev, *Quantum measurements and the abelian stabilizer problem*, Electron. Colloquium Comput. Complex. **TR96-003** (1996)

[Laa15] Thijs Laarhoven, *Search problems in cryptography*, Ph.D. thesis, Eindhoven University of Technology, 2015

[LLJL82] Arjen K. Lenstra, Hendrik W. Lenstra Jr., and László Lovász, *Factoring polynomials with rational coefficients*, Mathematische Annalen **261** (1982), 515–534

[Mon18] Ashley Montanaro, *Quantum-walk speedup of backtracking algorithms*, Theory of Computing **14** (2018), no. 15, 1–24

[MR04] Daniele Micciancio and Oded Regev, *Worst-case to average-case reductions based on Gaussian measures*, 45th FOCS, IEEE Computer Society Press, October 2004, pp. 372–381

[MR20] Simon Martiel and Maxime Remaud, *Practical implementation of a quantum backtracking algorithm*, SOFSEM 2020: Theory and Practice of Computer Science (Cham) (Alexander Chatzigeorgiou, Riccardo Dondi, Herodotos Herodotou, Christos Kapoutsis, Yannis Manolopoulos, George A. Papadopoulos, and Florian Sikora, eds.), Springer International Publishing, 2020, pp. 597–606

[MRBAG16] Jarrod R McClean, Jonathan Romero, Ryan Babbush, and Alán Aspuru-Guzik, *The theory of variational hybrid quantum-classical algorithms*, New Journal of Physics **18** (2016), no. 2, 023023

[MV10a] Daniele Micciancio and Panagiotis Voulgaris, *A deterministic single exponential time algorithm for most lattice problems based on voronoi cell computations*, 42nd ACM STOC (Leonard J. Schulman, ed.), ACM Press, June 2010, pp. 351–358

[MV10b] ——, *Faster exponential time algorithms for the shortest vector problem*, 21st SODA (Moses Charika, ed.), ACM-SIAM, January 2010, pp. 1468–1480

[MW16] Daniele Micciancio and Michael Walter, *Practical, predictable lattice basis reduction*, in Fischlin and Coron [FC16], pp. 820–849

[NC11] Michael A. Nielsen and Isaac L. Chuang, *Quantum computation and quantum information: 10th anniversary edition*, Cambridge University Press, 2011

[NIS16] NIST, *National institute of standards and technology's Post-Quantum Cryptography Standardization*, 2016, https://csrc.nist.gov/projects/post-quantum-cryptography

[NS05] Phong Q. Nguyen and Damien Stehlé, *Floating-point LLL revisited*, EUROCRYPT 2005 (Ronald Cramer, ed.), LNCS, vol. 3494, Springer, Heidelberg, May 2005, pp. 215–233

[NS06] Phong Q. Nguyen and Damien Stehlé, *LLL on the average*, Proceedings of the 7th International Conference on Algorithmic Number Theory (Berlin, Heidelberg), ANTS'06, Springer-Verlag, 2006, p. 238–256

[NV08] P. Q. Nguyen and T. Vidick, *Sieve algorithms for the shortest vector problem are practical*, Journal of Mathematical Cryptology **2** (2008), no. 2

[PLP16] Rafael Pino, Vadim Lyubashevsky, and David Pointcheval, *The whole is less than the sum of its parts: Constructing more efficient lattice-based akes*, Proceedings of the 10th International Conference on Security and Cryptography for Networks - Volume 9841 (Berlin, Heidelberg), Springer-Verlag, 2016, p. 273–291

[PMS+14] Alberto Peruzzo, Jarrod McClean, Peter Shadbolt, Man-Hong Yung, Xiao-Qi Zhou, Peter J. Love, Alán Aspuru-Guzik, and Jeremy L. O'Brien, *A variational eigenvalue solver on a photonic quantum processor*, Nature Communications **5** (2014), no. 1

[PRM17] Alex Parent, Martin Roetteler, and Michele Mosca, *Improved reversible and quantum circuits for karatsuba-based integer multiplication*, 12th Conference on the Theory of Quantum Computation, Communication and Cryptography, TQC 2017, June 14-16, 2017, Paris, France (Mark M. Wilde, ed.), LIPIcs, vol. 73, Schloss Dagstuhl - Leibniz-Zentrum für Informatik, 2017, pp. 7:1–7:15

[PS08] Xavier Pujol and Damien Stehlé, *Rigorous and efficient short lattice vectors enumeration*, ASIACRYPT 2008 (Josef Pieprzyk, ed.), LNCS, vol. 5350, Springer, Heidelberg, December 2008, pp. 390–405

[Reg05] Oded Regev, *On lattices, learning with errors, random linear codes, and cryptography*, 37th ACM STOC (Harold N. Gabow and Ronald Fagin, eds.), ACM Press, May 2005, pp. 84–93

[RNSL17] Martin Roetteler, Michael Naehrig, Krysta M. Svore, and Kristin E. Lauter, *Quantum resource estimates for computing elliptic curve discrete logarithms*, ASIACRYPT 2017, Part II (Tsuyoshi Takagi and Thomas Peyrin, eds.), LNCS, vol. 10625, Springer, Heidelberg, December 2017, pp. 241–270

[RS16] Neil J Ross and Peter Selinger, *Optimal ancilla-free Clifford+ T approximation of z-rotations.*, Quantum Inf. Comput. **16** (2016), no. 11&12, 901–953

[Sch87] Claus-Peter Schnorr, *A hierarchy of polynomial time lattice basis reduction algorithms*, Theoretical Computer Science **53** (1987), no. 2-3, 201–224

[Sch03] Claus-Peter Schnorr, *Lattice reduction by random sampling and birthday methods*, STACS, Springer, 2003, pp. 145–156

[SE94] Claus-Peter Schnorr and Michael Euchner, *Lattice basis reduction : improved practical algorithms and solving subset sum problems*, Mathematics of Programming **66** (1994), 181–199

[Sel13] Peter Selinger, *Quantum circuits o t-depth one*, Phys. Rev. A **87** (2013), 042302

[Sel15] Peter Selinger, *Efficient clifford+t approximation of single-qubit operators*, Quantum Inf. Comput. **15** (2015), no. 1-2, 159–180

[SH95] Claus-Peter Schnorr and Horst Helmut Hörner, *Attacking the Chor-Rivest cryptosystem by improved lattice reduction*, EUROCRYPT'95 (Louis C. Guillou and Jean-Jacques Quisquater, eds.), LNCS, vol. 921, Springer, Heidelberg, May 1995, pp. 1–12

[SRWDM17] Mathias Soeken, Martin Roetteler, Nathan Wiebe, and Giovanni De Micheli, *Hierarchical reversible logic synthesis using luts*, Proceedings of the 54th Annual Design Automation Conference 2017 (New York, NY, USA), DAC '17, Association for Computing Machinery, 2017

[STO96] *28th acm stoc*, ACM Press, May 1996

[TTK10] Yasuhiro Takahashi, Seiichiro Tani, and Noboru Kunihiro, *Quantum addition circuits and unbounded fan-out*, Quantum Info. Comput. **10** (2010), no. 9, 872–890

Symmetric-Key Cryptanalysis

Forgery Attacks on Several Beyond-Birthday-Bound Secure MACs

Yaobin Shen[1], François-Xavier Standaert[1(✉)], and Lei Wang[2(✉)]

[1] UCLouvain, ICTEAM, Crypto Group, Louvain-la-Neuve, Belgium
{yaobin.shen,fstandae}@uclouvain.be
[2] Shanghai Jiao Tong University, Shanghai, China
wanglei_hb@sjtu.edu.cn

Abstract. At CRYPTO'18, Datta et al. proposed nPolyMAC and proved the security up to $2^{2n/3}$ authentication queries and 2^n verification queries. At EUROCRYPT'19, Dutta et al. proposed CWC+ and showed the security up to $2^{2n/3}$ queries. At FSE'19, Datta et al. proposed Poly-MAC and its key-reduced variant 2k-PolyMAC, and showed the security up to $2^{2n/3}$ queries. This security bound was then improved by Kim et al. (EUROCRYPT'20) and Datta et al. (FSE'23) respectively to $2^{3n/4}$ and in the multi-user setting. At FSE'20, Chakraborti et al. proposed PDM*MAC and 1k-PDM*MAC, and showed the security up to $2^{2n/3}$ queries. Recently, Chen et al. proposed nEHtM$_p^+$ and showed the security up to $2^{2n/3}$ queries. In this paper, we show forgery attacks on nPolyMAC, CWC+, PolyMAC, 2k-PolyMAC, PDM*MAC, 1k-PDM*MAC and nEHtM$_p^+$. Our attacks exploit some vulnerability in the underlying polynomial hash function Poly, and (i) require only one authentication query and one verification query; (ii) are nonce-respecting; (iii) succeed with probability 1. Thus, our attacks disprove the provable high security claims of these schemes. We then revisit their security analyses and identify what went wrong. Finally, we propose two solutions that can restore the beyond-birthday-bound security.

Keywords: Message authentication code · Beyond-birthday-bound security · Polynomial hash function · Forgery attack

1 Introduction

Message authentication codes (MAC) are symmetric cryptographic primitives that allow senders and receivers who share a common secret key to ensure integrity and authenticity of a transmitted message. A MAC is typically designed from block ciphers, from hash functions or from universal hash functions. In this paper, we focus on the third class. The most widely used schemes are designed following the Wegman-Carter paradigm [35]: the input message is first mapped to a fixed-length string using a universal hash function indexed by a secret key, and then the resulting string is masked with a one-time pad. The one-time pad

© International Association for Cryptologic Research 2023
J. Guo and R. Steinfeld (Eds.): ASIACRYPT 2023, LNCS 14440, pp. 169–189, 2023.
https://doi.org/10.1007/978-981-99-8727-6_6

is typically achieved by using a block cipher with a unique nonce each time, e.g., the mechanism used in GMAC/GCM [1,2,21,28,30]. This method is simple and efficient, yet the security vanishes when the nonces are misused since the hash key can then be recovered. On the other hand, when the nonces are unique as required, its security caps at the so-called birthday bound $2^{n/2}$, i.e., resisting against at most $2^{n/2}$ queries. Indeed, the outputs of a random permutation can be distinguished from random strings within roughly $2^{n/2}$ queries. This bound is not always satisfying in practical applications. For conventional platforms where block ciphers like the AES are used with $n = 128$, it implies that we need to renew the key when the number of authentication queries exceeds 2^{32} if we want to maintain the forgery advantage of an adversary below $1/2^{32}$. For resource-constrained environments, where lightweight block ciphers with 64-bit block or even shorter [3,8–10] are likely to implemented, the bound becomes•2^{32} and is vulnerable in certain applications [6].

To go beyond the birthday bound and resist against nonce misuse, Cogliati and Seurin [13] proposed a scheme called Encrypted Wegman-Carter with Davies-Meyer (EWCDM) that requires one universal hash function and two block cipher calls with independent keys. They instantiated the one-time pad with the Davies-Meyer construction and encrypted the output of the Wegman-Carter construction with another block cipher call. They showed that this scheme is provably secure up to $2^{2n/3}$ authentication queries and 2^n verification queries against nonce-respecting adversaries, and secure up to $2^{n/2}$ authentication and verification queries against nonce-misusing adversaries[1]. Later, Mennink and Neves [31] improved this security bound to the optimal 2^n in the nonce-respecting setting using the mirror theory. To reduce the number of keys, Datta el al. [16] then proposed Decrypted Wegman-Carter with Davies-Meyer (DWCDM), which is similar to EWCDM except that the outer encryption call is replaced by a decryption call. The advantage of DWCDM is that the two block cipher calls can use the same key. It even becomes a truly single-key MAC if the hash key is derived as $K_h = E_K(0^{n-1} \parallel 1)$. They proved that DWCDM can achieve the security up to $2^{2n/3}$ authentication queries and 2^n verification queries against nonce-respecting adversaries, and remains secure up to $2^{n/2}$ authentication queries and 2^n verification queries against nonce-misusing adversaries. They then proposed nPolyMAC, a concrete instance of DWCDM by realizing the universal hash function with a polynomial hash, and proved that nPolyMAC enjoys the same beyond-birthday-bound security as DWCDM. Recently, Chakraborti [11] proposed PDM*MAC and 1k-PDM*MAC, a permutation-based variant of DWCDM and its single-key version, and proved that these two schemes are both secure up to $2^{2n/3}$ queries against nonce-respecting adversaries, which is tight as illustrated with a matching attack.

Another popular approach to achieve the beyond-birthday-bound security and maintain security against nonce misuse is to use the nonce-based Enhanced

---

[1] An adversary is said to be nonce-respecting if she does not repeat nonces in authentication queries, and is said to be nonce-misusing if she repeats nonces in authentication queries.

Hash-then-Mask (nEHtM) paradigm. The Enhanced Hash-then-Mask (EHtM) method was originally proposed by Minematsu [32] to construct a probabilistic MAC with beyond-birthday-bound security. It requires an n-bit salt, two independent pseudorandom functions and a universal hash function, and is proved to achieve a tight $2^{3n/4}$ security [18]. Dutta et al. [19] turned this method into a nonce-based MAC named nEHtM where (i) the random salt is replaced by the nonce; (ii) the two independent pseudorandom functions are replaced by a single-key block cipher with domain separation. They showed that nEHtM has beyond-birthday-bound security that gracefully degrades under nonce misuse. They then proposed a nonce-based AE coined CWC+ by combining nEHtM with the encryption mode CENC [24]. They proved that CWC+ provides the authenticity up to $2^{2n/3}$ queries against nonce-respecting adversaries and maintains gracefully degrading security up to $2^{n/2}$ queries against nonce-misusing adversaries. Recently, Chen et al. [12] proposed nEHtM$_p^+$, a permutation-based variant of nEHtM, and proved that it is secure up to $2^{2n/3}$ authentication and verification queries in both single-user and multi-user settings.

There is also another approach called Double-block Hash-then-Sum (DbHtS) [14] to provide beyond-birthday-bound security without a nonce. It requires two n-bit universal hash functions, and thus is less efficient than the above two methods that require a single n-bit universal hash when nonces are available. Nevertheless, it enjoys high provable security guarantees. A notable example is PolyMAC that is built from two polynomial hash functions and two block cipher calls. A series of works showed that PolyMAC and its key-reduced variant 2k-PolyMAC are provably highly secure in both single-user and multi-user settings. Datta et al. [14] proved that both PolyMAC and 2k-PolyMAC can achieve $2^{2n/3}$ security. Kim et al. [27] improved the security bound of PolyMAC to $2^{3n/4}$. Recently, Datta et al. [15] further showed that 2k-PolyMAC can achieve $2^{3n/4}$ security in the multi-user setting.

OUR CONTRIBUTION. In this paper, we show forgery attacks on beyond-birthday-bound secure schemes, including nPolyMAC [16], CWC+ [20], Poly-MAC [14,27], 2k-PolyMAC [14,15], PDM*MAC [11], 1k-PDM*MAC [11], and nEHtM$_p^+$ [12]. Interestingly, all of these schemes use the same polynomial hash function called Poly [11,12,14–16,20,27] to handle arbitrary length messages. This polynomial hash function is supposed to hash a message efficiently and securely, and is backed up with security proofs. Yet, as we discovered, it has some vulnerability. Although Poly implicitly encodes the length of a message as a parameter in the polynomial by $M_i \cdot K_h^{\ell+1-i}$, these terms can be zeroed out if we choose $M_i = 0^n$. Hence, it allows length-extension attack by prepending arbitrary number of 0^n blocks while the hashed value remains the same. By exploiting this vulnerability, we thus mount forgery attacks against all of these schemes. Notably, our attacks (i) require only one authentication query and one verification query; (ii) are nonce-respecting; (iii) succeed with probability 1. Thus, our attacks disprove their high provable security claims.

We remark that all of forgery attacks against these schemes follow the same principle. If we abstract these schemes by a single construction $\text{MAC}(N, M) =$

$F(N, \mathsf{Poly}(M))$ where F is a function, Poly the polynomial hash function, M the message, and N the nonce (there is no nonce in PolyMAC), then this attack principle can be summarized as follows: first query $T = \mathrm{MAC}(N, M) = F(N, \mathsf{Poly}(M))$, and then $(N, (0^n)_i \| M, T)$ is a valid forgery against these schemes for any $i \geq 1$ as $\mathsf{Poly}(M) = \mathsf{Poly}((0^n)_i \| M)$ always holds, where $(0^n)_i$ denotes the i-time concatenation of string 0^n.

We then revisit their security analyses to see what went wrong. Their beyond-birthday-bound security analyses require the underlying polynomial hash to be (i) ϵ_1-regular, namely for any message, the probability that the hashed value equals to any constant value should be negligible; (ii) ϵ_2-almost-xor-universal, namely for any two distinct messages, the probability that the difference of these two hashed values equals to any constant value should be negligible; (iii) ϵ_3-3-way-regular, namely for any three distinct messages, the probability that the sum of these three hashed values equals to a non-zero constant value should be negligible, when the hash key is uniformly chosen from the key space. Note that the almost-xor-universal property is required in security analyses of all these constructions, while the regular property is needed in nPolyMAC, PDM*MAC, 1k-PDM*MAC and nEHtM$_p^{+2}$, and the 3-way-regular property is needed in nPoly-MAC, PDM*MAC and 1k-PDM*MAC. Apparently, Poly does not meet the second property since the difference of two hashed values is always 0^n for any two messages M and M' where M' is obtained by prepending arbitrary 0^n blocks to M. Thus, the proposition [15–17] that showed Poly meets these three properties is flawed and cannot be fixed. Consequently, the security analyses of the schemes nPolyMAC, CWC+, PolyMAC, 2k-PolyMAC, PDM*MAC, 1k-PDM*MAC and nEHtM$_p^+$ that rely on this result to prove the beyond-birthday-bound security are flawed.

Finally, we propose two polynomial hash functions called PolyX and GHASHX that both meet regular, almost-xor-universal and 3-way-regular properties. The first one, PolyX, is a variant of Poly by reversing the order of a message in the polynomial. By doing so, the length-dependent term $M_\ell 10^* \cdot K_h^\ell$ in the polynomial will never be zeroed out since $M_\ell 10^*$ is always a non-zero value. We then prove that PolyX is ϵ_1-regular, ϵ_2-almost-xor-universal, and ϵ_3-3-way-regular, where $\epsilon_1 = \epsilon_2 = \epsilon_3 = \ell_{\max}/2^n$ and $\ell_{\max}$ is the maximum number of n-bits blocks of a message. The second one, GHASHX, is a variant of GHASH [28–30] by replacing the 0^* padding with 10^*. Although GHASH is well-known to be a ϵ_2-almost-xor-universal hash where $\epsilon_2 = (\ell_{\max} + 1)/2^n$, it is not regular since for an empty message $M = \varepsilon$, the hashed value always equals to 0^n. Even worse, if we instantiate nPolyMAC with GHASH, then it will result in a forgery attack. The 10^* padding can avoid this issue as it always appends a 1 first. We then prove that GHASHX is ϵ_1-regular, ϵ_2-almost-xor-universal, and ϵ_3-3-way regular where $\epsilon_1 = \epsilon_2 = \epsilon_3 = (\ell_{\max} + 1)/2^n$. Hence, by instantiating nPolyMAC, CWC+, PolyMAC, 2k-PolyMAC, PDM*MAC, 1k-PDM*MAC and nEHtM$_p^+$ with either of PolyX and GHASHX, we can restore their beyond-birthday-bound security.

---

[2] The regular property is also required in the multi-user security analysis of 2k-PolyMAC [15] and is not mandatory in its single-user security analysis.

ORGANIZATION. We first introduce notations and security notions in Sect. 2. We then show forgery attacks on nPolyMAC, CWC+, PolyMAC, 2k-PolyMAC, PDM*MAC, 1k-PDM*MAC and nEHtM$_p^+$ in Sect. 3. Next, we discuss the issues in their security analyses and propose two solutions that can restore their beyond-birthday-bound security in Sect. 4. Finally, we conclude the paper in Sect. 5. We also provide an overview of how Poly is used in these schemes in Appendix A.

2 Preliminaries

NOTATION.. Let ε denote the empty string. Let $\{0,1\}^*$ be the set of all finite bit strings including the empty string ε. For a finite set $\mathcal{X}$, we let $X \leftarrow_s \mathcal{X}$ denote the uniform sampling from $\mathcal{X}$ and assigning the value to X. Let $|X|$ denote the length of string X. Let $|X|_n$ denote the n-bit encoding of the length of string X. Concatenation of strings X and Y is written as $X \parallel Y$ or simply XY. $X10^*$ denotes the padding that appended with a single 1 and as few 0 bits so that the length of string to be a multiple of n. We let $Y \leftarrow \mathcal{A}(X_1, \ldots; r)$ denote running algorithm $\mathcal{A}$ with randomness r on inputs $X_1, \ldots$ and assigning the output to Y. We let $Y \leftarrow_s \mathcal{A}(X_1, \ldots)$ be the result of picking r at random and letting $Y \leftarrow \mathcal{A}(X_1, \ldots; r)$. Let Perm$(n)$ denote the set of all permutations over $\{0,1\}^n$, and let Func$(*, n)$ denote the set of all functions from $\{0,1\}^*$ to $\{0,1\}^n$. For a string $X \in \{0,1\}^*$, let $(X)_i$ denote concatenating X itself by i times, namely $(X)_i = X \parallel \ldots \parallel X$ where X repeats i times.

BLOCK CIPHERS AND PRFS. An adversary $\mathcal{A}$ is a probabilistic algorithm that has access to one or more oracles. Let $\mathcal{A}^{O_1, O_2, \cdots}$ denote an adversary $\mathcal{A}$ interacting with oracles $O_1, O_2, \ldots$, and $\mathcal{A}^{O_1, O_2, \cdots} = 1$ denote the event that $\mathcal{A}$ outputs 1 after interacting with $O_1, O_2, \ldots$. The resources of $\mathcal{A}$ are measured in terms of time and query complexities. Let $E : \{0,1\}^k \times \{0,1\}^n \to \{0,1\}^n$ be a block cipher. Let $\pi \leftarrow_s$ Perm(n) be a random permutation. The advantage of $\mathcal{A}$ against the PRP security of E is defined as

$$\mathsf{Adv}_E^{\mathrm{prp}}(\mathcal{A}) = \left| \Pr\left[\mathcal{A}^{E_K} = 1 \right] - \Pr\left[\mathcal{A}^\pi = 1 \right] \right|$$

where K is chosen uniformly at random from $\{0,1\}^k$. The block cipher E is said to be a (q, t, ϵ)-secure PRP if $\mathsf{Adv}_E^{\mathrm{prp}}(q, t) = \max_\mathcal{A} \mathsf{Adv}_E^{\mathrm{prp}}(\mathcal{A}) \leq \epsilon$ where the maximum is taken over all adversaries $\mathcal{A}$ that makes at most q queries and runs in time at most t.

Let $F : \mathcal{K} \times \{0,1\}^* \to \{0,1\}^n$ be a keyed function. Let $\mathcal{R} \leftarrow_s$ Func$(*, n)$ be a random function. The advantage of $\mathcal{A}$ against the PRF security of F is defined as

$$\mathsf{Adv}_F^{\mathrm{prf}}(\mathcal{A}) = \left| \Pr\left[\mathcal{A}^{F_K} = 1 \right] - \Pr\left[\mathcal{A}^\mathcal{R} = 1 \right] \right|$$

where K is chosen uniformly at random from $\mathcal{K}$. The function F is said to be a (q, t, ϵ)-secure PRF if $\mathsf{Adv}_F^{\mathrm{prf}}(q, t) = \max_\mathcal{A} \mathsf{Adv}_F^{\mathrm{prf}}(\mathcal{A}) \leq \epsilon$ where the maximum is taken over all adversaries $\mathcal{A}$ that makes at most q queries and runs in time at most t.

MESSAGE AUTHENTICATION CODE. A message authentication code (MAC) scheme Π is a triplet of algorithms (Gen, Auth, Ver), where Gen is the key-generation algorithm, Auth is the authentication algorithm, and Ver is the verification algorithm. The key-generation algorithm Gen samples a key K uniformly at random from the key space $\mathcal{K}$. The authentication algorithm Auth takes as input a key $K \in \mathcal{K}$ and a message $M \in \mathcal{M}$, and outputs a tag $T \in \{0,1\}^\tau$ where $T \leftarrow \mathrm{Auth}_K(M)$. The verification algorithm takes as input a key $K \in \mathcal{K}$, a message $M \in \mathcal{M}$ and a tag $T \in \{0,1\}^\tau$, and outputs 1 if $\mathrm{Auth}_K(M) = T$ and otherwise a symbol $\perp$ indicating invalidity.

An adversary $\mathcal{A}$ has oracle access to Auth_K and Ver_K, and attempts to forge a pair of message and tag against the MAC scheme Π. We say $\mathcal{A}$ forges successfully if she outputs a pair of (M, T) that can pass the verification oracle Ver_K and M has not been queried to Auth_K before. The advantage of $\mathcal{A}$ against the unforgeability of Π is defined as

$$\mathsf{Adv}_\Pi^{\mathrm{mac}}(\mathcal{A}) = \Pr\left[\mathcal{A}^{\mathrm{Auth}_K, \mathrm{Ver}_K} \text{ forges}\right]$$

where K is chosen uniformly at random from $\mathcal{K}$. The scheme Π is said to be a (q_m, q_v, t, ϵ)-secure MAC if $\mathsf{Adv}_\Pi^{\mathrm{mac}}(q_m, q_v, t) = \max_{\mathcal{A}} \mathsf{Adv}_\Pi^{\mathrm{mac}}(\mathcal{A}) \le \epsilon$ where the maximum is taken over all adversaries $\mathcal{A}$ that makes at most q_m authentication queries, q_v verification queries, and runs in time at most t.

NONCE-BASED MAC. A nonce-based MAC scheme Π takes an additional parameter called nonce $N \in \mathcal{N}$. The key-generation algorithm Gen samples a key K uniformly at random from the key space $\mathcal{K}$. The authentication algorithm Auth takes as input a key $K \in \mathcal{K}$, a nonce $N \in \mathcal{N}$ and a message $M \in \mathcal{M}$, and outputs a tag $T \in \{0,1\}^\tau$ where $T \leftarrow \mathrm{Auth}_K(N, M)$. The verification algorithm takes as input a key $K \in \mathcal{K}$, a nonce $N \in \mathcal{N}$, a message $M \in \mathcal{M}$ and a tag $T \in \{0,1\}^\tau$, and outputs 1 if $\mathrm{Auth}_K(N, M, T) = T$ and otherwise a symbol $\perp$ indicating invalidity.

The adversary is said to be nonce-respecting if she does not repeat nonces in authentication queries, and is said to be nonce-misusing if she repeats nonces in authentication queries. However, in both cases, the adversary can always repeat nonces in verification queries, either using the same nonce in two verification queries or repeating the nonce between a verification query and a authentication query. We say $\mathcal{A}$ forges successfully if she outputs a tuple of (N, M, T) that can pass the verification oracle Ver_K and (N, M) has not been queried to Auth_K before. The advantage of $\mathcal{A}$ against the unforgeability of Π is defined as

$$\mathsf{Adv}_\Pi^{\mathrm{mac}}(\mathcal{A}) = \Pr\left[\mathcal{A}^{\mathrm{Auth}_K, \mathrm{Ver}_K} \text{ forges}\right]$$

where K is chosen uniformly at random from $\mathcal{K}$. The scheme Π is said to be a (q_m, q_v, t, ϵ)-secure MAC if $\mathsf{Adv}_\Pi^{\mathrm{mac}}(q_m, q_v, t) = \max_{\mathcal{A}} \mathsf{Adv}_\Pi^{\mathrm{mac}}(\mathcal{A}) \le \epsilon$ where the maximum is taken over all adversaries $\mathcal{A}$ that makes at most q_m authentication queries, q_v verification queries, and runs in time at most t.

AUTHENTICATED ENCRYPTION. An authenticated encryption (AE) scheme Π is a triplet of algorithms (Gen, Enc, Dec), where Gen is the key-generation algorithm, Enc the encryption algorithm and Dec the decryption algorithm. The key-generation algorithm Gen samples a key K uniformly at random from the key space $\mathcal{K}$. The encryption algorithm Enc takes as input a key $K \in \mathcal{K}$, a nonce $N \in \mathcal{N}$, an associated data $A \in \{0,1\}^*$ and a message $M \in \mathcal{M}$, and returns a pair of ciphertext and tag $(C, T) \in \{0,1\}^{|M|+\tau}$ where $(C, T) \leftarrow \text{Enc}_K(N, A, M)$. The decryption algorithm takes as input a key $K \in \mathcal{K}$, a nonce $N \in \mathcal{N}$, an associated data $A \in \{0,1\}^*$, a ciphertext $C \in \{0,1\}^*$ and a tag $T \in \{0,1\}^\tau$, and returns either a message $M \in \{0,1\}^*$ or a symbol $\perp$ indicating invalidity. For correctness, we assume that if $(C, T) \leftarrow \text{Enc}_K(N, A, M)$, then $M \leftarrow \text{Dec}_K(N, A, C, T)$. Note that the message M is encrypted and authenticated simultaneously, while the associated data A is only authenticated.

Similarly, the adversary is said to be nonce-respecting if she does not repeat nonces in encryption queries, and is said to be nonce-misusing if she repeats nonces in encryption queries. In both cases, the adversary can always repeat nonces in decryption queries. An AE scheme Π should provide both authenticity and confidentiality. In this paper, we only consider the adversary against the authenticity of Π. We say $\mathcal{A}$ forges successfully if she outputs a tuple of (N, A, C, T) that can pass the decryption oracle Dec_K and (N, A, C, T) has not been obtained from queries to Enc_K before. The advantage of $\mathcal{A}$ against the authenticity of Π is defined as

$$\text{Adv}_\Pi^{\text{Auth}}(\mathcal{A}) = \Pr\left[\mathcal{A}^{\text{Enc}_K, \text{Dec}_K} \text{ forges}\right]$$

where K is chosen uniformly at random from $\mathcal{K}$. The scheme Π is said to be a (q_e, q_d, t, ϵ)-secure authenticator if $\text{Adv}_\Pi^{\text{Auth}}(q_e, q_d, t) = \max_\mathcal{A} \text{Adv}_\Pi^{\text{Auth}}(\mathcal{A}) \leq \epsilon$ where the maximum is taken over all adversaries $\mathcal{A}$ that makes at most q_e encryption queries, q_d decryption queries, and runs in time at most t.

3   Forgery Attacks on Polynomial-Based Constructions

In this section, we show forgery attacks on several polynomial-based MACs that are claimed to achieve beyond-birthday-bound security, including nPolyMAC, CWC+, PolyMAC, 2k-PolyMAC, PDM*MAC, 1k-PDM*MAC and nEHtM$_p^+$. Our attacks (i) require only one authentication query and one verification query; (ii) are nonce-respecting; (iii) succeed with the probability 1.

All of these attacks are due to the polynomial hash function chosen in those schemes and follow the attack principle outlined in introduction: assuming a construction $\text{MAC}(N, M) = \text{F}(N, \text{Poly}(M))$ where F is a function, Poly the polynomial hash function, M the message and N the nonce (there is no nonce in PolyMAC), the attack works by querying $T = \text{MAC}(N, M) = \text{F}(N, \text{Poly}(M))$ and observing that $(N, (0^n)_i \parallel M, T)$ is then a valid forgery for any $i \geq 1$ as $\text{Poly}(M) = \text{Poly}((0^n)_i \parallel M)$ always holds.

We do an exhaustive description of how this attack principle results in forgery attacks against these schemes and postpone a more general discussion about the source of these attacks and how to fix them to the next section. We also provide a brief summary of how the polynomial hash function Poly is used in these schemes in Appendix A.

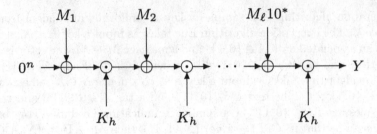

Fig. 1. The polynomial hash function Poly for a message $M = M_1 \| \ldots \| M_\ell$ with a hash key K_h.

3.1 Attack on nPolyMAC

nPolyMAC is an instance of DWCDM construction that is proved to achieve beyond-birthday-bound security [16,17]. It is built from a polynomial hash function Poly : $\mathcal{K}_h \times \{0,1\}^* \to \{0,1\}^n$ and a block cipher $E : \{0,1\}^k \times \{0,1\}^n \to \{0,1\}^n$, and can authenticate a message $M \in \{0,1\}^*$ of variable length. Given a message $M = M_1 \| M_2 \| \ldots \| M_\ell$ where $|M_i| = n$ and $0 \leq M_\ell \leq n - 1$, the 10^* padding[3] is first applied to make the total string length of M a multiple of n. The polynomial hash Poly is defined as

$$\mathsf{Poly}_{K_h}(M) = M_1 \cdot K_h^\ell \oplus M_2 \cdot K_h^{\ell-1} \oplus \ldots \oplus M_\ell 10^* \cdot K_h \ , \tag{1}$$

where $K_h \in \mathcal{K}_h$ is the hash key. See Fig. 1 for a pictorial illustration of Poly [4]. Then nPolyMAC is defined as

$$\mathsf{nPolyMAC}[\mathsf{Poly}, E](N, M) = E_K^{-1}(E_K(N) \oplus N \oplus \mathsf{Poly}_{K_h}(M))$$

where $N \in \{0,1\}^n$ is the nonce, $M \in \{0,1\}^*$ is the message.

In Theorem 4 of [16,17], it is proved that nPolyMAC is secure up to $2^{2n/3}$ authentication queries and 2^n verification queries against nonce-respecting adversaries, and remains secure up to $2^{n/2}$ authentication queries and 2^n verification queries against nonce-misusing adversaries. In the following, we show a forgery attack against nPolyMAC in the nonce-respecting setting that requires only one authentication query and one verification query, and succeeds with probability 1. Thus, the attack disproves the security claim of nPolyMAC.

The adversary can mount an attack against nPolyMAC as follows. She chooses an arbitrary message $M \in \{0,1\}^*$ and a nonce N, and queries (N, M) to obtain the tag T where

$$T = E_K^{-1}(E_K(N) \oplus N \oplus \mathsf{Poly}_{K_h}(M)) \ ,$$

and

$$\mathsf{Poly}_{K_h}(M) = M_1 \cdot K_h^\ell \oplus M_2 \cdot K_h^{\ell-1} \oplus \ldots \oplus M_\ell 10^* \cdot K_h \ .$$

---

[3] The 10^* padding is explicitly used as an injective padding method for Poly in [11, 12,14–17,19,20].

[4] Part of this figure is inspired by IACR TikZ [26].

Then the tuple (N, M', T) where $M' = (0^n)_i \parallel M$ is a valid forgery for any $i \geq 1$ since the equation $\mathsf{Poly}_{K_h}(M') = \mathsf{Poly}_{K_h}(M)$ always holds as

$$\mathsf{Poly}_{K_h}(M') = 0^n \cdot K_h^{\ell+i} \oplus \ldots \oplus 0^n \cdot K_h^{\ell+1} \oplus M_1 \cdot K_h^{\ell} \oplus \ldots \oplus M_\ell 10^* \cdot K_h = \mathsf{Poly}_{K_h}(M) \ .$$

This attack thus invalidates the beyond-birthday-bound security claim of nPoly-MAC.

REMARK 1. The reason why this attack works is that (i) the finite field multiplication has a fixed point 0^n, namely for any K_h, the result of $0^n \cdot K_h^{\ell+i}$ is always 0^n; (ii) although the design of Poly_{K_h} implicitly encodes the length of the messages as a parameter by $M_i \cdot K_h^{\ell+1-i}$, these terms will be canceled out if we choose M_i to be 0^n. Thus, we can prepend arbitrary number of 0^n blocks to a message while the hash value of this message remains the same. This attack looks simple but can be harmful, since the adversary can choose any message M that may contain some information that is unwilling to repeat again, and extend the number of 0^n blocks so that the message is always regarded as new and accepted by the receiver with probability 1.

3.2 Attack on CWC+

CWC+ [20] is a nonce-based authenticated encryption following the Encrypt-then-MAC paradigm [4]. The encryption of CWC+ is based on a variant of CENC [25] encryption scheme called $\mathsf{CENC_{max}}$ [7]. Taking as input a block cipher key $K \in \{0,1\}^k$, a nonce $N \in \{0,1\}^n$, and a length parameter $\ell < 2^{n/4}$, $\mathsf{CENC_{max}}$ outputs a sequence of key stream blocks $(S_1, \ldots, S_\ell)$, where the i-th key stream block is defined as

$$S_i = E_K(N) \oplus E_K(N + i) \ .$$

The authentication of CWC+ is built from a beyond-birthday-bound secure MAC algorithm called nEHtM [20]. Taking as input a block cipher key $K \in \{0,1\}^k$, a hash key $K_h \in \mathcal{K}_h$, a nonce $N \in \{0,1\}^{n-1}$ and a message $M \in \{0,1\}^*$, nEHtM is defined as

$$\mathsf{nEHtM}[E, H](N, M) = E_K(0 \parallel N) \oplus E_K(1 \parallel (N \oplus H_{K_h}(M))) \ .$$

The $(n-1)$-bit hash function H is realized by truncating the first bit of polynomial hash Poly defined in Eq. 1. The specification of CWC+ is given by combining $\mathsf{CENC_{max}}$, nEHtM and Poly that is illustrated in Fig. 2.

The Theorem 2 of [19,20] shows that CWC+ provides security up to $2^{2n/3}$ queries for both authenticity and confidentiality against nonce-respecting adversaries, and maintains graceful birthday-bound security against nonce-misusing adversaries. In the following, we show a forgery attack against the authenticity of CWC+ in the nonce-respecting setting that requires only one encryption query and one decryption query and succeeds with probability 1. Thus, this attack disproves the security claim of CWC+ regarding the authenticity.

procedure $\text{Enc}(K, N, A, M)$	**procedure** $\text{Dec}(K, N, A, C, T)$
$L \leftarrow E_K(0^n); N' \leftarrow N \parallel 0^{n/4-1}$	$L \leftarrow E_K(0^n); N' \leftarrow N \parallel 0^{n/4-1}$
$\ell \leftarrow \lceil |M|/n \rceil$	$\ell \leftarrow \lceil |C|/n \rceil$
$S \leftarrow \text{CENC}_{\max}(K, 0 \parallel N', \ell)$	$\widetilde{T}' \leftarrow \text{nEHtM}[E, \text{Poly}_L](N', C \parallel A)$
$C \leftarrow M \oplus \text{first}(S, |M|)$	**if** $\text{chop}_\tau \lceil \widetilde{T}' \rceil \neq T$ **then return** $\perp$
$\widetilde{T} \leftarrow \text{nEHtM}[E, \text{Poly}_L](N', C \parallel A)$	$S \leftarrow \text{CENC}_{\max}(K, 0 \parallel N', \ell)$
$T \leftarrow \text{chop}_\tau \lceil \widetilde{T} \rceil; \textbf{return } (C, T)$	$M \leftarrow C \oplus \text{first}(S, |C|); \textbf{return } M$

Fig. 2. Encryption and decryption procedures of CWC+. Here the nonce N is a $3n/4$-bit string. $\text{first}(S, |M|)$ denotes the first $|M|$ bits of the string S. $\text{chop}_\tau \lceil \cdot \rceil$ is a function that truncates the last $n - \tau$ bits of its input.

Since the adversary can arbitrarily choose a message M and an associated data A, she can simply set the message M to the empty string ε and choose an arbitrary associated data $A \in \{0,1\}^*$. Then the attack idea is similar to the one for nPolyMAC. In detail, the adversary can mount an attack against the authenticity of CWC+ as follows. She sets the message M to the empty string ε and chooses an arbitrary associated data $A \in \{0,1\}^*$ and a nonce $N \in \{0,1\}^{3n/4}$. She queries (N, A, ε) to obtain the tag T where

$$T = E_K(0 \parallel N') \oplus E_K(1 \parallel (N' \oplus \text{chop}_{n-1} \lfloor \text{Poly}_L(A) \rfloor)) \ ,$$

and $N' = N \parallel 0^{n/4-1}$, $L = E_K(0^n)$, $\text{chop}_{n-1} \lfloor \cdot \rfloor$ is a function that truncates the first bit of its input. Then the tuple (N, A', ε, T) where $A' = (0^n)_i \parallel A$ is a valid forgery against CWC+ for any $i \geq 1$ since $\text{Poly}_L(A) = \text{Poly}_L(A')$ always holds. Note that similar forgery attack also applies to nEHtM [20] when the hash function is instantiated with Poly.

3.3   Attacks on PolyMAC and 2k-PolyMAC

PolyMAC is a MAC algorithm built from the polynomial hash $\text{Poly} : \mathcal{K}_h \times \{0,1\}^* \rightarrow \{0,1\}^n$ defined in Eq. 1 and two block ciphers $E : \{0,1\}^k \times \{0,1\}^n \rightarrow \{0,1\}^n$ as follows

$$\text{PolyMAC}[\text{Poly}, E](M) = E_{K_1}(\text{Poly}_{K_{h_1}}(M)) \oplus E_{K_2}(\text{Poly}_{K_{h_2}}(M)) \ .$$

Its key-reduced variant 2k-PolyMAC is defined as

$$\text{2k-PolyMAC}[\text{Poly}, E](M) = E_K(\text{fix}_0(\text{Poly}_{K_{h_1}}(M))) \oplus E_K(\text{fix}_1(\text{Poly}_{K_{h_2}}(M))) \ ,$$

where the domain separating functions fix_0 and fix_1 fix the least significant bit of a string to be 0 and 1 respectively.

A series of works show that PolyMAC and its key-reduced variant 2k-PolyMAC enjoy provably high security in both single-user and multi-user settings. Datta et al. [14] proved that both PolyMAC and 2k-PolyMAC can achieve $2^{2n/3}$ security. Later, Kim et al. [27] improved the security bound of PolyMAC to be $2^{3n/4}$

by assuming an injective padding method. Recently, Datta et al. [15] further showed that 2k-PolyMAC can achieve $2^{3n/4}$ security in the multi-user setting. In the following, we show a forgery attack against PolyMAC that requires only one authentication query and one verification query and succeeds with probability 1. Similar attack also applies to 2k-PolyMAC. Thus, our attack disproves the security claim of both PolyMAC and 2k-PolyMAC.

The adversary can mount an attack against PolyMAC as follows. She first chooses an arbitrary message $M \in \{0,1\}^*$. She queries M to obtain T where

$$T = E_{K_1}(\mathsf{Poly}_{K_{h_1}}(M)) \oplus E_{K_2}(\mathsf{Poly}_{K_{h_2}}(M)) \ .$$

Then the pair of (M',T) is a valid forgery against PolyMAC where $M' = (0^n)_i \| M$ for any $i \geq 1$, since equations $\mathsf{Poly}_{K_{h_1}}(M') = \mathsf{Poly}_{K_{h_1}}(M)$ and $\mathsf{Poly}_{K_{h_2}}(M') = \mathsf{Poly}_{K_{h_2}}(M)$ always hold.

3.4 Attack on PDM*MAC and 1k-PDM*MAC

PDM*MAC [11] is a permutation-based Davis-Meyer MAC that is proved to achieve beyond-birthday-bound security. Given a key $K \in \{0,1\}^n$, a hash key $K_h \in \mathcal{K}_h$, an n-bit nonce N and a message $M \in \{0,1\}^*$, it computes a tag as follows

$$\mathsf{PDM^*MAC}[H, \pi] = \pi^{-1}(\pi(K \oplus N) \oplus 3K \oplus N \oplus H_{K_h}(M)) \oplus 2K$$

where $H : \mathcal{K}_h \times \{0,1\}^* \to \{0,1\}^n$ is a hash function and π is a public permutation over $\{0,1\}^n$. The hash function H is instantiated with Poly as defined in Eq. 1.

Theorem 2 of [11] shows that PDM*MAC is secure up to $2^{2n/3}$ queries against nonce-respecting adversaries and this security bound is tight illustrated with a matching attack. In the following, we show a forgery attack against PDM*MAC. Our attack requires only one authentication query and one verification query and succeeds with probability 1. Thus, our attack disproves the security claim of PDM*MAC instantiated with Poly.

The adversary can mount an attack against PDM*MAC as follows. She first chooses an arbitrary message $M \in \{0,1\}^*$. She asks M to PDM*MAC and obtains the tag T that is computed as

$$T = \pi^{-1}(\pi(K \oplus N) \oplus 3K \oplus N \oplus \mathsf{Poly}_{K_h}(M)) \oplus 2K \ .$$

Then the pair of (M',T) is a valid forgery against PDM*MAC where $M' = (0^n)_i \| M$ for any $i \geq 1$ since $\mathsf{Poly}_{K_h}(M') = \mathsf{Poly}_{K_h}(M)$ always holds. This attack also applies to 1k-PDM*MAC instantiated with Poly in [11], which is a single-key version of PDM*MAC and is proved in Theorem 3 [11] to achieve beyond-birthday-bound security.

3.5 Attack on nEHtM$_p^+$

nEHtM$_p^+$ [12] is a concrete instance of a permutation-based MAC called nEHtM$_p^*$ that is proved to achieve beyond-birthday-bound security. It is built from a

$(n-1)$-bit hash function $H : \mathcal{K}_h \times \{0,1\}^* \to \{0,1\}^{n-1}$ and a public permutation π over $\{0,1\}^n$ as follows:

$$\mathsf{nEHtM}_p^+[H,\pi](N,M) = \pi(0 \parallel N \oplus K) \oplus \pi(1 \parallel N \oplus K \oplus H_{\mathcal{K}_h}(M))$$

where $K \in \{0,1\}^n$ is the key, $N \in \{0,1\}^{n-1}$ the nonce, $M \in \{0,1\}^*$ the message, and $H_{\mathcal{K}_h}(M)$ is instantiated by truncating the first bit of $\mathsf{Poly}_{K_h}(M)$ as defined in Eq. 1.

It is proved in [12] that nEHtM_p^+ is secure up to $2^{2n/3}$ authentication queries and $2^{2n/3}$ verification queries in both single-user and multi-user settings. In the following we show a forgery attack that disproves this security claim.

Similarly to previous attacks, the adversary can mount an attack against nEHtM_p^+ as follows. She first chooses an arbitrary message $M \in \{0,1\}^*$ and a nonce N. She queries (N,M) to obtain the tag T where

$$T = \pi(0 \parallel N \oplus K) \oplus \pi(1 \parallel N \oplus K \oplus \mathsf{chop}_{n-1}\lfloor\mathsf{Poly}_{K_h}(M)\rfloor)$$

and $\mathsf{chop}_{n-1}\lfloor\cdot\rfloor$ is a function that truncates the first bit of its input. Then the tuple (N, M', T) is a valid forgery against nEHtM_p^+ where $M' = (0^n)_i \parallel M$ for any $i \geq 1$ since $\mathsf{Poly}_{K_h}(M') = \mathsf{Poly}_{K_h}(M)$ always holds.

REMARK 2. Our attacks do not apply to EWCDM [13] or EHtM [32] since they assumed using an almost-xor-universal hash and didn't propose concrete instance of the hash function. Their schemes are secure as claimed when instantiating with a proper hash function.

4   Issues in Previous Analyses and Possible Fixes

In this section, we first revisit the properties of the underlying hash function that are required in security analyses of constructions nPolyMAC, CWC+, Poly-MAC, 2k-PolyMAC, PDM*MAC, 1k-PDM*MAC and nEHtM_p^+, and show that the polynomial hash Poly fails to meet some of these properties. The failure of Poly is the source reason that their security analyses are flawed since all of their beyond-birthday-bound proofs rely on these properties. We then propose two polynomial hash functions called PolyX and GHASHX, and prove that they satisfy these properties. By instantiating these constructions with either of these two hash functions, their beyond-birthday-bound security can be restored.

4.1   Properties of the Hash Function

There are three properties that are required for the underlying hash function, namely regular, almost xor universal and 3-way regular properties. The almost-xor-universal property is required in security analyses of all constructions, i.e., nPolyMAC, CWC+, PolyMAC, 2k-PolyMAC, PDM*MAC, 1k-PDM*MAC and nEHtM_p^+, while the regular property is needed in nPolyMAC, PDM*MAC, 1k-PDM*MAC, nEHtM_p^+ and multi-user 2k-PolyMAC, and the 3-way-regular property is needed in nPolyMAC, PDM*MAC and 1k-PDM*MAC. We introduce them as follows.

Definition 1 (regular). *Let $\mathcal{K}_h$ and $\mathcal{X}$ be two non-empty finite sets. A keyed hash function $H : \mathcal{K}_h \times \mathcal{X} \rightarrow \{0,1\}^n$ is said to be ϵ_1-regular, if for any $X \in \mathcal{X}$ and $\Delta \in \{0,1\}^n$,*

$$\Pr[K_h \leftarrow_\$ \mathcal{K}_h : H_{K_h}(X) = \Delta] \leq \epsilon_1 .$$

Definition 2 (almost xor universal). [5] *Let $\mathcal{K}_h$ and $\mathcal{X}$ be two non-empty finite sets. A keyed hash function $H : \mathcal{K}_h \times \mathcal{X} \rightarrow \{0,1\}^n$ is said to be ϵ_2-almost-xor-universal, if for any distinct $X_1, X_2 \in \mathcal{X}$ and for any $\Delta \in \{0,1\}^n$,*

$$\Pr[K_h \leftarrow_\$ \mathcal{K}_h : H_{K_h}(X_1) \oplus H_{K_h}(X_2) = \Delta] \leq \epsilon_2 .$$

Definition 3 (3-way regular). *Let $\mathcal{K}_h$ and $\mathcal{X}$ be two non-empty finite sets. A keyed hash function $H : \mathcal{K}_h \times \mathcal{X} \rightarrow \{0,1\}^n$ is said to be ϵ_3-3-way-regular, if for any distinct $X_1, X_2, X_3 \in \mathcal{X}$ and for any non-zero $\Delta \in \{0,1\}^n$,*

$$\Pr[K_h \leftarrow_\$ \mathcal{K}_h : H_{K_h}(X_1) \oplus H_{K_h}(X_2) \oplus H_{K_h}(X_3) = \Delta] \leq \epsilon_3 .$$

We then recall a proposition in [14–17] that erroneously shows that Poly meets all of these three properties and discuss what is wrong.

Proposition 1. [16,17][6] *Let $\mathsf{Poly} : \{0,1\}^n \times \{0,1\}^* \rightarrow \{0,1\}^n$ be a hash function defined as follows: For a key $K_h \in \{0,1\}^n$ and a message $M \in \{0,1\}^*$, we first apply an injective padding such as 10^*, i.e., pad 1 followed by minimum number of zeros so that the total number of bits in the padded message becomes multiple of n. Let the padded message be $M^* = M_1 \| M_2 \| \ldots \| M_\ell$ where $|M_i| = n$ for each i. Then we define*

$$\mathsf{Poly}_{K_h}(M) = M_1 \cdot K_h^\ell \oplus M_2 \cdot K_h^{\ell-1} \oplus \ldots \oplus M_\ell \cdot K_h ,$$

where ℓ is the number of n-bit blocks. Then, Poly is ϵ_1-regular, ϵ_2-almost-xor-universal, and ϵ_3-3-way-regular where $\epsilon_1 = \epsilon_2 = \epsilon_3 = \ell_{\max}/2^n$ and $\ell_{\max}$ denotes the maximum number of n-bit blocks of a message.

However, Poly is not almost xor universal as shown by the following counterexample. For any two distinct messages M and M' such that $M \in \{0,1\}^*$ and $M' = (0^n)_i \| M$ for any $i \geq 1$, the equation $\mathsf{Poly}_{K_h}(M) \oplus \mathsf{Poly}_{K_h}(M') = 0^n$ always holds since

$$\mathsf{Poly}_{K_h}(M') = 0^n \cdot K_h^{\ell+i} \oplus \ldots \oplus 0^n \cdot K_h^{\ell+1} \oplus M_1 \cdot K_h^\ell \oplus \ldots \oplus M_\ell 10^* \cdot K_h = \mathsf{Poly}_{K_h}(M) .$$

---

[5] In [27], it only requires the polynomial hash function to be universal, namely the probability that $H_{K_h}(X_1) = H_{K_h}(X_2)$ is negligible for two different messages X_1 and X_2. The almost xor universal implies universal since we can choose $\Delta = 0^n$.

[6] This proposition appears as Lemma 4 in [15] without the ϵ_3-3-way-regular property.

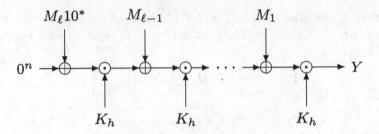

Fig. 3. The polynomial hash function PolyX for a message $M = M_1 \| \ldots \| M_\ell$ with a hash key K_h.

In the proof of Proposition 1 [15–17], the authors argued that the equation $\mathsf{Poly}_{K_h}(M) \oplus \mathsf{Poly}_{K_h}(M') \oplus \Delta = 0^n$ is a non-trivial polynomial of K_h with degree at most ℓ and thus the maximum number of roots of this polynomial is ℓ. They then claimed that the almost-xor-universal advantage of Poly is $\ell/2^n$. However, they overlooked the fact that the multiplication has a fixed point 0^n. By prepanding arbitrary 0^n blocks to the message M to become another message M', the above equation becomes trivial and always holds for $\Delta = 0^n$ regardless of the value of K_h. All the security analyses of constructions, i.e., nPolyMAC, CWC+, PolyMAC, 2k-PolyMAC, PDM*MAC, 1k-PDM*MAC and nEHtM$_p^+$, rely on this result to prove the beyond-birthday-bound security, and thus are flawed.

REMARK 3. There is another polynomial hash function proposed by Minematsu and Iwata [33] that is different from Poly. Given a message $M = M_1 \| M_2 \| \ldots \| M_\ell$ where $|M_i| = n$ for $1 \leq i \leq \ell - 1$ and $0 \leq |M_\ell| \leq n$, it is defined as

$$\mathsf{Poly}'_{K_h}(M) = M_1 \cdot K_h^\ell \oplus M_2 \cdot K_h^{\ell-1} \oplus \ldots \oplus M_\ell 0^* \cdot K_h$$

where 0^* denotes the padding that appends as few 0 bits so that the length of string to be a multiple of n. As emphasized by the authors [33], this hash function is $\ell/2^n$-almost-xor-universal only for fixed-length inputs. Thus, it cannot be used for variable-length messages.

4.2 Two Possible Fixes

We now propose two polynomial hash functions and prove that they meet the above three properties. Thus, by using either of these two hash functions, the beyond-birthday-bound security of these constructions can be restored.

THE FIRST HASH FUNCTION called PolyX is a variant of Poly that reverses the order of a message in the polynomial. Let the message be $M = M_1 \| M_2 \| \ldots \| M_\ell$ where $|M_i| = n$ for $1 \leq i \leq \ell - 1$ and $0 \leq |M_\ell| \leq n - 1$. Then given a key $K_h \in \{0,1\}^n$ and using 10^* padding, we define

$$\mathsf{PolyX}_{K_h}(M) = M_1 \cdot K_h \oplus M_2 \cdot K_h^2 \oplus \ldots \oplus M_\ell 10^* \cdot K_h^\ell . \tag{2}$$

A pictorial illustration of PolyX is given in Fig. 3. Compared to Poly, a notable difference is that the length-dependent term $M_\ell 10^* \cdot K_h^\ell$ will never be zeroed out since $M_\ell 10^*$ is always a non-zero value. Hence, it prevents the attacks shown in Sect. 3 since extending the number of 0^n blocks implicitly changes the length of a message and thus the value of $M_\ell 10^* \cdot K_h^\ell$. The following lemma shows that indeed PolyX meets regular, almost xor universal and 3-way regular properties.

Lemma 1. *Let* PolyX $: \{0,1\}^n \times \{0,1\}^* \to \{0,1\}^n$ *be defined by Eq. 2. Then* PolyX *is ϵ_1-regular, ϵ_2-almost-xor-universal, and ϵ_3-3-way-regular where $\epsilon_1 = \epsilon_2 = \epsilon_3 = \ell_{\max}/2^n$ and $\ell_{\max}$ is the maximum number of n-bit blocks of a message.*

Proof. We first consider the regular property. Given a message $M \in \{0,1\}^*$ and a constant value $\Delta \in \{0,1\}^n$, it requires the equation $\text{PolyX}_{K_h}(M) \oplus \Delta = 0^n$ holds, namely

$$M_1 \cdot K_h \oplus M_2 \cdot K_h^2 \oplus \ldots \oplus M_\ell 10^* \cdot K_h^\ell \oplus \Delta = 0^n \ .$$

This is a non-trivial polynomial of K_h of degree ℓ, since the coefficient $M_\ell 10^*$ of K_h^ℓ is always non-zero. Hence the maximum number of roots of this polynomial is ℓ. Thus, the regular advantage becomes $\ell/2^n \leq \ell_{\max}/2^n$ since the hash key K_h is chosen uniformly at random from the set $\{0,1\}^n$.

We then analyze the almost xor universal property. Given two distinct messages $M, M' \in \{0,1\}^*$ and a constant value $\Delta \in \{0,1\}^n$, it implies the equation $\text{PolyX}_{K_h}(M) \oplus \text{PolyX}_{K_h}(M') \oplus \Delta = 0^n$, i.e.,

$$M_1 \cdot K_h \oplus \ldots \oplus M_\ell 10^* \cdot K_h^\ell \oplus M_1' \cdot K_h \oplus \ldots \oplus M_{\ell'}' 10^* \cdot K_h^{\ell'} \oplus \Delta = 0^n \ .$$

If $\ell = \ell'$, then either there exists some $1 \leq i \leq \ell - 1$ such that $M_i \neq M_i'$ or $M_\ell 10^* \neq M_{\ell'}' 10^*$. Hence this is a non-trivial polynomial of K_h of degree at most ℓ, since either the coefficient $M_i \oplus M_i'$ of K_h^i or the coefficient $M_\ell 10^* \oplus M_\ell' 10^*$ of K_h^ℓ is non-zero. Thus, the almost xor universal advantage is at most $\ell/2^n \leq \ell_{\max}/2^n$. If $\ell \neq \ell'$, without loss of generality, we assume $\ell > \ell'$. Then the coefficient $M_\ell 10^*$ of K_h^ℓ is non-zero that implies this is a non-trivial polynomial of K_h of degree ℓ. Hence the almost xor universal advantage is again at most $\ell/2^n \leq \ell_{\max}/2^n$.

Finally we consider the 3-way regular property. Given three distinct messages $M, M', M'' \in \{0,1\}^*$ and a *non-zero* constant $\Delta \in \{0,1\}^n$, it requires the equation $\text{PolyX}_{K_h}(M) \oplus \text{PolyX}_{K_h}(M') \oplus \text{PolyX}_{K_h}(M'') = \Delta$ holds. If the left part reduces to a zero polynomial such that each coefficient is zero, which is possible by certain choice of messages, e.g., $M = M' \oplus M''$, then the 3-way regular advantage is 0 since $\Delta \neq 0^n$. Otherwise, the left part is a non-trivial polynomial since there is at least one K_h^i whose coefficient is non-zero. Hence, the 3-way regular advantage is at most $\max\{\ell, \ell', \ell''\}/2^n \leq \ell_{\max}/2^n$.

THE SECOND HASH FUNCTION called GHASHX is a variant of GHASH [28–30] by replacing the 0^* padding with the 10^* padding. Before that, we first recall the definition of GHASH and show that it cannot meet the regular property, and thus cannot be used in nPolyMAC, PDM*MAC, 1k-PDM*MAC, nEHtM$_p^+$ and multi-user 2k-PolyMAC to restore the beyond-birthday-bound security. Let the message be $M = M_1 \| M_2 \| \ldots \| M_\ell$ where $|M_i| = n$ for $1 \leq i \leq \ell - 1$ and $0 \leq |M_\ell| \leq n$. Given a hash key $K_h \in \{0,1\}^n$, GHASH is defined as follows:

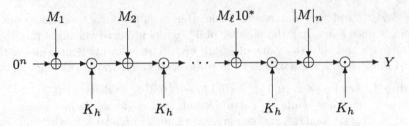

Fig. 4. The polynomial hash function GHASHX for a message $M = M_1 \| \ldots \| M_\ell$ with a hash key K_h.eps

$$\mathsf{GHASH}_{K_h}(M) = M_1 \cdot K_h^{\ell+1} \oplus M_2 \cdot K_h^\ell \oplus \ldots \oplus M_\ell 0^* \cdot K_h^2 \oplus |M|_n \cdot K_h \quad (3)$$

where 0^* is the padding method that appends as few zeros to make the total string length a multiple of n^7, and $|M|_n$ is the n-bit encoding of the length of message M. Note that GHASH explicitly multiplies the n-bit encoding of the length of a message $|M|_h$ by K_h. Hence, it can prevent the attack of prepending arbitrary 0^n blocks in Sect. 3 since then the length will change. McGrew and Viega [28,29] showed that GHASH is a ϵ_2-almost-xor-universal hash where $\epsilon_2 = (\ell_{\max} + 1)/2^n$ and $\ell_{\max}$ is the maximum number of n-bit blocks of a message. Hence, GHASH can be used in nEHtM, CWC+, PolyMAC, and 2k-PolyMAC to restore their beyond-birthday-bound security since for these constructions, they only require the underlying hash function to be almost-xor-universal. However, for nPolyMAC, PDM*MAC, 1k-PDM*MAC, nEHtM$_p^+$ and multi-user 2k-PolyMAC, their security analyses require that the underlying hash function should be also regular. Apparently, GHASH is not regular since for an empty string $M = \varepsilon$, $\mathsf{GHASH}_{K_h}(\varepsilon) = 0$ always holds. Hence, we cannot use GHASH in these three constructions otherwise it will violate their security analyses. Even worse, if we use GHASH in nPolyMAC, then there is a forgery attack since the tuple $(N, M, T) = (0^n, \varepsilon, 0^n)$ can always pass the decryption oracle without queried before.

Now we define GHASHX that is a variant of GHASH by replacing the 0^* padding with 10^* padding. Given a hash key $K_h \in \{0,1\}^n$ and a message $M = M_1 \| M_2 \| \ldots \| M_\ell$ where $|M_i| = n$ for $1 \le i \le \ell - 1$ and $0 \le |M_\ell| \le n - 1$, GHASHX is defines as follows:

$$\mathsf{GHASHX}_{K_h}(M) = M_1 \cdot K_h^{\ell+1} \oplus M_2 \cdot K_h^\ell \oplus \ldots \oplus M_\ell 10^* \cdot K_h^2 \oplus |M|_n \cdot K_h \quad (4)$$

where 10^* is the padding method that first appends a single 1 followed by as few zeros to make the total string length a multiple of n. A pictorial illustration of GHASHX is given in Fig. 4. The following lemma shows that GHASHX meets regular, almost-xor-universal and 3-way-regular properties, and thus can

---

[7] The number of zeros padded is 0 if the length of original message is already a multiple of n.

be instantiated in all of these constructions to restore their beyond-birthday-bound security. The proof of this lemma is similar to the one of Lemma 2. For the sake of completeness, we provide it in Appendix B.

Lemma 2. *Let* GHASHX $: \{0,1\}^n \times \{0,1\}^* \rightarrow \{0,1\}^n$ *be defined by Eq. 4. Then* GHASHX *is* ϵ_1*-regular,* ϵ_2*-almost-xor-universal, and* ϵ_3*-3-way-regular where* $\epsilon_1 = \epsilon_2 = \epsilon_3 = (\ell_{max} + 1)/2^n$ *and* ℓ_{max} *is the maximum number of n-bit blocks of a message.*

REMARK 4. Compared to GHASHX, PolyX uses the reverse order of a message to implicitly encode the length of a message as a parameter in the polynomial that will not be zeroed out. While GHASHX explicitly multiplies the length of a message by K_h, and thus requires one additional multiplication. On the other hand, GHASHX can be computed efficiently in the on-the-fly manner by using Honer's rule [34]. But if we want to compute PolyX efficiently by using Honer's rule, then we need to wait until the last block of a message arrives.

REMARK 5. Note that both PolyX and GHASHX are 1-key n-multiplication polynomial hash functions over $GF(2^n)$, the same as Poly. There are other types of polynomial hash functions requiring multiple keys, using $n/2$ multiplications, or over prime fields. We refer to [5,22] for a detailed discussion of these polynomial hash functions. Since our main focus is to propose some possible fixes by using 1-key n-multiplication polynomial hash function over $GF(2^n)$ as Poly, we leave it as the future work to investigate whether these hash functions can meet all of these three properties that are discussed in this section. Moreover, as the security and the performance of polynomial hash functions could have a significant impact on actual deployment, we leave it as another interesting and important future work to comparing these two newly proposed polynomial hash functions with existing ones (e.g., [5,22] or the international standard ISO/IEC 9797-3:2011 [23]).

5   Conclusion

In this paper, we demonstrate forgery attacks on several polynomial-hash-based MACs with provably beyond-birthday-bound security, namely nPolyMAC, CWC+, PolyMAC, 2k-PolyMAC, PDM*MAC, 1k-PDM*MAC and nEHtM$_p^+$. Our attacks exploit vulnerabilities in the underlying polynomial hash function, and require only one authentication query and one verification query with succeed probability of 1. Thus, our attacks disprove their high security claims. We then propose two new polynomial hash functions called PolyX and GHASHX, and prove that using either of two hash functions can fix the issues in these schemes, and thus can restore their beyond-birthday-bound security.

Acknowledgments. François-Xavier Standaert is senior research associate of the Belgian Fund for Scientific Research (F.R.S.-FNRS). This work has been funded in parts by the ERC consolidator grant 724725 (acronym SWORD), the ERC Advanced Grant

101096871 (acronym BRIDGE), and by National Key Research and Development Program of China (No. 2019YFB2101600). Views and opinions expressed are those of the author(s) only and do not necessarily reflect those of the European Union or the European Research Council. Neither the European Union nor the granting authority can be held responsible for them.

A   Overview of the Usage of Polynomial Hash Function

In this section, we briefly recall how the polynomial hash function Poly defined in Eq. 1 is used in schemes nPolyMAC [16], CWC+ [20], PolyMAC [14,27], 2k-PolyMAC [14,15], PDM*MAC [11], 1k-PDM*MAC [11], and nEHtM$_p^+$ [12]. In [16], the authors first showed the beyond-birthday-bound security of construction DWCDM. They then proposed nPolyMAC as a concrete instance of DWCDM by using Poly as the underlying hash function. They proved the beyond-birthday-bound security of nPolyMAC by combining the result of DWCDM and the properties of Poly. The required properties of Poly are ϵ_1-regular, ϵ_2-almost-xor-universal and ϵ_3-3-way-regular, and are proved in [16,17, Proposition 1]. In [20], the polynomial hash Poly was directly integrated into CWC+. The beyond-birthday-bound security analysis of CWC+ relies on the ϵ_2-almost-xor-universal property of Poly. In both PolyMAC and 2k-PolyMAC [14,15,27], the polynomial hash Poly was the main component of these two schemes. The beyond-birthday-bound security analyses of PolyMAC and 2k-PolyMAC require Poly to be ϵ_2-almost-xor-universal, while the multi-user beyond-birthday-bound security analysis of 2k-PolyMAC additionally requires Poly to be ϵ_1-regular. The authors [15, Lemma 4] proved that Poly was ϵ_1-regular and ϵ_2-almost-xor-universal. In [11], the authors first proved the beyond-birthday-bound security of PDM*MAC and 1k-PDM*MAC. They then explicitly used Poly to instantiate these two schemes to achieve the beyond-birthday-bound security. The required properties of Poly are ϵ_1-regular, ϵ_2-almost-xor-universal and ϵ_3-3-way-regular. In [12], the authors first showed the beyond-birthday-bound security of nEHtM$_p^*$. They then proposed nEHtM$_p^+$ as a concrete instance of nEHtM$_p^*$ by using Poly as the underlying hash function. They proved the beyond-birthday-bound security of nEHtM$_p^+$ by combining the result of nEHtM$_p^*$ and the ϵ_2-almost-xor-universal property of Poly.

B   Proof of Lemma 2

We first consider the regular property. Given a message $M \in \{0,1\}^*$ and a constant value $\Delta \in \{0,1\}^n$, it requires the equation $\mathsf{GHASHX}_{K_h}(M) \oplus \Delta = 0^n$ holds, namely

$$M_1 \cdot K_h^{\ell+1} \oplus M_2 \cdot K_h^{\ell} \oplus \ldots \oplus M_\ell 10^* \cdot K_h^2 \oplus |M| \cdot K_h \oplus \Delta = 0^n \ .$$

This is a non-trivial polynomial of K_h of degree at most $\ell + 1$ because the coefficient $M_\ell 10^*$ of K_h^2 is always non-zero. The number of roots of this polynomial is at most $\ell + 1$. Hence, the regular advantage is $(\ell+1)/2^n \leq (\ell_{\max}+1)/2^n$ since the hash key K_h is chosen uniformly at random from the set $\{0,1\}^n$.

We then analyze the almost xor universal property. Given two distinct messages $M, M' \in \{0,1\}^*$ and a constant value $\Delta \in \{0,1\}^n$, it implies the equation $\mathsf{GHASHX}_{K_h}(M) \oplus \mathsf{GHASHX}_{K_h}(M') \oplus \Delta = 0^n$, i.e.,

$$M_1 \cdot K_h^{\ell+1} \oplus \ldots \oplus M_\ell 10^* \cdot K_h^2 \oplus |M| \cdot K_h \oplus M_1' \cdot K_h^{\ell'+1} \oplus \ldots \oplus M_{\ell'}' 10^* \cdot K_h^2 \oplus |M'| \cdot K_h \oplus \Delta = 0^n .$$

If $\ell = \ell'$, then either there exists some $1 \le i \le \ell - 1$ such that $M_i \ne M_i'$ or $M_\ell 10^* \ne M_{\ell'}' 10^*$. Hence this is a non-trivial polynomial of K_h of degree at most $\ell + 1$, since either the coefficient $M_i \oplus M_i'$ of $K_h^{\ell+2-i}$ or the coefficient $M_\ell 10^* \oplus M_{\ell'}' 10^*$ of K_h^2 is non-zero. Thus, the almost xor universal advantage is at most $(\ell + 1)/2^n \le (\ell_{\max} + 1)/2^n$. If $\ell \ne \ell'$, then the coefficient $|M|_n \oplus |M'|_n$ of K_h is non-zero that implies this is a non-trivial polynomial of K_h of degree at most $\ell+1$. Hence the almost xor universal advantage is again at most $(\ell+1)/2^n \le (\ell_{\max} + 1)/2^n$.

Finally we consider the 3-way regular property. Given three distinct messages $M, M', M'' \in \{0,1\}^*$ and a *non-zero* constant $\Delta \in \{0,1\}^n$, it requires the equation $\mathsf{GHASHX}_{K_h}(M) \oplus \mathsf{GHASHX}_{K_h}(M') \oplus \mathsf{GHASHX}_{K_h}(M'') = \Delta$ holds. If the left part reduces to a zero polynomial, then the 3-way regular advantage is 0 since $\Delta \ne 0^n$. Otherwise, the left part is a non-trivial polynomial since there is at least one K_h^i whose coefficient is non-zero. Hence, the 3-way regular advantage is at most $\max\{\ell + 1, \ell' + 1, \ell'' + 1\}/2^n \le (\ell_{\max} + 1)/2^n$.

References

1. Iso/iec 9797-3:2011 information technology - security techniques - message authentication codes (macs) - part 3: Mechanisms using a universal hash-function. International Standard ISO/IEC 9797-3 (2011)
2. Iso/iec 19772:2020 information security - authenticated encryption. International Standard ISO/IEC 19772 (2020)
3. Banik, S., Pandey, S.K., Peyrin, T., Sasaki, Yu., Sim, S.M., Todo, Y.: GIFT: a small present - towards reaching the limit of lightweight encryption. In: Fischer, W., Homma, N. (eds.) CHES 2017. LNCS, vol. 10529, pp. 321–345. Springer, Cham (2017). https://doi.org/10.1007/978-3-319-66787-4_16
4. Bellare, M., Namprempre, C.: Authenticated encryption: relations among notions and analysis of the generic composition paradigm. In: Okamoto, T. (ed.) ASIACRYPT 2000. LNCS, vol. 1976, pp. 531–545. Springer, Heidelberg (2000). https://doi.org/10.1007/3-540-44448-3_41
5. Bernstein, D.J.: Polynomial evaluation and message authentication. http://cr.yp.to/papers.html#pema.IDb1ef3f2d385a926123e1517392e20f8c. Citations in this document 2 (2007)
6. Bhargavan, K., Leurent, G.: On the practical (in-)security of 64-bit block ciphers: collision attacks on HTTP over TLS and openvpn. In: Proceedings of the 2016 ACM SIGSAC Conference on Computer and Communications Security, Vienna, Austria, October 24–28, 2016, pp. 456–467 (2016). https://doi.org/10.1145/2976749.2978423
7. Bhattacharya, S., Nandi, M.: Revisiting variable output length XOR pseudorandom function. IACR Trans. Symmetric Cryptol. **2018**(1), 314–335 (2018). https://doi.org/10.13154/tosc.v2018.i1.314-335

8. Bogdanov, A., et al.: PRESENT: an ultra-lightweight block cipher. In: Paillier, P., Verbauwhede, I. (eds.) CHES 2007. LNCS, vol. 4727, pp. 450–466. Springer, Heidelberg (2007). https://doi.org/10.1007/978-3-540-74735-2_31

9. Borghoff, J., Canteaut, A., Güneysu, T., Kavun, E.B., Knezevic, M., Knudsen, L.R., Leander, G., Nikov, V., Paar, C., Rechberger, C., Rombouts, P., Thomsen, S.S., Yalçın, T.: PRINCE – a low-latency block cipher for pervasive computing applications. In: Wang, X., Sako, K. (eds.) ASIACRYPT 2012. LNCS, vol. 7658, pp. 208–225. Springer, Heidelberg (2012). https://doi.org/10.1007/978-3-642-34961-4_14

10. De Cannière, C., Dunkelman, O., Knežević, M.: KATAN and KTANTAN — a family of small and efficient hardware-oriented block ciphers. In: Clavier, C., Gaj, K. (eds.) CHES 2009. LNCS, vol. 5747, pp. 272–288. Springer, Heidelberg (2009). https://doi.org/10.1007/978-3-642-04138-9_20

11. Chakraborti, A., Nandi, M., Talnikar, S., Yasuda, K.: On the composition of single-keyed tweakable even-mansour for achieving BBB security. IACR Trans. Symmetric Cryptol. **2020**(2), 1–39 (2020). https://doi.org/10.13154/tosc.v2020.i2.1-39

12. Chen, Y.L., Dutta, A., Nandi, M.: Multi-user BBB security of public permutations based MAC. Cryptogr. Commun. **14**(5), 1145–1177 (2022). https://doi.org/10.1007/s12095-022-00571-w

13. Cogliati, B., Seurin, Y.: EWCDM: an efficient, beyond-birthday secure, nonce-misuse resistant MAC. In: Robshaw, M., Katz, J. (eds.) CRYPTO 2016. LNCS, vol. 9814, pp. 121–149. Springer, Heidelberg (2016). https://doi.org/10.1007/978-3-662-53018-4_5

14. Datta, N., Dutta, A., Nandi, M., Paul, G.: Double-block hash-then-sum: a paradigm for constructing BBB secure PRF. IACR Trans. Symmetric Cryptol. **2018**(3), 36–92 (2018). https://doi.org/10.13154/tosc.v2018.i3.36-92

15. Datta, N., Dutta, A., Nandi, M., Talnikar, S.: Tight multi-user security bound of sfdbhts. IACR Trans. Symmetric Cryptol. 2023(1), 192–223 (2023), https://doi.org/10.46586/tosc.v2023.i1.192-223

16. Datta, N., Dutta, A., Nandi, M., Yasuda, K.: Encrypt or decrypt? to make a single-key beyond birthday secure nonce-based MAC. In: Shacham, H., Boldyreva, A. (eds.) CRYPTO 2018. LNCS, vol. 10991, pp. 631–661. Springer, Cham (2018). https://doi.org/10.1007/978-3-319-96884-1_21

17. Datta, N., Dutta, A., Nandi, M., Yasuda, K.: Encrypt or decrypt? to make a single-key beyond birthday secure nonce-based MAC. IACR Cryptol. ePrint Arch. p. 500 (2018). https://eprint.iacr.org/2018/500

18. Dutta, A., Jha, A., Nandi, M.: Tight security analysis of ehtm MAC. IACR Trans. Symmetric Cryptol. **2017**(3), 130–150 (2017). https://doi.org/10.13154/tosc.v2017.i3.130-150

19. Dutta, A., Nandi, M., Talnikar, S.: Beyond birthday bound secure MAC in faulty nonce model. IACR Cryptol. ePrint Arch., p. 127 (2019). https://eprint.iacr.org/2019/127

20. Dutta, A., Nandi, M., Talnikar, S.: Beyond birthday bound secure MAC in faulty nonce model. In: Ishai, Y., Rijmen, V. (eds.) EUROCRYPT 2019. LNCS, vol. 11476, pp. 437–466. Springer, Cham (2019). https://doi.org/10.1007/978-3-030-17653-2_15

21. Dworkin, M.: Recommendation for block cipher modes of operation: Galois/counter mode (gcm) and gmac. NIST Special Publication 800–38D (2007)

22. Handschuh, H., Preneel, B.: Key-recovery attacks on universal hash function based MAC algorithms. In: Wagner, D. (ed.) CRYPTO 2008. LNCS, vol. 5157, pp. 144–161. Springer, Heidelberg (2008). https://doi.org/10.1007/978-3-540-85174-5_9

23. Information technology - Security techniques - Message Authentication Codes (MACs) - Part 3: Mechanisms using a universal hash-function. Iso/iec 9797-3:2011 (2011)

24. Iwata, T.: New blockcipher modes of operation with beyond the birthday bound security. In: Fast Software Encryption, 13th International Workshop, FSE 2006, Graz, Austria, March 15–17, 2006, Revised Selected Papers, pp. 310–327 (2006). https://doi.org/10.1007/11799313_20

25. Iwata, T.: New blockcipher modes of operation with beyond the birthday bound security. IACR Cryptol. ePrint Arch., p. 188 (2006). http://eprint.iacr.org/2006/188

26. Jean, J.: TikZ for Cryptographers (2023). https://www.iacr.org/authors/tikz/

27. Kim, S., Lee, B., Lee, J.: Tight security bounds for double-block hash-then-sum MACs. In: Canteaut, A., Ishai, Y. (eds.) EUROCRYPT 2020. LNCS, vol. 12105, pp. 435–465. Springer, Cham (2020). https://doi.org/10.1007/978-3-030-45721-1_16

28. McGrew, D.A., Viega, J.: The security and performance of the galois/counter mode (GCM) of operation. In: Canteaut, A., Viswanathan, K. (eds.) INDOCRYPT 2004. LNCS, vol. 3348, pp. 343–355. Springer, Heidelberg (2004). https://doi.org/10.1007/978-3-540-30556-9_27

29. McGrew, D.A., Viega, J.: The security and performance of the galois/counter mode of operation (full version). IACR Cryptol. ePrint Arch., p. 193 (2004). http://eprint.iacr.org/2004/193

30. McGrew, D.A., Viega, J.: The use of galois message authentication code (GMAC) in ipsec ESP and AH. RFC 4543, 1–14 (2006). https://doi.org/10.17487/RFC4543

31. Mennink, B., Neves, S.: Encrypted Davies-Meyer and its dual: towards optimal security using mirror theory. In: Katz, J., Shacham, H. (eds.) CRYPTO 2017. LNCS, vol. 10403, pp. 556–583. Springer, Cham (2017). https://doi.org/10.1007/978-3-319-63697-9_19

32. Minematsu, K.: How to thwart birthday attacks against macs via small randomness. In: Fast Software Encryption, 17th International Workshop, FSE 2010, Seoul, Korea, February 7–10, 2010, Revised Selected Papers, pp. 230–249 (2010). https://doi.org/10.1007/978-3-642-13858-4_13

33. Minematsu, K., Iwata, T.: Building blockcipher from tweakable blockcipher: extending FSE 2009 proposal. In: Chen, L. (ed.) IMACC 2011. LNCS, vol. 7089, pp. 391–412. Springer, Heidelberg (2011). https://doi.org/10.1007/978-3-642-25516-8_24

34. Shoup, V.: On fast and provably secure message authentication based on universal hashing. In: Koblitz, N. (ed.) CRYPTO 1996. LNCS, vol. 1109, pp. 313–328. Springer, Heidelberg (1996). https://doi.org/10.1007/3-540-68697-5_24

35. Wegman, M.N., Carter, L.: New hash functions and their use in authentication and set equality. J. Comput. Syst. Sci. 22(3), 265–279 (1981). https://doi.org/10.1016/0022-0000(81)90033-7

Correlation Cube Attack Revisited
Improved Cube Search and Superpoly Recovery Techniques

Jianhua Wang[1]([✉])([iD]), Lu Qin[2,3]([✉])([iD]), and Baofeng Wu[4,5]([✉])([iD])

[1] Key Laboratory of Mathematics Mechanization,
Academy of Mathematics and Systems Science, Chinese Academy of Sciences,
Beijing, China
wangjianhua@amss.ac.cn
[2] China UnionPay Co., Ltd., Shanghai, China
qinlu@unionpay.com
[3] School of Electronic Information and Electrical Engineering,
Shanghai Jiao Tong University, Shanghai, China
[4] Institute of Information Engineering, Chinese Academy of Sciences,
Beijing, China
wubaofeng@iie.ac.cn
[5] School of Cyber Security,
University of Chinese Academy of Sciences, Beijing, China

Abstract. In this paper, we improve the cube attack by exploiting low-degree factors of the superpoly w.r.t. certain *"special"* index set of cube (*ISoC*). This can be viewed as a special case of the correlation cube attack proposed at Eurocrypt 2018, but under our framework more beneficial equations on the key variables can be obtained in the key-recovery phase. To mount our attack, one has two challenging problems: (1) effectively recover algebraic normal form of the superpoly and extract out its low-degree factors; and (2) efficiently search a large quantity of good *ISoC*s. We bring in new techniques to solve both of them.

First, we propose the *variable substitution technique* for middle rounds of a cipher, in which polynomials on the key variables in the algebraic expressions of internal states are substituted by new variables. This will improve computational complexity of the superpoly recovery and promise more compact superpolys that can be easily decomposed with respect to the new variables. Second, we propose the *vector numeric mapping technique*, which seeks out a tradeoff between efficiency of the numeric mapping technique (Crypto 2019) and accuracy of the monomial prediction technique (Asiacrypt 2020) in degree evaluation of superpolys. Combining with this technique, a fast pruning method is given and modeled by MILP to filter good *ISoC*s of which the algebraic degree satisfies some fixed threshold. Thanks to automated MILP solvers, it becomes practical to comprehensively search for good cubes across the entire search space.

To illustrate the power of our techniques, we apply all of them to Trivium stream cipher. As a result, we have recovered the superpolys

Supported by National Natural Science Foundation of China (Grant No. 61972393).

J. Guo and R. Steinfeld (Eds.): ASIACRYPT 2023, LNCS 14440, pp. 190–222, 2023.
https://doi.org/10.1007/978-981-99-8727-6_7

of three cubes given by Kesarwani et al. in 2020, only to find they do not have `zero-sum` property up to 842 rounds as claimed in their paper. To our knowledge, the previous best practical key recovery attack was on 820-round Trivium with complexity $2^{53.17}$. We put forward 820-, 825- and 830-round practical key-recovery attacks, in which there are $2^{80} \times 87.8\%$, $2^{80} \times 83\%$ and $2^{80} \times 65.7\%$ keys that could be practically recovered, respectively, if we consider 2^{60} as the upper bound for practical computational complexity. Besides, even for computers with computational power not exceeding 2^{52} (resp. 2^{55}), we can still recover 58% (resp. 46.6%) of the keys in the key space for 820 rounds (resp. 830 rounds). Our attacks have led 10 rounds more than the previous best practical attack.

Keywords: Correlation cube attack · Variable substitution · Vector numeric mapping · MILP · Trivium

1   Introduction

Cube attack was introduced by Dinur and Shamir [8] at Eurocrypt 2009, which is a chosen plaintext key-recovery attack. In performing such an attack, one would like to express the outputs of a cryptosystem as Boolean functions on the inputs, namely, key bits and plaintext bits (say, IV bits for stream ciphers). By examining the integral properties of the outputs over some cubes, i.e., some indices of plaintext variables, one can obtain equations for the so-called superpolys over certain key bits of the cipher. After the introduction of cube attack, several variants of it were proposed, including cube testers [1], dynamic cube attack [9], conditional cube attack [16], division-property-based cube attack [22] and correlation cube attack [19]. Among these, correlation cube attack was proposed at Eurocrypt 2018 by Liu et al. [19]. It exploits correlations between the superpoly f_I of a cube and the so-called *basis* Q_I, which is a set of low-degree Boolean functions over key bits such that f_I can be expanded over them in terms of $f_I = \bigoplus_{h \in Q_I} h \cdot q_h$. Then the adversary could utilize the obtained equations regarding h to extract information about the encryption key.

Superpoly recovery has always been the most important step in a cube attack. At the beginning, one can only guess the superpolys by performing experiments, such as linearity tests [8] and degree tests [10]. It only became possible to recover the exact expressions of superpolys for some cubes when the division property was introduced to cube attacks.

Division property was introduced by Todo [21] in 2015, which turned out to be a generalization of the integral property. The main idea is, according to the parity of x^u for all x in a multiset $\mathbb{X}$ is even or unknown, one can divide the set of u's into two parts. By applying the division property, Todo [21] improved the integral distinguishers for some specific cryptographic primitives, such as KECCAK-f [3], Serpent [4] and the Simon family [2]. Then, the bit-based division property was proposed in 2016 [24], which aimed at cryptographic primitives only performing bit operations. It was also generalized to the three subsets setting to describe the parity of x^u for all x in $\mathbb{X}$ as not only even or unknown but also odd. Since it is more refined than the conventional division property, integral cryptanalysis against the Simon family of block ciphers was further improved. Afterwards, Xiang et al. [28] firstly transformed the propagation of bit-based division property into a mixed integer linear programming (MILP) model, and since then, one could search integral distinguishers by using off-the-shelf MILP solvers.

At Crypto 2017, cube attack based on the division property was proposed by Todo et al. [22]. One can evaluate values of the key bits that are not involved in the superpoly of a cube by using the division property. If we already know the superpoly is independent of most key bits, then we can recover the superpoly by trying out all possible combinations of other key variables which may be involved. At Crypto 2018, Wang et al. [26] improved the division-property-based cube attack in both complexity and accuracy. They reduced the complexity of recovering a superpoly by evaluating the upper bound of its degree. In addition, they improved the preciseness of the MILP model by using the "flag" technique so that one could obtain a non-zero superpoly. However, with these techniques, it remains impossible to recover superpolys with high degrees or superpolys for large-size cubes, as the time complexity grows exponentially in both cases.

Wang et al. [27] transformed the problem of superpoly recovery into evaluating the trails of division property with three subsets, and one could recover superpolys practically thanks to a breadth-first search algorithm and the pruning technique. As a result, they successfully recovered the superpolys of large-size *ISoCs* for 839- and 840-round Trivium practically, but only gave a theoretical attack against 841-round Trivium. In [11], Hao et al. pointed out that the pruning technique is not always so efficient. Therefore, instead of a breadth-first search algorithm, they simply utilized an MILP model for three-subset division property without unknown subset. As a result, they successfully recovered the superpoly of 840-, 841- and 842-round Trivium with the aid of an off-the-shelf MILP solver. At Asiacrypt 2020, Hu et al. [15] introduced the monomial prediction technique to describe the division property and provided deeper insights to understand it. They also established the equivalence between three-subset division property without unknown subsets and monomial predictions, showing both of them were perfectly accurate. However, the complexity of both techniques are very dependent on the efficiency of the MILP solvers. Once the number of division trails is very large, it is hard to recover superpolys by these two techniques, since the MILP solver may not find all solutions in an acceptable time. Afterwards, Hu et al. [14] proposed an improved framework called nested monomial prediction to recover massive superpolys. Recently, based on this technique, He et al. [13] proposed a new framework which contains two main steps: one is to obtain the so-called valuable terms which contributes to the superpoly in the middle rounds, and the other is to compute the coefficients of these valuable terms. To recover the valuable terms, non-zero bit-based division property (NBDP) and core monomial prediction (CMP) were introduced, which promoted great improvement to the computational complexity of superpoly recovery.

In addition to superpoly recovery, degree evaluation of cryptosystems is also an important issue in cube attacks, since the algebraic degree is usually used to judge whether the superpoly is zero and to search for good $ISoC$s. In [18], Liu introduced the numeric mapping technique and proposed an algorithm for degree evaluation of nonlinear feedback shift register (NFSR) based cryptosystems, which could give upper bounds of the degree. This method has low complexity but the estimation is less accurate generally. For example, it performs badly for Trivium-like ciphers when there exist adjacent indices in an $ISoC$. On the other hand, Hu et al.'s monomial prediction technique [15] can promise accurate degree evaluation, but the time consumption is too considerable which limits its application in large-scale search. An algorithm seeking a trade-off between accuracy and efficiency in degree evaluation has been missing in the literature.

The Trivium cipher [7], a notable member of the eSTREAM portfolio, has consistently been a primary target for cube attacks. Notably, the advances in cube attacks in recent years were significantly propelled by analysis of this cipher [5,13,14]. When it comes to theoretical attacks on 840 rounds of Trivium and beyond, the key challenge is to identify balanced superpolys. These superpolys often encompass millions to billions of terms, generally involving the majority of key bits. Due to the infeasibility of solving these high-degree equations, researchers have resorted to exhaustively enumerating most potential keys. This process simplifies the equations but often only results in the recovery of a handful of key bits. When it comes to practical attacks, we can look at the attacks mentioned in [5]. Here, a thorough search for $ISoC$s with simpler superpolys, such as linear or quadratic polynomials, is necessary. However, as the number of rounds increases, smaller $ISoC$s increasingly produce complex superpolys, making higher-round attacks infeasible. These complexities in superpolys obstruct effective key recovery attacks, leading us to the question that how can we gain more key information from the equation system to enhance the attack. In this work, we propose methods to address this challenge.

Our Contributions. To handle complex superpolys, leveraging the correlation between superpolys and low-degree Boolean functions is a promising approach for key recovery. In this paper, we revisit the correlation cube attack and propose an improvement by utilizing a significant number of so-called "special" $ISoC$s whose superpolys have low-degree Boolean factors, improving both the quantity and quality of equations obtained in the online phase. However, this approach introduces two challenges: superpoly recovery and the search for good $ISoC$s.

For superpoly recovery, we propose a novel and effective variable substitution technique. By introducing new variables to replace complex expressions of key bits and eliminating trails in intermediate states, we achieve a more compact representation of the superpoly on these new variables, making it easier to factorize. This technique also improves the computational complexity of superpoly recovery, enabling us to effectively identify special $ISoC$s.

To search good $ISoC$s, a common method is to filter $ISoC$s based on a comparison between the estimated algebraic degree and a fixed threshold. We introduce the concept of *vector degree* for a Boolean function, which contains more information than the conventional algebraic degree. We further employ a new technique called "vector numeric mapping" to depict the propagation of vector degrees in compositions of Boolean functions. As a result, we can iteratively estimate an upper bound for the vector degree of the entire composite function. Our vector numeric mapping technique outperforms Liu's numeric mapping in accuracy.

Furthermore, by studying properties of the vector numeric mapping, we introduce a pruning technique to quickly filter out good *ISoC*s whose superpolys have estimated degrees satisfying a threshold. We also construct an MILP model to describe this process, promissing an efficient automated selection of good *ISoC*s.

Our techniques are applied to the Trivium stream cipher. Initially, we apply our algorithms to three *ISoC*s proposed in [17], which were claimed to have zero-sum distinguishers up to 842 rounds. However, it is verified that these three *ISoC*s do not possess zero-sum properties for certain numbers of rounds. Nevertheless, two of them still exhibit the 841-round zero-sum property, which is the maximum number of rounds discovered so far for Trivium. Leveraging our good *ISoC* search technique and superpoly recovery with variable substitution technique, we mount correlation cube attacks against Trivium with **820**, **825** and **830** rounds, respectively. As a result, there are $2^{80} \times \mathbf{87.8\%}$, $2^{80} \times \mathbf{83\%}$ and $2^{80} \times \mathbf{65.7\%}$ keys that can be practically recovered, respectively, if we consider 2^{60} as the upper bound for practical computational complexity. Besides, even for computers with computational power not exceeding 2^{52}, we can still recover **58%** of the keys in the key space for 820 rounds. For computers with computational power not exceeding 2^{55}, we can recover **46.6%** of the keys in the key space for 830 rounds. Our attacks have achieved a significant improvement compared to the previous best practical attack [5], with up to 10 additional rounds recovered. Furthermore, for the first time, the complexity for recovering 830 rounds is less than 2^{75}, even surpassing the threshold of 2^{60}. Previous results on key recovery attacks against Trivium and our results are compared in Table 1.

Organization. The rest of this paper is organized as follows. In Sect. 2, we give some preliminaries including some notations and concepts. In Sect. 3, we review correlation cube attack and propose strategies to improve it. In Sect. 4, we propose the variable substitution technique to improve the superpoly recovery. In Sect. 5, we introduce the definition of vector degree for any Boolean function and present an improved technique for degree evaluation. Then we introduce an *ISoC* search method. In Sect. 6, we apply our techniques to Trivium. Conclusions are given in Sect. 7.

For the full version of this paper, please refer to [25].

2   Preliminaries

2.1   Notations

Let $\boldsymbol{v} = (v_0, \cdots, v_{n-1})$ be an n-dimensional vector. For any $\boldsymbol{v}, \boldsymbol{u} \in \mathbb{F}_2^n$, denote $\prod_{i=0}^{n-1} v_i^{u_i}$ by $\boldsymbol{v}^{\boldsymbol{u}}$ or $\pi_{\boldsymbol{u}}(\boldsymbol{v})$, and define an order $\boldsymbol{v} \preccurlyeq \boldsymbol{u}$ ($\boldsymbol{v} \succcurlyeq \boldsymbol{u}$, resp.), which

Table 1. A summary of key-recovery attacks against Trivium

| Attack type | # of Round | Off-line phase | | On-line phase | Total time | # of keys | Ref. |
		size of *ISoC*	# of *ISoCs*				
Practical	672	12	63	2^{17}	$2^{18.56}$	2^{80}	[8]
	767	28–31	35	2^{45}	$2^{45.00}$	2^{80}	[8]
	784	30–33	42	2^{38}	$2^{39.00}$	2^{80}	[10]
	805	32–38	42	2^{38}	$2^{41.40}$	2^{80}	[31]
	806	34–37	29	2^{35}	$2^{39.88}$	2^{80}	[20]
	808	39–41	37	2^{43}	$2^{44.58}$	2^{80}	[20]
	815	44–46	35	2^{45}	$2^{47.32}$	2^{80}	[5]
	820	48–51	30	2^{50}	$2^{53.17}$	2^{80}	[5]
	820	38	2^{13}	2^{51}	2^{52}	$2^{79.2}$	Sect. 6.5
	820	38	2^{13}	2^{51}	2^{60}	$2^{79.8}$	Sect. 6.5
	825	41	2^{12}	2^{53}	2^{54}	$2^{79.3}$	Sect. 6.5
	825	41	2^{12}	2^{53}	2^{60}	$2^{79.7}$	Sect. 6.5
	830	41	2^{13}	2^{54}	2^{55}	$2^{78.9}$	Sect. 6.5
	830	41	2^{13}	2^{54}	2^{60}	$2^{79.4}$	Sect. 6.5
Theoretical	799	32–37	18	2^{62}	$2^{62.00}$	2^{80}	[10]
	802	34–37	8	2^{72}	$2^{72.00}$	2^{80}	[29]
	805	28	28	2^{73}	$2^{73.00}$	2^{80}	[19]
	832	72	1	2^{79}	$2^{79.01}$	2^{80}	[22]
	832	72	1	2^{79}	$2^{79.01}$	2^{80}	[23]
	832	72	1	2^{79}	$2^{79.01}$	2^{80}	[27]
	835	72	4	2^{79}	$< 2^{79.01}$	2^{80}	[30]
	835	35	41	2^{75}	$2^{75.00}$	2^{80}	[19]
	840	75	3	2^{77}	$2^{77.32}$	2^{80}	[15]
	840	78	2	2^{79}	$2^{79.58}$	2^{80}	[11]
	841	78	2	2^{79}	$2^{79.58}$	2^{80}	[11]
	841	76	2	2^{78}	$2^{78.58}$	2^{80}	[15]
	842	76	2	2^{79}	$2^{78.58}$	2^{80}	[15]
	842	78	2	2^{79}	$2^{79.58}$	2^{80}	[12]
	843	54–57,76	5	2^{75}	$2^{76.58}$	2^{80}	[14]
	843	78	2	2^{79}	$2^{79.58}$	2^{80}	[20]
	844	54–55	2	2^{78}	$2^{78.00}$	2^{80}	[14]
	845	54–55	2	2^{78}	$2^{78.00}$	2^{80}	[14]
	846	51–54	6	2^{51}	$2^{79.00}$	2^{80}	[13]
	847	52–53	2	2^{52}	$2^{79.00}$	2^{80}	[13]
	848	52	1	2^{52}	$2^{79.00}$	2^{80}	[13]

means $v_i \leq u_i$ ($v_i \geq u_i$, resp.) for all $0 \leq i \leq n-1$. For any $\boldsymbol{u}_0, \cdots, \boldsymbol{u}_{m-1} \in \mathbb{F}_2^n$, we use $\boldsymbol{u} = \bigvee_{i=0}^{m-1} \boldsymbol{u}_i \in \mathbb{F}_2^n$ to represent the bitwise logical OR operation, that is, for $0 \leq j \leq n-1$, $u_j = 1$ if and only if there exists an $\boldsymbol{u}_i$ whose j-th bit equal to 1. Use $\boldsymbol{1}$ and $\boldsymbol{0}$ to represent the all-one and all-zero vector, respectively.

For a set I, denote its cardinality by $|I|$. For $I \subset [n] = \{0, 1, \cdots, n-1\}$, let I^c be its complement. For an n-dimensional vector $\boldsymbol{x}$, let $\boldsymbol{x}_I$ represent the $|I|$-dimensional vector $(x_{i_0}, \cdots, x_{i_{|I|-1}})$ for $I = \{i_0, \cdots, i_{|I|-1}\}$. Note that we always list the elements of I in an increasing order to eliminate ambiguity.

In this paper, we always distinguish $j \in \mathbb{Z}_{2^d}$ with a d-bit vector $\boldsymbol{u}$ in the sense that $\sum_{k=0}^{d-1} u_k 2^k = j$.

2.2 Algebraic Normal Form and Algebraic Degree of Boolean Functions

An n-variable Boolean function f can be uniquely written in the form $f(\boldsymbol{x}) = \bigoplus_{\boldsymbol{u} \in \mathbb{F}_2^n} a_{\boldsymbol{u}} \boldsymbol{x}^{\boldsymbol{u}}$, which is called the algebraic normal form (ANF) of f. If the term $\boldsymbol{x}^{\boldsymbol{u}}$ appears in f, i.e., $a_{\boldsymbol{u}} = 1$, we denote $\boldsymbol{x}^{\boldsymbol{u}} \to f$. Otherwise, denote $\boldsymbol{x}^{\boldsymbol{u}} \nrightarrow f$.

For an index set $I \subset [n]$ with size d, if $\boldsymbol{x}_I$ are considered as variables and $\boldsymbol{x}_{I^c}$ are considered as parameters in f, we can write the ANF of f w.r.t. $\boldsymbol{x}_I$ as

$$f(\boldsymbol{x}) = \bigoplus_{\boldsymbol{v} \in \mathbb{F}_2^d} g_{\boldsymbol{v}}(\boldsymbol{x}_{I^c}) \boldsymbol{x}_I^{\boldsymbol{v}},$$

where $g_{\boldsymbol{v}}(\boldsymbol{x}_{I^c}) = \bigoplus_{\{\boldsymbol{u} \in \mathbb{F}_2^n | \boldsymbol{u}_I = \boldsymbol{v}\}} a_{\boldsymbol{u}} \boldsymbol{x}_{I^c}^{\boldsymbol{u}_{I^c}}$.

The algebraic degree of f w.r.t. $\boldsymbol{x}_I$ is defined as

$$\deg(f)_{\boldsymbol{x}_I} = \max_{\boldsymbol{v} \in \mathbb{F}_2^d} \{\mathrm{wt}(\boldsymbol{v}) \mid g_{\boldsymbol{v}}(\boldsymbol{x}_{I^c}) \neq 0\},$$

where $\mathrm{wt}(\boldsymbol{v})$ is the Hamming weight of $\boldsymbol{v}$.

2.3 Cube Attack

The cube attack was proposed by Dinur and Shamir in [8], which is essentially an extension of the higher-order differential attack. Given a Boolean function f whose inputs are $\boldsymbol{x} \in \mathbb{F}_2^n$ and $\boldsymbol{k} \in \mathbb{F}_2^m$, and given a subset $I = \{i_0, \cdots, i_{d-1}\} \subset [n]$, we can write f as

$$f(\boldsymbol{x}, \boldsymbol{k}) = f_I(\boldsymbol{x}_{I^c}, \boldsymbol{k}) \cdot \boldsymbol{x}_I^1 + q_I(\boldsymbol{x}_{I^c}, \boldsymbol{k}),$$

where each term in q_I is not divisible by $\boldsymbol{x}_I^1$. Let C_I, called a cube (defined by I), be the set of vectors $\boldsymbol{x}$ whose components w.r.t. the index set I take all possible 2^d values and other components are undetermined. I is called the index set of the cube (*ISoC*). For each $\boldsymbol{y} \in C_I$, there will be a Boolean function with $n-d$ variables derived from f. Summing all these 2^d derived functions, we have

$$\bigoplus_{C_I} f(\boldsymbol{x}, \boldsymbol{k}) = f_I(\boldsymbol{x}_{I^c}, \boldsymbol{k}).$$

The polynomial f_I is called the superpoly of the cube C_I or of the *ISoC I*. Actually, f_I is the coefficient of $\boldsymbol{x}_I^1$ in the ANF of f w.r.t. $\boldsymbol{x}_I$. If we assign all the values of $\boldsymbol{x}_{I^c}$ to 0, f_I becomes the coefficient of $\boldsymbol{x}^u$ in f, which is a Boolean function in $\boldsymbol{k}$, where $u_i = 1$ if and only if $i \in I$. We denote it by $\mathtt{Coe}(f, \boldsymbol{x}^u)$.

2.4   Correlation Cube Attack

The correlation cube attack was proposed at Eurocrypt 2018 by Liu et al. [19]. The objective and high-level idea of this attack is to obtain key information by exploiting the correlations between superpolys and their low-degree basis, thereby deriving equations for the basis rather than the superpolys.

In mathematical terms, for an *ISoC I*, denote the basis of a superpoly f_I as $Q_I = \{h_1, \cdots, h_r\}$, such that h_i has low degree w.r.t. $\boldsymbol{k}$ and

$$f_I(\boldsymbol{x}_J, \boldsymbol{k}) = \bigoplus_{i=1}^{r} h_i q_i,$$

where $J \subset I^c$. This attack primarily works in two phases:

1. **Preprocessing phase** (see [25, Algorithm 4]): In this stage, the adversary tries to obtain a basis Q_I of the superpoly f_I and add the tuples (I, h_i, b) leading to $\Pr(h_i = b \mid f_I)$ greater than a threshold p into Ω, where $\Pr(h_i = b \mid f_I)$ is the probability of $h_i = 0$ (or $h_i = 1$) given that f_I is zero constant (or not) on $\boldsymbol{x}_J$ for a random fixed key, respectively.
2. **Online phase** (see [25, Algorithm 5]): The adversary randomly chooses α values for non-cube public bits, and computes corresponding values of the superpoly f_I to check whether it is zero constant or not. If all the values of f_I are zero, for each $(I, h_i, 0)$ in Ω the equation $h_i = 0$ holds with probability greater than p. Otherwise, for each $(I, h_i, 1)$ in Ω the equation $h_i = 1$ holds with probability greater than p. If all the h_i's are balanced and independent with each other, the adversary would recover r-bit key information with a probability greater than p^r by solving these r equations.

This method, though intricate, provides a solution for dealing with high-degree superpolys, and has demonstrated effectiveness in extending theoretical attacks on Trivium to more rounds.

2.5   Superpoly Recovery with Monomial Prediction/Three-Subset Division Property Without Unknown Subset

In [15], Hu et al. established the equivalence between monomial prediction and three-subset division property without unknown subset [11], showing both techniques could give accurate criterion on the existence of a monomial in f. Here we take the monomial prediction technique as an example to explain how to recover a superpoly.

For a vector Boolean function $f = f_{r-1} \circ \cdots \circ f_0$, denote the input and output of f_i by x_i and x_{i+1} respectively. If any $\pi_{u_i}(x_i) \to \pi_{u_{i+1}}(x_{i+1})$, i.e., the coefficient of $\pi_{u_i}(x_i)$ in $\pi_{u_{i+1}}(x_{i+1})$ is nonzero, then we call

$$\pi_{u_0}(x_0) \to \pi_{u_1}(x_1) \to \cdots \to \pi_{u_{r-1}}(x_{r-1})$$

a monomial trail from $\pi_{u_0}(x_0)$ to $\pi_{u_{r-1}}(x_{r-1})$, denoted by $\pi_{u_0}(x_0) \rightsquigarrow \pi_{u_{r-1}}(x_{r-1})$. If there is no trail from $\pi_{u_0}(x_0)$ to $\pi_{u_{r-1}}(x_{r-1})$, we denote $\pi_{u_0}(x_0) \not\rightsquigarrow \pi_{u_{r-1}}(x_{r-1})$. The set of all trails from $\pi_{u_0}(x_0)$ to $\pi_{u_{r-1}}(x_{r-1})$ are denoted by $\pi_{u_0}(x_0) \bowtie \pi_{u_{r-1}}(x_{r-1})$. Obviously, for any $0 < i < r - 1$, it holds that

$$|\pi_{u_0}(x_0) \bowtie \pi_{u_{r-1}}(x_{r-1})| = \sum_{u_i} |\pi_{u_0}(x_0) \bowtie \pi_{u_i}(x_i)| \cdot |\pi_{u_i}(x_i) \bowtie \pi_{u_{r-1}}(x_{r-1})|.$$

Theorem 1 (Monomial prediction[11,15]). *We have $\pi_{u_0}(x_0) \to \pi_{u_{r-1}}(x_{r-1})$ if and only if*

$$|\pi_{u_0}(x_0) \bowtie \pi_{u_{r-1}}(x_{r-1})| \equiv 1 \pmod 2.$$

That is, $\pi_{u_0}(x_0) \to \pi_{u_{r-1}}(x_{r-1})$ if and only if, for any $0 < i < r - 1$,

$$|\pi_{u_0}(x_0) \bowtie \pi_{u_{r-1}}(x_{r-1})| \equiv \sum_{\pi_{u_i}(x_i) \to \pi_{u_{r-1}}(x_{r-1})} |\pi_{u_0}(x_0) \bowtie \pi_{u_i}(x_i)| \pmod 2.$$

Theorem 2 (Superpoly recovery [11,15]). *Let f be a Boolean function with input x and k, and $f = f_{r-1} \circ f_{r-2} \circ \cdots \circ f_0(x, k)$. When setting $x_{I^c} = 0$, the superpoly of an ISoC I is*

$$\mathsf{Coe}(f, x^u) = \bigoplus_{|k^w x^u \bowtie f| \equiv 1 \pmod 2} k^w,$$

where $u_I = 1$ and $u_{I^c} = 0$.

MILP Model for Monomial Trails. It is a difficult task to search all the monomial trails manually. Since Xiang et al. [28] first transformed the propagation of bit-based division property into an MILP model, it only becomes possible to solve such searching problems by using off-the-shelf MILP solvers. To construct an MILP model for the monomial trail of a Boolean function, one needs only to model three basic operations, i.e., COPY, AND and XOR. Please refer to Appendix A in [25] for details.

2.6   Nested Monomial Prediction with NBDP and CMP Techniques

At Asiacrypt 2021, Hu et al. [14] proposed a framework, called nested monomial prediction, to exactly recover superpolys. For a Boolean function $f(x, k) = f_{r-1} \circ f_{r-2} \circ \cdots \circ f_0(x, k)$, denote the input and output of f_i by y_i and y_{i+1} respectively. To compute $\mathsf{Coe}(f, x^u)$, the process is as follows:

1. Set $n = r - 1$, $Y_n = \{f\}$ and set a polynomial $p = 0$.
2. Choose l such that $0 < l < n$ with certain criterion, and set $Y_l = \emptyset$ and $T_l = \emptyset$.
3. Express each term in Y_n with $\boldsymbol{y}_l$ by constructing and solving MILP model of monomial prediction and save the terms $\pi_{\boldsymbol{u}_l}(\boldsymbol{y}_l)$ satisfying that the size of $\{\pi_{\boldsymbol{u}_n}(\boldsymbol{y}_n) \in Y_n \mid \pi_{\boldsymbol{u}_l}(\boldsymbol{y}_l) \to \pi_{\boldsymbol{u}_n}(\boldsymbol{y}_n)\}$ is odd into T_l.
4. For each $\pi_{\boldsymbol{u}_l}(\boldsymbol{y}_l) \in T_l$, compute $\mathsf{Coe}(\pi_{\boldsymbol{u}_l}(\boldsymbol{y}_l), \boldsymbol{x}^{\boldsymbol{u}})$ by constructing and solving MILP model of monomial prediction. If the model about $\pi_{\boldsymbol{u}_l}(\boldsymbol{y}_l)$ is successfully solved with acceptable time, update p by $p \oplus \mathsf{Coe}(\pi_{\boldsymbol{u}_l}(\boldsymbol{y}_l), \boldsymbol{x}^{\boldsymbol{u}})$ and save the unsolved $\pi_{\boldsymbol{u}_l}(\boldsymbol{y}_l)$ into Y_l.
5. If $Y_l \neq \emptyset$, set $n = l$ and go to Step 2. Otherwise, return the polynomial p.

The idea of Step 3 and Step 4 comes from Theorem 1 and Theorem 2, i.e.,

$$\mathsf{Coe}(f, \boldsymbol{x}^{\boldsymbol{u}}) = \bigoplus_{\pi_{\boldsymbol{u}_n}(\boldsymbol{y}_n) \to f} \mathsf{Coe}(\pi_{\boldsymbol{u}_n}(\boldsymbol{y}_n), \boldsymbol{x}^{\boldsymbol{u}}) \tag{1}$$

$$= \bigoplus_{\pi_{\boldsymbol{u}_n}(\boldsymbol{y}_n) \to f} \bigoplus_{\pi_{\boldsymbol{u}_l}(\boldsymbol{y}_l) \to \boldsymbol{y}_n} \mathsf{Coe}(\pi_{\boldsymbol{u}_l}(\boldsymbol{y}_l), \boldsymbol{x}^{\boldsymbol{u}}) \tag{2}$$

$$= \bigoplus_{\pi_{\boldsymbol{u}_l}(\boldsymbol{y}_l) \in T_l} \mathsf{Coe}(\pi_{\boldsymbol{u}_l}(\boldsymbol{y}_l), \boldsymbol{x}^{\boldsymbol{u}}) \tag{3}$$

$$= p \oplus \left(\bigoplus_{\pi_{\boldsymbol{u}_l}(\boldsymbol{y}_l) \in Y_l} \mathsf{Coe}(\pi_{\boldsymbol{u}_l}(\boldsymbol{y}_l), \boldsymbol{x}^{\boldsymbol{u}}) \right). \tag{4}$$

Since the number of monomial trails grows sharply as the number of rounds of a cipher increases, it becomes infeasible to compute a superpoly for a high number of rounds with nested monomial prediction. At Asiacrypt 2022, He et al. [13] proposed new techniques to improve the nested monomial prediction. They no longer took the way of trying to solve out the coefficient of $\boldsymbol{x}^{\boldsymbol{u}}$ in $\pi_{\boldsymbol{u}_l}(\boldsymbol{y}_l)$ at multiple numbers of middle rounds. Instead, for a fixed number of middle round r_m, they focused on recovering a set of *valuable terms* (see Definition 1), denoted by VT_{r_m}, and then computing coefficient of $\boldsymbol{x}^{\boldsymbol{u}}$ in every *valuable term*. They discard the terms $\pi_{\boldsymbol{u}_{r_m}}(\boldsymbol{y}_{r_m})$ satisfying there exists no $\boldsymbol{k}^{\boldsymbol{w}}$ such that $\boldsymbol{k}^{\boldsymbol{w}}\boldsymbol{x}^{\boldsymbol{u}} \rightsquigarrow \pi_{\boldsymbol{u}_{r_m}}(\boldsymbol{y}_{r_m})$, i.e., $\mathsf{Coe}(\pi_{\boldsymbol{u}_{r_m}}(\boldsymbol{y}_{r_m}), \boldsymbol{x}^{\boldsymbol{u}}) = 0$ in Eq. (1) for $n = r_m$. The framework of this technique is as follows:

1. Try to recover VT_{r_m}. If the model is solved within an acceptable time, go to Step 2.
2. For each term $\pi_{\boldsymbol{u}_{r_m}}(\boldsymbol{y}_{r_m})$ in VT_{r_m}, compute $\mathsf{Coe}(\pi_{\boldsymbol{u}_{r_m}}(\boldsymbol{y}_{r_m}), \boldsymbol{x}^{\boldsymbol{u}})$ and then sum all of them.

To recover VT_{r_m}, He et al. proposed two techniques: non-zero bit-based division property (NBDP) and core monomial prediction (CMP), which led to great improvement of the complexity of recovering the *valuable terms* compared to nested monomial prediction. For details, please refer [13].

Definition 1 (Valuable terms [13]). *For a Boolean function $f(\boldsymbol{x}, \boldsymbol{k}) = f_{r-1} \circ f_{r-2} \circ \cdots \circ f_0(\boldsymbol{x}, \boldsymbol{k})$, denote the input and output of $\boldsymbol{f}_i$ by $\boldsymbol{y}_i$ and $\boldsymbol{y}_{i+1}$, respectively. Given $0 \le r_m < r$, if a term $\pi_{u_{r_m}}(\boldsymbol{y}_{r_m})$ satisfies (1) $\pi_{u_{r_m}}(\boldsymbol{y}_{r_m}) \to f$ and (2) $\exists \boldsymbol{k}^w$ such that $\boldsymbol{k}^w \boldsymbol{x}^u \rightsquigarrow \pi_{u_{r_m}}(\boldsymbol{y}_{r_m})$, then it is called a valuable term of $\mathrm{Coe}(f, \boldsymbol{x}^u)$ at round r_m.*

3　Improvements to Correlation Cube Attack

As the number of rounds of a cipher increases, it becomes infeasible to search small-size *ISoC*s with low-degree superpolys. Correlation cube attack [19] provides a viable solution to recover keys by using the correlation property between keys and superpolys, allowing for the use of high-degree superpolys. However, the correlation cube attack has not shown significant improvements or practical applications since its introduction. We revisit this attack first and then propose strategies to improve it.

For convenience, we will continue to use the notations from Sect. 2.4, where

$$f_I(\boldsymbol{x}_J, \boldsymbol{k}) = \bigoplus_{i=1}^{r} h_i q_i.$$

In the online phase of a correlation cube attack, the adversary computes the values of f_I for all possible values of $\boldsymbol{x}_J$. Using these values, the adversary can make guesses about the value of h_i in Q_I. The guessing strategy is as follows: for the tuple $(I, h_i, 1)$ satisfying $\Pr(h_i = 1 \mid f_I) > p$, if there exists a value of f_I is 1, guess $h_i = 1$; for the tuple $(I, h_i, 0)$ satisfying $\Pr(h_i = 0 \mid f_I) > p$, if $f_I \equiv 0$, guess $h_i = 0$. Therefore, the adversary can obtain some low-degree equations over $\boldsymbol{k}$.

Now we examine the probability of one such equation being correct. For certain i, in the first case, the success probability is $\Pr(h_i = 1 \mid f_I \not\equiv 0)$. If $r > 1$, and $f_I = 1$, $q_i = 1$ and $\bigoplus_{j \ne i} h_j q_j = 1$ for some value of $\boldsymbol{x}_{I^c}$, then we have $h_i = 0$. That is, the guess about h_i is incorrect. In the second case, the success probability is $\Pr(h_i = 0 \mid f_I \equiv 0)$. If $r > 1$ and $f_I \equiv 0$, there still exists the possibility that $h_i = 1$ and $q_i = \bigoplus_{j \ne i} h_j q_j$, leading to incorrect guess of h_i.

Therefore, since in the case $r > 1$ only probabilistic equations can be obtained, we first improve the strategy by constraining $r = 1$. That is, we consider the case

$$f_I = hq,$$

and call the *ISoC* I satisfying this condition a "special" *ISoC*. Note that now the success probability becomes 1 for the first case, and the fail probability for the second case is actually equal to $\Pr(h = 1, q \equiv 0)$. Considering there are a set of special *ISoC*s $\{I_1, \cdots, I_m\}$ such that $f_{I_i} = hq_i$, we can modify the strategy as follows: if $\exists i$ such that $f_{I_i} \not\equiv 0$, guess $h = 1$; otherwise, guess $h = 0$. The success probability is still 1 for the first case. The fail probability for the second case is now reduced to $\Pr(h = 1, q_1 \equiv 0, \ldots, q_m \equiv 0)$. In summary, we can improve the success probability of the guessing by searching for a large number of special $ISoC$s.

Based on the above observations, we propose the improved correlation cube attack in Algorithm 1 and Algorithm 2. This attack is executed in two phases:

1. **Preprocessing phase:**
   a. Identify special $ISoC$s.
   b. For each h, gather all the special $ISoC$ I for which h is a factor of f_I into a set T_h.
   c. To reduce the number of equations derived from wrong guesses of h, for those h whose success probability in the second case is at or below a threshold p, they will be exclusively guessed in the first case. Their associated T_h are then added to a set $\mathcal{T}_1$.
   d. The remaining h will be guessed in both cases with their associated T_h forming a set $\mathcal{T}$.
2. **Online phase:**
   a. Computes the value of f_I for each $ISoC$ I.
   b. For every T_h in $\mathcal{T}$, make a guess on the value of h based on f_I's value for all I in T_h.
   c. If for any T_h in $\mathcal{T}_1$, the values of f_I for all I in T_h satisfy the condition in the first case, then $h = 1$. Otherwise, no guess is formulated concerning h.
   d. Store the equations $h = 1$ in to a set G_1, while store the other equations into a set G_0. Note that only equations in G_0 may be incorrect.
   e. Using these derived equations along with partial key guesses, we can try to obtain a candidate of the key. If verifications for all partial key guesses do not yield a valid key, it indicates that there exist incorrect equations. In this case, modify some equations from G_0 and solve again until a valid key is obtained. Repeat this iteration until the correct key is ascertained.

A crucial factor for the success of this attack is to acquire a significant number of special $ISoC$s. To achieve this goal, the first step is to search for a large number of good $ISoC$s and recover their corresponding superpolys. Then, low-degree factors of these superpolys need to be computed.

Using degree estimation techniques is one of the common methods for searching cubes. In Sect. 5, we will first introduce a vector numeric mapping technique to improve the accuracy of degree estimation. By combining this attack, we will propose an algorithm for fast search of lots of good $ISoC$s on a large scale.

To our knowledge, it is difficult to decompose a complicated Boolean polynomial. To solve this problem, we propose a novel and effective technique to recover superpolys in Sect. 4. Using this technique, not only the computational complexity for recovering superpolys can be reduced, making it feasible to recover a large number of superpolys, but also it allows for obtaining compact superpolys that are easy to decompose.

Algorithm 1: Preprocessing Phase of Improved Correlation Cube Attacks

---

1 Generate a set $\mathcal{I}$ of $ISoC$'s;
2 $\mathcal{T} = \emptyset$, and $\mathcal{T}_1 = \emptyset$;
3 **for** *each ISoC I in $\mathcal{I}$* **do**
4 | Recover the superpoly f_I;
5 | **for** *each low-degree factor h of f_I* **do**
6 | | If $T_h \in \mathcal{T}$, set $T_h = T_h \cup \{I\}$; Otherwise, insert $T_h = \{I\}$ into $\mathcal{T}$;
7 | **end**
8 **end**
9 **for** T_h *in $\mathcal{T}$* **do**
10 | Estimate the conditional probability $\Pr(h = 0 \mid f_I = 0$ for $\forall I \in T_h)$; If its value is $<= p$, insert T_h into $\mathcal{T}_1$ and remove T_h from $\mathcal{T}$.
11 **end**
12 **return** $\mathcal{T}$ *and $\mathcal{T}_1$*.

Algorithm 2: Online Phase of Improved Correlation Cube Attacks

---

1 **Require:** $\mathcal{T}$ and $\mathcal{T}_1$;
2 $\mathcal{I} = \bigcup_{T_h \in \mathcal{T} \cup \mathcal{T}_1} T_h$
3 $G_0 = \emptyset$ and $G_1 = \emptyset$;
4 **for** *each ISoC I in $\mathcal{I}$* **do**
5 | Compute the sum of the output function f over all values in the cube C_I, i.e., the value of the superpoly f_I;
6 **end**
7 **for** T_h *in $\mathcal{T}$* **do**
8 | **if** *for any $I \in T_h$ the value of f_I is equal to 0* **then**
9 | | Set $G_0 = G_0 \cup \{h = 0\}$;
10 | **else**
11 | | Set $G_1 = G_1 \cup \{h = 1\}$;
12 | **end**
13 **end**
14 **for** T_h *in $\mathcal{T}_1$* **do**
15 | **if** *there exists $I \in T_h$ s.t. the value of f_I is equal to 1* **then**
16 | | Set $G_1 = G_1 \cup \{h = 1\}$;
17 | **end**
18 **end**
19 Set $e = 0$;
20 **for** *all possible choices of e equations from G_0* **do**
21 | Reset $h = 1$ for these e equations, and remain others in G_0;
22 | Solve these $|G_0| + |G_1|$ equations and check whether the solutions are correct;
23 **end**
24 If none of the solutions is correct, set $e = e + 1$ and go to Step 20.

---

4 Recover Superpolys from a Novel Perspective

4.1 Motivation

As discussed in Sect. 3, we need lots of special *ISoC*s to improve the correlation cube attack. On the one hand, it is still difficult to compute the factor of a complicated polynomial effectively with current techniques to our best knowledge. On the other hand, the efficiency of recovering superpolys needs to be improved in order to recover a large number of superpolys within an acceptable time. Therefore, we propose new techniques to address the aforementioned issues. Let $f(x, k) = f_{r-1} \circ f_{r-2} \circ \cdots \circ f_0(x, k)$ and denote the input and output of f_i by y_i and y_{i+1}, respectively. Here we adopt the notations used in the monomial prediction technique (see Sect. 2.5). Since

$$
\mathrm{Coe}(f, x^u) = \bigoplus_{\pi_{u_{r_m}}(y_{r_m})} \mathrm{Coe}(f, \pi_{u_{r_m}}(y_{r_m})) \mathrm{Coe}(\pi_{u_{r_m}}(y_{r_m}), x^u)
$$

$$
= \bigoplus_{\pi_{u_{r_m}}(y_{r_m}) \to f} \mathrm{Coe}(\pi_{u_{r_m}}(y_{r_m}), x^u)
$$

$$
= \bigoplus_{\pi_{u_{r_m}}(y_{r_m}) \to f \text{ and } \exists w \text{ s.t. } k^w x^u \leadsto \pi_{u_{r_m}}(y_{r_m})} \mathrm{Coe}(\pi_{u_{r_m}}(y_{r_m}), x^u).
$$

By Definition 1, the superpoly is equal to

$$
\mathrm{Coe}(f, x^u) = \bigoplus_{\pi_{u_{r_m}}(y_{r_m}) \in \mathrm{VT}_{r_m}} \mathrm{Coe}(\pi_{u_{r_m}}(y_{r_m}), x^u).
$$

Therefore, recovering a superpoly requires two steps: obtaining the *valuable terms* VT_{r_m} and recovering the coefficients $\mathrm{Coe}(\pi_{u_{r_m}}(y_{r_m}), x^u)$. The specific steps are as follows:

1. Try to obtain VT_{r_m}. If the model is solved within an acceptable time, go to Step 2.
2. For each term $\pi_{u_{r_m}}(y_{r_m})$ in VT_{r_m}, compute $\mathrm{Coe}(\pi_{u_{r_m}}(y_{r_m}), x^u)$ with our new techniques and sum them.

We will provide a detailed explanation of the procedures for each step.

4.2 Obtain Valuable Terms

One important item to note about the widely used MILP solver, the Gurobi optimizer, is that model modifications are done in a lazy fashion, meaning that effects of modifications of a model are not seen immediately. We can set up an MILP model with callback function indicating whether the optimizer finds a new solution. The following shows the process of how to obtain the r_m-round *Valuable Terms*; see [25, Algorithm 6].

1. Establish a model $\mathcal{M}$ to search for all trails $k^w x^u \leadsto \pi_{u_{r_1}}(y_{r_1}) \leadsto \cdots \leadsto f$.

2. Solve the model $\mathcal{M}$. Once a trail is found, go to Step 3. If there is no solution, go to Step 4.

3. (VTCallbackFun) Determine whether $\pi_{u_{r_m}}(y_{r_m}) \to f$ by the parity of the number of trails $\pi_{u_{r_m}}(y_{r_m}) \rightsquigarrow f$. If $\pi_{u_{r_m}}(y_{r_m}) \to f$, add $\pi_{u_{r_m}}(y_{r_m})$ to the set VT_{r_m}. Remove all trails from $\mathcal{M}$ that satisfy $k^w x^u \rightsquigarrow \pi_{u_{r_m}}(y_{r_m}) \rightsquigarrow f$. Go to the Step 2.

4. Return the *Valuable Terms* VT_{r_m}.

Note that for each $\pi_{u_{r_m}}(y_{r_m})$ satisfying $\pi_{u_{r_m}}(y_{r_m}) \rightsquigarrow f$, the parity of the number of trails is calculated only once due to the removal of all trails satisfying $k^w x^u \rightsquigarrow \pi_{u_{r_m}}(y_{r_m}) \rightsquigarrow f$.

He et al. [13] also applied the same framework, but they used different techniques. By combining their NBDP and DBP techniques, we can further improve the efficiency of recovering VT_{r_m}. We will show the results of experiments in Sect. 6.

4.3 Variable Substitution Technique for Coefficient Recovery

For a Boolean function $f(x, k) = f_{r-1} \circ f_{r-2} \circ \cdots \circ f_0(x, k)$ whose inputs are $x \in \mathbb{F}_2^n$ and $k \in \mathbb{F}_2^m$, denote the input and output of f_i by y_i and y_{i+1}, respectively. We study about the problem of recovering $\mathrm{Coe}(\pi_{u_{r_m}}(y_{r_m}), x^u)$ at middle rounds from an algebraic perspective. Let $\overleftarrow{f_{r_m}}$ denote $f_{r_m-1} \circ \cdots \circ f_0$, i.e., $y_{r_m} = \overleftarrow{f_{r_m}}(x, k)$. Assume the algebraic normal form of $\overleftarrow{f_{r_m}}$ in x is

$$\overleftarrow{f_{r_m}} = \bigoplus_{v \in \mathbb{F}_2^n} h_v(k) x^v.$$

Then one could get that $\mathrm{Coe}(\pi_{u_{r_m}}(y_{r_m}), x^u)$ is an XOR of some products over $h_v(k)$. Assume that the number of different non-constant $h_v[j]$'s is t for all v and j, where $h_v[j]$ represents the j-th component of h_v. Now we introduce new intermediates denoted by z to substitute these t $h_v[j]$'s. Without loss of generality, assume $z = d(k)$, where $d[i]$ is equal to a certain non-constant $h_v[j]$. From the ANF of $\overleftarrow{f_{r_m}}$, it is natural to derive the vectorial Boolean function g_{r_m} such that $y_{r_m} = g_{r_m}(x, z)$, whose ANF in x and z can be written as

$$g_{r_m}[j] = \bigoplus_v a_{v,j} z^{c_{v,j}} x^v,$$

where $g_{r_m}[j]$ represents j-th component of g_{r_m}, and $a_{v,j} \in \mathbb{F}_2$ and $c_{v,j} \in \mathbb{F}_2^t$ are both determined by v and j.

Example 1 serves as an illustration of the process of variable substitution. The transition from round 0 to round r_m with $(k_0 k_1 \oplus k_2 k_5 \oplus k_9 + k_{10})(k_2 k_7 \oplus k_8) x_0 x_2 x_3$ will have at least $4 * 2 = 8$ monomial trails. But after variable substitution, there remains only one trail $z_0 z_2 x_0 x_2 x_3$, which means we have consolidated 8 monomial trails into a single one. As the coefficients become more intricate and the number of terms in the product increases, the magnitude of this reduction becomes more pronounced. Additionally, it is evident that this also makes the superpoly more concise. In general, the more compact the superpoly is, the easier it is to factorize.

Example 1. Assume $y_{r_m} = g_{r_m}(x, k) = [(k_0 k_1 \oplus k_2 k_5 \oplus k_9 + k_{10}) x_0 x_2 \oplus (k_3 \oplus k_6) x_5, (k_2 k_7 \oplus k_8) x_3 \oplus x_6 x_7]$. Through variable substitution, all coefficients within y_{r_m}, including $k_0 k_1 \oplus k_2 k_5 \oplus k_9 + k_{10}$, $k_3 \oplus k_6$, and $k_2 k_7 \oplus k_8$, will be replaced with new variables z_0, z_1, and z_2, respectively. Then y_{r_m} could be rewritten as $y_{r_m} = g_{r_m}(x, z) = [z_0 x_0 x_2 \oplus z_1 x_5, z_2 x_3 \oplus x_6 x_7]$.

Therefore, we take such a way of substituting variables at the middle round r_m to recover $\mathsf{Coe}(\pi_{u_{r_m}}(y_{r_m}), x^u)$, and the process is as follows:

1. Compute the ANF of y_{r_m} in x.
2. Substitute all different non-constant $h_v[j]$ for all v and j by new variables z.
3. Recover $\mathsf{Coe}(\pi_{u_{r_m}}(y_{r_m}), x^u)$ in z by monomial prediction.

In fact, to solve $\mathsf{Coe}(\pi_{u_{r_m}}(y_{r_m}), x^u)$ in z by monomial prediction is equivalent to find all possible monomial trails $z^c x^u \rightsquigarrow \pi_{u_{r_m}}(y_{r_m})$ about c. We can construct an MILP model to describe all feasible trails.

Model for Recovering $\mathsf{Coe}(\pi_{u_{r_m}}(y_{r_m}), x^u)$ in z. To describe monomial prediction into an MILP model, we actually need only to construct an MILP model to describe all the trails for g_{r_m}. Since the ANF of g_{r_m} is known, three consecutive operations Copy $\rightarrow$ And $\rightarrow$ XOR are sufficient to describe g_{r_m}. The process is as follows:

- [Copy] For each x_i (resp. z_i), the number of copies is equal to the number of monomials divisible by x_i (resp. z_i) contained in $g_{r_m}[j]$ for all j.
- [And] Generate all monomials contained in $g_{r_m}[j]$ for all j.
- [XOR] According to the ANF of each $g_{r_m}[j]$, collect monomials using XOR to form $g_{r_m}[j]$.

We give an example to show how to describe g_{r_m} by Copy $\rightarrow$ And $\rightarrow$ XOR. The algorithm for recovering $\mathsf{Coe}(\pi_{u_{r_m}}(y_{r_m}), x^u)$ can be found in Algorithm 3.

Example 2. If $y_{r_m} = g_{r_m}(x, z) = (x_0 x_1 x_2 \oplus x_0 z_0 \oplus z_1, x_2 \oplus z_0 z_1 \oplus z_0)$, we can describe g_{r_m} by the following three steps.

$$(x_0, x_1, x_2, z_0, z_1) \xrightarrow{\text{Copy}} (x_0, x_0, x_1, x_2, x_2, z_0, z_0, z_0, z_1, z_1) \xrightarrow{\text{And}}$$
$$(x_0 x_1 x_2, x_0 z_0, z_1, x_2, z_0 z_1, z_0) \xrightarrow{\text{XOR}} (x_0 x_1 x_2 \oplus x_0 z_0 \oplus z_1, x_2 \oplus z_0 z_1 \oplus z_0)$$

Discussion. We have given a method of describing g_{r_m} into an MILP model, which is easy to understand and implement. In general, there may be other ways to construct the MILP model for a concrete g_{r_m}. Of course, different ways do not affect the correctness of the coefficients recovered. It is difficult to find theoretical methods to illustrate what kind of way of modeling g_{r_m} is easier to solve. In order to verify the improvement of our variable substitution technique over previous methods, we will compare the performance by some experiments.

Algorithm 3: Coefficient Recovery with Variable Substitution

Input: u, u_{r_m} and the ANF of g_{r_m}
Output: $q = \mathrm{Coe}(\pi_{u_{r_m}}(y_{r_m}), x^u)$

1   Declare an empty MILP model $\mathcal{M}$. Let $\mathbf{a}$ be $n + t$ MILP variables of $\mathcal{M}$
    corresponding to the $n + t$ components of $x \| z$.

2   $\mathcal{M}.con \leftarrow a_i = u_i$ for all $i \in [n]$.

3   Update $\mathcal{M}$ according to the function g_{r_m} and denote $\mathbf{b}$ as the output state of
    g_{r_m}.

4   $\mathcal{M}.con \leftarrow b_i = u_{r_m}[i]$ for all i.

5   $\mathcal{M}.optimize()$.

6   Prepare a hash table H whose key is t-bit string and value is counter.

7   **for** *each feasible solution of* $\mathcal{M}$ **do**

8   Let c denote the solution $(a_n, \cdots, a_{n+t-1})$.

9       $H[c] \leftarrow H[c] + 1$.

10 **end**

11 Prepare a polynomial $q \leftarrow 0$.

12 **for** *each* c *satisfying* $H[c]$ *is odd* **do**

13       $q \leftarrow q \oplus z^c$.

14 **end**

---

5   Improved Method for Searching a Large Scale of Cubes

The search of *ISoC*s in cube attacks often involves degree evaluations of cryptosystems. While the numeric mapping technique [18] offers lower complexity, it performs not well for Trivium-like ciphers when dealing with sets of adjacent indices. This limitation arises from the repeated accumulation of estimated degrees due to the multiplications of adjacent indices during updates. Although the monomial prediction technique [15] provides exact results, it is time-intensive. Thus, efficiently obtaining the exact degree of a cryptosystem remains a challenge. To efficiently search for promising cubes with adjacent indices on a large scale, we propose a compromise approach for degree evaluation called the "vector numeric mapping" technique. This technique yields a tighter upper bound than the numeric mapping technique while maintaining lower time complexity than monomial prediction. Additionally, we have developed an efficient algorithm based on an MILP model for large-scale search of *ISoC*s.

5.1   The Numeric Mapping

Let $\mathbb{B}_n$ be the set consisting of all n-variable Boolean functions. The numeric mapping [18], denoted by DEG, is defined as

$$\mathrm{DEG}: \quad \mathbb{B}_n \times \mathbb{Z}^n \longrightarrow \mathbb{Z}$$

$$(f, d) \longmapsto \max_{a_u \neq 0} \left\{ \sum_{i=0}^{n-1} u[i] d[i] \right\},$$

where a_u is the coefficient of the term x^u in the ANF of f.

Let $g = (g_1, \ldots, g_n)$ be an (m, n)-vectorial Boolean function, i.e. $g_i \in \mathbb{B}_m$, $1 \leq i \leq n$. Then for $f \in \mathbb{B}_n$, the numeric degree of the composite function $h = f \circ g = f(g_1, \ldots, g_n)$, denoted by $\mathtt{DEG}(h)$, is defined as $\mathtt{DEG}(f, d_g)$, where $d_g[i] \geq \deg(g[i])$ for all $0 \leq i \leq n-1$. The algebraic degree of h is always no greater than $\mathtt{DEG}(h)$, therefore, the algebraic degrees of internal states of an NFSR-based cryptosystem can be estimated iteratively by using the numeric mapping.

5.2 The Vector Numeric Mapping

Firstly, we introduce the definition of vector degree of a Boolean function, from which we will easily understand the motivation of the vector numeric mapping. For the sake of simplicity, let $\deg(g_1, \ldots, g_n)$ represent $(\deg(g_1), \ldots, \deg(g_n))$.

Definition 2 (Vector Degree). *Let f be an n-variable Boolean function represented w.r.t. $\boldsymbol{x}_I$ as*

$$f(\boldsymbol{x}) = \bigoplus_{\boldsymbol{u} \in \mathbb{F}_2^d} g_u(\boldsymbol{x}_{I^c}) \boldsymbol{x}_I^u,$$

where $I \subset [n]$, $|I| = d$. The vector degree of f w.r.t. $\boldsymbol{x}$ and the index set I, denoted by $\mathbf{vdeg}_{[I,x]}$, is defined as

$$\mathbf{vdeg}_{[I,x]}(f) = \deg(g_{u_0}, g_{u_1}, \ldots, g_{u_{2^d-1}})_{\boldsymbol{x}_{I^c}} = \left(\deg(g_{u_0})_{\boldsymbol{x}_{I^c}}, \ldots, \deg(g_{u_{2^d-1}})_{\boldsymbol{x}_{I^c}} \right),$$

where $\boldsymbol{u}_j$ satisfies $\sum_{k=0}^{d-1} \boldsymbol{u}_j[k] 2^k = j$, $0 \leq j \leq 2^d - 1$.

When we do not emphasize I and $\boldsymbol{x}$, we abbreviate $\mathbf{vdeg}_{[I,x]}$ as $\mathbf{vdeg}_I$ or $\mathbf{vdeg}$. Similarly, for a vectorial Boolean function $\boldsymbol{g} = (g_1, \ldots, g_n)$, we denote the vector degree of $\boldsymbol{g}$ by $\mathbf{vdeg}(\boldsymbol{g}) = (\mathbf{vdeg}(g_1), \ldots, \mathbf{vdeg}(g_n))$.

According to Definition 2, it is straightforward to get an upper bound of the vector degree of f, which is shown in Proposition 1.

Proposition 1. *For any $0 \leq j < 2^{|I|}$, $\mathbf{vdeg}_{[I,x]}(f)[j] \leq n - |I|$.*

Moreover, it is obvious that the vector degree of f contains more information about f than the algebraic degree. We can also derive the algebraic degree of f from its vector degree, that is,

$$\deg(f) = \max_{0 \leq j < 2^{|I|}} \{ \mathbf{vdeg}_I(f)[j] + \mathrm{wt}(j) \}.$$

Therefore, the upper bound of the algebraic degree can be estimated by the upper bound of the vector degree.

Corollary 1. *Let $\boldsymbol{v}$ be an upper bound of the vector degree of f, i.e., $\mathbf{vdeg}_{[I,x]}(f) \preccurlyeq \boldsymbol{v}$. Then we have*

$$\deg(f) \leq \max_{0 \leq j < 2^{|I|}} \{ \min \{ \boldsymbol{v}[j], n - |I| \} + \mathrm{wt}(j) \}.$$

In fact, the algebraic degree of f is the degenerate form of the vector degree of f w.r.t. $I = \emptyset$. Moreover, if $I_1 \subset I_2$, the vector degree of f w.r.t. I_1 can be deduced from the vector degree of f w.r.t. I_2, that is,

$$\mathbf{vdeg}_{I_1}(f)[j] = \max_{0 \leq j' < 2^{|I_2| - |I_1|}} \left\{ \mathbf{vdeg}_{I_2}(f)[j' \cdot 2^{|I_1|} + j] + \mathrm{wt}(j') \right\} \tag{5}$$

for any $0 \leq j < 2^{|I_1|}$.

In order to estimate the vector degree of composite functions, we propose the concept of vector numeric mapping.

Definition 3 (Vector Numeric Mapping). *Let $d \geq 0$. The vector numeric mapping, denoted by VDEG_d, is defined as*

$$\mathrm{VDEG}_d : \quad \mathbb{B}_n \times \mathbb{Z}^{n \times 2^d} \longrightarrow \mathbb{Z}^{2^d}$$
$$(f, V) \longmapsto \boldsymbol{w},$$

where $f = \bigoplus_{\boldsymbol{u} \in \mathbb{F}_2^n} a_{\boldsymbol{u}} \boldsymbol{x}^{\boldsymbol{u}}$ and for any $0 \leq j < 2^d$,

$$\boldsymbol{w}[j] := \max_{a_{\boldsymbol{u}} \neq 0} \max_{\substack{j_0, \cdots, j_{n-1} \\ 0 \leq j_i \leq \boldsymbol{u}[i](2^d - 1) \\ j = \vee_{i=0}^{n-1} \boldsymbol{u}[i] j_i}} \left\{ \sum_{i=0}^{n-1} \boldsymbol{u}[i] V[i][j_i] \right\}.$$

For an (m, n)-vectorial Boolean function $\boldsymbol{g} = (g_0, \ldots, g_{n-1})$, we define its vector numeric mapping as $\mathrm{VDEG}(\boldsymbol{g}, V) = (\mathrm{VDEG}(g_0, V), \ldots, \mathrm{VDEG}(g_{n-1}, V))$.

Theorem 3. *Let f be an n-variable Boolean function and $\boldsymbol{g}$ be an (m, n)-vectorial Boolean function. Assume $\mathbf{vdeg}_I(g_i) \preccurlyeq \boldsymbol{v}_i$ for all $0 \leq i \leq n - 1$ w.r.t. an index set I. Then each component of the vector degree of $f \circ \boldsymbol{g}$ is less than or equal to the corresponding component of $\mathrm{VDEG}_I(f, V)$, where $V = (\boldsymbol{v}_0, \cdots, \boldsymbol{v}_{n-1})$.*

The proof of Theorem 3 can be found in [25, Appendix D]. By Theorem 3, we know that the vector numeric mapping $\mathrm{VDEG}(f, V)$ gives an upper bound of the vector degree of the composite function $f \circ \boldsymbol{g}$ when V is the upper bound of the vector degree of the vectorial Boolean function $\boldsymbol{g}$.

For a Boolean function $f(\boldsymbol{x}) = f_{r-1} \circ f_{r-2} \circ \cdots \circ f_0(\boldsymbol{x})$, let I be the index set. We denoted the upper bound of the vector degree of f w.r.t. $\boldsymbol{x}$ and I by

$$\widehat{\mathbf{vdeg}}_{[I, \boldsymbol{x}]}(f) = \mathrm{VDEG}(f_{r-1}, V_{r-2}),$$

where $V_i = \mathrm{VDEG}(\boldsymbol{f}_i, V_{i-1})$, $0 < i \leq r - 2$, and $V_0 = \mathbf{vdeg}_{[I, \boldsymbol{x}]}(\boldsymbol{f}_0)$.

According to Proposition 1 and Corollary 1, the estimation of algebraic degree of f w.r.t. $\boldsymbol{x}$ and I, denoted by $\widehat{\deg}_{[I, \boldsymbol{x}]}(f)$, can be derived from $\widehat{\mathbf{vdeg}}_{[I, \boldsymbol{x}]}(f)$. To meet different goals in various scenes, we give the following three modes to get $\widehat{\deg}_{[I, \boldsymbol{x}]}(f)$:

Mode 1. $\widehat{\deg}_{[I, \boldsymbol{x}]}(f) = \max_{0 \leq j < 2^{|I|}} \{ \min\{\widehat{\mathbf{vdeg}}_{[I, \boldsymbol{x}]}(f)[j], n - |I|\} + \mathrm{wt}(j) \}.$

Mode 2. $\widehat{\mathbf{deg}}_{[I,x]}(f) = \widehat{\mathbf{vdeg}}_{[I,x]}(f)[2^{|I|} - 1] + |I|$.

Mode 3. $\widehat{\mathbf{deg}}_{[I,x]}(f) = \max_{0 \le j < 2^{|I|}} \{\widehat{\mathbf{vdeg}}_{[I,x]}(f)[j] + \mathrm{wt}(j)\}$.

Mode 1 gives the estimated degree that can be totally derived from previous discussions, which is most precise. Mode 2 focuses on the value of the last coordinate of $\widehat{\mathbf{vdeg}}_{[I,x]}(f)$, which may tell us whether the algebraic degree can reach the maximum value. Mode 3 gives the estimated degree without revision, which will be used when choosing the index set of the vector degree.

Since the index set I is an important parameter when estimating the vector degree of f, we learn about how different choices of the index set influence the estimation of the vector degree. Then, we give the relationship between numeric mapping and vector numeric mapping.

Theorem 4. *Let $f \in \mathbb{B}_n$ and I_1 and I_2 be two index sets with $|I_1| = k$, $|I_2| = d$ and $I_1 \subset I_2$. If $V_1 \in \mathbb{Z}^{n \times 2^k}$ and $V_2 \in \mathbb{Z}^{n \times 2^d}$ satisfy*

$$V_1[i][j] \ge \max_{0 \le j' < 2^{d-k}} \left\{ V_2[i][j' \cdot 2^k + j] + wt(j') \right\} \tag{6}$$

for any $0 \le i \le n - 1$ and $0 \le j < 2^k$, then we have

$$\mathrm{VDEG}_k(f, V_1)[j] \ge \max_{0 \le j' < 2^{d-k}} \left\{ \mathrm{VDEG}_d(f, V_2)[j' \cdot 2^k + j] + wt(j') \right\} \tag{7}$$

for any $0 \le j < 2^k$.

The proof of Theorem 4 can be found in [25, Appendix E]. Let $V_i \succcurlyeq \mathbf{vdeg}_{I_i}(g)$ for $i = 1, 2$ in Theorem 4, and assume that they satisfy the inequality (6). Since $\mathrm{VDEG}_d(f, V_2) \succcurlyeq \mathbf{vdeg}_{I_2}(f \circ g)$ by Theorem 3, we can see that the RHS of (7) is larger than or equal to $\mathbf{vdeg}_{I_1}(f \circ g)[j]$ from (5). It implies that the RHS of (7) gives a tighter upper bound of $\mathbf{vdeg}_{I_1}(f \circ g)[j]$ than the LHS of (7). Moreover, the relation in (6) would be maintained after iterations of the vector numeric mapping by Theorem 4.

In fact, the numeric mapping is the degenerate form of the vector numeric mapping in the sense of $d = 0$. Therefore, we can assert that $\deg(g_r \cdots g_1)$ derived from the iterations of the vector numeric mapping $\mathrm{VDEG}(g_i, V_i)$ leads to a tighter upper bound than the iterations of the numeric mapping $\mathrm{DEG}(g_i, d_i)$. An example can be found in [25, Appendix F].

How to choose a suitable index set of the vector degree? One can consider the index set $I = [m]$, where m is the size of the input of the function g. Of course, it is the best set by Theorem 4 if we only consider the accuracy of the estimated degree. However, the space and time complexity of the vector numeric mapping is exponential w.r.t. such a set. Therefore, we should choose the index set of the vector degree carefully. We will put forward some heuristic ideas for the Trivium cipher in Sect. 6.

5.3   Algorithm for Searching Good ISoCs

As mentioned in Sect. 3, finding a large scale of special *ISoCs* is quite important in improving correlation cube attacks. Indeed, we observe that if the estimated algebraic degree of f over an *ISoC* exceeds the size of it, the higher the estimated algebraic degree is, the more complex the corresponding superpoly tends to. Therefore, when searching *ISoCs* of a fixed size, imposing the constraint that the estimated algebraic degree of f is below a threshold may significantly increase the likelihood of obtaining a relatively simple superpoly. Then, we heuristically convert our goal of finding large scale of special *ISoCs* to finding large scale of good *ISoCs* whose corresponding estimated algebraic degrees of f are lower than a threshold d.

In the following, we propose an efficient algorithm for searching large scale of such good *ISoCs*.

Theorem 5. *Let* $f(x, k) = f_{r-1} \circ f_{r-2} \circ \cdots \circ f_0(x, k)$ *be a Boolean function, where* $x \in \mathbb{F}_2^n$ *represents the initial vector and* $k \in \mathbb{F}_2^m$ *represents the key. Let* $J \subset [n]$ *be an index set for vector degree and* I *and* K *be two ISoCs satisfying* $J \subset K \subset I$. *Then we have*

$$\widehat{\mathbf{vdeg}}_{[J, x_K]}(f|_{x_{K^c}=0}) \preccurlyeq \widehat{\mathbf{vdeg}}_{[J, x_I]}(f|_{x_{I^c}=0}).$$

Proof. Let $U_0 = \mathbf{vdeg}_{[J, x_K]}(f_0|_{x_{K^c}=0})$, $V_0 = \mathbf{vdeg}_{[J, x_I]}(f_0|_{x_{I^c}=0})$, and $U_t = \mathrm{VDEG}(f_t, U_{t-1})$, $V_t = \mathrm{VDEG}(f_t, V_{t-1})$ for $1 \le t \le r-2$. Then $\widehat{\mathbf{vdeg}}_{[J, x_K]}(f|_{x_{K^c}=0}) = \mathrm{VDEG}(f, U_{r-2})$, $\widehat{\mathbf{vdeg}}_{[J, x_I]}(f|_{x_{I^c}=0}) = \mathrm{VDEG}(f, V_{r-2})$.

It is obvious that the set of monomials in $f_0|_{x_{I^c}=0}$ is a superset of the set of monomials in $f_0|_{x_{K^c}=0}$ since $I^c \subset K^c$. Thus, we can get $U_0 \preccurlyeq V_0$ from Definition 2. According to Definition 3, we can iteratively get $U_i \preccurlyeq V_i$ for all $1 \le i \le r-2$, which leads to $\widehat{\mathbf{vdeg}}_{[J, x_K]}(f|_{x_{K^c}=0}) \preccurlyeq \widehat{\mathbf{vdeg}}_{[J, x_I]}(f|_{x_{I^c}=0})$.

Corollary 2. *Let* $f(x, k) = f_{r-1} \circ f_{r-2} \circ \cdots \circ f_0(x, k)$ *be a Boolean function. Let* J *be an index set of vector degree,* $d > |J|$ *be a threshold of algebraic degree, and* K *be an ISoC satisfying* $J \subset K$. *If* $\widehat{\deg}_{[J, x_K]}(f|_{x_{K^c}=0}) \ge d$, *then* $\widehat{\deg}_{[J, x_I]}(f|_{x_{I^c}=0}) \ge d$ *for all ISoCs* I *satisfying* $K \subset I$.

Corollary 2 can be derived from Theorem 5 directly. Theorem 5 shows a relationship between the estimated vector degrees of f w.r.t. a fixed index set J for two *ISoCs* containing J. According to Corollary 2, we can delete all the sets I containing an *ISoC* K from the searching space of *ISoCs* if K satisfies $\widehat{\deg}_{[J, x_K]}(f|_{x_{K^c}=0}) \ge d$. Therefore, in order to delete more "bad" *ISoCs* from the searching space, we can try to find such an *ISoC* K as small as possible.

For a given *ISoC* I satisfying $\widehat{\deg}_{[J, x_I]}(f|_{x_{I^c}=0}) \ge d$, we can iteratively choose a series of *ISoCs* $I \supsetneq I_1 \supsetneq \cdots \supsetneq I_q \supset J$ such that $\widehat{\deg}_{[J, x_{I_i}]}(f|_{x_{I_i^c}=0}) \ge d$ for all $1 \le i \le q$ and $\widehat{\deg}_{[J, x_{I'}]}(f|_{x_{I'^c}=0}) < d$ for any $I' \subsetneq I_q$. Note that this process can terminate with a smallest *ISoC* I_q from I since $\widehat{\deg}_{[J, x_J]}(f|_{x_{J^c}=0}) \le |J| < d$.

Next, we give a new algorithm according to previous discussions for searching a large scale of good *ISoCs*.

Process of Searching Good *ISoC*s. Let J be a given index set, Ω be the set of all subsets of $[n]$ containing J and with size k, d be a threshold of degree, and a be the number of repeating times. The main steps are:

1. Prepare an empty set $\mathcal{I}$.
2. Select an element I from Ω as an *ISoC*.
3. Estimate the algebraic degree of f w.r.t. the variable $\boldsymbol{x}_I$ and the index set J, denoted by d_I. If $d_I < d$, then add I to $\mathcal{I}$ and go to Step 5; otherwise, set $count = 0$ and go to Step 4.
4. Set $count = count + 1$. Let $I' = I$, randomly remove an element $i \in I' \setminus J$ from I' and let $x_i = 0$. Then, estimate the algebraic degree of f w.r.t. the variable $\boldsymbol{x}_{I'}$. If the degree is less than d and $count < a$, continue to execute Step 4; if the degree is less than d and $count \geq a$, go to step 5; if the degree is greater than or equal to d, let $I = I'$ and go to Step 3.
5. Remove all the sets containing I from Ω. If $\Omega \neq \emptyset$, go to Step 2; otherwise, output $\mathcal{I}$.

The output $\mathcal{I}$ is the set of all good *ISoC*s we want. In the algorithm, Step 4 shows the process of finding a "bad" *ISoC* as small as possible. Since the index i we choose to remove from I' is random every time, we use a counter to record the number of repeating times and set the number a as an upper bound of it to ensure that the algorithm can continue to run.

To implement the algorithm efficiently, we establish an MILP model and use the automated searching tool Gurobi to solve the model, and then we can get a large scale of good *ISoC*s that are needed.

MILP Model for Searching Good *ISoC*s. In order to evaluate the elements of Ω more clearly, we use linear inequalities over integers to describe Ω. We use a binary variables b_i to express whether to choose v_i as a cube variable, namely, $b_i = 1$ iff v_i is chosen as a cube variable, $0 \leq i \leq n-1$. Then the sub-models are established as follows:

Model 1. *To describe that the size of each element of Ω is equal to k, we use*

$$\sum_{i=0}^{n-1} b_i = k.$$

Model 2. *To describe that each element of Ω includes the set J, we use*

$$b_j = 1 \text{ for } \forall j \in J.$$

Model 3. *To describe removing all the sets that contain I from Ω, we use*

$$\sum_{i \in I} b_i < |I|.$$

Since some *ISoC*s are deleted in Step 5 during the searching process, we need to adjust the MILP model continuously. Thus we can use the *Callback* function of Gurobi to implement this process. In fact, using *Callback* function to adjust the model will not repeat the test for excluded nodes that do not meet the conditions, and will continue to search for nodes that have not been traversed, so the whole process of adjusting the model will not cause the repetition of the solving process, and will not result in a waste of time.

According to the above descriptions and the MILP model we have already established, we give an algorithm for searching good *ISoC*s. The algorithm includes two parts which are called the main procedure and the callback function, and the complete algorithm can be found in [25, Appendix G].

6   Application to Trivium

In this section, we apply all of our techniques to Trivium, including degree estimation, superpoly recovery and improved correlation cube attack. We set $r_m = 200$ in the experiment of recovering superpolys below, and expression of the states after 200-round initialization of Trivium has been computed and rewritten in new variables as described in Sect. 4, where the ANF of new variables in the key k is also determined. For details, please visit the git repository https://github.com/faniw3i2nmsro3nfa94n/Results. All experiments are completed on a personal computer due to the promotion of the algorithms.

6.1   Description of Trivium Stream Cipher

Trivium [7] consists of three nonlinear feedback shift registers whose size is 93, 84, 111, denoted by r_0, r_1, r_2, respectively. Their internal states, denoted by s with a size of 288, are initialized by loading 80-bit key k_i into s_i and 80-bit IV x_i into s_{i+93}, $0 \leq i \leq 79$, and other bits are set to 0 except for the last three bits of the third register. During the initialization stage, the algorithm would not output any keystream bit until the internal states are updated for 1152 rounds. The linear components of the three update functions are denoted by ℓ_1, ℓ_2 and ℓ_3, respectively, and the update process can be described as

$$s_{n_i} = s_{n_i-1} \cdot s_{n_i-2} \oplus \ell_i(s) \quad \text{for} \quad i = 1, 2, 3,$$
$$s \leftarrow (s_{287}, s_0, s_1, \cdots, s_{286}),$$

(8)

where n_1, n_2, n_3 are equal to $92, 176, 287$, respectively. Denote z to be the output bit of Trivium. Then the output function is $z = s_{65} \oplus s_{92} \oplus s_{161} \oplus s_{176} \oplus s_{242} \oplus s_{287}$.

6.2   Practical Verification for Known Cube Distinguishers

In [17], Kesarwani et al. found three *ISoC*s having Zero-Sum properties till 842 initialization rounds of Trivium by cube tester experiments. These *ISoC*s are listed in [25, Appendix H], denoted by I_1, I_2, I_3. We apply the superpoly recovery algorithm proposed in Sect. 4 to these *ISoC*s. It turns out that the declared Zero-Sum properties of these *ISoC*s is incorrect, which is due to the randomness of experiments on a small portion of the keys. The correct results are listed in Table 2, where "Y" represents the corresponding $ISoC$ has Zero-Sum property, while "N" represents the opposite. For more details about the superpolys of these $ISoC$s, please refer to our git repository. We also give some values of the key for which the value of non-zero superpolys is equal to 1, listed in [25, Appendix I].

Table 2. Verification of Zero-Sum properties in [17]

Rounds	≤ 835	836	837–839	840	841	842
I_1	Y	N	N	N	Y	N
I_2	Y	N	N	N	N	N
I_3	Y	Y	N	Y	Y	N

Comparison of Computational Complexity for Superpoly Recovery. For comparison, we recover superpoly of the $ISoC$ I_2 for 838 rounds by nested monomial prediction, nested monomial prediction with NBDP and CMP techniques, and nested monomial prediction with our variable substitution technique, respectively, where the number of middle rounds is set to $r_m = 200$ for the last two techniques. As a result, it takes more than one day for superpoly recovery by nested monomial prediction, about 13 min by NBDP and CMP techniques, and 15 min by our method. It implies that variable substitution technique plays a role as important as the NBDP and CMP techniques in improving the complexity of superpoly recovery. Further, by combining our methods with NBDP and CMP techniques to obtain *valuable terms*, it takes about 2 min to recover this superpoly. Thus, it is the best choice to combine our variable substitution technique with NBDP and CMP in superploy recovery.

6.3 Estimation of Vector Degree of Trivium

Recall the algorithm proposed by Liu in [18] for estimating the degree of Trivium-like ciphers. We replace the numeric mapping with the vector numeric mapping. The reason is that vector numeric mapping can perform well for the $ISoC$s containing adjacent indices but numeric mapping cannot.

The algorithm for estimation of the vector degree of Trivium is detailed in [25, Algorithm 11] and [25, Algorithm 12]. The main idea is the same as [18, Algorithm 2], but the numeric mapping is replaced. For the sake of simplicity, we denote $\text{VDEG}(\prod_{i=1}^{k} x[i], (v_1, \cdots, v_k))$ as $\text{VDEGM}(v_1, \cdots, v_k)$ in the algorithms.

Heuristics Method for Choosing Indices of Vector Degree. As we discussed earlier, the size of the index set of vector degree should not be too large, and we usually set the size less than 13. How to choose the indices to obtain a good degree evaluation? We give the following two heuristic strategies.

1. Check whether there are adjacent elements in the *ISoC* I. If yes, add all the adjacent elements into the index set J. When the size of the set J exceeds a preset threshold, randomly remove elements from J until its size is equal to the threshold. Otherwise, set $I = I \setminus J$ and execute Strategy 2.
2. Run our vector degree estimation algorithm ([25, Algorithm 11]) with the input $(s^0, I_i, \emptyset, R, 3)$ for all $i \in I$, where $I_i = \{i\}$. Remove the index with the largest degree evaluation of the R-round output bit from I every time, and add it to J until the size of J is equal to the preset threshold. If there exist multiple choices that have equal degree evaluation, randomly pick one of them.

After applying the above two strategies, we will get an index set of vector degree. Since there are two adjacent states multiplied in the trivium update function, the variables with adjacent indices may be multiplied many times. So in Strategy 1, we choose adjacent indices in I and add them to the index set of vector degree. In Strategy 2, we compute the degree evaluation of the R-round output bit by setting the degree of x_j to be zero for all $j \in I$ except i. Although the exact degree of the output bit is less than or equal to 1, the evaluation is usually much larger than 1. This is because the variable x_i is multiplied by itself many times and the estimated degree is added repeatedly. So we choose these variables, whose estimated degrees are too large, as the index of vector degree. Once we fix a threshold of the size of the index set of vector degree, we can obtain the index set by these two strategies.

Degree of Trivium on All IV Bits. We have estimated the upper bound of the degree of the output bit on all IV bits for R-round Trivium by our vector degree estimation algorithm ([25, Algorithm 11]) with $mode = 1$. Every time we set the threshold to be 8 to obtain the index set of vector degree and run the procedure of degree estimation with the index set. We repeat 200 times and choose the minimum value as the upper bound of the output bit's degree. The results compared with the numeric mapping technique are illustrated in Fig. 1. In our experiments, the upper bound of the output bit's degree reaches the maximum degree 80 till 805 rounds using vector numeric mapping, while till 794 rounds using numeric mapping. Besides, the exact degree [6] exhibits the behavior of a decrease when the number of rounds increases at certain points. The vector numeric mapping can also capture this phenomenon, whereas numerical mapping cannot. This is because the vector numeric mapping can eliminate the repeated degree estimation of variables whose indices are in the index set of vector degree.

Degree of Trivium on Partial IV Bits. In fact, the degree evaluation algorithm will perform better when there are a few adjacent indices in the *ISoC*. We generate the *ISoC* in the following way. Firstly, randomly generate a set $I_0 \subset [n]$ with size 36 which does not contain adjacent indices. Next, find a set $I_0 \subset I$ with size $36 + l$ such that there are exactly l pairs adjacent indices in I. Then, one can

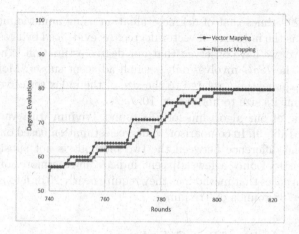

Fig. 1. Degree evaluations by vector numeric mapping and numeric mapping

estimate the degree for the *ISoC I* by numeric mapping technique and vector numeric mapping technique, where the size of the index set of vector degree is set to 8, and calculate the difference of a maximum number of zero-sum rounds between these two techniques. For each l, we repeat 200 times and record the average of the differences; see Table 3 for details.

Table 3. Average improved number of rounds by vector numeric mapping relative to numeric mapping technique

l	0	1	2	3	4	5	6	7	8
Number	6.8	27.8	41.0	44.7	45.4	39.4	34.6	31.5	29.7

It is obvious that when the *ISoC* contains adjacent indices, the vector numeric mapping technique can improve more than 27 rounds compared with the numerical mapping technique on average, even to 45 rounds. When there are no adjacent index or few adjacent indices, the difference between degree evaluations by numerical mapping technique and vector mapping technique is small. It implies the reason for the success of degree evaluation for cubes with no adjacent index by numeric mapping in [18]. As l increases, the improved number of rounds first increases and then slowly decreases. This is because the index set of vector degree cannot contain all adjacent indices when l is large. But the vector numeric mapping technique compared with the numeric mapping technique can still improve by about 30 rounds.

Complexity and Precision Comparison of Degree Evaluation. In theory, the complexity of degree evaluation using vector numeric mapping technique is no more than $2^{|J|}$ times that of degree evaluation using numeric mapping technique, where J is the index set of vector degree. As evidenced by the experiments conducted above, we have observed that our degree estimation is notably more accurate when the $ISoC$ involves only a small adjacent subset. Moreover, since complexity is exponentially related to the size of the index set of vector degree, we typically limit its size to not exceed 10.

The runtime of our algorithm for 788-round Trivium with various sizes is detailed in [25, Table 9]. In comparison to degree estimation based on the division property [6], the difference between the two methods is not substantial when the $ISoC$ consists of only a few adjacent indices. Furthermore, our algorithm significantly outpaces that method, as they require nearly 20 min to return degree evaluations for 788 rounds of Trivium.

6.4   The Complexity of Fast Cube Search

To validate the effectiveness of our pruning technique, we conducted a comparative experiment. As a comparison, we replicated a partial experiment by Liu [18], which involved searching for 837-round distinguishers using cubes of size 37 with non-adjacent indices. As a result, our search algorithm made a total of 9296 calls to the degree estimation algorithm to complete the search of entire space, while exhaustive search required over 38320568 calls to the degree estimation algorithm. This clearly demonstrates the effectiveness of our pruning technique.

6.5   Practical Key Recovery Attacks

Benefiting from the new framework of superpoly recovery and the $ISoC$ search technique, we could obtain a large scale of special $ISoC$s within an acceptable time so that we can mount practical correlation cube attacks against Trivium with large number of rounds. For correlation cube attacks, we choose the threshold of the conditional probability as $p = 0.77$. We will not elaborate further on these parameters.

Practical Key Recovery Attacks Against 820-Round Trivium

Parameter Settings. Set Ω to be the total space of the $ISoC$ with size $k = 38$. Set the index set $J = \{0, 1, 2, i, i + 1\}$, the threshold of degree d to be 41 in the $ISoC$ search algorithm in Sect. 5.3, where i ranges from 3 to 26. We call the search algorithms in parallel for different i.

Attacks. We have finally obtained 27428 special $ISoC$s with size 38, whose concrete information can be found in our git repository, including the $ISoC$s, superpolys, factors and balancedness of superpolys, where the balancedness of each superpoly is estimated by randomly testing 10000 keys. Besides, these $ISoC$s are sorted by balancedness of superpolys in descending order. Finally, we choose the first 2^{13} $ISoC$s to mount key recovery attacks.

For the first 2^{13} *ISoC*s, we call Algorithm 1 to generate the sets $\mathcal{T}$ and $\mathcal{T}_1$ whose elements are pairs composed of the factor of superpoly and the corresponding special *ISoC*, and sizes are 30 and 31, respectively. The results are listed in [25, Appendix L], where the probabilities are estimated by randomly testing 10000 keys. The details about the *ISoC* corresponding to each factor h are listed in our git repository.

In the online phase, after computing all the values of the superpolys, one obtain the set of equations G_0 and G_1. To make full use of the equations, one should recover keys as follows:

1. For all $54 \leq i \leq 79$, guess the value of k_i if the equation for k_i is not in $G_0 \cup G_1$.
2. For i from 53 to 0, if the equation for $k_i + k_{i+25}k_{i+26} + k_{i+27}$ or $k_i + k_{i+25}k_{i+26}$ is in $G_0 \cup G_1$, recover the value of k_i. Otherwise, guess the value of k_i.
3. Go through over all possible values of k_i guessed in Step 1 and Step 2, and repeat Step 1 until the solution is correct.
4. If none of the solutions is correct, adjust the equations in G_0 according to Step 20 in Algorithm 2 and go to Step 1.

Note that the complexity of recovering the value of k_i for $i < 53$ is $\mathcal{O}(1)$, since the values of k_{i+25}, k_{i+26} and k_{i+27} are known before. In our experiments, the factors are all chosen in the form $k_i + k_{i+25}k_{i+26} + k_{i+27}$ for $0 \leq i \leq 52$ or $k_{53} + k_{78}k_{79}$ or k_i for $54 \leq i \leq 65$. Thus the number of key bits obtained by the equations is always equal to the number of equations.

Now we talk about computing the complexity of our improved correlation cube attack. Since the set $\mathcal{I}$ of *ISoC*s is fixed, for each fixed key $\mathbf{k}$, the corresponding values of the superpolys of all *ISoC*s are determined. Therefore, we can calculate the time complexity of recovering this $\mathbf{k}$ using the following method. The complexity for computing the values of superpolys remains the same, which is $\mathcal{O}(2^{13} \cdot 2^{38})$. For brute force key recovery, the complexity can be determined by combining the values of the superpolys with the guessing strategy, allowing us to obtain the number of equations in G_0 and G_1, say, a_k and b_k, respectively, as well as the numbers of incorrect equations in G_0, denoted by e_k. It then enables us to determine the complexity of the preprocessing phase to be $2^{80-a_k-b_k} \cdot \left(\sum_{i=0}^{e_k} \binom{a_k}{i} \right)$. Thus, the complexity for recovering $\mathbf{k}$ is

$$\mathcal{C}_k = \mathcal{O}(2^{13} \cdot 2^{38}) + \mathcal{O}\left(2^{80-a_k-b_k} \cdot \left(\sum_{i=0}^{e_k} \binom{a_k}{i} \right) \right).$$

We estimated the proportion of keys with a complexity not larger than $\mathcal{C}$ by randomly selecting 10,000 keys, namely, $|\{\mathbf{k} : \mathcal{C}_k \leq \mathcal{C}\}|/10000$, and the result is listed in Table 4. Due to the extensive key space, we have performed a hypothesis testing in [25, Appendix O] to assess whether these proportions can accurately approximate the true proportions. In conclusion, our findings indicate a very strong correlation between them. From Table 4, it can be seen that 87.8% of the keys can be practically recovered by the attack. In particular, 58.0% of keys can be recovered with a complexity of only $\mathcal{O}(2^{52})$.

Table 4. The proportion of keys with attack complexities not exceeding C for 820 rounds

C	2^{52}	2^{54}	2^{56}	2^{58}	2^{60}
proportion	58.0%	69.2%	77.0%	82.8%	87.8%

Practical Key Recovery Attacks Against 825-Round Trivium

Parameter Settings. Set Ω to be the total space of *ISoC* with size 41. Set the index set $J = \{0, 1, \cdots, 10\} \setminus \{j_0, j_1, j_2\}$, the threshold of degree d to be 44 in the *ISoC* search algorithm in Sect. 5.3, where $j_0 > 2$, $j_1 > j_0+1$ and $j_1+1 < j_2 < 11$. We call the search algorithms in parallel for different tuples (j_0, j_1, j_2).

Attacks. We finally obtained 12354 special *ISoCs* with size 41, and we provide their concrete information in our git repository. Besides, these *ISoCs* are sorted by balancedness of superpolys in descending order, where the balancedness is estimated by randomly testing 10000 keys. We choose the first 2^{12} *ISoCs* to mount key recovery attacks.

For the first 2^{12} *ISoCs*, we call Algorithm 1 to generate the sets T and T_1 whose elements are pairs composed of the factor of superpoly and the corresponding special *ISoC*, and the sizes are 31 and 30, respectively. The results are listed in [25, Appendix M], where the probabilities are estimated by randomly testing 10000 keys. The details about the *ISoC* corresponding to each factor h are listed in our git repository.

We estimate the proportion of keys with a complexity not larger than C by randomly selecting 10,000 keys, and the result is listed in Table 5. From Table 5, it can be seen that 83% of the keys can be practically recovered by the attack. In particular, 60.9% of keys can be recovered with a complexity of only $\mathcal{O}(2^{54})$.

Table 5. The proportion of keys with attack complexities not exceeding C for 825 rounds

C	2^{54}	2^{56}	2^{58}	2^{60}
proportion	60.9%	70.7%	77.7%	83.0%

Practical Key Recovery Attacks Against 830-Round Trivium

Parameter Settings. The parameter settings are the same as that of 825 rounds, except the threshold of degree d is set to 45 here. We also call the search algorithms in parallel for different tuples (j_0, j_1, j_2).

Attacks. We finally obtained 11099 special *ISoC*s with size 41, whose concrete information can be found in our git repository. Besides these *ISoC*s are sorted by balancedness of superpolys in descending order, where the balancedness is estimated by randomly testing 10000 keys. We choose the first 2^{13} *ISoC*s to mount key recovery attacks.

For the first 2^{13} *ISoC*s, we call Algorithm 1 to generate the sets $\mathcal{T}$ and $\mathcal{T}_1$, with sizes 25 and 41, respectively. The results are listed in [25, Appendix N], where the probabilities are estimated by randomly testing 10000 keys. The details about the *ISoC* corresponding to each factor h are listed in our git repository.

We also estimate the proportion of keys with a complexity not larger than $\mathcal{C}$ by randomly selecting 10000 keys, and the result is listed in Table 6. From Table 6, it can be seen that 65.7% of the keys can be practically recovered by the attack. In particular, 46.6% of keys can be recovered with a complexity of only $\mathcal{O}(2^{55})$.

Table 6. The proportion of keys with attack complexities not exceeding $\mathcal{C}$ for 830 rounds

$\mathcal{C}$	2^{55}	2^{56}	2^{57}	2^{58}	2^{59}	2^{60}
proportion	46.6%	50.6%	54.2%	58.0%	61.9%	65.7%

Due to limited computational resources, we were unable to conduct practical validations of key recovery attacks. Instead, we randomly selected some generated superpolys and verified the model's accuracy through cross-validation, utilizing publicly accessible code for superpoly recovery. Furthermore, we have performed practical validations for the non-zero-sum case presented in [25, Table 8] to corroborate the accuracy of our model. In addition, as mentioned in [5], attempting to recover keys would take approximately two weeks on a PC equipped with two RTX3090 GPUs when the complexity reaches $\mathcal{O}(2^{53})$. Therefore, for servers with multiple GPUs and nodes, it is feasible to recover a 830-round key within a practical time.

Discussion About the Parameter Selections. Parameter selection is a nuanced process. The number of middle rounds r_m is determined by the complexity of computing the expression of g_{r_m}. Once r_m exceeds 200, the expression for g_{r_m} becomes intricate and challenging to compute, and overly complex expressions also hinder efficient computation of $\mathtt{Coe}(\pi_{u_{r_m}}(y_{r_m}), x^u)$ for MILP solvers. For *ISoC*s, we chose their size not exceeding 45 to maintain manageable complexity. We focused on smaller adjacent indices as bases when searching for *ISoC*s. The decision is based on the observation that smaller indices become involved later in the update process of Trivium. Consequently, this usually results in comparatively simpler superpolys. We directly selected these preset index sets as index of set for vector degree. When determining the threshold for searching good *ISoC*s, we noticed that a higher threshold tended to result in more complex superpolys. Thus, we typically set the threshold slightly above the size of the *ISoC*s. In the improved correlation cube attacks, the probability threshold significantly affects the complexity. Too low threshold will increase the number of incorrect guessed bits e_k, raising the complexity. Conversely, an excessively high threshold reduces the number of equations in G_0, i.e., a_k, prolonging the brute-force search. One can modify the p-value to obtain a relative high success probability.

Comparison with Other Attacks. From the perspective of key recovery, our correlation cube attack differs from attacks in [5,13,14] in how we leverage key information from the superpolys. We obtain equations from the superpolys' factors through their correlations with superpolys, whereas [5,13,14] directly utilize the equations of the superpolys. This allows us to extract key information even from high-degree complex superpolys. We also expect that this approach will be effective for theoretical attacks and find applications in improving theoretical attacks to more extended rounds.

7   Conclusions

In this paper, we propose a variable substitution technique for cube attacks, which makes great improvement to the computational complexity of superpoly recovery and can provide more concrete superpolys in new variables. To search good cubes, we give a generalized definition of degree of Boolean function and give out a degree evaluation method with the vector numeric mapping technique. Moreover, we introduce a pruning technique to fast filter the *ISoC*s and describe it into an MILP model to search automatically. It turn out that, these techniques perform well in cube attacks. We also propose practical verifications for some former work by other authors and perform practical key recovery attacks on 820-, 825- and 830-round Trivium cipher, promoting up to 10 more rounds than previous best practical attacks as we know. In the future study, we will apply our techniques to more ciphers to show their power.

References

1. Aumasson, J.-P., Dinur, I., Meier, W., Shamir, A.: Cube testers and key recovery attacks on reduced-round MD6 and trivium. In: Dunkelman, O. (ed.) FSE 2009. LNCS, vol. 5665, pp. 1–22. Springer, Heidelberg (2009). https://doi.org/10.1007/978-3-642-03317-9_1
2. Beaulieu, R., Shors, D., Smith, J., Treatman-Clark, S., Weeks, B., Wingers, L.: The Simon and speck lightweight block ciphers. In: Proceedings of the 52nd Annual Design Automation Conference. DAC '15, Association for Computing Machinery, New York, NY, USA (2015). https://doi.org/10.1145/2744769.2747946
3. Bertoni, G., Daemen, J., Peeters, M., Van Assche, G.: Keccak. In: Johansson, T., Nguyen, P.Q. (eds.) EUROCRYPT 2013. LNCS, vol. 7881, pp. 313–314. Springer, Heidelberg (2013). https://doi.org/10.1007/978-3-642-38348-9_19

4. Biham, E., Anderson, R., Knudsen, L.: Serpent: a new block cipher proposal. In: Vaudenay, S. (ed.) FSE 1998. LNCS, vol. 1372, pp. 222–238. Springer, Heidelberg (1998). https://doi.org/10.1007/3-540-69710-1_15

5. Che, C., Tian, T.: An experimentally verified attack on 820-round trivium. In: Deng, Y., Yung, M. (eds.) Inscrypt 2022. LNCS, vol. 13837, pp. 357–369. Springer, Cham (2022). https://doi.org/10.1007/978-3-031-26553-2_19

6. Chen, S., Xiang, Z., Zeng, X., Zhang, S.: On the relationships between different methods for degree evaluation. IACR Trans. Symm. Cryptol. **2021**(1), 411–442 (2021). https://doi.org/10.46586/tosc.v2021.i1.411-442

7. Cannière, C.: TRIVIUM: a stream cipher construction inspired by block cipher design principles. In: Katsikas, S.K., López, J., Backes, M., Gritzalis, S., Preneel, B. (eds.) ISC 2006. LNCS, vol. 4176, pp. 171–186. Springer, Heidelberg (2006). https://doi.org/10.1007/11836810_13

8. Dinur, I., Shamir, A.: Cube attacks on tweakable black box polynomials. In: Joux, A. (ed.) EUROCRYPT 2009. LNCS, vol. 5479, pp. 278–299. Springer, Heidelberg (2009). https://doi.org/10.1007/978-3-642-01001-9_16

9. Dinur, I., Shamir, A.: Breaking grain-128 with dynamic cube attacks. In: Joux, A. (ed.) FSE 2011. LNCS, vol. 6733, pp. 167–187. Springer, Heidelberg (2011). https://doi.org/10.1007/978-3-642-21702-9_10

10. Fouque, P.-A., Vannet, T.: Improving key recovery to 784 and 799 rounds of trivium using optimized cube attacks. In: Moriai, S. (ed.) FSE 2013. LNCS, vol. 8424, pp. 502–517. Springer, Heidelberg (2014). https://doi.org/10.1007/978-3-662-43933-3_26

11. Hao, Y., Leander, G., Meier, W., Todo, Y., Wang, Q.: Modeling for three-subset division property without unknown subset. In: Canteaut, A., Ishai, Y. (eds.) EUROCRYPT 2020. LNCS, vol. 12105, pp. 466–495. Springer, Cham (2020). https://doi.org/10.1007/978-3-030-45721-1_17

12. Hao, Y., Leander, G., Meier, W., Todo, Y., Wang, Q.: Modeling for three-subset division property without unknown subset. J. Cryptol. **34**(3), 22 (2021). https://doi.org/10.1007/s00145-021-09383-2

13. He, J., Hu, K., Preneel, B., Wang, M.: Stretching cube attacks: Improved methods to recover massive superpolies. In: Agrawal, S., Lin, D. (eds.) ASIACRYPT 2022. LNCS, vol. 13794, pp. 537–566. Springer, Cham (2022). https://doi.org/10.1007/978-3-031-22972-5_19

14. Hu, K., Sun, S., Todo, Y., Wang, M., Wang, Q.: Massive superpoly recovery with nested monomial predictions. In: Tibouchi, M., Wang, H. (eds.) ASIACRYPT 2021. LNCS, vol. 13090, pp. 392–421. Springer, Cham (2021). https://doi.org/10.1007/978-3-030-92062-3_14

15. Hu, K., Sun, S., Wang, M., Wang, Q.: An algebraic formulation of the division property: revisiting degree evaluations, cube attacks, and key-independent sums. In: Moriai, S., Wang, H. (eds.) ASIACRYPT 2020. LNCS, vol. 12491, pp. 446–476. Springer, Cham (2020). https://doi.org/10.1007/978-3-030-64837-4_15

16. Huang, S., Wang, X., Xu, G., Wang, M., Zhao, J.: Conditional cube attack on reduced-round Keccak sponge function. In: Coron, J.-S., Nielsen, J.B. (eds.) EUROCRYPT 2017. LNCS, vol. 10211, pp. 259–288. Springer, Cham (2017). https://doi.org/10.1007/978-3-319-56614-6_9

17. Kesarwani, A., Roy, D., Sarkar, S., Meier, W.: New cube distinguishers on NFSR-based stream ciphers. Des. Codes Cryptogr. **88**(1), 173–199 (2020). https://doi.org/10.1007/s10623-019-00674-1

18. Liu, M.: Degree evaluation of NFSR-based cryptosystems. In: Katz, J., Shacham, H. (eds.) CRYPTO 2017. LNCS, vol. 10403, pp. 227–249. Springer, Cham (2017). https://doi.org/10.1007/978-3-319-63697-9_8

19. Liu, M., Yang, J., Wang, W., Lin, D.: Correlation cube attacks: from weak-key distinguisher to key recovery. In: Nielsen, J.B., Rijmen, V. (eds.) EUROCRYPT 2018. LNCS, vol. 10821, pp. 715–744. Springer, Cham (2018). https://doi.org/10.1007/978-3-319-78375-8_23

20. Sun, Y.: Automatic search of cubes for attacking stream ciphers. IACR Trans. Symm. Cryptol. **2021**(4), 100–123 (2021). https://doi.org/10.46586/tosc.v2021.i4.100-123

21. Todo, Y.: Structural evaluation by generalized integral property. In: Oswald, E., Fischlin, M. (eds.) EUROCRYPT 2015. LNCS, vol. 9056, pp. 287–314. Springer, Heidelberg (2015). https://doi.org/10.1007/978-3-662-46800-5_12

22. Todo, Y., Isobe, T., Hao, Y., Meier, W.: Cube attacks on non-blackbox polynomials based on division property. In: Katz, J., Shacham, H. (eds.) CRYPTO 2017. LNCS, vol. 10403, pp. 250–279. Springer, Cham (2017). https://doi.org/10.1007/978-3-319-63697-9_9

23. Todo, Y., Isobe, T., Hao, Y., Meier, W.: Cube attacks on non-blackbox polynomials based on division property. IEEE Trans. Comput. **67**(12), 1720–1736 (2018). https://doi.org/10.1109/TC.2018.2835480

24. Todo, Y., Morii, M.: Bit-based division property and application to SIMON family. In: Peyrin, T. (ed.) FSE 2016. LNCS, vol. 9783, pp. 357–377. Springer, Heidelberg (2016). https://doi.org/10.1007/978-3-662-52993-5_18

25. Wang, J., Qin, L., Wu, B.: Correlation cube attack revisited: improved cube search and superpoly recovery techniques (2023). https://arxiv.org/abs/2201.06394

26. Wang, Q., Hao, Y., Todo, Y., Li, C., Isobe, T., Meier, W.: Improved division property based cube attacks exploiting algebraic properties of superpoly. In: Shacham, H., Boldyreva, A. (eds.) CRYPTO 2018. LNCS, vol. 10991, pp. 275–305. Springer, Cham (2018). https://doi.org/10.1007/978-3-319-96884-1_10

27. Wang, S., Hu, B., Guan, J., Zhang, K., Shi, T.: MILP-aided method of searching division property using three subsets and applications. In: Galbraith, S.D., Moriai, S. (eds.) ASIACRYPT 2019. LNCS, vol. 11923, pp. 398–427. Springer, Cham (2019). https://doi.org/10.1007/978-3-030-34618-8_14

28. Xiang, Z., Zhang, W., Bao, Z., Lin, D.: Applying MILP method to searching integral distinguishers based on division property for 6 lightweight block ciphers. In: Cheon, J.H., Takagi, T. (eds.) ASIACRYPT 2016. LNCS, vol. 10031, pp. 648–678. Springer, Heidelberg (2016). https://doi.org/10.1007/978-3-662-53887-6_24

29. Ye, C., Tian, T.: A new framework for finding nonlinear superpolies in cube attacks against trivium-like ciphers. In: Susilo, W., Yang, G. (eds.) ACISP 2018. LNCS, vol. 10946, pp. 172–187. Springer, Cham (2018). https://doi.org/10.1007/978-3-319-93638-3_11

30. Ye, C., Tian, T.: Algebraic method to recover superpolies in cube attacks. IET Inf. Secur. **14**(4), 430–441 (2020). https://doi.org/10.1049/iet-ifs.2019.0323

31. Ye, C.-D., Tian, T.: A practical key-recovery attack on 805-round trivium. In: Tibouchi, M., Wang, H. (eds.) ASIACRYPT 2021. LNCS, vol. 13090, pp. 187–213. Springer, Cham (2021). https://doi.org/10.1007/978-3-030-92062-3_7

Differential-Linear Approximation Semi-unconstrained Searching and Partition Tree: Application to LEA and Speck

Yi Chen[1], Zhenzhen Bao[2,4], and Hongbo Yu[3,4(✉)]

[1] Institute for Advanced Study, Tsinghua University, Beijing, China
chenyi2023@mail.tsinghua.edu.cn
[2] Institute for Network Sciences and Cyberspace, BNRist, Tsinghua University, Beijing, China
zzbao@mail.tsinghua.edu.cn
[3] Department of Computer Science and Technology, Tsinghua University, Beijing, China
yuhongbo@mail.tsinghua.edu.cn
[4] Zhongguancun Laboratory, Beijing, China

Abstract. The differential-linear attack is one of the most effective attacks against ARX ciphers. However, two technical problems are preventing it from being more effective and having more applications: (1) there is no efficient method to search for good differential-linear approximations. Existing methods either have many constraints or are currently inefficient. (2) partitioning technique has great potential to reduce the time complexity of the key-recovery attack, but there is no general tool to construct partitions for ARX ciphers. In this work, we step forward in solving the two problems. First, we propose a novel idea for generating new good differential-linear approximations from known ones, based on which new searching algorithms are designed. Second, we propose a general tool named partition tree, for constructing partitions for ARX ciphers. Based on these new techniques, we present better attacks for two ISO/IEC standards, i.e., LEA and Speck. For LEA, we present the first 17-round distinguisher which is 1 round longer than the previous best distinguisher. Furthermore, we present the first key recovery attacks on 17-round LEA-128, 18-round LEA-192, and 18-round LEA-256, which attack 3, 4, and 3 rounds more than the previous best attacks. For Speck, we find better differential-linear distinguishers for Speck48 and Speck64. The first differential-linear distinguishers for Speck96 and Speck128 are also presented.

Keywords: Differential-Linear Attack · Partition · LEA · Speck

1 Introduction

Differential cryptanalysis [11] and linear cryptanalysis [24] are the two best-known cryptanalysis techniques in symmetric cryptography. The preliminary

© International Association for Cryptologic Research 2023
J. Guo and R. Steinfeld (Eds.): ASIACRYPT 2023, LNCS 14440, pp. 223–255, 2023.
https://doi.org/10.1007/978-981-99-8727-6_8

step of differential cryptanalysis (respectively, linear cryptanalysis) is to search for high probability (resp. correlation) differential distinguishers (resp. linear distinguishers). In the last decade, a mainstream direction is developing efficient methods to automatically search for differential or linear distinguishers, such as the work in [22,26,27,32]. The larger space these methods can search in a practical time, the more firm our confidence in a cipher's resistance against differential or linear cryptanalysis is.

For some block ciphers, within a few rounds, it is easy to find high probability (resp. correlation) differential distinguishers (resp. linear distinguishers); however, with the increase in the number of rounds, differential and linear cryptanalysis simultaneously lose their power. Differential-linear attack is a technique that combines differential cryptanalysis with linear cryptanalysis such that their individual power over a small number of rounds can be joined to efficiently attack more rounds. It is first introduced by Langford and Hellman [20] in 1994 and has been applied to the security evaluation of various ciphers (e.g., IDEA [17], Serpent [16], COCUNUT98 [10], and Chaskey [21], etc.).

In differential-linear attacks, a preliminary step is to search for differential-linear distinguishers (denoted by $\Delta_{in} \rightarrow \gamma_{out}$) with high correlation. The development of automatic searching for differential-linear distinguishers has almost been at a virtual standstill for the past 20 years. Before 2023, researchers usually search for differential-linear distinguishers in a three-stage way: (1) experimentally verify short differential-linear distinguishers denoted by $\Delta_m \rightarrow \gamma_m$ (2) search short differential distinguishers (denoted by $\Delta_{in} \rightarrow \Delta_m$) and linear distinguishers (denoted by $\gamma_m \rightarrow \gamma_{out}$), (3) concatenate three short distinguishers into a long differential-linear distinguisher $\Delta_{in} \rightarrow \Delta_m \rightarrow \gamma_m \rightarrow \gamma_{out}$. Although there have been many improvements [2,5,10,21] to key recovery attacks based on differential-linear distinguishers, there is no efficient method to search for short differential-linear distinguishers $\Delta_m \rightarrow \gamma_m$. Thus, in practice, for a difference Δ_m, the search space is severely limited to the case of a linear mask γ_m of Hamming weight 1 or 2 [5,16,28], which is a long-term pain point since the extremely limited search space will weaken our confidence in a cipher's resistance to differential-linear attacks. In March 2023, using Mixed-Integer Quadratic Constraint Programming (MIQCP) and Mixed-Integer Linear Programming (MILP) techniques, Bellini et al. [6] and Lv et al. [23] both propose an automatic search method respectively, which is good progress. However, as the authors admit, the efficiency of their methods is currently not high [6,23], which is further demonstrated by the comparison (see Table 9) with our search method proposed in this paper.

Building symmetric-key primitives with modular additions, rotations, and XORs is a common practice. The resulting primitives are named ARX ciphers and their representatives can be found everywhere, including block ciphers (e.g., LEA [18] and Speck [3]), stream ciphers (e.g., Salsa20 [7]), MAC algorithms (e.g., Chaskey [25]), and so on. Differential-linear attack is one of the best attacks against ARX ciphers, such as the work in [4,5,21]. Recently, Beierle et al. proposed several improvements to the framework of differential-linear attacks with a special focus on ARX ciphers [4,5]. Among these improvements, building partitions for complex encryption functions is very helpful to reduce the key bits to be guessed. However, except for introducing the final partitions of a special example, the authors in [4,5] give no general tools to build partitions for other encryption functions, which is also a pain point since it hinders researchers from further applying the partitioning technique to other ARX ciphers.

Contribution. First, we propose a novel idea for searching for good differential-linear approximations, based on which we design new search algorithms that have no constraints on the intermediate linear mask and are efficient. We apply the search algorithms to LEA and Speck, and have found many better distinguishers. Table 1 summarizes the comparison of distinguishers. For Speck, only the 11-round differential-linear distinguisher of Speck48 is reported in Table 1, since it is the best distinguisher so far. Actually, we have found the first differential-linear distinguishers for 13-round Speck64, 15-round Speck96, and 18-round Speck128, respectively. Refer to Tables 8 and 9 for more details.

Table 1. The comparison of distinguishers. Cor: correlation, Pr: Probability.

Cipher	Type	Round	Cor/Pr	Source
LEA	Differential	13	$Pr = 2^{-123.79}$	[30]
	Impossible Differential	10	$Pr = 0$	[18]
	Boomerang	16	$Pr = 2^{-117.1114}$	[19]
	Differential-Linear	17	$Cor = -2^{-59.04}$	**This Paper**
Speck48	Differential	11	$Pr = 2^{-44.31}$	[30]
	Differential-Linear	11	$Cor = -2^{-17.55}$	[23]
	Differential-Linear	11	$Cor = -2^{-17.40}$	**This Paper**

Second, we propose a general tool named partition tree for building partitions for ARX encryption functions. Using this tool, we build dynamic partitions for parallel modular additions, based on which best key recovery attacks on round reduced LEA are obtained. Table 2 summarizes the key recovery attacks. The designers claim that the secure number of rounds is 17 for LEA-128, 18 for LEA-192, and 19 for LEA-256 [18].

Note that the 17-round key recovery attack as shown in Table 2 is based on the attack framework introduced in [4,5], and the 18-round key recovery attack is obtained by using the classical attack framework summarized in [12]. Due to the limitation in the differential part, we can only attack 17-round LEA using the attack framework in [4,5].

Table 2. Key recovery attacks on round-reduced LEA. R.A.: Rounds Attacked, T.R.: Total Rounds, D.T.: Distinguisher Type, CP: Chosen-Plaintexts.

Variant	R.A./T.R.	D.T.	Time	Data (CP)	Reference
LEA-128	14/24	Differential	$2^{124.79}$	$2^{124.79}$	[30]
	17/24	Differential-Linear	$2^{82.9}$	$2^{70.9}$	**This Paper**
LEA-192	14/28	Differential	$2^{124.79}$	$2^{124.79}$	[30]
	17/28	Differential-Linear	$2^{82.9}$	$2^{70.9}$	**This Paper**
	18/28	Differential-Linear	$2^{189.63}$	$2^{126.63}$	**This Paper**
LEA-256	15/32	Differential	$2^{252.79}$	$2^{124.79}$	[30]
	17/32	Differential-Linear	$2^{82.9}$	$2^{70.9}$	**This Paper**
	18/32	Differential-Linear	$2^{189.63}$	$2^{126.63}$	**This Paper**

2   Preliminaries

Given a set $S \subseteq \mathbb{F}_2^n$ and a Boolean function $f : \mathbb{F}_2^n \to \mathbb{F}_2$, we define the correlation

$$\mathbf{Cor}_{x \in S}[f(x)] := \frac{1}{|S|} \sum_{x \in S} (-1)^{f(x)}. \tag{1}$$

We denote the XOR operation by $\oplus$, the j-th unit vector of a binary vector space by $[j]$, and the sum of unit vectors $[j_1] \oplus [j_2] \oplus \cdots \oplus [j_t]$ by $[j_1, j_2, \cdots, j_t]$. Given a vector $x \in \mathbb{F}_2^n$, $x[j]$ denotes the j-th bit of x. For $x, \lambda \in \mathbb{F}_2^n$, we define the inner product by $\langle \lambda, x \rangle = \oplus_{j=0}^{n-1} \lambda[j]x[j]$.

2.1   Differential-Linear Distinguisher

Figure 1 shows the latest structure of differential-linear distinguishers [2]. The cipher E is divided into three sub-ciphers E_1, E_m, and E_2, such that $E = E_2 \circ E_m \circ E_1$. A differential distinguisher and a linear distinguisher are applied to E_1 and E_2 successively.

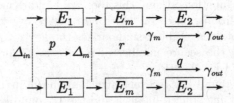

Fig. 1. The latest structure of differential-linear distinguishers.

Assume that the differential $\Delta_{\mathrm{in}} \xrightarrow{E_1} \Delta_m$ holds with probability p, the linear approximation $\gamma_m \xrightarrow{E_2} \gamma_{\mathrm{out}}$ has correlation q, and the experimental correlation of the middle part $\Delta_m \xrightarrow{E_m} \gamma_m$ is r, i.e.,

$$\mathbf{Pr}_{x \in \mathbb{F}_2^n} [E_1(x) \oplus E_1(x \oplus \Delta_{\text{in}}) = \Delta_m] = p,$$
$$\mathbf{Cor}_{x \in \mathbb{F}_2^n} [\langle \gamma_m, x \rangle \oplus \langle \gamma_{\text{out}}, E_2(x) \rangle] = q, \qquad (2)$$
$$\mathbf{Cor}_{x \in \mathcal{S}} [\langle \gamma_m, E_m(x) \rangle \oplus \langle \gamma_m, E_m(x \oplus \Delta_m) \rangle] = r,$$

where $\mathcal{S}$ denotes the set of samples over which the correlation is computed [1]. Then the total correlation of the differential-linear distinguisher $\Delta_{\text{in}} \xrightarrow{E} \gamma_{\text{out}}$ is estimated as

$$\mathbf{Cor}_{x \in \mathbb{F}_2^n} [\langle \gamma_{\text{out}}, E(x) \rangle \oplus \langle \gamma_{\text{out}}, E(x \oplus \Delta_{\text{in}}) \rangle] = prq^2. \qquad (3)$$

Therefore, by preparing $\epsilon p^{-2} r^{-2} q^{-4}$ pairs of chosen plaintexts $(x, x \oplus \Delta_{\text{in}})$, where ϵ is a small non-negative constant, one can distinguish the cipher from a pseudorandom permutation.

Recently, Beierle et al. proposed a technique to reduce the complexity [5]. The high-level idea of the technique is as follows. Denote the set of all right pairs for the differential $\Delta_{\text{in}} \xrightarrow{E_1} \Delta_m$ by $\mathcal{X}$. To amplify the correlation of the distinguisher $\Delta_{\text{in}} \xrightarrow{E_1} \gamma_{\text{out}}$, we choose $\epsilon r^{-2} q^{-4}$ right pairs in the set $\mathcal{X}$ to observe its correlation. To efficiently get the right pairs, we exploit the structure of the set $\mathcal{X}$. Concretely, the set $\mathcal{X}$ might have a special structure, such that for any $x \in \mathcal{X}$, one can obtain a set $X = \{(x \oplus u, x \oplus u \oplus \Delta_{\text{in}}) | u \in \mathcal{U}\}$, where $\mathcal{U}$ is a subspace, such that all elements in X are the right pairs for the differential $\Delta_{\text{in}} \to \Delta_m$. For a differential whose set of right pairs has such a special structure, once one right pair is obtained, one can generate a set of $2^{\dim \mathcal{U}}$ right pairs for free. To find such subspace $\mathcal{U}$ for a differential, one can use the concept of the differential's neutral bits [9]. In particular, we require $2^{\dim \mathcal{U}} \geqslant \epsilon r^{-2} q^{-4}$. For some differentials for which obtaining a large enough $\mathcal{U}$ is difficult, one might use a probabilistic approach related to the concept of probabilistic neutral bits [1]. Assume that the probability that a randomly generated input x belongs to $\mathcal{X}$ is $\overline{p}$. Then the complexity of the distinguisher is $\epsilon \overline{p}^{-1} r^{-2} q^{-4}$.

2.2   Partitioning Technique for Key Recovery

The partitioning technique is first proposed by Biham and Carmeli [8] to amplify the bias of a linear approximation of addition. It is then improved and used by Gaëtan in differential-linear attacks and helps improve data complexity significantly [21]. Recently, Beierle et al. not only further propose improved partitioning techniques for a modular addition, but also introduce a partition technique for complex ARX encryption function that contains two consecutive modular additions [4,5]. The basic idea of these partitioning techniques is to partition the data into several subsets according to some ciphertext bits. In each subset,

---

[1] When E_m involves round keys, the correlation r is estimated using N samples and M random keys, i.e., computing an empirical value using a random key and repeating for M times. The final value of r is set to the median (or mean) of the obtained M values [2,12,16].

one can observe a high correlation of a specific approximation. Besides, with partitioning technique, partial key guessing is more feasible.

The partition is done according to the property of modular addition. Specifically, consider two n-bit words x and z, and a modular addition operation

$$\mathbb{F}_2^{2n} \to \mathbb{F}_2^n, \quad (x, z) \mapsto y = x \boxplus z,$$

as depicted in Fig. 2. In [4], Beierle et al. introduce Lemma 1 to compute the value of $z[i]$ and $z[i] \oplus z[i-1]$.

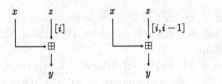

Fig. 2. One modular addition. We are interested in the value of $z[i]$ or $z[i] \oplus z[i-1]$.

Lemma 1. [4] Let $s = y \oplus x$ and let $i \geqslant 3$. Let $S_{b_0 b_1} := \{(x, y) \in \mathbb{F}_2^{2n} | s[i-1] = b_0$ and $s[i-2] = b_1\}$. We have

$$z[i] = \begin{cases} x[i] \oplus y[i] \oplus y[i-1] \oplus 1, & \text{with corr. 1, if } (x, y) \in S_{1*} \\ x[i] \oplus y[i] \oplus y[i-2] \oplus 1, & \text{with corr. 1, if } (x, y) \in S_{01} \\ x[i] \oplus y[i] \oplus y[i-3] \oplus 1, & \text{with corr. 0.5, if } (x, y) \in S_{00}, \end{cases} \quad (4)$$

$$z[i] \oplus z[i-1] = \begin{cases} x[i] \oplus y[i], & \text{with corr. 1, if } (x, y) \in S_{0*} \\ x[i] \oplus y[i] \oplus y[i-1] \oplus y[i-2] \oplus 1, & \text{with corr. 1, if } (x, y) \in S_{11} \\ x[i] \oplus y[i] \oplus y[i-1] \oplus y[i-3] \oplus 1, & \text{with corr. 0.5, if } (x, y) \in S_{10}, \end{cases}$$

where $S_{1*} = S_{10} \cup S_{11}$, and $S_{0*} = S_{00} \cup S_{01}$.

In the attacks presented later, we also adopt another way to compute the value of $z[i]$, see Lemma 2.

Lemma 2. Let $s = y \oplus x$ and let $i \geqslant 3$. Let $S_{b_0 b_1} := \{(x, y) \in \mathbb{F}_2^{2n} | s[i-1] = b_0$ and $s[i-2] = b_1\}$. We have

$$z[i] = \begin{cases} y[i] \oplus x[i] \oplus x[i-1], & \text{with corr. 1, if } (x, y) \in S_{1*} \\ y[i] \oplus x[i] \oplus x[i-2], & \text{with corr. 1, if } (x, y) \in S_{01} \\ y[i] \oplus x[i] \oplus x[i-3], & \text{with corr. 0.5, if } (x, y) \in S_{00} \end{cases}$$

where $S_{1*} = S_{10} \cup S_{11}$.

For the convenience of applying Lemmas 1 and 2 in the rest of this paper, we denote by $v \langle i_1, \cdots, i_m \rangle$ the value $\langle \gamma, v[i_1] || \cdots || v[i_m] \rangle$ in the case of an indeterministic linear mask γ. For example, formula 4 is rewritten as $z[i] = x[i] \oplus y \langle i, i-1, i-2, i-3 \rangle \oplus 1$.

3   Differential-Linear Approximations Searching

Consider the middle part E_m which is verified experimentally. Given a difference Δ_m, we will first introduce a new method to search for differential-linear approximations $\Delta_m \to \gamma_m$ with a correlation higher than a threshold. Then it is extended to search for differential-linear approximations $\Delta_m \to \gamma_{\text{out}}$ of $E_2 \circ E_m$.

3.1   Core Idea and Motivation

Core Idea. Figure 3 depicts the core idea of our search methods. Assume that the correlations of two differential-linear approximations are known. We can generate a new differential-linear approximation by the XOR operation, e.g., $\gamma_3 = \gamma_1 \oplus \gamma_2$ or $\gamma_6 = \gamma_4 \oplus \gamma_5$. Assume that the absolute correlation of $\Delta \to \gamma_i$ for $i \in \{1, 2\}$ exceeds a threshold, and the absolute correlation of $\Delta \to \gamma_j$ for $j \in \{4, 5\}$ does not exceed the threshold. Then we preferentially test $\Delta \to \gamma_3$ due to the motivation introduced later.

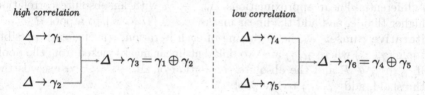

Fig. 3. The core idea of our differential-linear approximation searching methods. We preferentially verify the correlation of $\Delta \to \gamma_3$ which is generated from two differential-linear approximations with high correlation.

Motivation. The motivation behind our idea is relatively intuitive. Given a differential-linear approximation $\Delta \to \gamma$ of an encryption function E, we define a variable

$$z_\gamma = \langle E(P) \oplus E(P \oplus \Delta), \gamma \rangle \tag{5}$$

where $P \in \mathbb{F}_2^n$ is the plaintext and $z_\gamma \in \mathbb{F}_2$. Assume that $z_\gamma = 0$ holds with probability p, i.e., $\mathbf{Pr}_{P \in \mathbb{F}_2^n}[z_\gamma = 0] = p$. As a result, the correlation of $\Delta \to \gamma$ is:

$$\mathbf{Cor}_{P \in \mathbb{F}_2^n}[z_\gamma] = \frac{1}{|2^n|} \sum_{P \in \mathbb{F}_2^n} (-1)^{z_\gamma} = 2p - 1. \tag{6}$$

For convenience, denote by $G(z_\gamma)$ the correlation, i.e., $G(z_\gamma) = 2p - 1$.

Suppose that $G(z_{\gamma_i})$ is the correlation of $\Delta \to \gamma_i$ (see Fig. 3). Under the assumption that the two variables z_{γ_1} and z_{γ_2} (resp. z_{γ_4} and z_{γ_5}) are independent, we have

$$G(z_{\gamma_3}) = G(z_{\gamma_1}) \times G(z_{\gamma_2}), \quad G(z_{\gamma_6}) = G(z_{\gamma_4}) \times G(z_{\gamma_5}), \tag{7}$$

due to the piling-up lemma [24]. If $|G(z_{\gamma_i})| > c, i \in \{1, 2\}$ and $|G(z_{\gamma_j})| < c, i \in \{4, 5\}$ hold simultaneously where c is a threshold, then $|G(z_{\gamma_3})| > |G(z_{\gamma_6})|$ will hold too.

Thus, there is a heuristic conclusion: compared with two differential-linear approximations with a low absolute correlation, two ones with a high absolute correlation would be more likely to generate another relatively good differential-linear approximation. Although the assumption that the two variables are independent may not hold in a real scenario, this conclusion still shows a surprisingly positive influence in the support experiment introduced in Sect. 3.2.

3.2   Iterative Search

Based on the heuristic conclusion, an iterative search algorithm is designed to search for differential-linear approximations $\Delta_m \xrightarrow{E_m} \gamma_m$ (see Fig. 1).

The iterative search algorithm contains two phases:

1. **Initialization phase:** Preset a difference Δ_m and a threshold c. Then select t differential-linear approximations $\Delta_m \rightarrow \gamma_i$ with an absolute correlation higher than c, and add the linear masks $\gamma_i, i \in \{1, \cdots, t\}$ to a pool $\mathcal{P}$.
2. **iterative phase:** at the beginning of each iteration, traverse each possible tuple (γ_i, γ_j) where γ_i, γ_j are two different linear masks picked from the pool. If $\gamma_i \oplus \gamma_j \notin \mathcal{P}$ and the absolute correlation of $\Delta_m \rightarrow \gamma_i \oplus \gamma_j$ exceeds the threshold, add $\gamma_i \oplus \gamma_j$ to the pool.

Since the XOR operation (i.e., $\gamma_i \oplus \gamma_j$) is a linear operation, the search space of the iterative algorithm is decided by the t linear masks added to the pool in the initialization phase. Denote by $\overrightarrow{\gamma}_i$ the row vector transformed from the linear mask γ_i, i.e., $\overrightarrow{\gamma}_i[j] = \gamma_i[n - 1 - j]$. Let $\boldsymbol{\gamma} = [\overrightarrow{\gamma}_1, \cdots, \overrightarrow{\gamma}_t]^{\top}$ denote the $t \times n$ matrix composed of the t vectors. Apparently, the search space is decided by the rank of $\boldsymbol{\gamma}$. If the rank is t, i.e., the t row vectors are linearly independent, the size of the search space of the iterative algorithm is 2^t.

To ensure the vectors corresponding to the t linear masks are linearly independent, we focus on linear masks of Hamming weight 1 in the initialization phase. For the convenience of further introducing the iterative algorithm, two concepts named *strong unbalanced bit* and *weak unbalanced bit* are adopted, see Definition 1.

Definition 1. *For a preset difference Δ and a threshold c, suppose that the linear mask is $\gamma = [i], i \in \{0, \cdots, n - 1\}$ where n is the blocksize, if the absolute correlation of the differential-linear approximation $\Delta \rightarrow \gamma$ exceeds c, the i-th ciphertext bit is called a **strong unbalanced bit**. Otherwise, it is called a **weak unbalanced bit**.*

Suppose that $\mathcal{B}_S$ is the strong unbalanced bit set and $\mathcal{B}_W$ is the weak unbalanced bit set for the given difference Δ. In the initialization phase, all the linear masks $[i]$ for $i \in \mathcal{B}_S$ are added to the pool. Then the size of the search space is $2^{|\mathcal{B}_S|}$. Algorithm 1 summarizes the iterative search algorithm.

Algorithm 1. Search $\Delta_m \xrightarrow{E_m} \gamma_m$ in an iterative way

---

Require: A difference, Δ_m; A threshold, c; Number of iterations, Ni; Sample size, N.
Ensure: A list of linear masks $\gamma_m \in \mathbb{F}_2^n$.
1: $\mathcal{P} \leftarrow []$;
2: Randomly generate N plaintexts $P_i, i \in \{1, \cdots, N\}$;
3: Collect N ciphertext pairs $(E_m(P_i), E_m(P_i \oplus \Delta_m))$ for $i \in \{1, \cdots, N\}$.
4: **Initialization phase:**
5: **for** $i \in \{0, \cdots, n-1\}$ **do**
6:    $\gamma_m \leftarrow [i]$;
7:    Compute the correlation **Cor** of $\Delta_m \rightarrow \gamma_m$ over the N ciphertext pairs.
8:    **if** $|\text{\bf Cor}| \geqslant c$ **then**
9:      Add $[i]$ to $\mathcal{P}$;
10:    **end if**
11: **end for**
12: **Iterative phase:**
13: **for** $i \in \{1, \cdots, Ni\}$ **do**
14:    $\mathcal{Q} \leftarrow []$;
15:    Traverse each possible tuple (γ_1, γ_2) where $\gamma_1, \gamma_2 \in \mathcal{P}$. If $\gamma_1 \oplus \gamma_2 \notin \mathcal{P} \cup \mathcal{Q}$, compute the correlation of $\Delta_m \rightarrow \gamma_1 \oplus \gamma_2$ over the N ciphertext pairs. If the absolute correlation exceeds c, add $\gamma_1 \oplus \gamma_2$ to $\mathcal{Q}$;
16:    $\mathcal{P} \leftarrow \mathcal{P} \cup \mathcal{Q}$; /*Merge two sets $\mathcal{P}$ and $\mathcal{Q}$ */
17: **end for**

A Support Experiment. We have performed an experiment on two ciphers (i.e., 8-round LEA and 5-round Speck32) to support the previous heuristic conclusion and verify the iterative search, i.e., Algorithm 1.

Consider an encryption function $E_m : \mathbb{F}_2^n \rightarrow \mathbb{F}_2^n$ and an input difference Δ_m. Set an absolute correlation threshold c to identify the strong (weak) unbalanced bit set $\mathcal{B}_\mathcal{S}$ ($\mathcal{B}_\mathcal{W}$). We focus on differential-linear approximations $\Delta_m \xrightarrow{E_m} \gamma_m$ with an absolute correlation higher than the threshold c, and are interested in their distributions in two spaces $\mathcal{X}_1$ and $\mathcal{X}_2$, where $\mathcal{X}_1$ and $\mathcal{X}_2$ are defined as:

$$\mathcal{X}_1 = \{\Delta_m \xrightarrow{E_m} \gamma_m \,|\, 0 < HW(\gamma_m) \leqslant d\},$$

$$\mathcal{X}_2 = \{\Delta_m \xrightarrow{E_m} \gamma_m \,|\, 0 < HW(\gamma_m) \leqslant d; \gamma_m[i] = 0 \text{ for } i \notin \mathcal{B}_\mathcal{S}\},$$

where $HW(\gamma_m)$ denotes the Hamming weight of γ_m, and d is the Hamming weight threshold. We traverse the space $\mathcal{X}_1$ and denote by $\mathcal{G}$ all the found differential-linear approximations with an absolute correlation higher than c.

At first, we let $c = 2^{-4}$, set $d = 2$ for 8-round LEA and $d = 4$ for 5-round Speck32. If we set a larger d, the experiment takes too long. Table 3 summarizes the settings and experiment results. For 8-round LEA (respectively, 5-round Speck32/64), we find a total of 72 (resp. 785) differential-linear approximations with a correlation higher than 2^{-4}, and 43 (resp. 311) out of which belong to the space $\mathcal{X}_2$. Thus, if we randomly pick a sample $x \in \mathcal{X}_1$, the probability that $x \in \mathcal{G}$ is 0.0087 (resp. 0.0189). However, if we randomly pick a sample $x \in \mathcal{X}_2$, the

Table 3. Comparison of differential-linear approximations in two spaces.

E_m	n	Δ_m	c	$|\mathcal{B}_S|$	d	$|\mathcal{X}_1|$	$|\mathcal{X}_2|$	$|\mathcal{G}|$	$|\mathcal{G} \cap \mathcal{X}_2|$	$\frac{|\mathcal{G}|}{|\mathcal{X}_1|}$	$\frac{|\mathcal{G} \cap \mathcal{X}_2|}{|\mathcal{X}_2|}$
8-round LEA	128	[31]	2^{-4}	14	2	8256	105	72	43	0.0087	0.4095
5-round Speck32	32	[22]	2^{-4}	10	4	41448	385	785	311	0.0189	0.8078
					3	5488	175	250	146	0.0456	0.8343

a $|X|$: the size of set X; $X \cap Y$: the intersection of sets X and Y.

b $|\mathcal{X}_1| = \sum_{i \in \{1, \cdots, d\}} \binom{n}{i}$; $|\mathcal{X}_2| = \sum_{i \in \{1, \cdots, d\}} \binom{|\mathcal{B}_S|}{i}$.

corresponding probability is $0.4095 \approx 47 \times 0.0087$ (resp. $0.8078 \approx 42 \times 0.0189$). The advantage is extremely significant [2]. We wonder whether increasing d will weaken the advantage. Thus, we set $d = 3$ for 5-round Speck32 and perform the experiment again. Interestingly, the advantage becomes even more significant when d increases from 3 to 4, due to the size (i.e., $|\mathcal{X}_1|$) of the first space $\mathcal{X}_1$ increasing too sharply (see the second and third row of Table 3).

Next, we run Algorithm 1 by setting the same difference Δ_m (i.e., [31] for 8-round LEA and [22] for 5-round Speck32/64) and threshold $c = 2^{-4}$. Finally, for 8-round LEA (respectively, 5-round Speck32/64), all the 43 (resp. 311) differential-linear approximations are found within $Ni = 1$ (resp. 2) iterations.

3.3 Meet-in-the-Middle Search

Consider $E_2 \circ E_m$ and a given difference Δ_m. Based on each linear mask γ_m returned by Algorithm 1, one can search linear approximations $\gamma_m \xrightarrow{E_2} \gamma_{\text{out}}$ using an automatic search tool (e.g., [31]), and obtain a differential-linear approximation $\Delta_m \xrightarrow{E_2 \circ E_m} \gamma_{\text{out}}$ by connecting $\Delta_m \xrightarrow{E_m} \gamma_m$ and $\gamma_m \xrightarrow{E_2} \gamma_{\text{out}}$.

However, Algorithm 1 is time-consuming. Moreover, in distinguishing attacks or key recovery attacks, there are usually some requirements about the linear approximation $\gamma_m \to \gamma_{\text{out}}$, such as the upper bound of the correlation or the Hamming weight of γ_{out}. If the value of γ_m is fixed to a concrete value in advance, it is likely to be inefficient to find linear approximations $\gamma_m \to \gamma_{\text{out}}$ satisfying the requirements.

Hence, a meet-in-the-middle search algorithm is designed to search differential-linear approximations $\Delta_m \xrightarrow{E_2 \circ E_m} \gamma_{\text{out}}$. At a high-level view, we first search the linear approximations $\gamma_m \xrightarrow{E_2} \gamma_{\text{out}}$ without setting the value of γ_m. For each returned γ_m, check whether it is in the list returned by Algorithm 1.

Two tricks are applied to reduce the time consumption of the meet-in-the-middle search. First, in order to accelerate the matching of linear mask γ_m, we add the following necessary conditions when searching $\gamma_m \to \gamma_{\text{out}}$:

$$\gamma_m[i] = 0, \ i \in \mathcal{B}_{\mathcal{W}} \tag{8}$$

---

[2] The support experiment is also performed on 5-round PRESENT and 4-round DES, and the advantage is significant too. More details are available at https://github. com/AI-Lab-Y/DLA_search_and_partition_tree

where $\mathcal{B}_\mathcal{W}$ is the *weak unbalanced bit* set. Second, compute the experimental correlation of $\Delta_m \rightarrow \gamma_m$ after a linear approximation $\gamma_m \rightarrow \gamma_{out}$ is returned, instead of running Algorithm 1 to get the list of γ_m at the beginning. Algorithm 2 summarizes the meet-in-the-middle search algorithm.

Algorithm 2. Search $\Delta_m \xrightarrow{E_m} \gamma_m \xrightarrow{E_2} \gamma_{out}$ in a meet-in-the-middle way

---

Require: A difference, Δ_m; A threshold, c; Sample size, N.
Ensure: A list of linear mask tuples (γ_m, γ_{out}) where $\gamma_m, \gamma_{out} \in \mathbb{F}_2^n$.
1: $\mathcal{P} \leftarrow []$; $\mathcal{B}_S \leftarrow []$;
2: Randomly generate N plaintexts $P_i, i \in \{1, \cdots, N\}$;
3: Collect N pseudo-ciphertext pairs $(E_m(P_i), E_m(P_i \oplus \Delta_m))$ for $i \in \{1, \cdots, N\}$.
4: **Stage 1 (initialization phase in Algorithm 1):**
5: **for** $i \in \{0, \cdots, n-1\}$ **do**
6:     $\gamma_m \leftarrow [i]$;
7:     Compute the correlation **Cor** of $\Delta_m \rightarrow \gamma_m$ over the N pseudo-ciphertext pairs.
8:     **if** $|\mathbf{Cor}| \geqslant c$ **then**
9:         Add i to $\mathcal{B}_S$;
10:     **end if**
11: **end for**
12: **Stage 2 (search $\gamma_m \rightarrow \gamma_{out}$):**
13: **for** $i \in \{0, \cdots, n-1\}$ and $i \notin \mathcal{B}_S$ **do**
14:     Add a condition $\gamma_m[i] = 0$ to **Model()** ; /***Model()** is the automatic search model of linear approximations $\gamma_m \rightarrow \gamma_{out}$ */
15: **end for**
16: Collect linear mask tuples (γ_m, γ_{out}) by running **Model()**; /* filter tuples with duplicate mask γ_m before Stage 3 */
17: **Stage 3 (compute the correlation of $\Delta_m \rightarrow \gamma_m$):**
18: **for** each returned tuple (γ_m, γ_{out}) **do**
19:     Compute the correlation **Cor** of $\Delta_m \rightarrow \gamma_m$ over the N pseudo-ciphertext pairs.

20:     **if** $|\mathbf{Cor}| \geqslant c$ **then**
21:         Add (γ_m, γ_{out}) to $\mathcal{P}$;
22:     **end if**
23: **end for**

Remark 1. In order to apply Algorithm 2, one needs to determine the number of rounds (denoted by r_m) covered by the middle part E_m. If r_m is too large, the strong unbalanced bit set $\mathcal{B}_S$ corresponding to a given difference Δ_m may be an empty set, which will reduce the search space of Algorithm 2.

To avoid this problem and take full advantage of Algorithm 2, we provide an empirical rule on setting r_m as follows. Consider a pre-defined set (denoted by $\mathcal{D}_m$) of differences Δ_m to be searched. For most (for example, three-fourths) elements $\Delta_m = v \in \mathcal{D}_m$, the setting r_m should make sure that the corresponding strong unbalanced bit sets $\mathcal{B}_{S_v}$ are non-empty sets. This is based on our experience from searching for differential-linear approximations of LEA and Speck.

4   Partition Tree

In this section, we present a generic tool named *partition tree* to generate partitions for ARX encryption functions, starting from basic concepts.

4.1   Basic Concepts

A partition tree is a tree that describes the partition conditions and approximations simultaneously. In a partition tree, each non-leaf node stands for one object whose value is unknown, and each leaf node stands for one object whose value is known.

To build such a tree, some necessary concepts are proposed.

- *Partition Edge:* Denote by $A \dashrightarrow B$ (with a red dashed arrow) a partition edge, which means that we need to divide all the data into multiple partitions according to the value of B, for computing the value of A.
- *Approximation Edge:* Denote by $A \xrightarrow{X} B$ (with a black arrow) an approximation edge, which means that $A = X \oplus B$ where the value of X is known and the value of B is unknown. Similarly, the approximation edge $A \to B$ stands for $A = B$.

4.2   Building Process and Usage

In this subsection, we introduce the process of building a partition tree, and show how to derive the final partitions from the partition tree. For a more intuitive and deeper understanding, partition trees related to two encryption functions are first presented directly.

Partition Trees Related to Two Encryption Functions. The first encryption function is the single modular addition as shown in Fig. 2, i.e., $y = z \boxplus x$. Again, we are interested in the value of $z[i]$ or $z[i, i-1]$. Three partition trees are shown in Fig. 4.

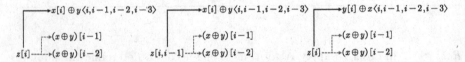

Fig. 4. Partition trees related to one modular addition. The left and middle partition trees correspond to Lemma 1. The right one corresponds to Lemma 2.

The second encryption function is the two consecutive modular additions as shown in the left picture in Fig. 5. The right picture shows a partition tree related to it. In [4,5], the authors have presented the final partitions and approximations of $z_1[i]$. Later, we will explain how to obtain the results presented in [4,5] using the partition tree.

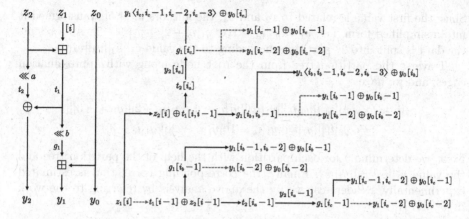

Fig. 5. Partition tree for two consecutive modular additions. The left picture shows the encryption function. The right picture shows the partition tree. Notice that $i_a = (i + a) \bmod n$, $i_b = (i + b) \bmod n$, $i_c = (i + a + b) \bmod n$, and n is the word size.

Building Process. At a high level, we build a partition tree by simulating the propagation of linear approximation. First, create a root node standing for the target bit (e.g. $z[i], z[i, i-1]$ in Fig. 4). Second, propagate the approximation. When meeting a modular addition, we choose partition conditions (eg. $(x \oplus y)[i-1]$ and $(x \oplus y)[i-2]$ in Fig. 4) for creating partition edges, and choose an approximation for creating an approximation edge. The available partition conditions and approximations refer to Lemma 1 and Lemma 2. When meeting other linear operations, we just need to create approximation edges. In an iterative way, we expand the tree until each leaf node is only related to objects whose values are known.

When meeting a modular addition, one can flexibly choose the partition conditions and approximations. For example, we always choose two partition conditions and an approximation with an indeterministic linear mask in Fig. 4. In Fig. 5, for computing $z_1[i]$, we choose only one partition condition and a deterministic approximation. The choice depends on the concrete encryption function.

Usage. Once a partition tree is built, we can obtain the final partitions and approximations. Take the partition tree as shown in Fig. 5 as an example.

In the partition tree, there are 7 partition edges that contain five different partition conditions. The related five values are v_i for $i \in \{1, 2, 3, 4, 5\}$:

$$
\begin{aligned}
v_1 &= t_1[i-1] \oplus z_2[i-1] \\
&= (y_2[i_a - 1] \oplus y_1[i_b - 2] \oplus y_1[i_c - 2]) \oplus \\
&\quad (y_1[i_b - 1] \oplus y_0[i_b - 1]) \oplus (y_1[i_c - 1] \oplus y_0[i_c - 1]); \quad (9) \\
v_2 &= y_1[i_b - 1] \oplus y_0[i_b - 1]; \quad v_3 = y_1[i_b - 2] \oplus y_0[i_b - 2]; \\
v_4 &= y_1[i_c - 1] \oplus y_0[i_c - 1]; \quad v_5 = y_1[i_c - 2] \oplus y_0[i_c - 2].
\end{aligned}
$$

Since the first value is related to v_2 and v_4, the authors in [4,5] transformed it into a simplified form, i.e., $v_1 = y_2[i_a - 1] \oplus y_1[i_b - 2] \oplus y_1[i_c - 2]$. As a result, the data is split into 2^5 partitions according to the value $v_1||v_2||v_3||v_4||v_5$.

Traverse the partition tree from the root node along with approximation edges, and we have

$$z_1[i] \approx \langle \gamma \, , \, y_2[i_a]||y_0[i_b]||y_1[i_b]||y_1[i_b - 1]||y_1[i_b - 2]||y_1[i_b - 3]||$$
$$y_0[i_c]||y_1[i_c]||y_1[i_c - 1]||y_1[i_c - 2]|| \, y_1[i_c - 3]\rangle \, .$$

Next, we determine γ for each partition with the help of the partition tree and the value $v_1||v_2||v_3||v_4||v_5$. Finally, the corresponding correlation is estimated experimentally. Readers can verify the above analysis by referring to the work in [5] and [4].

4.3   Dynamic Partitioning Technique

To make the key recovery attack achieve a good performance, for a given encryption function, the correlation corresponding to each partition should be nonzero [4]. When the encryption function is relatively complex, we may need to dynamically choose the partition conditions for each data to achieve the target.

In this section, we introduce the dynamic partitions for parallel modular additions as depicted in Fig. 6, which are used in attacks on LEA.

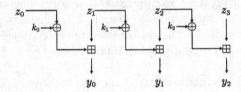

Fig. 6. Parallel modular additions. We assume that the values of the three keys k_0, k_1, k_2, and the input word z_0 are known. The values of the other three input words z_1, z_2, z_3 are unknown.

Partition Tree for Three Parallel Modular Additions. At first, we are interested in the value $z_3[i]$. Figure 7 shows a partition tree.

The data is split into 64 partitions in the following way

$$\mathcal{T}_{b_0 b_1 b_2 b_3 b_4 b_5} = \{(z_0, y_0, y_1, y_2, k_0, k_1, k_2) \in (\mathbb{F}_2^n)^7) \, |b_0 b_1 b_2 b_3 b_4 b_5 = v_1||v_2||v_3||v_4||v_5||v_6 \},$$

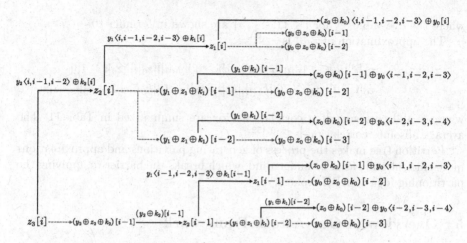

Fig. 7. A partition tree for three parallel modular additions.

where the six partition conditions v_i for $i \in \{1, \cdots, 6\}$ are:

$$v_1 = (y_0 \oplus z_0 \oplus k_0)[i-1];$$

$$v_2 = (y_0 \oplus z_0 \oplus k_0)[i-2]; \quad v_3 = (y_0 \oplus z_0 \oplus k_0)[i-3];$$

$$v_4 = \begin{cases} (y_1 \oplus k_1)[i-1] \oplus y_0[i-2], & \text{if } v_2 = 1; \\ (y_1 \oplus k_1)[i-1] \oplus y_0[i-3], & \text{if } v_2 = 0. \end{cases}$$

$$v_5 = \begin{cases} (y_1 \oplus k_1)[i-2] \oplus y_0[i-3], & \text{if } v_3 = 1; \\ (y_1 \oplus k_1)[i-2] \oplus y_0[i-4], & \text{if } v_3 = 0; \end{cases} \qquad (10)$$

$$v_6 = \begin{cases} (y_2 \oplus k_2)[i-1] \oplus y_1[i-2], & \text{if } v_2 \oplus v_5 = 0; \\ (y_2 \oplus k_2)[i-1] \oplus y_1[i-3], & \text{if } v_2 \oplus v_5 = 1; \end{cases}$$

The approximation of $z_3[i]$ is

$$z_3[i] \approx \langle \gamma, \; y_2[i]||y_2[i-1]||y_2[i-2]||y_1[i]||y_1[i-1]||y_1[i-2]||y_1[i-3]|| \\ y_0[i]||z_0[i]||z_0[i-1]||z_0[i-2]||z_0[i-3]||k_2[i]||k_1[i]||k_0[i]|| \\ k_0[i-1]||k_0[i-2]|| k_0[i-3] \rangle,$$

where γ and corresponding correlation **Cor** are summarized in Table 10. The average absolute correlation is $2^{-0.868}$.

To identify the belonging partition for data, one needs to dynamically choose the approximations of v_4, v_5, and v_6. If any one of v_4, v_5, v_6 is computed using a fixed approximation, the correlation corresponding to some partitions will be 0.

Partition Trees for Two Parallel Modular Additions. In the key recovery attacks introduced later, we are interested in the value $z_2[i]$ too. We directly adopt the subtree (see Fig. 7) that takes $z_2[i]$ as the root node.

The data is split into 32 partitions in the following way:

$$\mathcal{T}_{b_0b_1b_2b_3b_4} = \{(z_0, y_0, y_1, k_0, k_1) \in (\mathbb{F}_2^n)^5 \,|\, b_0b_1b_2b_3b_4 = v_1||v_2||v_3||v_4||v_5 \},$$

where the five values v_i for $i \in \{1, \cdots, 5\}$ are shown in formula 10.

The approximation of $z_2[i]$ is

$$z_2[i] \approx \langle \gamma,\ y_1[i]||y_1[i-1]||y_1[i-2]||y_1[i-3]||y_0[i]||z_0[i]||z_0[i-1]|| \\ z_0[i-2]||z_0[i-3]||k_1[i]||k_0[i]||k_0[i-1]||k_0[i-2]||\ k_0[i-3]\rangle,$$

where γ and corresponding correlation **Cor** are summarized in Table 11. The average absolute correlation is $2^{-0.452}$.

Partition tree makes the process of generating partitions and approximations more efficient and easier to understand, which breaks the barrier to applying the partitioning idea to ARX ciphers.

5   Overview of Our Attack Framework

This paper mainly focuses on the attack framework which is first proposed in [5] at CRYPTO 2020 and further improved in [4]. The framework has a constraint on how the secret key to be recovered is operated in the encryption process, which is removed in this section. Figure 8 (the left picture) shows our attack framework. Here the encryption function F uses the secret key k to encrypt its input. In [4,5], the secret key is used as the last whitening key (see the right picture), which is the core difference. Our aim is to recover parts of the secret key k by using a distinguisher $\Delta_{\text{in}} \to \gamma_{\text{out}}$.

In the following, we assume that the ciphertext-key (i.e., the concatenation $c||k$ of the ciphertext and key) space $\mathbb{F}_2^n$ is split into a direct sum $\mathcal{P} \oplus \mathcal{R}$ with $n_{\mathcal{P}} := \dim \mathcal{P}$ and $n_{\mathcal{R}} := n - n_{\mathcal{P}}$, so that the partitions will be given by the cosets $\mathcal{T}_{p_i} = p_i \oplus \mathcal{R}$ for any $p_i \in \mathcal{P}$ (i.e., p_i represents a set of the partition). Therefore, we can uniquely express $c||k$ as $(c||k)_{\mathcal{P}} \oplus (c||k)_{\mathcal{R}}$, where $(c||k)_{\mathcal{P}} \in \mathcal{P}$ and $(c||k)_{\mathcal{R}} \in \mathcal{R}$. Then, for any $p_i \in \mathcal{P}$, the partition $\mathcal{T}_{p_i} \subset \mathbb{F}_2^n$ is defined as $\mathcal{T}_{p_i} = \{(c||k) \in \mathbb{F}_2^n \,|\, (c||k)_{\mathcal{P}} = p_i\}$.

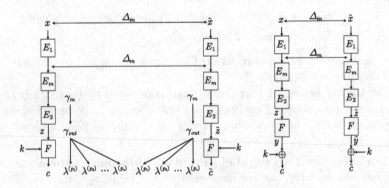

Fig. 8. The schematic diagram of the key recovery attack framework.

The idea is to identify several tuples $\left(\mathcal{T}_{p_i}, \lambda^{(p_i)}\right), i \in \{1, \cdots, s\}$, for which we can observe a high absolute correlation

$$\varepsilon_i := \mathbf{Cor}_{(c||k) \in \mathcal{T}_{p_i}} \left[\langle \gamma_{\text{out}}, z \rangle \oplus \left\langle \lambda^{(p_i)}, c||k \right\rangle \right],$$

where $\lambda^{(p_i)}$ is the linear mask of $c||k$ when $(c||k)_{\mathcal{P}} = p_i$. We finally observe the following correlation for $(c, \tilde{c})$ by guessing the secret key k, and the final correlation is defined as

$$\rho_{i,j} := \mathbf{Cor}_{(c||k, \tilde{c}||k) \in \mathcal{T}_{p_i} \times \mathcal{T}_{p_j}} \left[\left\langle \lambda^{(p_i)}, c||k \right\rangle \oplus \left\langle \lambda^{(p_j)}, \tilde{c}||k \right\rangle \right]. \tag{11}$$

According to the analysis in [4], the correlation $\rho_{i,j}$ can be estimated as

$$\rho_{i,j} = \varepsilon_i \varepsilon_j \mathbf{Cor}_{(x, \tilde{x}) \in (\mathbb{F}_2^n)^2} \left[\langle \gamma_{\text{out}}, z \oplus \tilde{z} \rangle \right]. \tag{12}$$

Next, let us consider the differential-linear attack using N pairs. Let $(c, \tilde{c})$ be the lth pair and assume that c and $\tilde{c}$ belong to the ith and jth partitions, respectively, i.e., $(c||k)_{\mathcal{P}} = p_i$ and $(\tilde{c}||k)_{\mathcal{P}} = p_j$ (for ease of notation, we do not make the dependency of c, $\tilde{c}$, i, j on l explicit). Then we get the 1-bit representation

$$w_l = \left\langle \lambda^{(p_i)}, c||k \right\rangle \oplus \left\langle \lambda^{(p_j)}, \tilde{c}||k \right\rangle$$

and let $C_l = \rho_{i,j}$ where $\rho_{i,j}$ is the correlation for the lth pair when the ith and jth partitions are used for this pair.

Compute the following log-likelihood ratio (LLR) statistic:

$$\text{LLR} = \frac{1}{2} \sum_{l=1}^{N} \ln \left(1 - C_l^2 \right) + \frac{1}{2} \sum_{l=1}^{N} \ln \left(\frac{1 + C_l}{1 - C_l} \right) (-1)^{w_l}. \tag{13}$$

According to the analysis in [4], the LLR statistic follows normal distribution $\mathcal{N}(\mu_0, \sigma_0^2)$ and $\mathcal{N}(\mu_1, \sigma_1^2)$ when the correct and wrong keys are guessed, respectively. The corresponding distribution parameters are

$$\mu_0 = -\mu_1 = \frac{1}{2} \sum_{l=1}^{N} C_l^2 = \frac{N}{2} \overline{C}, \qquad \sigma_0^2 = \sigma_1^2 = \sum_{l=1}^{N} C_l^2 = N \overline{C}.$$

Thus, one can recover the correct key by distinguishing between $\mathcal{N}(\mu_0, \sigma_0^2)$ and $\mathcal{N}(\mu_1, \sigma_1^2)$.

To compute the LLR statistic, we need to calculate C_l and w_l. At first, the key denoted by $k_{\mathcal{P}}$ is guessed to identify the partition. After guessing $k_{\mathcal{P}}$, the first term of the LLR statistic, i.e., $\alpha := \frac{1}{2} \sum_{l=1}^{N} \ln \left(1 - C_l^2 \right)$, is constant and independent of w_l. Then, we may need to guess some key bits denoted by $k_{\mathcal{L}}$ to compute w_l, and further compute the second term of the LLR statistic.

Divide the linear mask $\lambda^{(p_i)}$ and $\lambda^{(p_j)}$ into two parts, i.e., $\lambda^{(p_i)} = g^{(p_i)} || \Gamma^{(p_i)}$ and $\lambda^{(p_j)} = g^{(p_j)} || \Gamma^{(p_j)}$, such that

$$\left\langle \lambda^{(p_i)}, c||k \right\rangle = \left\langle g^{(p_i)}, c \right\rangle \oplus \left\langle \Gamma^{(p_i)}, k \right\rangle, \quad \left\langle \lambda^{(p_j)}, \tilde{c}||k \right\rangle = \left\langle g^{(p_j)}, \tilde{c} \right\rangle \oplus \left\langle \Gamma^{(p_j)}, k \right\rangle, \tag{14}$$

Then $k_{\mathcal{L}}$ is determined by $\Gamma^{(p_i)} \oplus \Gamma^{(p_j)}$. The size of $k_{\mathcal{L}}$ is $\dim W$ where a linear subspace W is defined by $W := Span\{\Gamma^{(p_i)} \oplus \Gamma^{(p_j)} | i, j \in \{1, \cdots, s\}\}$.

The computation of the second term of the LLR statistic is further accelerated by using the Fast Walsh-Hadamard transform (FWHT) [13], like the work in [4]. In some cases, due to the XOR operation $k \oplus \chi$ in F where k is the secret key and χ is an intermediate state, the linear masks $g^{(p_i)}$ and $g^{(p_j)}$ can be further divided into two parts, i.e., $g^{(p_i)} = \phi^{(p_i)} || \Gamma^{(p_i)}$, and $g^{(p_j)} = \phi^{(p_j)} || \Gamma^{(p_j)}$.

Next, we use an array β, whose element $\beta(\Gamma)$ is defined as

$$\beta(\Gamma) := \frac{1}{2} \sum_{l=1: \Gamma = \Gamma^{(p_i)} \oplus \Gamma^{(p_j)}}^{N} \ln \left(\frac{1 + C_l}{1 - C_l} \right) (-1)^{\langle \phi^{(p_i)} || \Gamma^{(p_i)}, c \rangle \oplus \langle \phi^{(p_j)} || \Gamma^{(p_j)}, \bar{c} \rangle}.$$

Then, the second term of the LLR statistic is computed as

$$\text{LLR}' = \frac{1}{2} \sum_{l=1}^{N} \ln \left(\frac{1 + C_l}{1 - C_l} \right) (-1)^{w_l} = \sum_{\Gamma \in W} \beta(\Gamma) \times (-1)^{\langle \Gamma, k \rangle}.$$

Using the FWHT, one can evaluate LLR' for each $\Gamma, k \in \mathbb{F}_2^{\dim W}$ with a time complexity $\dim W \cdot 2^{\dim W}$.

Algorithm 3 summarizes the attack procedure using the FWHT. We first collect N ciphertext pairs, guess $k_{\mathcal{P}}$, and prepare a real number α and the array of real numbers β to compute the LLR statistic. For every ciphertext pair, we identify partitions, get corresponding correlation $\rho_{i,j}$ and linear mask, and update α and β accordingly. We finally apply the FWHT to β and the LLR statistic is computed as $\alpha + \tilde{\beta}(k_{\mathcal{L}})$. The overall running time is estimated as $2^{n_{\mathcal{P}}}(2N + \dim W \cdot 2^{\dim W})$, where $n_{\mathcal{P}}$ is the bit length of $k_{\mathcal{P}}$. A total of $n_{\mathcal{P}} + \dim W$ key bits are recovered. Besides, one can deduce the following proposition.

Proposition 1. [4] *After running Algorithm 3 for p^{-1} times where p is the probability of the prepended differential $\Delta_{\text{in}} \to \Delta_m$, the probability that the correct key is among the key candidate is*

$$p_{\text{success}} \geqslant \frac{1}{2} \mathbf{Pr}[C(k_{\mathcal{P}}, k_{\mathcal{L}}) \geqslant \Theta] = \frac{1}{2} \left(1 - \Phi \left(\frac{\Theta - \frac{N}{2}\overline{C}}{\sqrt{N\overline{C}}} \right) \right),$$

where Φ is the cumulative distribution of the standard normal distribution $\mathcal{N}(0,1)$. The expected number of wrong keys is $\frac{2^{n_{\mathcal{P}} + \dim W}}{p} \times \left(1 - \Phi \left(\frac{\Theta + \frac{N}{2}\overline{C}}{\sqrt{N\overline{C}}} \right) \right)$.

6   Application to LEA

In 2013, the LEA family of block ciphers is published at WISA [18], expected to provide confidentiality in both high-speed and lightweight environments. In 2016, it is established as the national standard of Republic of Korea (KS X

Algorithm 3. Key recovery

Require: Cipher E, sample size N, threshold Θ.
Ensure: List of key candidates $(k_\mathcal{P}, k_\mathcal{L})$ for $n_\mathcal{P} + \dim W$ bit of information on k.

1: **for** $l \in \{1, \cdots, N\}$ **do**
2:     $x \xleftarrow{\$} \mathcal{U} \oplus a;$
3:     $(c(l), \tilde{c}(l)) \leftarrow (E(x), E(x \oplus \Delta_{in}))$
4: **end for**
5: **for** each possible $k'_\mathcal{P}$ **do**
6:     $\alpha \leftarrow 0$
7:     **for** $\Gamma \in W$ **do**
8:         $\beta(\Gamma) \leftarrow 0$
9:     **end for**
10:    **for** $l \in \{1, \cdots, N\}$ **do**
11:        $(c, \tilde{c}) \leftarrow (c(l), \tilde{c}(l))$
12:        Compute $(c\|k)_\mathcal{P}$ and $(\tilde{c}\|k)_\mathcal{P}$ to identify partitions.
13:        Identify $\mathcal{T}_i \times \mathcal{T}_j$ for $((c\|k)_\mathcal{P}, (\tilde{c}\|k)_\mathcal{P})$ and get corresponding correlation $\rho_{i,j}$.
14:        $\Gamma \leftarrow \Gamma^{(c\|k)_\mathcal{P}} \oplus \Gamma^{(\tilde{c}\|k)_\mathcal{P}}$
15:        $\alpha \leftarrow \alpha + \frac{1}{2}\ln(1 - \rho_{i,j}^2)$
16:        $\beta(\Gamma) \leftarrow \beta(\Gamma) + \frac{1}{2}\ln\left(\frac{1+\rho_{i,j}}{1-\rho_{i,j}}\right)(-1)^{\langle g^{(c\|k)_\mathcal{P}}, c\rangle \oplus \langle g^{(\tilde{c}\|k)_\mathcal{P}}, \tilde{c}\rangle}$
17:    **end for**
18:    Compute $\hat{\beta}$ by using the FAST Walsh-Hadamard Transform.
19:    $C(k'_\mathcal{P}, k'_\mathcal{L}) \leftarrow \alpha + \hat{\beta}(k_{\mathcal{L}'})$
20:    **if** $C(k'_\mathcal{P}, k'_\mathcal{L}) > \Theta$ **then**
21:        Save $(k'_\mathcal{P}, k'_\mathcal{L})$ as a key candidate.
22:    **end if**
23: **end for**

3246). After six years of public evaluation, it is included in the ISO/IEC 29192-2:2019 standard (Information security - Lightweight cryptography - Part 2: Block ciphers). The LEA family has three members with a common block size of 128 bits and three different key sizes of 128, 192, and 256 bits, denoted by LEA-128, LEA-192, and LEA-256, respectively.

Round Function. The encryption of LEA maps a plaintext of four 32-bit words $(x_0^0, x_1^0, x_2^0, x_3^0)$ into a ciphertext $(x_0^r, x_1^r, x_2^r, x_3^r)$ using a sequence of r rounds, where $r = 24$ for LEA-128, $r = 28$ for LEA-192 and $r = 32$ for LEA-256. Figure 9 provides a schematic view of the round function of LEA.

In [18], the designers claim that the actual differential-linear characteristics should be much shorter than 14 rounds or have a bias (equal to half of the correlation) whose absolute value is significantly smaller than 2^{-57}. Moreover, the designers claim that the secure number of rounds is 17 for LEA-128, 18 for LEA-192, and 19 for LEA-256.

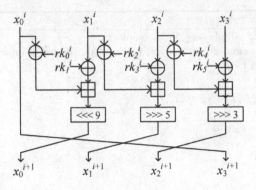

Fig. 9. The round function of LEA.

6.1 Differential-Linear Approximations

We first report differential-linear approximations that are searched using the methods introduced in Sect. 3.

Let r_1, r_m, r_2 denote the number of rounds covered by E_1, E_m, E_2 respectively. The differential-linear approximation $\Delta_m \xrightarrow{E_m} \gamma_m$ and linear approximation $\gamma_m \xrightarrow{E_2} \gamma_{out}$ are first searched together using Algorithm 2. Then a prepend differential $\Delta_{in} \xrightarrow{E_1} \Delta_m$ is added. Since it is practically infeasible to test all the differences Δ_m, we restricted ourselves to the case of a difference Δ_m of the form $[i]$ or $[i, i+1]$, i.e., 1-bit or consecutive 2-bit differences. We set $c = 2^{-8}$ (the correlation threshold) for Algorithm 2. Table 4 summarizes three differential-linear approximations searched by the above setting, which will be used in key recovery attacks.

Table 4. Differential-Linear approximations of round reduced LEA.

(r_m, r_2)	$\Delta_m \rightarrow \gamma_m \rightarrow \gamma_{out}$	Cor of $\Delta_m \rightarrow \gamma_{out}$
$(8,3)$	$[26] \rightarrow \sum \rightarrow [0,9,61,91,105]$	$2^{-4.679}$
$(8,4)$	$[31] \rightarrow \sum \rightarrow [0,9,61,91,105]$	$-2^{-10.970}$
$(8,5)$	$[31] \rightarrow [8,41,42,73,74] \rightarrow$ $[0,29,37,38,61,68,88,91,101,102,105,114]$	$-2^{-6.04} \times 2^{-10 \times 2}$

[a] $\sum$: all the possible linear masks γ_m are considered. Since many distinguishers returned by Algorithm 2 share the same linear mask γ_{out}, we directly estimate the experimental correlation of $\Delta_m \rightarrow \gamma_{out}$.
[b] The three correlations $2^{-4.679}$, $-2^{-10.970}$, $-2^{-6.04}$ are estimated again using N plaintext pairs and 100 keys. The three values are the median of 100 experimental correlations. For $2^{-4.679}$ and $-2^{-6.04}$, $N = 2^{24}$. For $-2^{-10.970}$, $N = 2^{32}$. The number 2^{-10} in the third row is the correlation of the linear approximation $\gamma_m \rightarrow \gamma_{out}$.

Table 5 shows one of the optimal 4-round differential characteristics whose output difference is $\Delta_m = [31]$. By placing it before the 12-round or 13-round differential-linear approximation as shown in Table 4, we obtain a 16-round or 17-round distinguisher for LEA. The 17-round distinguisher with a correlation $2^{-33} \times (-2^{-6.04}) \times 2^{-10 \times 2} = -2^{-59.04}$ is the best distinguisher so far. The previous best distinguisher is the 16-round Boomerang distinguisher with a probability $2^{-117.2}$ [19].

Table 5. An 4-round differential characteristic with an output difference $\Delta_m = [31]$.

r	Δ	$\mathbf{Pr}$
0	$(0x8a000080, 0x80402080, 0x80402210, 0xc0402234)$	
1	$(0x80400014, 0x80000014, 0x88000004, 0x8a000080)$	2^{-17}
2	$(0x80000000, 0x80400000, 0x80400010, 0x80400014)$	2^{-10}
3	$(0x80000000, 0x80000000, 0x80000000, 0x80000000)$	2^{-6}
4	$[31]$	1

6.2 Detecting Subspaces

For the 4-round differential characteristic as shown in Table 5, we need to detect a subspace $\mathcal{U}$ of the input space such that $E_1(P \oplus u) \oplus E_1(P \oplus u \oplus \Delta_{\text{in}}) = \Delta_m$ for all $u \in \mathcal{U}$ if $E_1(P) \oplus E_1(P \oplus \Delta_{\text{in}}) = \Delta_m$. To detect such a subspace, we first collect 2^{10} plaintext pairs conforming to the differential characteristic using the fast method introduced in [14].

The subspace is searched as follows: (1) Traverse $i \in \{0, \cdots, 127\}$, flip the ith bit of each pair $(P, \overline{P})$ and compute the probability $\mathbf{Pr}$ that the new pair $(P \oplus [i], \overline{P} \oplus [i])$ still conforms to the 4-round differential characteristic. If $\mathbf{Pr} \geqslant 0.7$, save i as a basis element. (2) Traverse each possible tuple $(i_1, \cdots, i_k)$ for $k \leqslant 3$ where $i_j, j \in \{1, \cdots, k\}$ is not a basis element, and check whether $[i_1, \cdots, i_k]$ can be a basis element by flipping the k bits of each pair simultaneously.

Table 6. Probability that adding one basis element doesn't affect the output difference.

Probability	Basis	Number
$\mathbf{Pr} = 1$	$[2], [4, 36], [22, 54, 86], [31]$	4
$0.9 \leqslant \mathbf{Pr} < 1$	$[14], [15], [16], [17], [18], [19], [20], [21], [50, 82], [51], [52]$	
	$[63, 95], [110], [111], [112], [113], [114], [124], [125], [126], [127]$	21
$0.8 \leqslant \mathbf{Pr} < 0.9$	$[23], [46, 78], [53], [83], [104], [105], [115]$	7
$0.7 \leqslant \mathbf{Pr} < 0.8$	$[24], [47, 79]$	2

Table 6 summarizes the result of the search. Given any plaintext pair $(P, P \oplus \Delta_{in})$ conforming to the 4-round differential characteristic as shown in Table 5, using the 34 basis elements, one can create from the plaintext pair a plaintext structure consisting of 2^{34} plaintext pairs. These 2^{34} plaintext pairs are expected to pass the differential characteristic together, with a theoretical probability $2^{-3.7}$ under the assumption that the effects of the 34 basis elements are independent. For verifying the theoretical probability $2^{-3.7}$, we generate 2^{10} plaintext pairs conforming to the 4-round differential characteristic, and find that the empirical probability is $2^{-3.18}$ (resp. $2^{-3.17}$, $2^{-3.33}$) for LEA-128 (resp. LEA-192, LEA-256) [3]. Thus, we obtain Lemma 3. The 17-round key recovery attack introduced later uses this linear subspace.

Lemma 3. *There is a set $\mathcal{X} \subseteq \mathbb{F}_2^{128}$ of size $2^{128-33-3.7}$ and a 34-dimensional linear subspace $\mathcal{U}$, such that for any element $x \in \mathcal{X}$ and any $u \in \mathcal{U}$ it holds that $E_1(x \oplus u) \oplus E_1(x \oplus u \oplus \Delta_{in}) = \Delta_m$ where E_1 denotes 4 rounds of LEA.*

6.3 The 17-Round Key Recovery Attack

The 16-round differential-linear approximation introduced in Sect. 6.1 is used to attack 17-round LEA by guessing the last round key. Look at the LEA round function as shown in Fig. 9. For the convenience of introducing the 17-round key recovery attack, we make the following transformation:

$$(z_0, z_1, z_2, z_3) := (x_0^{16}, x_1^{16} \oplus rk_1^{16}, x_2^{16} \oplus rk_3^{16}, x_3^{16} \oplus rk_5^{16});$$
$$(k_0, k_1, k_2) := (rk_0^{16}, rk_1^{16} \oplus rk_2^{16}, rk_3^{16} \oplus rk_4^{16}); \tag{15}$$
$$(y_0, y_1, y_2, y_3) := (x_0^{17} \ggg 9, x_1^{17} \lll 5, x_2^{17} \lll 3, x_3^{17}).$$

Now, the notations are consistent with those used in Fig. 6.

Consider the linear mask is $[0, 9, 61, 91, 105]$. The corresponding five bits to be computed are $z_3[0]$, $z_3[9]$, $z_2[29]$, $z_1[27]$, and $z_0[9]$. For $z_3[0]$ and $z_0[9]$, there are two deterministic relation:

$$z_3[0] = (z_0 \oplus y_0 \oplus y_1 \oplus y_2)[0] \oplus (k_0 \oplus k_1 \oplus k_2)[0]; \quad z_0[9] = y_3[9]. \tag{16}$$

Notice that the key bit $(k_0 \oplus k_1 \oplus k_2)[0]$ will be canceled in the key recovery stage. Thus, only the remaining three bits need to be computed by guessing key bits and using the partitioning technique.

Table 7 summarizes the approximations and partition conditions related to $z_3[9]$, $z_2[29]$, $z_1[27]$. To identify the partition, we need to know

$$s[26], s[25], s[28], s[27], g[28] \oplus y_0 \langle 27, 26 \rangle, g[27] \oplus y_0 \langle 26, 25 \rangle,$$
$$s[8], s[7], s[6], g[8] \oplus y_0 \langle 7, 6 \rangle, g[7] \oplus y_0 \langle 6, 5 \rangle, h[8] \oplus y_1 \langle 7, 6 \rangle$$

and 12-bit key guessing is enough, where $s = z_0 \oplus k_0 \oplus y_0$ and $g = y_1 \oplus k_1$ and $h = y_2 \oplus k_2$.

---

[3] The code for verifying the theoretical probability $2^{-3.7}$ is available at https://github. com/AI-Lab-Y/DLA_search_and_partition_tree

Table 7. Approximations and partition conditions related to $z_3[9]$, $z_2[29]$, $z_1[27]$.

ζ_1	Choice: $z_1[27]$
	$\mathcal{P}_1 \ni p_i \cong (s[26], s[25])$
	Linear: $y_0[27]$, $z_0[27]$, $z_0[26]$, $z_0[25]$, $z_0[24]$, $k_0[27]$, $k_0[26]$, $k_0[25]$, $k_0[24]$
ζ_2	Choice: $z_2[29]$
	$\mathcal{P}_2 \ni p_i \cong (s[28], s[27], s[26], g[28] \oplus y_0 \langle 27, 26 \rangle, g[27] \oplus y_0 \langle 26, 25 \rangle)$
	Linear: $y_1[29]$, $y_1[28]$, $y_1[27]$, $y_1[26]$, $y_0[29]$, $z_0[29]$, $z_0[28]$, $z_0[27]$, $z_0[26]$
	$k_1[29]$, $k_0[29]$, $k_0[28]$, $k_0[27]$, $k_0[26]$
ζ_3	Choice: $z_3[9]$
	$\mathcal{P}_3 \ni p_i \cong (s[8], s[7], s[6], g[8] \oplus y_0 \langle 7, 6 \rangle, g[7] \oplus y_0 \langle 6, 5 \rangle, h[8] \oplus y_1 \langle 7, 6 \rangle)$
	Linear: $y_2[9]$, $y_2[8]$, $y_2[7]$, $y_1[9]$, $y_1[8]$, $y_1[7]$, $y_1[6]$, $y_0[9]$, $z_0[9]$, $z_0[8]$,
	$z_0[7]$, $z_0[6]$, $k_2[9]$, $k_1[9]$, $k_0[9]$, $k_0[8]$, $k_0[7]$, $k_0[6]$

After guessing the 12-bit key, we identify 3×2 partitions for a ciphertext pair, and access corresponding linear masks and correlations. Suppose that the six correlations are $\mathbf{Cor}_i$ for $i \in \{1, \cdots, 6\}$. We have

$$\rho = -2^{-10.97} \times \prod_{i=1}^{6} \mathbf{Cor}_i \tag{17}$$

under the assumption that the six differential-linear approximations are independent, where ρ is used to calculate the LLR statistic for key recovery.

Experimental Reports. Before estimating the complexity of the 17-round attack, we first execute a practical auxiliary experiment. Look at the two differential-linear approximations as shown in the first and second rows of Table 4. They have the same output linear mask γ_{out}. Since the correlation of $[26] \rightarrow [0, 9, 61, 91, 105]$ is very high, we use it to verify our attack procedure. The right pair and the correct key are used to observe the LLR statistic for the correct case.

The LLR statistic depends on the sum of the squared correlation $N\overline{C} = \sum_{l=1}^{N} c_l^2$. We estimated $\overline{C} \approx 2^{-14.052}$ and $N\overline{C} \approx 61.74$ when $N = 2^{20}$ pairs are used. Figure 10 shows the comparison of the LLR statistics, where the theoretical distribution is drawn by the normal distribution with mean $\frac{N\overline{C}}{2}$ (for a correct case) and $-\frac{N\overline{C}}{2}$ (for a wrong case) and the standard deviation $\sqrt{N\overline{C}}$. By repeating the attack 512 times, two experimental histograms are drawn. In each trial, we ensure that the correlation of $\Delta_m \rightarrow \gamma_{\text{out}}$ approximately equals $2^{-4.679}$. Note that the experimental one is more biased than the theoretical estimation in the correct case. We expect that the reason comes from the additional auto-correlation-linear hull [4] that we do not take into account. The auxiliary experiment well verifies our attack procedure.

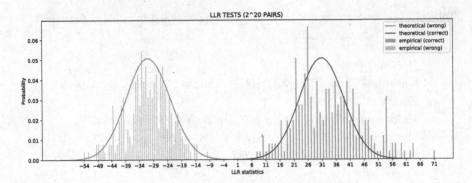

Fig. 10. Comparison with LLR statistics.

For the 17-round attack, we estimated $\overline{C} \approx 2^{-26.334}$ and $N\overline{C} \approx 50.77$ when $N = 2^{32}$ pairs are used. We finally estimate the data complexity and time complexity of this attack. To identify the partition, we need to guess the 12-bit key. We also enumerated elements of the linear subspace W and computed the basis using Gaussian elimination. As a result, the dimension of W is 9. To find a right pair, we need $2^{33+3.7}$ iterations because of Lemma 3. Thus, there are about $2^{12+9+33+3.7} = 2^{57.7}$ wrong cases. When $2^{33.2}$ pairs are used, we have $N\overline{C} \approx 116.16$. With a success probability of 90%, we can construct a 69.6-bit filter, which is enough to remove $2^{57.7}$ wrong cases. We finally estimate the time complexity by using the following formula [4]:

$$T = p^{-1} \times 2^{n_P} \times \left(2N + \dim W 2^{\dim W}\right)$$
$$= 2^{33+3.7} \times 2^{12} \times \left(2 \times 2^{33.2} + 9 \times 2^9\right) \approx 2^{82.9}.$$

6.4   The 18-Round Key Recovery Attack

The 17-round differential-linear approximation introduced in Sect. 6.1 is used to attack 18-round LEA. Since the correlation of the differential-linear approximation of $E_2 \circ E_m$ is too low, the LLR-based key recovery technique is not applicable. Hence, the classical key recovery algorithm introduced in Appendix A is adopted. For convenience, the transformation as shown in formula 15 is adopted.

The correlation of the 17-round distinguisher is $-2^{-59.04}$. Let the advantage be $a = 50$ and the success probability be 0.99, the required data complexity is $N = 2^{124.8}$ chosen-plaintext pairs. Consider the output linear mask

$$\gamma_{\text{out}} = [0, 29, 37, 38, 61, 68, 88, 91, 101, 102, 105, 114].$$

If no partition techniques are applied, in order to obtain the above bits, we need to guess $30 \times 3 = 90$ key bits, i.e., the least significant 30 bits of k_0 and k_1 and k_2. This will make the time complexity $2^{124.8+1+90} = 2^{215.8}$.

---

[4]   Notice that the required time complexity will be lower when the absolute correlation of $\Delta_m \to \gamma_{\text{out}}$ exceeds $2^{-10.97}$.

To make the 18-round attack apply to LEA-192, we make an improvement to this attack. Concretely, we compute $z_3[29]$ (i.e., bit 29) using the first two partitions (with correlation 1) as shown in Lemma 1 or Lemma 2. As a result, for the key k_2, we just need to guess three bits $k_2[29]$ and $k_2[28]$ and $k_2[27]$, instead of 30 bits. In other words, the improved attack guesses $30 \times 2 + 3 = 63$ key bits. Notice that only $\frac{3}{4} \times \frac{3}{4} \times N \approx 2^{-0.83} N$ chosen-plaintext pairs are useful now. Thus, the new data complexity should be $2^{124.8} \times 2^{0.83} = 2^{125.63}$ chosen plaintext pairs. The improved time complexity is $2^{125.63+1+63} = 2^{189.63} < 2^{192}$.

7   Application to Speck

Speck is a family of lightweight block ciphers designed by researchers from the U.S. National Security Agency (NSA) [3]. The Speck family has been a part of the RFID air interface standard (ISO/IEC 29167-22).

The Speck family contains ten members, each of which is characterized by its block size $2n$ and key size mn, thus is named Speck$2n/mn$. All the members with the same block size are also named Speck$2n$, i.e., Speck32, Speck48, Speck64, Speck96 and Speck128 respectively. The round function of Speck is shown in Fig. 11. For Speck32, two parameters are $R = 7$ and $L = 2$. For the remaining members, two parameters are $R = 8$ and $L = 3$.

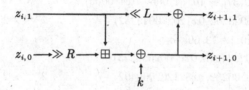

Fig. 11. The Speck round function.

Although the Speck family has been proposed for about ten years, there are few public papers on its resistance against differential-linear attacks. To our knowledge, there are no reports on differential-linear distinguishers of Speck96 and Speck128.

If we set aside the distinguishers given by fully automatic differential-linear approximation searching methods [6,23], the previous best distinguishers are: (1) 10-round differential-linear distinguisher (with a correlation $2^{-13.90}$) [28] for Speck32; (2) 11-round (with a probability $2^{-44.31}$), 15-round, 17-round, and 20-round differential distinguishers [30] for Speck48, Speck64, Speck96, Speck128 respectively. The results in [6,23] will be introduced and compared later.

Differential-Linear Approximations of Speck. Using Algorithm 2, we have found many differential-linear distinguishers for the Speck family.

Again, let r_1, r_m, r_2 denote the number of rounds covered by E_1, E_m, E_2 respectively. For all the members, the absolute correlation threshold used in Algorithm 2 is 2^{-8}. Moreover, we restricted ourselves to the case of a difference Δ_m of the form $[i]$ or $[i, i+1]$. Table 8 summarizes some differential-linear approximations that we have found. For convenience, we put the three numbers (i.e., r_1, r_m, r_2) on the arrows.

Table 8. Differential-Linear approximations of round-reduced Speck.

Member	$\Delta_{\text{in}} \xrightarrow{r_1} \Delta_m \xrightarrow{r_m} \gamma_m \xrightarrow{r_2} \gamma_{\text{out}}$	**Cor** of $\Delta_{\text{in}} \to \gamma_{\text{out}}$
Speck32	$(0x2800, 0x10) \xrightarrow{1} [22] \xrightarrow{6}$ $\sum \xrightarrow{3} (0x2300, 0x4380)$	$2^{-2} \times (-2^{-10.2})$
Speck48	$(0x20082, 0x120200) \xrightarrow{2} [39] \xrightarrow{6}$ $[2] \xrightarrow{3} (0xc2801, 0xd0800)^*$	$2^{-5} \times (-2^{-6.40}) \times 2^{-3 \times 2}$
	$(0x20082, 0x120200) \xrightarrow{2} [39] \xrightarrow{6}$ $[1, 2, 5, 37] \xrightarrow{3} (0xc00c0d, 0xc0c)$	$2^{-5} \times (-2^{-10.51}) \times 2^{-2 \times 2}$
Speck64	$(0x102490, 0x10801004)^* \xrightarrow{3} [53] \xrightarrow{6}$ $[0, 29, 40] \xrightarrow{4} (0x420c0200, 0x2400200)^*$	$2^{-11} \times 2^{-9.15} \times 2^{-4 \times 2}$
	$(0x40004092, 0x10420040)^* \xrightarrow{3} [47] \xrightarrow{6}$ $[25, 26, 29, 37] \xrightarrow{4} (0xc410060, 0x480060)^*$	$2^{-11} \times 2^{-9.63} \times 2^{-5 \times 2}$
Speck96	$(0x20020028202, 0x120200049282) \xrightarrow{4}$ $[93] \xrightarrow{6} [10, 12, 13, 69] \xrightarrow{5}$ $(0x4d000203422b, 0xc0002030223)^*$	$2^{-20} \times 2^{-5.72} \times 2^{-8 \times 2}$
	$(0x20200200282, 0x821202000492) \xrightarrow{4}$ $[85] \xrightarrow{6} [4, 41, 44, 51, 52, 59, 60] \xrightarrow{5}$ $(0x201234d00000, 0x201630c00000)^*$	$2^{-20} \times 2^{-8.59} \times 2^{-9 \times 2}$
Speck128	$(0x40002403c012, 0x10020040000400c2)^* \xrightarrow{5}$ $[117] \xrightarrow{8} [5, 77] \xrightarrow{5}$ $(0xa49000000020343, 0x208000000020303)^*$	$2^{-30} \times 2^{-5.81} \times 2^{-10 \times 2}$
	$(0x2000120120090, 0x8010020000200610)^* \xrightarrow{5}$ $[120] \xrightarrow{8} [7, 79] \xrightarrow{5}$ $(0x82802c000000808, 0x829a40000000809)^*$	$2^{-30} \times 2^{-7.70} \times 2^{-11 \times 2}$

[a] $\sum$: all the possible γ_m are considered for Speck32. Since many distinguishers returned by Algorithm 2 share the same linear mask γ_{out}, we directly estimate the experimental correlation (i.e., $-2^{-10.2}$) of $\Delta_m \to \gamma_{\text{out}}$.

[b] $*$: There are many optional choices.

[c] The total correlation of $\Delta_{\text{in}} \to \gamma_{\text{out}}$ is $X \times Y \times Z^2$ where X is the probability of $\Delta_{\text{in}} \to \Delta_m$, Y is the experimental correlation (estimated using 2^{30} pairs and 100 keys) of $\Delta_m \to \gamma_m$, and Z is the correlation of $\gamma_m \to \gamma_{\text{out}}$.

We are the first to report differential-linear distinguishers for Speck96 and Speck128. Moreover, when the results in [6,23] are not considered, the two distinguishers (with a correlation $-2^{-12.2}$ and $-2^{-17.40}$) in the second and third rows of Table 8 are the best distinguishers for Speck32 and Speck48 respectively.

Comparison with Fully Automatic Search Methods in [6,23]**.** The authors in [6,23] both searched differential-linear approximations of Speck using their fully automatic MIQCP/MILP-based methods. We have compared our search method, i.e., meet-in-the-middle search (Algorithm 2) with the methods in [6,23]. Table 9 presents the comparison results.

Table 9. Comparison of three search methods.

Method	Differential-linear approximation				
	Speck32	Speck48	Speck64	Speck96	Speck128
MIQCP/MILP [6]	$A_{10}(-12.0)$	×	×	×	×
MIQCP/MILP [23]	$A_{10}(-11.58)$	$A_{11}(-17.55)$	$A_{12}(-26.93)$	×	×
Algorithm 2	$A_{10}(-12.2)$	$A_{11}(-17.40)$	$A_{13}(-28.15)$	$A_{15}(-41.72)$	$A_{18}(-55.81)$

[a] × : not reported. $A_r(X)$: an r-round differential-linear approximation with an absolute correlation 2^X.

It is clear that our method performs better when applied to Speck48, Speck64, Speck96, and Speck128. In [6], the authors explained that their MIQCP/MILP-based method is currently slow, which is the bottleneck of the method in [23] too. Besides, our method selects good differential-linear approximation $\Delta_m \xrightarrow{E_m} \gamma_m$ by the experimental correlation while the methods in [6,23] do this by the theoretical correlation. Since the theoretical correlation is less accurate than the experimental correlation (see the data in [6,23]), we guess that the MIQCP/MILP-based methods may neglect some good differential-linear approximations, e.g., those we have found in this paper.

Now, consider the key recovery attack. The previous best key recovery attack against round-reduced Speck is the differential attack proposed by Dinur in [15]. Based on an h-round differential with a probability p, the adversary can attack $(h + 2)$-round Speck with a time complexity p^{-1} using the method in [15]. We do not find differential-linear distinguishers which cover more rounds than the previous best differential distinguisher in this paper. As a result, based on the differential-linear approximations presented in Tables 8, we do not obtain key recovery attacks which attack more rounds than previous best attacks.

8   Conclusions

In this paper, based on a novel idea, we have proposed new algorithms to search for differential-linear approximations with a high correlation. Besides, a generic tool named partition tree is proposed to efficiently generate partitions for complex ARX encryption functions. Based on our work, the cryptanalyst is able to better evaluate a cipher's resistance to differential-linear attacks. Moreover, the powerful attack framework proposed in [5] can be applied to more ciphers. The applications to LEA and Speck have demonstrated the potential and positive influence of our work.

In our search algorithms, we can not traverse all the possible differences Δ_m, which is still a bottleneck. We believe that it is possible to combine the advantages of our method and MIQCP/MILP-based methods, for accelerating MIQCP/MILP-based methods or making our method totally unconstrained (i.e., have no constraints on the difference Δ_m too). This topic could be a future research direction. Another direction is further explaining the heuristic conclusion presented in Sect. 2 under no assumptions, i.e., considering various possible dependencies between different differential-linear approximations.

Acknowledgments. We thank the anonymous reviewers for their detailed and helpful comments. This work was supported by the National Natural Science Foundation of China (Nos. 62072270), the National Key R&D Program of China (2018YFA0704701, 2020YFA0309705), Shandong Key Research and Development Program (2020ZLYS09), the Major Scientific and Technological Innovation Project of Shandong, China (2019JZZY010133), the Major Program of Guangdong Basic and Applied Research (2019B030302008), the High Performance Computing Center of Tsinghua University. Y. Chen was also supported by the Shuimu Tsinghua Scholar Program.

A   Classical Key Recovery Attack

Consider an $(h+1)$-round encryption function E. Using an h-round differential-linear distinguisher $\Delta \rightarrow \gamma$ of E, one can recover the round key $rk \in \mathbb{F}_2^n$ at round $h + 1$. Without loss of generality, assume that **Cor** > 0 where **Cor** is the correlation of the distinguisher $\Delta \rightarrow \gamma$.

Algorithm 4 summarizes the attack procedure. If N is sufficiently large, c_{rk} will be the largest one among 2^n correlations, where rk is the round key. There is a trade-off between N and the rank of c_{rk}. In [12], Blondeau et al. presented a theoretical analysis of the relation between N and the rank of c_{rk}.

Algorithm 4. Key recovery

Require: $(h+1)$-round encryption function E, sample size N;
   h-round differential-linear distinguisher $\Delta \to \gamma$;
Ensure: List of 2^n corrrelations $\{c_0, \cdots, c_{2^n-1}\}$.
1: $c_i \leftarrow 0$ for $i \in \{0, \cdots, 2^n - 1\}$;
2: **for** $j \in \{1, \cdots, N\}$ **do**
3:    Randomly choose a plaintext x;
4:    $(C^j_{h+1,0}, C^j_{h+1,1}) \leftarrow (E(x), E(x \oplus \Delta))$;
5:    **for** $i \in \{0, \cdots, 2^n - 1\}$ **do**
6:       $(C^j_{h,0}, C^j_{h,1}) \leftarrow (\text{ORD}(C^j_{h+1,0}, i), \text{ORD}(C^j_{h+1,1}, i))$;
       /* $\text{ORD}(C, i)$ stands for one round decryption and i is the key guess. */
7:       $c_i \leftarrow c_i + (-1)^{\langle \gamma, C^j_{h,0} \rangle \oplus \langle \gamma, C^j_{h,1} \rangle}$;
8:    **end for**
9: **end for**

The theoretical analysis in [12] is based on a concept named *advantage* introduced in [29]. If an attack on an n-bit key (eg. Algorithm 4) gets the correct value ranked among the top s out of 2^n possible candidates, we say the attack obtained an $(n - \log_2(s))$-bit *advantage* over the exhaustive search. Then the case where c_{rk} is the largest one among 2^n correlations corresponds to obtaining an n-bit advantage over an n-bit key.

If an attack obtains a preset advantage, we say the attack succeeded. In [12], Blondeau et al. presented that the success probability of the attack is:

$$P_S = \Phi \left(2\sqrt{N}\varepsilon - \Phi^{-1} \left(1 - 2^{-a}\right) \right),$$

where Φ is the cumulative distribution function of the standard normal distribution, a is the preset advantage of the attack in bits, and ε is the bias of the differential-linear distinguisher $\Delta \to \gamma$. Note that $\varepsilon = \frac{1}{2}\mathbf{Cor}$ where $\mathbf{Cor}$ is the correlation of $\Delta \to \gamma$. From this estimate, the data complexity of the differential-linear attack is deduced.

Lemma 4. [12] *Given the bias $\varepsilon = \frac{1}{2}\mathbf{Cor}$ of a differential-linear approximation, the data complexity of a key-recovery attack with advantage a and success probability P_S can be given as*

$$N = \frac{\left(\Phi^{-1}\left(P_S\right) + \Phi^{-1}\left(1 - 2^{-a}\right)\right)^2}{4\varepsilon^2}.$$

B   Partitions for Parallel Modular Additions

Table 10. The partitions for three parallel modular additions.

$b_0b_1b_2b_3b_4b_5$	$z_3[i]$ γ	Cor	$b_0b_1b_2b_3b_4b_5$	$z_3[i]$ γ	Cor
000000	101110011001111001	$2^{-2.194}$	100000	110101011100111100	$-2^{-1.178}$
000001	110110011001111001	$2^{-1.217}$	100001	101101011100111100	$-2^{-2.182}$
000010	101110011001111001	$2^{-2.647}$	100010	110100111100111100	$-2^{-1.534}$
000011	110110011001111001	$2^{-1.509}$	100011	101100111100111100	$-2^{-2.556}$
000100	110101011001111001	$2^{-1.184}$	100100	101110011100111100	$-2^{-2.165}$
000101	101101011001111001	$2^{-2.174}$	100101	110110011100111100	$-2^{-1.178}$
000110	110100111001111001	$2^{-1.539}$	100110	101110011100111100	$-2^{-2.479}$
000111	101100111001111001	$2^{-2.574}$	100111	110110011100111100	$-2^{-1.626}$
001000	101110011001111001	$-2^{-1.017}$	101000	110101011100111100	-1
001001	110110011001111001	-1	101001	101101011100111100	$-2^{-1.015}$
001010	101110011001111001	$-2^{-1.428}$	101010	110100111100111100	$-2^{-0.417}$
001011	110110011001111001	$-2^{-0.401}$	101011	101100111100111100	$-2^{-1.412}$
001100	110101011001111001	-1	101100	101110011100111100	$-2^{-0.988}$
001101	101101011001111001	$-2^{-0.989}$	101101	110110011100111100	-1
001110	110100111001111001	$-2^{-0.408}$	101110	101110011100111100	$-2^{-1.424}$
001111	101100111001111001	$-2^{-1.478}$	101111	110110011100111100	$-2^{-0.392}$
010000	101110011010111010	$-2^{-1.522}$	110000	110100111100111100	$-2^{-0.546}$
010001	110110011010111010	$-2^{-0.547}$	110001	101100111100111100	$-2^{-1.519}$
010010	101110011010111010	$-2^{-1.203}$	110010	110101011100111100	$-2^{-0.176}$
010011	110110011010111010	$-2^{-0.191}$	110011	101101011100111100	$-2^{-1.179}$
010100	110100111010111010	$-2^{-0.53}$	110100	101110011100111100	$-2^{-1.623}$
010101	101100111010111010	$-2^{-1.558}$	110101	110110011100111100	$-2^{-0.531}$
010110	110101011010111010	$-2^{-0.191}$	110110	101110011100111100	$-2^{-1.158}$
010111	101101011010111010	$-2^{-1.181}$	110111	110110011100111100	$-2^{-0.193}$
011000	101110011010111010	$-2^{-1.388}$	111000	110100111100111100	$-2^{-0.419}$
011001	110110011010111010	$-2^{-0.411}$	111001	101100111100111100	$-2^{-1.452}$
011010	101110011010111010	$-2^{-0.967}$	111010	110101011100111100	-1
011011	110110011010111010	-1	111011	101101011100111100	$-2^{-0.987}$
011100	110100111010111010	$-2^{-0.406}$	111100	101110011100111100	$-2^{-1.433}$
011101	101100111010111010	$-2^{-1.405}$	111101	110110011100111100	$-2^{-0.415}$
011110	110101011010111010	-1	111110	101110011100111100	$-2^{-1.004}$
011111	101101011010111010	$-2^{-1.012}$	111111	110110011100111100	-1

Table 11. The partitions for two parallel modular additions.

$b_0b_1b_2b_3b_4$	$z_2[i]$ γ	Cor	$b_0b_1b_2b_3b_4$	$z_2[i]$ γ	Cor
00000	11001100111001	$2^{-1.009}$	10000	10101110011100	$-2^{-1.408}$
00001	11001100111001	$2^{-0.964}$	10001	10011110011100	$-2^{-2.546}$
00010	10101100111001	$2^{-1.389}$	10010	11001110011100	$-2^{-0.994}$
00011	10011100111001	$2^{-2.379}$	10011	11001110011100	$-2^{-0.997}$
00100	11001100111001	-1	10100	10101110011100	-1
00101	11001100111001	-1	10101	10011110011100	$-2^{-0.993}$
00110	10101100111001	-1	10110	11001110011100	-1
00111	10011100111001	$-2^{-0.984}$	10111	11001110011100	-1
01000	11001101011010	-1	11000	10011110011100	$-2^{-1.416}$
01001	11001101011010	-1	11001	10101110011100	$-2^{-0.419}$
01010	10011101011010	$-2^{-1.416}$	11010	11001110011100	-1
01011	10101101011010	$-2^{-0.406}$	11011	11001110011100	-1
01100	11001101011010	-1	11100	10011110011100	$-2^{-0.996}$
01101	11001101011010	-1	11101	10101110011100	-1
01110	10011101011010	$-2^{-1.009}$	11110	11001110011100	-1
01111	10101101011010	-1	11111	11001110011100	-1

References

1. Aumasson, J.-P., Fischer, S., Khazaei, S., Meier, W., Rechberger, C.: New Features of Latin Dances: Analysis of Salsa, ChaCha, and Rumba. In: Nyberg, K. (ed.) FSE 2008. LNCS, vol. 5086, pp. 470–488. Springer, Heidelberg (2008). https://doi.org/10.1007/978-3-540-71039-4_30

2. Bar-On, A., Dunkelman, O., Keller, N., Weizman, A.: DLCT: a new tool for differential-linear cryptanalysis. In: Ishai, Y., Rijmen, V. (eds.) EUROCRYPT 2019. LNCS, vol. 11476, pp. 313–342. Springer, Cham (2019). https://doi.org/10.1007/978-3-030-17653-2_11

3. Beaulieu, R., Shors, D., Smith, J., Treatman-Clark, S., Weeks, B., Wingers, L.: The SIMON and SPECK lightweight block ciphers. In: DAC 2015, Proceedings, pp. 175:1–175:6. ACM (2015)

4. Beierle, C., et al.: Improved differential-linear attacks with applications to ARX ciphers. J. Cryptol. **35**(4), 29 (2022)

5. Beierle, C., Leander, G., Todo, Y.: Improved differential-linear attacks with applications to ARX ciphers. In: Micciancio, D., Ristenpart, T. (eds.) CRYPTO 2020. LNCS, vol. 12172, pp. 329–358. Springer, Cham (2020). https://doi.org/10.1007/978-3-030-56877-1_12

6. Bellini, E., Gérault, D., Grados, J., Makarim, R.H., Peyrin, T.: Fully automated differential-linear attacks against ARX ciphers. In: Rosulek, M. (ed.) CT-RSA 2023, Proceedings. LNCS, vol. 13871, pp. 252–276. Springer (2023)

7. Bernstein, D.J.: The Salsa20 family of stream ciphers. In: Robshaw, M., Billet, O. (eds.) New Stream Cipher Designs. LNCS, vol. 4986, pp. 84–97. Springer, Heidelberg (2008). https://doi.org/10.1007/978-3-540-68351-3_8

8. Biham, E., Carmeli, Y.: An improvement of linear cryptanalysis with addition operations with applications to FEAL-8X. In: Joux, A., Youssef, A. (eds.) SAC 2014. LNCS, vol. 8781, pp. 59–76. Springer, Cham (2014). https://doi.org/10.1007/978-3-319-13051-4_4

9. Biham, E., Chen, R.: Near-collisions of SHA-0. In: Franklin, M. (ed.) CRYPTO 2004. LNCS, vol. 3152, pp. 290–305. Springer, Heidelberg (2004). https://doi.org/10.1007/978-3-540-28628-8_18

10. Biham, E., Dunkelman, O., Keller, N.: Enhancing differential-linear cryptanalysis. In: Zheng, Y. (ed.) ASIACRYPT 2002. LNCS, vol. 2501, pp. 254–266. Springer, Heidelberg (2002). https://doi.org/10.1007/3-540-36178-2_16

11. Biham, E., Shamir, A.: Differential cryptanalysis of DES-like cryptosystems. In: Menezes, A.J., Vanstone, S.A. (eds.) CRYPTO 1990. LNCS, vol. 537, pp. 2–21. Springer, Heidelberg (1991). https://doi.org/10.1007/3-540-38424-3_1

12. Blondeau, C., Leander, G., Nyberg, K.: Differential-linear cryptanalysis revisited. J. Cryptol. **30**(3), 859–888 (2017)

13. Carlet, C. (ed.): Boolean Functions for Cryptography and Coding Theory. Cambridge University Press (2020)

14. Chen, Y., Bao, Z., Shen, Y., Yu, H.: A deep learning aided key recovery framework for large-state block ciphers. Cryptology ePrint Archive, Paper 2022/1659 (2022)

15. Dinur, I.: Improved differential cryptanalysis of round-reduced speck. In: Joux, A., Youssef, A. (eds.) SAC 2014. LNCS, vol. 8781, pp. 147–164. Springer, Cham (2014). https://doi.org/10.1007/978-3-319-13051-4_9

16. Dunkelman, O., Indesteege, S., Keller, N.: A differential-linear attack on 12-round serpent. In: Chowdhury, D.R., Rijmen, V., Das, A. (eds.) INDOCRYPT 2008. LNCS, vol. 5365, pp. 308–321. Springer, Heidelberg (2008). https://doi.org/10.1007/978-3-540-89754-5_24

17. Hawkes, P.: Differential-linear weak key classes of IDEA. In: Nyberg, K. (ed.) EUROCRYPT 1998. LNCS, vol. 1403, pp. 112–126. Springer, Heidelberg (1998). https://doi.org/10.1007/BFb0054121

18. Hong, D., Lee, J.-K., Kim, D.-C., Kwon, D., Ryu, K.H., Lee, D.-G.: LEA: a 128-bit block cipher for fast encryption on common processors. In: Kim, Y., Lee, H., Perrig, A. (eds.) WISA 2013. LNCS, vol. 8267, pp. 3–27. Springer, Cham (2014). https://doi.org/10.1007/978-3-319-05149-9_1

19. Kim, D., Kwon, D., Song, J.: Efficient computation of boomerang connection probability for arx-based block ciphers with application to SPECK and LEA. IEICE Trans. Fundam. Electron. Commun. Comput. Sci. **103-A**(4), 677–685 (2020)

20. Langford, S.K., Hellman, M.E.: Differential-linear cryptanalysis. In: Desmedt, Y.G. (ed.) CRYPTO 1994. LNCS, vol. 839, pp. 17–25. Springer, Heidelberg (1994). https://doi.org/10.1007/3-540-48658-5_3

21. Leurent, G.: Improved differential-linear cryptanalysis of 7-round chaskey with partitioning. In: Fischlin, M., Coron, J.-S. (eds.) EUROCRYPT 2016. LNCS, vol. 9665, pp. 344–371. Springer, Heidelberg (2016). https://doi.org/10.1007/978-3-662-49890-3_14

22. Liu, Y., Wang, Q., Rijmen, V.: Automatic search of linear trails in ARX with applications to SPECK and Chaskey. In: Manulis, M., Sadeghi, A.-R., Schneider, S. (eds.) ACNS 2016. LNCS, vol. 9696, pp. 485–499. Springer, Cham (2016). https://doi.org/10.1007/978-3-319-39555-5_26

23. Lv, G., Jin, C., Cui, T.: A miqcp-based automatic search algorithm for differential-linear trails of arx ciphers(long paper). Cryptology ePrint Archive, Paper 2023/259 (2023). https://eprint.iacr.org/2023/259

24. Matsui, M.: Linear cryptanalysis method for DES cipher. In: Helleseth, T. (ed.) EUROCRYPT 1993. LNCS, vol. 765, pp. 386–397. Springer, Heidelberg (1994). https://doi.org/10.1007/3-540-48285-7_33

25. Mouha, N., Mennink, B., Van Herrewege, A., Watanabe, D., Preneel, B., Verbauwhede, I.: Chaskey: an efficient MAC algorithm for 32-bit microcontrollers. In: Joux, A., Youssef, A. (eds.) SAC 2014. LNCS, vol. 8781, pp. 306–323. Springer, Cham (2014). https://doi.org/10.1007/978-3-319-13051-4_19

26. Mouha, N., Preneel, B.: Towards finding optimal differential characteristics for arx: Application to salsa20. Cryptology ePrint Archive, Paper 2013/328 (2013)

27. Mouha, N., Wang, Q., Gu, D., Preneel, B.: Differential and linear cryptanalysis using mixed-integer linear programming. In: Wu, C.-K., Yung, M., Lin, D. (eds.) Inscrypt 2011. LNCS, vol. 7537, pp. 57–76. Springer, Heidelberg (2012). https://doi.org/10.1007/978-3-642-34704-7_5

28. Niu, Z., Sun, S., Liu, Y., Li, C.: Rotational differential-linear distinguishers of ARX ciphers with arbitrary output linear masks. In: Dodis, Y., Shrimpton, T. (eds.) CRYPTO 2022, Proceedings

29. Selçuk, A.A.: On probability of success in linear and differential cryptanalysis. J. Cryptol. **21**(1), 131–147 (2008)

30. Song, L., Huang, Z., Yang, Q.: Automatic differential analysis of ARX block ciphers with application to SPECK and LEA. In: Liu, J.K., Steinfeld, R. (eds.) ACISP 2016, Proceedings

31. Sun, L., Wang, W., Wang, M.: Accelerating the search of differential and linear characteristics with the SAT method. IACR Trans. Symmetric Cryptol. **2021**(1), 269–315 (2021)

32. Sun, S., Hu, L., Wang, P., Qiao, K., Ma, X., Song, L.: Automatic security evaluation and (related-key) differential characteristic search: application to SIMON, PRESENT, LBlock, DES(L) and Other Bit-Oriented Block Ciphers. In: Sarkar, P., Iwata, T. (eds.) ASIACRYPT 2014. LNCS, vol. 8873, pp. 158–178. Springer, Heidelberg (2014). https://doi.org/10.1007/978-3-662-45611-8_9

Cryptanalysis of Elisabeth-4

Henri Gilbert[1,2], Rachelle Heim Boissier[2(✉)], Jérémy Jean[1],
and Jean-René Reinhard[1]

[1] ANSSI, Paris, France
[2] Université Paris-Saclay, UVSQ, CNRS,
Laboratoire de mathématiques de Versailles, Versailles, France
rachelle.heim@uvsq.fr

Abstract. Elisabeth-4 is a stream cipher tailored for usage in hybrid homomorphic encryption applications that has been introduced by Cosseron et al. at ASIACRYPT 2022. In this paper, we present several variants of a key-recovery attack on the full Elisabeth-4 that break the 128-bit security claim of that cipher. Our most optimized attack is a chosen-IV attack with a time complexity of 2^{88} elementary operations, a memory complexity of 2^{54} bits and a data complexity of 2^{41} bits.

Our attack applies the linearization technique to a nonlinear system of equations relating some keystream bits to the key bits and exploits specificities of the cipher to solve the resulting linear system efficiently. First, due to the structure of the cipher, the system to solve happens to be very sparse, which enables to rely on sparse linear algebra and most notably on the Block Wiedemann algorithm. Secondly, the algebraic properties of the two nonlinear ingredients of the filtering function cause rank defects which can be leveraged to solve the linearized system more efficiently with a decreased data and time complexity.

We have implemented our attack on a toy version of Elisabeth-4 to verify its correctness. It uses the efficient implementation of the Block Wiedemann algorithm of CADO-NFS for the sparse linear algebra.

1 Introduction

Hybrid Homomorphic Encryption (HHE) is an efficient technique for improving the performance of Fully Homomorphic Encryption (FHE) by combining the use of a FHE scheme with the one of a symmetric cipher, e.g., a stream cipher or the combination of a block cipher and an encryption mode of operation. The conducting idea of HHE can be roughly outlined as follows: instead of homomorphically encrypting some data in order to enable their remote processing in an untrusted environment (e.g., a server), a user first encrypts her data using a *classical* symmetric encryption algorithm under a key k and sends a *homomorphic* encryption of k to the remote party. At the cost of an extra computation by the remote party called *transciphering*, this allows to save computation power and bandwidth on the user side as compared with mere FHE, since the ciphertext to

© International Association for Cryptologic Research 2023
J. Guo and R. Steinfeld (Eds.): ASIACRYPT 2023, LNCS 14440, pp. 256–284, 2023.
https://doi.org/10.1007/978-981-99-8727-6_9

plaintext size ratio equals one and at the exception of the homomorphic encryption of k, only symmetric encryption is performed. The transciphering operated on the remote side transforms the symmetric ciphertext into a homomorphic encryption of the original plaintext under the FHE by running the decryption circuit homomorphically under k.

In this context, Elisabeth-4 is a HHE-friendly stream cipher introduced by Cosseron et al. at ASIACRYPT 2022 [3]. It is the only fully specified instance of a larger family of HHE-friendly stream ciphers named Elisabeth. It is parameterized by a 1024-bit key and an IV of unspecified length. The claimed security level for Elisabeth-4 is 128 bits. The design of Elisabeth extends a few other similar stream ciphers, more specifically FLIP [13] and FiLIP [12], which have been the subject of a couple of cryptanalytic works, e.g., [5] on FLIP.

Stream ciphers in the Elisabeth family follow the so-called *Group Filter Permutator* (GFP) paradigm: each keystream symbol belongs to an additive group $\mathbb{G}$ and is derived from a large key by a filtering function that operates on $\mathbb{G}$. Unlike for traditional filtered-LFSR stream ciphers, the filtering function used in Elisabeth is differentiated at each clock, most notably in the values of additive constants called *masks*. In the case of Elisabeth-4, the group $\mathbb{G}$ equals $(\mathbb{Z}/16\mathbb{Z}, +)$ and we will denote it $(\mathbb{Z}_{16}, +)$ for simplicity.

Two major design goals of the Elisabeth ciphers are to optimize the efficiency of the homomorphic decryption and to optimize the efficiency of subsequent format conversions and homomorphic data processings for typical use cases. The distinctive property of Elisabeth stream ciphers that they operate in an additive group such as $(\mathbb{Z}_{16}, +)$ rather than extensions of $\mathbb{F}_2$ like in more traditional symmetric ciphers was shown by the designers to play an important role in achieving these designs goals.

Our Contribution. In this paper, we present key-recovery attacks on the full Elisabeth-4. The starting point for our attack is the observation that over $\mathbb{F}_2$, the least significant bits (LSBs) of all keystream symbols can be expressed as polynomials in the key bits that involve a surprisingly low number of monomials. This observation on the algebraic normal form (ANF) of these keystream bits can be leveraged to mount a simple known-IV linearization attack and reach a first upper bound on the complexity of the key-recovery attack. We then show that various specificities of the Elisabeth-4 stream cipher allow to substantially reduce the complexity of a more involved linearization-based attack; we list them below.

1. We observe that interactions between the algebraic properties of the two $\mathbb{F}_2$-nonlinear ingredients of the Elisabeth-4 filtering function (namely, additions over $\mathbb{Z}_{16}$ and *negacyclic* $\mathbb{Z}_{16}$ to $\mathbb{Z}_{16}$ S-boxes) cause *degree and rank defects* in the polynomial equations over $\mathbb{F}_2$ of the LSBs of the keystream symbols. While the attack complexity is only negligibly affected by the defect in the degree of the ANF of the LSB of the keystream symbols (that is shown to be bounded by 12 instead of 16), it is significantly reduced by the highlighted rank defect phenomenon. In order to take into account and leverage the rank

defect phenomenon, the linearized equations have to be rewritten in a basis that consists of polynomials that are not all monomials. This can be viewed as a natural extension of the original linearization technique.

2. We analyze how to leverage the high sparsity of the linearized system (that is not affected by the former rank reduction considerations) in order to reduce the complexity of the key recovery using sparse linear algebra techniques, namely the Block Wiedemann algorithm.

3. We also show that a filtering of the collected equations allows to reduce the size of the linearized system. This decreases the memory complexity of the attack, and the overall time complexity for building and solving the system. In a known IV setting, this is achievable at the cost of an increased data complexity. In a chosen IV setting, this is achieved by a precomputation-based trade-off and allows to decrease the data complexity.

The combination of all these optimizations allows to mount a chosen-IV attack of overall time, data and memory complexity about 2^{88} elementary operations, about 2^{37} nibbles and 2^{54} bits. We list in Table 1 the various attacks described in this paper.

Table 1. Complexities of the key-recovery attacks presented in this paper.

Model	Time (operations)	Data (nibbles)	Memory (bits)	Reference
Known IV	2^{124}	2^{43}	2^{87}	Section 3
Known IV	2^{116}	2^{41}	2^{81}	Section 4
Known IV	2^{94}	2^{41}	2^{57}	Section 5
Known IV	2^{88}	2^{87}	2^{54}	Section 6.1
Chosen IV	2^{88}	2^{37}	2^{54}	Section 6.2

In order to corroborate our claims regarding the applicability of rank reduction and Block Wiedemann techniques, etc., we have implemented our attack on a small-scale variant of `Elisabeth-4`. Although this toy cipher is considerably weaker than the original one,[1] it nevertheless preserves most of the structure of the linearized equations of the LSBs of the keystream elements. Our implementation therefore gives some experimental evidence of the validity of our attack. We conducted this practical experiment to reach partial key recovery using the CADO-NFS library [4] and in particular its Block Wiedemann implementation. We have published the code of our implementation on GitHub and provided a Dockerfile to simplify reproducibility:

https://github.com/jj-anssi/asiacrypt2023-cryptanalysis-elisabeth4

---

[1] This toy cipher is not only vulnerable to linearization attacks but also other classes of attacks such as statistical cryptanalysis.

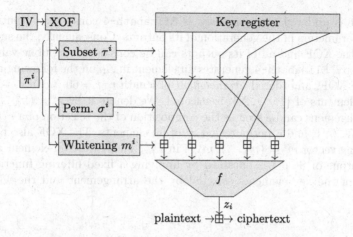

Fig. 1. Overall structure of `Elisabeth-4` (figure from [3]). A XOF generates a sequence of parameters from the IV that selects at every step an ordered subset of the secret key register and masks this selection before applying a fixed filtering function to compute the output of `Elisabeth-4` at this step.

Organization. The rest of this paper is organized as follows. We first describe the `Elisabeth-4` stream cipher in Sect. 2. In Sect. 3, we present an observation on the number of monomials involved in the ANF of the LSB of all keystream symbols and a simple linearization attack that leverages this observation. In Sects. 4, 5 and 6, we present improvements on this basic attack allowed respectively by a rank defect phenomenon, a sparsity of the considered linearized systems and further optimizations of the time and data complexities allowed by restricting the equations considered to build the linearized system. We conclude in Sect. 7 with the results of our small-scale experiments.

2   Description of `Elisabeth-4`

`Elisabeth-4` is a stream cipher designed by Cosseron et al. and published at ASIACRYPT 2022 [3]. The original specifications introduce a family of stream ciphers, but, for clarity, we only describe the only fully specified instance `Elisabeth-4`, which is the topic of this paper. It is optimized for Hybrid Homomorphic Encryption and the authors claim a security level of 128 bits. The architecture of `Elisabeth-4` (see Fig. 1) extends the Improved Filter Permutator principle [13].

Overview. `Elisabeth-4` operates on elements in $\mathbb{Z}/16\mathbb{Z}$, denoted here by $\mathbb{Z}_{16}$. Its state has two components. First, it contains a fixed register loaded with the stream cipher secret key. It is viewed as an array of length $N = 256$ of elements in $\mathbb{Z}/16\mathbb{Z}$, $k = (k_1, \ldots, k_N)$. Secondly, it contains the state of an *extendable output function* (XOF) that is initialized with the stream cipher initialization vector IV.

This state is updated autonomously as `Elisabeth-4` consumes outputs of the XOF as parameters in the generation of its outputs. Consequently, the successive states of the XOF and all of its outputs can be considered as public values.

At Step i, `Elisabeth-4` generates an element in $\mathbb{Z}_{16}$ in the following manner. Using the XOF, an ordered *arrangement* of length $r \cdot t = 60$, *i.e.* a $r \cdot t$-tuple of distinct elements of $\{1, \ldots, N\}$, is selected. We denote it by $\pi^i = (\pi_1^i, \ldots, \pi_{r \cdot t}^i)$. This arrangement can be seen as the composition of the selection of a $r \cdot t$-subset τ^i of $\{1, \ldots, N\}$, and a permutation σ^i of its elements. The XOF also produces a whitening vector $m^i = (m_1^i, \ldots, m_{r \cdot t}^i)$ in $\mathbb{Z}_{16}^{r \cdot t}$. The keystream element $z_i \in \mathbb{Z}_{16}$ at the output of Step i is obtained by applying a fixed filtering function f to the sum of the key elements selected by the arrangement and the whitening elements:

$$z_i = f(k_{\pi_1^i} + m_1^i, \ldots, k_{\pi_{r \cdot t}^i} + m_{r \cdot t}^i).$$

The Filtering Function f. The filtering function f internally uses $t = 12$ parallel calls to a function g applied on $r = 5$ elements. The r outputs are elements of $\mathbb{Z}_{16}$ and are summed together to produce the output of f (see Fig. 2). The function g itself uses a nonlinear function h that we describe below.

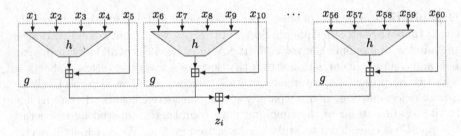

Fig. 2. The function f in `Elisabeth-4` internally uses $t = 12$ calls to g, which is in turn defined using the nonlinear function h. Every element belongs to $\mathbb{Z}_{16}$.

The Function g. The 5-to-1 function g is constructed as the sum of a nonlinear 4-to-1 function h and a linear function of the remaining variable (see Fig. 2):

$$g : \quad \mathbb{Z}_{16}^5 \quad \longrightarrow \quad \mathbb{Z}_{16}$$
$$(x_1, \ldots, x_5) \longmapsto h(x_1, x_2, x_3, x_4) + x_5.$$

The construction of the filtering function f over h is depicted in Fig. 2. The function h uses eight *negacyclic* look-up tables $S_1, \ldots, S_8$ over $\mathbb{Z}_{16}$ (see Fig. 3). These NLUTs were selected at random by the designers [3]. They are given in Appendix A.

Definition 1. *A negacyclic lookup table (NLUT) [1] over $\mathbb{Z}/2^\ell\mathbb{Z}$ is a lookup table S of length 2^ℓ that verifies the following property:*

$$\forall i \in [0, 2^{\ell-1} - 1], \quad S[i + 2^{\ell-1}] = -S[i].$$

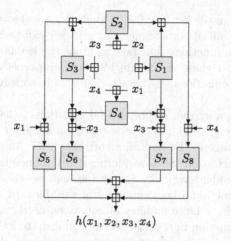

$$h(x_1, x_2, x_3, x_4)$$

Fig. 3. The function h uses eight NLUTs S_i to map the four variables (x_1, x_2, x_3, x_4) to $h(x_1, x_2, x_3, x_4)$.

3 Basic Attack

In this section, we present a general overview of the linearization principle before describing a basic application to the cryptanalysis of `Elisabeth-4`.

3.1 Linearization Technique

Algebraic cryptanalysis is a classical cryptanalysis paradigm. It consists in writing multivariate polynomial equations linking the secrets of a cryptographic mechanism (e.g., its key) and what is known to the attacker (e.g., IV bits, keystream bits, plaintext, ciphertext, etc.), and then solving this system of algebraic equations to recover the secrets. In principle, this can always be achieved by putting into equations the relations stemming from the specification of the cryptographic mechanism. The resulting equations can be difficult to write and/or store in practice, or require to introduce intermediate variables, but in the case where it is possible, the complexity of solving a large nonlinear multivariate system of equations in a large number of variables is often impractical. Let us consider the following formalization. Let us denote $\mathbb{Z}/2\mathbb{Z}$ by $\mathbb{Z}_2$. We denote the n-bit secret the cryptanalyst aims at deriving by $(x_1, \ldots, x_n) \in \mathbb{F}_2^n$. For any element $u = (u_1, \ldots, u_n) \in \mathbb{Z}_2^n$, we denote by x^u the monomial $x_1^{u_1} \cdots x_n^{u_n}$. Due to the field equation $x^2 = x$ over $\mathbb{F}_2$, any Boolean function p in n variables can be written uniquely as a sum of such monomials:

$$p(x_1, \ldots, x_n) = \sum_{u \in \mathbb{Z}_2^n} a_u x^u, \quad a_u \in \mathbb{F}_2.$$

This representation is the *algebraic normal form* (ANF) of p. In the case of a stream cipher generating a binary keystream, every keystream bit provides a polynomial equation in the key bits (or, in another typical setting not considered in the sequel, in the initial state value). An attacker can therefore compute the ANFs of the Boolean functions that take as input the key bits and return given keystream bits, collect these keystream bits, and construct an overdetermined system of nonlinear equations. If the attacker is able to solve this system, she recovers the key.

Although solving a system of polynomial equations is hard in general, several methods exist, e.g. solving methods based on Gröbner basis computation technique such as Faugères' F4 and F5 algorithms [6,7]. An elementary method of resolution is linearization [8]. Considering every monomial appearing in the system as an independent variable, the system can be viewed as a linear system of equations involving a larger number of variables. In order for the linear system to be solvable, a large number of equations needs to be available. The ANF of a Boolean function in n variables can count up to 2^n monomials, so this technique cannot be applied with profit in the general case. However, in the case of a stream cipher whose design is based on the filtering of a linear register, two factors make it worth pursuing this type of attacks. First, the degree of the ANF of the equations relating key bits and keystream bits does not grow and stays bounded by the degree of the filtering function. This enforces an upper bound μ on the number of monomials involved in the system, and thus on the number of variables in the linearized system. This number of monomials can be further restricted by the structure of the polynomial function. Secondly, the number of available equations is not limited since the size of the keystream can in general be adapted to collect enough equations, without requiring the introduction of additional variables, to reach a full-rank linear system with good probability. This system can then be solved in about μ^ω operations, where $2 \leq \omega \leq 3$ is the linear algebra exponent representing the complexity of matrix multiplication. In particular, for μ such that $\mu^\omega < 2^\kappa$ with κ the security parameter in bits, an attack is found.

Suppose the attacker has collected δ keystream bits z_i, $1 \leq i \leq \delta$, and computed the corresponding δ ANFs which we denote by $p_i(x_1, \ldots, x_n) = \sum_{u \in \mathbb{Z}_2^n} a_u^i x^u$ involving at most μ monomials. We let $\mathbf{z} \in \mathbb{F}_2^\delta$ denote the vector of keystream bits and $\mathbf{A}$ to be the $\mathbb{F}_2$-matrix of size $\delta \times \mu$ constructed as $\mathbf{A}[i, u] = a_u^i$. Finding the solutions to the matrix equation $\mathbf{A}\mathbf{x} = \mathbf{z}$ enables to recover monomials in the key bits, and the key itself since the key bits are in general part of the monomial basis.

3.2 Basic Linearization Attack on Elisabeth-4

Our attack on Elisabeth-4 relies on solving a system of Boolean polynomial equations on the key bits using the linearization method described in Sect. 3.1.

Without loss of generality, we consider a keystream generated from a single known IV. At iteration i of the keystream generator, a subset τ^i of the key register, a permutation σ^i of this subset and a whitening vector m^i are derived from the IV. Then, the filtering function f is applied. We can thus consider the ANF of each Boolean function that takes as input the vector of $r \cdot t = 60$ key nibbles and returns one of the bits of the keystream element. In particular, in our attack, we consider the Boolean function f_i that returns the least significant bit (LSB) of the keystream element. We indeed observe that the LSB of the addition in $\mathbb{Z}_{16}$ behaves linearly in $\mathbb{F}_2$. Thus, since f is constructed as the modular sum of $t = 12$ applications of the function g, where g is constructed as the sum of h, a nonlinear function of $r - 1 = 4$ elements, and a fifth element, the ANF of each f_i can be written as the sum of

- the least significant bits of the 12 key nibbles selected for the final addition in the g function (see Fig. 2),
- the algebraic normal form of 12 Boolean *variations* of the function h, restricted to the LSB of its output, and parameterized by the whitening mask values applied on the selected ordered 4-tuple of key elements.

If we fix any unordered quartet $\{x_1, x_2, x_3, x_4\}$ of four distinct key elements, the possible variations of h that take the elements of this set as inputs can be described as the set of Boolean functions $\{h_{m,\sigma}\}_{m \in \mathbb{Z}_{16}^4, \sigma \in \mathfrak{S}_4}$, with $m = (m_1, m_2, m_2, m_3) \in \mathbb{Z}_{16}^4$, $\mathfrak{S}_4$ the permutation group over four elements, and

$$h_{m,\sigma}: \quad \mathbb{Z}_{16}^4 \quad \longrightarrow \quad \mathbb{F}_2$$
$$(x_1, \ldots, x_4) \longmapsto \mathrm{LSB}(h(x_{\sigma(1)} + m_1, x_{\sigma(2)} + m_2, x_{\sigma(3)} + m_3, x_{\sigma(4)} + m_4)).$$

In the following, note that while Elisabeth-4 relies on operations defined on $\mathbb{Z}_{16}$, we write the algebraic modelization in $\mathbb{F}_2$, using the LSB of each keystream element.

Bounding the Number of Monomials. Since each element in $\mathbb{Z}_{16}$ is written on four bits, the observation above shows that the degree of the ANF of each f_i is bounded by $4 \cdot 4 = 16$. Moreover, the number of monomials required to describe the ANF of all LSB of the outputs of Elisabeth-4 is further reduced by the element-wise structure of the cipher. Indeed, no monomial can involve key variables appearing in more than four key elements, since the only $\mathbb{F}_2$-nonlinear functions involved are h variations that depend on four key elements. The four variables are written on a total of 16 bits. Thus, at most 2^{16} monomials can be formed with the bits of every selection of an unordered quartet of key elements regardless of the h variation $h_{m,\sigma}$ applied to this unordered quartet. This implies that the number of monomials to consider can be upper bounded by $\binom{256}{4} \cdot 2^{16} = 2^{43.4}$ monomials.[2]

Construction of the Linearized System. We describe here the construction of the matrix $\mathbf{A}$. We begin by the precomputation of the ANFs of the $2^{16} \cdot 4!$

---

[2] This direct bound can be further refined by taking into account that monomials involving less than four elements are counted multiple times. Observing that the number of monomials involving variables from exactly j elements is 15^j, a finer bound on the number of monomials is $\sum_{j=0}^4 \binom{256}{j} 15^j \approx 2^{43.0}$.

variations $h_{m,\sigma}$ of h by computing their truth table and applying the fast Möbius transform. This step has a complexity of around $4! \cdot 2^{32} \approx 2^{36.6}$ applications of the h function to compute the truth table, $4! \cdot 2^{16} \cdot \log(2^{16}) \cdot 2^{16} \approx 2^{40.6}$ elementary operations to compute the fast Möbius transform, and storing the result requires $2^{36.6}$ bits of memory. To build the matrix $\mathbf{A}$ of the linearized system, we associate to every unordered quartet of key elements a dedicated set of 2^{16} monomials.[3] Thus, the matrix $\mathbf{A}$ has $\mu = \binom{256}{4} \cdot 2^{16}$ columns. The matrix $\mathbf{A}$ is then built row by row, by considering successively least significant bits of the keystream. For a given row and for each of the $t = 12$ applications of the g function:

- we determine from the XOF outputs the unordered quartet τ of key elements on which a variation of function h is applied, and its parameters m and σ. The columns of monomials associated to the set of elements τ are set in the row of the matrix A according to the precomputed ANF of $h_{m,\sigma}$.
- we determine the key element that is linearly added to the output of h (see Fig. 2) and set a column associated with the LSB of this element in the set of monomials associated to a quartet containing this key element.

Finally, the sum of the LSB values of the whitening masks added to the fifth inputs of the g function calls determine whether an additional column corresponding to a constant monomial should be set in the row. Thus, at most $t \cdot (2^{16} + 1) + 1$ bits are non-zero in every row. Building the matrix $\mathbf{A}$ requires around $\delta \cdot t \cdot 2^{16}$ elementary operations.

Description of the Attack. We set $\delta \gtrsim \mu$. The data complexity of the attack is thus $\delta \approx 2^{43.3}$ nibbles and the time complexity of building the matrix is around $2^{62.9}$ elementary operations. The system is then solved by standard linear algebra techniques for a cost μ^ω. With straightforward Gaussian elimination ($\omega = 3$), the time complexity of the resolution is 2^{129} elementary operations, and its memory complexity, which corresponds to the cost of storing $\mathbf{A}$, is about $\delta \cdot \mu = 2^{87}$ bits. Using Strassen algorithm where $\omega = \log_2(7)$ and a small multiplicative constant < 6 needs to be taken into account [14], the time complexity can be brought down to less than $2^{124.14}$ elementary operations. We make the (customary in linearization attacks) assumption that the extra cost of recovering the key bits after recovering the affine space of solutions is negligible.[4]

This basic attack is a known-IV attack. It can be modified into a chosen-IV attack with a significantly improved online time complexity but similar total time and memory complexity. Indeed, one can simply precompute the matrix $\mathbf{A}$ and its Gaussian elimination (or LU decomposition in the case of Strassen

---

[3] In the finer monomial representation, without monomial duplication, the association between the parameters of the h function and the set of monomials is more complex, but can still be achieved with some indexes bookkeeping.

[4] We do not enter here into a discussion on the dimension of the found affine space of solutions and how a large number of key bits can be derived from any particular solution and leveraged to efficiently recover the missing key bits since this would largely amount to anticipating the analysis of the next section.

algorithm) before gathering the data and computing the solutions via a matrix-vector multiplication.

4 Improving the Attack Using Rank Defects

In this section, we identify an unexpected rank defect of the $2^{16} \cdot 4! \times 2^{16}$ matrix whose rows are the ANFs of the functions $h_{m,\sigma}$. We then discuss the impact of this rank defect on the linearization attack described in Sect. 3, namely a lowering of its expected complexity. Finally, we partially explain this rank defect with theoretical arguments, relating it to the use of negacyclic Sboxes.

4.1 Identification of a Rank Defect

As mentioned in Sect. 3, the ANFs of the $2^{16} \cdot 4!$ variations of h can be precomputed and stored in a matrix denoted here by $\mathbf{H}$ at a practical cost. Since the rank of $\mathbf{A}$ is related to the dimension of the vector space spanned by these ANFs seen as vectors of coefficients, we have computed the rank of the matrix $\mathbf{H}$ and obtained $\rho = 8705 \approx 2^{13.1}$, which is lower that the expected 2^{16}. Performing a reduced row echelon form computation, we can write

$$\mathbf{L}\mathbf{H} = \begin{bmatrix} \mathbf{P} \\ 0 \end{bmatrix}, \quad \mathbf{H} = \mathbf{L}'\mathbf{P},$$

with $\mathbf{P}$ an upper triangular matrix of size $\rho \times 2^{16}$, $\mathbf{L}$ a square invertible matrix of size $2^{16} \cdot 4!$ that is the product of elementary matrices and $\mathbf{L}'$ is the $2^{16} \cdot 4! \times \rho$ matrix obtained as the first ρ columns of the inverse of the matrix $\mathbf{L}$. $\mathbf{P}$ can be seen as a change of 'basis' matrix: its rows define ρ linear combinations of the monomials which are sufficient to describe the rows of matrix $\mathbf{H}$. We will refer to these combinations as the *polynomial basis*.

Given the greater value of small degree monomials, we adopt a degree monomial order and reorder the columns of $\mathbf{H}$ accordingly before performing the reduced row echelon reduction. With this choice, we observe that the polynomial basis contains 12 monomials corresponding to input bits to the h function. The most significant bits (MSBs) of the 4 input elements of h however do not belong to the span of the polynomial basis.

4.2 Impact on the Linearization Attack

Since the variations $h_{m,\sigma}$ of the h functions only linearly depend on the ρ polynomials of the polynomial basis, we adapt the linearization attack in a straightforward way. Instead of associating to every unordered quartets a set of 2^{16} monomial variables, we associate a set of ρ polynomial variables. Thus, the number of columns of the matrix $\mathbf{A}$ decreases to $\mu = \binom{256}{4} \cdot \rho \approx 2^{40.5}$, and the matrix can be built in the same way as before by using the rows of the matrix $\mathbf{L}'$ instead of those of the matrix $\mathbf{H}$. Linear terms corresponding to the LSBs of the fifth input to the function g can be handled as before since they are part of the polynomial basis. The number of equations required for the system to be solvable is reduced accordingly to $\delta \gtrsim \mu$ using heuristics that the dimension of the affine space of solutions is thereby reduced to a sufficiently small number of vectors. This is discussed in Appendix D and backed-up by the experimental results described in Sect. 7.

Thus, the rank defect lowers the complexity of solving the linear system and consequently the overall time complexity of the attack. The computation of the row echelon form of $\mathbf{H}$ and the subsequent computation of $\mathbf{L}'$ require about $\rho \cdot 2^{16} \cdot 4! \cdot 2^{16} \approx 2^{48.43}$ operations. The data complexity of the attack is $\mu \approx 2^{40.5}$, its time complexity is μ^ω, which is about $2^{121.4}$ elementary operations using Gaussian elimination and $2^{116.2}$ elementary operations using Strassen algorithm, and its memory complexity is $\mu^2 \approx 2^{80.9}$.

The resolution of the system enables to recover for all the unordered quartets of key elements the values taken by the polynomials of the polynomial basis applied to the relevant key bits. As seen above, this directly provides the key bits, except for the most significant bits of the key elements. These can be recovered quartet by quartet by small 2^4 exhaustive searches considering the system of ρ algebraic equations provided by the polynomial basis. In total, this adds $\binom{256}{4} 2^4$ elementary operations to our time complexity.

4.3   Explaining the Rank Defect

In this section, we provide a partial explanation for the rank defect of the matrix $\mathbf{H}$ whose rows correspond to the ANFs of the $2^{16} \cdot 4!$ variations $\{h_{m,\sigma}\}_{m \in \mathbb{Z}_{16}^4, \sigma \in \mathfrak{S}_4}$ of h. We find that this phenomenon is largely due to the interaction between modular addition and negacyclic look-up tables. Whilst analyzing said interaction, we also proved that the degree of the LSB at the output of the function h is bounded by 12 rather than 16, and thus that the degree of the LSB of the keystream is also bounded by 12. Although this result did not lead to a significant improvement of our linearization attack,[5] we provide its proof in Annex B.[6] Note that this proof uses definitions and propositions introduced in the rest of this section.

On Negacyclic Look-Up Tables. We start with two observations on negacyclic look-up tables over $\mathbb{Z}_{2^\ell}$. In Elisabeth-4, negacyclic look-up tables are applied to the sum of a key word and a whitening word. The following proposition shows that the composition of an addition with a negacyclic look-up table (NLUT) does not change its negacyclic nature: the composition is still a NLUT.

---

[5] Indeed, the number of monomials in 16 variables of degree at most 12 is equal to $\sum_{i=0}^{12} \binom{256}{i} = 2^{15.98}$ which is not significantly smaller than 2^{16}.

[6] Note that an observation made thanks to experiments on the degree of the keystream LSB for some mask values had already been made by the authors of Elisabeth-4 [3], but here we provide a proof that holds for any mask.

Proposition 1. *Let ℓ be an integer and let S be a NLUT over $\mathbb{Z}_{2^\ell}$. For any $\tilde{x} \in \mathbb{Z}_{2^\ell}$, the look-up table S' defined as $S'[x] := S[x + \tilde{x}]$ for all $x \in \mathbb{Z}_{2^\ell}$ is negacyclic.*

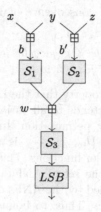

Fig. 4. The Antler function $H_{\mathcal{S}_1, \mathcal{S}_2, \mathcal{S}_3}$.

Proof. For all $x \in \mathbb{Z}_{2^\ell}$, $S'[x + 2^{\ell-1}] = S[x + \tilde{x} + 2^{\ell-1}] = -S[x + \tilde{x}] = -S'[x]$. □

The next proposition highlights a property of NLUTs that we will show to be largely responsible for the rank (and degree) defect(s).

Proposition 2. *Let ℓ be an integer and let S be a negacyclic look-up table over $\mathbb{Z}_{2^\ell}$. The Boolean function $x \mapsto LSB(S[x])$ does not depend on the MSB of x.*

Proof. For any $y \in \mathbb{Z}_{2^\ell}$, y and $-y$ have the same parity and thus the same LSB. As a consequence, for any $x \in \mathbb{Z}_{2^\ell}$, $S[x]$ and $S[x + 2^{\ell-1}] = -S[x]$ have the same LSB. Since x and $x + 2^{\ell-1}$ have all their bits equal except for their MSB, the proposition holds. □

On Antler Functions. In the sequel, we rely on the analysis of a family of 16-bit to 1-bit functions with a 2-round, triangular structure that we propose to name *Antler functions* (see Fig. 4). This is because the LSB of the function h and, as we will see in the sequel, the LSB of any of its variations $h_{m,\sigma}$, can be easily shown to be the sum of four Antler functions. Antler functions can be defined as follows.

Definition 2. *Let $\mathcal{S}_1, \mathcal{S}_2, \mathcal{S}_3$ be 3 negacyclic look-up tables. The Antler function associated to $\mathcal{S}_1, \mathcal{S}_2, \mathcal{S}_3$ is defined as*

$$H_{\mathcal{S}_1, \mathcal{S}_2, \mathcal{S}_3} : \quad \mathbb{Z}_{16}^4 \quad \longrightarrow \quad \mathbb{F}_2$$
$$(x, y, z, w) \longmapsto LSB(\mathcal{S}_3 \, [\mathcal{S}_1[x + y] + \mathcal{S}_2[y + z] + w]).$$

Although Antler functions are defined with domain $\mathbb{Z}_{16}^4$, we view them as Boolean functions by considering the binary representation of elements in $\mathbb{Z}_{16}$ and thus assimilating $\mathbb{Z}_{16}^4$ to 16-bit words or equivalently elements in $\mathbb{F}_2^{16}$. Generally, in the following, we assimilate elements in $\mathbb{Z}_{16}^n$ to $4n$-bit words or equivalently elements in $\mathbb{F}_2^{4n}$. Antler functions possess properties inherited from NLUTs. In particular, a direct consequence of Proposition 1 is the following proposition.

Proposition 3. *Let* $\mathcal{S}_1, \mathcal{S}_2, \mathcal{S}_3$ *be 3 negacyclic look-up tables and* $(\tilde{x}, \tilde{y}, \tilde{z}, \tilde{w}) \in \mathbb{Z}_{16}^4$. *Then,* $H_{\mathcal{S}_1, \mathcal{S}_2, \mathcal{S}_3}(x + \tilde{x}, y + \tilde{y}, z + \tilde{z}, w + \tilde{w})$ *is also an Antler function.*

Proposition 3 shows that the property that the LSB of h can be expressed as a sum of four Antler functions extends to all variations in the set $\{h_{m,id}\}_{m \in \mathbb{Z}_{16}^4}$, where $id \in \mathfrak{S}_4$ is the identity permutation. In particular, the vector space spanned by the set of ANFs of $\{h_{m,id}\}_{m \in \mathbb{Z}_{16}^4}$ is a subspace of the vector space spanned by the ANFs of all Antler functions. This can be generalized as follows. The vector space spanned by the set of ANFs of $\{h_{m,\sigma}\}_{m \in \mathbb{Z}_{16}^4, \sigma \in \Sigma_4}$ is a subspace of the vector space spanned by the ANFs of all Antler functions for any ordering of their input variables. Thus, to bound the dimension of the vector space spanned by $\{h_{m,\sigma}\}_{m \in \mathbb{Z}_{16}^4, \sigma \in \mathfrak{S}_4}$, we first exhibit a bound on the dimension of the vector space spanned by all Antler functions.

In the sequel, we will exhibit upper bounds on the dimension of some vector spaces of Boolean functions. We introduce the following definition.

Definition 3. *The rank of a set* $\{H_i\}_{i \in I}$ *of Boolean functions in n binary variables is defined as the dimension of the vector space of functions spanned by this set.*

For example, the rank of the set of variations $h_{m,\sigma}$ of h is the rank of **H**.

Bounding the Rank of the Set of Antler Functions

Proposition 4. *The rank of the set of Antler functions is bounded by* $2^{10.43}$.

To prove this proposition, we rely on the following lemma.

Lemma 1. *Let* $\mathcal{S}_1, \mathcal{S}_2, \mathcal{S}_3$ *be 3 negacyclic look-up tables. Let* $G_{\mathcal{S}_1, \mathcal{S}_2, \mathcal{S}_3}$ *be the Boolean function defined as*

$$G_{\mathcal{S}_1, \mathcal{S}_2, \mathcal{S}_3} \quad : \quad \mathbb{Z}_{16}^3 \quad \longrightarrow \quad \mathbb{F}_2$$
$$(b, b', w) \longmapsto LSB(\mathcal{S}_3 [\mathcal{S}_1[b] + \mathcal{S}_2[b'] + w]).$$

Then, the rank of the set of Antler functions is bounded by the dimension of the vector space spanned by all functions $G_{\mathcal{S}_1, \mathcal{S}_2, \mathcal{S}_3}$.

Sketch of Proof. Let S_1, S_2, S_3 be 3 negacyclic look-up tables. It is easy to see that $H_{S_1,S_2,S_3} = G_{S_1,S_2,S_3} \circ F$ where F is defined as

$$F \quad : \quad \mathbb{Z}_{16}^4 \longrightarrow \mathbb{Z}_{16}^3$$
$$(x, y, z, w) \longmapsto (b = x + y, b' = y + z, w = w).$$

Thus, consider a basis of the set of all functions of the form G_{S_1,S_2,S_3}. It is easy to see that the set of all functions constructed as the composition of F with a function in this basis generates the vector space spanned by Antler functions. Lemma 1 is thus shown. □

To prove Proposition 4, we thus only need showing that the rank of the set of all functions G_{S_1,S_2,S_3} is bounded by $2^{10.43}$. In this section, we only demonstrate a simpler result, namely, a bound 2^{11} on the dimension, since it gives a first intuition of the causes of the rank defects but remains simple to explain. We refer to Annex C for a full proof for the bound $2^{10.43}$ of Proposition 4. We believe the actual rank to be even lower, namely $1088 = 2^{10.09}$, as suggested by our experiments. We did not manage to explain theoretically this tighter bound.

Proof of the Bound 2^{11}. Notice that G_{S_1,S_2,S_3} has domain $\mathbb{Z}_{16}^3$. However, by Proposition 2, the output of G_{S_1,S_2,S_3} does not depend on the most significant bit of w. Thus, it can be seen as a Boolean function that takes as input 11 bits. This trivially implies that the dimension of the space spanned by all functions G_{S_1,S_2,S_3} is at most 2^{11}. □

Bounding the Rank of H. We have shown that the rank of the set of Antler functions for a fixed ordering of the input variables is bounded by $2^{10.43}$. Since these functions take as input four elements in $\mathbb{Z}_{16}$, the rank of this set for any ordering is at most $4! \cdot 2^{10.43}$. However, the vector space spanned by the set containing the functions H_{S_1,S_2,S_3} for all NLUTs (S_1, S_2, S_3) is equal to the vector space spanned by the compositions $(x, y, z, w) \mapsto H_{S_1,S_2,S_3}(z, y, x, w)$ of H_{S_1,S_2,S_3} with a transposition of x and z. Thus, the vector space spanned by all Antler functions and for any ordering of their variables has dimension at most $\frac{4!}{2} 2^{10.43} \approx 2^{14.01}$. Thus, the rank of the set $\{h_{m,id}\}_{m \in \mathbb{Z}_{16}^4, \sigma \in \mathfrak{S}_4}$ is at most $2^{14.01}$.

As mentioned above, using experiments, we found that the rank of an Antler function is in fact bounded by 1088. This gives a bound of $\frac{4!}{2} \cdot 1088 \approx 2^{13.67}$ for the rank of $\{H_{S_1,S_2,S_3} \circ \sigma\}$ for all NLUTs and all permutations, which can be considered close to the bound $8705 \approx 2^{13.1}$ as this bound holds for the particular case of `Elisabeth-4` (in which NLUTs are repeated across applications of Antler functions within h).

5   Solving Sparse Linear Systems

A matrix is said to be *sparse* if the number of its nonzero coefficients is small with regards to the total number of coefficients. The matrix **A** of size $\delta \times \binom{256}{4}$ ·

ρ obtained in our attack is sparse since it has at most $t(\rho + 1) \ll \binom{256}{4} \cdot \rho$ nonzero coefficients per $\binom{256}{4} \cdot \rho$-bit row. Binary sparse matrices can be stored in a compressed form, e.g., by storing for every row the indexes of the columns containing a nonzero coefficient. Further, sparse linear algebra algorithms can take advantage of this property of the matrix to solve classic linear algebra problems at a lower complexity.

In this section, we describe methods that allow to efficiently solve sparse linear algebra problems before detailing an improved linearization attack.

5.1   Efficient Methods for Sparse Linear Algebra

As mentioned above, sparse linear algebra problems can be solved more efficiently than general linear algebra problems. A well-known efficient method to solve sparse linear problems is the 1986 Wiedemann algorithm [15]. This algorithm, which exploits the cheapness of sparse matrix-vector products, has been widely studied [2,9,10]. In our attack, we use a variant of Wiedemann algorithm, the Block Wiedemann algorithm (BW) [2]. This algorithm introduced by Coppersmith in 1994 converts Wiedemann algorithm to a block form, allowing to process several bits at the same time. In this section, we begin with a brief description of the Wiedemann and BW algorithms before computing the improved complexity of our attack.

In the following, we let $\mathbf{M}$ be a square $\mathbb{F}_2$-matrix of dimension n and $\mathbf{y}$ be a vector in $\mathbb{F}_2^n$. We assume that $\mathbf{M}$ is sparse, i.e. that the number of nonzero coefficients per row is bounded by $s \ll n$. We wish to find a solution to the equation

$$\mathbf{M}\mathbf{x} = \mathbf{y}. \tag{1}$$

Wiedemann Algorithm. We begin with a brief overview of the Wiedemann algorithm [15]. We refer to specialized papers for a more comprehensive description of this algorithm, e.g., [2,9,10,15]. Wiedemann algorithm must be fed a square matrix $\mathbf{M}$ of size $n \times n$ and a vector $\mathbf{y}$ and returns a solution $\mathbf{x}^0$ or the error symbol. It requires at most $3n$ multiplications of the matrix $\mathbf{M}$ with a vector, $\mathcal{O}(n^2 \log(n))$ other operations, and a limited amount of storage in addition to the cost of storing $\mathbf{M}$ (see [10]).

This algorithm is divided into two main steps. In a first step, the algorithm recovers the minimal polynomial $f_\mathbf{M}$ of the matrix $\mathbf{M}$. Then, it uses this minimal polynomial to recover a solution to (1). Indeed, recovering $f_\mathbf{M}$ provides nontrivial coefficients $(c_i)_{0 \leq i \leq n}$ such that

$$\sum_{i=0}^{n} c_i \mathbf{M}^i = 0. \tag{2}$$

If $\mathbf{M}$ is nonsingular, then necessarily $c_0 \neq 0$. The unique solution can then be expressed as $\mathbf{x} = -(1/c_0) \sum_{i=1}^{n} c_i \mathbf{M}^{i-1} \mathbf{y}$. On the other hand, if $\mathbf{M}$ is known to be singular and $\mathbf{y} = \mathbf{0}$, the algorithm finds a vector in the kernel of $\mathbf{M}$ in the following manner. Since $\mathbf{M}$ is singular, $c_0 = 0$. Letting c_δ be the first nonzero coefficient and $\mathbf{r}$ be a random vector, it comes that computing the successive vectors $\mathbf{M}^i \left(\sum_{i=0}^n c_i \mathbf{M}^{i-\delta} \mathbf{r} \right)$ for $i = 1, \ldots, \delta$ yields a kernel element as long as $\mathbf{r}$ is not in the kernel of the non-null matrix $\sum_{i=0}^n c_i \mathbf{M}^{i-\delta} \mathbf{r}$, which happens with probability greater than $1/2$. Since $\mathbf{M}$ is s-sparse, a matrix-vector multiplication costs at most $2sn$ operations. The total complexity of this step can thus be bounded by $n(2sn + 2n) = 2(s+1)n^2$ operations.

To recover the minimal polynomial $f_{\mathbf{M}}$ of the matrix $\mathbf{M}$, the algorithm uses the sequence $(\mathbf{u}^T \mathbf{M}^i \mathbf{v})_{i \geq 0}$ for some random $\mathbf{u}$ and $\mathbf{v}$.[7] Since $\sum_{i=0}^n c_i \mathbf{M}^i \mathbf{v} = \mathbf{0}$, a fortiori, for any vectors $\mathbf{u}, \mathbf{v}$ and any integer j, $\sum_{i=0}^n c_i \mathbf{u}^T \mathbf{M}^{i+j} \mathbf{v} = 0$. Therefore, the sequence $(\mathbf{u}^T \mathbf{M}^i \mathbf{v})_{i \geq 0}$ is a linear recurrent sequence of degree smaller or equal to n. Thus, one can compute its first $2n$ first terms, feed them to the Berlekamp-Massey algorithm [11] and obtain the minimal polynomial f_1 of this sequence. Since $f_{\mathbf{M}}$ cancels this sequence, it comes that $f_1 | f_{\mathbf{M}}$. In fact, one can show that with high probability, $f_1 = f_{\mathbf{M}}$ After a few tries using different random vectors, the algorithm recovers $f_{\mathbf{M}}$ and thus provides a solution to (1).[8]

Block-Wiedemann Algorithm. Coppersmith's Block-Wiedemann algorithm [2] is a probabilistic algorithm that allows to parallelize or distribute the Wiedemann algorithm. It takes as input a square matrix $\mathbf{M}$ and returns a solution of the equation $\mathbf{M}\mathbf{x} = \mathbf{0}$ or the error symbol. In this algorithm, one draws simultaneously l_1 random vectors for $\mathbf{u}$ and l_2 random vectors for $\mathbf{v}$ and considers the sequence $(\mathbf{M}_i)_{i \geq 0}$ such that

$$\mathbf{M}_i = \mathbf{U}^T \mathbf{M}^i \mathbf{V} \in \mathbf{F}_2^{l_1 \times l_2} \text{ where } \mathbf{U}^T \in \mathbf{F}_2^{l_1 \times n} \text{ and } \mathbf{V} \in \mathbf{F}_2^{n \times l_2}.$$

In practice, we will set $l_1 = l_2$ and this parameter is usually equal to the size of a word on the processor considered. In the binary case, the implementation can also take advantage of the degree of parallelism offered by the execution of binary instructions on the bits of a word by a processor. Thus we typically use $l_1 = 64$. Coppersmith proposes a generalization of the Berlekamp-Massey algorithm that allows to compute a linear recurrence that generates this sequence. He then notices that the sequence of $(\mathbf{M}_i)_{i \geq 0}$ is in fact determined by its first $n/l_1 + n/l_2 + \mathcal{O}(1)$ elements rather than $2n$. This algorithm allows to compute a solution to an homogeneous sparse linear system in time $3n/l_1$ matrix-vector products, which cost at most $2sn$, which must be added to a small term in $\mathcal{O}(n^2)$ operations [2]. The total complexity can thus be approximated by $6sn^2/l_1$ operations.

Solving Arbitrary Sparse Linear Systems. It is always possible to transform the problem of solving the equation $\mathbf{M}\mathbf{x} = \mathbf{y}$ for arbitrary $\mathbf{M}$ (in particular

---

[7] In practice, if $\mathbf{M}$ is known to be nonsingular, one uses $\mathbf{v} = \mathbf{y}$.

[8] Although the algorithm is in practice slightly more complicated, we do not go into details as this is not the core of the article.

M non-square) and $\mathbf{y}$, into a problem that can be fed to either algorithms. If $\mathbf{M}$ is not square, several methods (some heuristic, some not) allow to transform the problem into a problem where the matrix considered is square, and in a way such that a solution to the square problem will provide a solution to the original problem with high probability [9]. We will not go into details about how these methods work. Further, to transform a non-homogeneous system into a homogeneous one, one can simply consider the equivalent problem of finding the solutions $\mathbf{x}^0$ to the equation

$$(\mathbf{M}|\mathbf{y})\mathbf{x} = 0$$

such that $\mathbf{x}_n^0 \neq 0$. If the matrix $(\mathbf{M}|\mathbf{y})$ is not square, one must then transform it into a square matrix using the methods mentioned above.

5.2 Improved Attack

The matrix $\mathbf{A}$ is a sparse matrix of size $\delta \times \mu$, where $\mu = \binom{N}{4} \cdot \rho$, $\delta \gtrsim \mu$ and the number of nonzero coefficients per row is bounded by $s = t \cdot (\rho + 1) + 1 \approx t \cdot \rho$. In our attack, we wish to recover the kernel of the matrix $\mathbf{A}|\mathbf{z}$. After extending $\mathbf{A}|\mathbf{z}$ to a square matrix of size about δ for a negligible cost, recovering vectors in its kernel has complexity $6 \cdot s \cdot \delta^2 / l_1$ elementary operations. With $l_1 = 64$, we improve the time complexity of the attack described in Sect. 4.2 from $2^{116.2}$ elementary operations using Strassen algorithm to $2^{94.2}$ using the Block Wiedemann algorithm. The memory complexity is also improved from $2^{80.9}$ to $s \cdot \delta \approx 2^{57.14}$, as the matrix can be stored more efficiently using its sparsity. The data complexity is not affected.

6 Filtering the Equations Used by the Linearization Attack

In this section, we propose a final improvement to our initial attack by filtering the collected equations in order to reduce the number of variables in the considered linearized systems. This leads to a known-IV time-data tradeoff, that reduces the time complexity of the attack at the cost of an increased data complexity, and a chosen-IV attack with a decreased time and data complexity thanks to an offline precomputation selecting appropriate IVs.

Contexts where a chosen-IV attack is possible usually correspond to a scenario where the attacker has access to a chosen ciphertext decryption/verification oracle. In the HHE context, a client must not only be able to encrypt some data using HHE (with IVs they choose themselves), but also to recover some information from the server later on. Such a scenario is thus not precluded. For example, we can consider a malicious server using the client as a chosen ciphertext decryption/verification oracle. This could happen in a Bleichenbacher type scenario where a client sends back a bit depending on the success of plaintext parsing (the malicious server has access to a symmetric decryption oracle), or a scenario where the server has access to the public result of a computation (access to a homomorphic decryption oracle).

6.1   Known-IV Attack

In this section, as in the case of the attacks described previously, the attacker has access to a long keystream generated from a single known-IV. However, she will only consider some useful positions in this keystream. This allows to restrict the equations considered in the system to particular equations involving nonlinearly only key elements in a proper subset of size N', where N' is comprised between $(r-1) \cdot t = 4t$ and N, of the set of all key elements, of size N. To produce a keystream element, the XOF selects $(r-1) \cdot t$ key nibbles at the input of the $t = 12$ applications of h. For instance, we could only keep equations where those key nibbles entering the h functions are all picked in the first half of the key register (see Fig. 5).

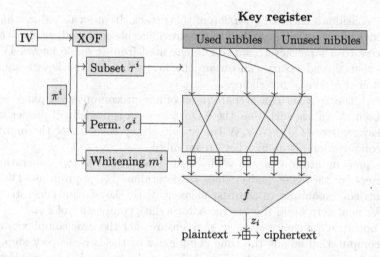

Fig. 5. Selected equations chosen so that the inputs to the h functions correspond to key nibbles from the first half of the key register.

Working under this principle, the number of variables in the linearized system is reduced to $\mu_{N'} = \binom{N'}{4}\rho + (N - N')$, since the $N - N'$ LSBs of the key elements that appear only linearly through g still need to be considered. The number of particular equations to collect is of the same order $\delta_{N'} \gtrsim \mu_{N'}$. Assuming that the XOF outputs are well distributed, the probability that all the key nibbles appearing at the input of the h functions belong to a subset of size N' is given by $p_{N'} = \binom{N'}{(r-1)\cdot t} / \binom{N}{(r-1)\cdot t}$. Thus the number of equations to obtain in order to get enough particular equations after filtering is $\delta_{N'}/p_{N'}$. This constitutes the data complexity of this attack. The time complexity of building the matrix $\mathbf{A}$ is now dominated by the cost of filtering the equations to keep only the particular equations. The time complexity is $\delta_{N'}/p_{N'}$ generations of parameters by the XOF. Then, the time complexity of the Block Wiedemann algorithm equals $\frac{6}{l_1} \cdot s \cdot \delta_{N'}^2$ operations, where 6 and l_1 are the same constants as in the previous Sect. 5.2. This enables the attacker to recover the N' key elements and the $N - N'$ LSBs of the other key elements using the previously described attack. Recovering the remaining $3(N - N')$ bits is an easier problem which can be linearized at a smaller cost.

Using the parameters from Elisabeth-4, we choose the size N' of the target subset so that the time complexity of the system construction and the time complexity of its resolution are similar. We find $N' = 137$, which makes the data complexity about 2^{87} nibbles and the time complexity about $2 \times 2^{87} = 2^{88}$ operations. Finally, the memory complexity is also improved, as storing $\mathbf{A}$ only requires about $t \cdot \rho \cdot \delta_{N'} = 2^{54}$ bits.

6.2   Chosen-IV Attack

We now consider a chosen-IV version of this attack. In order to reduce the data complexity of the attack described in the previous subsection where the attacker had access to a large keystream (e.g., generated from a single known IV), we assume that the adversary can obtain the first nibble of the keystream for a large number of IVs of her choice.

Indeed, the attacker can prepare in an offline precomputation phase several well-chosen IV values such that the XOF selects in a predefined proper subset of the key register of size $N' < N$ the $(r - 1) \cdot t$ key elements at the input of h in the computation of the first keystream nibble.

The precomputation of the well-chosen IVs costs $\delta_{N'}/p_{N'}$ generations of parameters by the XOF and enables to determine $\delta_{N'}$ appropriate IVs. The equations corresponding to the first element of the keystream generated from these IVs enable to build the matrix $\mathbf{A}$ for a data complexity of $\delta_{N'}$.

We optimize the choice of N' so as to ensure that the time complexity of the IV precomputation equals the time complexity of the key-recovery step. This results in the same optimal value $N' = 137$ as in the known-IV setting. The time complexity of the IV precomputation is then 2^{87} generations of parameters by the XOF, the data complexity is only $\mu_{N'} = 2^{37}$ elements, the time complexity of the construction and resolution of the linear system is 2^{87} elementary operations. The memory complexity of the attack is about $t \cdot \rho \cdot \delta_{N'} = 2^{54}$ bits.

7   Small-Scale Experiments

In order to illustrate the linearization attacks presented in this paper, and to validate their correctness, we implemented an attack on a reduced version of Elisabeth-4. In this section, we describe the reduced version we considered for our tests and report on the results we obtained. The implementation of our experiments can be found at the following address:

https://github.com/jj-anssi/asiacrypt2023-cryptanalysis-elisabeth4

7.1 Elisabeth-4 Reduced Version

Elisabeth-4 design is highly parameterizable, which enables to easily define reduced versions. In order to implement practically the attacks presented in this paper, we need to reduce the size of the cipher, but we want to do so in a way that remains representative of the structure of the cipher. We emphasize that we not make any claim of resistance of the reduced version of Elisabeth-4 considered here against any kind of attack.

In order to retain the effects of the rank defect discussed in Sect. 4, we choose not to modify the structure of the function g. Also, we require $t \geq 2$, since there is some decoupling in the linear system between the components related to different key quartets when $t = 1$. Consequently, we need $N \geq t \cdot r = 10$. Since the memory size of the sparse matrix $\mathbf{A}$ is already quite large at this point, namely $\binom{10}{4} \cdot t \cdot \rho^2 \approx 2^{35}$, we reduce further the design by considering 3-bit elements. Our reduced variants thus operates in $\mathbb{Z}_8$, and eight arbitrary negacyclic Sboxes are selected (see Table 2). We continue to observe a rank defect in this case with $\rho = 254 \ll 2^{12}$. This allows to increase the number N of key elements and the number t of parallel calls to g in the filtering function f.

Table 2. Comparison of the parameters of the original Elisabeth-4 cipher and the toy cipher introduced in this paper for experimental verifications.

Elisabeth-4	N	t	r	Sboxes	Group	ρ
Original	256	12	5	4-bit	$\mathbb{Z}_{16}$	8705
Toy	32	2	5	3-bit	$\mathbb{Z}_8$	254

While implementing this reduced version, we were under the impression that the XOF of Elisabeth-4 is not precisely defined in [3]. It refers to [13] as a source for the definition of a *forward secure PRG*, but the correspondence from random bits to random integers encoded in a function next_int [3, Algorithm 2] is not clearly explicited. Furthermore, the Rust implementation of Elisabeth-4[9] directly uses a RandomGenerator object from the concrete-core Rust library. In order to ensure interoperability, the XOF function should be explicitly and unambiguously defined. In our implementation, we try to fill the gaps in a sensible way. For more details on how we defined the XOF in our implementation, we refer the reader to Annex E and to our code (of which the link can be found at the beginning of this section). Please note that our cryptanalysis does not depend on the details of the XOF and of the functions that produce the round parameters of Elisabeth-4 from the output of the XOF.

7.2 Implemented Attack

We have implemented the linearization attack, taking into account the analysis performed in Sects. 4 and 5.

---

[9] https://github.com/princess-elisabeth/Elisabeth.

In order to implement the resolution of the sparse linear system, we used the implementation of the Block Wiedemann algorithm provided by the CADO-NFS project [4]. CADO-NFS is an open-source tool enabling to factor large integers using the state-of-the-art factorization algorithms [4]. It has been used to achieve factorization records in past years. A resource intensive phase of the factorization algorithm consists in finding a vector in the kernel of a large sparse matrix, thus CADO-NFS provides a state-of-the-art, parallelisable and distributable implementation of the Block Wiedemann algorithm, linalg/bwc. This implementation routinely solves linear algebra problems with sparse matrices with millions of rows and about a hundred nonzero entries per rows.

During our experiments, we encountered issues using linalg/bwc. We realized that this implementation is tailored to the case of matrices encountered in the context of the NFS algorithm. More precisely, linalg/bwc solves $x.A = 0$, with matrix A whose number of rows exceeds its number of columns, whereas considering an overdetermined system A places us in the case where the number or rows is less that the number of columns. There seems to be some issue with the padding of matrix A to a square matrix, since the gather program which is part of linalg/bwc reports nonzero coordinates in the padding part. In order to bypass these issues, we fallback to generating square A matrices, embedding the vector z as a column in the matrix A. In other words, we are using exactly $\delta = \mu + 1$. This constraint is not prohibitive as confirmed by the experimental results below. Further investigations of the encountered issues in linalg/bwc and solving them in order to get a general purpose implementation of the Block Wiedemann algorithm is left as an open problem.

Results. The goal of our experiment was to check that the improved attack of Sect. 5.2 works rather than experimentally evaluating its complexity. Our experiment showed that it is possible to solve an Elisabeth-4 type linear system using BW algorithm and that solving this linear system allows to recover the secret key. Indeed, we managed to run the linearization attack successfully on a reduced version of Elisabeth-4 (with 3-bit Sboxes, $N = 32$ and $t = 2$), and recovered the key from a found kernel vector. This result gives some confidence in the correctness of the attack.

As detailed in Sect. 5.2, the most expensive part of the attack performed is the Block-Wiedemann step. Its theoretical complexity is $6 \cdot t \cdot \binom{N}{4}^2 \cdot \rho^3/l_1$. As in our experiment, $t = 2$, $N = 32$, $\rho = 254$, $l_1 = 64$, we obtain a theoretical complexity of $2^{51.8}$ elementary operations. On the multicore platform that was used for the experiment, the attack required 44 h. Yet, we highlight that, due to the impact of an increased memory complexity, it is difficult to assess how these results scale when considering larger instances.

Acknowledgement. This work is partially supported by the French Agence Nationale de la Recherche through the SWAP project under Contract ANR-21-CE39-0012.

A   Sboxes

See Table 3.

Table 3. Sboxes used in Elisabeth-4 in hexadecimal notations.

	0	1	2	3	4	5	6	7	8	9	a	b	c	d	e	f
S_1	3	2	6	c	a	0	1	b	d	e	a	4	6	0	f	5
S_2	4	b	4	4	4	f	9	c	c	5	c	c	c	1	7	4
S_3	b	a	c	2	2	b	d	e	5	6	4	e	e	5	3	2
S_4	5	9	d	2	b	a	c	5	b	7	3	e	5	6	4	b
S_5	3	0	b	8	d	e	d	b	d	0	5	8	3	2	3	5
S_6	8	d	c	c	3	f	c	7	8	3	4	4	d	1	4	9
S_7	4	2	9	d	a	c	a	7	c	e	7	3	6	4	6	9
S_8	a	2	5	5	3	d	f	1	6	e	b	b	d	3	1	f

B   Degree of the Least Significant Bit

In this section, we show that at any iteration j of the keystream generator, the ANF of the Boolean function f_j that takes as input the key bits and returns the least significant bit of the keystream element is bounded by 12. We remind the reader that this proof uses definitions and propositions introduced in Sect. 4.3.

We showed that at any iteration j, the Boolean function f_j can be written as the sum of $t = 12$ Boolean variations of h and the least significant bits of some key elements (see Sect. 3). Thus, the degree of f_j is bounded by the maximum degree of a variation of h. Further, in Sect. 4.3, we showed that any Boolean variation of h can be written as the sum of four Antler functions. Thus, the maximum degree of any variation of h, and thus the degree of f_j, is bounded by the maximum degree of an Antler function. The following Theorem and its proof thus suffice to upper bound the degree of f_j.

Theorem 1. *For any 3 negacyclic look-up tables* S_1, S_2, S_3, *the ANF of* H_{S_1}, S_2, S_3 *has degree at most 12.*

Proof of Theorem 1. In order to study H_{S_1, S_2, S_3}, we introduce the following definitions (see Fig. 6):

$$u := S_1[b] = S_1[x + y]$$
$$v := S_2[b'] = S_2[y + z]$$
$$\beta := S_1[b] + S_2[b'] + w.$$

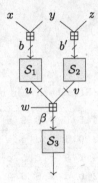

Fig. 6. The Antler function H_{S_1,S_2,S_3}.

Each bit of b (resp. b', $u+v$) can be expressed as a polynomial in the sum of the bits of x and y (resp. y and z, u and v) and in the product of the bits of x and y (resp. y and z, u and v). This property reflects the symmetric nature of the modular addition. Thus, for $0 \leq i \leq 3$, we also define

$$s_i := x_i \oplus y_i, s'_i = y_i \oplus z_i$$
$$p_i := x_i \cdot y_i, s'_i = y_i \cdot z_i$$
$$\sigma_i := u_i \oplus v_i$$
$$\pi_i := u_i \cdot v_i.$$

For any $0 \leq i \leq 3$, the following equations are verified

$$p_i s_i = 0$$
$$p'_i s'_i = 0$$
$$\pi_i \sigma_i = 0.$$

As a consequence, by applying the definition of the modular addition to $b = x+y$, we get

$$b_0 = s_0$$
$$b_1 = p_0 + s_1$$
$$b_2 = p_0 s_1 + p_1 + s_2$$
$$b_3 = p_0 s_1 s_2 + p_1 s_2 + p_2 + s_3.$$

The exact same equations hold for b'. Similarly, the bits of $u+v$ can be expressed as polynomials in the σ_i's and π_i's.

Going back to the proof, the main idea is to show that the monomials in x_i, y_i, z_i, w_i for $0 \leq i \leq 3$ that can appear in the ANF of $H_{S_1,S_2,S_3}(x,y,z,w)$ have their degree bounded by 12. The first property we use is that $H_{S_1,S_2,S_3}(x,y,z,t)$ does not depend on β_3. This is a direct consequence of Proposition 2. On the other hand, $H_{S_1,S_2,S_3}(x,y,z,t)$ can be expressed as a sum of monomials in the

β_i's for $i = 0, 1, 2$. In order to prove the theorem, we thus simply need to show that any monomial in $\beta_0, \beta_1, \beta_2$ can be expressed as a sum of monomials in x_i, y_i, z_i, w_i for $0 \leq i \leq 3$ that all have degree at most 12.

To do so, we first need to express β_0, β_1, β_2 as polynomials in the σ_i's, π_i's and the w_i's. By applying the modular addition to $\beta = u + v + w$, we obtain

$$\beta_0 = w_0 + \sigma_0$$
$$\beta_1 = w_1 + w_0\sigma_0 + \pi_0 + \sigma_1$$
$$\beta_2 = w_2 + w_0w_1\sigma_0 + w_1(\pi_0 + \sigma_1) + w_0\sigma_0\sigma_1 + \pi_0\sigma_1 + \pi_1 + \sigma_2.$$

Considering monomials in the β_i's for $i = 0, 1, 2$, we study which monomials in the σ_i's, π_i's and the w_i's can appear in their polynomial expression. For example, the monomial $\beta_0\beta_1$ can be expressed as

$$\beta_0\beta_1 = w_0w_1 + w_1\sigma_0 + w_0\pi_0 + w_0\sigma_1 + \sigma_0\sigma_1$$

and thus contains the monomials w_0w_1, $w_1\sigma_0$, $w_0\pi_0$, $w_0\sigma_1$ and $\sigma_0\sigma_1$. We show that the only monomial that can appear in the polynomial expression of a monomial in the β_i's, $0 \leq i \leq 2$ that depends on the three variables w_0, w_1 and w_2 is $w_0w_1w_2$. β_2 is the only variable that depends on w_2, β_0 does not depend on w_1 and β_1 depends only linearly on w_1. Thus, for a monomial in the three variables w_0, w_1 and w_2 to appear in the expression of a monomial in the β_i's, one must consider $\beta_0\beta_1\beta_2$, in which only the monomial $w_0w_1w_2$ depends on all three variables. Since only $w_0w_1w_2$ can appear, any monomial that depends on the σ_i's and π_i's depends on at most two of the w_i's. We will now show that the monomials in the σ_i's and π_i's expressed as polynomials in the x_i's, y_i's and z_i's are of degree at most 10, which will conclude the proof of the theorem.

The σ_i's and π_i's, as well as any monomial in these variables, can be expressed as a function of b and b'. In turn, b and b', as well as any monomial in these variables, can be expressed as a sum of monomials in the p_i's, s_i's, p_i''s and s_i''s. Since p_3 (resp. p_3') does not appear in the expression of b_i (resp. b_i'), $0 \leq i \leq 3$, the monomials that can appear in the expression of a monomial in the σ_i's and π_i's do not depend on p_3. Further, recall that $p_i s_i = p_i' s_i'$. Thus, the monomials cannot depend on both p_i and s_i (resp. p_i' and s_i'). Last but not least, note that any $p_i p_i' = x_i y_i z_i$ is of degree 3. At first sight, the monomial of highest degree that can be formed is $s_3 s_3' \prod_{i=0}^{2} p_i p_i'$. This monomial has degree 11, and is the only monomial of degree 11 that respects the constraints we have put forward. However, it turns out that this monomial cannot appear. Indeed, only b_3 (resp. b_3') is the depends on s_3 and p_2 (resp. s_3' and p_2'). Further, in the polynomial expression of b_3 (resp. b_3'), these variables are added to each other. It comes that in the polynomial expression of any monomial in the b_i's, these variables cannot be multiplied with each other. Thus, the monomials of highest degree that can be formed have degree 10. We have thus shown the theorem.

C   Proof of Proposition 4

By Lemma 1, we only need showing that the rank of the set of functions G_{S_1,S_2,S_3} has its dimension bounded by $2^{10.43}$. It is straightforward that the vector space spanned by all functions G_{S_1,S_2,S_3} is a linear subspace of a vector space of the form $B_0 + w_0 B_1 + w_1 B_2 + w_2 B_3 + w_0 w_1 B_4 + w_0 w_2 B_5 + w_1 w_2 B_6 + w_0 w_1 w_2 B_7$ where each B_i is a linear subspace of the linear space of dimension 2^8 spanned by the monomials in the bits of b and b'. The dimension of this vector space can thus be upper bounded by the sum $\sum_{i=0}^{7} \dim(B_i)$. We provide an upper bound on $\dim(B_i)$ for each i. We remind the reader of the following notations (see Fig. 7):

$$u := S_1[b]$$
$$v := S_2[b']$$
$$\beta := S_1[b] + S_2[b'] + w$$
$$\sigma_i := u_i \oplus v_i$$
$$\pi_i := u_i \cdot v_i.$$

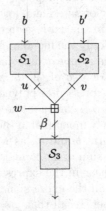

Fig. 7. The function G_{S_1,S_2,S_3}.

We also remind the reader of the expression of the value of the bits β_0, β_1 and β_2 as polynomials in the σ_i's, π_i's and w_i's.

$$\beta_0 = w_0 + \sigma_0$$
$$\beta_1 = w_1 + w_0 \sigma_0 + \pi_0 + \sigma_1$$
$$\beta_2 = w_2 + w_0 w_1 \sigma_0 + w_1 (\pi_0 + \sigma_1) + w_0 \sigma_0 \sigma_1 + \pi_0 \sigma_1 + \pi_1 + \sigma_2.$$

The least significant bit of h is a linear combination of monomials in β_i for $i = 0, 1, 2$. First, we consider B_7, which corresponds to $w_0 w_1 w_2$. The only monomial in the β_i's that contains a monomial dividable by $w_0 w_1 w_2$ is $\beta_0 \beta_1 \beta_2$. Further, the only monomial that can appear is $w_0w_1w_2$. Thus, B_7 has dimension 1. Next, we consider B_6, which corresponds to w_1w_2. The only two monomials in the β_i's that contain monomials dividable by w_1w_2 are $\beta_1\beta_2$ and $\beta_0\beta_1\beta_2$. We now consider the monomials dividable by w_1w_2 but not dividable by w_0 that appear in $\beta_1\beta_2$ and $\beta_0\beta_1\beta_2$. We obtain the set $\{w_1w_2, w_1w_2\sigma_0\}$. By Proposition 2, σ_0 is the sum of two bits that depend on 3 bits each and thus the rank of the set of σ_0 has rank $2^3 + 2^3 = 2^4$. It comes that B_6 has dimension at most 2^4. Lastly, we consider B_5, which corresponds to w_0w_2. Three monomials in the β_i's contain monomials dividable by w_0w_2, namely $\beta_0\beta_2$, $\beta_1\beta_2$ and $\beta_0\beta_1\beta_2$. We now consider the monomials dividable by w_0w_2 but not dividable by w_1 that appear in these three monomials. We obtain the set $\{w_0w_2, w_0w_2\sigma_0, w_0w_2\pi_0, w_0w_2\sigma_1\}$. By Proposition 2, the set of π_0 functions has rank at most $2^3 \times 2^3 = 2^6$. Further, it contains the linear subspace spanned by the σ_0 functions. The set of σ_1 functions has dimension $2^4 + 2^4 = 2^5$ and also contains the linear subspace spanned by the σ_0 functions. Thus, B_5 has dimension at most $2^6 + 2^5 - 2^4$. It comes that a bound on the rank of the LSB of h is $\sum_{i=0}^{7} \dim(B_i) \leq 5 \times 2^8 + 2^6 + 2^5 - 2^4 + 2^4 + 1 \approx 2^{10.43}$.

D   On the Dimension of the Affine Space of Solutions

In this section, we discuss the dimension of the affine space of solutions to the matrix equation $\mathbf{A}\mathbf{x} = \mathbf{z}$ for a matrix $\mathbf{A}$ constructed as described in Sect. 4 and Sect. 6. In particular, $\mathbf{A}$ is a matrix of size $\delta \times \binom{N'}{4}\rho$ where $\delta \gtrsim \binom{N'}{4}\rho$ and where $N' = N$ in Section Sect. 4 and $N' < N$ in Section Sect. 6. Ignoring a few lone nonzero bits from the final linear contribution to g, each row of $\mathbf{A}$ has less than $t \cdot \rho$ active bits, organized into $t = 12$ sets of ρ active bits. A necessary condition for the affine space of solutions to have dimension 1 is that each of the $\binom{N'}{4}$ submatrices of size $\delta \times \rho$ of $\mathbf{A}$, constructed by extracting the ρ columns corresponding to an unordered quartet of key element positions, is non-singular.

The concern that the matrix equation $\mathbf{A}\mathbf{x} = \mathbf{z}$ could have an affine space of solutions with a problematically large dimension, which would be highly unlikely for a random matrix, stems from the fact that $\mathbf{A}$ has the following structure: each row is nonzero in only t distinct sets of columns. If t was 'too' small, e.g. $t = 1$, then this necessary condition might not have been fulfilled: each submatrix would have on average just about ρ nonzero rows, and thus, the probability that all $\binom{N'}{4}$ submatrices have full rank would be rather low. For $t = 12$, on the other hand, we provide a proof that this necessary condition is satisfied with overwhelming probability for the values N' we consider in our attacks. In other words, the structure of $\mathbf{A}$ produces no oblivious rank deficiency as compared with the behaviour of a random matrix.

We consider a submatrix of size $\delta \times \rho$ extracted from $\mathbf{A}$ as described above. We let p_1 be the probability that after gathering δ equations, this submatrix has less than $2 \cdot \rho$ nonzero rows. This probability is strictly smaller than the probability that after gathering $\binom{N'}{4}\rho =_{def} \delta_1 < \delta$ equations, this submatrix has less than $2 \cdot \rho$ nonzero rows. We compute this latter probability. For a fixed submatrice, we can view the construction of $\mathbf{A}$ as drawing $\delta_1 = \binom{N'}{4}\rho$ rows such that for each row, the probability that this row is nonzero is $p_t = t/\binom{N'}{4}$. The number X of nonzero rows thus follows a binomial law with parameters $\delta_1 = \binom{N'}{4} \cdot \rho$ and p_t, $X \sim B(\delta_1, p_t)$. Thus, the probability that after $\binom{N'}{4} \cdot \rho$ equations, the submatrix has less than $2 \cdot \rho$ nonzero rows is $\mathbb{P}(X \leq 2 \cdot \rho)$. Since $\delta_1 \cdot p_t \cdot (1 - p_t) \gg 10$, we use the approximation of the binomial distribution by the normal distribution given by the Moivre-Laplace theorem:

$$\mathbb{P}(X \leq 2 \cdot \rho) \approx \mathbb{P}\left(Y \leq \frac{2 \cdot \rho - \delta_1 \cdot p_t}{\sqrt{\delta_1 \cdot p_t \cdot (1 - p_t)}}\right),$$

where $Y \sim \mathcal{N}(0,1)$. For $N' = N = 256$ and $N' = 137$, this probability can be shown to be at most $\frac{e^{-269^2}}{538\sqrt{\pi}}$.

We now compute the probability p_2 that a submatrix containing at least $2 \cdot \rho$ equations does not have full rank ρ. We approximate this probability by the probability that a random $2 \cdot \rho \times \rho$ matrix does not have full rank. It can be shown by induction that the probability that a random $\mathbb{F}_2$-matrix of size $2 \cdot \rho \times \rho$ has full rank ρ is at least $e^{-\frac{\rho}{2^{\rho+1}}}$. This implies that $p_2 \leq 1 - e^{-\frac{\rho}{2^{\rho+1}}}$.

For a fixed submatrice, p_1 is the probability that after gathering δ equations, this submatrix has less than $2 \cdot \rho$ nonzero rows whilst p_2 is the probability that a submatrix containing at least $2 \cdot \rho$ equations does not have full rank. Thus, the probability that a fixed submatrix is singular is at most $p_1 + p_2$. Since there are $\binom{N'}{4}$ submatrices, the probability that at least one submatrix is singular is at most $\binom{N'}{4}(p_1 + p_2)$. In particular, for $N' = N = 256$ and $N' = 137$, each submatrix is non-singular with probability at least $1 - \binom{N'}{4}(p_1 + p_2) > 0.99$.

E   Description of the XOF

The XOF state contains an AES key. It is initialized with the IV. During operation, a block of output is produced by encrypting a fixed constant using the key in the XOF state. The updated state is obtained by encrypting another fixed constant using the same XOF state as key. This enables to produce a sequence of bits of arbitrary length. From this sequence we extract bit sequences to generate masking values and integers to generate an ordered arrangement. In order to generate an integer uniformly at random in $\{0, .., n-1\}$, we apply rejection sampling. We form an integer from k bits of the XOF output, where k is the bitlength of n. While this candidate integer is greater or equal that n, we discard it and take a new candidate. In the other case we use this integer as the output. This defines a procedure $next\_int(n)$. Note that the state of the XOF is updated as bits of its output sequence are consumed.

Using this building block, we follow exactly Algorithm 2 of [3]. Note that the generation procedure of parameters π^i and m^i is stateful: a current permutation of $\{1, .., N\}$ and an array of N masking values is maintained. At every step, we need to extract $r \cdot t$ ($= 60$ for Elisabeth-4, $= 10$ in our toy version) key nibbles. We do so by performing an 'aborted Knuth shuffle': for i in $\{1, \cdots, r \cdot t\}$, we compose the current permutation with the transposition $(i, i + x)$ where x is an output of $next\_int(N - i)$. At the end of the loop, the $r \cdot t$ first positions of the current permutation contain an uniformly distributed ordered arrangement of $\{1, .., N\}$. For every position determined by this arrangement, we add in the array of masking values a fresh group element, generated through $next\_int(16)$.

References

1. Chillotti, I., Joye, M., Paillier, P.: Programmable bootstrapping enables efficient homomorphic inference of deep neural networks. In: Dolev, S., Margalit, O., Pinkas, B., Schwarzmann, A. (eds.) CSCML 2021. LNCS, vol. 12716, pp. 1–19. Springer, Cham (2021). https://doi.org/10.1007/978-3-030-78086-9_1
2. Coppersmith, D.: Solving homogeneous linear equations over gf(2) via block Wiedemann algorithm. Math. Comput. **62**(205), 333–350 (1994). http://www.jstor.org/stable/2153413
3. Cosseron, O., Hoffmann, C., Méaux, P., Standaert, F.X.: Towards globally optimized hybrid homomorphic encryption - featuring the Elisabeth stream cipher. In: ASIACRYPT 2022, Taipei, Taiwan (2022). http://hal.inria.fr/hal-03905546
4. cado-nfs Development Team, T.: cado-nfs, an implementation of the number field sieve algorithm (2017). http://cado-nfs.inria.fr/, release 2.3.0
5. Duval, S., Lallemand, V., Rotella, Y.: Cryptanalysis of the FLIP family of stream ciphers. In: Robshaw, M., Katz, J. (eds.) CRYPTO 2016, Part I. LNCS, vol. 9814, pp. 457–475. Springer, Heidelberg (2016). https://doi.org/10.1007/978-3-662-53018-4_17
6. Faugère, J.C.: A new efficient algorithm for computing Gröbner bases without reduction to zero (f5). In: Proceedings of the 2002 International Symposium on Symbolic and Algebraic Computation. ISSAC '02, pp. 75–83. Association for Computing Machinery, New York, NY, USA (2002). https://doi.org/10.1145/780506.780516
7. Faugére, J.C.: A new efficient algorithm for computing Gröbner bases (f4). J. Pure Appl. Algebra **139**(1), 61–88 (1999). https://www.sciencedirect.com/science/article/pii/S0022404999000055, https://doi.org/10.1016/S0022-4049(99)00005-5,
8. Joux, A.: Algorithmic Cryptanalysis. Cryptography and Network Security Series. Chapman & Hall/CRC, Taylor & Francis, Boca Raton (2009). https://books.google.fr/books?id=dyavmAEACAAJ
9. Joux, A., Pierrot, C.: Nearly sparse linear algebra and application to discrete logarithms computations. In: Contemporary Developments in Finite Fields and Applications, pp. 119–144. World Scientific (2016)
10. Kaltofen, E.: Analysis of Coppersmith's block Wiedemann algorithm for the parallel solution of sparse linear systems. In: Cohen, G., Mora, T., Moreno, O. (eds.) AAECC 1993. LNCS, vol. 673, pp. 195–212. Springer, Heidelberg (1993). https://doi.org/10.1007/3-540-56686-4_44
11. Massey, J.: Shift-register synthesis and bch decoding. IEEE Trans. Inf. Theory **15**(1), 122–127 (1969)
12. Méaux, P., Carlet, C., Journault, A., Standaert, F.-X.: Improved filter permutators for efficient FHE: better instances and implementations. In: Hao, F., Ruj, S., Sen Gupta, S. (eds.) INDOCRYPT 2019. LNCS, vol. 11898, pp. 68–91. Springer, Cham (2019). https://doi.org/10.1007/978-3-030-35423-7_4

13. Méaux, P., Journault, A., Standaert, F.-X., Carlet, C.: Towards stream ciphers for efficient FHE with low-noise ciphertexts. In: Fischlin, M., Coron, J.-S. (eds.) EUROCRYPT 2016, Part I. LNCS, vol. 9665, pp. 311–343. Springer, Heidelberg (2016). https://doi.org/10.1007/978-3-662-49890-3_13

14. Strassen, V.: Gaussian elimination is not optimal. Numer. Math. **13**, 354–356 (1969)

15. Wiedemann, D.: Solving sparse linear equations over finite fields. IEEE Trans. Inf. Theory **32**(1), 54–62 (1986)

Algebraic Attacks on Round-Reduced Rain and Full AIM-III

Kaiyi Zhang[1]([✉])[iD], Qingju Wang[2][iD], Yu Yu[1,3][iD], Chun Guo[4,5,6][iD],
and Hongrui Cui[1][iD]

[1] Shanghai Jiao Tong University, Shanghai, China
{kzoacn,yyuu,rickfreeman}@sjtu.edu.cn
[2] Telecom Paris, Institut Polytechnique de Paris, Palaiseau, France
qingju.wang@telecom-paris.fr
[3] Shanghai Qi Zhi Institute, Shanghai, China
[4] School of Cyber Science and Technology, Shandong University, Qingdao,
Shandong, China
[5] Key Laboratory of Cryptologic Technology and Information Security of Ministry of
Education, Shandong University, Qingdao, Shandong 266237, China
[6] Shandong Research Institute of Industrial Technology, Jinan, Shandong 250102,
China

Abstract. Picnic is a NIST PQC Round 3 Alternate signature candidate that builds upon symmetric primitives following the MPC-in-the-head paradigm. Recently, researchers have been exploring more secure/efficient signature schemes from conservative one-way functions based on AES, or new low-complexity one-way functions like Rain (CCS 2022) and AIM (CCS 2023 and Round 1 Additional Signatures announced by NIST PQC). The signature schemes based on Rain and AIM are currently the most efficient among MPC-in-the-head-based schemes, making them promising post-quantum digital signature candidates.

However, the exact hardness of these new one-way functions deserves further study and scrutiny. This work presents algebraic attacks on Rain and AIM for certain instances, where one-round Rain can be compromised in $2^{n/2}$ for security parameter $n \in \{128, 192, 256\}$, and two-round Rain can be broken in $2^{120.3}$, $2^{180.4}$, and $2^{243.1}$ encryptions, respectively. Additionally, we demonstrate an attack on AIM-III (which aims at 192-bit security) with a complexity of $2^{186.5}$ encryptions. These attacks exploit the algebraic structure of the power function over fields with characteristic 2, which provides potential insights into the algebraic structures of some symmetric primitives and thus might be of independent interest.

Keywords: Algebraic Attacks · Power Mapping · Arithmetization Oriented Primitives · Rain · AIM

1 Introduction

With significant advancements in quantum computing over the past decades, the security threats of quantum computers are increasingly becoming a reality. As a

© International Association for Cryptologic Research 2023
J. Guo and R. Steinfeld (Eds.): ASIACRYPT 2023, LNCS 14440, pp. 285–310, 2023.
https://doi.org/10.1007/978-981-99-8727-6_10

response, the cryptographic community is seeking post-quantum alternatives to the widely deployed public-key cryptography algorithms, the most noteworthy of which is NIST's post-quantum cryptography (PQC) standardization process.[1] This has motivated numerous novel designs as well as analyses of the underlying hardness assumptions.

Towards post-quantum digital signatures, a popular approach is to employ the MPC-in-the-Head (MPCitH) paradigm, proposed by Ishai et al. [24]. In detail, MPCitH provides a general construction of a zero-knowledge proof for an NP relation by making a black-box use of any secure multi-party computation protocol for a related functionality. A major application of the MPCitH paradigm is to construct post-quantum digital signatures, which are essentially a non-interactive zero-knowledge proof of knowledge (NIZKPoK) that the input of a specific one-way function (secret key of the signature) corresponds to the one-way function's output (public key of the signature). Note that the message to be signed is involved in the challenge generation of NIZKPoK. The NIZKPoK, when based on quantum-resistant one-way functions, gives rise to promising candidates for post-quantum signatures. Chase et al. [7,25] pioneered NIZKPoK-based signatures, and they designed the Picnic scheme that advanced to the third round of the NIST PQC standardization process.

Subsequent improvements to MPCitH-based signatures follow two approaches. The first approach [6,14,15] sticks to standard primitives such as the AES, and focuses on improving the efficiency of the zero-knowledge proof. Concretely, such designs instantiate the block cipher-based OWF $H(k) = E_k(P)$ (with P a public constant) with AES.[2] Since the performance of MPCitH-based signatures is typically closely tied to the number of non-linear operations in the circuit of the underlying one-way function, the large circuit size of AES constitutes the bottleneck. Generally, symmetric primitives, which aim to minimize the cost related to the number of non-linear operations, are called *arithmetization-oriented* symmetric primitives. With this in mind, the second approach is devoted to designing efficient arithmetization-oriented block ciphers for $H(k) = E_k(P)$ or even new one-way functions. In fact, Picnic already employed this idea and instantiated $H(k) = E_k(P)$ with an MPC-friendly block cipher LowMC, which aims to minimize the number of AND gates over $\mathbb{F}_2$. The idea was further extended by Dobraunig et al. [20] and Kim et al. [26]. Dobraunig et al. proposed a novel block cipher to instantiate $H(k) = E_k(P)$. More detailedly, RAIN may be viewed as an iterated Even-Mansour scheme with round permutation defined upon inversions in $\mathbb{F}_{2^n}$ and random matrices in $\mathbb{F}_2^{n \times n}$, where n is the block size. Such round permutations may also be viewed as generalizations of the AES S-box. Kim et al. [26] made a step further and proposed a "tweakable" OWF AIM that is built upon a novel construction and employs the Mersenne power function as its S-box. Both RAIN and AIM maintained to reduce the number of multiplications over $\mathbb{F}_{2^n}$, and they enjoy the shortest

---

[1] https://csrc.nist.gov/projects/post-quantum-cryptography.

[2] The one-wayness of $H(k) = E_k(P)$ is equivalent to the key recovery security of E with a single plaintext/ciphertext pair: see [20] for a proof.

signature size as well as comparable signing/verification time among MPCitH-based signatures (to the best of our knowledge). In July 2023, AIMer has been submitted as one of the NIST PQC Round 1 Additional Signatures in the category of Symmetric-based Signatures.[3]

We remark that the block cipher RAIN is only intended to be used in the OWF construction $H_k = E_k(P)$, the security of which is equivalent to the key recovery security of E with a single plaintext/ciphertext pair. Therefore, classical attacks involving multiple data, including statistical attacks like the differential attack, are not immediately relevant in this setting.

The MPC-friendly primitive-based approach proves a huge success w.r.t. performance: all of the aforementioned designs, i.e., (LowMC-based) Picnic, RAIN-based RAINIER and AIM-based AIMer, managed to reduce multiplications (over $\mathbb{F}_2$ or $\mathbb{F}_{2^n}$) as well as the signature size (as mentioned). On the other hand, classical cryptanalytic methods (e.g., differential and linear attacks) are mostly inapplicable due to the limited available data. These have motivated investigating dedicated cryptanalytic methods and deepening the understanding of such designs. For example, since proposed, LowMC has undergone quite some cryptanalysis [5,18,19,28,30,32,38]. In this work we focus on RAIN and AIM and design novel algebraic attacks breaking the one-wayness of certain instances, as elaborated below.

1.1 Our Contributions

Here we give an overview of our attacks and propose possible countermeasures.

Overview of the New Algebraic Attacks. RAIN employs the same kind of S-box as the AES, which is the multiplicative inverse function over $\mathbb{F}_{2^n}$ (with zero mapped to zero). Our initial focus was to linearize this S-box. We progress in this direction by discovering the following fact:

$$x^{254} = (x^{17})^{14} \cdot x^{16}$$

where x^{254} is the non-linear layer of AES and the formula is over $\mathbb{F}_{2^8}$. For the two terms of the formula:

- In the first term, 17 is a divisor of 255, meaning that x^{17} has only $255/17 = 15$ possible choices for $x \in \mathbb{F}_{2^8} \backslash \{0\}$.
- In the second term, the square function over $\mathbb{F}_{2^n}$ is linear, which means that square function x^2 can be represented by matrix multiplication as $x^2 = Mx$ for an invertible matrix $M \in \mathbb{F}_2^{8 \times 8}$. Hence, the mapping $x \mapsto x^{16}$ can be expressed as $x \mapsto M'x$ for $M' = M^4$.

Therefore, if we guess the value of $x^{17} = \alpha$ from 15 possible choices, we can express x^{254} as $x^{254} = \alpha^{14} \cdot x^{16} = M''x$ for some M''. This linearizes the non-linear layer of AES, but unfortunately, no attacks better than the current state-of-the-art has been found based on this fact.

---

[3] https://csrc.nist.gov/Projects/pqc-dig-sig/round-1-additional-signatures.

However, RAIN also uses the multiplicative inverse function over $\mathbb{F}_{2^n}$ as its non-linear layer. For an even n, we decompose it similarly to the AES as

$$x^{2^n-2} = (x^{2^{n/2}+1})^{2^{n/2}-2} \cdot x^{2^{n/2}}.$$

As can be seen, $d = 2^{n/2} + 1$ is a divisor of $2^n - 1$. In other words, $\{x^d : x \in \mathbb{F}_{2^n} \backslash \{0\}\}$ is a subgroup of the multiplicative group $\mathbb{F}_{2^n}^*$ of the finite field $\mathbb{F}_{2^n}$. Therefore x^d has only $|\mathbb{F}_{2^n}^*|/d = (2^n - 1)/(2^{n/2} + 1) = 2^{n/2} - 1$ possible choices. Secondly, $x \mapsto x^{2^{n/2}}$ is a linear function over $\mathbb{F}_2$. Guessing at most $2^{n/2} - 1$ possible choices in a similar way, allows the adversary to linearize the non-linear layer. Using this method, we can recover the key of one-round RAIN in $2^{n/2}$ encryptions.

When we move to two-round RAIN, this method will not work directly. Inspired by [30], we introduce quadratic equations into our attack, and propose a new method of deriving quadratic equations from two S-boxes in the form of power mappings. More specifically, in the first step, by linearizing the S-box in the first non-linear layer, we obtain independent linear equations, and free variables for the secret key bits. In the next step, we construct quadratic equations from the second S-box. By substituting unknown variables with free variables obtained in the previous step, we get a sufficient number of linearly independent quadratic equations so that all free variables can be solved efficiently.

Our Attacks on RAIN and AIM. We demonstrate that one-round RAIN can be compromised in $2^{n/2}$ number of encryptions, for $n \in \{128, 192, 256\}$, while two-round RAIN can be broken in $2^{120.3}$, $2^{180.4}$, and $2^{243.1}$ encryptions, respectively. Furthermore, we also show an attack on full AIM-III (which aims at 192-bit security) with $2^{186.5}$ encryptions. Notably, all these attacks are conducted in the one-way function setting, where the adversary has access to only one plaintext/ciphertext pair or one ciphertext in the case of AIM. Besides, the memory cost of our attacks is negligible. Finally, we implement attacks on two-round RAIN and AIM-III, practically showing that there are sufficiently enough linearly independent equations to solve unknown variables. Our implementation can be found at

https://github.com/kzoacn/LargeSbox/.

At present, these attacks do not affect the security of the signature scheme which uses three- or more-round RAIN. Moreover, the security of AIM-I (which aims at 128-bit security) and AIM-V (which aims at 256-bit security) are not significantly affected by our attack.

Our attack exploits the algebraic structure of the power function over the binary Galois field, which is widely used in the design of symmetric primitives suitable for MPCitH-based signature schemes. Therefore, our findings provide new insights into the algebraic structures of these primitives, which might be of independent interest.

Restoring the Security of AIM. Lastly, in Sect. 5.2 we discuss some countermeasures that allow AIM to regain security. These include countermeasures avoiding the simultaneous linearization of two S-boxes, restricting of the order n of extension field $\mathbb{F}_{2^n}$ to be odd, and increasing the number of rounds.

1.2   Related Work

Post-quantum signatures can be built upon other hardness assumptions as well, including lattice assumptions (e.g., CRYSTALS-Dilithium [33] and Falcon [37]), the intractability of Multivariate Quadratic (MQ) problems, etc. Some representative schemes such as SPHINCS$^+$ [23] are solely based on cryptographic hash functions (but rely on much stronger assumptions than the one-wayness of the hash functions). We refer to [39] for a survey.

Since RAIN is an instance of the iterated Even-Mansour scheme, we refer to [13,16,17,21,36] for generic key recovery attacks. Though, with just one plaintext/ciphertext pair, such generic attacks are either inapplicable (on two rounds) or less efficient than ours (on one round).

During the submission of this work, Liu and Mahzoun proposed attacks on 2-round RAIN and full-round AIM [29]. Since the natural isomorphism between $\mathbb{F}_2^n$ and $\mathbb{F}_{2^n}$, both RAIN and AIM defined over $\mathbb{F}_{2^n}$, can be represented as relatively low-degree polynomials over $\mathbb{F}_2^n$. They proposed highly refined techniques to solve systems of low-degree equations, while we more focus on the essential property of power mapping S-boxes in this work.

1.3   Paper Organization

In Sect. 2, we define notations and give background information for the linearization techniques used in this paper. We present our first attack on one-round RAIN in Sect. 3. In order to attack more rounds of RAIN, we first propose a general algebraic attack framework at the beginning of Sect. 4. Under this framework, we achieve attacks on two-round RAIN and the full rounds of AIM-III. We discuss some countermeasures that allow AIM to reestablish security in Sect. 5. We conclude this paper in Sect. 6.

2   Preliminaries

2.1   Notations

Let p be a prime number, and $q = p^n$ for a positive integer n. Let $\mathbb{F}_p$ denote a finite field with p elements, and let $\mathbb{F}_q = \mathbb{F}_{p^n}$ denote a finite field with characteristic p. The multiplicative group of $\mathbb{F}_q$ is denoted by $\mathbb{F}_q^* = \mathbb{F}_q \backslash \{0\}$. We use $[m]$ to denote the set $\{0, 1, \ldots, m-1\}$ for $m \in \mathbb{N}^+$. We use n as both the security parameter and the block size, since for both RAIN and AIM the block size equals the security parameter. The size of a set S is denoted by $|S|$. The n-dim identity matrix is denoted by I.

2.2   Finite Field

Theorem 1 (e.g., Theorem 2.1.37 from [34]). *The multiplicative group* $\mathbb{F}_q^*$ *of a finite field* $\mathbb{F}_q$ *is cyclic.*

Definition 1. *A generator g of a multiplicative group $\mathbb{F}_q^*$ is called a primitive element of the field $\mathbb{F}_q$. It is denoted as $\mathbb{F}_q^* = \langle g \rangle$.*

Theorem 2. *Let d be a divisor of $|\mathbb{F}_q^*| = p^n - 1$, and let $X \stackrel{\text{def}}{=} \{x^d : x \in \mathbb{F}_q^*\}$. The size of X is $|X| = |\mathbb{F}_q^*|/d = (p^n - 1)/d$.*

Theorem 2 tells us that for any appropriate $d > 1$ with $d|(p^n - 1)$, the power function $x \mapsto x^d$ maps inputs from $\mathbb{F}_q^*$ to a proper subset of $\mathbb{F}_q^*$.

2.3   Linearized Polynomial

Definition 2 (linearized polynomial). *A linearized polynomial is defined as $L(x) \stackrel{\text{def}}{=} \sum_{i \in [n]} a_i x^{p^i}$, where $a_i \in \mathbb{F}_{p^n}$ for some prime p.*

Let $L(x)$ be a linearized polynomial over a finite field $\mathbb{F}_p$. The map $x \mapsto L(x)$ is a linear map over $\mathbb{F}_p$, i.e., for all $a, b \in \mathbb{F}_{p^n}$ and $c \in \mathbb{F}_p$, we have $L(a + b) = L(a) + L(b)$ and $c \cdot L(a) = L(c \cdot a)$. Due to the existence of a vector space isomorphism $\mathbb{F}_p^n \cong \mathbb{F}_{p^n}$, we can naturally view an element $x \in \mathbb{F}_{p^n}$ as a vector $\hat{x} \in \mathbb{F}_p^n$. More specifically, there must exist a matrix $M \in \mathbb{F}_p^{n \times n}$ such that $L(x) = M\hat{x}$. For simplicity, we interchangeably view x as an element of $\mathbb{F}_{p^n}$ or a vector $x \in \mathbb{F}_p^n$, so that we can write $L(x) = Mx$.

In the case of the bijective mapping $\mathbb{F}_{2^n} \to \mathbb{F}_{2^n} : x \mapsto x^{2^k}$, we can represent it as $\mathbb{F}_2^n \to \mathbb{F}_2^n : x \mapsto Mx$ for some invertible binary matrix M.

2.4   Linearization and Multivariate Quadratic Equations over Finite Field

Linearization Attacks. Solving multivariate equations is regarded as an NP-hard problem in general. However, in some special cases, multivariate polynomial systems of equations over finite fields can be solved in polynomial time (see e.g., [27]). The core idea of linearization is to turn a system of non-linear equations into a linear system by treating each monomial as a separate variable. In general, the method generates polynomials of some degree, up to the point where the number of equations exceeds the number of monomials so a solution can be obtained by some linear algebra. In symmetric cryptography, it is usually assumed that the attackers have access to sufficiently many equations to linearize the system. Recall that the number of possible monomials in a degree d polynomial in $\mathbb{F}[x_1, \ldots, x_n]$, where $|\mathbb{F}| > d$, is $\mathcal{B}_{n,d} = \binom{n+d}{d}$. The linearization attack requires $\mathcal{O}(\mathcal{B}_{n,d}^\omega)$ multiplications in $\mathbb{F}$, where $2 < \omega \leq 3$, $\mathcal{O}(\mathcal{B}_{n,d})$ data complexity, and $\mathcal{O}(\mathcal{B}_{n,d}^2)$ memory complexity.

Multivariate Quadratic Equations Over $\mathbb{F}_2$. In this paper, the main focus is the quadratic multivariate equations. A set of multivariate quadratic equations consists of equations of the form

$$\sum_{i,j\in[n]} a_{i,j}x_ix_j + \sum_{i\in[n]} b_ix_i + c = 0,$$

where $a_{i,j}, b_i, c \in \mathbb{F}_2$ are constants, and $x_1, x_2, \ldots, x_n$ are the unknown variables. When applying the linearization technique to the quadratic case, it simply involves replacing each quadratic term with a new separate variable. Suppose we want to replace x_ix_j with a new variable $y_k = x_ix_j$. Note that in $\mathbb{F}_2$, $x_i^2 = x_i$ for any i always holds. Therefore the only possible quadratic terms are of the form $y_k = x_ix_j$ with $i < j$, which lead to $n(n-1)/2$ instead of $n(n+1)/2$ new variables. Therefore, combined with the n variables x_i's, the total number of variables will be $m = n + n(n-1)/2$.

While there are more sophisticated methods available, such as relinearization [27] or XL [11], the linearization technique suffices for our attacks.

3   Preliminary Algebraic Attack on One-Round RAIN

In this section, we present the algebraic attack on one-round RAIN. We first start with the specification of the target cipher.

3.1   Description of RAIN

RAIN is the one-way function designed for the signature scheme Rainier. RAIN is denoted as a keyed permutation $E_k(P) = C$, where the input P and the output C are public, and the secret key k is private. As a one-way function used in the signature scheme, it is $H(k) = E_k(P)$. The keyed permutation is a concatenation of r round functions R_i. For each round $1 \le i < r$, the round function R_i is defined by

$$R_i(x) = M_i(S(x + k + c^{(i)}))$$

and the last round function is

$$R_r(x) = k + S(x + k + c^{(r)}),$$

where $c^{(i)} \in \mathbb{F}_2^n$ is the round constant, and $M_i \in \mathbb{F}_2^{n\times n}$ is the linear layer matrix used in the i-th round. Each M_i can be represented as a linearized polynomial over $\mathbb{F}_{2^n}$ as defined in Definition 2. The details for the generation of the round constants and matrices are referred to in the design paper [20]. The non-linear layer of RAIN is defined as $S : \mathbb{F}_{2^n} \to \mathbb{F}_{2^n}$ such that

$$S(x) = x^{2^n-2} = \begin{cases} x^{-1}, & x \ne 0 \\ 0, & x = 0 \end{cases}$$

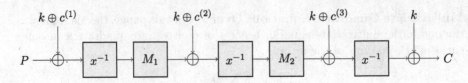

Fig. 1. RAIN permutation with $r = 3$.

A graphical overview of the construction with the round number $r = 3$ is shown in Fig. 1.

Parameter Sets. The block size of RAIN is $n \in \{128, 192, 256\}$. Two variants for each block size are recommended with the round number $r = 3, 4$, which are used in the signature Rainier$_r$-n. We denote the one-way function with the block size n as RAIN-n in our presentation, neglecting the number of rounds r.

The finite field and irreducible polynomials of RAIN are defined as follows:

- For 128-bit security, the finite field is $\mathbb{F}_{2^{128}}$ with irreducible polynomial $X^{128} + X^7 + X^2 + X + 1$.
- For 192-bit security, the finite field is $\mathbb{F}_{2^{192}}$ with irreducible polynomial $X^{192} + X^7 + X^2 + X + 1$.
- For 256-bit security, the finite field is $\mathbb{F}_{2^{256}}$ with irreducible polynomial $X^{256} + X^{10} + X^5 + X^2 + 1$.

3.2 Attack on One-Round RAIN

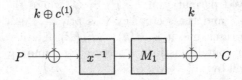

Fig. 2. RAIN permutation with $r = 1$.

In this subsection, we describe our attacks on one-round RAIN (Fig. 2). Here, one round of RAIN means a regular round, i.e., it consists of the nonlinear operation S-box, and the linear operation M_1. The relation of the public input P and public output C, and the secret key k can be expressed as

$$M_1(P + k + c^{(1)})^{-1} + k = C. \tag{1}$$

To recover the key k is to find the root of Eq. (1).

Before giving the procedures of our attack, we first explain some observations about the multiplicative inverse function (S-box) that the attack relies on.

Proposition 1. *For an even n, the multiplicative inverse function x^{-1} over $\mathbb{F}_{2^n}$ can be linearized by guessing $2^{n/2} - 1$ possible values for x^d, where $d = 2^{n/2} + 1$.*

Proof. For an even n, the multiplicative inverse function over $\mathbb{F}_{2^n}$ can be represented as

$$x^{2^n - 2} = (x^{2^{n/2}+1})^{2^{n/2}-2} \cdot x^{2^{n/2}} . \tag{2}$$

Let $d = 2^{n/2} + 1$, $s = 2^{n/2} - 2$, and $t = n/2$, Eq. (2) can be simplified as

$$x^{2^n - 2} = (x^d)^s \cdot x^{2^t} . \tag{3}$$

We proceed to performing an individual analysis of both terms within the simplified expression in Eq. (3) as follows:

i) According to Theorem 2, d is a divisor of $2^n - 1$, x^d takes only $(2^n - 1)/d = 2^{n/2} - 1$ possible values.
ii) According to Sect. 2.3, $x \mapsto x^{2^t}$ is equivalent to $x \mapsto Mx$ for an invertible matrix M.

It means that we can linearize the multiplicative inverse function over $\mathbb{F}_{2^n}$ (for even n) by guessing $2^{n/2} - 1$ possible values for x^d. ∎

Based on Proposition 1, we give the detailed steps of our attack as follows:

1. Enumerate an element α from the set $D = \{x^d : x \in \mathbb{F}_{2^n}^*\}$, then let the value of $(P + k + c^{(1)})^d$ be α.
2. Compute $(P + k + c^{(1)})^{-1} = \alpha^s \cdot (P + k + c^{(1)})^{2^t} = Mk + b$ for a matrix $M \in \mathbb{F}_2^{n \times n}$ and a vector $b \in \mathbb{F}_2^n$.
3. Substitute $(P + k + c^{(1)})^{-1}$ in Eq. (1) with $Mk + b$ and obtain $M'k + b' = 0$, where $M' = M_1 M + I$ and $b' = M_1 b + C$.
4. Use Gaussian elimination to solve $M'k + b' = 0$ and obtain k^* as the solution for k.
5. Check if k^* is the correct key by checking if $R_1(k^*, P) + k^* = C$. If not, we repeat Step 1.

Enumerating α. Let g be a generator of $\mathbb{F}_{2^n}^*$. According to Theorem 1, g generates the entire $\mathbb{F}_{2^n}^*$, i.e., any element $x \in \mathbb{F}_{2^n}^*$ can be represented as $x = g^i$ for $0 \leq i \leq 2^n - 1$. It follows that $D = \{x^d : x \in \mathbb{F}_{2^n}^*\} = \{g^{i \cdot d} : i = 0, 1, \ldots, (2^n - 1)/d - 1\}$. Therefore, we can generate the desired set D by enumerating $i \in \{0, 1, \ldots, (2^n - 1)/d - 1\}$ and compute $g^{i \cdot d}$.

Complexity Analysis. There are $(|\mathbb{F}_{2^n}| - 1)/d$ possible choices of α. For each guess, it takes $\mathcal{O}(n^3)$ time to solve the linear equations. Therefore, the time complexity of this attack is $T_{\text{bit}} = (2^n - 1)/d \cdot n^3$ in terms of bit operations. To convert the time complexity in a number of encryptions, we re-calculate it as $T = T_{\text{bit}}/n^3$. This is a useful conversion because it allows us to directly compare the complexity of this attack to that of a brute force attack, which has a complexity of exactly 2^n. The memory complexity of our approach is negligible since we only need to store the equations.

Table 1. Results for one-round RAIN. n is the block size and the security parameter, r is the number of rounds attacked, d is the divisor we use to determine the guess of $\alpha (= x^d)$, t determines the linear term in the decomposition of $2^n - 2$, and T is the time complexity of the attack.

Scheme	n	r	d	t	T
RAIN-128	128	1	$2^{64} + 1$	64	2^{64}
RAIN-192	192	1	$2^{96} + 1$	96	2^{96}
RAIN-256	256	1	$2^{128} + 1$	128	2^{128}

Parameter Sets of Our Attack. The detailed parameters of our attack on one-round RAIN are given in Table 1.

Toy Example. We provide a concrete example for the attack on one-round RAIN, which can be found in Appendix A.1.

4   Algebraic Attack Framework and Its Application to Two-Round RAIN and Full AIM-III

In the attack on one-round RAIN, we use a linearization technique to handle the non-linear S-box. With a carefully chosen divisor d of n, we guess the value of x^d and then decompose x^{-1} as a product of $(x^d)^s$ and x^{2^t}, where the former is a constant and the latter is linear.

In order to attack more rounds of RAIN, our initial attempt was to straightforwardly linearize more than one S-box using this method. We note that the complexity of the linearization of one S-box in such a way is roughly $(|\mathbb{F}_{2^n}|-1)/d$, so the larger the divisor d is, the smaller the complexity is. However, the largest possible divisor d that can be used to linearize x^{-1} is $2^{n/2}+1$, therefore the cost of this technique is at least $(|\mathbb{F}_{2^n}|-1)/d \approx 2^{n/2}$ for each S-box. Consequently, the unfavorable ramification for linearizing more than one S-box is that the overall complexity will not be superior to the brute force. Therefore, we must explore alternative techniques to tackle the two-round RAIN.

4.1   Algebraic Attack Framework

We devote ourselves to the algebraic attacks on more than one round of RAIN, i.e., more than one S-box. The efficiency of algebraic cryptanalysis heavily depends on the number of variables, the number of equations, and the degrees for the system of equations. Numerous efforts have been undertaken to investigate the number of linearly independent quadratic equations obtained from power functions over $\mathbb{F}_{2^n}$ [8,10,22,35]. For instance, it has been pointed out that for the inverse mapping which is the S-box employed in RAIN, this number is $5n$ [8,10]; for the power mapping with the exponentiation as a Mersenne number such as x^{2^e-1}, this number is $3n$ [35]. The security of RAIN and AIM against attacks exploiting algebraic properties such as Gröbner basis attack, is carefully evaluated by representing primitives in equations over both $\mathbb{F}_2$ and $\mathbb{F}_{2^n}$ of the highest degree to ensure the algebraic analysis infeasible.

In this subsection, we further leverage Proposition 1, and propose a new method of deriving quadratic equations from two S-boxes in the form of power mappings. More specifically, in the first step, by linearizing the S-box in the first non-linear layer, we obtain independent linear equations, and free variables for the secret key bits. In the next step, we construct quadratic equations from the second S-box. By substituting unknown variables with free variables obtained in the previous step, we get a sufficient number of linearly independent quadratic equations, enabling us to solve all free variables.

In the following, we describe details on how to construct linear equations and quadratic equations from the S-boxes of power mappings.

Deriving Linear Equations from x^d. Recall that d is one divisor of $2^n - 1$. We observe that for such a d, we can obtain linearly independent equations from $x^d = \alpha$. For example, let the field be $\mathbb{F}_{2^8}$. If we guess $x^5 = 1$, then we can obtain the equation $x^{16} + x = 0$ because $x^{16} = (x^5)^3 \cdot \dot{x} = x$. Representing the map $x \mapsto x^{16}$ as a matrix multiplication $x \mapsto Mx$, we can find that 4 out of 8 equations from $Mx + x = 0$ are linearly independent, which can be used to solve for x.

Suppose $d \cdot s_1 + 2^{t_1} = d \cdot s_2 + 2^{t_2}$, by guessing $x^d = \alpha$, we can obtain one linear equation $\alpha^{s_1} \cdot x^{2^{t_1}} + \alpha^{s_2} \cdot x^{2^{t_2}} = 0$ because $(x^d)^{s_1} \cdot x^{2^{t_1}} = (x^d)^{s_2} \cdot x^{2^{t_2}}$. The number of linearly independent equations (denoted by γ) can be found by experiment.

Deriving Quadratic Equations from x^d. We notice that when guessing $x^5 = 1$, we obtain the quadratic equation $x^4 \cdot x + 1 = 0$. More generally, we can obtain quadratic equations from expressions of the form x^d as follows.

Suppose $d \cdot s_1 + 2^{t_1} + 2^{t_2} = d \cdot s_2 + 2^{t_3} + 2^{t_4}$, we have quadratic equations $\alpha^{s_1} \cdot x^{2^{t_1}} \cdot x^{2^{t_2}} + \alpha^{s_2} \cdot x^{2^{t_3}} \cdot x^{2^{t_4}} = 0$ because $(x^d)^{s_1} \cdot x^{2^{t_1}} \cdot x^{2^{t_2}} = (x^d)^{s_2} \cdot x^{2^{t_3}} \cdot x^{2^{t_4}}$.

Deriving Equations for the S-Boxes. The S-boxes in both RAIN and AIM are power functions of the form $S(x) = x^h$. These functions can be leveraged in two ways to exploit their algebraic structures.

The first method involves linearizing x^h by making a guess for x^d and using the expression $x^h = (x^d)^s \cdot x^{2^t}$. The output of the S-box can be denoted as y, and this technique can be used to simplify the algebraic representation of $S(x)$.

The second method involves representing both S-boxes as quadratic equations. Subsequent subsections will provide more details on this approach.

Attack Framework. To summarize, our attacks on RAIN and AIM follow a similar framework, which can be outlined as follows:

1. Guess the value of x^d, where x and d are carefully chosen bases and exponents, respectively.
2. Derive a sufficient number of linear and quadratic equations over $\mathbb{F}_2$ from x^d and the internal relations of RAIN/AIM.

3. Solve the equations using linearization techniques and Gaussian elimination.

Under the new general algebraic attack framework, we will demonstrate the effectiveness of our attacks by applying it to two-round RAIN and full rounds of AIM-III in the following subsections.

4.2   Attack on Two-Round RAIN

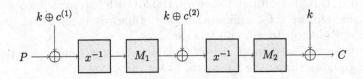

Fig. 3. RAIN permutation with $r = 2$.

The structure of the two-round RAIN is illustrated in Fig. 3. Once more, by two-round RAIN we mean two regular rounds of the RAIN permutation.

For an even value n, an (partially) integer factorization of $2^n - 1$ can be obtained by repeatedly applying the squared difference formula:

$$2^n - 1 = (2^{n/2} + 1) \cdot (2^{n/4} + 1) \cdots (2^{n/2^t} - 1),$$

where t is the maximum i such that 2^i is a divisor of n. In our parameter sets for the attack on two-round RAIN cipher, the divisor d is always of the form $2^w + 1$, where w is a positive integer.

Linearization of the First S-Box. The first step in our attack involves guessing the value of $(P + k + c^{(1)})^d = \alpha$, which linearizes the expression of the first S-box by $(P+k+c^{(1)})^{-1} = ((P+k+c^{(1)})^d)^s \cdot (P+k+c^{(1)})^{2^t} = \alpha^s \cdot (P+k+c^{(1)})^{2^t}$, because the first term is constant and the second one is linear. We then obtain γ linearly independent equations about the variables $\{k_i\}_{i \in [n]}$ from the equation $(P+k+c^{(1)})^{2^{2w}} = (P+k+c^{(1)})^{(2^w+1)(2^w-1)} \cdot (P+k+c^{(1)}) = \alpha^{2^w-1} \cdot (P+k+c^{(1)})$. Based on experimental evidence, the value of γ is always $n - 2w$. Consequently, each variable $\{k_i\}_{i \in [n]}$ can be expressed as a linear combination of $n - \gamma = 2w$ free variables $v \triangleq \{v_i\}_{i \in [2w]}$. The degree of freedom in this case is $|v| = 2w$.

Deriving Quadratic Equations from the Second S-Box. We can express the input of the second S-box as a linear combination of v. Similarly, the output of the second S-box, which can be obtained by computing $M_2^{-1}(k+C)$ backward, can also be expressed as a linear combination of v. For convenience, we denote the input and the output of the second S-box as $L_1(v)$ and $L_2(v)$, respectively. It is well-known that one can find overdefined quadratic equations from the multiplicative inverse function over $\mathbb{F}_{2^n}$ [12]. Thus we can then derive $3n$ quadratic equations:

$$L_1(v) \cdot L_2(v) = 1, \quad L_1^2(v) \cdot L_2(v) = L_1(v), \quad L_1(v) \cdot L_2^2(v) = L_2(v). \quad (4)$$

After substituting the variables $\{k_i\}_{i \in [n]}$ with $|v|$ new free variables v_i, we obtain $3n$ quadratic equations. Let m denote the number of linearly independent quadratic equations. If we choose the parameters appropriately such that $m = |v| + |v|(|v|-1)/2$, we can solve these equations using the linearization technique.

The Cost of Expressing Quadratic Equations by Free Variables. We first discuss the number of terms in the multiplication of two polynomials modulo an irreducible polynomial.

Let $a(x) = \sum_{i \in [n]} a_i x^i$ and $b(x) = \sum_{i \in [n]} b_i x^i$ be two polynomials, where the coefficients a_i, b_i are defined over some field $\mathbb{F}$, and x is called the indeterminate. If we consider the polynomials as abstract entities only, which are never evaluated, then the product $a(x) \cdot b(x) = \sum_{i \in [n], j \in [n]} a_i b_j x^{i+j}$ has exactly n^2 terms. However, when applying modular reduction operations by an irreducible polynomial, the number of terms in the product may increase, which makes it difficult to provide a formula to calculate the exact number of terms. In RAIN, the irreducible polynomials for the three security parameters are fixed (they are exactly the same for AIM), so we can compute the exact terms of the multiplication modulo the corresponding irreducible polynomials. Our computed results for the number of terms in the modulo multiplication over the three finite fields $\mathbb{F}_{2^n}$, $n \in \{128, 192, 256\}$, are presented in Table 2. Based on our findings, we are able to safely assume that the number of terms after applying modulo operations will not exceed $3n^2$.

Table 2. Number of terms in multiplication modulo irreducible polynomials for RAIN and AIM.

Finite Field	n	n^2	#Terms
$\mathbb{F}_{2^{128}}$	128	16,384	40,832
$\mathbb{F}_{2^{192}}$	192	36,864	91,936
$\mathbb{F}_{2^{256}}$	256	65,536	163,580

Let us backtrack to the phase of deriving quadratic equations for the second S-box. We observe that we can rewrite the quadratic equations in Eq. (4) uniformly as

$$\mathcal{L}_1(v) \cdot \mathcal{L}_2(v) = \mathcal{L}_3(v)$$

where $\mathcal{L}_i(v)$ $(i = 1, 2, 3)$ is a set of linear functions of free variables v. This means that the maximum number of terms that we will need to represent using new free variables is $3n^2|v|^2 + n|v|$. In the following complexity estimation, the cost of this step will be estimated as $\mathcal{O}(n^2|v|^2)$. However, we will provide a discussion on the impact of the hidden constant in the big $\mathcal{O}$ notation on the complexity of our attack.

Complexity Analysis. There are $(|\mathbb{F}_{2^n}| - 1)/d$ possible choices for the guess of α. For each guess, it takes $\mathcal{O}(n^3)$ time to find the free variables. Then it costs $\mathcal{O}(n^2|v|^2)$ time to express the $3n$ quadratic equations in terms of the free variables. Finally, we find and solve m linearly independent quadratic equations in $\mathcal{O}(m^3)$ time. The total time complexity is counted as $T_{\text{bit}} = (2^n - 1)/d \cdot \max\{n^3, n^2|v|^2, m^3\}$. To express the complexity in terms of the number of encryptions, we divide by n^3 to obtain $T = T_{\text{bit}}/n^3$. Since our approach only requires storing the equations, the memory complexity can be omitted.

Parameter Sets of Our Attacks. Our detailed results on all three versions of two-round RAIN are listed in Table 3. We note that parameter s is involved in the equation $2^n - 2 = d \cdot s + 2^t$, thus can easily be obtained by checking $(2^n - 2 - 2^t) \mod d = 0$. Due to its excessive length and it is not directly involved in the formula for the computation of complexity, we omit s from Table 3.

Table 3. Results for two-round RAIN. n denotes both the block size and the security parameter, r is the number of algorithmic rounds, $d = 2^w + 1$ represents a divisor of $2^n - 1$, t is defined by $d \cdot s + 2^t = 2^n - 2$, $|v|$ denotes the number of free variables, m denotes the number of variables in linearized quadratic equations, and T is the recalculated time complexity of our attack.

Scheme	n	r	d	t	w	$|v|$	m	T
RAIN-128	128	2	$2^8 + 1$	8	8	16	136	$2^{120.3}$
RAIN-192	192	2	$2^{16} + 1$	16	16	32	528	$2^{180.4}$
RAIN-256	256	2	$2^{16} + 1$	16	16	32	528	$2^{243.1}$

The Hidden Constant Factor in Big $\mathcal{O}$ and the Impacts. In the estimation of the time complexity of our attack, we omit the constant factor behind the big $\mathcal{O}$ notations and consider the most dominant part only. We argue that such estimation is proper both in theory and in practice.

In the step of expressing the quadratic equations with new free variables, the maximum number of terms that we will need to represent is $3n^2|v|^2 + n|v|$. Therefore, to express three sets of equations as free variables in the RAIN, the cost will be

$$3 \times (3n^2|v|^2 + n|v|) = 9n^2|v|^2 + 3n|v| \leq 10n^2|v|^2. \tag{5}$$

The steps of deriving free variables and solving quadratic equations are basically the execution of Gaussian elimination. We estimate the concrete bit complexity as n^3 and m^3, respectively. However, we point out they can be solved in $\mathcal{O}(n^\omega)$ and $\mathcal{O}(m^\omega)$ time respectively by using more sophisticated methods, such as the Strassen algorithm [40] ($\omega \approx 2.807$) or Coppersmith-Winograd algorithm [9] ($\omega \approx 2.376$). In recent algebraic attacks, both $\omega = 2.37$ and 2.8 are used [1,31].

On the one hand, the constant in Eq. (5) is just an upper bound which is quite loose. Besides, the constants are affected by many factors, such as the algorithm, the implementation, and the computing architecture. So it is meaningful to estimate the time complexity by ignoring constants and focusing on the most dominant part.

Toy Example. We provide a concrete example for the attack on two-round RAIN, which can be found in Appendix A.2.

Negligible Failure Probability. It is worth pointing out that the equation $y = x^{|\mathbb{F}|-2}$ can be represented as $xy = 1$ only when $x \neq 0$. Fortunately, this probability is exponentially small. In particular, in the context of an MPC-in-the-head-based signature scheme such as [6,14,15,20,26], the input of the S-box must be non-zero, or else it would be rejected and re-sample again. Therefore, this issue is minor and can be safely ignored.

On Three- or More-Round RAIN. At present, our attack strategy is not effective for three or more rounds of RAIN. Following the strategy of our attack for reduced rounds of RAIN, we linearize the S-box in the first round as before. In order to express the relation between the S-boxes in the second and the last round, the introduction of new variables is required. As a result, the resulting equations become too complex to be solved efficiently because the number of unknown variables increases significantly.

4.3 Description of AIM

Let x, y be the input and output respectively. Let ℓ be the number of S-boxes of the first layer. Let $e_1, \ldots, e_\ell, e_* \in \mathbb{N}$ be some constant. The S-boxes of AIM are exponentiation by Mersenne numbers, denoted as $\mathsf{Mer}[e] : \mathbb{F}_{2^n} \to \mathbb{F}_{2^n}$. More precisely, it is

$$\mathsf{Mer}[e](x) = x^{2^e - 1}.$$

As an extension, $\mathsf{Mer}[e_1, \ldots, e_\ell] : \mathbb{F}_{2^n} \to \mathbb{F}_{2^n}^\ell$ is defined by

$$\mathsf{Mer}[e_1, \ldots, e_\ell](x) = \mathsf{Mer}[e_1](x) \| \ldots \| \mathsf{Mer}[e_\ell](x).$$

The affine layer, denoted as Lin, is multiplication by an $n \times \ell n$ random binary matrix A_{iv} followed by an addition of a random constant $b_{\mathrm{iv}} \in \mathbb{F}_{2^n}$. Both A_{iv} and b_{iv} are generated by an extendable output function (XOF) with a (public) initial vector iv.

Overall, the $\mathsf{AIM}_{\mathrm{iv}} : \mathbb{F}_{2^n} \to \mathbb{F}_{2^n}$ function is defined by

$$\mathsf{AIM}_{\mathrm{iv}}(x) = \mathsf{Mer}[e_*] \circ \mathsf{Lin}[\mathrm{iv}] \circ \mathsf{Mer}[e_1, \cdots, e_\ell](x) \oplus x.$$

A graphical overview of the construction is shown in Fig. 4.

Parameter Sets. The recommended sets of parameters of AIM are listed in Table 4. As a one-way function used in signature schemes, y and iv are public, x is private. The irreducible polynomials for extension fields $\mathbb{F}_{2^{128}}$, $\mathbb{F}_{2^{192}}$ and $\mathbb{F}_{2^{256}}$ are the same as those used in RAIN.

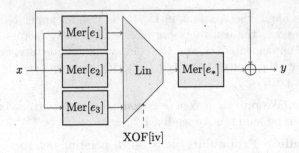

Fig. 4. The AIM-based one-way function with $\ell = 3$.

Table 4. Recommended sets of parameters of AIM.

Scheme	n	ℓ	e_1	e_2	e_3	e_*
AIM-I	128	2	3	27	–	5
AIM-III	192	2	5	29	–	7
AIM-V	256	3	3	53	7	5

4.4   Attack on AIM-III

We discovered a flaw in the design of AIM: the inputs of the S-boxes in the first nonlinear layer are identical, with no offset. This makes it possible for an attacker to linearize all the S-boxes in the first nonlinear layer at the same time. For AIM-III (the 192-bit version), we are able to exploit this flaw to mount a non-trivial attack.

In AIM-III, the first nonlinear layer comprises two S-boxes, namely $x^{2^{e_1}-1}$ and $x^{2^{e_2}-1}$, where $e_1 = 5$ and $e_2 = 29$. By guessing the value of $x^d = \alpha$ for $d = 45$, we can linearize these S-boxes using $x^{2^{e_i}-1} = (x^d)^{s_i} \cdot x^{2^{t_i}}, i \in \{1,2\}$. (Note that $x^{2^{e_1}-1} = x^{2^{e_1}-1+|\mathbb{F}_{2^n}|-1}$)

The subsequent steps of the attack are similar to those used for the two-round RAIN. We can obtain $\gamma = 180$ linearly independent equations involving variables $\{x_i\}_{i \in [n]}$ from the equations $x^{2^{12}} = (x^{45})^{91} \cdot x = \alpha^{91} \cdot x$. Thus, we can express each $\{x_i\}_{i \in [n]}$ as a linear combination of $n - \gamma = 12$ free variables, denoted as $v \triangleq \{v_i\}_{i \in [12]}$. Consequently, the degree of freedom is $|v| = 12$.

The input of the second non-linear layer can be expressed as a linear combination of the free variables v. Similarly, the output of the second non-linear layer, obtained by computing $x + y$ in the backward pass, can also be expressed as a linear combination of v. Let us denote the input and output of the second non-linear layer as $L_1(v)$ and $L_2(v)$ respectively. Then, we can write n quadratic equations:

$$L_1(v) \cdot L_2(v) = L_1(v)^{2^{e_*}}$$

To solve the system of n quadratic equations, we can substitute the variables $\{x_i\}$ with $|v|$ new free variables $\{v_i\}$. This results in n quadratic equations in the variables v_i. Let the number of linearly independent quadratic equations be denoted by m. We have found that $m = |v| + |v|(|v| - 1)/2$. Hence, we can use linearization techniques to solve these equations.

Complexity Analysis. The analysis is almost identical to the one for the attack on two-round RAIN. The only difference for AIM resides in the cost of expressing the quadratic equations arising from the second S-box by free variables. Following the analysis method for RAIN in Sect. 4, we conclude that the new cost of expressing the quadratic equations is $3n^2|v|^2 + n|v| \leq 4n^2|v|^2$.

Parameter Sets of Our Attack. Our results on AIM are listed in Table 5. We omit the parameter s_i due to its excessive length. We note that s_i is related to the equation $2^{e_i} - 1 = d \cdot s_i + 2^{t_i}$, where $(2^{e_i} - 1 - 2^{t_i}) \bmod d = 0$, can be easily verified.

Table 5. Results for AIM. n denotes both the block size and the security parameter, $d = 2^w + 1$ represents a divisor of $2^n - 1$, t_i is defined by $d \cdot s_i + 2^{t_i} = 2^{e_i} - 1$ for $i = 1, 2$, $|v|$ denotes the number of free variables, m denotes the number of variables in linearized quadratic equations, and T is the recalculated time complexity of our attack.

Scheme	n	d	t_1	t_2	$|v|$	m	T
AIM-I	128	5	1	1	4	10	$2^{125.7}$
AIM-III	192	45	8	8	12	78	$2^{186.5}$
AIM-V	256	3	0	0	2	3	$2^{254.4}$

On AIM-I and AIM-V. We also analyzed the security of AIM-I and AIM-V using a similar technique for RAIN. We found that only $d = 3$ or $d = 5$ is a suitable choice of the divisor of $2^n - 1$. By substituting these parameters into the complexity formula, we obtain complexity estimations for AIM-I and AIM-V as $2^{125.7}$ and $2^{254.4}$ encryptions respectively. These complexities are only about $3 \sim 5$ times better than a brute-force attack, which is not considered as significant, so we do not take them as our contribution.

5 Implementation and Final Remarks

5.1 Experimental Verification of Our Attacks

We implement attacks on two-round RAIN and AIM-III described in Sect. 4. As mentioned earlier, our attacks require a sufficient number of linearly independent linear equations and quadratic equations. However, providing an explicit formula for determining the number of linearly independent equations from the equation

$x^d = \alpha$ is challenging. Therefore, we resort to programming to determine these equations. Our implementation can be found at

https://github.com/kzoacn/LargeSbox/.

In our code, we randomly sample an instance for either RAIN or AIM, which includes round constants and linear layers. We then randomly pick $\alpha \in \{x^d : x \in \mathbb{F}_{2^n}^*\}$ and determine the number of linearly independent linear equations in this instance. Next, we identify the free variables and substitute them into the final quadratic equations. Finally, we verify that the number of linearly independent quadratic equations is sufficient to solve all the unknown variables.

We also estimate the complexity concretely. Both of our approach and brute force follow the Guess-and-Determine framework, which allowed us to estimate the complexity by multiplying the duration of each trial by the total number of trials. The experimental outcomes align well with the theoretical predictions. However, it is worth pointing out that creating fair comparisons is challenging due to the impact of engineering optimizations on concrete complexity.[4]

5.2   Restoring the Security of AIM

Preventing the Simultaneous Linearization of Multiple S-boxes. Our attack on full AIM-III depends on that we can linearize both the S-boxes in the first non-linear layer simultaneously. Based on this, for the AIM cipher, we can easily recommend implementing a patch to enhance its resistance against our attack. The proposed patch involves incorporating offsets for each S-box in the first non-linear layer, for instance, XORing a random constant c_i before the operation of the S-box Mer$[e_i]$, as illustrated in Fig. 5. The constant c_i's might be generated by an XOF, which is of low cost. By applying this patch, our attack is effectively mitigated as we can no longer linearize the S-boxes in the first layer simultaneously. We are not aware of attacks arising from involving extra random constants before the S-boxes in the setting of a single plaintext/ciphertext pair. Moreover, this patch can be seamlessly integrated into the MPC-in-the-head paradigm with minimal additional cost.

Restricting n to be Odd. We are aware that our attack highly relies on a foundational fact that the power function in RAIN and AIM can be represented as $(x^d)^s \cdot x^{2^t}$, where d is a divisor of $2^n - 1$. Recall that for an even n, $2^n - 1$ has a special factorization $2^n - 1 = (2^{n/2} + 1) \cdot (2^{n/4} + 1) \cdots (2^{n/2^t} - 1)$, where t is the maximal value of i such that 2^i divides n. However, this factorization can not be applied to an odd n. Therefore, the easiest way to prevent our attack is simply restricting n to an odd number.

---

[4] We refer interested readers to a faster implementation utilizing SIMD instructions for RAIN (https://github.com/IAIK/rainier-signatures).

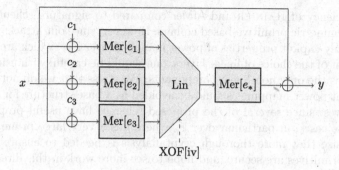

Fig. 5. Fixed AIM one way function with $\ell = 3$.

Increasing the Number of Rounds. A third alternative is to increase the number of rounds used in AIM, which can be achieved by appending more S-box operations after Mer$[e_*]$, such that the solving complexity of the system of equations is high enough to make the scheme secure against our attack. However, the main disadvantage of this approach is the loss of efficiency because applying more S-boxes would result in a higher number of multiplications, which might be detrimental for the signature schemes that are built upon AIM.

5.3 RAIN

As has been emphasized earlier, our attacks do not affect the security of the signature scheme RAINIER which uses three or more rounds of RAIN. However, we point out that for an even n, the essential decomposition of the multiplicative inverse function always holds. With a divisor d of $2^n - 1$, $\{x^d : x \in \mathbb{F}_{2^n} \setminus \{0\}\}$ is a subgroup of the multiplicative group $\mathbb{F}_{2^n}^*$ of the finite field $\mathbb{F}_{2^n}$. Therefore x^d has only $|\mathbb{F}_{2^n}^*|/d$ possible choices. Linearization of one round S-box can easily be accomplished. This might potentially be combined with other techniques, to threaten the security of RAIN.

5.4 On Other Relevant Symmetric Primitives

RAIN shares the similarity to MiMC [2], JARVIS [4] and instances of *Vision* [3], using a single large S-box covering the entire permutation state. While we have not discovered more novel attacks on the aforementioned ciphers based on the observation in this paper, we anticipate that it will contribute valuable insights to the understanding of these symmetric primitives.

6 Conclusion

In the past years, there have been remarkable advances in MPC-friendly symmetric primitive-based signatures. Constructing non-linear layers (S-boxes) by power mappings has proven advantageous in such signature schemes, exemplified by the efficiency of RAINIER and AIMer compared to signature schemes based on other symmetric primitive-based ciphers. However, since our attacks on RAIN and AIM only exploit properties of power mappings over $\mathbb{F}_{2^n}$, which are actually independent of the choice of linear layers, one should be careful with using power mappings as the only non-linear components. We stress that we do not mean to suggest that power mappings should be avoided as a base structure for symmetric primitives, since several of the proposed schemes have useful properties in relevant use cases, in particular over $\mathbb{F}_p$ where p is a very large prime. Rather, we emphasize that more thorough cryptanalysis is needed to ensure that the proposed primitives are secure, and hope to see more work in this direction.

Acknowledgments. Yu Yu was supported by the National Key Research and Development Program of China (Grant No. 2020YFA0309705) and the National Natural Science Foundation of China (Grant Nos. 62125204 and 92270201). This work was also supported in part by the National Key Research and Development Program of China (Grant No. 2018YFA0704701) and the Major Program of Guangdong Basic and Applied Research (Grant No. 2019B030302008). This work has been supported by the New Cornerstone Science Foundation through the XPLORER PRIZE.

A   Toy Examples of Attacks on Reduced-Round RAIN

In this section, we concretely present toy examples for one-round RAIN and two-round RAIN, which would help the readers understand our attacks via examples. We choose the field $\mathbb{F}_{2^4}$ with irreducible polynomial $f(x) = x^4 + x + 1$.

Notation. For an element $a_0 + a_1x + a_2x^2 + a_3x^3$ of field $\mathbb{F}_{2^4}$, $a_i \in \mathbb{F}_2$, we may express it in several equivalent forms:

1. Polynomial representation, i.e. $a_0 + a_1x + a_2x^2 + a_3x^3$.
2. Binary representation, i.e. $a_0a_1a_2a_3$.
3. Vector of $\mathbb{F}_2$, i.e. (a_0, a_1, a_2, a_3)

Concretely, $1 + x + x^3$ is equivalent to 1101 or $(1, 1, 0, 1)$. And 1 is equivalent to 1000 or $(1, 0, 0, 0)$. We also use the notation $(1, 1, 0, 1)^2 = (1 + x + x^3)^2 = 1 + x^3 = (1, 0, 0, 1)$

Power Function. We first show the square function over $\mathbb{F}_{2^4}$ is linear.

$$(a_0 + a_1x + a_2x^2 + a_3x^3)^2 \bmod f(x)$$
$$= (a_0 + a_1x^2 + a_2x^4 + a_3x^6) \bmod f(x)$$
$$= a_0 + a_1x^2 + a_2(x + 1) + a_3(x^3 + x^2)$$
$$= (a_0 + a_2) + a_2x + (a_1 + a_3)x^2 + a_3x^3$$

So we can use the notation $(a_0, a_1, a_2, a_3)^2 = (a_0 + a_2, a_2, a_1 + a_3, a_3)$. Similarly, we can have $(a_0, a_1, a_2, a_3)^4 = (a_0 + a_1 + a_2 + a_3, a_1 + a_3, a_2 + a_3, a_3)$.

Parameter Sets. We choose $P = 0000, c^{(1)} = 0010, c^{(2)} = 0001, k = 0100$ and

$$M_1 = \begin{bmatrix} 1\,0\,1\,0 \\ 0\,1\,0\,0 \\ 0\,0\,1\,0 \\ 1\,0\,0\,1 \end{bmatrix}, \quad M_2 = \begin{bmatrix} 1\,1\,0\,0 \\ 0\,0\,1\,0 \\ 0\,1\,0\,0 \\ 1\,0\,0\,1 \end{bmatrix}, \quad M_2^{-1} = \begin{bmatrix} 1\,0\,1\,0 \\ 0\,0\,1\,0 \\ 0\,1\,0\,0 \\ 1\,0\,1\,1 \end{bmatrix}.$$

For convenience, we precompute some values and list them on Table 6. Let $d = 3$. As you can see, $x^d, x \neq 0$ takes only $15/3 = 5$ possible choices.

Table 6. Table for $\mathbb{F}_{2^4}$.

x	x^{-1}	$M_1(x)$	$M_2(x)$	x^3
0000	0000	0000	0000	0000
1000	1000	1001	1001	1000
0100	1001	0100	1010	0001
1100	0111	1101	0011	1111
0010	1011	1010	0100	0011
1010	1101	0011	1101	0101
0110	1110	1110	1110	1000
1110	0110	0111	0111	1000
0001	1111	0001	0001	0101
1001	0100	1000	1000	1111
0101	0011	0101	1011	1111
1101	1010	1100	0010	0011
0011	0101	1011	0101	0001
1011	0010	0010	1100	0101
0111	1100	1111	1111	0001
1111	0001	0110	0110	0011

A.1   One-Round RAIN

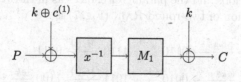

Fig. 6. RAIN permutation with $r = 1$.

The encryption of one-round RAIN (Fig. 6) is :

$$P = 0000 \xrightarrow{\oplus k \oplus c^{(1)}} 0110 \xrightarrow{x^{-1}} 1110 \xrightarrow{M_1(\cdot)} 0111 \xrightarrow{\oplus k} 0011 = C. \tag{6}$$

We guess the value of $(P + k + c^{(1)})^3$ over $(2^4 - 1)/3 = 5$ possible choices. Suppose we guess $(P + k + c^{(1)})^3 = 1$. The following steps will be repeated for each guess, here we only show the execution for the correct guess which is $(P + k + c^{(1)})^3 = 1$. So we have

$$
\begin{aligned}
(P + k + c^{(1)})^{-1} &= (P + k + c^{(1)})^{14} \\
&= (P + k + c^{(1)})^{3 \cdot 4} \cdot (P + k + c^{(1)})^2 \\
&= (P + k + c^{(1)})^2 \\
&= (k_0, k_1, k_2 + 1, k_3)^2 \\
&= (k_0 + k_2 + 1, k_2 + 1, k_1 + k_3, k_3)
\end{aligned} \tag{7}
$$

$$\xrightarrow{M_1(\cdot)} \quad (k_0 + k_1 + k_2 + k_3 + 1, k_2 + 1, k_1 + k_3, k_0 + k_2 + k_3 + 1)$$

$$\xrightarrow{\oplus k} \quad (k_1 + k_2 + k_3 + 1, k_1 + k_2 + 1, k_1 + k_2 + k_3, k_0 + k_2 + 1)$$

$$= (0, 0, 1, 1)$$

$$= C$$

By solving the linear equations, we can obtain two candidate keys $k^* = 0100$ and $k^{**} = 0010$. Given the public input P and output C, it is easy to check by executing the one-round encryption in Eq. (6) that k^* is the correct key.

A.2   Two-Round RAIN

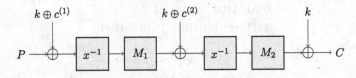

Fig. 7. RAIN permutation with $r = 2$.

We follow the notations and the parameter choices as in the attack on one-round RAIN. The encryption of two-round RAIN (Fig. 7) is :

$$P = 0000 \xrightarrow{\oplus k \oplus c^{(1)}} 0110 \xrightarrow{x^{-1}} 1110 \xrightarrow{M_1(\cdot)} 0111$$

$$\xrightarrow{\oplus k \oplus c^{(2)}} 0010 \xrightarrow{x^{-1}} 1011 \xrightarrow{M_2(\cdot)} 1100 \xrightarrow{\oplus k} 1000 = C.$$

– We linearize the first S-box by guessing $(P+k+c^{(1)})^3 = 1$ as in the previous attack on one-round. Then we have the following linear equations:

$$
\begin{aligned}
0 &= (P+k+c^{(1)})^4 + (P+k+c^{(1)}) \\
&= (k_0, k_1, k_2+1, k_3)^4 + (k_0, k_1, k_2+1, k_3) \\
&= (k_0+k_1+k_2+k_3+1, k_1+k_3, k_2+k_3+1, k_3) + (k_0, k_1, k_2+1, k_3) \\
&= (k_1+k_2+k_3+1, k_3, k_3, 0)
\end{aligned}
$$

This gives us two linearly independent equations:

$$
\begin{cases}
k_1 + k_2 = 1 \\
\quad\quad k_3 = 0
\end{cases}
$$

Consequently, we can decide on two free variables k_0, k_2 and two basic variables $k_1 = k_2 + 1, k_3 = 0$.

– Next, we compute the input of the second S-box $M_1(P+k+c^{(1)})^{-1}$. Substituting M_1 as we choose and substituting the expression of $(P+k+c^{(1)})^{-1}$ as in Eq. (7), we get the following

$$
M_1(P+k+c^{(1)})^{-1} = (k_0+k_1+k_2+k_3+1, k_2+1, k_1+k_3, k_0+k_2+k_3+1)
$$
$$
\xrightarrow{\oplus k \oplus c^{(2)}} (k_1+k_2+k_3+1, k_1+k_2+1, k_1+k_2+k_3, k_0+k_2)
$$
$$
\xrightarrow{\text{using free vars.}} (0, 0, 1, k_0+k_2)
$$

Backward, represent the output of the second S-box and we have

$$
M_2^{-1}(k+C) = (k_0+k_2+1, k_2, k_1, k_0+k_2+k_3+1)
$$
$$
\xrightarrow{\text{using free vars.}} (k_0+k_2+1, k_2, k_2+1, k_0+k_2+1)
$$

Because the multiplication of the input and the output of the second S-box equals 1, thus we can write down the following quadratic equations:

$$
(0, 0, 1, k_0+k_2) \cdot (k_0+k_2+1, k_2, k_2+1, k_0+k_2+1) = 1
$$
$$
\rightarrow (k_0 k_2 + 1, k_2, k_0 k_2 + k_0, k_2) = 1
$$

By solving the linear equation, we can obtain a candidate key $k^* = 0100$. Given the public input P and the output C, it is easy to check that k^* is the correct key by executing two-round RAIN encryption.

References

1. Albrecht, M.R., et al.: Algebraic cryptanalysis of STARK-friendly designs: application to MARVELLOUS and MiMC. In: Galbraith, S.D., Moriai, S. (eds.) ASIACRYPT 2019, Part III. LNCS, vol. 11923, pp. 371–397. Springer, Cham (2019). https://doi.org/10.1007/978-3-030-34618-8_13

2. Albrecht, M., Grassi, L., Rechberger, C., Roy, A., Tiessen, T.: MiMC: efficient encryption and cryptographic hashing with minimal multiplicative complexity. In: Cheon, J.H., Takagi, T. (eds.) ASIACRYPT 2016, Part I. LNCS, vol. 10031, pp. 191–219. Springer, Heidelberg (2016). https://doi.org/10.1007/978-3-662-53887-6_7

3. Aly, A., Ashur, T., Ben-Sasson, E., Dhooghe, S., Szepieniec, A.: Design of symmetric-key primitives for advanced cryptographic protocols. IACR Trans. Symm. Cryptol. 2020(3), 1–45 (2020). https://doi.org/10.13154/tosc.v2020.i3.1-45

4. Ashur, T., Dhooghe, S.: MARVELlous: a STARK-friendly family of cryptographic primitives. Cryptology ePrint Archive, Report 2018/1098 (2018). https://eprint.iacr.org/2018/1098

5. Banik, S., Barooti, K., Vaudenay, S., Yan, H.: New attacks on LowMC instances with a single plaintext/ciphertext pair. In: Tibouchi, M., Wang, H. (eds.) ASIACRYPT 2021, Part I. LNCS, vol. 13090, pp. 303–331. Springer, Cham (2021). https://doi.org/10.1007/978-3-030-92062-3_11

6. Baum, C., de Saint Guilhem, C.D., Kales, D., Orsini, E., Scholl, P., Zaverucha, G.: Banquet: short and fast signatures from AES. In: Garay, J.A. (ed.) PKC 2021, Part I. LNCS, vol. 12710, pp. 266–297. Springer, Cham (2021). https://doi.org/10.1007/978-3-030-75245-3_11

7. Chase, M., et al.: Post-quantum zero-knowledge and signatures from symmetric-key primitives. In: Thuraisingham, B.M., Evans, D., Malkin, T., Xu, D. (eds.) ACM CCS 2017, pp. 1825–1842. ACM Press (2017). https://doi.org/10.1145/3133956.3133997

8. Cheon, J.H., Lee, D.H.: Resistance of S-boxes against algebraic attacks. In: Roy, B., Meier, W. (eds.) FSE 2004. LNCS, vol. 3017, pp. 83–93. Springer, Heidelberg (2004). https://doi.org/10.1007/978-3-540-25937-4_6

9. Coppersmith, D., Winograd, S.: Matrix multiplication via arithmetic progressions. In: Proceedings of the Nineteenth Annual ACM Symposium on Theory of Computing, pp. 1–6 (1987)

10. Courtois, N., Debraize, B., Garrido, E.: On exact algebraic [non-]immunity of S-boxes based on power functions. In: Batten, L.M., Safavi-Naini, R. (eds.) ACISP 06. LNCS, vol. 4058, pp. 76–86. Springer, Heidelberg (Jul 2006)

11. Courtois, N., Klimov, A., Patarin, J., Shamir, A.: Efficient algorithms for solving overdefined systems of multivariate polynomial equations. In: Preneel, B. (ed.) EUROCRYPT 2000. LNCS, vol. 1807, pp. 392–407. Springer, Heidelberg (2000). https://doi.org/10.1007/3-540-45539-6_27

12. Courtois, N.T., Pieprzyk, J.: Cryptanalysis of block ciphers with overdefined systems of equations. In: Zheng, Y. (ed.) ASIACRYPT 2002. LNCS, vol. 2501, pp. 267–287. Springer, Heidelberg (2002). https://doi.org/10.1007/3-540-36178-2_17

13. Daemen, J.: Limitations of the even-Mansour construction. In: Imai, H., Rivest, R.L., Matsumoto, T. (eds.) ASIACRYPT 1991. LNCS, vol. 739, pp. 495–498. Springer, Heidelberg (1993). https://doi.org/10.1007/3-540-57332-1_46

14. de Saint Guilhem, C.D., De Meyer, L., Orsini, E., Smart, N.P.: BBQ: using AES in picnic signatures. In: Paterson, K.G., Stebila, D. (eds.) SAC 2019. LNCS, vol. 11959, pp. 669–692. Springer, Cham (2020). https://doi.org/10.1007/978-3-030-38471-5_27

15. de Saint Guilhem, C., Orsini, E., Tanguy, T.: Limbo: efficient zero-knowledge MPCitH-based arguments. In: Vigna, G., Shi, E. (eds.) ACM CCS 2021, pp. 3022–3036. ACM Press (2021). https://doi.org/10.1145/3460120.3484595

16. Dinur, I., Dunkelman, O., Keller, N., Shamir, A.: Key recovery attacks on 3-round Even-Mansour, 8-step LED-128, and full AES^2. In: Sako, K., Sarkar, P. (eds.) ASIACRYPT 2013, Part I. LNCS, vol. 8269, pp. 337–356. Springer, Heidelberg (2013). https://doi.org/10.1007/978-3-642-42033-7_18

17. Dinur, I., Dunkelman, O., Keller, N., Shamir, A.: Cryptanalysis of iterated even-Mansour schemes with two keys. In: Sarkar, P., Iwata, T. (eds.) ASIACRYPT 2014, Part I. LNCS, vol. 8873, pp. 439–457. Springer, Heidelberg (2014). https://doi.org/10.1007/978-3-662-45611-8_23

18. Dinur, I., Liu, Y., Meier, W., Wang, Q.: Optimized interpolation attacks on LowMC. In: Iwata, T., Cheon, J.H. (eds.) ASIACRYPT 2015, Part II. LNCS, vol. 9453, pp. 535–560. Springer, Heidelberg (2015). https://doi.org/10.1007/978-3-662-48800-3_22

19. Dobraunig, C., Eichlseder, M., Mendel, F.: Higher-order cryptanalysis of LowMC. In: Kwon, S., Yun, A. (eds.) ICISC 2015. LNCS, vol. 9558, pp. 87–101. Springer, Cham (2016). https://doi.org/10.1007/978-3-319-30840-1_6

20. Dobraunig, C., Kales, D., Rechberger, C., Schofnegger, M., Zaverucha, G.: Shorter signatures based on tailor-made minimalist symmetric-key crypto. In: Yin, H., Stavrou, A., Cremers, C., Shi, E. (eds.) ACM CCS 2022, pp. 843–857. ACM Press (2022). https://doi.org/10.1145/3548606.3559353

21. Dunkelman, O., Keller, N., Shamir, A.: Slidex attacks on the Even-Mansour encryption scheme. J. Cryptol. **28**(1), 1–28 (2015). https://doi.org/10.1007/s00145-013-9164-7

22. Gupta, K.C., Ray, I.G.: Finding biaffine and quadratic equations for s-boxes based on power mappings. IEEE Trans. Inf. Theory **61**(4), 2200–2209 (2015). https://doi.org/10.1109/TIT.2014.2387052

23. Hülsing, A., et al.: SPHINCS$^+$. Technical report, National Institute of Standards and Technology (2022). https://csrc.nist.gov/Projects/post-quantum-cryptography/selected-algorithms-2022

24. Ishai, Y., Kushilevitz, E., Ostrovsky, R., Sahai, A.: Zero-knowledge from secure multiparty computation. In: Johnson, D.S., Feige, U. (eds.) 39th ACM STOC, pp. 21–30. ACM Press (2007). https://doi.org/10.1145/1250790.1250794

25. Katz, J., Kolesnikov, V., Wang, X.: Improved non-interactive zero knowledge with applications to post-quantum signatures. In: Lie, D., Mannan, M., Backes, M., Wang, X. (eds.) ACM CCS 2018, pp. 525–537. ACM Press (2018). https://doi.org/10.1145/3243734.3243805

26. Kim, S., et al.: AIM: symmetric primitive for shorter signatures with stronger security. Cryptology ePrint Archive, Report 2022/1387 (2022). https://eprint.iacr.org/2022/1387

27. Kipnis, A., Shamir, A.: Cryptanalysis of the HFE public key cryptosystem by relinearization. In: Wiener, M. (ed.) CRYPTO 1999. LNCS, vol. 1666, pp. 19–30. Springer, Heidelberg (1999). https://doi.org/10.1007/3-540-48405-1_2

28. Liu, F., Isobe, T., Meier, W.: Cryptanalysis of full LowMC and LowMC-M with algebraic techniques. In: Malkin, T., Peikert, C. (eds.) CRYPTO 2021. LNCS, vol. 12827, pp. 368–401. Springer, Cham (2021). https://doi.org/10.1007/978-3-030-84252-9_13

29. Liu, F., Mahzoun, M.: Algebraic attacks on RAIN and AIM using equivalent representations. IACR Cryptol. ePrint Arch. p. 1133 (2023). https://eprint.iacr.org/2023/1133

30. Liu, F., Meier, W., Sarkar, S., Isobe, T.: New low-memory algebraic attacks on LowMC in the Picnic setting. IACR Trans. Symm. Cryptol. 2022(3), 102–122 (2022). https://doi.org/10.46586/tosc.v2022.i3.102-122

31. Liu, F., Sarkar, S., Meier, W., Isobe, T.: Algebraic attacks on rasta and dasta using low-degree equations. In: Tibouchi, M., Wang, H. (eds.) ASIACRYPT 2021, Part I. LNCS, vol. 13090, pp. 214–240. Springer, Cham (2021). https://doi.org/10.1007/978-3-030-92062-3_8

32. Liu, F., Sarkar, S., Wang, G., Meier, W., Isobe, T.: Algebraic meet-in-the-middle attack on LowMC. In: Agrawal, S., Lin, D. (eds.) ASIACRYPT 2022, Part I. LNCS, vol. 13791, pp. 225–255. Springer, Heidelberg (2022). https://doi.org/10.1007/978-3-031-22963-3_8

33. Lyubashevsky, V., et al.: CRYSTALS-DILITHIUM. Technical report, National Institute of Standards and Technology (2022). https://csrc.nist.gov/Projects/post-quantum-cryptography/selected-algorithms-2022

34. Mullen, G.L., Panario, D.: Handbook of Finite Fields. CRC Press, Boca Raton (2013)

35. Nawaz, Y., Gupta, K.C., Gong, G.: Algebraic immunity of s-boxes based on power mappings: analysis and construction. IEEE Trans. Inf. Theory **55**(9), 4263–4273 (2009). https://doi.org/10.1109/TIT.2009.2025534

36. Nikolić, Ivica, Wang, Lei, Wu, Shuang: Cryptanalysis of round-reduced LED. In: Moriai, Shiho (ed.) FSE 2013. LNCS, vol. 8424, pp. 112–129. Springer, Heidelberg (2014). https://doi.org/10.1007/978-3-662-43933-3_7

37. Prest, T., et al.: FALCON. Technical report, National Institute of Standards and Technology (2022), available at https://csrc.nist.gov/Projects/post-quantum-cryptography/selected-algorithms-2022

38. Rechberger, C., Soleimany, H., Tiessen, T.: Cryptanalysis of low-data instances of full LowMCv2. IACR Trans. Symm. Cryptol. 2018(3), 163–181 (2018). https://doi.org/10.13154/tosc.v2018.i3.163-181

39. Srivastava, V., Baksi, A., Debnath, S.K.: An overview of hash based signatures. IACR Cryptol. ePrint Arch. p. 411 (2023). https://eprint.iacr.org/2023/411

40. Strassen, V., et al.: Gaussian elimination is not optimal. Numer. Math. **13**(4), 354–356 (1969)

Quantum Speed-Up for Multidimensional (Zero Correlation) Linear Distinguishers

Akinori Hosoyamada[✉]

NTT Social Informatics Laboratories, Tokyo, Japan
akinori.hosoyamada@ntt.com

Abstract. This paper shows how to achieve a quantum speed-up for multidimensional (zero correlation) linear distinguishers. A previous work by Kaplan et al. has already shown a quantum quadratic speed-up for one-dimensional linear distinguishers. However, classical linear cryptanalysis often exploits multidimensional approximations to achieve more efficient attacks, and in fact it is highly non-trivial whether Kaplan et al.'s technique can be extended into the multidimensional case. To remedy this, we investigate a new quantum technique to speed-up multidimensional linear distinguishers. Firstly, we observe that there is a close relationship between the subroutine of Simon's algorithm and linear correlations via Fourier transform. Specifically, a slightly modified version of Simon's subroutine, which we call Correlation Extraction Algorithm (CEA), can be used to speed-up multidimensional linear distinguishers. CEA also leads to a speed-up for multidimensional zero correlation distinguishers, as well as some integral distinguishers through the correspondence of zero correlation and integral properties shown by Bogdanov et al. and Sun et al. Furthermore, we observe possibility of a more than quadratic speed-ups for some special types of integral distinguishers when *multiple* integral properties exist. Especially, we show a single-query distinguisher on a 4-bit cell SPN cipher with the same integral property as 2.5-round AES. Our attacks are the first to observe such a speed-up for classical cryptanalytic techniques without relying on hidden periods or shifts. By replacing the Hadamard transform in CEA with the general quantum Fourier transform, our technique also speeds-up generalized linear distinguishers on an arbitrary finite abelian group.

Keywords: symmetric-key cryptography · quantum cryptanalysis · linear cryptanalysis · integral cryptanalysis · more-than-quadratic speed-up

1 Introduction

Research in the past decade has revealed possible quantum attacks on symmetric cryptosystems are not limited to the exhaustive key search with Grover's algorithm [30] or the collision search by the BHT algorithm [19]. A notable line of research is the one initiated by Kuwakado and Morii showing that

© International Association for Cryptologic Research 2023
J. Guo and R. Steinfeld (Eds.): ASIACRYPT 2023, LNCS 14440, pp. 311–345, 2023.
https://doi.org/10.1007/978-981-99-8727-6_11

Simon's algorithm breaks lots of classically secure schemes in polynomial time [13,42,45,46]. Other previous works show how to speed-up classical crypt-analytic techniques such as differential and linear cryptanalysis, MITM, and integral attacks [15,37,43]. Some recent papers study dedicated quantum collision attacks on concrete hash functions such as SHA-2 and SHA-3 [28,31,38,39].

In this paper, we investigate the possibility to achieve more quantum speed-up for major classical cryptanalytic techniques than previous works.

Q1 and Q2. For quantum cryptanalysis on symmetric cryptosystems, there are two attack models called Q1 and Q2 [43]. The Q1 model assumes the existence of a quantum computer but oracles of keyed functions are classical[1], whereas Q2 assumes that oracles are also quantum[2]. For instance, a Q2 attack on a cipher is allowed to query quantum superposition of messages to the encryption oracle. Such an attack is called a Quantum Chosen-Plaintext Attack (QCPA). This paper studies attacks in the Q2 model.

Significance of Studying Q2 Attacks. The Q1 model is more realistic than Q2 in that oracles in Q1 are the same as classical ones, and thus Q1 attacks become real threats as soon as a large-scale fault-tolerant quantum computer is available. Still, studying Q2 attacks is important for the following two reasons. First, a new non-trivial Q1 attack may be found based on Q2 attacks. For instance, the so-called offline Simon's algorithm by Bonnetain et al. [12], which is a Q1 attack, is developed by modifying the Q2 attack by Leander and May [47]. Second, Q2 attacks can be converted into Q1 attacks when the key length is sufficiently long: Let E_K be an n-bit block cipher with k-bit keys. Suppose that $k > 2n$, and that there is a Q2 attack on E_K with time complexity $T < 2^{k/2}$. Now, assume we are in the Q1 model and run the following attack. First, query all the (classical) inputs to E_K, storing the results in a qRAM. Second, simulate the quantum oracle of E_K by accessing the qRAM, and execute the Q2 attack with the simulated oracle. This is a valid Q1 attack since the resulting complexity $T' = \max\{T, 2^n\}$ is less than $2^{k/2}$, the complexity of the exhaustive key-search by Grover's algorithm. Even if $k \leq 2n$, some Q2 attacks may similarly be converted into Q1 if quantum queries are required only on some small portion of inputs.

Quantum Speed-Up for Linear Cryptanalysis. Linear cryptanalysis [49] is one of the most fundamental techniques in symmetric cryptanalysis. Kaplan et al. [43] has already shown a quadratic quantum speed-up for linear attacks. However, their distinguisher uses only one-dimensional linear approximations, while classical attacks often exploit multidimensional linear approximations to reduce complexity [32–34]. In fact, it is unclear whether Kaplan et al.'s distinguisher

---

[1] Note that attacks that gather encrypted data now and execute quantum algorithms later (after the realization of a large-scale quantum computer) are also in Q1.

[2] When attack targets are primitives without secret keys, e.g. hash functions, it is reasonable to assume attackers can compute all functions in quantum superposition. Namely, attacks are always Q2, or there is no distinction between Q1 and Q2.

can be sped-up further even if multiple linear approximations are available, due to the following reason.

Kaplan et al.'s distinguisher relies on the quantum counting algorithm [18], which (approximately) counts the number of x satisfying $F(x) = 1$ for an (efficiently computable) Boolean function F. Since classical one-dimensional linear distinguishers work just by counting the number of messages satisfying a linear approximation, such F is naturally defined in the one-dimensional case, and the quantum counting algorithm can be applied.

Meanwhile, classical multidimensional linear distinguishers are based on sophisticated statistical tests exploiting a relationship between capacity and a sum of squared correlations in a clever way. It is highly unclear whether there exists an efficiently computable Boolean function F such that just counting the number of x satisfying $F(x) = 1$ corresponds to performing such statistical tests.

Thus it is natural to ask whether there exists another quantum technique for linear distinguishers running faster than Kaplan et al.'s when a multidimensional linear approximation is available.

Multidimensional linear cryptanalysis has many variants including (multidimensional) zero correlation linear cryptanalysis [9] and generalized linear cryptanalysis on an arbitrary finite abelian group [4]. However, no previous work has shown quantum speed-up for them. A technique speeding-up multidimensional linear distinguishers may lead to a speed-up for such variants, which is of another interest. It may also lead to a speed-up for some integral distinguishers, because a class of multidimensional zero correlation linear distinguishers corresponds to integral distinguishers based on balanced functions, as shown by Bogdanov et al. and Sun et al. [8,56].

Quadratic Barrier. Due to Grover's generic quadratic speed-up for exhaustive search, the only way to break more rounds in the quantum setting, especially for key-recovery and distinguishing attacks, is to achieve a super-quadratic speed-up[3]. Hence, such a speed-up is one of the main goals in quantum cryptanalysis on symmetric-key cryptosystems.

Some previous works have already achieved such a speed-up, even in the Q1 model [16], but the types of techniques are limited. All of them exploit algebraic structures such as *hidden periods* or *shifts* of target ciphers by using Simon's algorithm or a related algorithm solving an algebraic problem.

---

[3] The reason of this is as follows: Consider attacks on a k-bit-key block cipher. Assume that, in the classical setting, we know a valid dedicated attack (i.e., an attack faster than 2^k) on r rounds of the cipher, but know only an *invalid* attack (i.e., attack requiring time more than 2^k) for $(r+1)$-rounds. Especially, r rounds of the cipher are classically broken but $(r+1)$ rounds are not. Let T_c be the classical complexity of the invalid $(r+1)$-round attack. Since this attack is classically invalid, $T_c > 2^k$ holds. Suppose we achieve some quantum speed-up for the $(r+1)$-round attack and the resulting complexity is T_q. Then, since the generic complexity of key-recovery is $\sqrt{2^k}$ in the quantum setting (by the Grover search), the attack after quantum speed-up is valid (i.e., $T_q < \sqrt{2^k}$ and $(r+1)$ rounds are broken) only if the speed-up is more-than-quadratic and $T_q < \sqrt{T_c}$ holds.

Moreover, few previous works have succeeded to achieve a more than quadratic speed-up on classical cryptanalytic techniques such as differential, linear, or integral cryptanalysis. The only one exception is the quantum versions of (advanced) slide attacks [14,42], but they also rely on special algebraic structures like hidden periods. Whether a more than quadratic speed-up is possible for other major classical techniques (without relying on periods or shifts) has been an important open problem for years.

1.1 Our Contributions

This paper shows that quantum speed-up for multidimensional (zero correlation) linear and integral distinguisher can be achieved by using a modified version of the subroutine of Simon's algorithm, without exploiting hidden periods or shifts. Especially, we show that some special versions of integral distinguishers achieve a more-than-quadratic speed-up.

First, we observe that Simon's algorithm has a close relationship with linear correlations of functions via Fourier transform. Simon's algorithm iterates a subroutine, which is composed of the Hadamard transform and an oracle query to the target function. We find that, with a slight modification made, the subroutine outputs a pair of linear masks of the target function with probability proportional to the squared linear correlation. Since it extracts linear correlations of a function into quantum amplitude, we call the subroutine after the modification the *correlation extraction algorithm*, or CEA for short.

Second, we show that multidimensional linear distinguishers can be sped-up by combining CEA and the Quantum Amplitude Amplification (QAA) technique. As an application example, we show that the multidimensional distinguishers on FEA-1 and FEA-2 by Beyne [6] can be sped-up from $O(2^{(r/4-3/4)n})$ and $O(2^{(r/6-3/4)n})$ to $O(2^{(r/8-1/4)n})$ and $O(2^{(r/12-1/4)n})$, respectively, when messages are n bits and the number of rounds is r.

Then we show that CEA also leads to a speed-up for multidimensional zero correlation linear distinguishers. Our technique leads to quantum distinguishers on 5-round balanced Feistel running in time $O(2^{n/2})$ when round functions are bijections and the entire width of the cipher is n, and distinguishers on Type-I/II generalized Feistel structures. (See Table 2 of this paper's full version [36] for details.)

Finally, we show a speed-up for integral distinguishers. The speed-up is obtained via the correspondence of integral and zero correlation properties observed by Bogdanov et al. and Sun et al. [8,56], and applicable when integral properties are based on balanced functions. Especially, we observe the possibility of a more than quadratic speed-up when there are *multiple* integral properties on mutually orthogonal subspaces, which appear in some SPN ciphers such as the 3.5-round AES. As a notable example, we show that a toy 4-bit-cell SPN cipher having the same integral property as the 2.5-round AES is distinguished only by a *single* quantum query. Such a single-query attack is almost impossible in the classical setting (unless another weakness exists), and the example illustrates a new type of qualitative difference between classical and quantum computation that has not been observed before[4].

Note that all of our attacks do not require the target cipher to have algebraic structures such as hidden periods or shifts. It is somewhat surprising that (a modified) Simon's algorithm, which was primarily developed to solve an algebraic problem of hidden periods, leads to non-trivial speed-ups for various classical attacks not relying on hidden periods nor shifts.

Our technique extends to generalized linear distinguishers on arbitrary finite abelian groups [4] by replacing the Hadamard transform in CEA with the general Quantum Fourier Transform (QFT). As an application, we show a speed-up for the distinguisher by Beyne [6] on the FF3-1 structure. The amount of speed-up is the same as that for FEA-1.

A drawback of our technique is that it cannot be applied to integral distinguishers based on zero-sum properties, although zero-sum properties are usually used to extend distinguishers into key-recovery attacks on more rounds. Especially, it does not directly lead to breaking more rounds than classical attacks. Still, we believe that our techniques are novel and general, and will inspire other new types of quantum attacks in both of the Q1 and Q2 models.

1.2   Related Works

Quantum speed-up for integral attacks has already been studied in, e.g., [15], but zero-sum properties are used and the distinguisher part itself is not sped-up. A recent work by Shi et al. [54] also studies zero correlation linear attacks in the quantum setting, but it mainly focuses on how to find zero correlation linear approximations by using quantum computers, and does not have much overlap with our results.

Schrottenloher's Key-Recovery Attack. Another recent concurrent and independent work by Schrottenloher [53] showed how to obtain quantum speed-up for linear *key-recovery* attacks.

Classical linear distinguishers are often combined with efficient key-recovery attacks using the FFT [22,29,57]. What Schrottenloher did is to combine such classical techniques with the QFT. Computing convolution of some Boolean functions related to linear approximations in quantum superposition, Schrottenloher's algorithm produces some quantum superposition of *subkey candidates* in such a way that the quantum amplitude are proportional to their experimental correlations. Then the amplitude of the right key is amplified by QAA.

Note that our main interest is to achieve a speed-up for *multidimensional* (zero correlation) linear distinguishers. Schrottenloher's work [53] also deals with multiple linear approximations, but the existence of multiple approximations improves only precision of attack by a constant factor, and essentially does not

---

[4] Bonnetain showed a single query attack on the one-time pad encryption scheme by making quantum registers for messages and ciphertexts disentangled [11], but the attack target and technique are quite different from ours.

contribute much to reducing the time complexity. Additionally, zero correlation linear or integral attacks are not studied in [53].

One would expect that a more speed-up for key-recovery is obtained by combining our technique and Schrottenloher's. Still, the mechanism of the two techniques is quite different (Schrottenloher uses the QFT to compute convolution in superposition to obtain a superposition of key candidates, while we use it to extract correlations of multidimensional linear approximations), and so far we do not have any idea on how to combine them. Studying theoretical connection between them and reducing the time complexity of key-recovery exploiting (zero correlation) multidimensional linear approximations is definitely an important and interesting future work.

1.3 Organization

Section 2 introduces basic notions and facts. Section 3 reviews classical (multidimensional) linear distinguishers and Kaplan et al.'s quantum one-dimensional linear distinguisher. Section 4 studies relationships between the Simon's subroutine and linear correlations, and introduces CEA. Sections 5, 6, and 7 show how to achieve a quantum speed-up with CEA for multidimensional linear, zero correlation multidimensional linear, and integral distinguishers, respectively. Section 8 shows the extension to generalized linear distinguishers on an arbitrary finite abelian group. Section 9 concludes the paper.

2 Preliminaries

$\mathbb{F}_2$ denotes the Galois field of order two. We identify the set of n-bit strings $\{0,1\}^n$ and the n-dimensional $\mathbb{F}_2$-vector space $\mathbb{F}_2^n$. Especially, by "bit string" we denote an element of $\mathbb{F}_2^n$ for some n. By $\mathbf{e}_i$ we denote the n-bit string (for some n) of which the i-th bit is 1 and other bits are 0. $x \oplus y$ denotes the addition of x and y in $\mathbb{F}_2^n$, and $x||y$ denotes the concatenation as bit strings. For a bit string $x \in \mathbb{F}_2^n$, we denote the i-th bit (from the left) by x_i. Namely we represent x as $x = x_1||\cdots||x_n$. For $x, y \in \mathbb{F}_2^n$, the dot product of x and y is defined by $x \cdot y := (x_1 \cdot y_1) \oplus \cdots \oplus (x_n \cdot y_n)$. For a vector space $V \subset \mathbb{F}_2^n$ (resp., vector x), $V^\perp$ (resp., $x^\perp$) denotes the subspace that is composed of y satisfying $y \cdot x = 0$ for all $x \in V$ (resp., y satisfying $y \cdot x = 0$). For two vector spaces $V_1, V_2 \subset \mathbb{F}_2^n$, we write $V_1 \perp V_2$ if $v_1 \cdot v_2 = 0$ for all $v_1 \in V_1$ and $v_2 \in V_2$. The event that a (classical or quantum) algorithm $\mathcal{A}$ outputs a classical bit string x is denoted by $x \leftarrow \mathcal{A}$. For a bit string $x \in \mathbb{F}_2^n$ (resp., function $f : \mathbb{F}_2^m \to \mathbb{F}_2^n$), by $\mathsf{msb}_u[x]$ (resp., $\mathsf{msb}_u[f]$) we denote the most significant u bits of x (resp., the function that returns $\mathsf{msb}_u[f(x)]$ for each input x). The notations $\mathsf{lsb}_u[x]$ and $\mathsf{lsb}_u[f]$ are similarly defined for least significant u bits. For a distribution D and a real value X_w depending on a parameter w, $\mathbb{E}_{w \sim D}[X_w]$ denotes the expected value of X_w when w is sampled according to D. It is also denoted by $\mathbb{E}_w[X_w]$ or just $\mathbb{E}[X_w]$ if the distribution is clear from the context. Similar notations are used for variance and the probability of an event. For a unitary operator U, its adjoint is denoted by U^*. In cryptanalysis of a block cipher E, we regard the unit of time as the time to encrypt a message by E. We assume that readers are familiar with Pearson's chi-squared test of goodness-of-fit. For those who are not, we provide a brief overview about the relationship between the test and distinguishers in Section A of the full version of this paper [36].

2.1 Linear Approximations and Correlations

The (one-dimensional) linear approximation of a function $f : \mathbb{F}_2^m \to \mathbb{F}_2^n$ for an input mask $\alpha \in \mathbb{F}_2^m$ and output mask $\beta \in \mathbb{F}_2^n$ is the Boolean function defined by $x \mapsto (\alpha \cdot x) \oplus (\beta \cdot f(x))$. The correlation $\mathrm{Cor}(f; \alpha, \beta)$ of this linear approximation is defined by $\mathrm{Cor}(f; \alpha, \beta) := \Pr_x[\alpha \cdot x = \beta \cdot f(x)] - \Pr_x[\alpha \cdot x \neq \beta \cdot f(x)]$. It is well-known that the linear correlation satisfies

$$\mathrm{Cor}(f; \alpha, \beta) = \sum_{x \in \mathbb{F}_2^m} \frac{(-1)^{\alpha \cdot x \oplus \beta \cdot f(x)}}{2^m}. \tag{1}$$

In addition, we need the following claim for analysis of attacks.

Claim 1 (Distribution of capacity of a random permutation). *Let $V \subset \mathbb{F}_2^n \times \mathbb{F}_2^n$ be a vector space and S be an arbitrary basis of V. Then, for a randomly chosen permutation P, the value $2^n \cdot \sum_{(\alpha,\beta) \in V-\{0\}} \mathrm{Cor}(P; \alpha, \beta)^2$ approximately follows the χ^2 distribution with $2^v - 2^u - 2^w + 1$ degrees of freedom. Here, $v := \dim(V)$, $u := \dim(V \cap \mathbb{F}_2^n \times \{0^n\})$ and $w := \dim(V \cap \{0^n\} \times \mathbb{F}_2^n)$.*

This claim is conjectured in [2]. We do not have a formal proof, but explain why the claim is plausible in Section D of the full version of this paper [36].

2.2 Balanced Function and Zero-Sum Property

Integral cryptanalysis [44], which was initially proposed as a dedicated attack on the block cipher SQUARE [24], exploits the *zero-sum property* of (a part of) ciphers. Here, we say that a function $f : \mathbb{F}_2^m \to \mathbb{F}_2^n$ has the zero-sum property if $\sum_x f(x) = 0$. Moreover, we say that a function f is balanced if $|f^{-1}(y)| = |f^{-1}(y')|$ holds for any y, y' in the range of f. A balanced function has the zero-sum property but the converse does not necessarily hold. In some previous works, the zero-sum property is called "balanced property", but this paper uses the term "balanced" only when referring to a balanced function in the above sense.

2.3 Quantum Computation

We assume that the readers are familiar with quantum computation and linear algebra (see, e.g., [52] for basics of quantum computation). We adopt the standard quantum circuit model and do not take the cost of quantum error correction into account. I_m denotes the identity operator on an m-qubit system and H denotes the (1-qubit) Hadamard transform. For a function $f : \mathbb{F}_2^m \to \mathbb{F}_2^n$, U_f

denotes the unitary operator defined by $U_f : |x\rangle |y\rangle \mapsto |x\rangle |y \oplus f(x)\rangle$. Namely, U_f is the quantum oracle of f. All quantum attacks in this paper are Quantum Chosen-Plaintext Attacks (QCPAs, in the Q2 model), and the quantum encryption oracle U_{E_K} of a target cipher E_K is assumed to be available. If E_K is a tweakable block cipher, adversaries query tweaks also in quantum superposition.

Quantum Amplitude Amplification. Here we recall the Quantum Amplitude Amplification (QAA) technique [18], which is a generalization of Grover's algorithm [30]. Let $f : \mathbb{F}_2^m \to \mathbb{F}_2$ be a Boolean function, U be a unitary operator acting on an m-qubit system, and p denote the probability that we observe a bit string x satisfying $f(x) = 1$ when the state $U |0^m\rangle$ is measured by the computational basis. In addition, let $\mathcal{S}_f$ and $\mathcal{S}_0$ be the unitary operators acting on an m-qubit quantum system defined by $\mathcal{S}_f |x\rangle = (-1)^{f(x)} |x\rangle$ and $\mathcal{S}_0 |x\rangle = (-1)^{\delta_{0^m,x}} |x\rangle$, where $\delta_{0^m,x}$ is Kronecker's delta.

Proposition 1 (Quantum amplitude amplification). *In the above setting, let $Q(U,f) := -U\mathcal{S}_0 U^* \mathcal{S}_f$. When the state $Q(U,f)^i U |0^m\rangle$ is measured by the computational basis for some $i > 0$, an outcome x satisfying $f(x) = 1$ is obtained with probability $\sin^2((2i+1) \cdot \arcsin(\sqrt{p}))$. Especially, such an x is obtained with probability at least $\max\{p, 1-p\}$ by setting $i = \lceil \pi/4 \arcsin(\sqrt{p}) \rceil$.*

Grover's algorithm is obtained when $U = H^{\otimes m}$. Here, $p = |f^{-1}(1)|/2^m$ and an $x \in f^{-1}(1)$ is found by applying $Q(H^{\otimes m}, f)$ at most $\sqrt{2^m/|f^{-1}(1)|}$ times.

Applications to Distinguishers. A typical task in cryptanalysis is to distinguish two distributions of functions. That is, under the assumption that a function f is chosen from a distribution D_1 or D_2, an adversary tries to judge which distribution f is chosen from. For linear distinguishers, D_1 (resp., D_2) corresponds to a linear approximation of a real block cipher (resp., a random permutation).

A counterpart of such a task in the quantum setting is to distinguish two distributions of unitary operators. That is, under the assumption that a unitary operator U is chosen according to a distribution D_1 or D_2, an adversary tries to judge which distribution U is chosen from[5].

QAA can be used to solve such a task. Assume that an adversary has access to not only U but U^*, and that U acts on an n-qubit system[6]. Moreover, suppose that we know a Boolean function $F : \mathbb{F}_2^n \to \mathbb{F}_2$ satisfying the following conditions.

(1) If U is chosen from D_1, then the probability $p_U := \Pr\left[x \xleftarrow{\text{measure}} U |0^n\rangle : F(x) = 1\right]$ is relatively high on average.

(2) If U is chosen from D_2, then p_U is relatively low on average.

---

[5] A typical example is that D_1 corresponds to the quantum encryption oracle U_{E_K} of a block cipher E_K while D_2 to the oracle U_P of a random permutation P (choosing K or P randomly corresponds to sampling according to D_1 or D_2).

[6] If U is the quantum oracle U_f of a function f, then $U_f^* = U_f$ holds. Especially, an access to $U = U_f$ automatically means an access to U^*.

Specifically, assume we know a value t satisfying $\mathbb{E}_{U \sim D_1}[p_U] \geq t \gg \mathbb{E}_{U \sim D_2}[p_U]$. Then we can distinguish D_1 and D_2 by using QAA on U and F: If U is chosen from D_1, then QAA with $O(\sqrt{t^{-1}})$ applications of U, U^*, and $\mathcal{S}_F$ will find x satisfying $F(x) = 1$ because $p_U \geq t$. If U is chosen from D_2, such QAA will not find x because $t \gg p_U$ and the number of iterations is not large enough.

More precisely, since we know only the lower bound of $\mathbb{E}_{U \sim D_1}[p_U]$, we run multiple instances of QAAs with the number of iteration randomized as follows.

QAA for Distinguisher ($\mathcal{QD}$)

1. For $j = 1, \ldots, s$, do:
   (a) Choose i from the set of integers from 0 to $\left\lfloor \dfrac{1}{\sin\left(2 \cdot \arcsin\left(\sqrt{t}\right)\right)} \right\rfloor$ uniformly at random.
   (b) Apply $Q(U, F)^i U$ to $|0^n\rangle$ and measure the entire state by the computational basis, and let x be the outcome.
   (c) Compute $F(x)$. If $F(x) = 1$, return 1 and abort.
2. Return 0.

Here, s is a positive integer constant chosen depending on applications. We denote the above algorithm by $\mathcal{QD}$.

The idea of randomly choosing the number of iteration is just a straightforward adaptation of previous works on Grover's algorithm and QAA without knowing initial success probability [17,18].

Proposition 2. *With the above setting and notions, suppose $1/4 > t > 0$. Then, $\mathcal{QD}$ applies U, U^*, and $\mathcal{S}_F$ at most $s(\frac{1}{\sqrt{t}} + 1)$ times and (1) returns 1 with probability at least $(1 - (\frac{3}{4})^s) \cdot \Pr_{U \sim D_1}[1/4 > p_U \geq t]$ if U is chosen according to D_1 and (2) returns 1 with probability at most $s \cdot (\frac{16t'}{t} + \frac{20t'}{\sqrt{t}}) + \Pr_{U \sim D_2}[t' < p_U]$ for any $t' > 0$ satisfying $4\sqrt{t'/t} + 2\sqrt{t'} < \pi/2$ if U is chosen according to D_2.*

The interpretation of the proposition is as follows. Suppose that p_U is distributed around t (resp., t') if U is chosen according to D_1 (resp., D_2), and $1/4 > t \gg t'$ holds. For a sufficiently large constant s (e.g., $s = 3$), the proposition guarantees that $\mathcal{QD}$ returns 1 with probability $\geq 1/2$ (resp., only with a negligibly small probability) when U is chosen according to D_1 (resp., D_2). Hence D_1 is distinguished from D_2. The proof of Proposition 2 is a straightforward application of some lemmas in previous works [17,18], though, we provide a proof in Section B of the full version of this paper [36] for completeness.

Simon's Algorithm. Simon's quantum algorithm [55] finds a period of a periodic function. More precisely, it solves the following problem.

Problem 1. Let $s \in \mathbb{F}_2^m$ be a (secret) constant, and $f : \mathbb{F}_2^m \to \mathbb{F}_2^n$ be a function satisfying the following properties C1 and C2.

C1. $f(x \oplus s) = f(x)$ for all x. Namely, f is a periodic function with period s.

C2. $f(x) \neq f(y)$ if $x \neq y$ and $x \oplus s \neq y$.

Given the (quantum) oracle of f, find s.

The classical complexity to solve the problem is $\Theta(2^{m/2})$ but Simon's algorithm, which runs as follows, solves it in polynomial time with high probability.

1. For $i = 1, 2, \ldots, 2m$, execute the following subroutine (a)–(e).
   (a) Prepare the initial state $|0^m\rangle |0^n\rangle$.
   (b) Apply the m-qubit Hadamard transform $H^{\otimes m}$ on the first m qubits.
   (c) Apply U_f on the state (i.e., make a quantum query to f).
   (d) Apply the $H^{\otimes m} \otimes I_n$ on the state.
   (e) Measure the first m qubits by the computational basis, discard the remaining n-qubits, and return the observed m-bit string (denoted by α_i).
2. If $\dim(\mathrm{Span}_{\mathbb{F}_2}(\alpha_1, \ldots, \alpha_{2m})) = m - 1$, compute and output the unique $s' \in \mathbb{F}_2^m \setminus \{0^m\}$ such that $s' \cdot \alpha_i = 0$ for $i = 1, \ldots, 2m$. If $\dim(\mathrm{Span}_{\mathbb{F}_2}(\alpha_1, \ldots, \alpha_{2m})) \neq m - 1$, output $\perp$.

Simon showed that each α_i is uniformly distributed over the subspace $\{v \in \mathbb{F}_2^m | v \cdot s = 0\}$, and thus the algorithm returns the period s with high probability. We refer to the subroutine (a)–(e) as Simon's subroutine.

Many papers (e.g., [42, 45, 46]) showed polynomial-time quantum attacks on symmetric cryptosystems by using Simon's algorithm. In fact only C1 is satisfied in those applications and C2 is not necessarily satisfied. Still, C1 guarantees that the subroutine (a)–(e) always returns an α_i satisfying $\alpha_i \cdot s = 0$ [42].

3   Classical and Kaplan et al.'s Linear Distinguishers

Here we review classical (multidimensional) linear distinguishers and Kaplan et al.'s quantum one-dimensional linear distinguisher [43].

3.1   Classical One-Dimensional Linear Distinguisher

The linear correlation $\mathrm{Cor}(P; \alpha, \beta)$ of an n-bit random permutation P approximately follows the normal distribution $\mathcal{N}(0, 2^{-n})$ for an arbitrary mask (α, β) with $\alpha, \beta \neq 0^n$ [26]. Thus, if the correlation $\mathrm{Cor}(E_K; \alpha, \beta)$ for a block cipher E_K with $\alpha, \beta \neq 0^n$ significantly deviates from the segment $[-2^{-n/2}, 2^{-n/2}]$, then E_K can be distinguished by collecting a list $L = \{(P_1, C_1), \ldots, (P_N, C_N)\}$ for random $P_1, \ldots, P_N$, and checking if the estimated empirical correlation

$$\widehat{\mathrm{Cor}}(E_K; \alpha, \beta) = \frac{\#\{(P, C) \in L | \alpha \cdot P = \beta \cdot C\} - \#\{(P, C) \in L | \alpha \cdot P \neq \beta \cdot C\}}{N}$$

is far from $[-2^{-n/2}, 2^{-n/2}]$. The attack succeeds with a high probability if $N \gtrsim \mathrm{Cor}(E_K; \alpha, \beta)^{-2}$.

3.2   Classical Multidimensional Linear Distinguishers

A natural idea to enhance the power of linear distinguishers is to utilize multiple linear approximations. Some early works indeed show such attacks, assuming the existence of statistically independent multiple approximations [7,41]. However, the assumption does not necessarily hold in general [50]. Instead, Hermelin et al. [35] proposed to use multidimensional linear approximations, i.e., sets of linear approximations of which the input-output masks form a vector space.

Specifically, let $f : \mathbb{F}_2^m \to \mathbb{F}_2^n$ be a function, $V \subset \mathbb{F}_2^m \times \mathbb{F}_2^n$ be a set of input-output masks for f that is a vector space, and $S := \{(\alpha_1, \beta_1), \ldots, (\alpha_\ell, \beta_\ell)\}$ be a basis of V. Then the multidimensional linear approximation of f (w.r.t. (V, S)) is defined as the function $\mathsf{Lin}_S^f : \mathbb{F}_2^m \to \mathbb{F}_2^\ell$ such that

$$\mathsf{Lin}_S^f(x) = (\alpha_1 \cdot x \oplus \beta_1 \cdot f(x), \ldots, \alpha_\ell \cdot x \oplus \beta_\ell \cdot f(x)).$$

Define a distribution p_S^f on $\mathbb{F}_2^\ell$ by $p_S^f(z) := \Pr\left[x \xleftarrow{\$} \mathbb{F}_2^m : \mathsf{Lin}_S^f(x) = z\right]$.

Below we denote the zero vector $(0^m, 0^n)$ by $\mathbf{0}$. We say that the input and output masks are linearly independent if $V = V_1 \times V_2$ holds for some $V_1 \subset \mathbb{F}_2^m$ and $V_2 \subset \mathbb{F}_2^n$. Moreover, we say that the input and output masks are linearly completely dependent if there exists a basis $\{(\alpha_i, \beta_i)\}_{1 \leq i \leq \dim(V)}$ of V such that both of $\{\alpha_i\}_{1 \leq i \leq \dim(V)}$ and $\{\beta_i\}_{1 \leq i \leq \dim(V)}$ are linearly independent in $\mathbb{F}_2^n$.

The advantage of considering a set of masks forming a vector space is that we can utilize a link of the sum of the squared correlations to the *capacity* of p_S^f and Pearson's chi-squared test: Here, the capacity of a probability function (distribution) p over $\mathbb{F}_2^\ell$ is the value defined[7] by

$$\mathrm{Cap}(p) := 2^\ell \sum_{z \in \mathbb{F}_2^\ell} (p(z) - 2^{-\ell})^2.$$

The important well-known fact is that

$$\mathrm{Cap}(p_S^f) = \sum_{(\alpha, \beta) \in V - \{\mathbf{0}\}} \mathrm{Cor}(f; \alpha, \beta)^2 \tag{2}$$

holds for the multidimensional approximation of f. Moreover, suppose a list of random input-output pairs $L = \{(P_1, C_1), \ldots, (P_N, C_N)\}$ is given. Then the capacity $\mathrm{Cap}(\hat{p}_S^f)$ of the estimated empirical distribution $\hat{p}_S^f$ (defined by $\hat{p}_S^f(z) := \frac{\#\{(P,C) \in L | \mathsf{Lin}_S^f(P) = z\}}{N}$) multiplied by N is equal to the test statistic of the Pearson's chi-squared goodness-of-fit test (for testing the goodness-of-fit of p_S^f and the uniform distribution on $\mathbb{F}_2^\ell$).

The idea of multidimensional linear distinguishers for a block cipher E_K is that the distribution $p_S^{E_K}$ is far from uniform if the right hand side of Eq. (2) with $f = E_K$ is sufficiently large for random K, and thus E_K can be distinguished

---

[7] In fact this is the χ^2-divergence between p and the uniform distribution over $\mathbb{F}_2^\ell$. We use the term *capacity* following previous works on linear cryptanalysis.

from random by checking whether the test statistic of the Pearson's chi-squared test is larger than a certain threshold. Specifically, given a list of (real) random plaintext-ciphertext pairs $L = \{(P_1, C_1), \ldots, (P_N, C_N)\}$, we count $\mathsf{num}(z) := \{(P_i, C_i) \in L | \mathsf{Lin}_S^{E_K}(P_i) = z\}$ for each z, and compute the test statistic $\chi_{\mathrm{real}}^2 := N2^\ell \sum_z (\mathsf{num}(z)/N - 2^{-\ell})^2 = N \cdot \mathsf{Cap}(\hat{p}_S^{E_K})$. Then χ_{real}^2 is approximately distributed around $(2^\ell - 1) + N \sum_{(\alpha,\beta) \in V - \{0\}} \mathsf{Cor}(E_K; \alpha, \beta)^2$. If the plaintext-ciphertext pairs are generated from a random permutation, then $\mathsf{num}(z)$ approximately follows the uniform distribution. Thus, the similarly computed statistic χ_{ideal}^2 approximately follows the χ^2 distribution with $(2^\ell - 1)$ degrees of freedom (denoted by $\chi_{2^\ell-1}^2$), of which the standard deviation is $\sqrt{2(2^\ell - 1)}$. Hence E_K can be distinguished from a random permutation with a constant advantage when[8] $N \gg \sqrt{2^\ell} / \sum_{(\alpha,\beta) \in V - \{0\}} \mathsf{Cor}(E_K; \alpha, \beta)^2 = \sqrt{2^\ell} / \mathsf{Cap}(p_S^{E_K})$, by checking whether the test statistic is larger than $(2^\ell - 1) + \sqrt{2(2^\ell - 1)}$ or not.

Some Remarks. The arguments in the above paragraph are mainly based on [6, Section 4.3]. Strictly speaking, the statistic in the ideal world χ_{ideal}^2 does not follow $\chi_{2^\ell-1}^2$ actually because the squared correlation $\mathsf{Cor}(P; \alpha, \beta)^2$ is not zero on average even for a random permutation P for $\alpha, \beta \neq 0^n$. Still, the difference of χ_{ideal}^2 and $\chi_{2^\ell-1}^2$ is very small compared to the difference of χ_{real}^2 and $\chi_{2^\ell-1}^2$, and it is usually (and implicitly) assumed that the above arguments heuristically work in practice. Meanwhile, zero-correlation linear cryptanalysis *does* exploit such small difference, which we will explain later.

Some early works showed that distinguishers based on the Log Likelihood Ratio (LLR) test [3,32,33] requires only $O(1/\mathsf{Cap}(p_S^{E_K}))$ data instead of $O(\sqrt{2^\ell}/\mathsf{Cap}(p_S^{E_K}))$ of the χ^2-test-based distinguishers, and the LLR-test-based distinguishers perform better. However, the LLR test requires accurate knowledge on key-dependent distributions of multidimensional linear approximations, which is not often the case as pointed out by Cho [21].

3.3 Kaplan et al.'s Quantum One-Dimensional Linear Distinguisher

Kaplan et al. [43] observed that a quadratic quantum speed-up can be obtained for linear distinguishers by using the quantum counting algorithm [18].

Roughly speaking, the quantum counting algorithm achieves a quadratic speed-up to solve the problem of estimating $M := \#\{x | F(x) = 1\}$ for a Boolean function F. Making $O(q)$ quantum queries to F, it returns an approximation $\tilde{M}$ of M satisfying $|\tilde{M} - M| \leq O\left(\frac{\sqrt{M(2^n - M)}}{q} + \frac{2^n}{q^2}\right)$.

Now, suppose that there exists a linear approximation of an n-bit block cipher E_K satisfying $c := |\mathsf{Cor}(E_K; \alpha, \beta)| \gg 2^{-n/2}$ for a random key K, and let F be

---

[8] The squared correlation and capacity can significantly change depending on keys in general, but they are often estimated by their averages under the assumption that they concentrate around the mean. As the first step of achieving quantum speed-up for multidimensional linear attacks, we also assume this. An in-depth study about the key-dependence of complexity is an important future work.

the Boolean function such that $F(x) = 1$ iff $\alpha \cdot x \oplus \beta \cdot E_K(x) = 0$. Then, E_K can be distinguished by estimating $M = \#\{x | F(x) = 1\}$ and checking whether $|M - \frac{2^n}{2}| \gg 2^{n/2}$. Using the quantum counting algorithm, one can obtain an estimation of $\tilde{M}$ with sufficient precision for distinguisher ($|\tilde{M} - M| \leq \frac{M}{a}$ for a small integer $a > 0$) in time $O(1/c)$. Compared to the classical complexity of $O(1/c^2)$, a quadratic speed-up is achieved.

Extension to Multidimensional Linear Distinguishers? After seeing Kaplan et al.'s work, it is natural to ask whether their technique can be extended to multidimensional linear distinguishers. However, to apply the quantum counting algorithm to solve a problem, one has to construct an efficiently computable Boolean function F in such a way that counting the number of x satisfying $F(x) = 1$ solves the problem. In the one-dimensional case F is obtained in a quite natural way as explained above, but in the multidimensional case essentially we have to construct F in such a way to achieve a quadratic speed-up for Pearson's chi-squared test applied to the distribution $p_S^{E_K}$. It seems highly unclear whether such F exists, and thus we seek for another technique.

4 New Observation on Simon's Algorithm

As explained in Sect. 2, the subroutine of Simon's algorithm uses only the quantum oracle of a target function and the Hadamard transform, which is the Fourier transform over the group $(\mathbb{Z}/2\mathbb{Z})^n$. Meanwhile, a well-know fact is that linear correlations have strong relationships with Fourier transform. This section shows that a slightly modified version of Simon's subroutine, which we call CEA, returns input and output masks of a function with a probability proportional to the linear correlations. Later we show that CEA can be utilized to obtain speed-up for various techniques including multidimensional linear distinguishers. Since $\mathbb{F}_2^n$ is isomorphic to $(\mathbb{Z}/2\mathbb{Z})^n$ as Abelian groups, in what follows we identify $\mathbb{F}_2^n$ with $(\mathbb{Z}/2\mathbb{Z})^n$.

4.1 Fourier Transform

First, we recall the Fourier transform (over $(\mathbb{Z}/2\mathbb{Z})^n$) and its relationship with linear cryptanalysis and quantum computation. The Fourier transform of a function $F : \mathbb{F}_2^n \to \mathbb{C}$ is the function $\mathcal{F}F : \mathbb{F}_2^n \to \mathbb{C}$ defined by $\mathcal{F}F(x) := \sum_{y \in \mathbb{F}_2^n} \frac{(-1)^{x \cdot y} F(y)}{\sqrt{2^n}}$.

Relationship with Linear Correlations. It is well-known that the linear correlation of an arbitrary function f is obtained by applying the Fourier transform on a function naturally defined from f [23,58].

For arbitrary function $f : \mathbb{F}_2^m \to \mathbb{F}_2^n$, let $f_{\text{emb}} : \mathbb{F}_2^m \times \mathbb{F}_2^n \to \mathbb{C}$ be the function defined by $f_{\text{emb}}(x, y) = 1$ if $f(x) = y$ and $f_{\text{emb}}(x, y) = 0$ otherwise[9]. Then some straightforward calculation shows

---
[9] "emb" is an abbreviation of "embedding".

$$\mathcal{F} f_{\text{emb}}(\alpha, \beta) = \sqrt{2^{m-n}} \cdot \text{Cor}(f; \alpha, \beta). \tag{3}$$

Relationship with Quantum Computation. The relationship with quantum computation is quite clear. The Fourier transform on $\mathbb{F}_2^n$ exactly corresponds to the Hadamard operator $H^{\otimes n}$. For instance, let $\psi : \mathbb{F}_2^n \to \mathbb{C}$ and $|\psi\rangle := \sum_{x \in \mathbb{F}_2^n} \psi(x) |x\rangle$. Then

$$H^{\otimes n} |\psi\rangle = \sum_{y \in \mathbb{F}_2^n} \mathcal{F}\psi(y) |y\rangle \tag{4}$$

holds. (Note that this property holds regardless of the norm of $|\psi\rangle$.) In fact this is one of the most important sources of quantum speed-up: While the classical FFT requires time $O(n2^n)$ to compute the Fourier transform of a function, an application of the Hadamard transform to a quantum state requires time $O(1)$.

4.2   Extracting Correlations by (Modified) Simon's Subroutine

Here we show that Simon's subroutine with a slight modification returns input and output masks for linear approximations with high correlation. We call the resulting algorithm Correlation Extraction Algorithm (CEA) because it extracts linear correlations into the quantum amplitude of a state, and we denote it by CEA^f when applied to a function f. Specifically, the algorithm runs as follows.

Algorithm CEA^f

(a) Prepare the initial state $|0^m\rangle |0^n\rangle$.
(b) Apply the m-qubit Hadamard transform $H^{\otimes m}$ on the first m qubits.
(c) Apply U_f on the state (i.e., make a quantum query to f).
(d) Apply the $(m+n)$-qubit Hadamard transform $H^{\otimes(m+n)}$ on the state.
(e) Measure the entire $(m+n)$ qubits by the computational basis and return the observed $(m+n)$-bit string $\alpha\|\beta$ ($\alpha \in \mathbb{F}_2^m$ and $\beta \in \mathbb{F}_2^n$).

The underlines indicate the parts modified from the original Simon's subroutine on p.9. CEA^f is different from the original Simon's subroutine only in that CEA^f does not discard the last n qubits and measure them after applying $H^{\otimes n}$.

Note that this change does not affect the distribution of α in Step (e). Especially, α is just uniformly distributed over the subspace $\{v \in \mathbb{F}_2^m | v \cdot s = 0\}$ if f satisfies the conditions of Problem 1. Thus there is nothing new if we focus only on α. However, we observe that CEA^f shows an interesting link to linear correlations when β is taken into account, as in the following proposition.

Proposition 3. *The quantum state of* CEA^f *before the final measurement is*

$$\sum_{\alpha \in \mathbb{F}_2^m, \beta \in \mathbb{F}_2^n} \frac{\text{Cor}(f; \alpha, \beta)}{\sqrt{2^n}} |\alpha\rangle |\beta\rangle. \tag{5}$$

In particular, for any subset $S \subset \{0,1\}^m \times \{0,1\}^n$,

$$\Pr\left[(\alpha, \beta) \leftarrow \mathsf{CEA}^f : (\alpha, \beta) \in S\right] = \sum_{(\alpha,\beta) \in S} \frac{\mathrm{Cor}(f; \alpha, \beta)^2}{2^n} \tag{6}$$

holds.

Proof. The quantum state of CEA^f before the final measurement is

$$H^{\otimes(m+n)} U_f \left(H^{\otimes m} \otimes I_n\right) |0^m\rangle |0^n\rangle = H^{\otimes(m+n)} U_f \sum_{x \in \mathbb{F}_2^m} \frac{1}{\sqrt{2^m}} |x\rangle |0^n\rangle$$

$$= H^{\otimes(m+n)} \sum_{x \in \mathbb{F}_2^m} \frac{1}{\sqrt{2^m}} |x\rangle |f(x)\rangle$$

$$\overset{\text{Def. of } f_{\mathrm{emb}}}{=} H^{\otimes(m+n)} \sum_{x \in \mathbb{F}_2^m, y \in \mathbb{F}_2^n} \frac{f_{\mathrm{emb}}(x,y)}{\sqrt{2^m}} |x\rangle |y\rangle$$

$$\overset{\text{Eq. (4)}}{=} \sum_{\alpha \in \mathbb{F}_2^m, \beta \in \mathbb{F}_2^n} \frac{\mathcal{F} f_{\mathrm{emb}}(\alpha, \beta)}{\sqrt{2^m}} |\alpha\rangle |\beta\rangle$$

$$\overset{\text{Eq. (3)}}{=} \sum_{\alpha \in \mathbb{F}_2^m, \beta \in \mathbb{F}_2^n} \frac{\mathrm{Cor}(f; \alpha, \beta)}{\sqrt{2^n}} |\alpha\rangle |\beta\rangle.$$

Hence we have Eq. (5). Eq. (6) immediately follows from Eq. (5). □

Some Remarks. CEA is quite close to the Bernstein-Vazirani algorithm [5] when $n = 1$ and some previous works [20,59] already observes similar relationships between linear correlations and the Bernstein-Vazirani algorithm. Still, analysis in the previous works is done only in the case of $n = 1$. To obtain speed-up for multidimensional (zero correlation) linear and integral distinguishers, our analysis for general n involving both input and output masks is essential. Furthermore, we observe that a similar relationship holds for generalized linear correlations over an arbitrary finite abelian group and the general quantum Fourier transformation. See Sect. 8 for details.

5   Speed-Up for Multidimensional Linear Distinguishers

By using the CEA in the previous section, here we show quantum linear distinguishers achieving a bigger speed-up than Kaplan et al.'s when a multidimensional linear approximation with high correlations exists. Recall that what the algorithm CEA^f does is to apply the unitary operator $H^{\otimes(m+n)} U_f(H^{\otimes m} \otimes I_n)$ on $|0^m\rangle |0^n\rangle$ and measure the entire state by the computational basis. By abuse of notation, let CEA^f also denote the operator $H^{\otimes(m+n)} U_f(H^{\otimes m} \otimes I_n)$ itself.

We show three distinguishers[10] $\mathcal{A}_1$, $\mathcal{A}_2$, and $\mathcal{A}_3$. $\mathcal{A}_1$ is a general distinguisher applicable to arbitrary multidimensional linear approximations. $\mathcal{A}_2$ (resp., $\mathcal{A}_3$) is applicable only when the input and output masks are linearly independent (resp., completely dependent). Here are some remarks on notations and assumptions.

- We assume that $\sum_{(\alpha,\beta)\in V-\{0\}} \mathrm{Cor}(E_K;\alpha,\beta)^2 \geq c$ holds with a high probability for some $c > 0$, and that we know the value of c. $\mathcal{O}$ denotes the given oracle, which is either E_K for a random K or a random permutation P.
- (Notations for $\mathcal{A}_2$) When the input and output masks are linearly independent, i.e., $V = V_1 \times V_2$ holds for some subspaces $V_1, V_2 \subset \mathbb{F}_2^n$, we denote $\dim(V_1)$ and $\dim(V_2)$ by u and w, respectively. In addition, $S_1 := \{\alpha_1, \ldots, \alpha_u\}$ and $S_2 := \{\beta_1, \ldots, \beta_w\}$ denotes basis of V_1 and V_2. Without loss of generality, we assume $V_2 = \{\beta || 0^{n-w} | \beta \in \mathbb{F}_2^w\}$ and $\beta_i = \mathbf{e}_i$[11]. Especially, we regard V as a subspace of $\mathbb{F}_2^n \times \mathbb{F}_2^w$.
- (Notations for $\mathcal{A}_3$) When the input and output masks are linearly completely dependent, we fix a basis $S := \{(\alpha_i, \beta_i)\}_{1\leq i \leq \dim(V)}$ of V such that both of $\{\alpha_i\}_{1\leq i \leq \dim(V)}$ and $\{\beta_i\}_{1\leq i \leq \dim(V)}$ are linearly independent in $\mathbb{F}_2^n$. W.l.o.g., we assume $\beta_i = \mathbf{e}_i$[12]. Especially, we regard V as a subspace of $\mathbb{F}_2^n \times \mathbb{F}_2^{\dim(V)}$.

Distinguishers $\mathcal{A}_1$, $\mathcal{A}_2$, and $\mathcal{A}_3$. All the three distinguishers are obtained by applying the algorithm $\mathcal{QD}$ of Proposition 2. The difference between the distinguishers is the choice of the parameters s and t, the unitary operator U, and the Boolean function[13] F, which is as follows.

$\mathcal{A}_1$ **(general case):** $(s,t) := (3, c/2^n)$ and $U := \mathsf{CEA}^{\mathcal{O}}$. F is the Boolean function of which the domain is $\mathbb{F}_2^n \times \mathbb{F}_2^n$ and $F(\alpha,\beta) = 1$ iff $(\alpha,\beta) \in V - \{0\}$.

$\mathcal{A}_2$ **(linearly independent masks):** $(s,t) := (3, c/2^w)$ and $U := \mathsf{CEA}^{\mathsf{msb}_w[\mathcal{O}]}$. F is the Boolean function of which the domain is $\mathbb{F}_2^n \times \mathbb{F}_2^w$ and $F(\alpha,\beta) = 1$ iff $(\alpha,\beta) \in V - \{0\}$.

$\mathcal{A}_3$ **(linearly completely dependent masks):** $(s,t) := (3, c/2^{\dim(V)})$ and $U := \mathsf{CEA}^{\mathsf{msb}_{\dim(V)}[\mathcal{O}]}$. F is the Boolean function of which the domain is $\mathbb{F}_2^n \times \mathbb{F}_2^{\dim(V)}$ and $F(\alpha,\beta) = 1$ iff $(\alpha,\beta) \in V - \{0\}$.

Here, sampling a unitary U according to D_1 (resp., D_2) in Proposition 2 corresponds to sampling a random key K for a real cipher (resp., choosing an ideally random permutation P).

---

[10] The three distinguishers might be unified into a single one by restricting inputs and outputs appropriately. Still we focus on these cases because the three distinguishers are enough for the examples of interest shown later, and to avoid unnecessarily complex analysis.

[11] Let M be an arbitrary full-rank $n \times n$ matrix over $\mathbb{F}_2$ satisfying $M^T \mathbf{e}_i = \beta_i$. Then we have $\beta_i \cdot E_K(x) = (M^T \mathbf{e}_i) \cdot E_K(x) = \mathbf{e}_i \cdot M(E_K(x))$, and thus distinguishing E_K by using output mask β_i is equivalent to distinguishing $M \circ E_K$ by using output mask $\mathbf{e}_i$. Since E_K can be distinguished from a random permutation P iff $M \circ E_K$ can be distinguished, we can assume them without loss of generality.

[12] The reasoning is almost the same as before.

[13] See Section F of the full version [36] on how to efficiently compute F on a quantum circuit..

Analysis. If input and output masks are linearly independent, $\mathcal{A}_2$ distinguishes E_K and P in time $O(\sqrt{2^w/c})$ roughly due to the following reasoning. If the oracle given to $\mathcal{A}_2$ is E_K, the probability that we observe $(\alpha,\beta) \in F^{-1}(1)$ when measuring $\mathsf{CEA}^{\mathsf{msb}_w[E_K]} |0^n\rangle |0^w\rangle$ is approximately lower bounded by $c/2^w$. Hence, QAA on $\mathsf{CEA}^{\mathsf{msb}_w[E_K]}$ and F with $O(\sqrt{2^w/c})$ iterations returns $(\alpha,\beta) \in F^{-1}(1)$ (i.e., $\mathcal{A}_2$ returns 1) with high probability. On the other hand, if the oracle given to $\mathcal{A}_2$ is a random permutation P, from Claim 1 it follows that the probability that we observe $(\alpha,\beta) \in F^{-1}(1)$ when measuring $\mathsf{CEA}^{\mathsf{msb}_w[P]} |0^n\rangle |0^w\rangle$ is approximately upper bounded by $2^{\dim(V)}/2^{n+w}$. Especially, the probability that QAA on $\mathsf{CEA}^{\mathsf{msb}_w[P]}$ and F with $O(\sqrt{2^w/c})$ iterations returns $(\alpha,\beta) \in F^{-1}(1)$ (i.e., $\mathcal{A}_2$ returns 1) is negligibly small. For similar reasons, $\mathcal{A}_1$ and $\mathcal{A}_3$ distinguish E_K and P in time $O(\sqrt{2^n/c})$ and $O(\sqrt{2^{\dim(V)}/c})$, respectively.

More precisely, define parameters c_i, pb_i, and T_i for $i = 1, 2, 3$ as follows.

- $c_1 := c_3 = 2^{-n}$, $c_2 := 2^{-n-w+\dim(V)}$.
- $pb_1 := \dfrac{2^{\dim(V)+7}(n+1)}{2^{2n} \cdot c} + 2^{-\dim(V)+1} \cdot n^{-2}$, $pb_2 := \dfrac{2^{\dim(V)+7}(n+1)}{2^{n+w} \cdot c} + 2^{-\dim(V)+1} \cdot n^{-2}$, and $pb_3 := \dfrac{2^7(n+1)}{2^n \cdot c} + 2^{-\dim(V)+1} \cdot n^{-2}$.
- $T_1 := 6\sqrt{2^n/c}$, $T_2 := 6\sqrt{2^w/c}$, and $T_3 := 6\sqrt{2^{\dim(V)}/c}$.

Then the following proposition holds.

Proposition 4. *Let $i = 1, 2,$ or 3. Suppose that $c \gg c_i$, and that $1/4 > \sum_{(\alpha,\beta) \in V - \{0\}} \mathrm{Cor}(E_K; \alpha, \beta)^2 \geq c$ holds with a constant probability p when K is randomly chosen. If $\mathcal{A}_i$ runs relative to the real cipher E_K, then the probability that $\mathcal{A}_i$ outputs 1 is at least $p/2$. If $\mathcal{A}_i$ runs relative to a random permutation P, then the probability that $\mathcal{A}_i$ outputs 1 is approximately upper bounded by pb_i. In addition, the time complexity of $\mathcal{A}_i$ is at most T_i. (The probabilities are taken not only over the randomness of $\mathcal{A}_i$ but also over the randomness of choices of K or P.)*

This proposition can be proven by applying Proposition 2 and Claim 1 in a straightforward manner. Still, we provide a proof in Section C of the full version [36] for completeness.

Some Remarks. The speed-ups in this section are not always quadratic. Still, a quadratic speed-up is obtained in the specific case when input-output masks are linearly independent and $u = w$ (by applying $\mathcal{A}_2$). In this case, the classical complexity is about $2^{\ell/2}/(\text{capacity}) = 2^w/(\text{capacity})$ because $\ell = \dim(V) = \dim(V_1) + \dim(V_2) = u + w = 2w$. Meanwhile, if $\mathcal{A}_2$ is applied[14], the complexity drops to about $\sqrt{2^w}/(\text{capacity})$. For other cases, the speed-up is not quadratic in general, except for the one-dimensional case.

In the one-dimensional case, the asymptotic complexity of our technique is the same as Kaplan et al.'s, but the non-asymptotic complexity become smaller in a specific situation. For example, suppose that we have a one-dimensional

---

[14] $\mathcal{A}_1$ is also applicable here but performs worse than $\mathcal{A}_2$.

linear approximation of a cipher, and the absolute value of the linear correlation is concentrated in a very narrow range around a known value $c > 0$. Then, some analysis shows that the combination of CEA and QAA distinguishes the cipher by making $(\sqrt{2}\pi) \cdot (1/c)$ queries to the oracle. (This is faster than $\mathcal{A}_3$ in Proposition 4. Here, we consider to run QAA only once, whereas $\mathcal{A}_3$ runs QAA multiple times. A single run of QAA is sufficient here since the variance of the correlation is assumed to be small.) Meanwhile, Kaplan et al.'s distinguisher requires about $(2\sqrt{2}\pi) \cdot (1/c)$ queries. (See Appendix E of the full version [36] for details.) Thus our attack is about 2 times faster in this situation. For general cases where the variance of the correlation may be large, we do not observe evident difference between ours and Kaplan et al.'s because we have to run QAA multiple times (as $\mathcal{A}_3$ does).

So far we have discussed how to distinguish block ciphers from random permutations, but we expect the above distinguishers are also applicable to distinguish keyed functions from random functions of n-bit inputs, without changing the asymptotic complexity (in the same way as classical linear distinguishers work not only for permutations but Below we give some application examples, but they are essentially distinguishers on keyed functions from random functions, rather than block ciphers from random permutations.

5.1   Application Example: FEA-1 and FEA-2 Structures

FEA is a Korean standard (TTAK.KO-12.0275) for format preserving encryption [48], which has two variants named FEA-1 and FEA-2. Both variants adopt *tweakable* Feistel structures. Here we study linear distinguishers on these structures when round functions are ideally random.

The FEA-1 and FEA-2 structures look like Fig. 1. As in usual Feistel structures, plaintexts are divided into two parts. We focus on the case when the widths of the two branches are equal. A tweak T is also divided into two parts, denoted by T_L and T_R, and processed in an alternate manner. In FEA-1, the i-th round function takes T_L (resp., T_R) when $i \equiv 1$ (resp., $i \equiv 0$) mod 2. In FEA-2, the i-th round function takes T_L (resp., T_R) when $i \equiv 2$ (resp., $i \equiv 0$) mod 3. The $(3j + 1)$-th round function of FEA-1 does not take any tweak (or equivalently, take a constant value instead). For simplicity, we assume the tweak length is sufficiently large.

At CRYPTO 2021, Beyne showed multidimensional linear distinguishers on these structures [6]. The multidimensional linear approximation[15] for FEA-1 is a vector space V of completely linearly dependent input-output masks with $\dim(V) = n/2$ (when n is the block size of Feistel), and the sum of the squared correlations $\sum_{(\alpha,\beta) \in V} \mathrm{Cor}(\alpha, \beta)^2$ is equal to $2^{n(1-r/4)}$. Meanwhile, the approximation for FEA-2 is a vector space V' of linearly independent input-output masks with $\dim(V) = \dim(V_2') = n/2$ (here, we assume V' is decomposed as $V' = V_1' \times V_2'$), and the sum of the squared correlation is equal to $2^{n(1-r/6)}$.

---

[15] See the original paper [6] on details of linear approximations. What is significant here is only the dimensions of the approximations and the sum of the squared correlations.

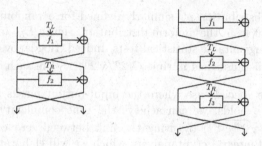

Fig. 1. The FEA-1 structure (left) and FEA-2 structure (right).

The classical distinguishing complexity is $O(2^{(r/4-3/4)n})$ for FEA-1 (resp., $O(2^{(r/6-3/4)n})$ for FEA-2). By applying our quantum distinguishers above, the complexity is reduced to $O(2^{(r/8-1/4)n})$ (resp., $O(2^{(r/12-1/4)n})$).

Remark 1. In [6], linear distinguishers are extended to message recovery attacks and key recovery attacks. Our distinguishers could also be extended to message or key recovery attacks in the quantum setting by just guessing the secret information with the Grover search, though, non-trivial extension of interest (beyond just applying Grover) would require another new idea and not be straightforward.

6 Speed-Up for Zero Correlation Linear Distinguishers

This section shows how CEA can be used to speed-up (multidimensional) zero correlation linear distinguishers [9]. We first recall the basic ideas of attacks in the classical setting.

6.1 Classical Zero Correlation Linear Distinguishers

Unlike linear cryptanalysis, zero correlation linear cryptanalysis exploits linear approximations of which the correlation is exactly zero.

For instance, let E_K be an n-bit block cipher and suppose $\mathrm{Cor}(E_K; \alpha, \beta) = 0$ holds for some input and output masks $\alpha, \beta \neq 0^n$. Then, $(\mathrm{Cor}(P; \alpha, \beta))^2$ for a random permutation P is distributed around 2^{-n} and non-zero with high probability. Hence we can distinguish E_K from P if we have sufficiently many ($\approx 2^n$) plaintext-ciphertext pairs by checking whether the estimated empirical correlation is zero or not.

This idea naturally extends to attacks exploiting multidimensional linear approximations of correlation zero (below we follow the notations of Sect. 3.2). Again, let E_K be an n-bit block cipher and $V \subset \mathbb{F}_2^n \times \mathbb{F}_2^n$ be a vector space such that $\mathrm{Cor}(E_K; \alpha, \beta) = 0$ for all $(\alpha, \beta) \in V$. Moreover, let S be an arbitrary basis of V. Then the distribution $p_S^{E_K}$ over $\mathbb{F}_2^{\dim(V)}$ defined by $p_S^{E_K}(z) := \mathrm{Pr}_x \left[\mathrm{Lin}_S^f(x) = z \right]$ exactly matches the uniform distribution. On the other hand, the distribution p_S^P similarly defined for a random permutation P is slightly different from the uniform distribution. Hence E_K and P can be distinguished by using suitable statistical tests. Indeed, Bogdanov et al. [8] showed that E_K can be distinguished in time $O(2^n/\sqrt{2^{\dim(V)}})$ in such a setting[16].

Remark 2. In the special case where the input-output masks are independent and $V = V_1 \times V_2$ holds, we can achieve the time complexity $O(2^n/2^{\dim(V_1)})$ instead of $O(2^n/\sqrt{2^{\dim(V)}})$ by using the link between zero correlation linear cryptanalysis and integral cryptanalysis, which we will elaborate in Sect. 7.

6.2   Quantum Speed-Up by CEA

Next, we study how to speed-up (multidimensional) zero correlation linear distinguishers by using CEA and QAA.

As well as linear distinguishers in Sect. 3.2, we introduce three distinguishers which we denote by $\mathcal{B}_1$, $\mathcal{B}_2$, and $\mathcal{B}_3$. $\mathcal{B}_1$ is a general distinguisher applicable to arbitrary multidimensional linear approximations. $\mathcal{B}_2$ (resp., $\mathcal{B}_3$) is applicable when the input and output masks are linearly independent (resp., completely dependent).

In what follows, we assume that $\mathrm{Cor}(E_K; \alpha, \beta)^2 = 0$ holds for all $(\alpha, \beta) \in V - \{\mathbf{0}\}$. $\mathcal{O}$ denotes the oracle, which is either E_K for a random K or a random permutation P. For notations related to $\mathcal{B}_2$ and $\mathcal{B}_3$, we use the same ones as those for $\mathcal{A}_2$ and $\mathcal{A}_3$ introduced on p.16.

Distinguisher $\mathcal{B}_1$ (General Case). When nothing can be assumed on linear dependence of masks, a natural way to mount a distinguisher by using QAA and CEA is to run the following procedure.

1. Let $F : \mathbb{F}_2^n \times \mathbb{F}_2^n \to \mathbb{F}_2$ be the Boolean function such that $F(\alpha, \beta) = 1$ iff $(\alpha, \beta) \in V - \{\mathbf{0}\}$.
2. Apply QAA on $\mathrm{CEA}^{\mathcal{O}}$ and F with the number of iterations $\lfloor \frac{\pi}{4}\sqrt{2^{2n-\dim(V)}} \rfloor$. Namely, let the unitary operator $Q(\mathrm{CEA}^{\mathcal{O}}, F)^i \mathrm{CEA}^{\mathcal{O}}$ act on $|0^n\rangle |0^n\rangle$ with $i = \lfloor \frac{\pi}{4}\sqrt{2^{2n-\dim(V)}} \rfloor$. Then, measure the resulting state by the computational basis and let (α, β) be the observed bit string.
3. If $F(\alpha, \beta) = 0$, return 1. Otherwise, return 0.

Some analysis shows that this algorithm distinguishes E_K and P with high probability. However, the running time of $\mathcal{B}_1$ is $O(\sqrt{2^{2n-\dim(V)}}) = O(2^n/\sqrt{2^{\dim(V)}})$, which is the same as the complexity of the classical distinguisher. Namely, $\mathcal{B}_1$ does not obtain any speed-up from classical attacks. Meanwhile, we can obtain some quantum speed-up when input-output masks are linearly independent or linearly completely dependent, which we explain below.

---

[16] Bogdanov and Wang showed a similar result assuming that many statistically independent linear approximations exist [10], but the assumption often does not hold.

Remark 3. $\mathcal{B}_1$ runs QAA only once, unlike $\mathcal{QD}$ of Proposition 2 (or its applications $\mathcal{A}_1$-$\mathcal{A}_3$) running QAA multiple times. This is because the probability $\Pr[F(\alpha, \beta) = 1]$ is exactly zero when (α, β) is obtained by measuring the state $\mathsf{CEA}^{E_K} |0^n\rangle |0^n\rangle$, and thus we can achieve a sufficiently high advantage with a single run of QAA.

Distinguishers $\mathcal{B}_2$ and $\mathcal{B}_3$. Here we show distinguishers $\mathcal{B}_2$ and $\mathcal{B}_3$ for linearly independent and completely dependent masks, respectively[17].

$\mathcal{B}_2$ is obtained by modifying the unitary operators and the number of iterations for QAA in $\mathcal{B}_1$. Specifically, we change

1. the unitary operator for QAA of $\mathcal{B}_1$ from $\mathsf{CEA}^{\mathcal{O}}$ to $\mathsf{CEA}^{\mathsf{msb}_w[\mathcal{O}]}$, and
2. the number of iterations from $\lfloor \frac{\pi}{4}\sqrt{2^{2n-\dim(V)}} \rfloor$ to $\lfloor \frac{\pi}{4}\sqrt{2^{n+w-\dim(V)}} \rfloor = \lfloor \frac{\pi}{4}\sqrt{2^{n-u}} \rfloor$.

$\mathcal{B}_3$ is obtained just by changing the parameter w appeared in $\mathcal{B}_2$ to $\dim(V)$.

$\mathcal{B}_2$ distinguishes E_K and P with high probability, roughly for the following reason: If the oracle given to $\mathcal{B}_2$ is E_K, $\mathcal{B}_2$ always returns 1. If the oracle given to $\mathcal{B}_2$ is a random permutation P, Claim 1 guarantees[18] that the probability that we observe $(\alpha, \beta) \in F^{-1}(1)$ when measuring $\mathsf{CEA}^{\mathsf{msb}_w[P]} |0^n\rangle |0^w\rangle$ is approximately equal to $2^{\dim(V)}/2^{n+w} = 2^{u-n}$. Hence the QAA with $O(\sqrt{2^{n-u}})$ iterations in Step 2 of $\mathcal{B}_2$ returns $(\alpha, \beta) \in F^{-1}(1)$ with high probability, and $\mathcal{B}_2$ returns 0. Thus $\mathcal{B}_2$ distinguishes E_K and P. Especially, $\mathcal{B}_2$ achieves a quadratic speed-up in the special case where $w = 1$ (see Remark 2). Similarly, $\mathcal{B}_3$ distinguishes E_K in time $O(\sqrt{2^n})$. More precisely, the following proposition holds.

Proposition 5. *If $\mathcal{B}_2$ (resp., $\mathcal{B}_3$) runs relative to E_K, then $\mathcal{B}_2$ (resp., $\mathcal{B}_3$) always outputs 1. If $\mathcal{B}_2$ (resp., $\mathcal{B}_3$) runs relative to a random permutation P, then the probability that $\mathcal{B}_2$ (resp., $\mathcal{B}_3$) outputs 0 is approximately lower bounded by $\frac{1}{2} \cdot (1 - 2^{-\dim(V)+1})$. In addition, the running time of $\mathcal{B}_2$ (resp., $\mathcal{B}_3$) is at most $2\lfloor \frac{\pi}{4}\sqrt{2^{n-u}} \rfloor + 1$ (resp., $2\lfloor \frac{\pi}{4}\sqrt{2^n} \rfloor + 1$) encryptions by E_K. (The probabilities are taken not only over the randomness of $\mathcal{B}_2$ or $\mathcal{B}_3$ but also over the randomness of choices of K or P.)*

A proof of the proposition is given in Section G of the full version [36].

6.3 Applications

Both of $\mathcal{B}_2$ and $\mathcal{B}_3$ have various immediate applications. For instance, Bogdanov and Rijmen showed multidimensional zero correlation linear approximations on the 5-round balanced Feistel structure, 18-round 4-branch Type-I generalized Feistel structure, and 9-round 4-branch Type-II generalized Feistel structure (see Fig. 2 and Table 1 of the full version [36]) when round functions are bijections. The input-output masks of the linear approximations are linearly completely

---

[17] Recall that we use the same notations as those for $\mathcal{A}_2$ and $\mathcal{A}_3$. See p.16 for details.
[18] Note that $2^n \cdot \sum_{(\alpha, \beta) \in V - \{0\}} \mathrm{Cor}(P; \alpha, \beta)^2$ in Claim 1 is equal to $2^n \cdot \mathrm{Cap}(p_S^P)$.

dependent. Thus $\mathcal{B}_3$ distinguishes these constructions in time $O(2^{n/2})$ (when inputs and outputs are n bits). In fact the linear approximations on the 4-branch Type-I/II generalized Feistel structures can be extended to k-branch structures for general[19] k in a straightforward manner, and $\mathcal{B}_3$ distinguishes $(k^2 + k - 2)$-round (resp., $(2k+1)$-round) k-branch Type-I (resp., Type-II) generalized Feistel structure in time $O(2^{n/2})$.

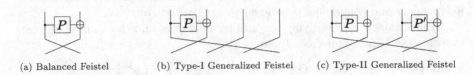

(a) Balanced Feistel   (b) Type-I Generalized Feistel   (c) Type-II Generalized Feistel

Fig. 2. One round of Balanced and (4-branch) generalized Feistel structures. What we assume is only that P and P' are bijections. Our attacks work regardless of whether P (and P') for different rounds are independent or not.

Table 1. Input-output mask patterns for balanced and generalized Feistel structures. $\alpha \in \mathbb{F}_2^{n/2}$ and $\beta \in \mathbb{F}^{n - \frac{n}{k}}$ are non-zero values. "0" for generalized Feistel structures denotes $0^{n/k} \in \mathbb{F}_2^{n/k}$.

Balanced	k-branch Type-I	k-branch Type-II
$(\alpha\|\|0^{n/2}, 0^{n/2}\|\|\alpha)$	$(\beta\|\|0\|\| \cdots \|\|0, 0\|\|\beta\|\|0\|\| \cdots \|\|0$	$(\alpha\|\|0\|\| \cdots \|\|0, 0\|\|0\|\| \cdots \|\|0\|\|\beta)$

Note that the numbers of rounds we attack here are larger than those broken by previous polynomial time attacks using Simon's algorithm in a black-box way. The number of rounds of balanced (resp., k-branch Type-I and Type-II) Feistel broken by previous polynomial time attacks is 4 [40] (resp., $k^2 - k + 1$ [51] and $k + 1$ [27]). See also Table 2 of the full version [36].

In fact, the complexity of our distinguishers may also be achieved just by speeding-up a one-dimensional zero-correlation linear distinguisher with simpler techniques. Still, to the authors' best knowledge, we are the first to point out the existence of attacks with such complexity.

There also exist lots of other previous works showing zero correlation approximations [1, 8–10, 56] and our $\mathcal{B}_2$ or $\mathcal{B}_3$ can be applied to all of them in principle. The amount of quantum speed-up compared to classical distinguishers depends on linear approximations, and we can achieve at most quadratic speed-up.

7   Speed-Up for Integral Distinguishers

This section shows applications of CEA to integral cryptanalysis. As shown by Bogdanov et al. [8] and Sun et al. [56], balanced property of a cipher is equivalent

---

[19] k must be even for Type-II structures.

to multidimensional zero correlation linear properties of which the input-output masks are linearly independent. Specifically, the following proposition holds[20].

Proposition 6 ([8,56]). *Let $F : \mathbb{F}_2^m \to \mathbb{F}_2^n$ be a function. Let $V_1 \subset \mathbb{F}_2^m, V_2 \subset \mathbb{F}_2^n$ be sub-vector spaces, and $V := V_1 \times V_2$. Then the following conditions are equivalent.*

1. *V is the set of input-output masks of a multidimensional zero correlation linear approximation of F, i.e., $\mathrm{Cor}(F; \alpha, \beta) = 0$ for all $(\alpha, \beta) \in V - \{\mathbf{0}\}$.*
2. *The function $G : x \mapsto \beta \cdot F(x \oplus \lambda)$ is balanced over $V_1^{\perp}$ for all $\lambda \in \mathbb{F}_2^m$ and $\beta \in V_2 - \{\mathbf{0}\}$.*

Remark 4. Note that this equivalence holds only for balanced property but not for zero-sum property. Our quantum attacks below also rely on the above equivalence. Especially, the attacks are applicable only if a balanced property exists.

Recall that the distinguisher $\mathcal{B}_2$ (Proposition 5) is applicable when a multidimensional zero correlation linear approximation exists and the input-output masks are linearly independent. Together with Proposition 6, this implies the following proposition.

Proposition 7. *Let E_K be an n-bit block cipher. Suppose some output bits of E_K are balanced over a vector space $V \subset \mathbb{F}_2^n$. (W.l.o.g., we assume the most significant w bits are balanced, and let $V' := \{x || 0^{n-w} | x \in \mathbb{F}_2^w \}$.) Then, by applying $\mathcal{B}_2$ on the zero correlation multidimensional linear approximations of $V^{\perp} \times V'$, we can distinguish E_K from P with time and query complexity at most $2\lfloor \frac{\pi}{4}\sqrt{2^{\dim(V)}} \rfloor + 1$. $\mathcal{B}_2$ always outputs 1 if the given encryption oracle is the real cipher E_K. If the oracle is a random permutation P, then $\mathcal{B}_2$ outputs 0 with probability at least $\frac{1}{2} \left(1 - 2^{-\dim(V)+1}\right)$.*

This proposition shows that we can obtain (almost) quadratic speed-up for integral distinguisher because the complexity of $\mathcal{B}_2$ is $\approx 1.6\sqrt{2^{\dim(V)}}$ while the complexity of the classical integral distinguisher is $2^{\dim(V)}$.

Still, this is at most quadratic speed-up. At first glance, achieving a more than quadratic speed-up seems impossible for integral distinguishers. However, we see possibility of a more than quadratic speed-up in some situations.

7.1 Possibility of More Than Quadratic Speed-Up

Roughly speaking, if a part of the outputs of a cipher (e.g., a specific byte of ciphertexts) is balanced on *multiple mutually orthogonal vector spaces* included in the input space, there exists possibility to achieve a more than quadratic quantum speed-up by using CEA.

Specifically, let $E_K : \mathbb{F}_2^n \to \mathbb{F}_2^n$ be a block cipher, and suppose there exist sub-vector spaces $V_1, \ldots, V_s \subset \mathbb{F}_2^m$ satisfying the following conditions.

---

[20] This equivalence was first shown by [8] and later refined by [56]. [56] proves the equivalence only in the special case $\dim(V_2) = 1$ but it immediately implies the equivalence for $\dim(V_2) > 1$.

1. $V_1, \ldots, V_s$ are mutually orthogonal, i.e., $V_i \perp V_j$ for $i \neq j$.
2. There exists some $d \leq n/2$ and $\dim(V_i) = d$ holds for all i.
3. A part of the outputs of E_K is balanced on $V_i \oplus \lambda$ for all $1 \leq i \leq s$ and arbitrary $\lambda \in \mathbb{F}_2^m$. (For ease of explanation, below we assume the most significant w bits of outputs of E_K are balanced.)

Then, by Proposition 6 we have $\mathrm{Cor}(\mathsf{msb}_w[E_K]; \alpha, \beta) = 0$ if $\alpha \in (V_1)^\perp \cup \cdots \cup (V_s)^\perp - \{\mathbf{0}\}$ and $(\alpha, \beta) \neq (0, 0)$. This means

$$\Pr_K \left[(\alpha, \beta) \leftarrow \mathsf{CEA}^{\mathsf{msb}_w[E_K]} : \alpha \perp V_i \text{ for some } i \text{ and } \alpha \neq 0 \text{ and } \beta \neq 0 \right] = 0.$$

Meanwhile, for a random permutation P we have

$$\Pr_P \left[(\alpha, \beta) \leftarrow \mathsf{CEA}^{\mathsf{msb}_w[P]} : \alpha \perp V_i \text{ for some } i \text{ and } \alpha \neq 0 \text{ and } \beta \neq 0 \right]$$

$$\overset{(*)}{=} \sum_{\substack{\alpha \neq 0, \beta \neq 0 \\ \alpha \perp V_i \text{ for some } i}} \mathbb{E}_P \left[\frac{\mathrm{Cor}(\mathsf{msb}_w[P]; \alpha, \beta)^2}{2^w} \right]$$

$$= \sum_{\substack{\alpha \neq 0, \beta \neq 0 \\ \alpha \perp V_i \text{ for some } i \\ \mathsf{lsb}_{n-w}[\beta] = 0}} \mathbb{E}_P \left[\frac{\mathrm{Cor}(P; \alpha, \beta)^2}{2^w} \right] \overset{(**)}{=} \sum_{\substack{\alpha \neq 0, \beta \neq 0 \\ \alpha \perp V_i \text{ for some } i \\ \mathsf{lsb}_{n-w}[\beta] = 0}} \frac{1}{2^w(2^n - 1)}$$

$$= \# \{ \alpha \in \mathbb{F}_2^n - \{\mathbf{0}\} \mid \alpha \perp V_i \text{ for some } i \} \cdot \frac{\# \{ \beta \in \mathbb{F}_2^n - \{\mathbf{0}\} \mid \mathsf{lsb}_{n-w}[\beta] = 0 \}}{2^w(2^n - 1)}$$

$$\geq \left(\sum_{1 \leq i \leq s} |V_i^\perp| - \sum_{1 \leq i < j \leq s} |V_i^\perp \cap V_j^\perp| - 1 \right) \cdot \frac{2^w - 1}{2^w(2^n - 1)}$$

$$\overset{V_i \perp V_j \text{ for } i \neq j}{\geq} \left(s2^{n-d} - s^2 2^{n-2d} - 1 \right) \cdot \frac{2^w - 1}{2^w(2^n - 1)} \approx \frac{s}{2^d}.$$

Here, $(*)$ (resp., $(**)$) follows from Proposition 3 (resp., Proposition 11 of the full version [36]).

Therefore, E_K can be distinguished from P in time about $\frac{\pi}{2} \sqrt{2^d/s}$ by applying QAA on $\mathsf{CEA}^{\mathsf{msb}_w[E_K]}$ (or $\mathsf{CEA}^{\mathsf{msb}_w[P]}$) and the Boolean function $F : \mathbb{F}_2^n \times \mathbb{F}_2^w \to \mathbb{F}_2$ such that $F(\alpha, \beta) = 1$ iff $\alpha \perp V_i$ for some $i = 1, \ldots, s$ and $\alpha \neq 0$ and $\beta \neq 0$.

This can lead to a more than quadratic speed-up compared to the corresponding classical integral distinguisher (when $s \geq 4$) because the classical complexity is 2^d: Even if we have such multiple spaces $V_1, \ldots, V_s$, what we can do in the classical setting is just to choose a single space V_i and check whether (a part of) E_K is balanced on that space, unless some additional properties can be assumed.

Application Examples. To see how the above distinguisher can be applied to concrete ciphers, let us recall the 3.5-round integral property of AES for an example [25]. If a tuple of certain four cells of inputs take all values while others being constant, we can make a single column after the first round take all values while others remain constant, and each cell after 3.5 rounds balanced (see Fig. 3). Since there are four choices on which tuple of four cells to activate (i.e., which column after the first round to activate), we are in the situation of the distinguisher explained above with $d = 32$ and $s = 4$ (V_i corresponds to a tuple of four active cells of inputs).

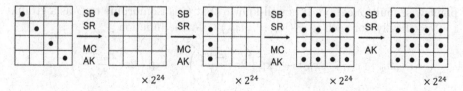

Fig. 3. The integral property of the 2.5-round AES. Cells with filled circles are those taking all values and others are constants. "$\times 2^{24}$" indicates that 2^{24} sets of the same active cell pattern shown in the figure is observed.

In fact this example itself is not so significant because more efficient distinguishers exist: If a tuple of four cells of inputs take all values like Fig. 3, actually a certain tuple of four cells of outputs take all values. This means that the integral property specifies a 32-bit permutation between part of inputs and outputs. Hence the 3.5-round AES is distinguished by checking if this part contains a collision in time $\approx \sqrt[3]{2^{32}}$ with the BHT algorithm [19].

Still, we observe an interesting attack when s is relatively large. For instance, suppose $s = 2^d$ holds. This situation happens if, e.g., E_K is a 4-bit cell SPN cipher with the same integral property as the 2.5-round AES (the latter 2.5 round of Fig. 3). Then $\Pr[F(\alpha, \beta) = 1] \approx s/2^d = 1$ holds when (α, β) is obtained by measuring $\mathsf{CEA}^{\mathsf{msb}_w}[P]$, while the probability is always zero for the real cipher E_K. Thus we can distinguish E_K only with a *single* quantum query, which apparently exhibits a more than quadratic speed-up.

The margin compared to the square-root of the classical complexity is not large, but this example is important in that a new-type example illustrating a qualitative difference between classical and quantum computation is achieved by using a classical cryptanalytic technique.

8   Extension to Generalized Linear Distinguishers

Linear cryptanalysis is useful when group operations are done in $\mathbb{Z}_2^n$, but some ciphers use other group operations such as modular additions (i.e., additions in $\mathbb{Z}/2^n\mathbb{Z}$), where generalized linear cryptanalysis on arbitrary finite groups [4] is more useful. Generalized linear cryptanalysis uses group characters instead of bit masks, but we observe again there exists a close relationship between (generalized) correlations and quantum computation via Fourier transform. This section shows how the technique of Sect. 5 extends to generalized linear distinguishers. In this section, the symbol "$\oplus$" denotes the direct sum of groups.

8.1   Fourier Transform on Arbitrary Finite Abelian Group

Let G be an arbitrary finite abelian group. Then, by the Chinese remainder theorem, there is a group isomorphism from G to $\mathbb{Z}/N_1\mathbb{Z} \oplus \cdots \oplus \mathbb{Z}/N_m\mathbb{Z}$ for some positive integers $N_1, \ldots, N_m$. We fix an isomorphism and identify the two groups. Recall that a character of a finite abelian group G is a group homomorphism $\phi : G \to \mathbb{C}^\times$. The set of characters of G is denoted by $\hat{G}$, which forms a group by point-wise multiplication. It is well-known that $\hat{G}$ is isomorphic to G as a group.

Specifically, for each $w = (w_1, \ldots, w_m) \in G$, the function

$$\mathsf{ch}_w : (x_1, \ldots, x_m) \mapsto \exp\left(2\pi i \frac{x_1 w_1}{N_1}\right) \cdots \exp\left(2\pi i \frac{x_m w_m}{N_m}\right)$$

is a character of G. In fact the map $w \mapsto \mathsf{ch}_w$ defines a group isomorphism from G to $\hat{G}$. We identify G with $\hat{G}$ by this isomorphism.

Let G be a finite abelian group and $F : G \to \mathbb{C}$ be a function. Then, the Fourier transform of F over G is a function $\mathcal{F}_G F : G \to \mathbb{C}$ defined by

$$\mathcal{F}_G F(w) := \sum_{x \in G} \frac{1}{\sqrt{|G|}} \cdot \overline{\mathsf{ch}_w(x)} \cdot F(x).$$

The inverse transform of $\mathcal{F}_G$, denoted by $\mathcal{F}_G^*$, is given by $\mathcal{F}_G^* F(x) = \sum_{w \in G} \frac{1}{\sqrt{|G|}} \cdot \mathsf{ch}_x(w) \cdot F(w)$.

We naturally identify a function from G to $\mathbb{C}$ (resp., the set of the functions from G to $\mathbb{C}$) with a vector in the $|G|$-dimensional vector space $\mathbb{C}^{|G|}$ (resp., the vector space $\mathbb{C}^{|G|}$). Moreover, we assume that $\mathbb{C}^{|G|}$ is endowed with the standard Hermitian inner product. Then $\mathcal{F}_G$ can be regarded as a unitary operator.

8.2   Linear Correlations

Let G, H be finite abelian groups and $f : G \to H$ be a function. For $\alpha \in G$ and $\beta \in H$, the (generalized) linear correlation $\mathrm{Cor}(f; \alpha, \beta)$ is defined as

$$\mathrm{Cor}(f; \alpha, \beta) := \sum_{x \in G} \frac{1}{|G|} \overline{\mathsf{ch}_\beta(f(x))} \cdot \mathsf{ch}_\alpha(x).$$

We call α (resp., β) an input mask (resp., output mask).

Let $f_{\mathrm{emb}} : G \oplus H \to \mathbb{C}$ be the function defined by $f_{\mathrm{emb}}(x, y) = 1$ if $y = f(x)$ and $f_{\mathrm{emb}}(x, y) = 0$ if $y \neq f(x)$. Then, some straightforward calculation shows that

$$((\mathcal{F}_G^* \otimes \mathcal{F}_H) f_{\mathrm{emb}})(\alpha, \beta) = \sqrt{|G|/|H|} \cdot \mathrm{Cor}(f; \alpha, \beta) \tag{7}$$

holds. (This corresponds to Eq. (3) for the linear cryptanalysis over $(\mathbb{Z}/2\mathbb{Z})^{\oplus n}$.)

8.3   Extension of CEA

For an arbitrary finite abelian group G, we assume that elements of G are appropriately encoded into n-bit strings for some n s.t. $|G| \le 2^n$. Let $\psi : G \to \mathbb{C}$ be a function satisfying $\sum_{x \in G} |\psi(x)|^2 = 1$, and $|\psi\rangle := \sum_x \psi(x) |x\rangle$. Recall that the Quantum Fourier Transform (QFT) over an abelian group G, denoted by QFT_G, is defined by

$$\mathrm{QFT}_G |\psi\rangle = \sum_x (\mathcal{F}_G^* \psi)(x) |x\rangle. \tag{8}$$

With these notations, the extension of CEA on a function $f : G \to H$ (G and H are finite abelian groups) is obtained by replacing the Hadamard transform in CEA with the QFT (or its inverse) over G and H. Specifically, the extended algorithm runs as follows.

Extended Version of CEA

(a) Prepare the initial state $|0_G\rangle |0_H\rangle$.
(b) Apply QFT_G on the first (left) register.
(c) Apply U_f on the state (i.e., make a quantum query to f).
(d) Apply $\mathrm{QFT}_G \otimes \mathrm{QFT}_H^*$ on the state.
(e) Measure the entire state by the computational basis and return the observed result $(\alpha, \beta) \in G \oplus H$.

We also use the symbol CEA^f to denote the extended algorithm.

The following proposition is an extension of Proposition 3.

Proposition 8. *The quantum state of* CEA^f *before the final measurement is*

$$\sum_{\alpha \in G, \beta \in H} \frac{\mathrm{Cor}(f; \alpha, \beta)}{\sqrt{|H|}} |\alpha\rangle |\beta\rangle. \tag{9}$$

In particular, for any subset $S \subset G \oplus H$,

$$\Pr\left[(\alpha, \beta) \leftarrow \mathrm{CEA}^f : (\alpha, \beta) \in S\right] = \sum_{(\alpha, \beta) \in S} \frac{\mathrm{Cor}(f; \alpha, \beta)^2}{|H|} \tag{10}$$

holds.

Proof. The quantum state of CEA^f before the final measurement is

$$(\mathrm{QFT}_G \otimes \mathrm{QFT}_H^*)U_f(\mathrm{QFT}_G \otimes I_n)|0_G\rangle|0_H\rangle$$

$$= (\mathrm{QFT}_G \otimes \mathrm{QFT}_H^*)U_f \sum_{x \in G} \frac{1}{\sqrt{|G|}}|x\rangle|0_H\rangle$$

$$= (\mathrm{QFT}_G \otimes \mathrm{QFT}_H^*) \sum_{x \in G} \frac{1}{\sqrt{|G|}}|x\rangle|f(x)\rangle$$

$$\overset{\text{Def. of } f_{\mathrm{emb}}}{=} (\mathrm{QFT}_G \otimes \mathrm{QFT}_H^*) \sum_{x \in G, y \in H} \frac{f_{\mathrm{emb}}(x,y)}{\sqrt{|G|}}|x\rangle|y\rangle$$

$$\overset{\text{Def. of QFT}}{=} \sum_{\alpha \in G, \beta \in H} \frac{((\mathcal{F}_G^* \otimes \mathcal{F}_H)f_{\mathrm{emb}})(\alpha, \beta)}{\sqrt{|G|}}|\alpha\rangle|\beta\rangle$$

$$\overset{\text{Eq. (7)}}{=} \sum_{\alpha \in G, \beta \in H} \frac{\mathrm{Cor}(f; \alpha, \beta)}{\sqrt{|H|}}|\alpha\rangle|\beta\rangle .$$

Hence we have Eq. (9). Equation (10) immediately follows from Eq. (9). □

8.4 Quantum Speed-Up for Generalized Linear Distinguishers

Let $f : G \to H$ be a function, where G and H are finite abelian groups. Here we define linearly independent masks and linearly completely dependent masks.

1. Suppose G and H are decomposed as $G = G_1 \oplus G_2$ and $H = H_1 \oplus H_2$. Then, we say the set $G_1 \oplus H_1 (\subset G \oplus H)$ is a set of linearly independent input-output masks.
2. Suppose again the decomposition $G = G_1 \oplus G_2$ and $H = H_1 \oplus H_2$, and assume that there is a group isomorphism $\phi : G_1 \to H_1$. Then we say that the set $\{(g, \phi(g))|g \in G_1\}$ is a set of linearly completely dependent input-output masks.

We show distinguishers when input-output masks are linearly independent or completely dependent, which correspond to $\mathcal{A}_2$ and $\mathcal{A}_3$ in Sect. 5. We provide only rough ideas and heuristic estimations, and omit detailed analysis.

Distinguisher for Linearly Independent Input-Output Masks. Suppose $f_K : G \to H$ is a keyed function, G and H are decomposed as $G = G_1 \oplus G_2$, $H = H_1 \oplus H_2$, and $\sum_{\alpha \in G_1, \beta \in H_1} \mathrm{Cor}(f_K; \alpha, \beta)^2/|H_1| \gg \frac{1}{|G_2|}$ holds. Let $f_K^{(1)} : G \to H_1$ be the projection of f_K onto H_1, and $F : G_1 \oplus H_1 \to \{0, 1\}$ be the Boolean function such that $F(\alpha, \beta) = 1$ iff $(\alpha, \beta) \in G_1 \oplus H_1$. Then,

$$p_{\mathrm{real}} := \Pr\left[(\alpha, \beta) \leftarrow \mathsf{CEA}^{f_K^{(1)}} : F(\alpha, \beta) = 1\right] = \sum_{(\alpha, \beta) \in G_1 \oplus H_1} \frac{\mathrm{Cor}(f_K; \alpha, \beta)^2}{|H_1|}$$

follows from Proposition 8. Meanwhile, for a random function $\text{RF} : G \to H$,

$$p_{\text{ideal}} := \Pr\left[(\alpha,\beta) \leftarrow \text{CEA}^{\text{RF}^{(1)}} : F(\alpha,\beta) = 1\right] = \sum_{(\alpha,\beta)\in G_1\oplus H_1} \frac{\text{Cor}(\text{RF};\alpha,\beta)^2}{|H_1|}$$

$$\approx \sum_{(\alpha,\beta)\in G_1\oplus H_1} \frac{1}{|G|} \cdot \frac{1}{|H_1|} = \frac{1}{|G_2|}.$$

(We heuristically assume the third equality approximately holds due to [6, Theorem 3.2].) Since $p_{\text{real}} \gg p_{\text{ideal}}$ by assumption, we can distinguish f_K from RF by applying the QAA on $\text{CEA}^{f_K^{(1)}}$ (or $\text{CEA}^{\text{RF}^{(1)}}$) and F with $O(\sqrt{1/p_{\text{real}}})$ iterations.

Distinguisher for Linearly Completely Dependent Input-Output Masks. Again, let $f_K : G \to H$ be a keyed function, G and H are decomposed as $G = G_1 \oplus G_2$, $H = H_1 \oplus H_2$. Moreover, assume there is a group isomorphism $\phi : G_1 \to H_1$ and $\sum_{\alpha\in G_1} \text{Cor}(f_K;\alpha,\phi(\alpha))^2/|H_1| \gg \frac{1}{|G|}$ holds. Let $F : G_1 \oplus H_1 \to \{0,1\}$ be the binary function such that $F(\alpha,\beta) = 1$ iff $\alpha \in G_1$ and $\beta = \phi(\alpha)$. Then, from Proposition 8,

$$p_{\text{real}} := \Pr\left[(\alpha,\beta) \leftarrow \text{CEA}^{f_K^{(1)}} : F(\alpha,\beta) = 1\right] = \sum_{\alpha\in G_1} \frac{\text{Cor}(f_K;\alpha,\phi(\alpha))^2}{|H_1|}$$

follows. On the other hand, for a random function $\text{RF} : G \to H$ we have

$$p_{\text{ideal}} := \Pr\left[(\alpha,\beta) \leftarrow \text{CEA}^{\text{RF}^{(1)}} : F(\alpha,\beta) = 1\right] = \sum_{\alpha\in G_1} \frac{\text{Cor}(\text{RF};\alpha,\phi(\alpha))^2}{|H_1|}$$

$$\approx \sum_{\alpha\in G_1} \frac{1}{|G|} \cdot \frac{1}{|H_1|} = \frac{1}{|G|}.$$

Since $p_{\text{real}} \gg p_{\text{ideal}}$ holds by assumption, we can distinguish f_K from RF by applying the QAA on $\text{CEA}^{f_K^{(1)}}$ (or $\text{CEA}^{\text{RF}^{(1)}}$) and F with $O(\sqrt{1/p_{\text{real}}})$ iterations.

Application to the FF3-1 Structure. Beyne [6] showed generalized linear distinguishers on the FF3-1 structure in addition to linear distinguishers on FEA. The FF3-1 structure is almost the same as the FEA-1 structure (see Fig. 1), but the XOR operations in FEA-1 are replaced with modular additions in FF3-1. Thus, generalized linear distinguisher is more suitable for the FF3-1 structure.

The (generalized) linear approximation for FF3-1 in [6] is similar to the multidimensional linear approximation for FEA-1, but underlying groups are different from $\mathbb{Z}_2^n$. In fact, firstly a keyed function $F_K : \mathbb{Z}/2^{n/2}\mathbb{Z} \oplus \mathbb{Z}_2^t \to \mathbb{Z}/2^{n/2}\mathbb{Z}$ is built from the FF3-1 structure by fixing some inputs (here, input means plaintext and tweak) and truncating some outputs, and the distinguisher is applied F_K. The set (sub-group) of input-output masks is given by $\{((\alpha,0),\alpha) \in (\mathbb{Z}/2^{n/2}\mathbb{Z} \oplus \mathbb{Z}_2^t) \oplus \mathbb{Z}/2^{n/2}\mathbb{Z} \,|\, \alpha \in \mathbb{Z}/2^{n/2}\mathbb{Z}\}$. In particular, the input-output masks are linearly completely dependent. The corresponding sum of the squared correlation is estimated as $\sum_{\alpha \in \mathbb{Z}/2^n/2\mathbb{Z}} \mathrm{Cor}(F_K; (\alpha, 0), \alpha)^2 \approx 2^{-n(r/4-1)}$, and the classical distinguishing complexity is $O(2^{(r/4-3/4)n})$.

On the other hand, if we apply the quantum distinguisher explained above, we achieve the complexity $O(2^{(r/8-1/4)n})$.

9   Concluding Remarks

This paper showed a quantum speed-up for the multidimensional (zero correlation) linear distinguishers for the first time in such a way to exploit multidimensional approximation in a non-trivial way. Firstly, we observed that there is a close relationship between the subroutine of Simon's algorithm and linear correlations of functions via Fourier transform. Specifically, a slightly modified version of the subroutine, which we call CEA, returns input and output linear masks of a target function with probability proportional to the squared linear correlation. Combining CEA with QAA, we achieved a quantum speed-up for multidimensional linear distinguishers. It is interesting that, only with a slight modification made, the subroutine of Simon's algorithm can be used to speed-up such a statistical attack. Our technique is naturally extended to generalized linear distinguishers on arbitrary finite abelian groups by replacing the Hadamard transform in CEA with general QFT. We also showed that CEA similarly speeds-up multidimensional zero correlation linear distinguishers, as well as some integral distinguishers via the correspondence shown by Bogdanov et al. and Sun et al [8,56]. Especially, we observe that a more than quadratic speed-up is possible if an integral property holds on multiple mutually orthogonal vector spaces of the same dimension, and even a single-query distinguisher for a toy example of a 4-bit cell SPN cipher with the same integral property as the 2.5-round AES.

Future Directions. An important future work is to investigate how to extend our technique to key-recovery attacks, or combine it with Schrottenloher's [53].

All the distinguishers in this paper can be extended to key-recovery attacks just by guessing sub-keys of additional rounds using Grover's algorithm. Suppose we would like to recover the key of an $(r + r')$-round cipher and there is a (quantum) r-round distinguisher on the cipher running in time T. In addition, assume that we can apply the distinguisher on the intermediate r rounds if we know a k-bit subkey K' in the remaining r'-rounds. Then, roughly speaking, by just guessing the subkey K' with the Grover search while checking if a key-guess is correct with the distinguisher, we achieve an $(r + r')$-round quantum key-recovery attack of time complexity $O(T \cdot 2^{k/2})$.

Still this idea is too naive, compared to classical key-recovery attacks using sophisticated techniques such as the FFT [22,29,57]. As mentioned in Sect. 1.2, the recent work by Schrottenloher [53] has shown how to combine such key-recovery techniques using the FFT with the QFT, taking multiple linear approximations into account. However, in Schrottenloher's attack, multiple approximations contribute to only the precision of the attack by a constant factor, and does not contribute much to reducing time complexity. It is definitely an important and interesting future work to investigate theoretical relationships between our technique with Schrottenloher's and study how to reduce the time complexity of key-recovery exploiting multidimensional approximations.

Another important future work is to study quantum speed-up for integral distinguishers based on zero-sum properties. As mentioned before, our quantum integral distinguishers are applicable only if the distinguishers are based on a balanced functions and not a zero-sum property. However, distinguishers based on zero-sum properties often break more rounds than those on balanced functions, especially when extended to key-recovery attacks. Since multiple integral properties sometimes could lead to a more than quadratic speed-up, a quantum attack breaking more rounds of a cipher than classical attacks may be found by investigating this direction.

It would be also of interest to investigate how the super-quadratic speed-up in Sect. 7.1 can be reproduced more broadly. We observe that the following two things are essential in achieving that speed-up: (i) There exist multiple properties that are similar to each other, but only one of them can be exploited at a time in the classical setting. (For the 2.5-round integral property of AES-like ciphers, there are 16 choices on which input cell to activate, but the existence of multiple choices is not exploited in the classical distinguisher.) (ii) The properties are translated/embedded into quantum amplitude in some sense (by using CEA, through the correspondence between integral and zero-correlation linear properties). So, if we find some classical properties satisfying (i) and a quantum technique enabling (ii), we might be able to reproduce similar quantum speed-ups, not only for linear/integral distinguishers but also for some other techniques.

References

1. Ankele, R., Dobraunig, C., Guo, J., Lambooij, E., Leander, G., Todo, Y.: Zero-correlation attacks on tweakable block ciphers with linear tweakey expansion. IACR Trans. Symmetric Cryptol. **2019**(1), 192–235 (2019)
2. Ashur, T., Khan, M., Nyberg, K.: Structural and statistical analysis of multidimensional linear approximations of random functions and permutations. IEEE Trans. Inf. Theory **68**(2), 1296–1315 (2022)
3. Baignères, T., Junod, P., Vaudenay, S.: How far can we go beyond linear cryptanalysis? In: Lee, P.J. (ed.) ASIACRYPT 2004. LNCS, vol. 3329, pp. 432–450. Springer, Heidelberg (2004). https://doi.org/10.1007/978-3-540-30539-2_31
4. Baignères, T., Stern, J., Vaudenay, S.: Linear cryptanalysis of non binary ciphers. In: Adams, C., Miri, A., Wiener, M. (eds.) SAC 2007. LNCS, vol. 4876, pp. 184–211. Springer, Heidelberg (2007). https://doi.org/10.1007/978-3-540-77360-3_13
5. Bernstein, E., Vazirani, U.V.: Quantum complexity theory. SIAM J. Comput. **26**(5), 1411–1473 (1997)
6. Beyne, T.: Linear cryptanalysis of FF3-1 and FEA. In: Malkin, T., Peikert, C. (eds.) CRYPTO 2021, Part I. LNCS, vol. 12825, pp. 41–69. Springer, Cham (2021). https://doi.org/10.1007/978-3-030-84242-0_3

7. Biryukov, A., De Cannière, C., Quisquater, M.: On multiple linear approximations. In: Franklin, M. (ed.) CRYPTO 2004. LNCS, vol. 3152, pp. 1–22. Springer, Heidelberg (2004). https://doi.org/10.1007/978-3-540-28628-8_1

8. Bogdanov, A., Leander, G., Nyberg, K., Wang, M.: Integral and multidimensional linear distinguishers with correlation zero. In: Wang, X., Sako, K. (eds.) ASIACRYPT 2012. LNCS, vol. 7658, pp. 244–261. Springer, Heidelberg (2012). https://doi.org/10.1007/978-3-642-34961-4_16

9. Bogdanov, A., Rijmen, V.: Linear hulls with correlation zero and linear cryptanalysis of block ciphers. Des. Codes Cryptogr. **70**(3), 369–383 (2014)

10. Bogdanov, A., Wang, M.: Zero correlation linear cryptanalysis with reduced data complexity. In: Canteaut, A. (ed.) FSE 2012. LNCS, vol. 7549, pp. 29–48. Springer, Heidelberg (2012). https://doi.org/10.1007/978-3-642-34047-5_3

11. Bonnetain, X.: Hidden structures and quantum cryptanalysis. Ph.D. thesis (2019)

12. Bonnetain, X., Hosoyamada, A., Naya-Plasencia, M., Sasaki, Yu., Schrottenloher, A.: Quantum attacks without superposition queries: the offline Simon's algorithm. In: Galbraith, S.D., Moriai, S. (eds.) ASIACRYPT 2019, Part I. LNCS, vol. 11921, pp. 552–583. Springer, Cham (2019). https://doi.org/10.1007/978-3-030-34578-5_20

13. Bonnetain, X., Leurent, G., Naya-Plasencia, M., Schrottenloher, A.: Quantum linearization attacks. In: Tibouchi, M., Wang, H. (eds.) ASIACRYPT 2021, Part I. LNCS, vol. 13090, pp. 422–452. Springer, Cham (2021). https://doi.org/10.1007/978-3-030-92062-3_15

14. Bonnetain, X., Naya-Plasencia, M., Schrottenloher, A.: On quantum slide attacks. In: Paterson, K.G., Stebila, D. (eds.) SAC 2019. LNCS, vol. 11959, pp. 492–519. Springer, Cham (2020). https://doi.org/10.1007/978-3-030-38471-5_20

15. Bonnetain, X., Naya-Plasencia, M., Schrottenloher, A.: Quantum security analysis of AES. IACR Trans. Symmetric Cryptol. **2019**(2), 55–93 (2019)

16. Bonnetain, X., Schrottenloher, A., Sibleyras, F.: Beyond quadratic speedups in quantum attacks on symmetric schemes. In: Dunkelman, O., Dziembowski, S. (eds.) EUROCRYPT 2022, Part III. LNCS, vol. 13277, pp. 315–344. Springer, Cham (2022). https://doi.org/10.1007/978-3-031-07082-2_12

17. Boyer, M., Brassard, G., Høyer, P., Tapp, A.: Tight bounds on quantum searching. Fortschritte der Physik: Progress Phys. **46**(4–5), 493–505 (1998)

18. Brassard, G., Hoyer, P., Mosca, M., Tapp, A.: Quantum amplitude amplification and estimation. Contemp. Math. **305**, 53–74 (2002)

19. Brassard, G., HØyer, P., Tapp, A.: Quantum cryptanalysis of hash and claw-free functions. In: Lucchesi, C.L., Moura, A.V. (eds.) LATIN 1998. LNCS, vol. 1380, pp. 163–169. Springer, Heidelberg (1998). https://doi.org/10.1007/BFb0054319

20. Canale, F., Leander, G., Stennes, L.: Simon's algorithm and symmetric crypto: generalizations and automatized applications (2022)

21. Cho, J.Y.: Linear cryptanalysis of reduced-round PRESENT. In: Pieprzyk, J. (ed.) CT-RSA 2010. LNCS, vol. 5985, pp. 302–317. Springer, Heidelberg (2010). https://doi.org/10.1007/978-3-642-11925-5_21

22. Collard, B., Standaert, F.-X., Quisquater, J.-J.: Improving the time complexity of Matsui's linear cryptanalysis. In: Nam, K.-H., Rhee, G. (eds.) ICISC 2007. LNCS, vol. 4817, pp. 77–88. Springer, Heidelberg (2007). https://doi.org/10.1007/978-3-540-76788-6_7

23. Daemen, J., Govaerts, R., Vandewalle, J.: Correlation matrices. In: Preneel, B. (ed.) FSE 1994. LNCS, vol. 1008, pp. 275–285. Springer, Heidelberg (1995). https://doi.org/10.1007/3-540-60590-8_21

24. Daemen, J., Knudsen, L., Rijmen, V.: The block cipher Square. In: Biham, E. (ed.) FSE 1997. LNCS, vol. 1267, pp. 149–165. Springer, Heidelberg (1997). https://doi. org/10.1007/BFb0052343

25. Daemen, J., Rijmen, V.: AES proposal: Rijndael (1999)

26. Daemen, J., Rijmen, V.: Probability distributions of correlation and differentials in block ciphers. J. Math. Cryptol. $1(3)$, 221–242 (2007)

27. Dong, X., Li, Z., Wang, X.: Quantum cryptanalysis on some generalized Feistel schemes. Sci. China Inf. Sci. $62(2)$, 22501:1–22501:12 (2019)

28. Dong, X., Sun, S., Shi, D., Gao, F., Wang, X., Hu, L.: Quantum collision attacks on AES-like hashing with low quantum random access memories. In: Moriai, S., Wang, H. (eds.) ASIACRYPT 2020, Part II. LNCS, vol. 12492, pp. 727–757. Springer, Cham (2020). https://doi.org/10.1007/978-3-030-64834-3_25

29. Flórez-Gutiérrez, A., Naya-Plasencia, M.: Improving key-recovery in linear attacks: application to 28-round PRESENT. In: Canteaut, A., Ishai, Y. (eds.) EURO- CRYPT 2020, Part I. LNCS, vol. 12105, pp. 221–249. Springer, Cham (2020). https://doi.org/10.1007/978-3-030-45721-1_9

30. Grover, L.K.: A fast quantum mechanical algorithm for database search. In: ACM STOC 1996, pp. 212–219. ACM (1996)

31. Guo, J., Liu, G., Song, L., Tu, Y.: Exploring SAT for cryptanalysis: (quantum) collision attacks against 6-round SHA-3. To appear at ASIACRYPT 2022

32. Hermelin, M., Cho, J.Y., Nyberg, K.: Multidimensional linear cryptanalysis of reduced round Serpent. In: Mu, Y., Susilo, W., Seberry, J. (eds.) ACISP 2008. LNCS, vol. 5107, pp. 203–215. Springer, Heidelberg (2008). https://doi.org/10. 1007/978-3-540-70500-0_15

33. Hermelin, M., Cho, J.Y., Nyberg, K.: Multidimensional extension of matsui's algorithm 2. In: Dunkelman, O. (ed.) FSE 2009. LNCS, vol. 5665, pp. 209–227. Springer, Heidelberg (2009). https://doi.org/10.1007/978-3-642-03317-9_13

34. Hermelin, M., Cho, J.Y., Nyberg, K.: Multidimensional linear cryptanalysis. J. Cryptol. $32(1)$, 1–34 (2019)

35. Hermelin, M., Nyberg, K.: Multidimensional linear distinguishing attacks and boolean functions. In: Fourth International Workshop on Boolean Functions: Cryp- tography and Applications (2008)

36. Hosoyamada, A.: Quantum speed-up for multidimensional (zero correlation) linear and integral distinguishers. IACR Cryptology ePrint Archive 2022/1558 (2022)

37. Hosoyamada, A., Sasaki, Yu.: Cryptanalysis against symmetric-key schemes with online classical queries and offline quantum computations. In: Smart, N.P. (ed.) CT-RSA 2018. LNCS, vol. 10808, pp. 198–218. Springer, Cham (2018). https:// doi.org/10.1007/978-3-319-76953-0_11

38. Hosoyamada, A., Sasaki, Yu.: Finding hash collisions with quantum computers by using differential trails with smaller probability than birthday bound. In: Canteaut, A., Ishai, Y. (eds.) EUROCRYPT 2020, Part II. LNCS, vol. 12106, pp. 249–279. Springer, Cham (2020). https://doi.org/10.1007/978-3-030-45724-2_9

39. Hosoyamada, A., Sasaki, Yu.: Quantum collision attacks on reduced SHA-256 and SHA-512. In: Malkin, T., Peikert, C. (eds.) CRYPTO 2021, Part I. LNCS, vol. 12825, pp. 616–646. Springer, Cham (2021). https://doi.org/10.1007/978-3-030- 84242-0_22

40. Ito, G., Hosoyamada, A., Matsumoto, R., Sasaki, Yu., Iwata, T.: Quantum chosen- ciphertext attacks against Feistel ciphers. In: Matsui, M. (ed.) CT-RSA 2019. LNCS, vol. 11405, pp. 391–411. Springer, Cham (2019). https://doi.org/10.1007/ 978-3-030-12612-4_20

41. Kaliski, B.S., Robshaw, M.J.B.: Linear cryptanalysis using multiple approximations. In: Desmedt, Y.G. (ed.) CRYPTO 1994. LNCS, vol. 839, pp. 26–39. Springer, Heidelberg (1994). https://doi.org/10.1007/3-540-48658-5_4

42. Kaplan, M., Leurent, G., Leverrier, A., Naya-Plasencia, M.: Breaking symmetric cryptosystems using quantum period finding. In: Robshaw, M., Katz, J. (eds.) CRYPTO 2016, Part II. LNCS, vol. 9815, pp. 207–237. Springer, Heidelberg (2016). https://doi.org/10.1007/978-3-662-53008-5_8

43. Kaplan, M., Leurent, G., Leverrier, A., Naya-Plasencia, M.: Quantum differential and linear cryptanalysis. IACR Trans. Symmetric Cryptol. **2016**(1), 71–94 (2016)

44. Knudsen, L., Wagner, D.: Integral cryptanalysis. In: Daemen, J., Rijmen, V. (eds.) FSE 2002. LNCS, vol. 2365, pp. 112–127. Springer, Heidelberg (2002). https://doi.org/10.1007/3-540-45661-9_9

45. Kuwakado, H., Morii, M.: Quantum distinguisher between the 3-round Feistel cipher and the random permutation. In: ISIT 2010, pp. 2682–2685. IEEE (2010)

46. Kuwakado, H., Morii, M.: Security on the quantum-type Even-Mansour cipher. In: ISITA 2012, pp. 312–316. IEEE (2012)

47. Leander, G., May, A.: Grover meets Simon – quantumly attacking the FX-construction. In: Takagi, T., Peyrin, T. (eds.) ASIACRYPT 2017. LNCS, vol. 10625, pp. 161–178. Springer, Cham (2017). https://doi.org/10.1007/978-3-319-70697-9_6

48. Lee, J.-K., Koo, B., Roh, D., Kim, W.-H., Kwon, D.: Format-preserving encryption algorithms using families of tweakable blockciphers. In: Lee, J., Kim, J. (eds.) ICISC 2014. LNCS, vol. 8949, pp. 132–159. Springer, Cham (2015). https://doi.org/10.1007/978-3-319-15943-0_9

49. Matsui, M.: Linear cryptanalysis method for DES cipher. In: Helleseth, T. (ed.) EUROCRYPT 1993. LNCS, vol. 765, pp. 386–397. Springer, Heidelberg (1994). https://doi.org/10.1007/3-540-48285-7_33

50. Murphy, S.: The independence of linear approximations in symmetric cryptanalysis. IEEE Trans. Inf. Theory **52**(12), 5510–5518 (2006)

51. Ni, B., Ito, G., Dong, X., Iwata, T.: Quantum attacks against type-1 generalized Feistel ciphers and applications to CAST-256. In: Hao, F., Ruj, S., Sen Gupta, S. (eds.) INDOCRYPT 2019. LNCS, vol. 11898, pp. 433–455. Springer, Cham (2019). https://doi.org/10.1007/978-3-030-35423-7_22

52. Nielsen, M.A., Chuang, I.L.: Quantum Computation and Quantum Information: 10th Anniversary Edition. Cambridge University Press, Cambridge (2010)

53. Schrottenloher, A.: Quantum linear key-recovery attacks using the QFT. IACR Cryptology ePrint Archive 2023/184 (2023)

54. Shi, R., Xie, H., Feng, H., Yuan, F., Liu, B.: Quantum zero correlation linear cryptanalysis. Quantum Inf. Process. **21**(8), 293 (2022)

55. Simon, D.R.: On the power of quantum computation. SIAM J. Comput. **26**(5), 1474–1483 (1997)

56. Sun, B., Liu, Z., Rijmen, V., Li, R., Cheng, L., Wang, Q., Alkhzaimi, H., Li, C.: Links among impossible differential, integral and zero correlation linear cryptanalysis. In: Gennaro, R., Robshaw, M. (eds.) CRYPTO 2015, Part I. LNCS, vol. 9215, pp. 95–115. Springer, Heidelberg (2015). https://doi.org/10.1007/978-3-662-47989-6_5

57. Todo, Y., Aoki, K.: Fast Fourier transform key recovery for integral attacks. IEICE Trans. Fundam. Electron. Commun. Comput. Sci. **98-A**(9), 1944–1952 (2015)
58. Xiao, G., Massey, J.L.: A spectral characterization of correlation-immune combining functions. IEEE Trans. Inf. Theory **34**(3), 569–571 (1988)
59. Xie, H., Yang, L.: Using Bernstein-Vazirani algorithm to attack block ciphers. Des. Codes Cryptogr. **87**(5), 1161–1182 (2019)

Exact Security Analysis of ASCON

Bishwajit Chakraborty[1,2], Chandranan Dhar[1(✉)], and Mridul Nandi[1,3]

[1] Indian Statistical Institute, Kolkata, India
chandranandhar@gmail.com
[2] Nanyang Technological University, Nanyang, Singapore
bishwajit.chakrabort@ntu.edu.sg
[3] Institute for Advancing Intelligence, TCG CREST, Kolkata, India

Abstract. The ASCON cipher suite, offering both authenticated encryption with associated data (AEAD) and hashing functionality, has recently emerged as the winner of the NIST Lightweight Cryptography (LwC) standardization process. The AEAD schemes within ASCON, namely ASCON-128 and ASCON-128a, have also been previously selected as the preferred lightweight authenticated encryption solutions in the CAESAR competition. In this paper, we present a tight and comprehensive security analysis of the ASCON AEAD schemes within the random permutation model. Existing integrity analyses of ASCON (and any Duplex AEAD scheme in general) commonly include the term $DT/2^c$, where D and T represent data and time complexities respectively, and c denotes the capacity of the underlying sponge. In this paper, we demonstrate that ASCON achieves AE security when T is bounded by $\min\{2^\kappa, 2^c\}$ (where κ is the key size), and DT is limited to 2^b (with b being the size of the underlying permutation, which is 320 for ASCON). Our findings indicate that in accordance with NIST requirements, ASCON allows for a tag size as low as 64 bits while enabling a higher rate of 192 bits, surpassing the recommended rate.

Keywords: ASCON · AEAD · tight security · lightweight cryptography

1 Introduction

The Sponge function, initially proposed by Bertoni et al. at the ECRYPT Hash Workshop [3], serves as a mode of operation for variable output-length hash functions and has gained significant popularity. This is evident from the numerous Sponge-based constructions submitted in the NIST SHA-3 competition, with Keccak [7] being the notable winner. At a high level, a Sponge construction utilizes a fixed permutation π of size b and a b-bit state, which is divided into a c-bit capacity and an $r := (b - c)$-bit rate for the Sponge. The Sponge construction begins by initializing the state to zero and padding the input message using a padding function, followed by dividing it into r-bit blocks. Then, the absorption phase of the Sponge construction commences, where the message is XOR-ed with the rate part of the sponge while interleaved with applications of π. Once

© International Association for Cryptologic Research 2023
J. Guo and R. Steinfeld (Eds.): ASIACRYPT 2023, LNCS 14440, pp. 346–369, 2023.
https://doi.org/10.1007/978-981-99-8727-6_12

the absorption phase is complete, the squeezing phase begins. In this phase, the first r bits of the state are outputted as output blocks, again interleaved with applications of π.

The Duplex construction [4] is a variant of the Sponge construction and serves as a widely used approach for constructing authenticated encryption schemes. The Duplex construction maintains a state between calls and processes input strings while producing output strings that depend on all previously received inputs. At a high level, the Duplex mode is a stateful construction that comprises an initialization interface and a duplexing interface. Initialization creates an initial state using the underlying permutation π, and each duplexing call to π absorbs and squeezes r bits of data. The usage of keyed Duplex approach in constructing authenticated encryption modes is evident from the numerous submissions in competitions like CAESAR (including the winner ASCON [13, 14]) and the recently concluded NIST LwC competition (with 26 total Duplex-type submissions, notably including the winner ASCON). The security analysis of keyed Duplex-type AEAD modes involves considering two parameters: the data complexity D (representing the total number of initialization and duplexing calls to π) and the time complexity T (representing the total number of direct calls to π).

1.1 ASCON

ASCON was initially introduced as a candidate in Round 1 of the CAESAR competition [11]. Subsequent versions (v1.1 and v1.2) incorporated minor modifications to the original design (version 1 [14]). The latest version (v1.2 [13]), declared as the winner of the NIST Lightweight Cryptography (LwC) project [20], includes the ASCON-128 and ASCON-128a authenticated ciphers, as well as the ASCON-HASH hash function and the ASCON-XOF extendable output function. All the schemes in the suite ensure 128-bit security and utilize a common 320-bit permutation internally, enabling the implementation of both duplex-based AEAD and sponge-based extendable-output hashing with a single lightweight primitive.

The authenticated encryption mode of ASCON is based on the duplex construction [4], specifically the MONKEYDUPLEX construction [6]. However, unlike MONKEYDUPLEX, ASCON's mode employs double-keyed initialization and double-keyed finalization to enhance its robustness. For a detailed description of the ASCON AEAD mode, please refer to Sect. 4.

1.2 Existing Security Analysis

It has come to our attention that previous analyses of ASCON predominantly regard it as a variant of the Duplex construction (as indicated in [13]), with no specific security analysis dedicated to ASCON available in the literature. Hence, we briefly discuss the security bounds of generic Duplex constructions here. At a high level, the Sponge construction is known to achieve $2^{c/2}$ bits security, where c is the capacity of the Sponge. This security level has been extended to its keyed variations, such as MONKEYDUPLEX. The first result which indicates that the duplex-based modes can provide security beyond the birthday bound on the capacity c, was by Bertoni et al. [5]. However, they could achieve this only when the time complexity (roughly, this is the number of permutation computations an adversary does) remains well below $2^{c/2}$. In fact, the dominating term in their security analysis was

$$\frac{D^2 + DT}{2^c},$$

where D is the data complexity and T is the time complexity. In 2014 [16], and later in 2019 [17], Jovanovic et al. achieve an improved security of the form

$$\frac{(D + T)q_d}{2^c}$$

where q_d is the number of decryption queries. Andreeva et al. [2] show that the time complexity can be made close to $2^c/\mu$ where μ is the total multiplicity (i.e., the number of queries with a repeated nonce). As the nonce is allowed to repeat in decryption queries, the μ can be as large as q_d (the number of decryption queries). Hence, their security bound is essentially of the form

$$\frac{q_d T}{2^c}.$$

Considering full-state keyed Duplex, Daemen et al. [12] establish stronger bounds for the Duplex mode of operation. These bounds are based on comparing the Duplex mode to an *Ideal Extendable Input Function (IXIF)*. They also do this in a multi-user setting and take into account both respectful and misusing adversaries. The results indicate that the data limit or key could potentially be increased further. One of the dominating terms in their security bound is $\frac{LT}{2^c}$ where L represents the number of construction queries that have some common prefix to some prior query. So, an adversary can easily achieve $L = q_d$ (the number of decryption queries) as nonce is allowed to repeat in decryption queries. So, their bound essentially reduces to $\frac{q_d T}{2^c}$.

Recently, Chakraborty et al. [9] introduced a generic AEAD construction called the Transform-then-Permute (TtP) construction. They demonstrated that well-known constructions such as the keyed Sponge Duplex construction, Beetle [8], and SpoC [1] can be viewed as specific examples of this generic construction. In their work, they provided rigorous proof for a tight security bound of the TtP construction in the form of $\frac{\mu_T D}{2^c} +$ other smaller order terms, where μ_T is a parameter defined in their paper [9]. For a special class of TtP constructions where the decryption feedback function (defined in their paper) is invertible, they showed that $\mu_T = \mathcal{O}\left(\max\{T/2^r, T/2^\tau, T^2/2^b\}\right)$. This result indicates that these constructions achieve security levels much higher than $q_d T/2^c$ when D (data complexity) is significantly smaller than T (time complexity). Importantly, this holds true for the upper limits of D and T as specified by the NIST guidelines for Lightweight Cryptography (LwC). However, for other TtP constructions, such as the keyed Sponge Duplex and ASCON constructions, where the decryption feedback function is not invertible, bounding μ_T was left as an open problem for future research.

In a concurrent work [18], Mennink and Lefevre also presented a dedicated security analysis of ASCON. While they focus on a different setting (authenticity under nonce misuse and state recovery, multi-user security), they could show the impact of strengthened initialization and finalization of ASCON in the case of authenticity under state recovery. However, in the case of conventional single-user nonce-based authenticity, their bounds reduce to $\frac{q_d T}{2^c}$.

As observed, a common constraint in the existing analyses of ASCON, as well as other Duplex constructions, is the condition $DT \ll 2^c$, or similar variants where D may be replaced by q_d. It is important to note that no forgery attack matching this bound has been discovered. Notably, the best-known attack on Duplex constructions by Gilbert et al. [15] establishes a lower bound of the form $DT \gg 2^{3c/2}$.

1.3 Our Contribution

In this paper, motivated by the recently concluded NIST LwC competition, we try to provide an improved security bound for the ASCON AEAD mode. As already stated above, previous analyses of ASCON have treated it as a variant of the Duplex construction, overlooking its unique key robustness features, namely the double-keyed initialization and double-keyed finalization.

Our analysis establishes a tight security bound, considering the tag size τ bits, key size κ bits, capacity c bits, and state size b bits. The derived bound is given by

$$\frac{T}{2^{\min\{\kappa,c\}}} + \frac{D}{2^{\min\{\tau,c\}}} + \frac{DT}{2^b}.$$

Comparing our result with the recent analysis by Gilbert et al. [15], it becomes evident that ASCON surpasses other generic Duplex constructions in terms of security, solidifying its status as a true champion. Notably, our proof leverages the double-keyed finalization process of ASCON during tag generation, which plays a vital role in achieving such a tight and improved security bound. It should be emphasized that our proof methodology is not applicable to classical sponge constructions, as they do not incorporate a key at the final stage. Furthermore, the recent attack by Gilbert et al. [15] conclusively demonstrates that ASCON consistently offers higher security than other sponge-based modes of operation.

Lastly, in the context of NIST LwC requirements ($D \leq 2^{53}, T \leq 2^{112}$, $\kappa \geq 128$, $\tau \geq 64$), our conclusion is that a capacity size of $c = 128$ (given $b = 320$) and $\tau = 64$ is sufficient to ensure adequate security for ASCON. This choice enables a higher rate of 192 bits, thereby significantly enhancing efficiency without compromising security within the random permutation model. We believe this represents a substantial improvement compared to existing analyses.

1.4   Organization of the Paper

In Sect. 2, we define the basic notations used in the paper. We give a brief description of the AEAD security in the random permutation model, and also briefly describe the H-coefficient technique. Additionally, in Sect. 3, we elaborate on function graph structures that play a crucial role in our subsequent analyses. Moving forward, in Sect. 4, we present a detailed examination of the ASCON AEAD scheme. We present our primary result, the security bound of ASCON, and establish its significance in relation to the NIST LwC criteria. To support our claims, we provide an interpretation of our findings within the context of the NIST guidelines. In Sect. 5, we present a rigorous proof of our main theorem, using the H-coefficient technique. Finally, in Sect. 6, we discuss the tightness of our bound, and conclude the paper.

2   Preliminaries

2.1   Notations

For all $a \leq b \in \mathbb{N}$, let $[b]$ and $[a, b]$ denote the sets $\{1, 2, \ldots, b\}$ and $\{a, a+1, \ldots, b\}$ respectively. For $n, k \in \mathbb{N}$, such that $n \geq k$, we define the falling factorial $(n)_k := n(n-1)\cdots(n-k+1)$. Note that $(n)_k \leq n^k$.

Let $\{0, 1\}^n$ denote the set of bit strings of length n, and $\{0, 1\}^+$ denote the set of bit strings of arbitrary length. Let λ denote the empty string and we write $\{0, 1\}^* = \{\lambda\} \cup \{0, 1\}^+$. For any bit string $x = x_1 x_2 \cdots x_k \in \{0, 1\}^k$ of length k, and for $n \leq k$, we write $\lceil x \rceil_n := x_1 \cdots x_n$ (resp. $\lfloor x \rfloor_n := x_{k-n+1} \cdots x_k$) to denote the most (resp. least) significant n bits of x. We use $\|$ to denote the bit concatenation operation. We also abuse the notation $(x_1, \ldots, x_r)$ to denote the bit concatenation operation $x_1 \| \cdots \| x_r$ where $x_i \in \{0, 1\}^*$. So, if $V := x \| z := (x, z) \in \{0, 1\}^r \times \{0, 1\}^c$ then $\lceil V \rceil_r = x$ and $\lfloor V \rfloor_c = z$. We use $\oplus$ to denote bitwise xor operation.

PADDING AND PARSING A BIT STRING. Let $r > 0$ be an integer and $X \in \{0, 1\}^*$. Let $d = |X| \bmod r$ (the remainder while dividing $|X|$ by r).

$$\mathsf{pad}_1(X) = \begin{cases} \lambda & \text{if } |X| = 0 \\ X \| 1 \| 0^{r-1-d} & \text{otherwise} \end{cases}$$

and

$$\mathsf{pad}_2(X) = X \| 1 \| 0^{r-1-d}.$$

Given $X \in \{0, 1\}^*$, let $x = \lceil \frac{|X|+1}{r} \rceil$. We define $(X_1, \ldots, X_x) \xleftarrow{r}_* X$ where $X_1 \| \cdots \| X_x = X$, $|X_1| = \cdots = |X_{x-1}| = r$ and

$$X_x = \begin{cases} \lambda & \text{if } |X| = r(x-1) \\ \lfloor X \rfloor_{|X|-r(x-1)} & \text{otherwise} \end{cases}.$$

2.2 Authenticated Encryption with Associated Data: Definition and Security Model

An authenticated encryption scheme with associated data functionality (called AEAD in short), is a tuple of algorithms $\mathsf{AE} = (\mathsf{E}, \mathsf{D})$, called the encryption and decryption algorithms, respectively, and defined over the *key space* $\mathcal{K}$, *nonce space* $\mathcal{N}$, *associated data space* $\mathcal{A}$, *message space* $\mathcal{M}$, *ciphertext space* $\mathcal{C}$, and *tag space* $\mathcal{T}$, where

$$\mathsf{E} : \mathcal{K} \times \mathcal{N} \times \mathcal{A} \times \mathcal{M} \to \mathcal{C} \times \mathcal{T} \quad \text{and} \quad \mathsf{D} : \mathcal{K} \times \mathcal{N} \times \mathcal{A} \times \mathcal{C} \times \mathcal{T} \to \mathcal{M} \cup \{\mathsf{rej}\}.$$

Here, rej indicates the tag-ciphertext pair is invalid and hence rejected. Further, we require the correctness condition: $\mathsf{D}(K, N, A, \mathsf{E}(K, N, A, M)) = M$ for any $(K, N, A, M) \in \mathcal{K} \times \mathcal{N} \times \mathcal{A} \times \mathcal{M}$. For all key $K \in \mathcal{K}$, we write $\mathsf{E}_K(\cdot)$ and $\mathsf{D}_K(\cdot)$ to denote $\mathsf{E}(K, \cdot)$ and $\mathsf{D}(K, \cdot)$, respectively. In this paper, we have $\mathcal{K} = \{0,1\}^\kappa, \mathcal{N} = \{0,1\}^\nu, \mathcal{T} = \{0,1\}^\tau$ and $\mathcal{A}, \mathcal{M} = \mathcal{C} \subseteq \{0,1\}^*$.

AEAD Security in the Random Permutation Model

For a finite set $\mathcal{X}$, $\mathsf{X} \xleftarrow{\$} \mathcal{X}$ denotes the uniform and random sampling of X from $\mathcal{X}$, and $\mathsf{X} \xleftarrow{\mathsf{wor}} \mathcal{X}$ denotes without replacement sampling of X from $\mathcal{X}$. Let $\mathsf{Perm}(b)$ denote the set of all permutations over $\{0,1\}^b$ and $\mathsf{Func}(\mathcal{N} \times \mathcal{A} \times \mathcal{M}, \mathcal{M} \times \mathcal{T})$ denote the set of all functions from (N, A, M) to (C, T) such that $|C| = |M|$. Let

- $\Pi \xleftarrow{\$} \mathsf{Perm}(b)$,
- $\Gamma \xleftarrow{\$} \mathsf{Func}(\mathcal{N} \times \mathcal{A} \times \mathcal{M}, \mathcal{M} \times \mathcal{T})$, and
- rej denotes the degenerate function from $(\mathcal{N}, \mathcal{A}, \mathcal{M}, \mathcal{T})$ to $\{\mathsf{rej}\}$.

We use the superscript $\pm$ to denote bidirectional access to Π.

Definition 1. *Let AE_Π be an AEAD scheme based on the random permutation Π, defined over $(\mathcal{K}, \mathcal{N}, \mathcal{A}, \mathcal{M}, \mathcal{T})$. The AEAD advantage of an adversary $\mathscr{A}$ against AE_Π is defined as*

$$\mathbf{Adv}_{\mathsf{AE}_\Pi}^{\mathsf{aead}}(\mathscr{A}) := \left| \Pr_{\substack{K \xleftarrow{\$} \mathcal{K} \\ \Pi^\pm}} \left[\mathscr{A}^{\mathsf{E}_K, \mathsf{D}_K, \Pi^\pm} = 1 \right] - \Pr_{\Gamma, \Pi^\pm} \left[\mathscr{A}^{\Gamma, \mathsf{rej}, \Pi^\pm} = 1 \right] \right|.$$

Here $\mathscr{A}^{\mathsf{E}_K, \mathsf{D}_K, \Pi^\pm}$ denotes $\mathscr{A}$'s response after its interaction with E_K, D_K, and $\Pi^\pm$ respectively. Similarly, $\mathscr{A}^{\Gamma, \mathsf{rej}, \Pi^\pm}$ denotes $\mathscr{A}$'s response after its interaction with Γ, rej, and $\Pi^\pm$ respectively.

In this paper, we assume that the adversary is adaptive, that is it neither makes any duplicate queries nor makes any query for which the response is already known due to some previous query. Let q_e, q_d and q_p denote the number of queries to $\mathsf{E}_K, \mathsf{D}_K$ and $\Pi^\pm$ respectively. Let σ_e and σ_d denote the sum of input (associated data and message) lengths across all encryption and decryption queries respectively. Also, let $\sigma := \sigma_e + \sigma_d$ denote the combined construction query resources.

Remark 1. Here σ corresponds to the online or data complexity, and q_p corresponds to the offline or time complexity of the adversary. Any adversary that adheres to the resource constraints mentioned above is called an $(q_p, \sigma_e, \sigma_d)$-adversary.

2.3   H-Coefficient Technique

Consider a deterministic and computationally unbounded adversary $\mathscr{A}$ trying to distinguish the real oracle (say $\mathcal{O}_{re}$) from the ideal oracle (say $\mathcal{O}_{id}$). Let the transcript ω denote the query-response tuple of $\mathscr{A}$'s interaction with its oracle. Sometimes, at the end of the query-response phase of the game, if the oracle chooses to reveal any additional information to the distinguisher, then the extended definition of the transcript may also include that information. Let Θ_{re} (resp. Θ_{id}) denote the random transcript variable when $\mathscr{A}$ interacts with $\mathcal{O}_{re}$ (resp. $\mathcal{O}_{id}$). The probability of realizing a given transcript ω in the security game with an oracle $\mathcal{O}$ is known as the *interpolation probability* of ω with respect to $\mathcal{O}$. Since $\mathscr{A}$ is deterministic, this probability depends only on the oracle $\mathcal{O}$ and the transcript ω. A transcript ω is said to be *realizable* if $\Pr[\Theta_{id} = \omega] > 0$. In this paper, $\mathcal{O}_{re} = (\mathsf{E_K}, \mathsf{D_K}, \Pi^{\pm})$, $\mathcal{O}_{id} = (\Gamma, \mathsf{rej}, \Pi^{\pm})$, and the adversary is trying to distinguish $\mathcal{O}_{re}$ from $\mathcal{O}_{id}$ in AEAD sense.

Theorem 1 (H-coefficient technique [21,22]). *Let Ω be the set of all realizable transcripts. For some $\epsilon_{bad}, \epsilon_{ratio} > 0$, suppose there is a set $\Omega_{bad} \subseteq \Omega$ satisfying the following:*

- $\Pr[\Theta_{id} \in \Omega_{bad}] \leq \epsilon_{bad}$;
- *For any $\omega \notin \Omega_{bad}$,*

$$\frac{\Pr[\Theta_{re} = \omega]}{\Pr[\Theta_{id} = \omega]} \geq 1 - \epsilon_{ratio}.$$

Then for any adversary $\mathscr{A}$, we have the following bound on its AEAD distinguishing advantage:

$$\mathbf{Adv}^{aead}_{\mathcal{O}_{re}}(\mathscr{A}) \leq \epsilon_{bad} + \epsilon_{ratio}.$$

A proof of Theorem 1 can be found in multiple papers including [10,19,22].

2.4   Expected Multicollision in a Uniform Random Sample

Let $S := (x_i)_{i \in I}$ be a tuple with elements from a set T. For any $x \in T$, we define $\mathsf{mcoll}_x(S) = |\{i \in I : x_i = x\}|$ (the number of times x appears in the tuple). Finally, we define multicollision of S as the $\mathsf{mcoll}(S) := \max_{x \in T} \mathsf{mcoll}_x(S)$. In this section, we revisit some multicollision results discussed in [9].

For $N \geq 4$, $n = \log_2 N$, we define

$$\mathsf{mcoll}(q, N) = \begin{cases} 3 & \text{if } 4 \leq q \leq \sqrt{N} \\ \frac{4\log_2 q}{\log_2 \log_2 q} & \text{if } \sqrt{N} < q \leq N \\ 5n \lceil \frac{q}{nN} \rceil & \text{if } N < q. \end{cases}$$

Lemma 1. *[9] Let $\mathcal{D}$ be a set of size $N \geq 4$, $n = \log_2 N$. Given random variables* $X_1, \ldots, X_q \xleftarrow{\$} \mathcal{D}$, *we have* $\mathbb{E}\left[\mathrm{mcoll}(X_1, \ldots, X_q)\right] \leq \mathrm{mcoll}(q, N)$.

Remark 2. Similar bounds as in the above Lemma 1 can be achieved in the case of non-uniform samplings. Let $Y_1, \ldots, Y_q \xleftarrow{\mathrm{wor}} \{0,1\}^b$ and define $X_i := \lceil Y_i \rceil_r$ for some $r < b$. If we take $N = 2^r$ for this truncated random sampling, then we have the same result as above for multicollisions among $X_1, \ldots, X_q$.

We also have the following general result:

Lemma 2 (general multicollision bound). *Let $\mathscr{A}$ be an adversary which makes queries to a b-bit random permutation $\Pi^{\pm}$ and τ-bit to τ-bit random function Γ. Let $(X_1, Y_1), \ldots, (X_{q_1}, Y_{q_1})$ and $(X_{q_1+1}, Y_{q_1+1}), \ldots, (X_{q_1+q_2}, Y_{q_1+q_2})$ be the tuples of input-output corresponding to Π and Γ respectively obtained by the $\mathscr{A}$. Let $q := q_1 + q_2 \leq 2^b$ and $Z_i := \mathrm{trunc}_\tau(X_i) \oplus \mathrm{trunc}_\tau(Y_i)$ for $i \in [q_1]$ and $Z_i := (X_i \oplus Y_i)$ for $i \in [q_1 + 1, q]$ where trunc_τ represents some τ-bit truncation. For $\tau \geq 2$,*

$$\mathbb{E}\left[\mathrm{mcoll}(Z^q)\right] \leq \mathrm{mcoll}(q, 2^\tau).$$

3 Function Graph Structures

3.1 Partial Function Graph

A *partial function* $\mathcal{L} : \{0,1\}^b \dashrightarrow \{0,1\}^c$ is a subset $\mathcal{L} = \{(p_1, q_1), \ldots, (p_t, q_t)\} \subseteq \{0,1\}^b \times \{0,1\}^c$ with distinct p_i values. We call it an *injective partial function* if q_i's are also distinct. We define

$$\mathrm{domain}(\mathcal{L}) = \{p_i : i \in [t]\}, \quad \mathrm{range}(\mathcal{L}) = \{q_i : i \in [t]\}.$$

We write $\mathcal{L}(p_i) = q_i$ and for all $p \notin \mathrm{domain}(\mathcal{L})$, $\mathcal{L}(p) = \bot$ (a special symbol to mean that the value is undefined).[1] For $f : \{0,1\}^b \dashrightarrow \{0,1\}^b$, $c \in [b-1]$, we define $\lfloor f \rfloor_c : \{0,1\}^b \dashrightarrow \{0,1\}^c$ such that $\lfloor f \rfloor_c(x) = \lfloor f(x) \rfloor_c$ whenever $f(x) \neq \bot$.

Definition 2. *Let $\mathcal{L} : \{0,1\}^b \dashrightarrow \{0,1\}^c$ for $r := b - c > 0$. We associate a labeled directed graph $G := G^{\mathcal{L}}$, called (labeled) partial function graph, over the set of vertices*

$$V := \lfloor \mathrm{domain}(\mathcal{L}) \rfloor_c \cup \mathrm{range}(\mathcal{L}) \subseteq \{0,1\}^c$$

with the label set $\{0,1\}^r$ and the following labeled edge set

$$E(G) := \{u \xrightarrow{x} v \mid \mathcal{L}(x \| u) = v\}.$$

We call it (labeled) function graph if $\mathcal{L}$ is known to be a function.

We write a walk

$$u_0 \xrightarrow{x_1} u_1 \xrightarrow{x_2} \cdots \xrightarrow{x_{l-1}} u_{l-1} \xrightarrow{x_l} u_l$$

simply as $u_0 \xrightarrow{x^l} u_l$. It is easy to see that if $u \xrightarrow{x} v_1$ and $u \xrightarrow{x} v_2$ then $v_1 = v_2$ (this follows from the fact that $\mathcal{L}$ is a partial function).

---

[1] A function is a partial function for which every output is defined.

3.2   Sampling Process of a Labeled Walk

Let $f : \{0,1\}^b \dashrightarrow \{0,1\}^b$, $x = x^k$ be a k-tuple label, $k \geq 0$, and $z_0 \in \{0,1\}^c$. We now describe a process that extends the partial function f to f' so that there is a walk

$$z_0 \xrightarrow{x_1} z_1 \xrightarrow{x_2} \cdots \xrightarrow{x_k} z_k$$

in the graph $G^{\lfloor f \rfloor_c}$. The process we define below is denoted as

$$\mathsf{Rand\_Extn}^f(z_0, x^k),$$

which randomly extends the elements of the partial function f whenever required to complete the walk.

$\underline{\mathsf{Rand\_Extn}^f(z_0, x^k):}$

Initialize $f' = f$.
For $j = 1$ to k:

1. $v_j = f'(x_j, z_{j-1})$.
2. If $v_j = \bot$ then
   - $v_j \xleftarrow{\$} \{0,1\}^b$ and
   - $f' \leftarrow f' \cup \{(x_j \| z_{j-1}, v_j)\}$
3. $z_j = \lfloor v_j \rfloor_c$.

The described process provides a clear and effective method for successfully completing a labeled walk. It operates based on a simple rule: when the current value falls within the defined domain, we utilize the corresponding output to progress further in the walk. In cases where the current value is outside the domain, we employ a random sampling approach to determine the next output. This ensures the completion of the walk.

3.3   Partial XOR-Function Graph

Now, consider a partial function $\mathcal{P} : \{0,1\}^b \dashrightarrow \{0,1\}^b$ and $r \in [b-1]$. We define a new partial function $\mathcal{P}^{\oplus} : \{0,1\}^b \times \{0,1\}^r \dashrightarrow \{0,1\}^b$ as follows. Let $u = u' \| u''$ where $u' \in \{0,1\}^r$. Now,

$$\mathcal{P}^{\oplus}(u, x) = \mathcal{P}((u' \oplus x) \| u'').$$

Note that the above may not be defined, in which case we define the output $\bot$ as before. We similarly define partial function graph $G^{\oplus} := G^{\mathcal{P}^{\oplus}}$ with label edges denoted as $u \xrightarrow{x}_{\oplus} v$ (whenever $\mathcal{P}^{\oplus}(u, x) = v$). A walk

$$u_0 \xrightarrow{x_1}_{\oplus} u_1 \xrightarrow{x_2}_{\oplus} \cdots \xrightarrow{x_{l-1}}_{\oplus} u_{l-1} \xrightarrow{x_l}_{\oplus} u_l$$

is denoted as $u_0 \xrightarrow{x^l}_{\oplus} u_l$. Similar to $\mathsf{Rand\_Extn}^f$ Algorithm, we now define a randomized extension algorithm for $\mathcal{P}^{\oplus}$, denoted as $\mathsf{xorRand\_Extn}^{\mathcal{P}}(v_0, x^k)$, $v_0 \in \{0,1\}^b, x_i \in \{0,1\}^r$.

$\underline{\mathsf{xorRand\_Extn}^{\mathcal{P}}(v_0, x^k)}:$

Initialaize $\mathcal{P}' = \mathcal{P}$.
For $j = 1$ to k:

1. $v_j = \mathcal{P}'(v_{j-1} \oplus (x_j \| 0^c))$.
2. If $v_j = \perp$ then

   $-$ $v_j \overset{\$}{\leftarrow} \{0,1\}^b$ and
   $-$ $\mathcal{P}' \leftarrow \mathcal{P}' \cup \{v_{j-1} \oplus (x_j \| 0^c), v_j)\}$

After this process, we obtain a modified partial function $\mathcal{P}' : \{0,1\}^b \dashrightarrow \{0,1\}^b$ for which we have the following walk:

$$v_0 \xrightarrow{x_1}_{\oplus} v_1 \xrightarrow{x_2}_{\oplus} \cdots \xrightarrow{x_{k-1}}_{\oplus} v_{k-1} \xrightarrow{x_k}_{\oplus} v_k$$

4   Ascon AEAD

In this section, we define the ASCON AEAD [13] construction. Note that the ASCON AEAD is a simple variation of the Duplex construction. Let b denote the state size of the underlying permutation Π and $0 < r < b$ be the number of bits of associated data/message processed per permutation call. We call r the rate of the ASCON construction, and $c = b - r$ is called the capacity. Let κ, ν, τ denote the key size, nonce size, and tag size respectively such that

$- \tau \leq \kappa \leq c$,
$- \kappa + \nu \leq b$,
$- \kappa + r \leq b$.

We fix an $IV \in \{0,1\}^{b-\kappa-\nu}$. The AEAD uses a permutation π (ASCON permutation), modeled to be the random permutation while we analyze its security.

Encryption Algorithm. It receives an input of the form $(N, A, M) \in \{0,1\}^\nu \times \{0,1\}^* \times \{0,1\}^*$ and a key $K \in \{0,1\}^\kappa$. Broadly we divide the encryption algorithm into three phases: (i) initialization, (ii) associated data and message processing, and (iii) tag generation, run sequentially.

INITIALIZATION. In this phase, we first apply the following function

$$\mathrm{INIT}^\pi(K, N) = \pi(IV \| K \| N) \oplus (0^{b-\kappa} \| K) := V_0.$$

Before we process associated data and messages, we first parse them:

$$(A_1, \ldots, A_a) \overset{r}{\leftarrow} \mathsf{pad}_1(A), (M_1, \ldots, M_m) \overset{r}{\leftarrow} \mathsf{pad}_2(M).$$

Note that a can be zero in which case it is parsed as an empty string. But $m \geq 1$.

ASSOCIATED DATA AND MESSAGE PROCESSING. Using the XOR-function graph corresponding to the function $\pi^{\oplus}$, we obtain a walk

$$V_0 \xrightarrow{A_1}_{\oplus} V_1 \xrightarrow{A_2}_{\oplus} \cdots \xrightarrow{A_a}_{\oplus} V_a, \quad V_a \oplus 0^*1 \xrightarrow{M_1}_{\oplus} V_{a+1} \cdots \xrightarrow{M_{m-1}}_{\oplus} V_{a+m-1}.$$

We define the ciphertext as follows:

$$C_i = \lceil V_{a+i-1} \rceil_r \oplus M_i, \quad \forall i \in [m], \quad C = \lceil C_1 \| \cdots \| C_m \rceil_{|M|}.$$

We denote the above process as

$$\mathsf{AM\_Proc}^\pi (V_0, A, M) \to \left(C, F := V_{t-1} \oplus (M_m \| 0^r)\right).$$

TAG GENERATION. Finally, we compute

$$T := \mathrm{TAG}^\pi(K, F) = \lfloor \pi\left(F \oplus (0^r \| K \| 0^{c-\kappa})\right)\rfloor_\tau \oplus \lfloor K \rfloor_\tau$$

The ASCON AEAD returns (C, T).

Remark 3. The ASCON construction uses two different permutations, p^a and p^b, where a and b indicate the specific rounds used for the underlying permutation p (called the ASCON permutation). In the ASCON implementation, p^a is employed during the initialization phase and for tag generation and verification. On the other hand, p^b is utilized for processing associated data, messages, and ciphertext. For instance, in the ASCON-128 construction, a is set to 12, while b is set to 6.

When modeling ASCON in the random permutation model, there are two options: either using the same permutation $\pi = p^a = p^b$, or utilizing independent permutations π_1 and π_2. Our analysis focuses on the assumption that the permutations are the same, which is generally more challenging to prove compared to assuming independent random permutations. A similar analysis (with bounds of the same order) can be made for the independent random permutation model.

Verification Algorithm. The decryption algorithm performs a verification process to ensure the correctness of the ciphertext and tag pair. If the verification is successful, the algorithm proceeds to generate the corresponding message. While the details of message computation are omitted in this analysis, readers can refer to [13] for a comprehensive explanation. It is important to note that our focus lies primarily on the verification process itself, rather than the specific steps involved in message computation. On receiving an input of the form $(N, A, C, T) \in \{0,1\}^\nu \times \{0,1\}^* \times \{0,1\}^* \times \{0,1\}^\tau$ and a key $K \in \{0,1\}^\kappa$, the steps of the verification process is outlined below:

1. $(A_1, \ldots, A_a) \xleftarrow{r} \mathsf{pad}_1(A)$ and $(C_1, \ldots, C_l) \xleftarrow{r} \mathsf{pad}_2(C)$.
2. Compute $V_0 := \mathrm{INIT}^\pi(K, N)$.
3. We compute the walk for the permutation π

$$V_0 \xrightarrow{A_1} \oplus V_1 \xrightarrow{A_2} \oplus \cdots \xrightarrow{A_a} \oplus V_a$$

4. Let $C_l = C_l' \| 10^*$ for some C_l' (may be the empty string) and $|C_l'| = d$. Let $z_a = \lfloor V_a \rfloor_c$.
   - Case $l = 1$: We define $F = C_l' \| (\lfloor V_a \rfloor_{b-d} \oplus 10^*1)$.
   - Case $l \geq 2$: We compute

$$z_a \oplus 0^*1 \xrightarrow{C_1} z_{a+1} \xrightarrow{C_2} \cdots \xrightarrow{C_{l-2}} z_{a+l-2}$$

   We define $F = C_l' \| (\lfloor \pi(C_{l-1} \| z_{a+l-2}) \rfloor_{b-d} \oplus 10^*)$.
5. Rejects if $T \neq \mathrm{TAG}^\pi(K, F)$, otherwise, it accepts.

4.1 Security Bound of ASCON

Theorem 2 (Main Theorem). *Consider a nonce-respecting AEAD adversary $\mathscr{A}$ making q_p permutation queries, q_e encryption queries with a total number of σ_e data blocks, and q_d decryption queries with a total number of σ_d data blocks. Define $\sigma := \sigma_e + \sigma_d$. Then, we can upper bound the AEAD advantage of $\mathscr{A}$ against ASCON as follows:*

$$\mathbf{Adv}_{\mathrm{ASCON}}^{\mathrm{AEAD}}(\mathscr{A}) \leq \frac{2q_d}{2^\tau} + \frac{\sigma_e^2}{2^b} + \frac{\sigma_d(q_p + \sigma_d)}{2^b} + \frac{\mathsf{mcoll}(\sigma_e, 2^r)(\sigma_d + q_p)}{2^c}$$
$$+ \frac{q_p + \sigma}{2^\kappa} + \frac{\mathsf{mcoll}(q_e, 2^r)q_d}{2^c} + \frac{q_e q_d + (q_e + q_d)(\sigma + q_p)}{2^b}$$
$$+ \frac{\mathsf{mcoll}(\sigma + q_p, 2^r)q_d}{2^\kappa}.$$

4.2 Interpretation of Theorem 2

We interpret our bound in light of the requirements proposed by NIST for the LwC competition, and the choices of the parameters, namely rate (and hence capacity) and tag size. ASCON operates with a state size (size of the permutation) $b = 320$ bits. We assume $q_p \leq 2^{112}$ and $r\sigma \leq 2^{53}$ as prescribed by NIST.

We give upper bounds to $\mathsf{mcoll}(\sigma_e, 2^r)$, $\mathsf{mcoll}(q_e, 2^r)$ and $\mathsf{mcoll}(\sigma + q_p, 2^r)$, depending on the choice of r and τ.

First, from the definition of $\mathsf{mcoll}(q, N)$, we have

$$\mathsf{mcoll}(\sigma_e, 2^r) \leq 3 \quad \forall r \geq 128.$$

Now, we fix two choices for tag size τ : 64 bits (the minimum tag size required by NIST) and 128 bits (the tag size recommended by the designers of ASCON). Again, from the definition of $\mathsf{mcoll}(q, N)$, we have

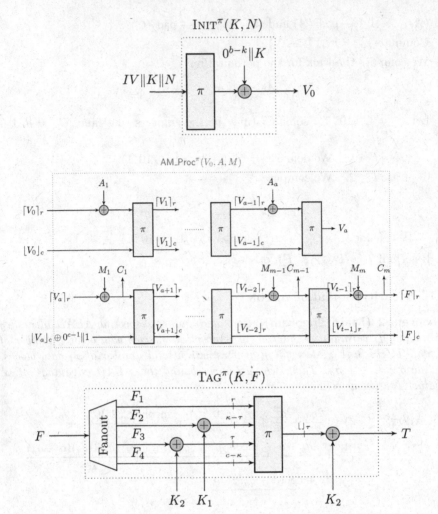

Fig. 1. Encryption in ASCON AEAD. The final ciphertext is $C = \lceil C_1 \| \cdots \| C_m \rceil_{|M|}$. Here $t := a+m$, $K_1 = \lceil K \rceil_{\kappa-\tau}$, $K_2 = \lfloor K \rfloor_\tau$. The Fanout operation parses $F = F_1 \| F_2 \| F_3 \| F_4$ such that $|F_1| = r$, $|F_2| = \kappa - \tau$, $|F_3| = \tau$ and $|F_4| = c - \kappa$. It is easy to follow that in the decryption protocol, the permutation input generated after processing C_1 is simply $C_i \| \lfloor V_{a+i-1} \oplus 0^{b-1} \| 1 \rfloor_{b-r}$. Similarly after the i-th ciphertext processing where $1 < i \leq m - 1$, the permutation input is simply $C_i \| \lfloor V_{a+i-1} \rfloor_{b-r}$. For processing the last block, the $|C| - r(m-1)$ most significant bits of M_m are calculated using V_{t-1} and C_m and then pad_2 is applied to determine the remaining bits of M_m. Finally, this M_m is used in the same way as the encryption protocol to generate F.

- For $\tau = 64$:

$$\mathsf{mcoll}(q_e, 2^\tau) \leq \frac{4\log_2 \sigma}{\log_2 \log_2 \sigma} < 40, \quad \text{and} \quad \mathsf{mcoll}(\sigma + q_p, 2^\tau) \leq \frac{5(q_p + \sigma)}{2^\tau}.$$

Here we assume $q_p \gg 2^\tau$.

- For $\tau = 128$:

$$\mathsf{mcoll}(q_e, 2^\tau) \leq 3, \quad \text{and} \quad \mathsf{mcoll}(\sigma + q_p, 2^\tau) \leq \frac{4\log_2(q_p + \sigma)}{\log_2\log_2(q_p + \sigma)} < 75.$$

So, if $r \geq 128, \tau = 64$, we have

$$\mathbf{Adv}_{\mathrm{ASCON}}^{\mathrm{AEAD}}(\mathscr{A}) \leq \frac{2q_d}{2^\tau} + \frac{\sigma_e^2}{2^b} + \frac{\sigma_d(q_p + \sigma_d)}{2^b} + \frac{3(\sigma_d + q_p)}{2^c} + \frac{40q_d}{2^c}$$
$$+ \frac{q_p + \sigma}{2^\kappa} + \frac{q_e q_d + (q_e + q_d)(\sigma + q_p)}{2^b} + \frac{5(q_p + \sigma_e)q_d}{2^{\kappa+\tau}}$$
$$= O(\frac{q_d}{2^\tau}) + O(\frac{\sigma q_p}{2^b}) + O(\frac{q_p}{2^\kappa}) + O(\frac{q_p}{2^c})$$

(assuming $\sigma \leq q_p$).

If $r \geq 128, \tau = 128$, we have

$$\mathbf{Adv}_{\mathrm{ASCON}}^{\mathrm{AEAD}}(\mathscr{A}) \leq \frac{2q_d}{2^\tau} + \frac{\sigma_e^2}{2^b} + \frac{\sigma_d(q_p + \sigma_d)}{2^b} + \frac{3(\sigma_d + q_p)}{2^c} + \frac{3q_d}{2^c}$$
$$+ \frac{q_p + \sigma}{2^\kappa} + \frac{q_e q_d + (q_e + q_d)(\sigma + q_p)}{2^b} + \frac{75q_d}{2^\kappa}$$
$$= O(\frac{q_d}{2^\tau}) + O(\frac{\sigma q_p}{2^b}) + O(\frac{q_p}{2^\kappa}) + O(\frac{q_p}{2^c}).$$

Thus, in terms of order, a tag size of 64 bits yields the same security as a tag size of 128 bits. Given that the key size κ is at least 128 bits (required by NIST), we can see that ASCON is secure even when $c = 128$ (implying $r = 192$), and $\tau = 64$.

Remark 4. Our assumption $\kappa \leq c$ is only for the sake of simplicity as this implies the key is always xor-ed in the capacity part. However, it can be easily verified that the analysis remains the same even when $\kappa > c$.

5   Proof of Theorem 2

5.1   Description of the Real World

The real-world samples $K \xleftarrow{\$} \{0,1\}^\kappa$ and a random permutation Π. All queries are then responded to honestly following ASCON AEAD as defined above (including direct primitive queries to Π). A transcript in the real world would be of the form

$$\Theta_{\mathrm{re,on}} = ((\mathsf{N}_i, \mathsf{A}_i, \mathsf{M}_i, \mathsf{C}_i, \mathsf{T}_i)_{i \in [q_e]}, \ (\mathsf{N}_i', \mathsf{A}_i', \mathsf{C}_i', \mathsf{T}_i', \mathsf{M}_i')_{i \in [q_d]}, \ \mathsf{P})$$

where P represents the query responses for primitive queries (represented in terms of the partial function for Π). When the i-th decryption query is rejected we write $M_i' = \mathsf{rej}$ (we keep this as one of the necessary conditions for a good transcript in the ideal world). After all queries have been made, all inputs-outputs used in Π for all encryption and decryption queries have been included in the offline transcript. Let $\mathsf{P_{fin}}$ denote the extended partial function and clearly, all encryption and decryption queries are determined by $\mathsf{P_{fin}}$. Note that the key K is also determined from the domain of $\mathsf{P_{fin}}$. It is implicitly understood that the domain and range elements of $\mathsf{P_{fin}}$ are given in order of the execution of the underlying permutation to compute all encryption and decryption queries. Let

$$\Theta_{\mathrm{re}} = \left((\mathsf{N}_i, \mathsf{A}_i, \mathsf{M}_i, \mathsf{C}_i, \mathsf{T}_i)_{i \in [q_e]}, \ (\mathsf{N}_i', \mathsf{A}_i', \mathsf{C}_i', \mathsf{T}_i', \mathsf{M}_i')_{i \in [q_d]}, \ \mathsf{P_{fin}}\right)$$

denote the extended real world transcript. For any real world realizable transcript $\theta = \left((N_i, A_i, M_i, C_i, T_i)_{i \in [q_e]}, \ (N_i', A_i', C_i', T_i', M_i')_{i \in [q_d]}, \ P_{fin}\right)$,

$$\Pr(\Theta_{\mathrm{re}} = \theta) = \Pr(P_{fin} \subseteq \Pi) = 1/(2^b)_{|P_{fin}|}$$

5.2 Description of the Ideal World

Now we describe how the ideal oracle behaves with the adversary $\mathscr{A}$. This description consists of two primary phases: (i) the online phase, which encompasses the actual interaction between the adversary and the ideal oracle, and (ii) the offline phase, which occurs after the online phase and involves the ideal oracle sampling intermediate variables to ensure compatibility with the ASCON construction.

The offline phase is further segmented into several stages, each dependent on events defined over the preceding stages. In the event of a bad event occurring at any stage, the ideal oracle has the option to either abort or exhibit arbitrary behavior. To effectively analyze the situation, we aim to establish an upper bound on the probability of all such bad events. Consequently, at any given stage, we assume that all prior bad events have not occurred. To simplify notation, we utilize the same notations for the transcripts in both the real and ideal worlds.

ONLINE PHASE. The adversary can make three types of queries in an interleaved manner without any repetition: (i) encryption queries (ii) decryption queries, and (iii) primitive queries.

- ON i-TH ENCRYPTION QUERY $(\mathsf{N}_i, \mathsf{A}_i, \mathsf{M}_i)$, $\forall i \in [q_e]$, RESPOND RANDOMLY:

$$\mathsf{C}_i \xleftarrow{\$} \{0,1\}^{|\mathsf{M}_i|}, \ \mathsf{T}_i \xleftarrow{\$} \{0,1\}^\tau, \ \mathsf{return}(\mathsf{C}_i, \mathsf{T}_i).$$

- ON i-TH DECRYPTION QUERY $(\mathsf{N}_i', \mathsf{A}_i', \mathsf{C}_i', \mathsf{T}_i')$, $i \in [q_d]$, REJECT STRAIGHT-AWAY: Ideal oracle returns rej for all decryption queries (here we assume that the adversary does not make any decryption query that is obtained from a previous encryption query).

- ON i-TH PRIMITIVE QUERY $(\mathsf{Q}_i, \mathsf{dir}_i) \in \{0,1\}^b \times \{+1, -1\}$, $i \in [q_p]$, RESPOND HONESTLY: We maintain a list P of responses of primitive queries, representing the partial (injective) function of a random permutation Π. Initially, $\mathsf{P} = \emptyset$.

1. If $dir_i = +1$, we set $U_i = Q_i$. Let $V_i \xleftarrow{\$} \{0,1\}^b \setminus range(P)$, $P \leftarrow P \cup \{(U_i, V_i)\}$, return V_i.

2. If $dir_i = -1$, we set $V_i = Q_i$. Let $U_i \xleftarrow{\$} \{0,1\}^b \setminus domain(P)$, $P \leftarrow P \cup \{(U_i, V_i)\}$, return U_i.

After all queries have been made we denote the online transcript (visible to the adversary) as

$$\Theta_{id,on} = \left((N_i, A_i, M_i, C_i, T_i)_{i \in [q_e]}, \; (N'_i, A'_i, C'_i, T'_i, rej)_{i \in [q_d]}, \; P\right)$$

BAD EVENT. We set $bad_1 = 1$, if

$$(N_i, A_i, C_i, T_i) = (N'_j, A'_j, C'_j, T'_j), \quad i \in [q_e], \; j \in [q_d]$$

for which the encryption query is made later. It is important to note that the adversary is not allowed to make a decryption query that matches a previous encryption query. However, there is a possibility that a decryption query accidentally matches an encryption query made subsequently. This situation is referred to as a "bad event" and is of concern. Since the adversary has the capability to make nonce-respecting encryption queries only, we can establish an upper bound for the probability of bad_1 as given in the Lemma below. Although the proof for this is omitted here, it can be straightforwardly derived from the description of the ideal world for encryption queries (by looking at the randomness of the tag values).

Lemma 3. $Pr(bad_1 = 1) \leq \frac{q_d}{2^\tau}$.

OFFLINE PHASE. The offline phase is divided into three stages, performed sequentially: (i) setting internal states of encryption queries, (ii) setting internal states of decryption queries, and (iii) sampling a key, and verifying compatibility with the online phase.

First, we set the input-output pairs for all permutations used in processing associated data and message part of each encryption query. For $i \in [q_e]$ (i.e., for i-th encryption query) we perform the following:

1. We first parse all data we have in the online transcript.

$$(A_{i,1}, \ldots, A_{i,a_i}) \xleftarrow{r} pad_1(A_i)$$
$$(M_{i,1}, \ldots, M_{i,m_i}) \xleftarrow{r}_* M_i$$
$$(C_{i,1}, \ldots, C_{i,m_i}) \xleftarrow{r}_* C_i$$

2. Let $t_i = a_i + m_i$, $d_i = |M_{i,m_i}| = |C_{i,m_i}|$. We now sample

$$V_{i,0}, \ldots, V_{i,a_i-1} \xleftarrow{\$} \{0,1\}^b$$
$$Z_{i,a_i}, \ldots, Z_{i,t_i-1} \xleftarrow{\$} \{0,1\}^c, \delta_i^* \xleftarrow{\$} \{0,1\}^{r-d_i}$$

The values of $V_{i,j}$ would determine all inputs and outputs for associate data processing. Similarly, $C_i, Z_{i,j}, \delta_i^*$ would determine the input and outputs for message processing.

3. We now set all inputs and outputs of the permutation used in associate data and message processing. Note that while $a_i = 0$ is possible, $m_i \geq 1$.

If $a_i > 0$, we define the following:
- $U_{i,j} = V_{i,j-1} \oplus (A_{i,j} \| 0^c)$, $\forall j \in [a_i]$.
- $V_{i,a_i} = (C_{i,1} \oplus M_{i,1}) \| Z_{i,a_i}$.

If $m_i \geq 2$:
- $U_{i,a_i+1} = C_{i,1} \| (Z_{i,a_i} \oplus 0^{c-1}1)$.
- $U_{i,a_i+j} = C_{i,j} \| Z_{i,a_i+j-1}, 2 \leq j \leq m_i - 1$.
- $V_{i,a_i+j} = (C_{i,j+1} \oplus M_{i,j+1}) \| Z_{i,a_i+j-1}, \forall j \in [m_i - 2]$.
- $V_{i,t_i-1} = (C_{i,m_i} \oplus M_{i,m_i}) \| \delta_i^* \| Z_{i,t_i-1}$.
- $F_i = C_{i,m_i} \| \delta_i^* \| Z_{i,t_i-1}$.

Otherwise:
- $F_i = C_{i,m_1} \| \delta_i^* \| (Z_{i,a_i} \oplus 0^{c-1}1)$.

We define P_E to be the partial function mapping $U_{i,j}$ to $V_{i,j}$ for all $i \in [q_e]$, $j \in [t_i - 1]$, provided all $U_{i,j}$'s are distinct. In this case, it is easy to see that

$$V_{i,0} \xrightarrow{A_{i,1}}_\oplus V_{i,1} \xrightarrow{A_{i,2}}_\oplus \cdots \xrightarrow{A_{i,a_i}}_\oplus V_{i,a_i}; V_{i,a_i} \oplus 0^{b-1}1 \xrightarrow{M_{i,1}}_\oplus V_{i,a_i+1} \cdots \xrightarrow{M_{i,m_i-1}}_\oplus V_{i,t_i-1}.$$

Moreover, P_E would be an injective partial function if $V_{i,j}$'s are all distinct.

BAD EVENT: P_E IS NOT AN INJECTIVE PARTIAL FUNCTION.   We set

1. $\mathsf{bad}_2 = 1$ if for some $(i,j) \neq (i',j')$, either $U_{i,j} = U_{i',j'}$ or $V_{i,j} = V_{i',j'}$,
2. $\mathsf{bad}_3 = 1$ if for some $i \neq i' \in [q_e]$, $F_i = F_{i'}$ (if this happens then it would force $T_i = T_{i'}$ to hold).

Lemma 4. $\Pr(\mathsf{bad}_2 = 1 \vee \mathsf{bad}_3 = 1) \leq \dfrac{\sigma_e^2}{2^b}$.

Proof. The proof of the above statement is straightforward as it is easy to see that $V_{i,j}$'s are randomly sampled and $U_{i,j}$'s are defined through a bijective mapping of $V_{i,j-1}$ values. The same applies to F_i values. Given that we have at most $\binom{\sigma_e}{2}$ choices for inputs and outputs, we get the above bound by simply using the union bound. ▢

Contingent on the condition that none of the aforementioned bad events occur, we would like to set the input-output pairs for all permutations used in associated data and ciphertext processing for all decryption queries. Here, we only use P to run the randomized extension. Later, we set a bad event if it is not disjoint (both from the domain and the range) with P_E. This would ensure the compatibility of $P_1 \sqcup P_E$ (where P_1 is the randomized extension of P) and would also help later in upper bounding the forging probability of a decryption query. For $i \in [q_d]$ (i.e., for the i-th decryption query) with $t_i \geq 2$, we perform the following:

We first parse all data as we have done for encryption queries:

$$(A'_{i,1}, \ldots, A'_{i,a'_i}) \xleftarrow{r} \mathsf{pad}_1(A'_i)$$
$$(C'_{i,1}, \ldots, C'_{i,c_i}) \xleftarrow{r}_* C'_i$$

Let $t'_i = a'_i + c_i$, $d'_i = |C_{i,c_i}|$. Now, we define p_i indicating the length of the longest common prefix of the i-th decryption query and an encryption query.

DEFINITION OF p_i, $i \in [q_d]$.

1. If there does not exist any $j \in [q_e]$ such that $N_j = N'_i$, we define $p_i = -1$.
2. Otherwise, there exists a unique j for which $N_j = N'_i$ (since the adversary is nonce-respecting and hence every nonce in encryption queries is distinct). Define p_i denote the length of the largest common prefix of
   - $(A'_{i,1}, \ldots, (A'_{i,a'_i}, *), C'_{i,1}, \ldots, C'_{i,c_i})$ and
   - $(A_{j,1}, \ldots, (A_{j,a_j}, *), C_{j,1}, \ldots, C_{j,m_i})$.
   Here $*$ is used to distinguish associate data blocks and ciphertext blocks.

Now, for each $i \in [q_d]$, depending on the value of p_i, we perform the following:

ASSOCIATED DATA AND CIPHERTEXT PROCESSING

1. For $i = 1$ to q_d with $p_i = -1$:
   - $V'_{i,0} \xleftarrow{\$} \{0,1\}^b$.
   - If $a'_i > 0$, run $\mathsf{xorRand\_Extn}^P(V'_{i,0}, (A'_{i,1}, \ldots, A'_{i,a'_i}))$ to obtain a walk

   $$V'_{i,0} \xrightarrow{A'_{i,1}}_{\oplus} V'_{i,1} \xrightarrow{A'_{i,2}}_{\oplus} \cdots \xrightarrow{A'_{i,a'_i}}_{\oplus} V'_{i,a'_i}.$$

   - If $c_i > 1$, run $\mathsf{Rand\_Extn}^P(V'_{i,a_i} \oplus 0^*1, C'_{i,1}\| \ldots \|C'_{i,c_i-1})$ to obtain a walk

   $$V'_{i,a'_i} \oplus 0^*1 \xrightarrow{C'_{i,1}} V'_{i,a'_i+1} \xrightarrow{C'_{i,2}} \cdots \xrightarrow{C'_{i,c_i-1}} V'_{i,a'_i+c_i-1}.$$

2. For $i = 1$ to q_d with $0 \leq p_i \leq a'_i$:
   - $V'_{i,p_i} := V_{j,p_i}$.
   - If $a'_i > p_i$, run $\mathsf{xorRand\_Extn}^P(V'_{i,p_i}, (A'_{i,p_i+1}, \ldots, A'_{i,a'_i}))$ to obtain a walk

   $$V'_{i,p_i} \xrightarrow{A'_{i,p_i+1}}_{\oplus} V'_{i,p_i+1} \xrightarrow{A'_{i,p_i+2}}_{\oplus} \cdots \xrightarrow{A'_{i,a'_i}}_{\oplus} V'_{i,a'_i}.$$

   - If $c_i > 1$, run $\mathsf{Rand\_Extn}^P(V'_{i,a_i} \oplus 0^*1, C'_{i,1}\| \ldots \|C'_{i,c_i-1})$ to obtain a walk

   $$V'_{i,a'_i} \oplus 0^*1 \xrightarrow{C'_{i,1}} V'_{i,a'_i+1} \xrightarrow{C'_{i,2}} \cdots \xrightarrow{C'_{i,c_i-1}} V'_{i,a'_i+c_i-1}.$$

3. For $i = 1$ to q_d with $a'_i < p_i < t_i$:
   - $\mathsf{V}'_{i,p_i} := \mathsf{V}_{j,p_i}$.
   - If $p_i < t_i - 1$, run $\mathsf{Rand\_Extn}^P(\mathsf{V}'_{i,p_i}, \mathsf{C}'_{i,p_i-a'_i+1} \| \cdots \| \mathsf{C}'_{i,c_i-1})$ to obtain a
     walk
     $$\mathsf{V}'_{i,p_i} \xrightarrow{\mathsf{C}'_{i,p_i-a'_i+1}} \mathsf{V}'_{i,p_i+1} \xrightarrow{\mathsf{C}'_{i,p_i-a'_i+2}} \cdots \xrightarrow{\mathsf{C}'_{i,c_i-1}} \mathsf{V}'_{i,a'_i+c_i-1}.$$
4. For $i = 1$ to q_d with $p_i = t_i$:
   - $\mathsf{V}'_{i,a'_i+c_i-1} := \mathsf{V}_{j,a'_i+c_i-1}$.

For all the cases above, we define

$$\mathsf{F}'_i = \begin{cases} \mathsf{C}'_{i,c_i} \| 10^* \| \lfloor \mathsf{V}'_{i,a'_i+c_i-1} \rfloor_c & \text{if } c_i \geq 2 \\ \mathsf{C}'_{i,c_i} \| 10^* \| (\lfloor \mathsf{V}'_{i,a'_i+c_i-1} \rfloor_c \oplus 0^{c-1}1) & \text{if } c_i = 1 \end{cases}.$$

Note that for each $i \in [q_d]$, P is updated by both the randomized extension algorithms, and although we start with a permutation, the resulting extended function P_1 need not be injective.

BAD EVENT: P_1 IS NOT AN INJECTIVE PARTIAL FUNCTION. We define $\mathsf{bad}_4 = 1$ if there exist (X, Y) and (X', Y') in the set P_1 such that $Y = Y'$. It is important to note that P is an injective partial function, and thus this bad event can only occur when at least one of the values Y or Y' is obtained during the offline phase. Considering that both inputs and outputs are uniformly sampled, the probability of bad_4 can be straightforwardly bounded using the union bound.

Lemma 5. $\Pr(\mathsf{bad}_4 = 1) \leq \dfrac{\sigma_d(q_p + \sigma_d)}{2^b}$.

BAD EVENT (PERMUTATION COMPATIBILITY OF $\mathsf{P_E}$ AND P_1). We now set $\mathsf{bad}_5 = 1$ if

$$\text{domain}(\mathsf{P}_1) \cap \text{domain}(\mathsf{P_E}) \neq \emptyset \text{ or } \text{range}(\mathsf{P}_1) \cap \text{range}(\mathsf{P_E}) \neq \emptyset.$$

Given that this bad event does not hold, $\mathsf{P_E} \cup \mathsf{P}_1$ is an injective partial function that is desired for a random permutation.

Lemma 6. $\Pr(\mathsf{bad}_5 = 1) \leq \dfrac{\mathsf{mcoll}(\sigma_e, 2^r) \times (\sigma_d + q_p)}{2^c}$.

Proof. Let ρ_1 (and ρ_2) denote the multicollision on the values of $\lceil x \rceil_r$, for all $x \in \text{domain}(\mathsf{P_E})$ (and for all $x \in \text{range}(\mathsf{P_E})$ respectively). Then, by the randomness of the randomized extension process and randomized xor-extension process, $\Pr(\mathsf{bad}_5 = 1 \mid \max\{\rho_1, \rho_2\} = \rho) \leq \rho(\sigma_d + q_p)/2^c$. Hence, using the expectation of $\max\{\rho_1, \rho_2\}$, and applying Lemma 1 and the remark following it, we get the above bound. $\square$

BAD EVENT (CORRECTLY FORGING).   We now set bad events whenever we have a correct forging in the ideal world based on the injective partial function $P_2 := P_1 \sqcup P_E$ constructed so far. We set $\mathsf{bad}_6 = 1$ if

$$(\mathsf{F}'_i, \mathsf{T}'_i) = (\mathsf{F}_j, \mathsf{T}_j), \quad i \in [q_d], \quad j \in [q_e].$$

This is similar to bad_3 as this would force a decryption query to be valid.

Lemma 7. $\Pr(\mathsf{bad}_6 = 1) \leq \dfrac{\mathsf{mcoll}(q_e, 2^\tau) q_d}{2^c}$.

Proof. We divide this into two cases. First, consider $p_i = c_i - 1$ and $\mathsf{T}'_i = \mathsf{T}_j$. Then $\mathsf{F}'_i \neq \mathsf{F}_j$, and hence bad_6 does not occur.

Next, we assume $p_i \neq c_i - 1$. Let ρ_3 denote the number of multicollision of T_j values. By using the randomness of Z_{j,t_i-1} and using the multicollision we have, $\Pr(\mathsf{bad}_6 = 1 \mid \rho_3 = \rho) \leq \frac{\rho q_d}{2^c}$. Hence, using the expectation of ρ_3, and applying Lemma 1, we have the above bound. □

We also have to consider some other ways to become a valid forgery. Now, we reach the time to sample the key

$$K = (K_1, K_2) \xleftarrow{\$} \{0,1\}^\kappa, \quad K_2 \in \{0,1\}^\tau.$$

Let

$$\mathcal{J} = \{j \in [q_d] : \mathsf{N}'_j \neq \mathsf{N}_i \ \forall i \in [q_e]\}.$$

Now, we can define all remaining input-outputs for the underlying permutation used in the initialization and tag generation phase as follows:

1. For all $i \in [q_e]$,
   - $\mathsf{I}_i := IV\|K\|\mathsf{N}_i$, $\mathsf{O}_i := \mathsf{V}_{i,0} \oplus 0^{b-\kappa}\|K$,
   - $\mathsf{X}_i := \mathsf{F}_i \oplus 0^r\|K\|0^{c-\kappa}$, $\mathsf{Y}_i := \alpha_i\|(\mathsf{T}_i \oplus K_2)$, where $\alpha_i \xleftarrow{\$} \{0,1\}^{b-\tau}$.
2. For all $j \in \mathcal{J}$,
   - $\mathsf{I}'_j := IV\|K\|\mathsf{N}'_j$ and $\mathsf{O}'_j := \mathsf{V}'_{j,0} \oplus 0^{b-\kappa}\|K$.
3. For all other $j \in [q_d]$, there exists $i \in [q_e]$ such that $\mathsf{N}'_j = \mathsf{N}_i$, and we define $\mathsf{I}'_j := \mathsf{I}_i$, $\mathsf{O}'_j := \mathsf{O}_i$.

Define $P_{\mathsf{in\text{-}tag}} = \left((\mathsf{I}_i, \mathsf{O}_i)_{i \in [q_e]}, \ (\mathsf{X}_i, \mathsf{Y}_i)_{i \in [q_e]}, \ (\mathsf{I}'_j, \mathsf{O}'_j)_{j \in \mathcal{J}}\right)$.

BAD EVENT (PERMUTATION COMPATIBILITY OF $P_{\mathsf{IN\text{-}TAG}}$ AND P_2). We define $\mathsf{bad}_7 = 1$ if one of the following holds:

1. $\mathsf{I}_i, \mathsf{I}'_j \in \mathsf{domain}(P_2)$ for some $i \in [q_e], j \in [q_d]$.
2. $\mathsf{O}_i = \mathsf{O}'_j$ for $i \in [q_e]$ and $j \in [q_d]$ such that $\mathsf{N}_i \neq \mathsf{N}'_j$.
3. $\mathsf{O}_i, \mathsf{O}'_j \in \mathsf{range}(P_2)$ for some $i \in [q_e], j \in [q_d]$.

Once again, if this bad event does not hold, $P_3 := P_2 \sqcup P_{\mathsf{in\text{-}tag}}$ is an injective partial function. By using the randomness of K, $\mathsf{V}_{i,0}$ and $\mathsf{V}'_{i,0}$ we can easily bound the probability of bad_7 as stated below.

Lemma 8. $\Pr(\mathsf{bad}_7 = 1) \leq \dfrac{q_p + \sigma}{2^\kappa} + \dfrac{q_e q_d + (q_e + q_d)(\sigma + q_p)}{2^b}.$

Finally, we settle the tag computation of all decryption queries and we set bad whenever a valid forgery occurs. For all $i \in [q_d]$, we define $\mathsf{X}'_i := \mathsf{F}'_i \oplus (0^r \| K \| 0^{c-\kappa})$. If $\mathsf{X}'_i \in \mathsf{domain}(\mathsf{P}_3)$ then we define $\mathsf{Y}'_i = \mathsf{P}_3(\mathsf{X}'_i)$. Else, $\mathsf{Y}'_i \xleftarrow{\$} \{0,1\}^b$.

BAD EVENT (DECRYPTION QUERIES ARE NOT REJECTED). We divide this into two cases depending on whether $\mathsf{X}'_i \in \mathsf{domain}(\mathsf{P}_3)$ or not:

- Let $\mathsf{F}'_i = (\beta'_i \| x'_i \| \gamma'_i)$, where $|\beta'_i| = r + \kappa - \tau$, $|x'_i| = \tau$ and $|\gamma'_i| = c - \kappa$. We set $\mathsf{bad}_8 = 1$ if

$$\exists i \in [q_d], \quad \mathsf{X}'_i \in \mathsf{domain}(\mathsf{P}_3) \ \wedge \ \lfloor \mathsf{P}_3(\mathsf{X}'_i) \rfloor_\tau \oplus K_2 = \mathsf{T}'_i.$$

If $\mathsf{bad}_8 = 1$, then
  (i) for some $(\beta_j \| x_j \| \gamma_j) \in \mathsf{domain}(\mathsf{P}_3)$, $\mathsf{X}'_i = (\beta_j \| x_j \| \gamma_j)$, $|\beta_j| = r + \kappa - \tau$, $|x_j| = \tau$ and $|\gamma_j| = c - \kappa$, and
  (ii) $x_j \oplus y_j = \mathsf{T}'_i \oplus x'_i$ where $y_j = \lfloor \mathsf{P}_3(\beta_j \| x_j \| \gamma_j) \rfloor_\tau$.
Let ρ_4 denote the multicollision on the values of $(x_a \oplus y_a)_a$ varying over all elements of P_3. Hence, the number of choices of j is at most ρ_4. Then, by the randomness of K,

$$\Pr(\mathsf{bad}_8 = 1 \mid \rho_4 = \rho) \leq \frac{\rho q_d}{2^\kappa}.$$

So, using the expectation of ρ_4, and applying Lemma 2, we have

Lemma 9. $\Pr(\mathsf{bad}_8 = 1) \leq \dfrac{\mathsf{mcoll}(\sigma + q_p, 2^\tau) q_d}{2^\kappa}.$

- $\mathsf{X}'_i \notin \mathsf{domain}(\mathsf{P}_3)$. Let $y_i = \lfloor \mathsf{Y}'_i \rfloor_\tau$. We set $\mathsf{bad}_9 = 1$ if there exists $i \in [q_d]$ such that $y_i \oplus K_2 = \mathsf{T}'_i$. Similarly, by the randomness of y_i, we have

Lemma 10. $\Pr(\mathsf{bad}_9 = 1) \leq \dfrac{q_d}{2^\tau}.$

Let bad denote the union of all bad events, namely $\cup_{i=1}^{9} \mathsf{bad}_i$. By Lemmas 3 through 10, we have shown that

$$\Pr(\mathsf{bad} = 1) \leq \frac{2q_d}{2^\tau} + \frac{\sigma_e^2}{2^b} + \frac{\sigma_d(q_p + \sigma_d)}{2^b} + \frac{\mathsf{mcoll}(\sigma_e, 2^\tau) \times (\sigma_d + q_p)}{2^c} + \frac{q_p + \sigma}{2^\kappa}$$
$$+ \frac{\mathsf{mcoll}(q_e, 2^\tau) q_d}{2^c} + \frac{q_e q_d + (q_e + q_d)(\sigma + q_p)}{2^b} + \frac{\mathsf{mcoll}(\sigma + q_p, 2^\tau) q_d}{2^\kappa}.$$

If all these bad events do not occur, then all the decryption queries are correctly rejected for the injective partial function P_3.

Let $\mathsf{P}_{\mathsf{fin}} := \mathsf{P}_3 \cup ((\mathsf{X}'_i, \mathsf{Y}'_i)_{i \in [q_d]})$. In the offline transcript, we provide all the input-outputs of $\mathsf{P}_{\mathsf{fin}}$. Then,

$$\Theta_{\mathsf{id}} = \big((\mathsf{N}_i, \mathsf{A}_i, \mathsf{M}_i, \mathsf{C}_i, \mathsf{T}_i)_{i \in [q_e]}, \ (\mathsf{N}'_i, \mathsf{A}'_i, \mathsf{C}'_i, \mathsf{T}'_i, \mathsf{rej})_{i \in [q_d]}, \ \mathsf{P}_{\mathsf{fin}}\big).$$

Let θ be a good transcript (no bad events occur). Note that we sample either inputs or outputs of $\mathsf{P_{fin}} \setminus \mathsf{P}$ uniformly. Thus,

$$\Pr(\Theta_{\mathrm{id}} = \theta) = \Pr(\mathsf{P} \subseteq \Pi) \times 2^{-b(|\mathsf{P_{fin}}| - |\mathsf{P}|)} \leq 1/(2^b)_{|\mathsf{P_{fin}}|} = \Pr(\Theta_{\mathrm{re}} = \theta)$$

By using the H-coefficient technique, we complete the proof of our main theorem.

6 Final Discussion

In this paper, we have proved a bound for ASCON AEAD, the winner of the recently concluded NIST LwC competition. This mode follows a Sponge type of construction. Notably, the inclusion of a key XOR operation during the Tag Generation phase allows us to derive a bound in the following form:

$$\frac{q_p}{2^\kappa} + \frac{q_p}{2^c} + \frac{q_d}{2^c} + \frac{\sigma_e^2}{2^b} + \frac{\sigma_d^2}{2^b} + \frac{q_d}{2^\tau} + \frac{q_p \sigma_d}{2^b} + \frac{q_d}{2^\kappa}$$

One can easily see that these bounds are tight:

- $\frac{q_p}{2^\kappa}, \frac{q_d}{2^\kappa}$ correspond to generic attacks which guess the key in primitive calls or decryption queries.
- $\frac{q_d}{2^\tau}$ is also a generic attack that guesses the tag in decryption queries.
- Attacks for the terms $\frac{\sigma_e^2}{2^b}, \frac{q_p}{2^c}, \frac{q_d}{2^c}, \frac{\sigma_d^2}{2^b}$ and $\frac{q_p \sigma_d}{2^b}$ can be constructed by observing state collisions in the encryption, primitive and decryption queries.

Further, when $\tau \leq \min\{\kappa, c\}$, the obtained security bound can be reduced to

$$\frac{T}{2^{\min\{\kappa,c\}}} + \frac{D}{2^\tau} + \frac{DT}{2^b}$$

where T is the time complexity and D is the data complexity of the adversary.

We would like to again emphasize that our analysis cannot be directly applied to general Sponge constructions without the double-keyed tag generation/verification protocol. Exploring the security of sponge constructions and achieving improved security, considering the gap between the current known security bounds and recent attacks [15], poses an interesting research problem.

Finally, in the multi-user setting, it is worth noting that our analysis indicates that the first term in the bound for bad_7 (Lemma 8) becomes $\frac{\mu(q_p + \sigma)}{2^\kappa}$, where μ denotes the number of users. Therefore, our current result does not directly extend to the multi-user setting, and a separate analysis would be required to address it.

References

1. AlTawy, R., et al.: Spoc. Submission to NIST LwC Standardization Process (Round 2) (2019)
2. Andreeva, E., Daemen, J., Mennink, B., Van Assche, G.: Security of keyed sponge constructions using a modular proof approach. In: Leander, G. (ed.) FSE 2015. LNCS, vol. 9054, pp. 364–384. Springer, Heidelberg (2015). https://doi.org/10.1007/978-3-662-48116-5_18
3. Bertoni, G., Daemen, J., Peeters, M., Assche, G.V.: Sponge functions. In: ECRYPT Hash Workshop 2007. Proceedings (2007)
4. Bertoni, G., Daemen, J., Peeters, M., Van Assche, G.: Duplexing the sponge: single-pass authenticated encryption and other applications. In: Miri, A., Vaudenay, S. (eds.) SAC 2011. LNCS, vol. 7118, pp. 320–337. Springer, Heidelberg (2012). https://doi.org/10.1007/978-3-642-28496-0_19
5. Bertoni, G., Daemen, J., Peeters, M., Assche, G.V.: On the security of the keyed sponge construction. In: Symmetric Key Encryption Workshop 2011. Proceedings (2011)
6. Bertoni, G., Daemen, J., Peeters, M., Assche, G.V.: Permutation-based encryption, authentication and authenticated encryption. In: DIAC 2012 (2012)
7. Bertoni, G., Daemen, J., Peeters, M., Assche, G.V.: Keccak. In: Advances in Cryptology - EUROCRYPT 2013. Proceedings, pp. 313–314 (2013)
8. Chakraborti, A., Datta, N., Nandi, M., Yasuda, K.: Beetle family of lightweight and secure authenticated encryption ciphers. Cryptology ePrint Archive (2018)
9. Chakraborty, B., Jha, A., Nandi, M.: On the security of sponge-type authenticated encryption modes. IACR Trans, Symmetric Cryptol., 93–119 (2020)
10. Chen, S., Steinberger, J.P.: Tight security bounds for key-alternating ciphers. In: Advances in Cryptology - EUROCRYPT 2014. Proceedings, pp. 327–350 (2014)
11. Committee, T.C.: Caesar: competition for authenticated encryption: security, applicability, and robustness (2014). https://competitions.cr.yp.to/caesar-submissions.html
12. Daemen, J., Mennink, B., Van Assche, G.: Full-state keyed duplex with built-in multi-user support. In: Takagi, T., Peyrin, T. (eds.) ASIACRYPT 2017. LNCS, vol. 10625, pp. 606–637. Springer, Cham (2017). https://doi.org/10.1007/978-3-319-70697-9_21
13. Dobraunig, C., Eichlseder, M., Mendel, F., Schläffer, M.: Ascon v1.2: lightweight authenticated encryption and hashing. J. Cryptol. **34**(3), 33 (2021). https://doi.org/10.1007/s00145-021-09398-9
14. Dobraunig, C., Eichlseder, M., Mendel, F., Schläffer, M.: ASCON v1. Submission to the CAESAR Competition (2014), https://competitions.cr.yp.to/round1/asconv1.pdf
15. Gilbert, H., Heim Boissier, R., Khati, L., Rotella, Y.: Generic attack on duplex-based aead modes using random function statistics. In: Advances in Cryptology-EUROCRYPT 2023: 42nd Annual International Conference on the Theory and Applications of Cryptographic Techniques, Lyon, France, April 23–27, 2023, Proceedings, Part IV, pp. 348–378. Springer (2023). https://doi.org/10.1007/978-3-031-30634-1_12
16. Jovanovic, P., Luykx, A., Mennink, B.: Beyond $2^{c/2}$ security in sponge-based authenticated encryption modes. In: Sarkar, P., Iwata, T. (eds.) ASIACRYPT 2014. LNCS, vol. 8873, pp. 85–104. Springer, Heidelberg (2014). https://doi.org/10.1007/978-3-662-45611-8_5

17. Jovanovic, P., Luykx, A., Mennink, B., Sasaki, Y., Yasuda, K.: Beyond conventional security in sponge-based authenticated encryption modes. J. Cryptology **32**(3), 895–940 (2019)
18. Mennink, B., Lefevre, C.: Generic security of the ascon mode: on the power of key blinding. IACR Cryptol. ePrint Arch. p. 796 (2023). https://eprint.iacr.org/2023/796
19. Mennink, B., Neves, S.: Encrypted davies-meyer and its dual: towards optimal security using mirror theory. In: Katz, J., Shacham, H. (eds.) CRYPTO 2017. LNCS, vol. 10403, pp. 556–583. Springer, Cham (2017). https://doi.org/10.1007/978-3-319-63697-9_19
20. NIST: Submission requirements and evaluation criteria for the Lightweight Cryptography Standardization Process (2018). https://csrc.nist.gov/CSRC/media/Projects/Lightweight-Cryptography/documents/final-lwc-submission-requirements-august2018.pdf
21. Patarin, J.: Etude des Générateurs de Permutations Pseudo-aléatoires Basés sur le Schéma du DES. Ph.D. thesis, Université de Paris (1991)
22. Patarin, J.: The "coefficients H" technique. In: Selected Areas in Cryptography - SAC 2008. Revised Selected Papers, pp. 328–345 (2008)

Automated Meet-in-the-Middle Attack
Goes to Feistel

Qingliang Hou[1,2], Xiaoyang Dong[3,6,7(✉)], Lingyue Qin[4,6(✉)],
Guoyan Zhang[1,5,7(✉)], and Xiaoyun Wang[1,3,5,6,7(✉)]

[1] School of Cyber Science and Technology, Shandong University, Qingdao, China
qinglianghou@mail.sdu.edu.cn, guoyanzhang@sdu.edu.cn
[2] State Key Laboratory of Cryptology, P.O. Box 5159, Beijing 100878, China
[3] Institute for Advanced Study, BNRist, Tsinghua University, Beijing, China
{xiaoyangdong,xiaoyunwang}@tsinghua.edu.cn
[4] BNRist, Tsinghua University, Beijing, China
qinly@tsinghua.edu.cn
[5] Key Laboratory of Cryptologic Technology and Information Security, Ministry of Education, Shandong University, Jinan, China
[6] Zhongguancun Laboratory, Beijing, China
[7] Shandong Institute of Blockchain, Jinan, China

Abstract. Feistel network and its generalizations (GFN) are another important building blocks for constructing hash functions, e.g., `Simpira v2`, `Areion`, and the ISO standard `Lesamnta-LW`. The Meet-in-the-Middle (MitM) is a general paradigm to build preimage and collision attacks on hash functions, which has been automated in several papers. However, those automatic tools mostly focus on the hash function with Substitution-Permutation network (SPN) as building blocks, and only one for Feistel network by Schrottenloher and Stevens (at CRYPTO 2022).

In this paper, we introduce a new automatic model for MitM attacks on Feistel networks by generalizing the traditional *direct or indirect partial matching strategies* and also Sasaki's multi-round matching strategy. Besides, we find the equivalent transformations of Feistel and GFN can significantly simplify the MILP model. Based on our automatic model, we improve the preimage attacks on `Feistel-SP-MMO`, `Simpira-2/-4-DM`, `Areion-256/-512-DM` by 1–2 rounds or significantly reduce the complexities. Furthermore, we fill in the gap left by Schrottenloher and Stevens at CRYPTO 2022 on the large branch ($b > 4$) `Simpira-b`'s attack and propose the first 11-round attack on `Simpira-6`. Besides, we significantly improve the collision attack on the ISO standard hash `Lesamnta-LW` by increasing the attacked round number from previous 11 to ours 17 rounds.

Keywords: MitM · Automatic Tool · Feistel · Simpira v2 · Lesamnta-LW · Areion

1 Introduction

The cryptographic hash function is one of the most important primitives, playing a vital role in digital signatures, message integrity, passwords, and proof-of-

J. Guo and R. Steinfeld (Eds.): ASIACRYPT 2023, LNCS 14440, pp. 370–404, 2023.
https://doi.org/10.1007/978-981-99-8727-6_13

work, etc. The collision resistance, preimage resistance, and second-preimage resistance are the three basic security requirements for cryptographic hash functions. Besides the well-known SHA-3 [12], another crucial design strategy is to build hash functions on block ciphers [38,43]. Typical examples are PGV-modes [43], Davies-Meyer (DM), Matyas-Meyer-Oseas (MMO), and Miyaguchi-Preneel (MP), etc., instantiated with AES [19] or other AES-like constructions, e.g., Whirlpool [8], Grøstl [28], ECHO [11], Haraka v2 [37]. Feistel network and generalized Feistel network (GFN) are important designs for block ciphers and permutations. To share the security proof and implementation benefit, building Feistel (or GFN) primitives with AES round function becomes popular in research communities, e.g., Simpira v2 [29], Areion [35], and the ISO lightweight hash function standard Lesamnta-LW [31], etc., which are the main targets of this paper.

The Meet-in-the-Middle (MitM) Attack is a time-memory trade-off cryptanalysis technique introduced by Diffie and Hellman to attack block cipher [22]. At SAC 2008, Aumasson, Meier, and Mendel [4] proposed the MitM preimage attacks on reduced MD5 and full 3-pass HAVAL. At ASIACRYPT 2008, Sasaki and Aoki formally combined the MitM and local-collision techniques to attack full 3, 4, and 5-pass HAVAL. Further, they proposed the *splice-and-cut* technique [3] and the *initial structure* [49] to strengthen MitM attack and successfully broke the preimage resistance of the full MD5. In the past decades, the MitM attack has been widely applied to the cryptanalysis on block ciphers [14,25,34,41] and hash functions [3,30,49]. Simultaneously, various techniques have been introduced to improve the framework of MitM attack, such as internal state guessing [25], splice-and-cut [3], initial structure [49], bicliques [13], 3-subset MitM [14], indirect-partial matching [3,49], sieve-in-the-middle [17], match-box [27], dissection [23], MitM with guess-and-determine [50], differential-aided MitM [16,26,36], algebraic MitM [40], two-stage MitM [5], quantum MitM [51], etc. Till now, the MitM attack and its variants have broken MD4 [30,39], MD5 [49], KeeLoq [33], HAVAL [4,48], GOST [34], GEA-1/2 [1,10], etc.

Automatic Tools are significantly boosting the MitM attacks, recently. At CRYPTO 2011 and 2016, several automatic tools [15,21] were proposed for MitM attacks on AES. At FSE 2012, Wu *et al.* [53] introduced a search algorithm for MitM attacks on Grøstl. In [45], Sasaki first programmed the MitM attack on GIFT into a dedicated Mixed-Integer-Linear-Programming (MILP) model. At EUROCRYPT 2021, Bao *et al.* [6] introduced the MILP-based automatic search framework for MitM preimage attacks on AES-like hashing, whose compression function is built from AES-like block cipher or permutation. At CRYPTO 2021, Dong *et al.* [24] further extended Bao *et al.*'s model into key-recovery and collision attacks. At CRYPTO 2022, Schrottenloher and Stevens [51] simplified the language of the automatic model and applied it in both classic and quantum settings. Bao *et al.* [7] considered the MitM attack in view of the superposition states. At EUROCRYPT 2023, Qin *et al.* [44] proposed MitM attacks and automatic tools on sponge-based hashing.

Most state-of-the-art automatic tools of MitM attacks are about AES-like substitution-permutation network (SPN) primitives [6,7,24]. For Feistel or GFN constructions, most MitM cryptanalysis results are achieved by hand, such as the attacks on MD-SHA hash functions [2,3,30,49]. At ACNS 2013, Sasaki *et al.* [47] studied the preimage attacks on hash functions based on Feistel constructions with substitution-permutation (SP) round function, i.e., Feistel-SP. At CRYPTO 2022, Schrottenloher and Stevens [51] introduced an efficient MitM automatic tool including the first application to Feistel constructions, e.g., Simpira v2 [29].

Our Contributions

In this paper, we focus on building a new MILP-based MitM automatic tool on hash functions with Feistel or GFN constructions.

For the first contribution, we first generalize the matching strategy for MitM attack. The essential idea of MitM attack is to find two neutral states (represented by ■ and ■ bytes), which are computed along two independent paths ('forward' and 'backward') that are then linked in the middle by deterministic relations, i.e. the matching point. The deterministic relations are usually of the form $f_\mathcal{B} = g_\mathcal{R}$, where $f_\mathcal{B}$ and $g_\mathcal{R}$ are determined by ■ and ■, respectively. In [3,49], the matching equation $f_\mathcal{B} = g_\mathcal{R}$ is usually part of the full state, which is then named as *partial matching*. If $f_\mathcal{B} = g_\mathcal{R}$ is derived directly, then it is a *direct partial matching* [3]. However, if $f_\mathcal{B} = g_\mathcal{R}$ is computed by a linear transformation on the outputs of forward and backward computation, then it is named as *indirect partial matching* [2,49]. For both direct and indirect partial matching, the relation $f_\mathcal{B} = g_\mathcal{R}$ is essential for MitM attacks. Almost all the recent MitM attacks and automatic models [6,7,24,44] leverage these two traditional matching strategies.

However, in this paper, we find the relations $f'_\mathcal{B} = g'_\mathcal{B}$ (or $f'_\mathcal{R} = g'_\mathcal{R}$) can also be used for matching, where $f'_\mathcal{B}$ and $g'_\mathcal{B}$ are determined only by ■ bytes. Together with the direct and indirect partial matching strategies, we propose a generalized matching strategy. After programming the new matching strategy into our MILP model, we significantly reduce the 5-round preimage attack on Areion-256 from 2^{248} [35] to 2^{193}, and improve the preimage attack on Simpira-2 from previous 5 rounds [51] to ours 7 rounds.

For the second contribution, We first generalize Sasaki's multi-round matching strategy for Feistel [47] into full-round matching. At ACNS 2013, Sasaki [47] proposed a matching strategy for Feistel-SP and GFN. For the Feistel-SP structure, it is hard to find any matching at first glance, but two-byte matching obviously appeared after applying a linear transformation to 4 consecutive rounds. In this paper, we find Sasaki's multi-round matching can be further extended into full-round matching. Therefore, the states involved in matching come from all round functions from the matching point to the initial structure. The full-round matching strategy may discover more useful matching equations than the multi-round matching. The reason is that in the multi-round matching, the involved states are first computed along forward and backward from the known bytes in the initial structure, and many bytes become unknown (i.e., depending on both ■ and ■ bytes, denoted as □ bytes), and then it is hard to derive any matching equations through the □ bytes. In full-round matching, matches are constructed by directly considering the fresh states from the initial structure.

Since many internal states are considered in full-round matching, it becomes hard to build MILP constraints for matching. To solve this problem, we find an equivalent transformation of Feistel and GFN that can significantly simplify the MILP programming of the full-round matching, where each byte of the full state can be programmed individually to determine if it is a one-byte matching.

Based on the above techniques, the achievements in this paper are listed below and also in Table 1.

- Based on the above techniques, we improve Sasaki's 11-round MitM attack [47] on Feistel-SP to ours 12 rounds with almost the same time complexity.
- We improve Schrottenloher and Stevens's MitM preimage attacks at CRYPTO 2022 [51] on Simpira v2 by improving the attack on Simpira-2 from 5 rounds [51] to ours 7 rounds, and improving the attack on Simpira-4 from 9 rounds [51] to ours 11 rounds. As stated by Schrottenloher and Stevens [52, Appendix B7], they can not attack on Simpira-b versions with $b \notin \{2, 3, 4\}$. We first fill the gap by introducing the 11-round MitM attack on Simpira-6.
- For the ISO standardized lightweight hash Lesamnta-LW [31], we significantly improve the collision attack from the previous 11-round attack to ours 17-round attack. Moreover, we also found a 20-round Lesamnta-LW MitM characteristic with time 2^{124} which is better than the generic birthday bound 2^{128}, but it's higher than the designers' security claim against collision attack, which is 2^{120}.
- For the hash function Areion [35] proposed at TCHES 2023, we improve the MitM preimage attack on Areion256-DM from the previous 5 rounds to ours 7 rounds, and improve the attack on Areion512-DM from previous 10 rounds to ours 11 rounds. For the source code, please refer to

https://github.com/Hql-code/MitM-Feistel

Comparison to Schrottenloher and Stevens's MitM Attack. At CRYPTO 2022, Schrottenloher and Stevens [51] introduced automatic MitM tools based on MILP, which are also applied to preimage attacks on Feistel constructions, i.e., Simpira v2 [29] and Sparkle [9]. Their model is a top-down model with a greatly simplified attack representation excluding many details. While our model in this paper follows the bottom-up approach, which has been used by Bao *et al.* [6,7] and Dong *et al.* [24]. Therefore, our model inherits the advantages of previous works [6,7,24], which is easy to understand and use by only specifying the admissible coloring transitions at each stage and computing the parameters which give the time and memory complexities of the MitM attack. On Simpira v2's attacks [51], to simplify the model, the attacks are of branch-level. However, in our model, all attacks are found at the byte-level, which is more fine-grained. Combined with our new model on the matching strategy, we can improve Schrottenloher and Stevens' attacks on `Simpira-2/-4` by up to 2 rounds. Also, we find an attack on 11-round `Simpira-6`, while Schrottenloher and Stevens stated that their attack can not apply to it [52, Appendix B7].

Table 1. A Summary of the Attacks.

Target	Attacks	Settings	Rounds	Time	Memory	Generic	Ref
Feistel-SP-128	Preimage	Classical	11	2^{112}	2^{24}	2^{128}	[47]
		Classical	12	2^{113}	2^{48}	2^{128}	Sect. 5
Simpira-2	Preimage	Classical	5	2^{128}	-	2^{256}	[51]
		Quantum	5	2^{64}	-	2^{128}	[51]
		Classical	7	2^{225}	2^{96}	2^{256}	Sect. 6.1
Simpira-4	Preimage	Classical	9	2^{128}	-	2^{256}	[51]
		Quantum	9	2^{64}	-	2^{128}	[51]
		Classical	11	2^{225}	2^{160}	2^{256}	Sect. 6.2
Simpira-6	Preimage	Classical	11	$2^{193.6}$	2^{193}	2^{256}	Full Ver. [32]
Lesamnta-LW	Collision	Classical	11	2^{97}	2^{96}	2^{128}	[31]
		Classical	17	$2^{113.58}$	2^{112}	2^{128}	Sect. 7
		Classical	20	2^{124}	2^{124}	2^{128}	Full Ver. [32]
Areion256-DM	Preimage	Classical	5	2^{248}	2^{8}	2^{256}	[35]
		Classical	5	2^{193}	2^{88}	2^{256}	Sect. 8
		Classical	7	2^{240}	2^{64}	2^{256}	Sect. 8
Areion512-DM	Preimage	Classical	10	2^{248}	2^{8}	2^{256}	[35]
		Classical	11	2^{241}	2^{48}	2^{256}	Sect. 8

2 Preliminaries

In the section, we first introduce the main notations used in the following paper, and briefly describe the Meet-in-the-Middle attack, the specification of `AES`, (Generalized) Feistel Networks, `Areion`, `Lesamnta-LW`, and the idea of Sasaki's preimage attack on Feistel-SP.

2.1 Notations

$A_{\text{SB}}^{(r)}$: the internal state after operation SB in round r, $r \geq 0$

$A_{\text{SB}}^{(r)}[i]$: the i-th byte of the internal state $A_{\text{SB}}^{(r)}$

■, $\mathcal{R}$: known byte with backward computation, $(x, y) = (0, 1)$

■, $\mathcal{B}$: known byte with forward computation, $(x, y) = (1, 0)$

■, $\mathcal{G}$: known byte with forward and backward computations, $(x, y) = (1, 1)$

□, $\mathcal{W}$: unknown byte in forward and backward computations, $(x, y) = (0, 0)$

$\lambda_{\mathcal{R}}$: the byte number of the ■ bytes in the starting state

$\lambda_{\mathcal{B}}$: the byte number of the ■ bytes in the starting state

DoF : degree of freedom in bytes

$\text{DoF}_{\mathcal{R}}$: the byte number of DoF of the ■ neutral words

$\text{DoF}_{\mathcal{B}}$: the byte number of DoF of the ■ neutral words

$l_{\mathcal{B}}$: the byte number of consumed DoF of the ■ bytes
$l_{\mathcal{R}}$: the byte number of consumed DoF of the ■ bytes
DoM : the byte number of DoF of the matching point
$End_{\mathcal{B}}$: the matching point determined by ■ bytes
$End_{\mathcal{R}}$: the matching point determined by ■ bytes

2.2   The Meet-in-the-Middle Attack

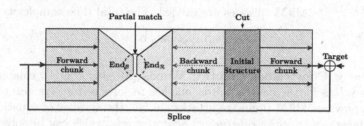

Fig. 1. The closed computation path of the MitM attack

Since the pioneering works on preimage attacks on Merkle-Damgård hashing, e.g. MD4, MD5, and HAVAL [3,30,39,49], techniques such as *splice-and-cut* [3], *initial structure* [49] and *(indirect-) partial matching* [2,49] have been invented to significantly improve the MitM approach. In Fig. 1, the compression function is divided at certain intermediate rounds (initial structure) into two chunks:

1. In the initial structure, a starting state is chosen with $\lambda_{\mathcal{R}}$ ■ bytes and $\lambda_{\mathcal{B}}$ ■ bytes, which are also denoted as the initial degree of freedom (DoF) of ■ and ■ bytes. The ■ and ■ bytes are then constrained linearly [46,47] or nonlinearly [24] by $l_{\mathcal{R}}$ and $l_{\mathcal{B}}$ byte equations, so that the two chunks can be computed independently on two distinct solution spaces of ■ and ■ derived by solving the constraint equations. The two solution spaces are named as *neutral space*. The DoFs of the ■ or ■ neutral space are denoted as $DoF_{\mathcal{R}}$ or $DoF_{\mathcal{B}}$.
2. The two *neutral spaces* are computed along two independent paths ('forward chunk' and 'backward chunk').
3. One chunk is computed across the first and last rounds via the *feed-forward mechanism* of the hashing mode, and they end at a common intermediate round (partial matching point) to derive the deterministic relation '$End_{\mathcal{B}} = End_{\mathcal{R}}$' for matching. The number of bytes for matching is denoted as the degree of matching (DoM).

Thereafter, a closed computation path of the MitM attack is derived. After setting up the configurations, the basic attack procedure goes as follows:

1. Choose constants for the initial structure.
2. For all $2^{8 \cdot DoF_{\mathcal{R}}}$ values of ■ neutral space, compute backward from the initial structure to the matching points $End_{\mathcal{R}}$ to generate a table $L_{\mathcal{R}}[End_{\mathcal{R}}]$.

3. Similarly, build L_B for $2^{8 \cdot \text{DoF}_B}$ values of ■ neutral space with forward computation.
4. Check for the DoM bytes match on indices between L_R and L_B.
5. For the pairs surviving the partial match, check for a full-state match.
6. Steps 1–5 form one MitM episode that will be repeated until a full match is found.

The attack complexity. An MitM episode ,is performed with time $2^{8 \cdot \max(\text{DoF}_R, \text{DoF}_B)} + 2^{8 \cdot (\text{DoF}_R + \text{DoF}_B - \text{DoM})}$. To find an h-bit target preimage, $2^{h - 8 \cdot (\text{DoF}_R + \text{DoF}_B)}$ MitM episodes are needed. The total time complexity of the attack is:

$$2^{h - 8 \cdot \min(\text{DoF}_R, \text{DoF}_B, \text{DoM})}. \tag{1}$$

Nonlinearly Constrained Neutral Words [24]. In order to compute the allowable values for the neutral words, one has to solve certain systems of equations. In previous MitM preimage attacks [46,50], the systems of equations are usually linear, i.e., *linearly constrained neutral words*, which can be solved with ease. At CRYPTO 2021, Dong *et al.* [24] found that the systems of equations can be nonlinear, which can not be solved directly like linear system. Therefore, Dong *et al.* proposed a table-based method to solve those *nonlinearly constrained neutral words*. Suppose in the starting state, there are λ_R ■ bytes and λ_B ■ bytes, and the number of nonlinear constraints are l_R and l_B for ■ and ■ bytes.

1. Fix the ■ bytes for the initial structure,
2. For 2^{λ_R} ■ values, compute the l_R bytes constraints (denoted as $c_R \in \mathbb{F}_2^{8 \cdot l_R}$), and store the λ_R ■ bytes in table $U_R[c_R]$,
3. For 2^{λ_B} ■ values, compute the l_B bytes constraints (denoted as $c_B \in \mathbb{F}_2^{8 \cdot l_B}$), and store the λ_B ■ bytes in table $U_B[c_B]$.

Then, for given c_R and c_B, the values in $U_R[c_R]$ and $U_B[c_B]$ can be computed independently (i.e., neutral) in one MitM episode. Therefore, we have $\text{DoF}_R = \lambda_R - l_R$ and $\text{DoF}_B = \lambda_B - l_B$. According to [24], both the time and memory complexities of one precomputation are $2^{\lambda_R} + 2^{\lambda_B}$. After the precomputation, $2^{l_R + l_B}$ MitM episodes are produced.

Automated MitM Based MILP. At EUROCRYPT 2021, Bao *et al.* [6] proposed the MILP-based automatic model for MitM preimage attacks on AES-like hashing. At CRYPTO 2021, Dong *et al.* extended the model into key-recovery and collision. At CRYPTO 2022, Bao *et al.* [7] proposed the superposition MitM attack, i.e., the ■ bytes and ■ bytes are handled independently in linear operations. A similar idea has been proposed and, called indirect-partial matching in 2009 [2]. In the superposition MitM attack framework, each state involved in a linear operation is separated into two virtual states, which are also called superposition states. One state preserves the ■ bytes, ■ bytes, and □ bytes in the original state, while the positions where ■ bytes are located turn ■. The other state can be obtained similarly but exchanging the ■ and ■ bytes. Therefore, two superposition states can be propagated equally and independently along the forward or backward computation paths through linear operations. The initial DoFs can be consumed in both directions. Then, two superposition states are finally combined before the next nonlinear operation after a series of linear operations. The color patterns and how the states are separated and combined are visualized in Fig. 2.

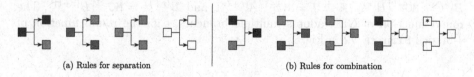

(a) Rules for separation   (b) Rules for combination

Fig. 2. Rules for separation and combination, where "$*$" means any color

The rules `MC-Rule` and `XOR-Rule` are first introduced in [6] to model the propagation rules of `MixColumn` and `AddRoundKey` in AES-like hashing. Since $\lambda_\mathcal{B}$ ■ bytes of the starting states are imposed $l_\mathcal{B}$ constraints (similar to ■), the rules `MC-Rule` and `XOR-Rule` are required to describe how the impacts from the neutral bytes in one chunk are limited on the opposite chunk. For more details on the two basic rules, please refer to [6] and also **Supplementary Material** A in our full version paper [32].

2.3 AES

To be concrete, we first recall the round function of `AES-128` [19]. It operates on a 16-byte state arranged into a 4×4 matrix and contains four operations as illustrated in Fig. 3: `SubBytes` (SB), `ShiftRows` (SR), `MixColumns` (MC), and `AddRoundKey` (AK). The `MixColumns` is to multiply an MDS matrix to each column of the state. Embedding a block cipher into the PGV hashing modes [43], such as Davies-Meyer (DM, Fig. 4), Matyas-Meyer-Oseas (MMO, Fig. 5) and Miyaguchi-Preneel (MP), is a common way to build the compression functions for hashing.

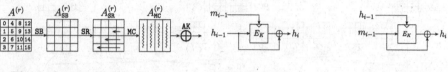

Fig. 3. One round AES   **Fig. 4.** DM   **Fig. 5.** MMO

2.4 (Generalized) Feistel Networks

Another widely used design approach is the Feistel network, which was first used in DES [18], and the generalized Feistel network (GFN) [54]. When the round function of Feistel adopts AddRoundKey (AK), SubBytes (SB), and a permutation layer, i.e., SP round function, the Feistel is named as Feistel-SP. In this paper, the permutation layer is a MixColumns (MC) with MDS, as shown in Fig. 6. Figure 7 is an equivalent transformation of Fig. 6, where $\tilde{A}^{(r)} = \text{MC}^{-1}(A^{(r)})$, $\tilde{B}^{(r)} = \text{MC}^{-1}(B^{(r)})$, $\tilde{A}^{(r+1)} = \text{MC}^{-1}(A^{(r+1)})$, and $\tilde{B}^{(r+1)} = \text{MC}^{-1}(B^{(r+1)})$. The round function of GFN adopts multiple branches, e.g., the round function of 4-branch Simpira v2 in Fig. 8.

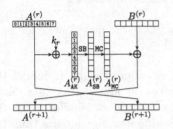
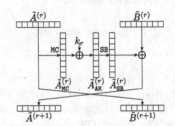

Fig. 6. One round Feistel-SP

Fig. 7. Equivalent transform of Feistel-SP

2.5 Simpira v2

Simpira v2 [29] is a family of cryptographic permutations that support inputs of $128 \times b$ bits, where b is the number of branches. When $b = 1$, Simpira v2 consists of 12 rounds AES with different constants. When $b \geq 2$, Simpira v2 is a Generalized Feistel Structure (GFS) with the F-function that consists of two rounds of AES. We denote Simpira v2 family members with b branches as Simpira-b. The total number of rounds is 15 for $b = 2$, $b = 4$ and $b = 6$, 21 for $b = 3$, and 18 for $b = 8$. Figure 8 shows the round function of Simpira-4.

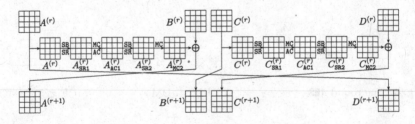

Fig. 8. The round function of Simpira-4

2.6 Areion

Areion [35] is a family of highly-efficient permutations based on AES instruction. It consists of two versions with 256-bit and 512-bit, named as Areion-256 (the round function is shown in Fig. 9) and Areion-512. Based on the two permutations, two hash functions with short input are designed with Davies-Meyer (DM) construction, i.e., Areion256-DM and Areion512-DM, which are our targets.

2.7 Lesamnta-LW

Lesamnta-LW is a lightweight 256-bit hash function proposed by Hirose *et al.* in 2010 [31], which has been specified in ISO/IEC 29192-5:2016. Lesamnta-LW is a Merkle-Damgård iterated hash function [20,42]. Figure 11 shows a hash with two message blocks, where the i-th compression function (CF) is $\mathrm{CF}(h_{i-1}, m_i) = E(h_{i-1}^0, m_i \| h_{i-1}^1) = h_i$, with $h_{i-1}^0, h_{i-1}^1, m_i \in \mathbb{F}_2^{128}$, $h_{i-1}, h_i \in \mathbb{F}_2^{256}$, and $h_{i-1} = h_{i-1}^0 \| h_{i-1}^1$. The initial h_0 is the initial vector and the last h_N is the 256-bit digest. The internal block cipher of CF is of 64 rounds with 256-bit plaintext and 32-bit round keys. Our attack is independent of the key schedule which is omitted. Figure 10 shows the round function, where $m_i = A^{(r)} \| B^{(r)}$, $h_{i-1}^1 = C^{(r)} \| D^{(r)}$. Lesamnta-LW uses AES's components, i.e., SB and MC, while P just permutes the bytes. Lesamnta-LW claims at least 2^{120} security levels against both collision and preimage attacks, and we target the MitM collision attack on Lesamnta-LW.

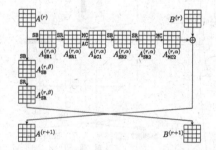
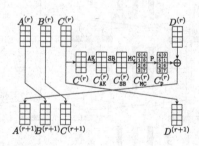

Fig. 9. One round Areion-256   **Fig. 10.** One round Lesamnta-LW

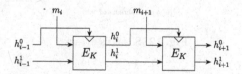

Fig. 11. Lesamnta-LW hash with two message blocks

2.8   Sasaki's Preimage Attack on Feistel-SP

At ACNS 2013, Sasaki [47] introduced the MitM preimage attacks on MMO hashing mode with Feistel-SP block ciphers by omitting the last network twist. In Fig. 12(a), $A_{\text{AK}}^{(6)}$ and $A_{\text{AK}}^{(7)}$ are chosen as the initial states with $\lambda_{\mathcal{R}} = 11$ and $\lambda_{\mathcal{B}} = 3$. The □ just represents the linear combination of ■ and ■ bytes. From $B^{(7)}$ to $A^{(8)}$, the consumed DoF of ■ is $l_{\mathcal{R}} = 8$. Therefore, the remaining DoFs of ■ and ■ are $\text{DoF}_{\mathcal{R}} = 11 - 8 = 3$ and $\text{DoF}_{\mathcal{B}} = 3$, respectively. In Fig. 12(b), by assigning conditions $k_0 = k_{10} \oplus H_A$ and $k_1 = k_9 \oplus H_B$, we have $A_{\text{MC}}^{(10)} = A_{\text{MC}}^{(0)}$ and $A_{\text{MC}}^{(9)} = A_{\text{MC}}^{(1)}$. Therefore, $A^{(2)} = B^{(9)} \oplus H_A$ and $B^{(2)} = A^{(9)} \oplus H_B$. In Fig. 12(c), Sasaki applied a linear transformation in the computation from $A_{\text{SB}}^{(3)}$ to $A_{\text{SB}}^{(5)}$ to derive a multi-round matching with DoM = 2 as shown in Fig. 13. The time complexity is $2^{8 \times (16 - \min\{3,3,2\})} = 2^{112}$.

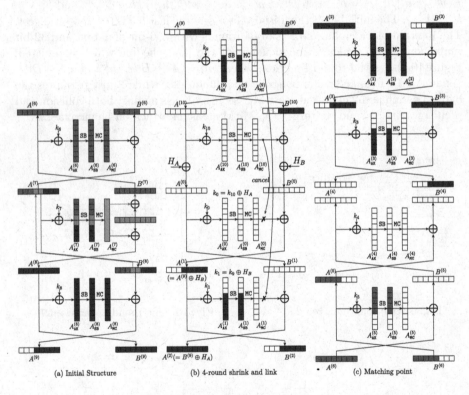

(a) Initial Structure   (b) 4-round shrink and link   (c) Matching point

Fig. 12. Sasaki's attack

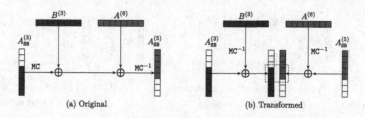

Fig. 13. Matching in Sasaki's attack

3 Generalization on Matching Strategy in MitM

In the matching point of the MitM attack, with forward and backward computations, if two matching states F^+ and F^- are determined only by the ■ and ▨, respectively, then, the relation $F^+ = F^-$ acts as a *direct partial matching*. This simple matching strategy is frequently used in previous works [46,49]. In ASIACRYPT 2009, Aoki *et al.* introduced the *indirect partial matching technique* [2], where F^+ can be expressed as $\phi_\mathcal{B} + \phi_\mathcal{R}$, and $F^- = \Phi_\mathcal{B} + \Phi_\mathcal{R}$. $\phi_\mathcal{B}$ and $\Phi_\mathcal{B}$ are determined by the ■ and ▨ bytes. $\phi_\mathcal{R}$ and $\Phi_\mathcal{R}$ are determined by the ■ and ▨ bytes. Therefore, the DoM-byte equation $\phi_\mathcal{B} + \Phi_\mathcal{B} = \phi_\mathcal{R} + \Phi_\mathcal{R}$ can be built from $F^+ = F^-$, which acts as the matching. In this paper, we denote $End_\mathcal{B} = \phi_\mathcal{B} + \Phi_\mathcal{B}$ and $End_\mathcal{R} = \phi_\mathcal{R} + \Phi_\mathcal{R}$.

In addition to the above two common matching strategies, we find that the byte equation determined only by one of the two colors (■, ▨) can also be used in the MitM attack. Taking the matching by combining MixColumn and XOR operations at MixColumns and AddRoundKey for AES as an example as shown in Fig. 14(a). Suppose from the matching states, there exist $M_\mathcal{R}$ byte-equations $\pi_\mathcal{R} = 0$, $M_\mathcal{B}$ byte-equations $\pi_\mathcal{B} = 0$, and DoM byte-equations $End_\mathcal{B} = End_\mathcal{R}$, where $End_\mathcal{R}$ and $\pi_\mathcal{R}$ are determined by ▨ and ■, $End_\mathcal{B}$ and $\pi_\mathcal{B}$ are determined by ■ and ▨. Figure 14(b) is a commonly used matching strategy (indirect partial matching) in previous MitM attacks [46,47], where there exists DoM = 1 byte matching equation $End_\mathcal{B} = End_\mathcal{R}$. Figure 14(c) is the new matching strategy, where there exists $M_\mathcal{R} = 1$ byte matching equation:

$$\pi_\mathcal{R} = 7\alpha[0] \oplus 11\alpha[1] \oplus 4\alpha[3] \oplus 3\gamma[0] \oplus 3\beta[0] \oplus \beta[1] \oplus \gamma[1] = 0.$$

This matching method in Fig. 14(c) can not be included in any of the two common matching strategies (direct or indirect partial matching), but can still lead to valid MitM attacks. With the new matching strategy, we introduce the new MitM procedures in the following:

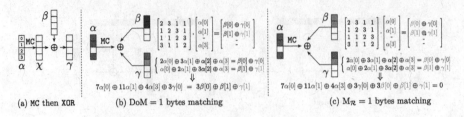

Fig. 14. Examples in Generalized Matching Strategy

(a) MC then XOR   (b) DoM = 1 bytes matching   (c) $M_{\mathcal{R}} = 1$ bytes matching

1. Choose constants for the initial structure.
2. For all $2^{8 \cdot \mathrm{DoF}_{\mathcal{R}}}$ values of ■ neutral space, compute from the initial structure to the matching points. If $\pi_{\mathcal{R}} = 0$ holds, store the $\mathrm{DoF}_{\mathcal{R}}$ ■ bytes in table $L_{\mathcal{R}}[End_{\mathcal{R}}]$.
3. For all $2^{8 \cdot \mathrm{DoF}_{\mathcal{B}}}$ values of ■ neutral space, compute from the initial structure to the matching points. If $\pi_{\mathcal{B}} = 0$ holds, store the $\mathrm{DoF}_{\mathcal{B}}$ ■ bytes in table $L_{\mathcal{B}}[End_{\mathcal{B}}]$.
4. Check for the DoM bytes matching with $End_{\mathcal{R}} = End_{\mathcal{B}}$ on indices between $L_{\mathcal{R}}$ and $L_{\mathcal{B}}$.
5. For the pairs surviving the partial matching, check for a full-state match.
6. Steps 1–5 form one MitM episode that will be repeated until a full match is found.

The Complexity. In one MitM episode, the time complexities of Step 2 and 3 are $2^{8 \cdot \mathrm{DoF}_{\mathcal{R}}}$ and $2^{8 \cdot \mathrm{DoF}_{\mathcal{B}}}$, respectively. The memory costs of Step 2 and 3 are $2^{8(\mathrm{DoF}_{\mathcal{R}} - M_{\mathcal{R}})}$ and $2^{8(\mathrm{DoF}_{\mathcal{B}} - M_{\mathcal{B}})}$. In Step 4 and 5, there expect $2^{8(\mathrm{DoF}_{\mathcal{R}} - M_{\mathcal{R}})} \cdot 2^{8(\mathrm{DoF}_{\mathcal{B}} - M_{\mathcal{B}}) - 8 \cdot \mathrm{DoM}}$ surviving pairs to check for a full-state match. Therefore, the time complexity of one MitM episode is

$$2^{8 \cdot \mathrm{DoF}_{\mathcal{R}}} + 2^{8 \cdot \mathrm{DoF}_{\mathcal{B}}} + 2^{8(\mathrm{DoF}_{\mathcal{R}} + \mathrm{DoF}_{\mathcal{B}} - M_{\mathcal{R}} - M_{\mathcal{B}} - \mathrm{DoM})}.$$

For a given h-bit target, $2^{h - 8(\mathrm{DoF}_{\mathcal{R}} + \mathrm{DoF}_{\mathcal{B}})}$ MitM episodes are needed to perform, and the total time complexity is

$$2^{h - 8 \cdot \min(\mathrm{DoF}_{\mathcal{R}}, \mathrm{DoF}_{\mathcal{B}}, M_{\mathcal{R}} + M_{\mathcal{B}} + \mathrm{DoM})}. \tag{2}$$

Remark 1. Compared with the attack framework proposed by Bao *et al.* [6], steps 2–3 in our framework will first filter the states that do not satisfy the matching equations containing only one color, and then store the remaining states in tables. The overall memory is $2^{8 \times \min\{\mathrm{DoF}_{\mathcal{R}} - M_{\mathcal{R}}, \mathrm{DoF}_{\mathcal{B}} - M_{\mathcal{B}}\}}$ which may be lower than the main memory cost in [6], i.e. $2^{8 \times \min\{\mathrm{DoF}_{\mathcal{R}}, \mathrm{DoF}_{\mathcal{B}}\}}$.

Modelling the Matching Point. For a given byte in Fig. 14, we introduce a Boolean variable ω, that $\omega = 1$ means this byte is □, otherwise $\omega = 0$. ω_i^{α}, ω_i^{β}, and ω_i^{γ} indicate whether the i-th byte in α, β, and γ is white respectively, and $\omega_i^{(\beta,\gamma)}$ is defined by $\mathtt{OR}(\omega_i^\beta, \omega_i^\gamma)$, i.e., $\omega_i^{(\beta,\gamma)} = 1$ if ω_i^β or ω_i^γ is 1. Besides, an auxiliary state χ is introduced in Fig. 14, where $\chi = \beta \oplus \gamma$. The rule to generate χ follows the $\mathtt{XOR\text{-}Rule}$ in [6], (i.e. ■ $\oplus$ ■ = □, ■ $\oplus$ ■ = ■, □ $\oplus$ ■ = □, etc.). Moreover, we introduce 4 general variables $n_\mathcal{B}^\alpha$, $n_\mathcal{R}^\alpha$, $n_\mathcal{B}^\chi$ and $n_\mathcal{R}^\chi$ to count the numbers of ■ cells and ■ cells or the number of ■ cells and ■ cells in α or χ. For example, $n_\mathcal{B}^\alpha$ is the number of ■ cells and ■ cells in α. Another general variable $n_\mathcal{G}$ is introduced to count the total number of ■ cells in α and χ. Suppose (x_i^α, y_i^α) and (x_i^χ, y_i^χ) denote the i-th cell in α and χ respectively, then we have

$$\begin{cases} n_\mathcal{B}^\alpha = \sum_{i=0}^{3} x_i^\alpha; \\ n_\mathcal{R}^\alpha = \sum_{i=0}^{3} y_i^\alpha; \end{cases} \quad \begin{cases} n_\mathcal{B}^\chi = \sum_{i=0}^{3} x_i^\chi; \\ n_\mathcal{R}^\chi = \sum_{i=0}^{3} y_i^\chi; \end{cases} \quad n_\mathcal{G} = \sum_{i=0}^{3} \mathtt{AND}(x_i^\alpha, y_i^\alpha) + \mathtt{AND}(x_i^\chi, y_i^\chi).$$

where $\mathtt{AND}(x_i, y_i) = 1$ if and only if $x_i = y_i = 1$. To avoid double counting the number of equations derived only by ■, let $\mathrm{M}_\mathcal{G} = \max\{0, n_\mathcal{G} - 4\}$ and exclude $\mathrm{M}_\mathcal{G}$ equations from $\pi_\mathcal{R} = 0$. Then, the number of equations in $\pi_\mathcal{B} = 0$ and $\pi_\mathcal{R} = 0$ can be calculated by

$$\mathrm{M}_\mathcal{B} = \max\{0, \ n_\mathcal{B}^\alpha + n_\mathcal{B}^\chi - 4\}, \quad \mathrm{M}_\mathcal{R} = \max\{0, \ n_\mathcal{R}^\alpha + n_\mathcal{R}^\chi - \mathrm{M}_\mathcal{G} - 4\}. \quad (3)$$

For the $\mathtt{MC}$ then $\mathtt{XOR}$ operations in Fig. 14, we can build $4 - \sum_{i=0}^{3}(\omega_i^{(\beta,\gamma)} + \omega_i^\alpha)$ linear equations which are determined by only known cells (■, ■, ■). Therefore, the number of byte equations $End_\mathcal{B} = End_\mathcal{R}$ is equal to the total linear equations minus $M_\mathcal{B}$ and $M_\mathcal{R}$ equations. We get

$$\mathrm{DoM} = \max\left\{0, \ 4 - \sum_{i=0}^{3}(\omega_i^{(\beta,\gamma)} + \omega_i^\alpha) - \mathrm{M}_\mathcal{B} - \mathrm{M}_\mathcal{R}\right\}. \quad (4)$$

4   Automatic Model for Transformed Feistel Structure

In this section, we first generalize Sasaki's multi-round matching strategy into full-round matching. Then, we introduce an equivalent transformation of Feistel and GFN, which is very friendly with the new proposed full-round matching strategy. At last, we construct the MILP constraints to describe the attributes propagation through transformed Feistel and how the full-round match is deployed. Combining the equivalent transformation and full-round match, the MILP model can be simplified and easy to program.

4.1   The Generalization of Sasaki's Matching Strategy for Feistel

In [47], Sasaki proposed a matching strategy for Feistel with a linear transformation. As shown in Fig. 13, it is hard to see any matching in the original Fig. 13(a). However, after a linear transformation in Fig. 13(b), the two-byte matching is obviously obtained. Besides the attack on balanced Feistel-SP, Sasaki [47] also built MitM attacks on GFN with SP round function, where the matching point covers 7 consecutive rounds. A similar linear transformation as in Fig. 13(b) is also applied, but involves more internal states.

Inspired by Sasaki's matching strategy [47], we generalize the matching strategy to full-round matching, i.e., the matching can happen by writing down the internal states involved from the *matching point* to the *initial structure*. For example, we can further extend Fig. 13(a) by replacing $B^{(3)}$ by $\mathrm{MC}(A_{\mathrm{SB}}^{(7)}) \oplus B^{(7)} \oplus H_A$ and replacing $A^{(6)}$ by $B^{(7)}$, where the internal states $A_{\mathrm{SB}}^{(7)}$ and $B^{(7)}$ come from the initial structure. Therefore, Fig. 13 becomes Fig. 15. The advantages of the generalized full-round matching are summarized below:

I Since the internal states from the initial structure preserve more useful information than other internal states (there are usually no □ bytes in the initial structure), a full-round matching may be more likely to produce a valid match than a local-round matching (e.g., 3 or 4 rounds). An example is found for `Simpira`-4 in Fig. 18, where the matching obviously exists for the full-round case, but disappears for certain local-round case.

II Also a linear transformation is applied to Fig. 15(a) to obtain Fig. 15(b). This is essential and can not be replaced by Bao *et al.*'s superposition MitM technique [7]. If we apply the superposition MitM technique in Fig. 15(a), $A_{\mathrm{SB}}^{(3)}$ will be separated into two states following the rules in Fig. 2, then one of the two states will be all □ after `MC`. Therefore, an unknown state will be XORed into the matching path, which leads to no matching at all.

If we apply a linear transformation to obtain Fig. 15(b), each byte of $A_{\mathrm{SB}}^{(3)}$ will be involved in the matching path individually. For example, considering the 4-th byte, there is a one-byte equation

$$\mathrm{MC}^{-1}\left(B^{(7)}\right)[3] \oplus A_{\mathrm{SB}}^{(7)}[3] \oplus A_{\mathrm{SB}}^{(3)}[3] \oplus A_{\mathrm{SB}}^{(5)}[3] = \mathrm{MC}^{-1}\left(B^{(7)} \oplus H_A\right)[3], \quad (5)$$

which is obviously a matching equation (no □ byte is involved).

III The transformed structure in Fig. 15(b) is easy to program in the automatic tool. As shown in Eq. (5), each byte can be individually considered, which is very friendly than the untransformed case in Fig. 15(a). As a matter of fact, this is very important when building the automatic tool, since for many (generalized) Feistel networks, the situation is much more complex than the very easy case for Feistel-SP. For example, in our 11-round attack on `Simpira`-4 (Fig. 23), there are more states involved in matching than that in Fig. 15(a). Therefore, if we do not apply the linear transformation, we have to program many `MC` operations into a whole matching rule, which is very complex or even infeasible for many ciphers like `Simpira`-4.

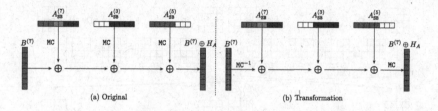

(a) Original   (b) Transformation

Fig. 15. Full-match in Feistel-SP

We find that the transformation in Fig. 15(b) can be directly obtained if we consider MitM attacks on an equivalent transformation of Feistel-SP, i.e., Fig. 6(b). To better understand this fact, we take the MILP-based MitM attack on transformed Simpira-4 as an example in the following part.

4.2 MILP-Based MitM Attack on Transformed Feistel

As shown in Fig. 8, the output $A^{(r+1)}$ is equivalent to $B^{(r)} \oplus \text{MC}(A^{(r)}_{\text{SR2}})$. With a linear transformation on $A^{(r+1)}$, we have $\text{MC}^{-1}(A^{(r+1)}) = \text{MC}^{-1}(B^{(r)}) \oplus A^{(r)}_{\text{SR2}}$. Similarly, $B^{(r+1)}, C^{(r+1)}$ and $D^{(r+1)}$ can be handled in the same way. For the sake of simplicity and intuition, we transform the Feistel network by putting the last MixColumn operation first in each round like Fig. 6(b). Then the output of each round is the state after the above linear transformation in the original structure. Therefore, we propose the following property.

Property 1. Simpira-4 is equivalent to the permutation with a round function

$$\mathcal{R}'_i = \text{SR} \circ \text{SB} \circ \text{AC} \circ \text{MC} \circ \text{SR} \circ \text{SB} \circ \text{MC},$$

except for replacing the input $(A^{(r)}, B^{(r)}, C^{(r)}, D^{(r)})$ by $(\tilde{A}^{(r)}, \tilde{B}^{(r)}, \tilde{C}^{(r)},$ $\tilde{D}^{(r)}) = (\text{MC}^{-1}(A^{(r)}), \text{MC}^{-1}(B^{(r)}), \text{MC}^{-1}(C^{(r)}), \text{MC}^{-1}(D^{(r)}))$, and the final output becomes $(\tilde{A}^{(r+1)}, \tilde{B}^{(r+1)}, \tilde{C}^{(r+1)}, \tilde{D}^{(r+1)})$.

Following Property 1, we represent the 3-round transformed Simpira-4 in Fig. 16, where $\tilde{A}^{(r+1)} = \tilde{B}^{(r)} \oplus \tilde{A}^{(r)}_{\text{SR2}}$. In this way, $\tilde{A}^{(r)}_{\text{MC1}} = \text{MC}(\tilde{A}^{(r)}) = A^{(r)}$, then $\tilde{A}^{(r)}_{\text{SR2}} = A^{(r)}_{\text{SR2}}$. According to the predefined $\tilde{B}^{(r)} = \text{MC}^{-1}(B^{(r)})$, $\tilde{A}^{(r+1)}$ is equivalent to $\text{MC}^{-1}(B^{(r)}) \oplus A^{(r)}_{\text{SR2}}$. Therefore, the output $\tilde{A}^{(r+1)}$ in the transformed Simpira-4 is actual the state $\text{MC}^{-1}(A^{(r+1)})$ in the original Simpira-4 (Fig. 8). This is also true for $\tilde{B}^{(r+1)}, \tilde{C}^{(r+1)}$ and $\tilde{D}^{(r+1)}$.

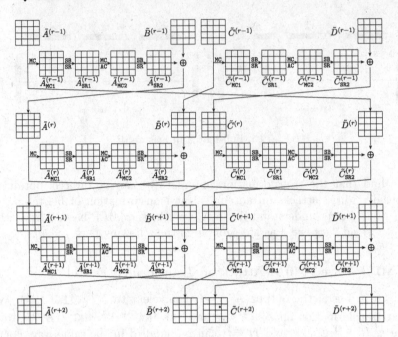

Fig. 16. Equivalent transform of Simpira-4

MILP Constraints for the Computation Paths. As shown in Fig. 16, $\tilde{A}_{MC1}^{(r+1)}$ can be computed by $MC\left(\tilde{A}_{SR2}^{(r)} \oplus \tilde{B}^{(r)}\right)$, where $\tilde{B}^{(r)}$ can be replaced by $MC^{-1}\left(\tilde{C}_{MC1}^{(r-1)}\right)$. Therefore, $\tilde{A}_{MC1}^{(r+1)} = MC\left(\tilde{A}_{SR2}^{(r)}\right) \oplus \tilde{C}_{MC1}^{(r-1)}$, which is also named as MC-then-XOR-Rule. In fact, if we sequentially compute the colors of $\tilde{A}_{MC1}^{(r+1)}$ by computing $\tilde{B}^{(r)} = MC^{-1}\left(\tilde{C}_{MC1}^{(r-1)}\right)$ and then $\tilde{A}_{MC1}^{(r+1)} = MC\left(\tilde{A}_{SR2}^{(r)} \oplus \tilde{B}^{(r)}\right)$, i.e., first apply MC-Rule, and then XOR-Rule, and then MC-Rule, we may lose many possible and useful color schemes even in the most advanced superposition MitM framework. An example is given in Fig. 17(a), when applying MC-Rule on the superposition states of $\tilde{C}_{MC1}^{(r-1)}$, it will lead to all □ cells. Subsequently, $\tilde{A}_{MC1}^{(r+1)}$ will end up with a full column of □ cells. However, if we apply the MC-then-XOR-Rule with superposition framework as shown in Fig. 17(b), three ■ cells will be preserved by consuming three ■ cells. This also fits our intuition, i.e. more linear operations yield a higher possibility of generating unknown cells.

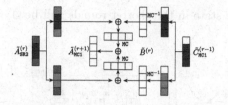

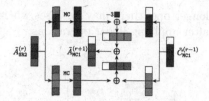

(a) Model MC-Rule and XOR-Rule separately   (b) Model the link by MC-then-XOR-Rule

Fig. 17. The advantage of modeling link by applying MC-then-XOR-Rule

MILP Constraints for the Full-Round Match. In Fig. 12(c), the ending states are $(A^{(4)}, B^{(4)})$ computed from two opposite directions. With a linear transformation, two-byte partial matching is deduced as shown in Fig. 13. The matching phase involves two rounds of forward and two rounds of backward, respectively. So we denote such multi-round matching as *(2+2)-round match*. Taking the transformed Simpira-4 as an example, assume that the output state $\tilde{A}^{(r+1)}$ is chosen to be the ending states in Fig. 16. We have

$$\tilde{A}^{(r+1)} = \tilde{A}^{(r)}_{\text{SR2}} \oplus \tilde{B}^{(r)}, \text{ where } \tilde{B}^{(r)} = \text{MC}^{-1}\left(\tilde{C}^{(r-1)}_{\text{MC1}}\right). \tag{6}$$

As mentioned above, $\tilde{C}^{(r-1)}_{\text{MC1}}$ can be computed directly by $\text{MC}\left(\tilde{C}^{(r-2)}_{\text{SR2}}\right) \oplus \tilde{A}^{(r-3)}_{\text{MC1}}$ in the transformed Simpira-4 model. Hence, $\tilde{B}^{(r)}$ can be replaced by $\tilde{C}^{(r-2)}_{\text{SR2}} \oplus \text{MC}^{-1}\left(\tilde{A}^{(r-3)}_{\text{MC1}}\right)$ in Eq. (6). Immediately, $\tilde{A}^{(r-3)}_{\text{MC1}}$ can also be replaced in the same way. Subsequently, this replacement is done round by round until the initial structure to build the so-called *full-round matching*. Take our 11-round attack (Fig. 23) on transformed Simpira-4 in Sect. 6.2 as an example. The ending state $\tilde{D}^{(2)}$ is computed forward and backward to the initial structure. The shortest round that a matching exists is the $(6, 4)$-round matching given in Fig. 18(a). If a shorter round is considered for matching, e.g., $(6, 2)$-round in Fig. 18(b), there will be no matching, since the state $\tilde{C}^{(3)}_{\text{MC1}}$ will be all □. If we extend the $(6, 4)$-round matching to the full-round matching, we get Fig. 18(c), where the two states applied MC^{-1} in both directions will eventually converge to an identical state $\tilde{C}^{(7)}_{\text{MC1}}$ in the initial structure. Figure 18(c) can also be displayed with the following full-round matching Eq. (7):

$$\text{MC}^{-1}\left(\tilde{C}^{(7)}_{\text{MC1}}\right) \oplus \tilde{A}^{(8)}_{\text{SR2}} \oplus \tilde{C}^{(10)}_{\text{SR2}} \oplus \tilde{A}^{(0)}_{\text{SR2}} \oplus \tilde{C}^{(2)}_{\text{SR2}} \oplus \tilde{A}^{(4)}_{\text{SR2}} \oplus \tilde{C}^{(6)}_{\text{SR2}} = \text{MC}^{-1}\left(\tilde{C}^{(7)}_{\text{MC1}} \oplus H_B\right), \tag{7}$$

where $\text{MC}^{-1}\left(\tilde{C}^{(7)}_{\text{MC1}}\right)$ can be cancelled in both sides. The reason follows the fact that the initial degrees of freedom of ■ and ■ cells will be consumed along the forward or backward computation path. The number of □ cells only becomes bigger through some linear or nonlinear operations. If the matching happens within shorter rounds, there will only be more matching cases after elongation. But on the contrary, while considering to find a shorter-round match from a longer one, there may be cases where the state in the shorter rounds will be $\square$ after applying linear operations.

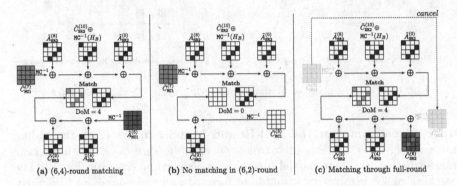

(a) (6,4)-round matching   (b) No matching in (6,2)-round   (c) Matching through full-round

- In 18(a), $\square$ cell is the linear combination of ■ cells and ■ cells.
- In 18(b), $\tilde{C}_{\text{MC1}}^{(3)}$ is computed by $\text{MC}^{-1}\left(\tilde{A}_{\text{SR2}}^{(4)}\right) \oplus \tilde{A}_{\text{MC1}}^{(5)}$ in 18(a). Since there are $\square$ cells in each column of $\tilde{A}_{\text{SR2}}^{(4)}$, the cells in $\tilde{C}_{\text{MC1}}^{(3)}$ become all unknown.
- In 18(c), $\text{MC}^{-1}\left(\tilde{A}_{\text{MC1}}^{(5)}\right)$ is replaced by $\text{MC}^{-1}\left(\tilde{C}_{\text{MC1}}^{(7)}\right) \oplus \tilde{C}_{\text{SR2}}^{(6)}$. The two states to perform MC^{-1} converge to $\tilde{C}_{\text{MC1}}^{(7)}$, so both of them can be canceled in two directions.

Fig. 18. The (6,4)-round match in Simpira-4, and its impacts on the match after being shortened or elongated

Following the above study, we only need to consider whether there exist match cells in the full-round matching. The two states to perform MC^{-1} will eventually converge into the starting states in the initial structure, or even can be canceled in both matching directions as shown in Fig. 18(c). For the general case, assume the matching phase consists of two starting states I_1 and I_2, e.g., in Fig. 18(c) $I_1 = I_2 = \tilde{C}_{\text{MC1}}^{(7)}$, and assume t internal states $X_1, X_2, \cdots, X_t$ are involved in the full-round matching equation. Similar to Eq. (7), the generic full-round matching equation can be written as

$$\text{MC}^{-1}(I_1) \oplus X_1 \oplus \cdots \oplus X_t = \text{MC}^{-1}(I_2). \tag{8}$$

The matching equation can be computed for each byte individually. In the i-th column and j-th row $(i, j = 0, 1, 2, 3)$, the byte matching equation is linearly computed from $X_k[4i + j]$ $(k = 1, \cdots, t)$ and $I_1[4i, 4i + 1, 4i + 2, 4i + 3]$ and $I_2[4i, 4i + 1, 4i + 2, 4i + 3]$. From our analysis on the generalization of matching in Sect. 3, if all these involved bytes are not $\square$ bytes, there will be valid matching for MitM attack. For j-th byte of X_k, we introduce a Boolean variable $\omega_j^{X_k}$, where $\omega_j^{X_k} = 1$ means this byte is $\square$, otherwise $\omega_j^{X_k} = 0$. Let

$$\omega_{4i+j} = \text{OR}\left(\omega_{4i+j}^{X_1}, \cdots, \omega_{4i+j}^{X_t}, \omega_{4i}^{I_1}, \cdots, \omega_{4i+3}^{I_1}, \omega_{4i}^{I_2}, \cdots, \omega_{4i+3}^{I_2}\right).$$

If $\omega_{4i+j} = 0$, then we get one valid matching byte for MitM in the i-th column and j-th row.

5   Meet-in-the-Middle Attack on Reduced Feistel-SP

With our new model, we find a 12-round preimage attack of `Feistel-SP-MMO` as shown in Fig. 19, which improves Sasaki's attack [47] by 1 round. The starting states are $\tilde{A}_{\text{MC}}^{(7)}$ and $\tilde{A}_{\text{MC}}^{(8)}$. The initial DoFs for $\blacksquare$ and $\blacksquare$ are $\lambda_\mathcal{B} = 14$, $\lambda_\mathcal{R} = 2$, respectively.

From $\tilde{A}_{\text{MC}}^{(9)}$, $\tilde{A}_{\text{MC}}^{(6)}$ and $\tilde{A}_{\text{MC}}^{(5)}$, we get 12 constraints on forward neutral words and 0 constraints on backward neutral words, i.e. $l_\mathcal{B} = 12$, $l_\mathcal{R} = 0$. Then we have $\text{DoF}_\mathcal{B} = 2$ and $\text{DoF}_\mathcal{R} = 2$. The matching points are $\tilde{A}^{(5)}$ and $\tilde{B}^{(5)}$. But only a full-round match is found through $\tilde{B}^{(5)}$, which is

$$\text{MC}^{-1}\left(\tilde{A}_{\text{MC}}^{(7)}\right) \oplus \tilde{A}_{\text{SB}}^{(8)} \oplus \text{MC}^{-1}(H_A) \oplus \tilde{A}_{\text{SB}}^{(3)} \oplus \tilde{A}_{\text{SB}}^{(5)} \oplus \tilde{A}_{\text{SB}}^{(7)} = \text{MC}^{-1}\left(\tilde{A}_{\text{MC}}^{(8)}\right), \quad (9)$$

with $\tilde{A}_{\text{SB}}^{(1)} = \tilde{A}_{\text{SB}}^{(10)}$ by assigning the same assumption to Sasaki's attack [47], i.e., $k_0 = k_{11} \oplus H_A$ and $k_1 = k_{10} \oplus H_B$. From Eq. (9), 2 bytes degree of match indexed by $[6, 7]$ are derived, i.e. $\text{DoM} = 2$. The 12-round MitM attack is given in Algorithm 1. The time complexity to precompute U is $2^{8 \cdot \lambda_\mathcal{B}} = 2^{112}$. The memory to store U is $2^{8 \cdot (\lambda_\mathcal{B} - 8)} = 2^{48}$. The final time complexity is

$$2^{64+48} + 2^{8 \times (16 - \min\{14 - 12, 2, 2\})} \approx 2^{113}.$$

6   Meet-in-the-Middle Attack on Reduced Simpira V2

For `Simpira v2` [29] with branch number $b > 2$, the designers suggested the permutation-based hashing based on Davies-Meyer (DM) construction: $\pi(x) \oplus x$, where π is `Simpira v2` permutation. For the common size of digest, i.e., 256 bits, the output of `Simpira v2` has to be truncated. For a fair comparison with Schrottenloher and Stevens' attacks [51], we follow the same way of truncation for `Simpira v2`. We introduce the first 7-round attack on `Simpira-2` and 11-round attack on `Simpira-4`. To fill a gap left by Schrottenloher and Stevens [51], we introduce the first attack on reduced `Simpira-6` in Supplementary Material C in our full version paper [32]. We also give an experiment based on a new 7-round MitM characteristic of `Simpira-2` in Supplementary Material F in [32].

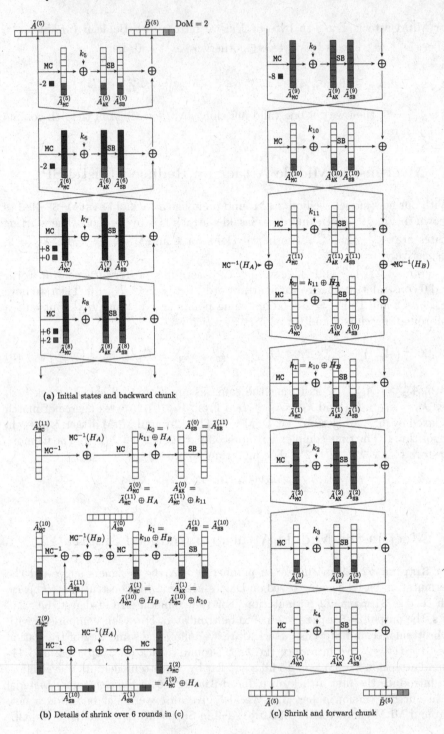

Fig. 19. MitM attack on 12-round Feistel-SP

Algorithm 1: Preimage Attack on 12-round `Feistel-SP`

---

1 Set constraints on key schedule $k_0 = k_{11} \oplus H_A$ and $k_1 = k_{10} \oplus H_B$

2 **for** $g_b \in \mathbb{F}_2^{64}$ /* $\texttt{MC}(\tilde{A}_{\texttt{SB}}^{(8)}[0\text{-}5]\|0\|0) \oplus \tilde{A}_{\texttt{MC}}^{(7)} = g_b$ */

3 **do**

4       $U \leftarrow [\cdot]$

5   **for** $v_B \in \mathbb{F}_2^{6 \times 8}$ *in* $\tilde{A}_{\texttt{SB}}^{(8)}[0\text{-}5]$ **do**

6           $\tilde{A}_{\texttt{MC}}^{(7)} \leftarrow \texttt{MC}(v_B\|0\|0) \oplus g_b$

7   Compute through AK and SB to get the values of ■ cells in $\tilde{A}_{\texttt{SB}}^{(7)}$

8           $c_0\|c_1 \leftarrow \texttt{MC}(\tilde{A}_{\texttt{SB}}^{(7)})[6,7]$ /* $\tilde{A}_{\texttt{MC}}^{(6)} = \texttt{MC}(\tilde{A}_{\texttt{SB}}^{(7)}) \oplus \tilde{A}_{\texttt{MC}}^{(8)}$ */

9   Compute ■ cells in $\tilde{A}_{\texttt{SB}}^{(6)}$

10          $c_2\|c_3 \leftarrow \texttt{MC}(\tilde{A}_{\texttt{SB}}^{(6)}[0\text{-}5]\|0\|0)[6,7] \oplus \tilde{A}_{\texttt{MC}}^{(7)}[6,7]$

11          $c_B \leftarrow c_0\|c_1\|c_2\|c_3$

12          $U[c_B] \leftarrow v_B$ /* There are 2^{16} elements in $U[c_B]$ given c_B */

13   **end**

14   **for** $c_B \in \mathbb{F}_2^{4 \times 8}$ **do**

15          $L \leftarrow [\,]$

16   **for** $v_B \in U[c_B]$ **do**

17   Compute backward to the ■ cells in $\tilde{A}_{\texttt{MC}}^{(6)}$. According to Fig. 19, derive 2 bytes End_B for matching by

18
$$End_B \leftarrow \texttt{MC}^{-1}\left(\tilde{A}_{\texttt{MC}}^{(6)}[0-5]\|0\|0\right)[6,7]$$

            $L[End_B] \leftarrow v_B$

19   **end**

20   **for** $2^{8\lambda_\mathcal{R}}$ *values* $v_\mathcal{R}$ *of the* ■ *bytes in* $\tilde{A}_{\texttt{MC}}^{(8)}$, $\lambda_\mathcal{R} = 2$ **do**

21   Compute backward to the ■ cells in $\tilde{A}_{\texttt{SB}}^{(5)}$

22   Due to the predefined constraints on key schedule, there always be $\tilde{A}_{\texttt{MC}}^{(1)} = \tilde{A}_{\texttt{MC}}^{(10)} \oplus H_B$ and $\tilde{A}_{\texttt{MC}}^{(2)} = \tilde{A}_{\texttt{MC}}^{(9)} \oplus H_A$

23   With $\tilde{A}_{\texttt{MC}}^{(1)}$ and $\tilde{A}_{\texttt{MC}}^{(2)}$, compute forward to the ■ cells in $\tilde{A}_{\texttt{SB}}^{(3)}$

24   From $\tilde{A}_{\texttt{MC}}^{(2)}$, $\tilde{A}_{\texttt{SB}}^{(3)}$ and $\tilde{A}_{\texttt{SB}}^{(5)}[6,7]$, derive 2 bytes $End_\mathcal{R}$ for matching by

$$End_\mathcal{R} \leftarrow \texttt{MC}^{-1}\left(\tilde{A}_{\texttt{MC}}^{(2)}\right)[6,7] \oplus \tilde{A}_{\texttt{SB}}^{(3)}[6,7] \oplus \tilde{A}_{\texttt{SB}}^{(5)}[6,7] \oplus \texttt{MC}^{-1}\left(0\|0\|0\|0\|0\|\tilde{A}_{\texttt{MC}}^{(6)}[6,7]\right)[6,7]$$

25   **for** $v_B \in L[End_\mathcal{R}]$ **do**

26   Reconstruct the (candidate) message X

27   **if** X *is a preimage* **then**

28   Output X and stop

29   **end**

30   **end**

31   **end**

32   **end**

33 **end**

6.1   Meet-in-the-Middle Attack on 7-Round `Simpira-2`

As shown in Fig. 20, we give a 7-round preimage attack on `Simpira-2`. The starting states are $\tilde{A}_{\texttt{MC1}}^{(3)}$ and $\tilde{A}_{\texttt{MC1}}^{(4)}$, where $\lambda_\mathcal{R} = 4$ and $\lambda_B = 28$. Along the forward and backward computation paths, there are 0 constraints on ■ and 20 constraints on ■, i.e. $l_\mathcal{R} = 0$ and $l_B = 20$ as shown in Fig. 21. Then, we have $\text{DoF}_\mathcal{R} = \lambda_\mathcal{R} - l_\mathcal{R} = 4$ and $\text{DoF}_B = \lambda_B - l_B = 8$. The matching points are $\tilde{A}^{(2)}$ and $\tilde{B}^{(2)}$ and the full-round matching equation is (10). Due to $\texttt{MC}^{-1}(\tilde{A}_{\texttt{MC1}}^{(3)})$ appears in both directions, $\text{MC}^{-1}(\tilde{A}_{\text{MC1}}^{(3)})$ makes no contribution to the match and can be canceled without influence as shown in Fig. 22.

$$\tilde{A}_{\text{SR2}}^{(2)} \oplus \tilde{A}_{\text{SR2}}^{(4)} \oplus \tilde{A}_{\text{SR2}}^{(6)} \oplus \text{MC}^{-1}(H_B) = \tilde{A}_{\text{SR2}}^{(0)}. \tag{10}$$

Then, 4 bytes for matching in the Eq. (10) indexed by $[3, 6, 9, 12]$ are only determined by the ■ bytes, i.e. $\text{M}_\mathcal{R} = 4$. The detailed attack procedure is shown in Algorithm 2. The time to construct U is $2^{8 \cdot \lambda_B} = 2^{224}$. The memory cost to store U is $2^{8 \cdot (\lambda_B - 16)} \approx 2^{96}$. According to Eq. (2), the overall time complexity to mount a MitM attack is

$$2^{224} + 2^{8 \times (32 - \min\{8,4,4\})} \approx 2^{225}.$$

The memory cost is about 2^{96} to store hash table U.

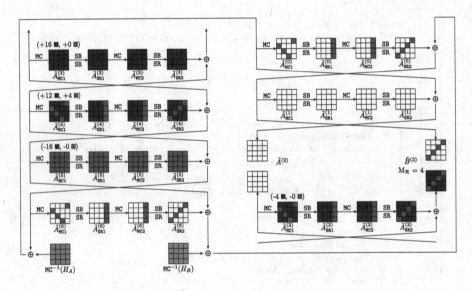

Fig. 20. MitM attack on 7-round Simpira-2

6.2   Meet-in-the-Middle Attack on 11-Round Simpira-4

Figure 23 is an 11-round MitM characteristic of Simpira-4. Figure 28 given in Supplementary Material B in our full version paper [32] is an alternative representation of the MitM characteristic with MC-then-XOR-Rule in superposition states. The starting states are $\tilde{A}_{\text{MC1}}^{(7)}$, $\tilde{C}_{\text{MC1}}^{(6)}$, $\tilde{A}_{\text{MC1}}^{(6)}$, and $\tilde{C}_{\text{MC1}}^{(7)}$. The initial DoFs for ■ and ■ are $\lambda_\mathcal{R} = 24$ and $\lambda_B = 4$, respectively. Along the forward and backward

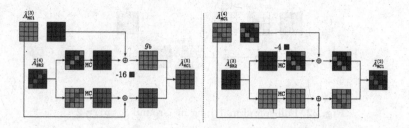

Fig. 21. The `MC-then-XOR-Rule` of `Simpira-2` in superposition framework

Algorithm 2: Preimage Attack on 7-round `Simpira-2`

1   **for** $g_b \in \mathbb{F}_2^{128}$ **do**
2      $U \leftarrow [\,]$
3   **for** $v_\mathcal{B} \in \mathbb{F}_2^{12 \times 8}$ *in* $\tilde{A}_{MC1}^{(4)}[0, 2\text{-}5, 7\text{-}10, 13\text{-}15]$ **do**
4   Compute the ■ cells in $\tilde{A}_{SR2}^{(4)}$ from $\tilde{A}_{MC1}^{(4)}$
5   Let $\tilde{A}_{SR2}^{(4)}[i] \leftarrow 0$, where $i \in [3, 6, 9, 12]$
6   Compute $\tilde{A}_{MC1}^{(3)}$ by $\mathrm{MC}(\tilde{A}_{SR2}^{(4)}) \oplus g_b$ /* **Left part of Fig. 21**   */
7   Compute $\tilde{A}_{SR2}^{(3)}$ from $\tilde{A}_{MC1}^{(3)}$
8        $c_0 \| c_1 \| c_2 \| c_3 \leftarrow \mathrm{MC}(\tilde{A}_{SR2}^{(3)})[1, 6, 11, 12]$ /* **Right part of Fig. 21**   */
9        $c_\mathcal{B} \leftarrow c_0 \| c_1 \| c_2 \| c_3$
10       $U[c_\mathcal{B}] \leftarrow v_\mathcal{B}$ /* **There are** $2^{8 \times 8}$ **elements** $U[c_\mathcal{B}]$ **given** $c_\mathcal{B}$ */
11   **end**
12   **for** $c_\mathcal{B} \in \mathbb{F}_2^{4 \times 8}$ **do**
13   Set $\mathcal{S}$ to be an empty set to store the compatible values of ■
14   **for** $2^{8\lambda_\mathcal{R}}$ *values* $v_\mathcal{R}$ *of the* ■ *bytes in* $\tilde{A}_{MC1}^{(4)}$, $\lambda_\mathcal{R} = 4$ **do**
15   Compute to the ■ cells in $\tilde{A}_{SR2}^{(0)}$, $\tilde{A}_{SR2}^{(2)}$, $\tilde{A}_{SR2}^{(4)}$ and $\tilde{A}_{SR2}^{(6)}$
16   As shown in Fig. 22, $\mathrm{M}_\mathcal{R} = 4$ bytes equations are derived by

$$\left(\tilde{A}_{SR2}^{(2)} \oplus \tilde{A}_{SR2}^{(4)} \oplus \tilde{A}_{SR2}^{(6)} \oplus \mathrm{MC}^{-1}(H_B) \right)[3, 6, 9, 12] = \tilde{A}_{SR2}^{(0)}[3, 6, 9, 12]$$

         Put the solution into $\mathcal{S}$
17   **end**
18   **for** $v_\mathcal{B} \in U[c_\mathcal{B}]$ **do**
19   Compute the ■ cells in $\tilde{A}_{MC1}^{(3)}$ as Line 6 **for** $v_\mathcal{R} \in \mathcal{S}$ **do**
20   Reconstruct the (candidate) message X **if** X *is a preimage* **then**
21   Output X and stop
22   **end**
23   **end**
24   **end**
25   **end**
26 **end**

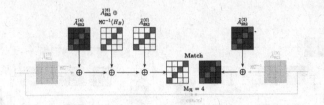

Fig. 22. Full-round matching in 7-round Simpira-2

computation paths, there are a total of 20 constraints on ■ and 0 constant constraints on ■, i.e., $l_{\mathcal{R}} = 20$ and $l_{\mathcal{B}} = 0$. Hence, we get $\text{DoF}_{\mathcal{R}} = \lambda_{\mathcal{R}} - l_{\mathcal{R}} = 4$ and $\text{DoF}_{\mathcal{B}} = \lambda_{\mathcal{B}} - l_{\mathcal{B}} = 4$. The matching points are $(\tilde{A}^{(2)}, \tilde{B}^{(2)}, \tilde{C}^{(2)}, \tilde{D}^{(2)})$. The full-matching equation is (11), where $\text{MC}^{-1}(\tilde{C}_{\text{MC1}}^{(7)})$ appears in both directions and can be cancelled.

$$\tilde{A}_{\text{SR2}}^{(8)} \oplus \tilde{C}_{\text{SR2}}^{(10)} \oplus \text{MC}^{-1}(H_B) \oplus \tilde{A}_{\text{SR2}}^{(0)} = \tilde{C}_{\text{SR2}}^{(6)} \oplus \tilde{A}_{\text{SR2}}^{(4)} \oplus \tilde{C}_{\text{SR2}}^{(2)}. \tag{11}$$

Then, 4 bytes in Eq. (11) indexed by $[0, 7, 10, 13]$ are derived as the degree of match, i.e. $\text{DoM} = 4$. The 11-round attack is given in Algorithm 3. The time to construct V is $2^{8 \cdot \lambda_{\mathcal{R}}} = 2^{192}$ and memory is $2^{8 \cdot (\lambda_{\mathcal{R}} - 4)} = 2^{160}$. We need to traverse 2^{32} values of the ■ in $\tilde{A}_{\text{MC1}}^{(6)}$, $\tilde{C}_{\text{MC1}}^{(6)}$ and $\tilde{C}_{\text{MC1}}^{(7)}$. Hence, the total time complexity can be computed by $2^{32} \times 2^{192} + 2^{8 \times (32 - \min\{24 - 20, 4, 4\})} \approx 2^{225}$. The overall memory is 2^{160} to store V.

7   Meet-in-the-Middle Attack on 17-Round Lesamnta-LW

We also apply our automated model to Lesamnta-LW [31]. Since the Lesamnta-LW does not have the feed-forward mechanism, there are only two forward chunks. We find a 17-round MitM characteristic for Lesamnta-LW without linear transformation, which is shown in Fig. 24. The initial DoFs for ■ and ■ are $\lambda_{\mathcal{B}} = 4$, $\lambda_{\mathcal{R}} = 4$, respectively. Without consuming DoF of ■/■ in the computation from round 0 to round 17, there is $\text{DoF}_{\mathcal{R}} = \text{DoF}_{\mathcal{B}} = 4$. The matching happens between $D^{(17)}$ and the targeted hash value, where $\text{DoM} = 8$. The attack procedure is given in Algorithm 4, where two message blocks (m_1, m_2) are needed as shown in Fig. 11. In this attack, we only use the first column of $D^{(17)}$ for matching. At first, we randomly fix the first 32-bit in $D^{(17)}$ as constant. Then, in one MitM episode, we can get $2^{32+32-32} = 2^{32}$ (m_1, m_2) satisfying the 32-bit partial target. When we find $2^{(256-32)/2} = 2^{112}$ different (m_1, m_2, h) with the same fixed 32-bit partial target, we can find a collision on the remaining $(256 - 32)$ bits of the full 256-bit target. The time complexity is $2^{16+64} \cdot (2^{32} + 2^{32} + 2^{32}) \approx 2^{113.58}$. The memory complexity is 2^{112}. The same time and memory cost can also be obtained when considering the linear transformation of collision.

Besides, we also found a 20-round MitM collision attack on Lesamnta-LW when targeting the linear transformation of collision, the overall time complexity is 2^{124} which is better than the generic birthday bound 2^{128}. However, it's not

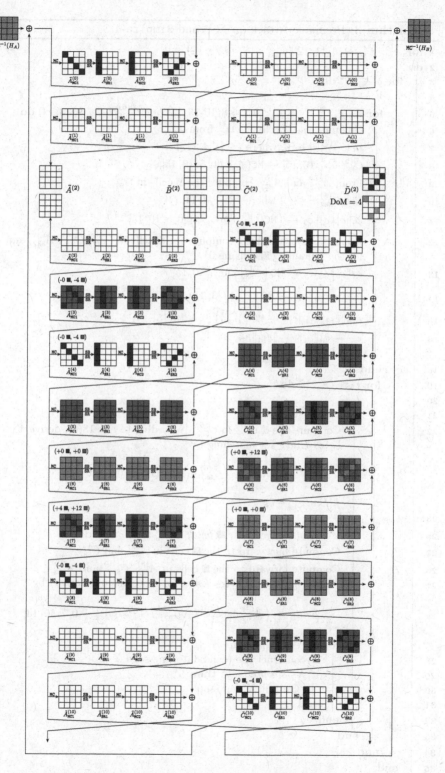

Fig. 23. MitM attack on 11-round Simpira-4

Algorithm 3: Preimage Attack on 11-round Simpira-4

---

1   **for** $\tilde{A}_{\text{MC1}}^{(6)} \| \tilde{C}_{\text{MC1}}^{(6)}[1,6,11,12] \| \tilde{C}_{\text{MC1}}^{(7)} \in \mathbb{G}$ /* $|\mathbb{G}| = 2^{32}$ */

2   **do**

3   **for** $g_r \in \mathbb{F}_2^{32}$ **do**

4      $V \leftarrow [\,]$

5   **for** $v_{\mathcal{R}} \in \mathbb{F}_2^{20 \times 8}$ *in* $\tilde{A}_{\text{MC1}}^{(7)}[0\text{-}2, 5\text{-}8, 10\text{-}13, 15]$ *and* $\tilde{C}_{\text{MC1}}^{(6)}[2\text{-}4, 7\text{-}9, 13, 14]$ **do**

6   Compute the ■ cells in $\tilde{A}_{\text{SR2}}^{(7)}$ from $\tilde{A}_{\text{MC1}}^{(7)}$

7   Let $\tilde{A}_{\text{SR2}}^{(7)}[i] \leftarrow 0$, where $i \in [1,4,11,14]$

8       $\tilde{C}_{\text{MC1}}^{(6)}[0,5,10,15] \leftarrow \text{MC}(\tilde{A}_{\text{SR2}}^{(7)})[0,5,10,15] \oplus g_r$

9   From $\tilde{A}_{\text{MC1}}^{(7)}$ and $\tilde{A}_{\text{MC1}}^{(6)}$, compute the ■ cells in $\tilde{C}_{\text{SR2}}^{(5)}$

10   Let $\tilde{C}_{\text{SR2}}^{(5)}[i] \leftarrow 0$, where $i \in [1,4,11,14]$

11      $c_0 \| c_1 \| c_2 \| c_3 \leftarrow \left(\text{MC}(\tilde{C}_{\text{SR2}}^{(5)}) \oplus \tilde{C}_{\text{MC1}}^{(6)} \right)[0,5,10,15]$

12   From the known values, compute the ■ cells in $\tilde{C}_{\text{SR2}}^{(9)}$, $\tilde{C}_{\text{SR2}}^{(4)}$, $\tilde{A}_{\text{SR2}}^{(3)}$, and let the remaining ■ cells be 0

13      $c_4 \| c_5 \| c_6 \| c_7 \leftarrow \text{MC}\left(\tilde{C}_{\text{SR2}}^{(9)} \right)[0,5,10,15]$

14      $c_8 \| c_9 \| c_{10} \| c_{11} \leftarrow \text{MC}\left(\tilde{C}_{\text{SR2}}^{(4)} \right)[3,4,9,14]$

15      $c_{12} \| c_{13} \| c_{14} \| c_{15} \leftarrow \text{MC}\left(\tilde{A}_{\text{SR2}}^{(3)} \right)[0,5,10,15]$

16      $\mathfrak{c}_{\mathcal{R}} \leftarrow c_0 \| c_1 \| \cdots \| c_{14} \| c_{15}$

17      $V[\mathfrak{c}_{\mathcal{R}}] \leftarrow v_{\mathcal{R}}$

18   **end**

19   **for** $\mathfrak{c}_{\mathcal{R}} \leftarrow \mathbb{F}_2^{16 \times 8}$ **do**

20      $L \leftarrow [\,]$

21   **for** $v_{\mathcal{R}} \in V[\mathfrak{c}_{\mathcal{R}}]$ **do**

22   Compute the ■ cells in $\tilde{C}_{\text{SR2}}^{(6)}$. According to Fig. 18(c), derive 4 bytes $End_{\mathcal{R}}$ for matching by

$$End_{\mathcal{R}} \leftarrow \left(\tilde{C}_{\text{SR2}}^{(6)} \oplus \text{MC}^{-1}(H_B) \right)[0,7,10,13]$$

       $L[End_{\mathcal{R}}] \leftarrow v_{\mathcal{R}}$

23   **end**

24   **for** $2^{8\lambda_B}$ *values* v_B *of the* ■ *bytes in* $\tilde{A}_{\text{MC1}}^{(7)}$, $\lambda_B = 4$ **do**

25   Compute backward to the ■ cells in $\tilde{A}_{\text{SR2}}^{(4)}$ and $\tilde{C}_{\text{SR2}}^{(2)}$

26   Compute forward to the ■ cells in $\tilde{A}_{\text{SR2}}^{(8)}$, $\tilde{C}_{\text{SR2}}^{(10)}$ and $\tilde{A}_{\text{SR2}}^{(0)}$

27   As in Fig. 18(c), 4 bytes End_B for matching are derived by

$$End_B \leftarrow \left(\tilde{A}_{\text{SR2}}^{(8)} \oplus \tilde{C}_{\text{SR2}}^{(10)} \oplus \tilde{A}_{\text{SR2}}^{(0)} \oplus \tilde{C}_{\text{SR2}}^{(2)} \oplus \tilde{A}_{\text{SR2}}^{(4)} \right)[0,7,10,13]$$

       for $v_{\mathcal{R}} \in L[End_B]$ **do**

28   Reconstruct the (candidate) message X

29   **if** X *is a preimage* **then**

30   Output X and stop

31   **end**

32   **end**

33   **end**

34   **end**

35   **end**

36 **end**

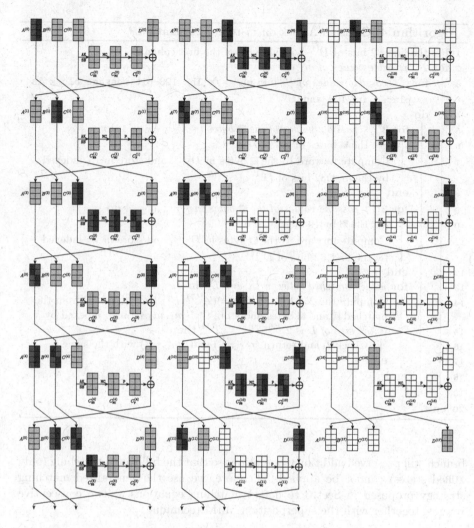

Fig. 24. MitM attack on 17-round Lesamnta-LW

better than the designers' security claim against collision attack, which is 2^{120}. We still put the 20-round MitM characteristic in Supplementary Material D in our full version paper [32] to clearly specify the superiority of our new model.

8   Meet-in-the-Middle Attack on Reduced Areion

Based on DM hashing mode, Isobe *et al.* [35] built hash functions Areion256-DM and Areion512-DM. This section studies the MitM preimage attacks on these two ciphers. However, in the left branch of Areion, there exist additional operations, such as SR ∘ SB for Areion-256. If we just transform it like Simpira, the left

---

Algorithm 4: Collision Attack on 17-round `Lesamnta-LW`

---

1 Fix the first 32 bits of $D^{(17)}$, i.e. 4 bytes of the first column

2 **for** 2^{16} *possible values of* m_1 **do**

3   **for** 2^{64} *possible values of* $B^{(0)}$ *in* m_2 /* The 128-bit message block is placed in $A^{(0)}$ and $B^{(0)}$ */

4   **do**

5   **for** $2^{8\lambda_{\mathcal{R}}}$ *possible values of the* ■ *bytes in* $A^{(0)}$, $\lambda_{\mathcal{R}} = 4$ **do**

6   Set the ■ bytes in $A^{(0)}$ to 0

7   Compute forward to the □ bytes in $D^{(17)}$, and store in L_1 indexed by the first 32 bits of $D^{(17)}$

8   **end**

9   **for** $2^{8\lambda_{\mathcal{B}}}$ *possible values of the* ■ *bytes in* $A^{(0)}$, $\lambda_{\mathcal{B}} = 4$ **do**

10   Set the ■ bytes in $A^{(0)}$ to 0

11   Compute forward to the □ bytes in $D^{(17)}$, and store in L_2 indexed by the first 32 bits of $D^{(17)}$

12   **end**

13   **for** *values matched between* L_1 *and* L_2 **do**

14   Compute the 256-bit target $h = (A^{(17)}, B^{(17)}, C^{(17)}, D^{(17)})$ from the matched ■ and ■ bytes and store the (m_1, m_2, h) in L indexed by h

15   **if** *the size of* L *is* $2^{(256-32)/2} = 2^{112}$ **then**

16   Check L and return (m_1, m_2) and (m_1', m_2') with the same h

17   **end**

18   **end**

19   **end**

20 **end**

---

branch still preserved additional operations so that the full-round matching (only XORed states) cannot be applied. Therefore, we use the generalized matching strategy proposed in Sect. 3 to detect matching equations at two consecutive rounds, together with the superposition MitM technique.

8.1 Meet-in-the-Middle Attack on 5-Round `Areion-256`

By applying the automatic MitM attack, we find a 5-round preimage attack on `Areion-256` as shown in Fig. 25. The starting states are $A^{(3)}$ and $B^{(3)}$. The initial DoFs for ■ and ■ are $\lambda_{\mathcal{R}} = 8$ and $\lambda_{\mathcal{B}} = 23$, respectively. The consuming degrees for backward and forward are 0 and 15, i.e. $l_{\mathcal{R}} = 0$ and $l_{\mathcal{B}} = 15$. Then we have $\text{DoF}_{\mathcal{R}} = \lambda_{\mathcal{R}} - l_{\mathcal{R}} = 8$ and $\text{DoF}_{\mathcal{B}} = \lambda_{\mathcal{B}} - l_{\mathcal{B}} = 8$. The matching happens between $A_{\text{SR2}}^{(1,\alpha)}$ and $B^{(1)} \oplus A^{(2)}$, by combining `MixColumn` and `XOR` operations as Fig. 14, where DoM = 6. According to Sect. 3, we get additional $M_{\mathcal{R}} = 2$ bytes from the last column of $B^{(1)} \oplus A^{(2)}$, which are determined only by ■ cells and can also be used in matching phase.

The new 5-round attack on `Areion-256` is given in Algorithm 7 in Supplementary Material E in our full version paper [32]. The time to construct table U is $2^{8 \cdot \lambda_B} = 2^{184}$. Hence, we have the time complexity $2^8 \cdot 2^{184} + 2^{8 \times (32 - \min\{23 - 15, 8, 8\})} \approx 2^{193}$. The overall memory complexity is 2^{88} to store U.

8.2   Meet-in-the-Middle Attack on 7-Round Areion-256

The attack figure and algorithm on 7-round Areion-256 are given in Fig. 34 and Algorithm 8 in Supplementary Material E in our full version paper [32]. The starting states are $A^{(4)}$ and $B^{(4)}$. The initial DoFs for ■ and ■ are $\lambda_R = 22$ and $\lambda_B = 4$, respectively. The consumed DoFs of ■ and ■ are $l_R = 20$ and $l_B = 2$, so there is $\mathrm{DoF}_R = \mathrm{DoF}_B = 2$. The matching happens between $A_{\mathrm{SR2}}^{(1, \alpha)}$ and $B^{(1)} \oplus A^{(2)}$, by combining MixColumn and XOR operations as Fig. 14, where $\mathrm{DoM} = 2$. The time to construct table V is $2^{8 \cdot \lambda_R} = 2^{176}$ and memory is $2^{8 \cdot (\lambda_R - 14)} = 2^{64}$. The overall time complexity is $2^{48} \cdot 2^{176} + 2^{8 \times (32 - \min\{22 - 20, 4 - 2, 2\})} \approx 2^{240}$. The memory cost is 2^{64} to store V.

8.3   Meet-in-the-Middle Attack on 11-Round Areion-512

The attack figure and algorithm on 11-round Areion-512 are given in Fig. 35, 36, and Algorithm 9 in Supplementary Material E in our full version paper [32]. The starting states are $A^{(3)}$, $B^{(3)}$, $C^{(3)}$ and $D^{(3)}$. The initial DoFs for ■ and ■ are $\lambda_R = 30$, $\lambda_B = 2$, respectively. The consuming DoF of backward and forward neutral words are $l_R = 28$ and $l_B = 0$. Then, we have $\mathrm{DoF}_R = \lambda_R - l_R = 2$ and $\mathrm{DoF}_B = \lambda_B - l_B = 2$. The matching phase happens between $C_{\mathrm{SR}}^{(9, \beta)}$ and $B^{(10)}$ through MixColumn, where $\mathrm{DoM} = 2$. The time complexity to precompute V is $2^{8 \cdot \lambda_R} = 2^{240}$. The time complexity is $2^{240} + 2^{8 \times (32 - \min\{30 - 28, 2, 2\})} \approx 2^{241}$. The overall memory complexity is 2^{48} to store V.

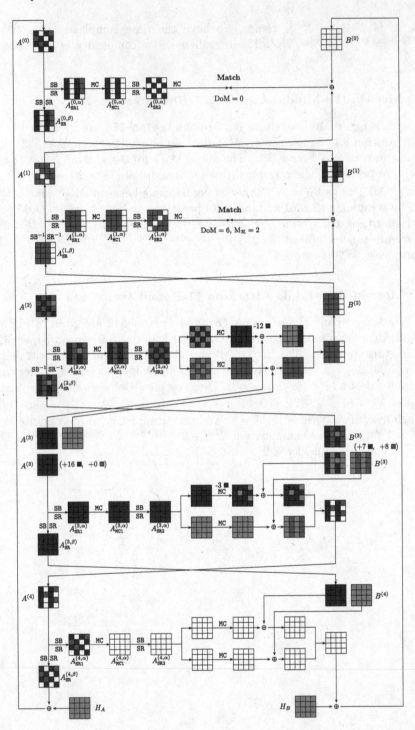

Fig. 25. MitM attack on 5-round `Areion-256`

9   Conclusion

In this paper, we build a new Meet-in-the-Middle automatic tool for Feistel networks. In our model, we generalize the traditional direct or indirect partial matching strategies and also Sasaki's multi-round matching strategy. We also find some equivalent transformations of Feistel and GFN to significantly simplify the MILP models. Applying our new models, we obtain improved preimage attacks on `Feistel-SP-MMO`, `Simpira-2/-4-DM,16` `Areion-256/-512-DM` and the first 11-round attack on `Simpira-6`. Besides, we significantly improve the collision attack on the ISO standard hash `Lesamnta-LW` by 6 rounds.

Acknowledgements. We thank the anonymous reviewers from ASIACRYPT 2023 for their insightful comments. This work is supported by the National Key R&D Program of China (2022YFB2702804, 2018YFA0704701), the Natural Science Foundation of China (62272257, 62302250, 62072270, 62072207), Shandong Key Research and Development Program (2020ZLYS09), the Major Scientific and Technological Innovation Project of Shandong, China (2019JZZY010133), the Major Program of Guangdong Basic and Applied Research (2019B030302008, 2022A1515140090), Key Research Project of Zhejiang Province, China (2023C01025).

References

1. Amzaleg, D., Dinur, I.: Refined cryptanalysis of the GPRS ciphers GEA-1 and GEA-2. IACR Cryptology ePrint Archive, Paper 2022/424 (2022)
2. Aoki, K., Guo, J., Matusiewicz, K., Sasaki, Yu., Wang, L.: Preimages for step-reduced SHA-2. In: Matsui, M. (ed.) ASIACRYPT 2009. LNCS, vol. 5912, pp. 578–597. Springer, Heidelberg (2009). https://doi.org/10.1007/978-3-642-10366-7_34
3. Aoki, K., Sasaki, Yu.: Preimage attacks on one-block MD4, 63-step MD5 and more. In: Avanzi, R.M., Keliher, L., Sica, F. (eds.) SAC 2008. LNCS, vol. 5381, pp. 103–119. Springer, Heidelberg (2009). https://doi.org/10.1007/978-3-642-04159-4_7
4. Aumasson, J.-P., Meier, W., Mendel, F.: Preimage attacks on 3-pass HAVAL and step-reduced MD5. In: Avanzi, R.M., Keliher, L., Sica, F. (eds.) SAC 2008. LNCS, vol. 5381, pp. 120–135. Springer, Heidelberg (2009). https://doi.org/10.1007/978-3-642-04159-4_8
5. Banik, S., Barooti, K., Vaudenay, S., Yan, H.: New attacks on LowMC instances with a single plaintext/ciphertext pair. In: Tibouchi, M., Wang, H. (eds.) ASIACRYPT 2021. LNCS, vol. 13090, pp. 303–331. Springer, Cham (2021). https://doi.org/10.1007/978-3-030-92062-3_11
6. Bao, Z., et al.: Automatic search of meet-in-the-middle preimage attacks on AES-like hashing. In: Canteaut, A., Standaert, F.-X. (eds.) EUROCRYPT 2021. LNCS, vol. 12696, pp. 771–804. Springer, Cham (2021). https://doi.org/10.1007/978-3-030-77870-5_27
7. Bao, Z., Guo, J., Shi, D., Tu, Y.: Superposition meet-in-the-middle attacks: updates on fundamental security of AES-like hashing. In: Dodis, Y., Shrimpton, T. (eds.) Advances in Cryptology, CRYPTO 2022. LNCS, vol. 13507, pp. 64–93. Springer, Cham (2022). https://doi.org/10.1007/978-3-031-15802-5_3
8. Barreto, P.S.L.M., Rijmen, V.: The WHIRLPOOL hashing function. Submitted to NESSIE (2000)

9. Beierle, C., et al.: Lightweight AEAD and hashing using the sparkle permutation family. IACR Trans. Symmetric Cryptol. **2020**(S1), 208–261 (2020)

10. Beierle, C., et al.: Cryptanalysis of the GPRS encryption algorithms GEA-1 and GEA-2. In: Canteaut, A., Standaert, F.-X. (eds.) EUROCRYPT 2021. LNCS, vol. 12697, pp. 155–183. Springer, Cham (2021). https://doi.org/10.1007/978-3-030-77886-6_6

11. Benadjila, R., et al.: SHA-3 proposal: ECHO. Submission to NIST (updated), p. 113 (2009)

12. Bertoni, G., Daemen, J., Peeters, M., Van Assche, G.: Keccak sponge function family main document. Submission to NIST (Round 2), vol. 3, no. 30, pp. 320–337 (2009)

13. Bogdanov, A., Khovratovich, D., Rechberger, C.: Biclique cryptanalysis of the full AES. In: Proceedings of the ASIACRYPT 2011, pp. 344–371 (2011)

14. Bogdanov, A., Rechberger, C.: A 3-subset meet-in-the-middle attack: cryptanalysis of the lightweight block cipher KTANTAN. In: Biryukov, A., Gong, G., Stinson, D.R. (eds.) SAC 2010. LNCS, vol. 6544, pp. 229–240. Springer, Heidelberg (2011). https://doi.org/10.1007/978-3-642-19574-7_16

15. Bouillaguet, C., Derbez, P., Fouque, P.-A.: Automatic search of attacks on round-reduced AES and applications. In: Rogaway, P. (ed.) CRYPTO 2011. LNCS, vol. 6841, pp. 169–187. Springer, Heidelberg (2011). https://doi.org/10.1007/978-3-642-22792-9_10

16. Boura, C., David, N., Derbez, P., Leander, G., Naya-Plasencia, M.: Differential meet-in-the-middle cryptanalysis. IACR Cryptology ePrint Archive, Paper 2022/1640 (2022)

17. Canteaut, A., Naya-Plasencia, M., Vayssière, B.: Sieve-in-the-middle: improved MITM attacks. In: Canetti, R., Garay, J.A. (eds.) CRYPTO 2013. LNCS, vol. 8042, pp. 222–240. Springer, Heidelberg (2013). https://doi.org/10.1007/978-3-642-40041-4_13

18. Coppersmith, D.: The data encryption standard (DES) and its strength against attacks. IBM J. Res. Dev. **38**(3), 243–250 (1994)

19. Daemen, J., Rijmen, V.: The Design of Rijndael: AES - The Advanced Encryption Standard. ISC, Springer, Heidelberg (2002). https://doi.org/10.1007/978-3-662-04722-4

20. Damgård, I.B.: A design principle for hash functions. In: Brassard, G. (ed.) CRYPTO 1989. LNCS, vol. 435, pp. 416–427. Springer, New York (1990). https://doi.org/10.1007/0-387-34805-0_39

21. Derbez, P., Fouque, P.-A.: Automatic search of meet-in-the-middle and impossible differential attacks. In: Robshaw, M., Katz, J. (eds.) CRYPTO 2016, Part II. LNCS, vol. 9815, pp. 157–184. Springer, Heidelberg (2016). https://doi.org/10.1007/978-3-662-53008-5_6

22. Diffie, W., Hellman, M.E.: Special feature exhaustive cryptanalysis of the NBS data encryption standard. Computer **10**(6), 74–84 (1977)

23. Dinur, I., Dunkelman, O., Keller, N., Shamir, A.: Efficient dissection of composite problems, with applications to cryptanalysis, knapsacks, and combinatorial search problems. In: Safavi-Naini, R., Canetti, R. (eds.) CRYPTO 2012. LNCS, vol. 7417, pp. 719–740. Springer, Heidelberg (2012). https://doi.org/10.1007/978-3-642-32009-5_42

24. Dong, X., Hua, J., Sun, S., Li, Z., Wang, X., Hu, L.: Meet-in-the-middle attacks revisited: key-recovery, collision, and preimage attacks. In: Malkin, T., Peikert, C. (eds.) CRYPTO 2021. LNCS, vol. 12827, pp. 278–308. Springer, Cham (2021). https://doi.org/10.1007/978-3-030-84252-9_10

25. Dunkelman, O., Sekar, G., Preneel, B.: Improved meet-in-the-middle attacks on reduced-round DES. In: Srinathan, K., Rangan, C.P., Yung, M. (eds.) INDOCRYPT 2007. LNCS, vol. 4859, pp. 86–100. Springer, Heidelberg (2007). https://doi.org/10.1007/978-3-540-77026-8_8

26. Espitau, T., Fouque, P.-A., Karpman, P.: Higher-order differential meet-in-the-middle preimage attacks on SHA-1 and BLAKE. In: Gennaro, R., Robshaw, M. (eds.) CRYPTO 2015, Part I. LNCS, vol. 9215, pp. 683–701. Springer, Heidelberg (2015). https://doi.org/10.1007/978-3-662-47989-6_33

27. Fuhr, T., Minaud, B.: Match box meet-in-the-middle attack against KATAN. In: Cid, C., Rechberger, C. (eds.) FSE 2014. LNCS, vol. 8540, pp. 61–81. Springer, Heidelberg (2015). https://doi.org/10.1007/978-3-662-46706-0_4

28. Gauravaram, P., Knudsen, L.R., Matusiewicz, K., Mendel, F., Rechberger, C., Schläffer, M., Thomsen, S.S.: Grøstl - a SHA-3 candidate. In: Symmetric Cryptography (2009)

29. Gueron, S., Mouha, N.: Simpira v2: a family of efficient permutations using the AES round function. In: Cheon, J.H., Takagi, T. (eds.) ASIACRYPT 2016, Part I. LNCS, vol. 10031, pp. 95–125. Springer, Heidelberg (2016). https://doi.org/10.1007/978-3-662-53887-6_4

30. Guo, J., Ling, S., Rechberger, C., Wang, H.: Advanced meet-in-the-middle preimage attacks: first results on full tiger, and improved results on MD4 and SHA-2. In: Abe, M. (ed.) ASIACRYPT 2010. LNCS, vol. 6477, pp. 56–75. Springer, Heidelberg (2010). https://doi.org/10.1007/978-3-642-17373-8_4

31. Hirose, S., Ideguchi, K., Kuwakado, H., Owada, T., Preneel, B., Yoshida, H.: A lightweight 256-bit hash function for hardware and low-end devices: Lesamnta-LW. In: Rhee, K.-H., Nyang, D.H. (eds.) ICISC 2010. LNCS, vol. 6829, pp. 151–168. Springer, Heidelberg (2011). https://doi.org/10.1007/978-3-642-24209-0_10

32. Hou, Q., Dong, X., Qin, L., Zhang, G., Wang, X.: Automated meet-in-the-middle attack goes to Feistel. Cryptology ePrint Archive, Paper 2023/1359 (2023). https://eprint.iacr.org/2023/1359

33. Indesteege, S., Keller, N., Dunkelman, O., Biham, E., Preneel, B.: A practical attack on KeeLoq. In: Smart, N. (ed.) EUROCRYPT 2008. LNCS, vol. 4965, pp. 1–18. Springer, Heidelberg (2008). https://doi.org/10.1007/978-3-540-78967-3_1

34. Isobe, T.: A single-key attack on the full GOST block cipher. J. Cryptol. 26(1), 172–189 (2013)

35. Isobe, T., et al.: Areion: highly-efficient permutations and its applications to hash functions for short input. IACR Trans. Cryptogr. Hardw. Embed. Syst. 2023(2), 115–154 (2023)

36. Knellwolf, S., Khovratovich, D.: New preimage attacks against reduced SHA-1. In: Safavi-Naini, R., Canetti, R. (eds.) CRYPTO 2012. LNCS, vol. 7417, pp. 367–383. Springer, Heidelberg (2012). https://doi.org/10.1007/978-3-642-32009-5_22

37. Kölbl, S., Lauridsen, M.M., Mendel, F., Rechberger, C.: Haraka v2 - efficient short-input hashing for post-quantum applications. IACR Trans. Symmetric Cryptol. 2016(2), 1–29 (2016)

38. Lai, X., Massey, J.L.: Hash functions based on block ciphers. In: Rueppel, R.A. (ed.) EUROCRYPT 1992. LNCS, vol. 658, pp. 55–70. Springer, Heidelberg (1993). https://doi.org/10.1007/3-540-47555-9_5

39. Leurent, G.: MD4 is not one-way. In: Nyberg, K. (ed.) FSE 2008. LNCS, vol. 5086, pp. 412–428. Springer, Heidelberg (2008). https://doi.org/10.1007/978-3-540-71039-4_26

40. Liu, F., Sarkar, S., Wang, G., Meier, W., Isobe, T.: Algebraic meet-in-the-middle attack on LowMC. In: Agrawal, S., Lin, D. (eds.) Advances in Cryptology, ASIACRYPT 2022, Part I. LNCS, vol. 13791, pp. 225–255. Springer, Cham (2022). https://doi.org/10.1007/978-3-031-22963-3_8

41. Lucks, S.: Attacking triple encryption. In: Vaudenay, S. (ed.) FSE 1998. LNCS, vol. 1372, pp. 239–253. Springer, Heidelberg (1998). https://doi.org/10.1007/3-540-69710-1_16

42. Merkle, R.C.: A certified digital signature. In: Brassard, G. (ed.) CRYPTO 1989. LNCS, vol. 435, pp. 218–238. Springer, New York (1990). https://doi.org/10.1007/0-387-34805-0_21

43. Preneel, B., Govaerts, R., Vandewalle, J.: Hash functions based on block ciphers: a synthetic approach. In: Stinson, D.R. (ed.) CRYPTO 1993. LNCS, vol. 773, pp. 368–378. Springer, Heidelberg (1994). https://doi.org/10.1007/3-540-48329-2_31

44. Qin, L., Hua, J., Dong, X., Yan, H., Wang, X.: Meet-in-the-middle preimage attacks on sponge-based hashing. In: Hazay, C., Stam, M. (eds.) Advances in Cryptology, EUROCRYPT 2023, Part IV. LNCS, vol. 14007, pp. 158–188. Springer, Cham (2023). https://doi.org/10.1007/978-3-031-30634-1_6

45. Sasaki, Yu.: Integer linear programming for three-subset meet-in-the-middle attacks: application to GIFT. In: Inomata, A., Yasuda, K. (eds.) IWSEC 2018. LNCS, vol. 11049, pp. 227–243. Springer, Cham (2018). https://doi.org/10.1007/978-3-319-97916-8_15

46. Sasaki, Yu.: Meet-in-the-middle preimage attacks on AES hashing modes and an application to Whirlpool. In: Joux, A. (ed.) FSE 2011. LNCS, vol. 6733, pp. 378–396. Springer, Heidelberg (2011). https://doi.org/10.1007/978-3-642-21702-9_22

47. Sasaki, Yu.: Preimage attacks on Feistel-SP functions: impact of omitting the last network twist. In: Jacobson, M., Locasto, M., Mohassel, P., Safavi-Naini, R. (eds.) ACNS 2013. LNCS, vol. 7954, pp. 170–185. Springer, Heidelberg (2013). https://doi.org/10.1007/978-3-642-38980-1_11

48. Sasaki, Yu., Aoki, K.: Preimage attacks on 3, 4, and 5-pass HAVAL. In: Pieprzyk, J. (ed.) ASIACRYPT 2008. LNCS, vol. 5350, pp. 253–271. Springer, Heidelberg (2008). https://doi.org/10.1007/978-3-540-89255-7_16

49. Sasaki, Yu., Aoki, K.: Finding preimages in full MD5 faster than exhaustive search. In: Joux, A. (ed.) EUROCRYPT 2009. LNCS, vol. 5479, pp. 134–152. Springer, Heidelberg (2009). https://doi.org/10.1007/978-3-642-01001-9_8

50. Sasaki, Yu., Wang, L., Wu, S., Wu, W.: Investigating fundamental security requirements on whirlpool: improved preimage and collision attacks. In: Wang, X., Sako, K. (eds.) ASIACRYPT 2012. LNCS, vol. 7658, pp. 562–579. Springer, Heidelberg (2012). https://doi.org/10.1007/978-3-642-34961-4_34

51. Schrottenloher, A., Stevens, M.: Simplified MITM modeling for permutations: new (quantum) attacks. In: Dodis, Y., Shrimpton, T. (eds.) Advances in Cryptology, CRYPTO 2022, Part III. LNCS, vol. 13509, pp. 717–747. Springer, Cham (2022). https://doi.org/10.1007/978-3-031-15982-4_24

52. Schrottenloher, A., Stevens, M.: Simplified MITM modeling for permutations: new (quantum) attacks. IACR Cryptology ePrint Archive, Paper 2022/189 (2022)

53. Wu, S., Feng, D., Wu, W., Guo, J., Dong, L., Zou, J.: (Pseudo) preimage attack on round-reduced Grøstl hash function and others. In: Canteaut, A. (ed.) FSE 2012. LNCS, vol. 7549, pp. 127–145. Springer, Heidelberg (2012). https://doi.org/10.1007/978-3-642-34047-5_8

54. Zheng, Y., Matsumoto, T., Imai, H.: On the construction of block ciphers provably secure and not relying on any unproved hypotheses. In: Brassard, G. (ed.) CRYPTO 1989. LNCS, vol. 435, pp. 461–480. Springer, New York (1990). https://doi.org/10.1007/0-387-34805-0_42

Revisiting Higher-Order Differential-Linear Attacks from an Algebraic Perspective

Kai Hu[✉], Thomas Peyrin, Quan Quan Tan, and Trevor Yap

School of Physical and Mathematical Sciences, Nanyang Technological University, Singapore, Singapore
kai.hu.sdu@gmail.com, {thomas.peyrin,trevor.yap}@ntu.edu.sg, quanquan001@e.ntu.edu.sg

Abstract. The Higher-order Differential-Linear (HDL) attack was introduced by Biham *et al.* at FSE 2005, where a linear approximation was appended to a Higher-order Differential (HD) transition. It is a natural generalization of the Differential-Linear (DL) attack. Due to some practical restrictions, however, HDL cryptanalysis has unfortunately attracted much less attention compared to its DL counterpart since its proposal.

In this paper, we revisit HD/HDL cryptanalysis from an algebraic perspective and provide two novel tools for detecting possible HD/HDL distinguishers, including: (a) Higher-order Algebraic Transitional Form (HATF) for probabilistic HD/HDL attacks; (b) Differential Supporting Function (DSF) for deterministic HD attacks. In general, the HATF can estimate the biases of ℓth-order HDL approximations with complexity $\mathcal{O}(2^{\ell+d2^{\ell}})$ where d is the algebraic degree of the function studied. If the function is quadratic, the complexity can be further reduced to $\mathcal{O}(2^{3.8\ell})$. HATF is therefore very useful in HDL cryptanalysis for ciphers with quadratic round functions, such as ASCON and XOODYAK. DSF provides a convenient way to find good linearizations on the input of a permutation, which facilitates the search for HD distinguishers.

Unsurprisingly, HD/HDL attacks have the potential to be more effective than their simpler differential/DL counterparts. Using HATF, we found many HDL approximations for round-reduced ASCON and XOODYAK initializations, with significantly larger biases than DL ones. For instance, there are deterministic 2nd-order/4th-order HDL approximations for ASCON/XOODYAK initializations, respectively (which is believed to be impossible in the simple DL case). We derived highly biased HDL approximations for 5-round ASCON up to 8th order, which improves the complexity of the distinguishing attack on 5-round ASCON from 2^{16} to 2^{12} calls. We also proposed HDL approximations for 6-round ASCON and 5-round XOODYAK (under the single-key model), which couldn't be reached with simple DL so far. For key recovery, HDL attacks are also more efficient than DL attacks, thanks to the larger biases of

---

The full version of this paper is [14].

© International Association for Cryptologic Research 2023
J. Guo and R. Steinfeld (Eds.): ASIACRYPT 2023, LNCS 14440, pp. 405–435, 2023.
https://doi.org/10.1007/978-981-99-8727-6_14

HDL approximations. Additionally, HATF works well for DL (1st-order HDL) attacks and some well-known DL biases of ASCON and XOODYAK that could only be obtained experimentally before can now be predicted theoretically.

With DSF, we propose a new distinguishing attack on 8-round ASCON permutation, with a complexity of 2^{48}. Also, we provide a new zero-sum distinguisher for the full 12-round ASCON permutation with 2^{55} time-/data complexity. We highlight that our cryptanalyses do not threaten the security of ASCON or XOODYAK.

Keywords: Higher-Order Differential · Higher-Order Differential-Linear · ASCON · XOODYAK

1   Introduction

1.1   Differential-Linear Cryptanalysis

Differential and linear cryptanalysis have been the fundamental methods for evaluating the security of a cipher [5,22]. Nowadays, all new schemes are requested to claim resistance against these two attacks. However, resistance against the plain differential and linear cryptanalysis does not necessarily lead to resistance against their variants. For example, despite its security proof against differential attacks, the cipher COCONUT98 [28] is vulnerable to boomerang and Differential-Linear (DL) cryptanalysis [3,29] which are two variants of the differential and linear attacks, leveraging a combined strategy.

Differential-linear cryptanalysis was proposed by Langford and Hellman in 1994 [18]. For a cipher E, let $C = E(P)$ and $C' = E(P')$. Given a difference-mask pair (Δ_I, λ_O), the bias q' of a DL approximation can be derived from the following equation

$$\Pr[\lambda_O \cdot (C \oplus C') = 0 \mid P \oplus P' = \Delta_I] = \frac{1}{2} + q'.$$

Similar to the case of linear cryptanalysis, if the bias $|q'|$ is significantly larger than 0, we can distinguish the cipher from a random permutation.

There are mainly two types of methods to estimate q' in the literature. In the classical DL cryptanalysis [3,18], a cipher E is decomposed into two sub-ciphers as $E = E_1 \circ E_0$, where a differential $\Delta_I \xrightarrow{p} \Delta_O$ for E_0 and a linear approximation $\lambda_I \xrightarrow{q} \lambda_O$ for E_1 are considered. The DL bias q' can be estimated by $q' = (-1)^{\Delta_O \cdot \lambda_I} 2pq^2$ under some independence assumptions.

As pointed out in [3], experiments are required to verify the estimated bias when possible because the underlying assumptions may fail. There are two main refined methods of classical DL attacks. One is from Blondeau et al. [6], where an accurate formula for q' is given under the sole assumption that E_0 and E_1 are independent. The other, proposed by Bar-On et al. [1] at EUROCRYPT 2019, is called the Differential-Linear Connectivity Table (DLCT) which overcomes the independence problem between E_0 and E_1. The drawback of the first method is that it is computationally impossible to apply the formula for practical use-cases, while the second method only works when a large-enough DLCT can be built efficiently.

A new method to estimate q' from an algebraic perspective has been proposed by Liu *et al.* [20] at CRYPTO 2021. If we define a Boolean function according to λ_O as $f_{\lambda_O} : \mathbb{F}_2^n \to \mathbb{F}_2, f_{\lambda_O}(u) = \lambda_O \cdot u$ and let $f = f_{\lambda_O} \circ E$, the bias of $\lambda_O \cdot (C \oplus C')$ is equivalent to the bias of the following Boolean function

$$\mathcal{D}_{\Delta_I} f(P) = f(P) \oplus f(P \oplus \Delta_I). \tag{1}$$

Then, they introduced another function with an auxiliary variable $x \in \mathbb{F}_2$ as

$$f_{\Delta_I}(P, x) = f(P \oplus x\Delta_I), \tag{2}$$

where $x\Delta_I \in \mathbb{F}_2^n$ means that x is multiplied with each coordinate of Δ_I, *i.e.*, $x\Delta_I = (x\Delta_I[0], \dots, x\Delta_I[n-1])$. Given a Boolean function $g(a_0, a_1, \dots, a_{n-1})$ with n variables and for a certain variable a_i (a_j for $j \neq i$ are viewed as parameters), we can write g as $g = g''a_i \oplus g'$ with g' and g'' being independent of a_i and where the partial derivative of g with respect to a_i is the polynomial g'', denoted by $D_{a_i}g$. Liu *et al.* gave the following observation linking Eqs. 1 and 2 (Eq. 3, as proposed in [20], was initially presented based on intuition, with the underlying rationale not explicitly discussed. A comprehensive explanation and detailed insight into the reasoning behind this formula will be provided in Sect. 3),

$$f'' = D_x f_{\Delta_I} = \mathcal{D}_{\Delta_I} f, \tag{3}$$

where $D_x f_{\Delta_I}$ is the partial derivative of f_{Δ_I} with respect to x. That is to say, considering Eqs. 1, 2, 3, in order to evaluate the bias of $\lambda_O \cdot (C \oplus C')$, we only need to evaluate the bias of the Boolean function $D_x f_{\Delta_I}$. This estimation from an algebraic perspective does not require any assumption in theory. However, it is extremely difficult to derive $D_x f_{\Delta_I}$ or evaluate its bias. To overcome this obstacle, Liu *et al.* introduced the so-called Algebraic Transitional Forms (ATF)[1] technique to construct a transitional expression of $D_x f_{\Delta_I}$. Then, the bias is estimated from this transitional expression.

1.2   Higher-Order Differential(-Linear) Cryptanalysis

Inspired by the boomerang and DL cryptanalysis, other combined attacks were studied by Biham, Dunkelman, and Keller [4]. These combined attacks include the differential-bilinear, Higher-order Differential-Linear (HDL), boomerang-linear attack, *etc.*

The Higher-order Differential (HD) was for the first time introduced by Lai in 1994 [30] and later studied by Knudsen [16]. It is a natural generalization of

---

[1] In [20], there is another terminology DATF when ATF is used to construct transitional expressions for f_Δ. In this paper, we directly use ATF for all kinds of Boolean functions no matter whether we target f or f_Δ.

the differential attack that takes advantage of having access to more plaintexts. Given an ℓth-order difference $\boldsymbol{\Delta}_I = (\Delta_0, \Delta_1, \ldots, \Delta_{\ell-1})$ where $\Delta_0, \Delta_1, \ldots, \Delta_{\ell-1}$ are linearly independent, the ℓth derivative of a (partial) cipher E with respect to $\boldsymbol{\Delta}_I$ studies the probability

$$p = \Pr\left[\bigoplus_{x \in X \oplus \mathcal{L}(\boldsymbol{\Delta}_I)} E(x) = \Delta_O\right],$$

where $\mathcal{L}(\boldsymbol{\Delta}_I)$ is the linear span of $(\Delta_0, \Delta_1, \ldots, \Delta_{\ell-1})$, the ℓ dimensional affine space $X \oplus \mathcal{L}(\boldsymbol{\Delta})$ is called the *input set* with respect to $\boldsymbol{\Delta}$, and Δ_O is called the output difference.

As the name higher-order differential-linear suggests, HDL cryptanalysis [4] studies the bias concerning an ℓth-order input difference $\boldsymbol{\Delta}_I$ and an output mask λ_O. The bias ε of an HDL approximation is derived from the following formulation:

$$\Pr\left[\lambda_O \cdot \left(\bigoplus_{x \in X \oplus \mathcal{L}(\boldsymbol{\Delta}_I)} E(x)\right) = 0\right] = \frac{1}{2} + \varepsilon.$$

Akin to the first kind of method to evaluate the bias in DL cryptanalysis, Biham *et al.* [4] gave an analysis based on viewing E as two sub-ciphers $E = E_1 \circ E_0$. Suppose that we know an ℓth derivative with probability p for E_0 and that E_1 has a linear approximation with bias equal to q, then the overall bias ε is estimated as $\varepsilon = 2^{2^\ell - 1} p q^{2^\ell}$. However, currently there is no effective method to trace the propagation of an HD or calculate its probability yet. Thus, Biham *et al.* had to restrain themselves to the integral property for E_0, which leads to $p = 1$. The integral property usually requires a large ℓ to attack an interesting number of rounds, but if $|q| \neq \frac{1}{2}$, ε will become extremely close to zero. As a result, we can only get an interesting HDL distinguisher when there is a linear approximation with bias $\pm\frac{1}{2}$ for E_1. In practice, some ciphers such as IDEA [17] allow weak-key linear approximations with bias $\frac{1}{2}$, which makes them vulnerable to HDL attacks [2,4].

1.3   Motivation and Contributions

Considering that DL attacks are efficient for many important primitives, such as ASCON [12] (recent winner of the NIST lightweight competition) and XOODYAK [9], we are naturally interested in whether the HDL attack could achieve even better performance. However, as we mentioned, we did not have any tool to study the probabilistic HD distinguishers and they were far less practical than their DL counterparts. How to handle the probabilistic HD/HDL cryptanalysis remains an open problem.

Recently, an algebraic perspective on DL attacks [20] opened up a new road to study the differential/DL attacks and achieved better precision for some important ciphers such as ASCON [12]. However, we note that their method is based on some intuitive observations and is limited to the first-order case. In this paper, we generalize and refine this algebraic method to higher-order cases.

Our Contributions. In this paper, we revisit the HD/HDL cryptanalysis of a Boolean function from an algebraic perspective, which provides novel methods to study HD and HDL cryptanalysis. Two tools for HD/HDL cryptanalysis are proposed based on this new perspective, one is the Higher-order Algebraic Transitional Form (HATF), which is used to detect probabilistic HDL approximations. The other is the Differential Supporting Function (DSF), which is useful to find deterministic HD distinguishers.

Table 1. Approximation Biases of the DL and HDL approximations for ASCON, XOODYAK and XOODOO. The column of Expr. shows the experimental biases.

Primitive	Round	Order	Bias Expr.	Theory	Method	Reference
ASCON Init.	4	1st	2^{-2}	2^{-20}	Classical	[11]
				2^{-5}	DLCT	[1]
				$2^{-2.365}$	ATF	[20]
				$\mathbf{2^{-2.09}}$	**HATF**	Section 5.1
		2nd	2^{-1}	$\mathbf{2^{-1}}$	**HATF**	Section 5.1
	5	1st	2^{-9}	–	Experimental	[11]
				$\mathbf{2^{-10}}$	**HATF**	Section 5.1
		2nd	$2^{-6.60}$	$\mathbf{2^{-7.05}}$	**HATF**	Section 5.1
		8th	$2^{-3.35}$	$\mathbf{2^{-4.73}}$	**HATF**	Section 5.1
	6	3rd	2^{-22}†	$\mathbf{2^{-25.97}}$†	**HATF**	Section 5.1
XOODYAK Init.	4	1st	$2^{-9.7}$	–	Experimental	[13]
				$\mathbf{2^{-9.67}}$	**HATF**	Section 6.1
			$-2^{-5.36}$‡	–	Experimental	[13]
				$\mathbf{-2^{-6.0}}$	**HATF**	Section 6.1
		2nd	$2^{-5.72}$	$\mathbf{2^{-5.72}}$	**HATF**	Section 6.1
		4th	2^{-1}	$\mathbf{2^{-1}}$	**HATF**	Section 6.1
	5	2nd	–	$\mathbf{2^{-45}}$	**HATF**	Section 6.1
XOODOO	4	-	2^{-1}	$\mathbf{2^{-1}}$	Rot. DL	[21]
		4th	2^{-1}	$\mathbf{2^{-1}}$	**HATF**	Section 6.1
	5	3rd	$2^{-8.79}$	$\mathbf{2^{-8.96}}$	**HATF**	Section 6.1

†This bias holds when 24 conditions are satisfied.
‡In [13], this 4-round DL distinguisher was extended to 5 rounds in a natural way, with an additional cost of 2^{-4}.

Higher-Order Algebraic Transitional Form (HATF). By transforming the input set of a Boolean function f from an ℓ dimensional affine space to an

ℓ dimensional linear space, we can transform a general HD attack to a standard integral/cube attack. The HD/HDL approximations are then the biases of the coefficient of the maxterm in f with the transformed inputs. Since almost all modern ciphers are built in a composite way, we can obtain the HD/HDL expressions in the form of a composite vectorial Boolean function, which is easier to study.

HATF is a way to estimate the biases of HDL approximations of ciphers (concretely, they are the expected biases among all input variabels). It is a two-step process: (a) constructing the composite formula of an HD/HDL expression for a cipher; (b) calculating the biases of state bits iteratively. The complexity of HATF is $\mathcal{O}(2^{\ell+d2^{\ell}})$ in general cases where ℓ is the HD/HDL order and d is the algebraic degree of the round function. However, for ciphers with quadratic round functions, the complexity is $\mathcal{O}(2^{3.8\ell})$. Thus, HATF is a very useful tool to study the HDL approximations of some permutation-based ciphers such as ASCON and XOODYAK.

Using HATF, we detected many highly biased HDL approximations for round-reduced ASCON, XOODYAK and XOODOO. For example, we propose deterministic HDL approximations for both ASCON and XOODYAK on 4 rounds. For 5-round ASCON, we give HDL approximations up to the 8th order. Based on these, we have improved the distinguishing attacks for 4- and 5-round ASCON and XOODYAK (see Table 2).

We can improve the precision of HATF with a so-called partitioning technique as compared to all previous detection tools for DL (first-order HDL) attacks. For instance, HATF estimates the bias of the well-studied 4-round ASCON's DL approximation as $2^{-2.09}$ (the experimental results is 2^{-2}), which is better than previous tools such as the DLCT [1] (2^{-5}) or the ATF [20] ($2^{-2.36}$). Also, for the first time we give the theoretical bias for the 5-round ASCON's DL approximation: the bias is estimated as 2^{-10} while the experimental value is 2^{-9}, no previous tool could predict this bias. For XOODYAK, HATF also gives precise theoretical predictions for two DL approximations found by experiments [13]. These results are shown in Table 1.

In addition, by injecting some conditions into HATF, we obtained the best key-recovery attack on 5-round ASCON with time/data complexity of 2^{22}, which is 16 times faster than the DL attacks [20] and 4 times faster than the conditional cube attacks [19]. For 4-round XOODYAK, the HDL attack is 4 times more efficient than the DL attack [13]. A summary of these key-recovery attacks is given in Table 2.

Finally, we make clear that HATF cannot give any lower or upper bound for HDL approximation biases in theory. However, empirically, it is quite precise to predict biased bits, as we show in our experiments. In cases where the reported bias is high, we note that it was always the case that the experimental bias was also observed as high (we have not seen any counterexample for this). We provide data and discuss the precision of HATF in the full version of this paper based on HDL cryptanalysis of ASCON.

Differential Supporting Function (DSF). Instead of using the degree evaluation of a cipher to derive deterministic HD distinguishers, we can evaluate the algebraic degree of its DSF. As we will see, the DSF is parameterized by the input value and the (higher-order) difference. Thus, a proper choice of the parameters could significantly reduce its algebraic degree, leading to a greater chance of detecting a deterministic HD distinguisher for the DSF. After that, we can conveniently transform it into an HD distinguisher for the original cipher. With this technique, we improve the best-known distinguishing attacks on round-reduced ASCON permutation [12]. A 46th-order HD will lead to a zero output difference (in 64 bits) for 8 rounds, *i.e.*, 2^{46} plaintexts are enough to distinguish an 8-round ASCON permutation from a random permutation (the previous best-known distinguisher requires 2^{130} computations [26]). With a similar method applied to the inverse ASCON permutation, we constructed a zero-sum distinguisher for a full 12-round ASCON permutation requiring only 2^{55} calls while the previous best zero-sum distinguisher costs 2^{130} calls. These distinguishers are demonstrated in Table 3.

Table 2. Summary of DL-like attacks on the ASCON and XOODYAK initializations. Cond. is short for conditional.

Type	Rnd	Data(log)	Time (log)	Method	Reference
ASCON Initialization					
Distinguisher	4	5	5	DL	[11]
		2	**2**	**2ⁿᵈ HDL**	**Section** 5.1
	5	18	18	DL	[11]
		12	**12**	**8ᵗʰ HDL**	**Section** 5.1
Key-Recovery	5	36	36	DL	[11]
		31.44	31.44	DL	[25]
		26	26	Cond. DL	[20]
		24	24	Cond. Cube	[19]
		22	**22**	**Cond. HDL**	**Section** 5.2
Best	7	77	103	Cond. Cube	[19]
	7	64	123	Cube	[23]
XOODYAK Initialization					
Key-Recovery	4	23	23	DL	[13]
		21	**21**	**Cond. HDL**	**Section** 6.2
	5	22	22	DL†	[13]
		70	**70**	**Cond. HDL**	**Section** 6.2
Best	6	43.8	43.8	Cond. Cube	[31]

† This attack is under the related-key model because they obtained the 5-round DL approximation by extending a 4-round one. Our attack is a single-key one, which means we have to choose the input differences from the beginning of 5 rounds.

Table 3. Summary of zero-sum attacks on ASCON permutation. We verified them up to 7 rounds by experiments.

Type	Rnd	Data(log)	Time (log)	Method	Reference
From Start	8	130	130	Integral	[26]
		48	48	**HD**	**Section 7**
Best	11	315	315	Integral	[26]
Inside out	12	130	130	Zero-Sum‡	[26]
		55	55	**Zero-Sum**	**Full Version** [14]

‡Their zero-sum distinguisher can be further extended to a zero-sum partition distinguisher, while ours cannot.

We emphasize that these results do not threaten the security of the ASCON and XOODYAK AEAD schemes.

Source Code. We implemented the HATF algorithms in C++ and DSF in Python, the source codes are provided in the git repository https://github.com/hukaisdu/HDL.git.

Outline. In Sect. 2, we briefly recall the main concepts of the HD and an algebraic perspective on the differential attack, and other useful background knowledge used in this paper. In Sect. 3, we provide an algebraic perspective on the HD/HDL. The HATF technique is introduced in Sect. 4. In the following sections, we describe the HDL attacks on ASCON and XOODYAK. In Sect. 7, we give the theory and results of DSF. Section 8 concludes this paper.

2   Preliminaries

2.1   Notations

We use italic lower-case letters such as x to represent elements in $\mathbb{F}_2^n, n \geq 1$. The jth bit of x is denoted by $x[j]$, $0 \leq j < n$, where $x[0]$ is the most significant (the leftmost) bit. The vectors of ℓ elements in $\mathbb{F}_2^n$ are denoted by $\boldsymbol{x} = (x_0, x_1, \ldots, x_{\ell-1}) \in (\mathbb{F}_2^n)^\ell$, the ith element of $\boldsymbol{x}$ is denoted by x_i (the jth bit of x_i is then denoted by $x_i[j]$). Given $x \in \mathbb{F}_2$ and $\Delta \in \mathbb{F}_2^n$, $x\Delta = (\Delta[0]x, \Delta[1]x, \ldots, \Delta[n-1]x)$. For $a, b \in \mathbb{F}_2^n$, $a||b \in \mathbb{F}_2^{2n}$ represents the concatenation of a and b, $a \cdot b$ stands for the product as $a \cdot b = \bigoplus_{0 \leq i < n} a[i]b[i]$.

In this paper, $\boldsymbol{x} = (x_0, x_1, \ldots, x_{n-1}) \in \mathbb{F}_2^n$ is usually used as symbolic variables. Given $u \in \mathbb{F}_2^n$, $\boldsymbol{x}^u$ is a monomial of $\boldsymbol{x}$ as $\boldsymbol{x}^u = \prod_i x_i^{u[i]}$. For a vectorial Boolean function $E : \mathbb{F}_2^n \to \mathbb{F}_2^n$, we use the $E[0], E[1], \ldots, E[n-1]$ to represent the Boolean functions of its bits.

2.2   Boolean Function

An n-variable Boolean function is a mapping from $\mathbb{F}_2^n$ to $\mathbb{F}_2$, which can be uniquely written as its Algebraic Normal Form (ANF) as a multivariate polynomial over $\mathbb{F}_2$ as (note the input $x \in \mathbb{F}_2^n$ of this Boolean function is written as $x \in (\mathbb{F}_2)^n$ to stress that the input can be seen as n bit variables)

$$f(x) = f(x_0, x_1, \ldots, x_{n-1}) = \bigoplus_{u \in \mathbb{F}_2^n} a_u x^u = \bigoplus_{u \in \mathbb{F}_2^n} a_u \prod_{i=0}^{n-1} x_i^{u[i]}, a_u \in \mathbb{F}_2.$$

The algebraic degree of f, denoted by $\deg(f)$ is defined as $\max_{a_u \neq 0}\{wt(u)\}$ for all $u \in \mathbb{F}_2^n$ in the above formula. The monomial $x_0 x_1 \cdots x_{n-1}$ is called the *maxterm* of f, denoted by $\pi(x)$. The coefficient of a monomial x^u of f is denoted by $\mathsf{Coe}(f, x^u)$. Each output bit of a cryptographic primitive can be written as a Boolean function of its public variables (such as plaintexts, initial values (IV), or nonces) and secret variables such as the key bits.

The bias and correlation are two ways of measuring the unbalancedness of an n-variable Boolean function f. The bias ε is defined as $\varepsilon = \frac{1}{2^n}|\{f(x) = 0\}| - \frac{1}{2} = \Pr[f = 0] - \frac{1}{2}$ while the correlation $c = \frac{1}{2^n}\sum_{x \in \mathbb{F}_2^n}(-1)^{f(x)}$. Actually, $c = 2\varepsilon$. In this paper, we will only use the bias ε to measure the unbalancedness.

2.3   Algebraic Perspective on DL

In [20], Liu *et al.* introduced a new algebraic method for the differential and DL cryptanalysis as we have already mentioned in Sect. 1. Recalling Eq. 1, the bias of a DL approximation is related to the differential bias of the Boolean function $f = f_{\lambda_O} \circ E$. Thus, to study the DL attack it is enough to focus on the differential property of a sole Boolean function. As explained in Sect. 1, Liu *et al.* proposed Eq. 3 ($f'' = D_x f_{\Delta_I} = \mathcal{D}_{\Delta_I} f$) based on some intuitive observations, but no formal proof nor clear motivation was given in their article. In the next section, we will make it clearer when introducing our algebraic perspective on the ℓth-order HD.

Basic Idea of Algebraic Transitional Forms. Eq. 3 tells us that if we can (a) calculate the ANF of $D_x f_\Delta$, (b) evaluate the bias of $D_x f_\Delta$, then we can directly know the bias of the output difference. Unfortunately, both tasks are computationally infeasible for modern cryptographic primitives. To overcome these two obstacles, Liu *et al.* introduced the ATF of the exact ANF of f_Δ. ATF of a Boolean function f is a composite representation of f, denoted by $\mathcal{A}$. From $\mathcal{A}(f_\Delta)$, we obtain a simpler expression of $D_x f_\Delta$, say $D_x \mathcal{A}(f_\Delta)$, whose bias will be regarded as an estimation of the real bias.

The core of ATF technique is to substitute some parts of a Boolean function with new variables to simplify its form. Finally, $D_x \mathcal{A}(f_\Delta)$ will be a simple formula of intermediate variables (some are variables introduced for substitution). The bias of $D_x \mathcal{A}(f_\Delta)$ is relatively easier to calculate.

In [20], Liu *et al.* proposed two methods to estimate the bias of $D_x \mathcal{A}(f_\Delta)$. Both methods are based on the following Lemma,

Lemma 1. (*[20]*). *Given a Boolean function* $f : \mathbb{F}_2^n \to \mathbb{F}_2^n$ *and* n *input bits* $x_0, x_1, \ldots, x_{n-1}$ *with biases* $\varepsilon_0, \varepsilon_1, \ldots, \varepsilon_{n-1}$ *respectively. Under the assumption that all inputs are independent, the bias of* f *is*

$$Bias(f) = \sum_{\substack{x_0, x_1, \ldots, x_{n-1} \\ s.t. f(x_0, \ldots, x_{n-1}) = 0}} \prod_{i=0}^{n-1} \left(\frac{1}{2} + (-1)^{x_i} \varepsilon_i \right) - \frac{1}{2}. \tag{4}$$

Equation 4 is derived from such an idea: the event of $f = 0$ happens means any of the input that makes $f = 0$ happens. The bias of x_i is ε_i, so it happens with probability of $\frac{1}{2} + \varepsilon_i$ when $x_i = 0$ or $\frac{1}{2} - \varepsilon_i$ when $x_i = 1$. Equation 4 follows. When using Eq. 4, we need to find out all inputs that make $f = 0$. Thus the complexity to calculate the bias of f is about $\mathcal{O}(2^n)$.

In the basic method, Liu *et al.* assume that all inputs of $D_x \mathcal{A}(f_\Delta)$ are uniformly random (*i.e.*, the biases of all inputs are exactly 0), the bias of $D_x \mathcal{A}(f_\Delta)$ is computed according to Lemma 1. The improved method is similar to the basic one, but the bias of the intermediate variables will be calculated in advance. Thus, the precision can be improved.

3   HD/HDL Cryptanalysis from an Algebraic Perspective

In this section, we give the theory about the ℓth derivative of a Boolean function f from an algebraic perspective. This is a general case of the algebraic perspective on DL proposed in [20]. It is well known that the cube/integral attacks are special cases of HD attacks with all ℓ linearly-independent differences being unit vectors. The expression of the HD derivative of f in this case is the coefficient of the so-called cube term [10]. The theory in this section answers such a question: given any ℓ linear-independent differences, what is the expression of the HD derivative of f?

Given a Boolean function $f : \mathbb{F}_2^n \to \mathbb{F}_2$ and an ℓth-order input difference $\mathbf{\Delta} = (\Delta_0, \Delta_1, \ldots, \Delta_{\ell-1}) \in (\mathbb{F}_2^n)^\ell$, the input set is $X \oplus \mathcal{L}(\mathbf{\Delta})$ for a certain input $X \in \mathbb{F}_2^n$. The ℓth derivative of f is calculated as

$$\mathcal{D}_{\mathbf{\Delta}} f(X) = \bigoplus_{a \in X \oplus \mathcal{L}(\mathbf{\Delta})} f(a).$$

Note that $\mathbb{A}^\ell = X \oplus \mathcal{L}(\mathbf{\Delta})$ is an ℓ-dimensional affine space, so we can link $\mathbb{A}^\ell$ to any another ℓ-dimensional affine space $(\mathbb{A}^\ell)'$ by a bijective mapping $\mathcal{M}$ that sends $(\mathbb{A}^\ell)'$ to $\mathbb{A}^\ell$. Not surprisingly, we tend to choose the simplest ℓ-dimensional affine space, *i.e.*, the ℓ-dimensional linear space $\mathbb{F}_2^\ell$. One choice of $\mathcal{M}$ can be

$$\mathcal{M} : \mathbb{F}_2^\ell \to \mathbb{A}^\ell$$
$$(x_0, x_1, \ldots, x_{\ell-1}) \mapsto X \oplus x_0 \Delta_0 \oplus x_1 \Delta_1 \oplus \cdots \oplus x_{\ell-1} \Delta_{\ell-1} \triangleq X \oplus \mathbf{x}\mathbf{\Delta} \tag{5}$$

We define a new function f_Δ from f with the transformed input set as[2]:

$$f_\Delta : \mathbb{F}_2^\ell \to \mathbb{F}_2, \quad x \mapsto f(X \oplus x\Delta).$$

If we let $D_x f_\Delta$ represent the coefficient of the maxterm in f_Δ, i.e., $D_x f_\Delta = \mathsf{Coe}\,(f\,(X \oplus x\Delta), \pi(x))$ (recall that the maxterm is $\pi(x) = \prod_{i=0}^{\ell-1} x_i$), we can give the following formal proposition,

Proposition 1 (Algebraic-Perspective on HD/HDL). *Given* $f : \mathbb{F}_2^n \to \mathbb{F}_2$ *and an* ℓ^{th}-*order difference* $\Delta \in (\mathbb{F}_2^n)^\ell$, $\mathcal{D}_\Delta f = D_x f_\Delta$.

Proof. With $\mathcal{M}$ as given in Eq. 5, for any X we have

$$\mathcal{D}_\Delta f(X) = \bigoplus_{a \in X \oplus \mathcal{L}(\Delta)} f(a) = \bigoplus_{x \in \mathbb{F}_2^\ell} f(\mathcal{M}(x)) = \bigoplus_{x \in \mathbb{F}_2^\ell} f(X \oplus x\Delta).$$

From the perspective of the Möbius transform, the sum over all $x \in \mathbb{F}_2^\ell$ is the coefficient of $\pi(x)$, i.e.,

$$\bigoplus_{x \in \mathbb{F}_2^\ell} f(X \oplus x\Delta) = \mathsf{Coe}\,(f(X \oplus x\Delta), \pi(x)) = D_x f_\Delta.$$

$\square$

4 Estimating HDL Approximation Biases Using HATF

On the basis of Sect. 3, we propose a technique to measure the bias of a probabilistic HDL approximation. The basic idea is inspired by the ATF technique introduced by Liu *et al.* for the DL cryptanalysis [20]: we construct a composite representation of the HDL approximation, then estimate the bias according to the composite representation. In Sect. 4.1, we construct the HATF for a cipher E, which is a composite representation of the ℓth derivative of E. In Sect. 4.2, we estimate the bias of the ℓth-order HDL based on HATF under some reasonable assumptions. In Sect. 4.4, the partitioning technique is introduced to further improve the precision of the HATF method.

4.1 Construction of the HATF

According to Proposition 1, if for a Boolean function f, we have the ability to calculate the bias of $D_x f_\Delta = \mathsf{Coe}\,(f(X \oplus x\Delta), \pi(x))$, then we will also have the bias of $\mathcal{D}_\Delta f$. However, $D_x f_\Delta$ is too complicated to derive, let alone calculate its bias. Considering that almost all modern ciphers are constructed as a composition of small functions whose ANFs are available, we can represent $D_x f_\Delta$ in a composite way. Based on the composite representation, it becomes possible to estimate its bias under some assumptions.

---

[2] Note that f_Δ is a Boolean function of $x = (x_0, x_1, \ldots, x_{\ell-1})$, X and Δ are regarded as parameters.

Suppose that an R-round cipher $E : \mathbb{F}_2^n \to \mathbb{F}_2^n$ is represented as the following composition,

$$E = E_{R-1} \circ E_{R-2} \circ \cdots \circ E_0, \quad E_r : \mathbb{F}_2^n \to \mathbb{F}_2^n, \qquad (6)$$

then, according to Proposition 1, to calculate the ℓth-order differential of E with the input difference $\boldsymbol{\Delta} = (\Delta_0, \Delta_1, \ldots, \Delta_{\ell-1})$, we can calculate $D_x E\left(X \oplus x\boldsymbol{\Delta}\right)$. Here E is a vectorial Boolean function as $E = (E[0], E[1], \ldots, E[n-1])$, so $D_x E\left(X \oplus x\boldsymbol{\Delta}\right) = \left(D_x E[0]\left(X \oplus x\boldsymbol{\Delta}\right), \ldots, D_x E[n-1]\left(X \oplus x\boldsymbol{\Delta}\right)\right)$.

In the following, we will write $X \oplus x\boldsymbol{\Delta}$ in a more general form. Let e_i be the unit vector with only the ith bit being 1 and $\mathbf{0}$ be the vector with all elements being zero, then

$$\alpha_u = \begin{cases} X, & \text{if } u = \mathbf{0} \\ \Delta_i, & \text{if } u = e_i \\ \mathbf{0}, & \text{otherwise} \end{cases},$$

then $X \oplus x\boldsymbol{\Delta} = X \oplus x_0\Delta_0 \oplus x_1\Delta_1 \oplus \cdots \oplus x_{\ell-1}\Delta_{\ell-1}$ can be written in an equivalent form as

$$X \oplus x\boldsymbol{\Delta} = \bigoplus_{u \in \mathbb{F}_2^\ell} \alpha_u x^u, \quad \alpha_u \in \mathbb{F}_2^n.$$

$x = (x_0, x_1, \ldots, x_{\ell-1})$ are ℓ symbolic variables in this representation. Hence, the input and output of E_r are both polynomials of x as follows,

$$\bigoplus_{u \in \mathbb{F}_2^\ell} \alpha_u^{(r+1)} x^u = E_r\left(\bigoplus_{u \in \mathbb{F}_2^\ell} \alpha_u^{(r)} x^u\right), \quad \alpha_u^{(r+1)}, \alpha_u^{(r)} \in \mathbb{F}_2^n.$$

Since $\alpha_u^{(r+1)}$ is a vectorial Boolean function with all $\alpha_u^{(r)}$ as input, we derive a new vectorial Boolean function from E_r:

$$\mathcal{E}_r^\ell : (\mathbb{F}_2^n)^{2^\ell} \to (\mathbb{F}_2^n)^{2^\ell}, \quad \left(\alpha_u^{(r)}, u \in \mathbb{F}_2^\ell\right) \mapsto \left(\alpha_u^{(r+1)}, u \in \mathbb{F}_2^\ell\right),$$

where

$$\alpha_u^{(r+1)} = f_u\left(\alpha_u^{(r)}, u \in \mathbb{F}_2^n\right) = \text{Coe}\left(E_r\left(\bigoplus_{u \in \mathbb{F}_2^n} \alpha_u^{(r)} x^u\right), x^u\right).$$

Connecting all $\mathcal{E}_r^\ell, 0 \le r < R$, we derive from E a composite function $\mathcal{E}^\ell$ (an example is illustrated in Fig. 1):

$$\mathcal{E}^\ell = \mathcal{E}_{R-1}^\ell \circ \mathcal{E}_{R-2}^\ell \circ \cdots \circ \mathcal{E}_0^\ell, \quad \mathcal{E}_r^\ell : (\mathbb{F}_2^n)^{2^\ell} \to (\mathbb{F}_2^n)^{2^\ell}. \qquad (7)$$

Definition 1. (ℓ^{th} Higher-order Algebraic Transitional Form (ℓ^{th} HATF)). *The composite function in Eq. 7 above is called the ℓth Higher-order Algebraic Transitional Form (ℓ^{th} HATF) of E. If the order information is clear from the context, we will omit the superscript ℓ for convenience.*

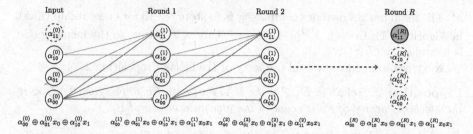

Fig. 1. An illustration of $\mathcal{E}^\ell$ when $\ell = 2$ (2nd HATF). The input is $X \oplus x_0 \Delta_0 \oplus x_1 \Delta_1 = \alpha_{00}^{(0)} \oplus \alpha_{01}^{(0)} x_0 \oplus \alpha_{10}^{(0)} x_1$. The outputs of the ith round of $\mathcal{E}^\ell$ are the constant monomial and coefficients of $x_0, x_1, x_0 x_1$. Finally, the R-round HDL bias is just the bias of $\alpha_{11}^{(R)}$.

Algorithm 1. Construction of the HATF $\mathcal{E}^\ell$ from a cipher E

Input: 1. the ANFs of components of $E = E_{R-1} \circ \cdots \circ E_0$,
        2. the order ℓ,
        3. the block size n,
        4. an ℓth-order difference $(\Delta_0, \ldots, \Delta_{\ell-1})$,
        5. an input value X
Output: the ℓth-order HATF $\mathcal{E}^\ell = \mathcal{E}_{R-1}^\ell \circ \cdots \circ \mathcal{E}_0^\ell$
1: Let $\alpha_0^{(0)} = X$, $\alpha_{e_i}^{(0)} = \Delta_i$, $\Delta_u^{(0)} = 0$ for all $wt(u) \geq 2$
2: **for** $0 \leq r < R$ **do**
3:     **for** $0 \leq i < n$ **do**
4:         Calculate $f = E_r[i]\left(\bigoplus_{u \in \mathbb{F}_2^n} \alpha_u^{(r)} \boldsymbol{x}^u\right)$
5:         **for** $0 \leq u < 2^\ell$ **do**
6:             Calculate $\alpha_u^{(r+1)}[i] = \mathsf{Coe}\,(f, \boldsymbol{x}^u)$
7:         **end for**
8:     **end for**
9: **end for**
10: **return** $\alpha_u^{(r)}$ for all $1 \leq r \leq R$ and $u \in \mathbb{F}_2^n$, which are actually $\mathcal{E}^\ell$

Algorithm 1 shows the detailed process of constructing a HATF. The time complexity of Algorithm 1 is dominated by line 4, *i.e.*, calculating $E_r[i]\left(\bigoplus_{u \in \mathbb{F}_2^n} \alpha_u \boldsymbol{x}^u\right)$. If $\deg(E_r) = d$, then the complexity of calculating $E_r[i]$ is dominated by the calculation of all the d-degree monomials in $E_r[i]$. For each d-degree monomial, we need to multiply d bits of $\bigoplus_{u \in \mathbb{F}_2^n} \alpha_u \boldsymbol{x}^u$. The complexity of computing a d-degree monomial is about $2^{d\ell}$ multiplications and $2^{d\ell}$ additions. Suppose there are t d-degree monomials in $E_r[i]$, the time complexity of computing all d-degree monomials is about $C_1 = 2 \cdot t \cdot 2^{d\ell}$. Then the complexity of computing an R-round cipher is approximately $C_h = 2 \cdot R \cdot n \cdot t \cdot 2^{d\ell}$ multiplications or additions. For a specific cipher, the round R, block size n, algebraic degree d and the number of d-degree monomials are all constants, thus the complexity of constructing the HATF is $\mathcal{O}(2^{d\ell})$.

The main part of memory complexity is to store $\alpha_u^{(r)}[i]$ for every round (line 6 in Algorithm 1). In each $\alpha_u^{(r)}[i]$, there are at most 2^ℓ terms, so the memory cost is bounded by $\mathcal{O}(2^{2\ell})$.

Next, we introduce a useful property of HATF as Proposition 2.

Proposition 2. *Let $\mathcal{E}^\ell$ in Eq. 7 be the HATF of E in Eq. 6. For each $0 \le r < R$, the algebraic degree of $\mathcal{E}_r^\ell$ is equal to the algebraic degree of E_r.*

Proof. Let $\deg(E_r) = d$ and consider the output of $\mathcal{E}_r^\ell$. Since

$$\alpha_u^{(r+1)} = \mathsf{Coe}\left(E_r\left(\bigoplus_{u \in \mathbb{F}_2^n} \alpha_u^{(r)} \boldsymbol{x}^u \right), \boldsymbol{x}^u \right),$$

each bit of $\alpha_u^{(r+1)} \boldsymbol{x}^u$ is obtained by multiplying at most d different bits of $\bigoplus_{u \in \mathbb{F}_2^n} \alpha_u^{(r)} \boldsymbol{x}^u$. Therefore, the algebraic degree of $\alpha_u^{(r+1)}$ is at most d. Finally, when $u = \mathbf{0}$, $\alpha_0^{(r+1)}$ is just the output of $E_r(\alpha_0^{(r)})$, so $\deg(\mathcal{E}_r^\ell) = \deg(E_r)$. $\qquad\square$

4.2   Estimation of the HDL Bias Based on HATF

Suppose we have obtained the ℓth HATF of a cipher $E = E_{R-1} \circ \cdots \circ E_0$ according to Algorithm 1. The biases of the ℓth-order HD/HDL approximations of all the output bits of E are biases of $\alpha_1^{(R)}$ (where $\mathbf{1}$ is the ℓ-bit vector with all elements being 1). From the HATF of E, we know the composite form of $\alpha_1^{(R)}$ is as follows,

$$\left(\alpha_u^{(0)}, u \in \mathbb{F}_2^n\right) \xrightarrow{\mathcal{E}_0} \left(\alpha_u^{(1)}, u \in \mathbb{F}_2^n\right) \xrightarrow{\mathcal{E}_1} \cdots \xrightarrow{\mathcal{E}_{R-2}} \left(\alpha_u^{(R-1)}, u \in \mathbb{F}_2^n\right) \xrightarrow{\mathcal{E}_{R-1}} \alpha_1^{(R)}.$$

Besides, the bias of $a_u^{(0)}, u \in \mathbb{F}_2^n$ is available since they are the input values by adversaries (under a chosen-plaintext attack)[3].

Under the assumption that all the bits of $\alpha_u^{(r)}, u \in \mathbb{F}_2^n$ are independent, the bias of $\alpha_u^{(r+1)}, u \in \mathbb{F}_2^n$ can be estimated according to Lemma 1. Therefore, we can calculate the bias of $\alpha_1^{(R)}$ from $\alpha_u^{(0)}, u \in \mathbb{F}_2^n$ iteratively.

The detailed process is shown in Algorithm 2 with blue words. According to Lemma 1, the time complexity of computing the bias of a Boolean function is exponentially related to the number of variables. For a fixed round r and index i, $\alpha_1^{(r+1)}[i]$ has the most number of variables as compared to $\alpha_u^{(r+1)}, u \ne \mathbf{1}$. If the algebraic degree of $\alpha_1^{(r+1)}[i]$ is d, then the number of variables in it is at most $d \times 2^\ell$, and the numbers of variables in other $\alpha_u^{(r)}[i], u \ne \mathbf{1}$ are significantly smaller. Therefore the time complexity of line 5 in Algorithm 2 is about $2^{d \times 2^\ell}$. The whole complexity is then approximately $R \cdot n \cdot 2^\ell \cdot 2^{d \times 2^\ell}$, which can be bounded by $\mathcal{O}(2^{\ell + d \times 2^\ell})$. The memory complexity is negligible.

---

[3] In all attacks of this paper, we simply use uniform $\alpha_u^{(0)}$, *i.e.*, the input values do not have biases.

Algorithm 2. Estimate the bias of $\alpha_1^{(R)}$

Input: 1. the HATF $\mathcal{E}^\ell = \mathcal{E}_{R-1}^\ell \circ \cdots \circ \mathcal{E}_0^\ell$,
  2. the bias of $\alpha_u^{(0)}[i]$ for all $0 \le i < n$ and $u \in \mathbb{F}_2^n$
Output: the ℓth-order HATF $\mathcal{E}^\ell = \mathcal{E}_{R-1}^\ell \circ \cdots \circ \mathcal{E}_0^\ell$

1: **for** $1 \le r < R$ **do**
2:   **for** $0 \le i < n$ **do**
3:     **for** $0 \le u < 2^\ell$ **do**
4:       /* For general cases */
5:       Compute the bias of $\alpha_u^{(r)}[i]$ using Lemma 1
6:       /* For quadratic cases */
7:       Find M so that $\alpha_u^{(r)}[i] = g \circ M^{-1}$ (Lemma 2)
8:       Compute the bias of $M^{-1}\left(\alpha_u^{(r)}, u \in \mathbb{F}_2^n\right)$ (Piling-up lemma [22])
9:       Compute the bias of $\alpha_u^{(r)}[i]$ with $g \circ M^{-1}$ (Lemma 3)
10:     **end for**
11:   **end for**
12: **end for**
13: **return** the bias of $\alpha_1^{(R)}[i]$ for $0 \le i < n$

Reducing the Complexity for Quadratic Boolean Functions. Since the complexity of estimating the bias from HATF is $\mathcal{O}(2^{\ell+d\times 2^\ell})$, even a small order will result in high complexity. In the following, we show that for ciphers whose round functions are quadratic, the complexity can be reduced from $\mathcal{O}(2^{\ell+d\times 2^\ell})$ to $\mathcal{O}(2^{3.8\ell})$.

Note that a Boolean function is quadratic if its algebraic degree is 2. A disjoint quadratic Boolean function is defined as follows,

Definition 2 (Disjoint quadratic Boolean function). *A quadratic Boolean function is disjoint if all its quadratic monomials do not share any common variables.*

Any quadratic Boolean functions can be decomposed into a disjoint form [15, P438]. In [24], Shi *et al.* applied this method to cryptanalysis of Morus. We omit the detailed algorithm here and only give a small example to show its core idea.

Example 1. Let $f = x_0x_1 \oplus x_0x_2 \oplus x_1x_2$. It is not disjoint, but we can convert it to a disjoint Boolean function with the following steps:

1. $f = x_0x_1 \oplus x_0x_2 \oplus x_1x_2 = x_0(x_1 \oplus x_2) \oplus x_1x_2$, we first let $x_1' = x_1 \oplus x_2$ to obtain $g = x_0x_1' + (x_1' \oplus x_2)x_2 = x_0x_1' \oplus x_1'x_2 \oplus x_2$.
2. $g = x_1'(x_0 \oplus x_2) + x_2$, we then let $x_0' = x_0 \oplus x_2$ and obtain $g = x_1'x_0' \oplus x_2$, then g is a disjoint quadratic Boolean function.

During the process, we do linear variable substitutions with $x_1' = x_1 \oplus x_2$ and $x_0' = x_0 \oplus x_2$. For sake of convenience, we let $x_2' = x_2$, so $g = f(M[x_0, x_1, x_2]^t)$ where $M = \begin{bmatrix} 1 & 0 & 1 \\ 0 & 1 & 1 \\ 0 & 0 & 1 \end{bmatrix}$. Equivalently, $f = g \circ M^{-1}$.

We write this method as a lemma for a convenient citation.

Lemma 2. (*[15]*). *A quadratic Boolean function* $f : \mathbb{F}_2^n \to \mathbb{F}_2^n$ *can be converted into a disjoint Boolean function* $g : \mathbb{F}_2^n \to \mathbb{F}_2^n$ *with* $g = f \circ M$ *where* $M \in \mathbb{F}_2^{n \times n}$ *is an invertible matrix. The time complexity is* $\mathcal{O}(n^{3.8})$ *and the memory complexity is* $\Omega(n^2)$.

The bias of a disjoint quadratic Boolean function can be computed with ease, as shown in Lemma 3.

Lemma 3. *Let* $g : \mathbb{F}_2^n \to \mathbb{F}_2$ *be a disjoint quadratic Boolean function as*

$$g = g_0 \oplus g_1 \oplus \cdots \oplus g_{T-1}$$

where all $g_i, 0 \leq i < T$ *do not share common variables, and the biases of all input variables of* g *are available. Then we can compute the bias of each* g_i *using Lemma 1 with small complexities. Finally, the bias of* g *can be computed with the piling-up lemma with biases of all* g_i.

According to Proposition 2, when a cipher uses quadratic round functions, the round functions of its HATF is also quadratic. For calculating the bias of $\alpha_u^{(r+1)}[i]$ (line 5 of Algorithm 2) from $\alpha_u^{(r)}$, we first find an invertible matrix M such that $g = \alpha_u^{(r+1)}[i] \circ M$ is disjoint according to Lemma 2. Equivalently, $\alpha_u^{(r+1)}[i] = g \circ M^{-1}(\alpha_u^{(r)}, u \in \mathbb{F}_2^n)$.[4] Based on the biases of $\alpha_u^{(r)}$, the bias of $M^{-1}\left(\alpha_u^{(r)}, u \in \mathbb{F}_2^n\right)$ can be calculated using the piling-up lemma. Applying the disjoint Boolean function g to the output of $M^{-1}\left(\alpha_u^{(r)}, u \in \mathbb{F}_2^n\right)$, the bias of $\alpha_u^{(r+1)}[i]$ can be obtained according to Lemma 3.

The process is also given in Algorithm 2, but with red words. The complexity is dominated by line 7, *i.e.*, converting $\alpha_u^{(r+1)}[i]$ to a disjoint quadratic form. Since the number of variables in $\alpha_u^{(r+1)}[i]$ is at most $2 \times 2^\ell$ (we are working on quadratic functions), the time complexity of line 7 is $\mathcal{O}(2^{3.8\ell})$, and the memory complexity is $\Omega(2^{2\ell})$.

Considering both Algorithms 1 and 2, the time complexity of computing the biases of the ℓth HDL approximations is $\mathcal{O}(2^{\ell+d\times 2^\ell})$ in general case, and $\mathcal{O}(2^{3.8\ell})$ for ciphers with quadratic round functions. The memory complexity is $\Omega(2^{2\ell})$.

4.3   Discussion on the Assumption of Independence and Precision

HATF works on the assumption that all bits of $\alpha_u^{(r)}, 0 \leq r < R, u \in \mathbb{F}_2^n$ are independent. If we directly use Algorithm 1 to construct the HATF, many related $\alpha_u^{(r+1)}[i]$ will be regarded as independent variables (line 6 of Algorithm 1), which makes our assumption less valid. Thus, we need to avoid such cases as much as possible. Methods that we use to avoid these related variables are introduced as follows, both of which are concerned about line 6 only

---

[4] Note that not all bits in $\alpha_u^{(r)}$, $u \in \mathbb{F}_2^n$ are input of $g \circ M^{-1}$. We write it in this way for convenience.

1. When $\deg(\alpha_u^{(r+1)}[i]) \leq 1$, we do not introduce a new variable $\alpha_u^{(r+1)}[i]$ to substitute $\mathsf{Coe}(f, \boldsymbol{x}^u)$, because variables in linear expressions are easier to be related with other variables. In this case, the following computation will depend on $\mathsf{Coe}(f, \boldsymbol{x}^u)$ directly rather than $\alpha_u^{(r+1)}[i]$.

2. We use a dictionary Q to store each variable substitution as

$$Q[\mathsf{Coe}(f, \boldsymbol{x}^u)] = \alpha_u^{(r+1)}[i],$$

then if $\mathsf{Coe}(f, \boldsymbol{x}^u)$ or $\mathsf{Coe}(f, \boldsymbol{x}^u) \oplus 1$ has been in Q, we do not need to introduce new variables, $\alpha_u^{(r+1)}[i]$ or $\alpha_u^{(r+1)}[i] \oplus 1$ can be reused.

By these two methods, we can avoid most simple related-bit cases. Other kinds of relations are relatively more complicated and are not considered in this paper. We hope that those bits with complicated relationships can be approximately treated as independent bits.

In terms of the time/memory complexities, the first method increases the number of variables linearly but does not affect its order of magnitude; the second method saves the number of new variables, so it actually reduces the complexity of Algorithm 2. Hence, the time/memory complexities of HATF remain unchanged up to the $\mathcal{O}/\Omega$ notations.

4.4 Improving the Precision with Partitioning Technique

As the order and rounds increase, the HATF systems become more and more complicated. The precision of HATF for complicated Boolean functions according to Lemma 1 or Lemma 3 drops accordingly. To mitigate the imprecision, we partition the whole input space (in the HDL distinguishers, the input includes both the public and secret variables) into several smaller *equal-size* subsets. Given a cipher E, suppose we have partitioned the whole input S into κ disjoint subsets as $S = S_0 + S_1 + \cdots + S_{\kappa-1}$ (we use "+" to stress that S_i are disjoint) where $S_i, 0 \leq i < \kappa$ have the same size. The bias of $\mathsf{Coe}(E, \boldsymbol{\pi}(\boldsymbol{x}))$ is the average value among the S. Note that $\mathsf{Coe}(E, \boldsymbol{\pi}(\boldsymbol{x}))$ is a Boolean function of values in S (recall Sect. 4.1). Let $|S_i| = w$ for $0 \leq i < \kappa$ and $|S| = \kappa w$, we have

$$
\begin{aligned}
\mathbf{Bias}\left(\mathsf{Coe}\left(\mathcal{E}, \boldsymbol{\pi}(\boldsymbol{x})\right)\right) &= \frac{\#\{\mathsf{Coe}\left(\mathcal{E}, \boldsymbol{\pi}(\boldsymbol{x})\right)(s) = 0 : s \in S\}}{\kappa w} - \frac{1}{2} \\
&= \frac{\sum_{i=0}^{\kappa-1} \#\{\mathsf{Coe}\left(\mathcal{E}_{S_i}, \boldsymbol{\pi}(\boldsymbol{x})\right)(s') = 0 : s' \in S_i\}}{\kappa w} - \frac{1}{2} \\
&= \frac{1}{\kappa} \sum_{i=0}^{\kappa-1} \frac{\#\{\mathsf{Coe}\left(\mathcal{E}_{S_i}, \boldsymbol{\pi}(\boldsymbol{x})\right)(s') = 0 : s' \in S_i\}}{w} - \frac{1}{2} \\
&= \frac{1}{\kappa} \sum_{i=0}^{\kappa-1} \left(\frac{\#\{\mathsf{Coe}\left(\mathcal{E}_{S_i}, \boldsymbol{\pi}(\boldsymbol{x})\right)(s') = 0 : s' \in S_i\}}{w} - \frac{1}{2} \right) \\
&= \frac{1}{\kappa} \sum_{i=0}^{\kappa-1} \left(\mathbf{Bias}\left(\mathsf{Coe}\left(\mathcal{E}_{S_i}, \boldsymbol{\pi}(\boldsymbol{x})\right)\right)\right),
\end{aligned}
\tag{8}
$$

where $\mathcal{E}_{S_i}$ is the HATF of E with the subset S_i as the input. As a result, for each of these subsets, we first apply our HATF technique to evaluate the bias for each S_i, then calculate the average bias among all these S_i. The partition simplifies the ANFs of $\mathcal{E}^\ell$, so for each subset, the precision can be improved. The methods of partitioning the input are chosen in different ways for different ciphers, which will be described in our applications.

4.5   Conditional HDL Cryptanalysis by Injecting Conditions

In [20], to improve the biases of DL approximations, Liu *et al.* imposed some conditions to the first R_0 rounds in the ATF. The basic principle is to zero the differences in the first R_0 rounds as much as possible. In our HDL attacks based on HATF, we can also use this method to obtain a set of conditions to improve the HDL biases.

In the construction of the first R_0-round HATF, we put the first non-constant $\alpha_u^{(r)}, r \le r_0, u \ne \mathbf{0}$ into a set I as ideal generators. Next, we reduce all the $\alpha_u^{(r)}$ over the ideal generated from I, denoted by "mod I". If a certain $\alpha_u^{(r)}$ cannot be reduced to a constant, we will add this $\alpha_u^{(r)}$ into I and use the updated I to reduce the remaining non-constant $\alpha_u^{(r)}$. Finally, all $\alpha_u^{(r)}, u \ne \mathbf{0}, r \le r_0$ are usually reduced to constants, and a system of equations $S = \{f = 0 \mid f \in I\}$ is obtained. When the conditions in I are satisfied, the HDL distinguisher will have a significantly higher bias. By checking these conditions, we can recover the secret keys. These conditions are also used for partitioning the input space.

5   Applications to Ascon Initialization

Ascon, designed by Dobraunig, Eichlseder, Mendel, and Schläffer, is a family of AEAD and hash algorithms [12]. It has been selected as the winner in the NIST Lightweight Cryptography competition. Due to page limits, the description of the Ascon AEAD and its permutation is provided in [14], we also recommend that readers refer to [12] for the whole specification.

Notations used for describing the Ascon initialization. For the Ascon initialization, the 320-bit output state after r rounds is denoted by

$$S^{(r)} = S^{(r)}[0]\|S^{(r)}[1]\|S^{(r)}[2]\|S^{(r)}[3]\|S^{(r)}[4],$$

where $S^{(r)}[i]$ is the ith word (the ith row) of $S^{(r)}$; $S^{(0)}$ is the input of the whole permutation. The jth bit of $S^{(r)}[i]$ is denoted by $S^{(r)}[i][j]$ where $0 \le i < 5, 0 \le j < 64$. $S^{(r)}[0][0]$ is the leftmost bit of the first row of the state matrix $S^{(r)}$. Let p_C, p_S, p_L represent the operations of *addition of constants, substitution layer, linear diffusion layer*, respectively. Then $S^{(r)} = (p_L \circ p_S \circ p_C)^r(S^{(0)})$. The adversary can only access the first word of the output state for Ascon-128, and the first two words for Ascon-128a (our cryptanalysis focuses on Ascon-128, so it is also applicable to Ascon-128a). Since the linear layer is applied to each row, we do not consider the linear layer of the last round.

Since p_S is quadratic, the time complexity for an ℓth-order HDL cryptanalysis of Ascon is $\mathcal{O}(2^{3.8\ell})$. To apply the HATF technique, we need to decompose the

R-round ASCON initialization into several small parts. In this paper, we take the same method to cut the ASCON functions as [20][5]. Firstly, we divide the Sbox of ASCON into two parts, p_{S_L} and p_{S_N}. The first part of the Sbox, p_{S_L}, is a linear operation

$$x_0 = x_0 \oplus x_4; \qquad x_4 = x_4 \oplus x_3; \qquad x_2 = x_2 \oplus x_1;$$

where $(x_0, x_1, x_2, x_3, x_4)$ is the input of p_{S_L}. The round function of the ASCON permutation is then divided into two parts, $p_A = p_{S_L} \circ p_{P_C}$ and $p_B = p_L \circ p_{S_N}$.

In Algorithm 1, we let $E^{(0)} = p_A$, and $E^{(r)} = p_A \circ p_B$ for $1 \leq r < R$, and $E^{(R)} = p_{S_N}$. Thus R-round ASCON is represented as

$$E = p_{S_N} \circ (p_A \circ p_B)^{R-1} \circ p_A$$

The 128-bit key and 128-bit nonce are set to 256 binary variables, the IV is set to the constant specified in [12].

When applying the ℓth-order HDL distinguishing attack on the ASCON initialization, we choose $\Delta_j, 0 \leq j < \ell$ as the ℓ linearly-independent differences, where Δ_j is active in the two nonce bits of the same Sbox, i.e., $S^{(0)}[3][i_j]$ and $S^{(0)}[4][i_j]$ ($0 \leq i_j < 64$). (We also tested other kinds of differences, but this setting brings the best results.) Then the input difference can be denoted by an ℓ-tuple, denoted by $\Delta(i_0, i_1, \ldots, i_{\ell-1})$. To simplify the ANFs, we by default always set $S^{(0)}[3][i_j] = S^{(0)}[4][i_j] = 0$. For R-round outputs, we consider the single-bit bias of the first word, i.e., $S^{(R)}[0][i], 0 \leq i < 64$. We choose such input differences because the input of ASCON comes into Sboxes directly and our choices of input can simplify the ANFs.

5.1   HDL Distinguishers for ASCON

Application 1: Revisiting the first-order DL distinguishers for 4- and 5-round ASCON. Our first application is to revisit two DL distinguishers on the 4- and 5-round initialization of ASCON. These two DL distinguishers were first found by the designers in [11] with experiments. The input difference was set as $\Delta(0)$. Although the classical DL attack theory predicted that the 4-round distinguisher has a bias of 2^{-20}, experiments showed that its real bias is about 2^{-2} which is significantly higher. Later, at EUROCRYPT 2019, Bar-On et al. [1] revisited this distinguisher and used the Differential-Linear Connectivity Table (DLCT) technique to give a higher theoretical estimation of 2^{-5}. Recently, at CRYPTO 2021, Liu et al. used the ATF to improve the theoretical bias to $2^{-2.36}$, which is the most precise value before this paper. However, none of the three methods can find any 5-round DL distinguisher.

Our HATF technique is a higher-order extension of the ATF technique, so it is also applicable to the first-order DL attack. With the partitioning technique, we achieved better estimation. Setting the input difference as $\Delta(0)$, the two key bits in the same Sbox, i.e., $S^{(0)}[1][0]$ and $S^{(0)}[2][0]$, are chosen to partition the

---

[5] Our experiments show such cutting can lead to slightly better results compared to the cutting method according to the rounds, in the case of HATF.

input space. Let $S^{(0)}[1][0]||S^{(0)}[2][0]$ be 00, 01, 10 and 10, we partition the input subspace to 4 equal-size subspaces. The bias of $S^{(4)}[0][54]$ is then

$$
\texttt{Bias}(S^{(4)}[0][54]) = \begin{cases} 2^{-2.678}, & \text{when } (S^{(0)}[1][0], S^{(0)}[2][0]) = 00 \\ 2^{-2.678}, & \text{when } (S^{(0)}[1][0], S^{(0)}[2][0]) = 01 \\ 2^{-1.678}, & \text{when } (S^{(0)}[1][0], S^{(0)}[2][0]) = 10 \\ 2^{-1.678}, & \text{when } (S^{(0)}[1][0], S^{(0)}[2][0]) = 11 \end{cases}
$$

According to the partitioning technique and Eq. 8,

$$
\texttt{Bias}(S^{(4)}[0][54]) = 2^{-2}(2^{-2.678} + 2^{-2.678} + 2^{-1.678} + 2^{-1.678}) \approx 2^{-2.09}.
$$

This theoretical bias is again closer to the experimental bias 2^{-2}.

For 5-round ASCON, the known DL distinguisher is also with the input difference $\Delta(0)$, the bias of $S^{(5)}[0][47]$ is about 2^{-9}.[6] With the above partition, the bias from the HATF is always 0, hence we need to partition the space into smaller ones to detect the bias. According to Sect. 4.5, we can derive a set of 7 conditions that affect the bias significantly. Since the 7 conditions are all balanced Boolean functions, by assigning all possible values to them (every Boolean function then has two statuses: true or false), we can partition the whole space into 128 subspaces[7]. Computing HATF for every individual subspace, we obtain the average bias of approximately 2^{-10}. This is the first theoretical method that can predict this 5-round DL bias.

Application 2: 2nd-order HDL distinguisher for 4-round ASCON. Our second application is the 2nd-order DL distinguisher for 4-round ASCON initialization. We exhaustively search through all possible $\Delta(0, i), 1 \le i < 64$ as our 2nd-order differences, all such differences lead to highly biased 4-round output bits. Especially, when $(i, j) = (0, 60)$, the bias of $S^{(4)}[0][50]$ is $\frac{1}{2}$, i.e., this is a deterministic 2nd-order DL bias. With 2^{26} randomly chosen samples, this deterministic distinguisher is fully verified. We plot the theoretical and experimental biases of the 64 bits of $S^{(4)}[0]$ as shown in Fig. 2a, and the concrete data is provided in the full version. The theoretical biases are very close to the experimental ones. According to these 2nd-order HDL biases, one sample, i.e., 2^2 chosen nonces is enough to distinguish the 4-round initialization.

Application 3: 2nd-order HDL distinguisher for 5-round ASCON. In our 2nd-order HDL distinguishing attack on the 5-round ASCON initialization, we also exhausted all possible $\Delta(0, i), 1 \le i < 64$ differences and checked every single bit output of $S^{(5)}[0]$, the most significant bias is $S^{(5)}[0][50]$ when $(i, j) = (0, 3)$ which is predicted to be $2^{-7.05}$ by HATF. We use 2^{26} samples to check this bias and find that it should be $2^{-6.60}$ approximately, which is slightly larger but still considerably close to our prediction.

---

[6] Under the default setting that $S^{(0)}[3][0] = S^{(0)}[4][0]$, see [11] for more information about this DL distinguisher.

[7] We also encourage readers to read our code to further understand how we use these conditions: https://github.com/hukaisdu/HDL/blob/main/HATF/ascon.cpp.

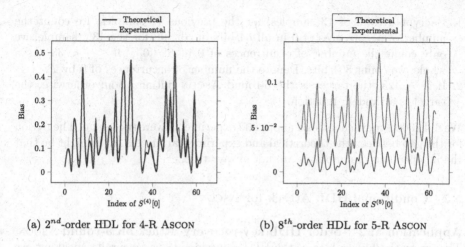

(a) 2nd-order HDL for 4-R Ascon   (b) 8th-order HDL for 5-R Ascon

Fig. 2. Theoretical and experimental biases for 4-round and 5-round Ascon

Application 4: 8th-order HDL distinguisher for 5-round Ascon.

Generally speaking, as the order increases, the biases become more and more significant according to HATF. Here we give the results of the 8th-order HDL distinguishing attack on the 5-round Ascon initialization. We randomly select 8 indexes $(i_0, i_1, \ldots, i_7) = (0, 8, 9, 13, 14, 26, 43, 60)$ as the 8th-order input differences $\Delta(0, 8, 9, 13, 14, 26, 43, 60)$. The 16 key bits in the same Sboxes with the input differences are used to partition the input space into 2^{16} subspaces. Applying HATF to each of the subspaces, and calculating the average bias, we find all single bits are highly biased. For example, HATF predicts that $\mathtt{Bias}(S^{(5)}[0][50]) = 2^{-4.73}$. With 2^{22} samples, experiments show that this bias is about $2^{-3.35}$. The average bias over the 64 output bits is predicted as $2^{-6.34}$, and the experimental result is $2^{-4.11}$. The theoretical and experimental biases of all 64 bits of $S^{(5)}[0]$ are shown in Fig. 2b, the concrete biases are provided in the full version.

We use this 8th-order HDL approximation to mount the best distinguishing attack on 5-round Ascon. Suppose that we encrypt N samples, we can observe $64N$ output bits in total. Regarding each bit of $S^{(5)}[0]$ as a Bernoulli experiment with expectation of $\frac{1}{2} + 2^{-4.11}$, The number of occurrences of 0 conforms to the binomial distribution $\mathcal{B}(64N, \frac{1}{2} + 2^{-4.11})$, which can be approximated by a normal distribution $\mathcal{N}(35.71N, 15.79N)$ for a convenient analysis. In a random case, the number of occurrences of 0 conforms to another binomial distribution $\mathcal{B}(64N, \frac{1}{2})$, which can be approximated by $\mathcal{N}(32N, 16N)$. The method to distinguish two normal distributions has been well-known in cryptanalysis, which is summarized in our full vesion. Setting that the probabilities for Type-I and Type-II errors to be $\alpha_0 = \alpha_1 = 0.05$, i.e., we require 95% success rate, we have $N \approx 3^{3.65}$, i.e., we need to check about 801 output bits. The threshold is $\tau \approx 424$. The time complexity is about $2^{11.65}$.

We can mount a distinguishing attack as follows,

1. Encrypt a total of 13 samples, for the previous 12 samples, we count the number of occurrences of 0 in all 64 bits of $S^{(5)}[0]$; for the 13th sample, we only count the number of occurrences of 0 in $S^{(5)}[0][j], 0 \leq j < 33$. As a whole, we count 801 bits. Denote the number of occurrences of 0 by T,
2. If $T \geq 423$, the target is the 5-round ASCON initialization; otherwise, the target is a random function.

We did 1000 experiments, and about 900 experiments were successful. The reason for the gap between the theoretical and experimental success rates might be that the independent assumptions are not always true.

5.2   Conditional HDL Attack for ASCON

Application 5: 2nd-order HDL key-recovery attack on 5-round ASCON. Thanks to the higher bias of the HDL approximations, generally speaking, we can mount key-recovery attacks more efficiently than DL attacks. In this paper, we use several 2nd-order HDL approximations to recover the secret keys from 5-round ASCON, which is the most efficient attack for 5-round ASCON thus far. The idea of this key-recovery attack is similar to the conditional DL attacks introduced in [20]. When applying the HATF, we inject the conditions for the first two rounds according to Sect. 4.5. By exhausting all possible 2nd-order differences $\Delta(i, j)$, all of them lead to at least one highly biased bit. The two most significant ones are listed as follows (readers can use our code to generate all of them),

1. When $\Delta(i,j) = \Delta(i', i' + 9), 0 \leq i' < 64$, under 14 conditions, $\texttt{Bias}(S^{(5)}[0][27 + i']) = 0.375$,
2. When $\Delta(i,j) = \Delta(i', i' + 24), 0 \leq i' < 64$, under 16 conditions, $\texttt{Bias}(S^{(5)}[0][51 + i']) = 0.313$.

Experiments with 2^{26} samples have fully verified these biased bits. With these two 2nd-order approximations, we can do the key-recovery attack with about 2^{22} computations. Since this attack is similar to the key-recovery attack on XOODYAK, we provide all the details in the full version of this paper.

Application 6: 3rd-order HDL approximation for 6-round ASCON. At the end of this section, we present a conditional 3rd-order HDL approximation for 6-round ASCON initialization. In [20], Liu *et al.* showed that there are no conditional DL approximations for 6-round ASCON initialization. As the order increases, it is not surprising that there are truly some HDL approximations for 6 (or even more) rounds. However, from the 5-round to the 6-round, the complexity required to find a highly biased approximation become significantly larger. In our conditional 3rd-order HDL approximation, we inject 24 conditions into the first two rounds of the HATF. The input difference is $\Delta(0, 30, 61)$, the bias occurs in $S^{(6)}[0][34]$ and is predicted as $2^{-25.97}$. It is difficult to verify this bias with experiments directly. However, since $S^{(6)}[0][34]$ is the output bit of the Sbox in the 6th round, we can verify the bias of bits in $S^{(5)}$. According to the linear approximation table (LAT) of ASCON's Sbox, there is a mask propagation 0x3 → 0x10 with a bias of -2^{-2}. Thus, $S^{(5)}[3][34] \oplus S^{(5)}[4][34]$ (the two bits are inputs of the Sbox related to $S^{(6)}[0][34]$) may have a high bias. We use 2^{30} samples to test it, the bias of $S^{(5)}[3][34] \oplus S^{(5)}[4][34]$ is about 2^{-14}. Considering the piling-up lemma [22] and we have 8 approximations, the bias of $S^{(6)}[0][34]$ should be around 2^{-22}. It means that the 6-round conditional 3rd HDL approximation is true.

6   Applications to XOODYAK INITIALIZATION AND XOODOO

XOODYAK is a cryptographic primitive for hashing, authenticated encryption, and MAC computation, and is one of the ten finalists of the NIST LWC competition [9]. XOODYAK uses XOODOO as its underlying cryptographic permutation, which is a family of 384-bit to 384-bit permutations [8]. The 384-bit state of XOODOO is arranged into a $4 \times 3 \times 32$ cube and a state bit is denoted by $S[x][y][z]$. When x and z are fixed, the three bits of $S[x][\cdot][z]$ are called a column; when y is fixed, the 128 bits of $S[\cdot][y][\cdot]$ are called a plane. The input and output states of the rth round are denoted by $S^{(r-1)}$ and $S^{(r)}$, respectively. The initial state is then denoted by $S^{(0)}$. One round of XOODOO consists of five operations as $\rho_{east} \circ \chi \circ \iota \circ \rho_{west} \circ \theta$.

$$\theta: \quad S[x][y][z] = S[x][y][z] \oplus \bigoplus_y S[x-1][y][z-5] \oplus \bigoplus_y S[x-1][y][z-14]$$

$$\rho_{west}: \quad S[x][1][z] = S[x-1][1][z], S[x][2][z] = S[x][2][z-11]$$

$$\iota: \quad S[0][0] = S[0][0] \oplus RC_i$$

$$\chi: \quad S[x][y][z] = S[x][y][z] \oplus ((S[x][y+1][z] \oplus 1) \cdot S[x][y+2][z])$$

$$\rho_{east}: \quad S[x][1][z] = S[x][1][z-1], S[x][2][z] = S[x-2][2][z-8]$$

RC_i in the ι operation is the i-round constant, which can be found in [8]. Note that χ is a quadratic function. XOODYAK AEAD supports three methods to handle the nonces. This paper focuses on the third method's initialization. In this mode, the 128-bit state of $S^{(0)}[x][0][z], 0 \leq x < 4, 0 \leq z < 32$ are initialized by an 128-bit key, denoted by k_i where $i = z + 32x$, and the remaining 256 bits of $S^{(0)}[x][y][z], 0 \leq x < 4, 1 \leq y < 3, 0 \leq z < 32$ by a 256-bit nonce, denoted by u_i where $i = z + 32(x + 4(y-1))$. Then, XOODOO is applied to the initialized state, and the first 192 bits are visible and XORed to the first block of the plaintext. The following HDL approximations for XOODYAK and XOODOO are found mainly by trying all low-weight difference-mask pairs.

6.1   HDL Distinguishers for XOODYAK AND XOODOO

Application 1: Revisiting the DL Distinguishers for 4-round XOODYAK. In [13], Dunkelman and Weizman gave the first DL attacks on 4-round XOODYAK under the single-key model and on 5-round XOODYAK under the related-key model. The two distinguishers used in the attacks are detected by experiments. HATF with the partitioning technique can easily give the theoretical biases for the two distinguishers.

For the 4 rounds, the input difference is in (u_0, u_{128}) (*i.e.*, $S^{(0)}[0][1][0]$ and $S^{(0)}[0][2][0]$), and the output bit of $S^{(4)}[0][1][15]$ has a bias of about $2^{-9.7}$. Applying our HATF technique to the 4-round XOODYAK, we first obtain a set of 4 conditions that are injected into the first round to zero all the differences after the first round according to Sect. 4.5. These 4 conditions are listed as follows,

$$u_{102} = k_{11} \oplus k_{102} \oplus k_{125} \oplus u_{125} \oplus u_{230} \oplus u_{253}$$
$$u_{70} = k_{70} \oplus k_{93} \oplus u_{93} \oplus u_{107} \oplus u_{198} \oplus u_{221} \oplus 1$$
$$u_7 = k_7 \oplus k_{16} \oplus u_{16} \oplus u_{135} \oplus u_{144} \oplus u_{181}$$
$$u_{18} = k_{18} \oplus k_{27} \oplus k_{32} \oplus u_{27} \oplus u_{146} \oplus u_{155} \oplus 1$$

Since these 4 conditions are all linear and independent, they can partition the whole input space into 16 subspaces by assigning all possible values to them. After applying the first-order HATF technique, the bias of $S^{(4)}[0][1][15]$ is

$$\text{Bias}(S^{(4)}[0][1][15]) = 2^{-9.67},$$

which is very close to the experimental results.

In the related-key DL attack on the 5-round XOODYAK, Dunkelman and Weizman used another 4-round DL distinguisher where the input difference is in (k_0, u_{128}) (*i.e.*, $S^{(0)}[0][0][0]$ and $S^{(0)}[0][2][0]$) and the output bias of $S^{(4)}[0][0][0]$ is about $-2^{-5.36}$ [13]. Again, this distinguisher was obtained by experiments. To apply HATF to it, we also obtain 4 equations by injecting conditions into the first round,

$$u_{103} = k_{103} \oplus k_{112} \oplus u_{112} \oplus u_{149} \oplus u_{231} \oplus u_{240} \oplus 1$$
$$u_{70} = k_{70} \oplus k_{93} \oplus u_{93} \oplus u_{107} \oplus u_{198} \oplus u_{221} \oplus 1$$
$$u_{102} = k_{11} \oplus k_{102} \oplus k_{125} \oplus u_{125} \oplus u_{230} \oplus u_{253}$$
$$u_{82} = k_{82} \oplus k_{91} \oplus u_{91} \oplus u_{96} \oplus u_{210} \oplus u_{219}$$

Another time, we obtain 16 subspaces. After applying the first-order HATF technique to each subspace, the bias of $S^{(4)}[0][0][0]$ is

$$\text{Bias}(S^{(4)}[0][0][0]) = -2^{-6},$$

which is very close to the experimental results.

Application 2: 2nd-order HDL distinguisher for 4-round XOODYAK. In our 2nd-order distinguisher, we choose the two differences as Δ_0 that is active in (u_0, u_{128}), Δ_1 that is active in (u_{47}, u_{175}). After 4-round XOODYAK initialization, our HATF technique shows that the bias of $S^{(4)}[0][0][12]$ is about $0.019 \approx 2^{-5.72}$. Experiments with 2^{26} randomly-selected samples show the real bias is also approximately $2^{-5.72}$.

Application 3: 4th-order HDL distinguisher for 4-round XOODYAK.
Unlike ASCON, the nonlinear function of XOODOO (χ) is after the linear operation. Hence if we select low-weight input differences before θ, the input differences into χ are complicated. Thus, we also tried selecting low-weight differences before χ, then we can compute the actual differences back through $(\theta \circ \rho_{west} \circ \iota)^{-1}$. In our 4th-order distinguisher, we choose four differences such as (Let S be the input state): Δ_0 is active in $(S[0][0][0], S[0][2][0])$, Δ_1 is active in $(S[2][0][7], S[2][2][7])$, Δ_2 is active in $(S[2][0][15], S[2][2][15])$, and Δ_3 is active in $(S[3][0][27], S[3][2][27])$. After 3.5 rounds of XOODYAK initialization ($\rho_{east} \circ \chi$ of the first round and the remaining three full rounds), our HATF technique shows that the bias of $S^{(4)}[0][1][1]$ is 2^{-1}. Thus, when the input difference of the 4-round XOODYAK is then $(\theta \circ \rho_{west} \circ \iota)^{-1}(\Delta_0, \Delta_1, \Delta_2, \Delta_3)$, the bias of $S^{(4)}[0][1][1]$ is 2^{-1}. Note that $(\theta \circ \rho_{west} \circ \iota)^{-1}(\Delta_0, \Delta_1, \Delta_2, \Delta_3)$ will be active in all three planes, so this HDL distinguisher is under the related-key model.

Application 4: 2nd-order HDL distinguisher for 5-round XOODYAK.
It becomes very difficult to detect useful HDL approximations for 5-round XOODYAK under the single-key model, we exhaust all possible 2nd-order differences that are active in (u_0, u_{128}) and (u_j, u_{j+128}). If we do not inject any conditions, the biases of all output bits from HATF are all 0. Hence, we first inject 8 conditions according to Sect. 4.5. When the input difference is active in (u_0, u_{128}) and (u_{34}, u_{162}), the highest bias occurs in $S^{(5)}[0][0][20]$ which is 2^{-37}. We then tried all 256 possibilities of the 8 conditions and found the average bias to be 2^{-45}.

Application 5: 2nd- and 3rd-order HDL distinguishers for 4- and 5-round XOODOO. Besides XOODYAK, XOODOO also plays an important role in other schemes such as XOOFFF [8]. Thus, it is also interesting to see if there are some HDL distinguishers for XOODOO. Since XOODOO is a public permutation, we do not need to consider the linear layers before the first nonlinear operations in the first round. Let S be the input state of the first χ. First, we let the 288 bits in $S[x], 1 \leq x < 4$ be zero. Next, for the remaining 96 bits in $S[0]$, we set $S[0][0][z] = S[0][2][z]$ and $S[0][1][z] = 0$ for $0 \leq z < 32$. For the ℓth-order HDL attack, we choose the input differences $\Delta(i_0, i_1, \ldots, i_{\ell-1})$ that have 2ℓ active bits of $S[0][0][i_j]$ and $S[0][2][i_j]$.

For 4-round XOODOO, we choose the input difference as $\Delta(0, 20)$, the bias of $S[0][0][0]$ after 4 rounds would be $\frac{1}{2}$. For 5-round XOODOO, we choose the input difference as $\Delta(0, 13, 14)$, and the bias of $S[1][1][28]$ is $2^{-8.96}$. We experimentally verified these two approximations, and found the 4-round distinguisher is truly deterministic and the 5-round 3rd-order HDL approximation has a bias of about $2^{-8.79}$ which is very close to our prediction. The big gap of biases between XOODYAK and XOODOO implies the XOODYAK gains some strength against HDL attacks by arranging χ after θ and ρ_{west}.

6.2 HDL Key-Recovery Attacks for XOODYAK

Application 6: 2nd-order HDL key-recovery attack on 4-round XOODYAK. In our 2nd-order key-recovery attack, we choose the two differences as Δ_0 is active in (u_0, u_{128}), Δ_1 is active in (u_{72}, u_{200}). We inject 8 conditions in the first round to cancel the differences. After 4-round XOODYAK initialization, our HATF technique shows that the bias of $S^{(4)}[0][0][14]$ is about 0.141 when all the conditions are satisfied. Experiments with 2^{26} randomly-selected samples show that the real bias is also 0.141 (up to 3 digits precision). The 8 conditions are listed as follows,

$$x_7 = k_7 \oplus k_{16} \oplus x_{16} \oplus x_{135} \oplus x_{144} \oplus x_{181}, x_{70} = k_{70} \oplus k_{93} \oplus x_{93} \oplus x_{107} \oplus x_{198} \oplus x_{221} \oplus 1$$
$$x_5 = k_5 \oplus k_{14} \oplus x_{14} \oplus x_{51} \oplus x_{133} \oplus x_{142} \oplus 1, x_{67} = k_{67} \oplus k_{90} \oplus k_{104} \oplus x_{90} \oplus x_{195} \oplus x_{218} \oplus 1$$
$$x_{18} = k_{18} \oplus k_{27} \oplus k_{32} \oplus x_{27} \oplus x_{146} \oplus x_{155} \oplus 1, x_{102} = k_{11} \oplus k_{102} \oplus k_{125} \oplus x_{125} \oplus x_{230} \oplus x_{253}$$
$$x_{37} = k_{37} \oplus k_{46} \oplus k_{83} \oplus x_{46} \oplus x_{165} \oplus x_{174}, x_{88} = k_{79} \oplus k_{88} \oplus x_{79} \oplus x_{207} \oplus x_{216} \oplus x_{253}$$

If not all the 8 conditions hold, the bias of $S^{(4)}[0][0][14]$ is at most 0.07. Thus, doing statistical tests can find the correct assignment of the 8 variables on the left side, and then 8 bits of key information. Firstly, we fixed all the nonce variables on the right side as 0, then we try all possible 2^8 values of the nonce bits on the left. The values making $S^{(4)}[0][0][14]$ most biased is the values of the key expressions in each condition. According to the method distinguishing two normal distributions, the complexity is about 2^9. Thus, the time/data complexity for recovering 8 bits of key information in the above conditions is about $2^{8+9} = 2^{17}$. We experimentally tested this attack, and among 100 experiments, we can recover the correct key 96 times. Due to the rotational-variance property of XOODOO, recovering all 128-bit keys needs about 2^{21} computations. This is about 4 times faster than the DL attacks in [13].

Application 7: Theoretical 3rd-order HDL key-recovery attack on 5-round XOODYAK under the single-key model. In [13], a related-key DL attack on 5-round ASCON was given by Dunkelman and Weizman. The authors built this related-key DL approximation from a 4-round one (the second DL approximation in Application 1 of this section). Until now, the conditional cube attack is still the only attack that can reach 5 rounds under the single-key model [31]. In this section, we give a 3rd-order HDL attack on 5-round XOODYAK under the single-key model.

We choose the 3rd-order difference as $(\Delta_0, \Delta_1, \Delta_2)$ where Δ_0 is active in (u_0, u_{128}), Δ_1 is active in (u_9, u_{137}), and Δ_2 is active in (u_{36}, u_{164}). We inject 12 conditions into the first round, then after 5 full rounds, the bias of $S^{(5)}[0][0][29]$ is predicted as $2^{-30.72}$. The 12 conditions are all linear and provided in the full version. We assume that if not all 12 conditions are true, the bias of $S^{(5)}[0][29]$ is close to 0. Thus, a statistical test with approximately 2^{64} samples is enough to distinguish them. Then we can use a similar strategy as the 4-round attack to recover 12 bits of key information. The complexity is about $12 \times 2^{64} \approx 2^{68}$. We can repeat this process for 5 other positions by rotation to recover 60 more bits of key information, the remaining keys can be searched by force. The whole time/data complex of recovering all key bits is about $2^{70.2}$.

7   HD Cryptanalysis Based on DSF Degree Estimation

According to Sect. 3, $f \circ \mathcal{M}$ plays an important role in (higher-order) differential cryptanalysis, thus we call it *differential supporting function* and give it a formal definition.

Definition 3. (Differential Supporting Function (DSF)). *Given a Boolean function* $f : \mathbb{F}_2^n \to \mathbb{F}_2$ *and an* ℓ^{th}*-order difference* $\boldsymbol{\Delta} = (\Delta_0, \Delta_1, \dots, \Delta_{\ell-1}) \in (\mathbb{F}_2^n)^\ell$, *the composite Boolean function*

$$\mathrm{DSF}_{f,X,\boldsymbol{\Delta}}^\ell(\boldsymbol{x}) = f \circ \mathcal{M}(\boldsymbol{x}) = f(X \oplus \boldsymbol{x}\boldsymbol{\Delta}), \boldsymbol{x} = (x_0, x_1, \dots, x_{\ell-1})$$

is called the ℓth*-order differential supporting function (DSF) of* f *with respect to* $(X, \boldsymbol{\Delta})$. *When the order* ℓ *is clear from context, we will ignore it in the notation, i.e.,* $\mathrm{DSF}_{f,X,\boldsymbol{\Delta}}(\boldsymbol{x})$.

The DSF provides a convenient way to find good *affine space* for the input that reduces the algebraic degree of the target cipher. In this paper, we take the ASCON permutation as an example to show the usage of the DSF. Until now, all attacks on the ASCON permutation with complexity less than or equal 2^{64} can only reach 7 rounds. The only integral distinguishers given by Todo [26] require more than 2^{130} calls to attack 8 and more rounds, already higher than ASCON's claimed security level (2^{128} calls). By analyzing the degree evolution of the DSF, we present a new HD distinguisher for 8 rounds requiring only 2^{46} complexity.

Basic Idea. Note that in the Definition 3, $\boldsymbol{x}$ are variables while X and $\boldsymbol{\Delta}$ are parameters (here the term "parameters" means X and $\boldsymbol{\Delta}$ should be fixed as a constant). Hence, different X and $\boldsymbol{\Delta}$ will lead to different DSF. So it is possible to find some proper $(X, \boldsymbol{\Delta})$ that reduce the algebraic degree of the DSF. More specifically, $\deg(\mathrm{DSF}_{f,X,\boldsymbol{\Delta}})$ may be reduced to some values smaller than the order ℓ. In this case, we derive an integral property for $\mathrm{DSF}_{f,X,\boldsymbol{\Delta}}$. Applying the inverse of $\mathcal{M}$, we immediately derive an ℓth-order difference yielding the following property, *i.e.*,

$$\mathcal{D}_{\boldsymbol{\Delta}}f(X) = \bigoplus_{x \in \mathbb{F}_2^\ell} \mathrm{DSF}_{f,X,\boldsymbol{\Delta}}(x) = 0.$$

To estimate the degree upper bound of a DSF, we cut a Boolean function into two phases as follows,

$$\mathrm{DSF}_{f,X,\boldsymbol{\Delta}}(\boldsymbol{x}) = f(X \oplus \boldsymbol{x}\boldsymbol{\Delta}) = f^1 \circ f^0(X \oplus \boldsymbol{x}\boldsymbol{\Delta}).$$

We let f^0 be simple so that we can compute out its exact ANFs as well as the exact degrees of the output of $f^0(X \oplus \boldsymbol{x}\boldsymbol{\Delta})$. Next, we update the obtained degrees by f^1 to obtain the degree upper bounds of the whole $\mathrm{DSF}_{f,X,\boldsymbol{\Delta}}$.

In terms of the r-round ASCON permutation, we choose its first $r_0 = 2.5$ rounds as f^0 for it achieves a balance between efficiency and precision[8]. The

---

[8] A larger r_0 will make the estimation of $\deg(\mathrm{DSF}_{f,X,\boldsymbol{\Delta}})$ more precise but more time-consuming to compute the ANFs, while a smaller r_0 may undermine the precision.

remaining $(r - 2.5)$-round permutation is seen as f^1, the degree update of f^1 can be done by methods such as the division properties [26,27] or any other suitable methods. In this paper, we use the method of the degree matrix to update the algebraic degree of f^1:

Definition 4 (Degree Matrix of $S^{(r)}$). *The algebraic degrees or their upper bounds of the bits in the state $S^{(r)}$ are called a degree matrix of $S^{(r)}$, denoted by*

$$\text{DM}(S^{(r)}) = \Big(\deg(S^{(r)}[i][j]), 0 \leq i < 5, 0 \leq j < 64\Big).$$

Given the degree matrix of $S^{(r)}$, we can quickly calculate the degree matrix of $S^{(r+1)}$ considering the ANFs of the p_S and p_L (see our full version). Our experiments show that the degree matrix method is not worse than the division property to calculate the upper bound on the algebraic degree of $\text{DSF}_{f,X,\Delta}$ for the case of ASCON permutation[9]. The only challenge now is to find a desirable combination of (X, Δ).

Heuristic Method of Choosing (X, Δ). To find a proper (X, Δ), a naive idea is to exhaust all possible values of (X, Δ), but the search space is clearly too large. For ASCON, we use the same notations as we do in Sect. 5. Considering the first operation of the ASCON permutation without p_C (we can safely ignore the first p_C operation since we target the permutation) is p_S which consists of 64 parallel small Sboxes. If we consider independent ℓ'^{th}-order differences for each Sbox $\mathcal{S}$, in total we are considering an $(\ell = 64\ell')^{th}$-order differences for the whole permutation. Our experiments show $\ell' = 1$ will achieve the best performance. This is not surprising, since $\ell' = 1$ means that we put one variable in each Sbox to linearize all Sboxes, similar ideas were already mentioned in some previous works such as [7]. With $\ell' = 1$, our 64th-order input difference is then denoted by $\Delta = (\Delta_0, \Delta_1, \ldots, \Delta_{63})$. Thus, we write $p_S(X \oplus x\Delta)$ as follows:

$$p_S(X \oplus x\Delta) = \mathcal{S}(X_0 \oplus x_0\Delta_0')||\mathcal{S}(X_1 \oplus x_1\Delta_1')|| \cdots ||\mathcal{S}(X_{63} \oplus x_{63}\Delta_{63}'),$$

where $X = X_0||X_1|| \cdots ||X_{63}$ and $\Delta_i = 0|| \cdots ||\Delta_i'|| \cdots ||0$ for $0 \leq i < 64$.

To further reduce the search space, we restrict the 64 X_i's and 64 Δ_i''s to be equal respectively, i.e., $(X_i, \Delta_i') = (\bar{X}, \bar{\Delta})$ for $0 \leq i < 64$. Therefore, we only need to consider 2^5 possibilities for $\bar{X}$ and 31 possibilities for $\bar{\Delta}$ (excluding the trivial case $\bar{\Delta} = 0$). The total search space is reduced to $32 \times 31 = 992$ different cases.

For each $(\bar{X}, \bar{\Delta}) \in \mathbb{F}_2^5 \times \mathbb{F}_2^5 \backslash \{0\}$, we calculate the ANFs of $f^0(X \oplus x\Delta)$, then derive the degree matrix of its output. After that we update the degree matrix according to [14] to calculate the degree matrix of $S^{(r)}$ (for $r \geq 4$) which is the degree upper bound of the corresponding DSF. If the degree of a certain DSF

---

[9] Note that the degree matrix method only happens to be as good as the division property in this specific case. We choose the degree matrix method simply because it can be more easily integrated into our algorithm. In general case, the division property has overwhelming advantages in accuracy and versatility.

Table 4. Upper bounds on the algebraic degree of the DSF of the ASCON permutation with (X, Δ) in Eq. 9. We experimentally verified all algebraic degrees up to 7 rounds.

Round r	Upper bounds on the algebraic degree				
	$S^{(r)}[0]$	$S^{(r)}[1]$	$S^{(r)}[2]$	$S^{(r)}[3]$	$S^{(r)}[4]$
4	3	3	2	2	3
5	6	5	5	6	6
6	11	11	12	12	11
7	23	24	23	23	22
8	47	47	45	46	47

is smaller than 64, we find useful 64th HD distinguishers for r-round ASCON permutation.

We found dozens of useful HD distinguishers with orders lower than 64 for up to 8 rounds. Among them, there are 8 optimal combinations of $(\bar{X}, \bar{\Delta})$ that make the algebraic degree of the third word of $S^{(8)}$ be only 45. They are

$$(\bar{X}, \bar{\Delta}) \in \left\{ \begin{array}{l} (\texttt{0x6}, \texttt{0x13}), (\texttt{0xa}, \texttt{0x13}), (\texttt{0xc}, \texttt{0x17}), (\texttt{0xf}, \texttt{0x18}), \\ (\texttt{0x15}, \texttt{0x13}), (\texttt{0x17}, \texttt{0x18}), (\texttt{0x19}, \texttt{0x13}), (\texttt{0x1b}, \texttt{0x17}) \end{array} \right\}. \qquad (9)$$

In Table 4, we list all the upper bounds on degrees of the DSF up to 8-round ASCON permutation with respect to (X, Δ) in Eq. 9. As is seen, for 7 rounds, the degree upper bound of $S^{(7)}$ is only 24, so 2^{25} chosen texts are enough to enforce the zero output difference. For the 8-round output, the algebraic degree is at most 47. Therefore if we choose 2^{48} plaintexts in any 48-dimensional affine space defined by values in Eq. 9, the summation of all ciphertexts will be zero. Given a random permutation, the probability that the summation of such 2^{48} ciphertexts will be zero is 2^{-320}. Thus, 2^{48} chosen plaintexts are enough to distinguish the 8-round ASCON permutation from a random permutation.

8   Conclusion and Discussion

In this paper, we revisited the HD/HDL cryptanalysis from an algebraic perspective. HATF and DSF are two tools for probabilistic and deterministic HDL/HD cryptanalysis, respectively. Improved results for ASCON and XOODYAK, as well as XOODOO are obtained from the two tools. We believe that the HDL cryptanalysis has more potential than expected, and deserves more attention.

In terms of HATF, it is the first theoretical tool for nondeterministic HDL cryptanalysis. It can predict the biases of an ℓth-order HDL approximations with a time complexity of $\mathcal{O}(2^{\ell+d2\ell})$ for ciphers with d-degree round functions. For ciphers with quadratic round functions, the time complexity can be reduced to $\mathcal{O}(2^{3.8\ell})$. Thus, HATF is very useful for HDL cryptanalysis of permutation-based ciphers such as ASCON and XOODYAK. The precision of HATF is supported by experiments (see [14]). When HATF predicts a biased bit, it is of a great probability that it is biased as far as our experiments show. Finally, we make it clear again that HATF does not guarantee any lower or upper bounds on the bias of a HDL approximation. Whenever possible, the theoretical results should be verified with experiments.

For DSF, it provides an intuitive method for detecting HD distinguishers for permutations. With proper choices of (X, Δ), the algebraic degree of a DSF might drop drastically. Therefore, we have a greater opportunity to find better HD distinguishers rather than to analyze the original Boolean function.

We have shown that a proper partitioning of the input space can improve the precision of HATF, how to find better or even optimal partitioning methods? Can we use the HDL cryptanalysis to propose best key-recovery attacks on some ciphers in terms of rounds? For DSF, our method to choose (X, Δ) is intuitive and actually considers only a small percentage of candidates, can we find better (X, Δ) leading to better HD distinguishers for ASCON permutation? These are interesting questions worth exploring that we leave as future work.

Acknowledgments. We are grateful to the anonymous referees for their comments that improved the quality of this article. Kai Hu thanks Yang Wang for the fruitful discussion. The authors are supported by the France-Singapore NRF-ANR research grant NRF2020-NRF-ANR072 and the Singapore NRF Investigatorship research grant NRF-NRFI08-2022-0013.

References

1. Bar-On, A., Dunkelman, O., Keller, N., Weizman, A.: DLCT: a new tool for differential-linear cryptanalysis. In: EUROCRYPT (2019)
2. Biham, E., Dunkelman, O., Keller, N.: A new attack on 6-round IDEA. In: FSE (2007)
3. Biham, E., Dunkelman, O., Keller, N.: Enhancing differential-linear cryptanalysis. In: ASIACRYPT (2002)
4. E. Biham, O. Dunkelman, Keller, N.: New combined attacks on block ciphers. In: FSE (2005)
5. Biham, E., Shamir, A.: Differential cryptanalysis of DES-like cryptosystems. In: CRYPTO (1990)
6. Blondeau, C., Leander, G., Nyberg, K.: Differential-linear cryptanalysis revisited. J. Cryptol. **30**(3), 859–888 (2017)
7. Bonnetain, X., Leurent, G., Naya-Plasencia, M., Schrottenloher, A.: Quantum linearization attacks. In: ASIACRYPT (2021)
8. Daemen, J., Hoffert, S., Assche, G., Keer, R.: The design of Xoodoo and Xoofff. IACR ToSC (4) (2018)
9. Daemen, J., Hoffert, S., Peeters, M., Assche, G., Keer, R.: Xoodyak, a lightweight cryptographic scheme. In: IACR ToSC, 2020(S1) (2020)
10. Dinur, I., Shamir, A.: Cube attacks on tweakable black box polynomials. In: EUROCRYPT (2009)
11. Dobraunig, C., Eichlseder, M., Mendel, F., Schläffer, M.: Cryptanalysis of Ascon. In: CT-RSA (2015)
12. Dobraunig, C., Eichlseder, M., Mendel, F., Schläffer, M.: Ascon v1.2: lightweight authenticated encryption and hashing. J. Cryptol. **34**(3), 33 (2021)

13. Dunkelman, O., Weizman, A.: Differential-linear cryptanalysis on Xoodyak. In: NIST Lightweight Cryptography Workshop (2022)
14. Hu, K., Peyrin, T., Tan, Q., Yap, T.: Revisiting Higher-Order Differential-Linear Attacks from an Algebraic Perspective. Cryptology ePrint Archive, 2022/1335
15. Florence Jessie, M., Neil James Alexander, S.: The Theory of Error-Correcting Codes, vol. 16. Elsevier (1977)
16. Knudsen, L.: Truncated and higher order differentials. In: FSE (1994)
17. Lai, X., Massey, J.: A proposal for a new block encryption standard. In: EURO-CRYPT (1990)
18. Langford, S., Hellman, M.: Differential-Linear cryptanalysis. In: CRYPTO (1994)
19. Li, Z., Dong, X., Wang, X.: Conditional cube attack on round-reduced ASCON. IACR ToSC, 2017(1) (2017)
20. Liu, M., Lu, X., Lin, D.: Differential-linear cryptanalysis from an algebraic perspective. In: CRYPTO (2021)
21. Liu, Y., Sun, S., Li, C.: Rotational cryptanalysis from a differential-linear perspective - practical distinguishers for round-reduced FRIET, Xoodoo, and Alzette. In: EUROCRYPT (2021)
22. Matsui, M.: Linear cryptanalysis method for DES cipher. In: EUROCRYPT (1993)
23. Rohit, R., Hu, K., Sarkar, S., Sun, S.: Misuse-free key-recovery and distinguishing attacks on 7-Round Ascon. IACR ToSC, 2021(1) (2021)
24. Shi, D., Sun, S., Sasaki, Y., Li, C., Hu, L.: Correlation of quadratic Boolean functions: cryptanalysis of all versions of full MORUS. In: CRYPTO (2019)
25. Tezcan, C.: Analysis of Ascon, DryGASCON, and Shamash Permutations. IACR Cryptol. ePrint Arch., 2020/1458
26. Todo, Y.: Structural evaluation by generalized integral property. In: EUROCRYPT (2015)
27. Todo, Y., Morii, M.: Bit-based division property and application to Simon family. In: FSE (2016)
28. Vaudenay, S.: Provable security for block ciphers by decorrelation. In: STACS (1998)
29. Wagner, D.: The Boomerang Attack. In: FSE (1999)
30. Xuejia, L.: Higher order derivatives and differential cryptanalysis. In: Communications and Cryptography, pp. 227–233 (1994)
31. Zhou, H., Li, Z., Dong, X., Jia, K., Meier, W.: Practical key-recovery attacks on round-reduced Ketje Jr, Xoodoo-AE and Xoodyak. Comput. J. **63**(8), 1231–1246 (2020)

More Insight on Deep Learning-Aided Cryptanalysis

Zhenzhen Bao[1,6(✉)] , Jinyu Lu[2,3(✉)] , Yiran Yao[3(✉)] ,
and Liu Zhang[3,4,5(✉)]

[1] Institute for Network Sciences and Cyberspace, BNRist,
Tsinghua University, Beijing, China
zzbao@tsinghua.edu.cn
[2] College of Sciences, National University of Defense Technology,
Changsha 410073, Hunan, China
[3] School of Physical and Mathematical Sciences,
Nanyang Technological University, Singapore, Singapore
yiran005@e.ntu.edu.sg
[4] School of Cyber Engineering, Xidian University, Xi'an, China
liuzhang@stu.xidian.edu.cn
[5] State Key Laboratory of Cryptology, P.O.Box 5159, Beijing 100878, China
[6] Zhongguancun Laboratory, Beijing, China

Abstract. In CRYPTO 2019, Gohr showed that well-trained neural networks could perform cryptanalytic distinguishing tasks superior to differential distribution table (DDT)-based distinguishers. This suggests that the differential-neural distinguisher ($\mathcal{ND}$) may use additional information besides pure ciphertext differences. However, the explicit knowledge beyond differential distribution is still unclear. In this work, we provide explicit rules that can be used alongside DDTs to enhance the effectiveness of distinguishers compared to pure DDT-based distinguishers. These rules are based on strong correlations between bit values in right pairs of XOR-differential propagation through addition modulo 2^n. Interestingly, they can be closely linked to the earlier study of the multi-bit constraints and the recent study of the fixed-key differential probability. In contrast, combining these rules does not improve the $\mathcal{ND}$s' performance. This suggests that these rules or their equivalent form have already been exploited by $\mathcal{ND}$s, highlighting the power of neural networks in cryptanalysis.

In addition, we find that to enhance the differential-neural distinguisher's accuracy and the number of rounds, regulating the differential propagation is imperative. Introducing differences into the keys is typically believed to help eliminate differences in encryption states, resulting in stronger differential propagations. However, differential-neural attacks differ from traditional ones as they don't specify output differences or follow a single differential trail. This questions the usefulness of introducing differences in a key in differential-neural attacks and the resistance of SPECK against such attacks in the related-key setting. This work shows that the power of differential-neural cryptanalysis in the related-key setting can exceed that in the single-key setting by successfully conducting a 14-round key recovery attack on SPECK32/64.

© International Association for Cryptologic Research 2023
J. Guo and R. Steinfeld (Eds.): ASIACRYPT 2023, LNCS 14440, pp. 436–467, 2023.
https://doi.org/10.1007/978-981-99-8727-6_15

Keywords: Neural Network · Interpretability · Modular Addition · Related-key · SPECK

1   Introduction

In 2019, Gohr [15] proposed differential-neural cryptanalysis, employing neural networks as superior distinguishers and exploiting them to perform efficient key recovery attacks. Impressively, the differential-neural distinguisher ($\mathcal{ND}$) outperformed the traditional pure differential distinguishers using full differential distribution tables (DDT). However, interpreting these neural network-based distinguishers remains challenging, hindering the comprehension of the additional knowledge learned by differential-neural distinguishers.

Despite the intricate nature of neural network interpretability, researchers have made primary progress in understanding the differential-neural distinguisher's inner workings. In EUROCRYPT 2021, Benamira *et al.* [7] proposed that Gohr's neural distinguisher effectively approximates the cipher's DDT during the learning phase. Moreover, the distinguisher relies on both the differential distribution of ciphertext pairs and that of the penultimate and antepenultimate rounds. Yet, the specific form of additional information remains undisclosed.

In AICrypt 2023, Gohr *et al.* [16] proved the differential-neural distinguisher for SIMON32/64 can use only differential features and achieve accuracy same as pure differential ones. Applying the same neural network to both SPECK and SIMON yields different conclusions: neural networks learned or did not learn features beyond full DDT. These intriguing findings motivate us to delve deeper into the neural network's mechanisms, aiming to comprehend the specific features underpinning its conclusions for each cipher and to improve and exploit further the neural distinguishers should additional features be captured.

Our Contributions. In this work, we conclude that $\mathcal{ND}$s' advantage over pure DDT-based distinguishers is in exploiting the differential distribution under the partially known value input to the last non-linear operation. Specifically, $\mathcal{ND}$s exploit the correlation between the ciphertexts' partial value, ciphertext pair's differences, and intermediate states' differences. Furthermore, our work shows that differential-neural cryptanalysis in the related-key ($\mathcal{RK}$) setting can attack more rounds than in the single-key setting, which was not apparent before. The concrete contributions include the following.

- **Improving full DDT-based distinguisher.** We observe that, apart from the information of differences, one knows the partial value of inputs, denoted by y, to the last modular addition of SPECK, leveraging by which one can improve DDT-based distinguishers. We show that the differential probability conditioned on a fixed value of y can differ from the average differential probability over all possible y. This insight enables more accurate classification based on the ciphertext pair's differences and the ciphertexts' partial value. The high-level idea is to consider conditional probabilities and specific cases where the fulfillment of the differential constraints can be predicted based on

Table 1. Summary of key recovery attacks on SPECK32/64

#R	Distinguisher	Configure	Time	Data	Succ. Rate	Key Space	Advantage	Ref.
	$\mathcal{DD}$	1+8+4	2^{57}	2^{25}	-	2^{64}	2^{7}	[12]
	$\mathcal{DD}$	1+8+3	$2^{55.58}$	$2^{24.26}$	-	2^{64}	$2^{8.42}$	[14]
	$\mathcal{DD}$	1+8+2+2	$2^{50.16}$	$2^{31.13}$	63%	2^{64}	$2^{13.84}$	[9]
13	$\mathcal{ND}$	1+3+8+1	$2^{50.17}$	2^{29}	82%	2^{63}	$2^{13.83}$	[3]
	$\mathcal{ND}$	1+3+8+1	$2^{44.36}$	2^{27}	21%	2^{63}	$2^{18.64}$	[26]
	$\mathcal{RK}\text{-}\mathcal{ND}$	1+2+9+1	$2^{34.57}$	2^{16}	54.29%	2^{50}	$2^{15.43}$	Sect. 5.2
	$\mathcal{RK}\text{-}\mathcal{ND}$	1+2+9+1	$2^{31.79}$	2^{10}	43.33%	2^{46}	$2^{14.21}$	Sect. 5.2
	$\mathcal{DD}$	1+9+4	2^{63}	2^{31}	-	2^{64}	2^{1}	[12]
	$\mathcal{DD}$	1+9+4	$2^{62.47}$	$2^{30.47}$	-	2^{64}	$2^{1.53}$	[24]
	$\mathcal{DD}$	1+9+2+2	$2^{60.99}$	$2^{31.75}$	63%	2^{64}	$2^{3.01}$	[9]
14	$\mathcal{DD}$	2+9+3	$2^{60.58}$	$2^{30.26}$	76.00%	2^{64}	$2^{3.42}$	[14]
	$\mathcal{ND}$	1+3+8+2	$2^{60.36}$	2^{27}	21%	2^{63}	$2^{2.64}$	[26]
	$\mathcal{RK}\text{-}\mathcal{ND}$	1+3+9+1	$\mathbf{2^{35.59}}$	$\mathbf{2^{16}}$	75.71%	2^{42}	$\mathbf{2^{6.41}}$	Sect. 5.2
	$\mathcal{RK}\text{-}\mathcal{ND}$	1+3+9+1	$\mathbf{2^{35.78}}$	$\mathbf{2^{15}}$	71.43%	2^{41}	$\mathbf{2^{5.22}}$	Sect. 5.2
15	$\mathcal{DD}$	1+10+4	$2^{63.39}$	$2^{30.39}$	-	2^{64}	$2^{0.61}$	[17]
	$\mathcal{DD}$	1+10+2+2	$2^{62.25}$	$2^{30.39}$	-	2^{64}	$2^{1.75}$	[9]

−: Not available; "Advantage" denotes the time complexity advantage over a brute force attack.

the value of y. The results indicate that it is highly likely that $\mathcal{ND}$s rely on these specific cases to outperform pure DDT-based distinguishers.

- **Optimizing the performance and training process of $\mathcal{ND}$s.** Addressing the challenge of training high-round, especially 8-round, $\mathcal{ND}$ of SPECK32/64, we introduce the Freezing Layer Method. By freezing all convolutional layers in a pre-trained 7-round $\mathcal{ND}$, we efficiently train an 8-round $\mathcal{ND}$ using simple basic training with unaltered hyperparameters. This method matches Gohr's accuracy but cuts training time and data.
- **Exploring differential-neural attacks in the related-key setting.** The conclusion that $\mathcal{ND}$s can efficiently capture features beyond full DDT encourages further exploration of $\mathcal{ND}$-based attacks. We observed that control over the differential propagation is vital for achieving effective high-round $\mathcal{ND}$s. Hence, we introduce related-key ($\mathcal{RK}$) differences to slow down the diffusion of differences, aiding in training $\mathcal{ND}$ for higher rounds. As a result, we achieve a 14-round key recovery attack on SPECK32/64 using related-key neural distinguishers ($\mathcal{RK}\text{-}\mathcal{ND}$s). Results are in Table 1. Furthermore, we constructed various distinguishers under various $\mathcal{RK}$ differential trails and conducted comprehensive comparisons, reinforcing $\mathcal{ND}$ explainability.

Organization. The paper's structure is as follows: Sect. 2 provides preliminaries. Section 3 provides insights on the $\mathcal{ND}$ explainability. Section 4 provides enhancements on the $\mathcal{ND}$ training. Section 5 details of related-key differential-neural cryptanalysis. The conclusion is presented in Sect. 6.

2   Preliminary

2.1   Notations

Denote by $C = (C_{n-1}, \ldots, C_0)$ the binary vector of n bits, where C_i is the bit at position i and C_0 is the least significant. Define n as the word size in bits and $2n$ as the state size. Let (C_L^r, C_R^r) represent left and right state branches after r rounds, and k^r the r-round subkey. Bitwise XOR is denoted by $\oplus$, addition modulo 2^n by $\boxplus$, bitwise AND by $\odot$, and bitwise right/left rotation by $\ggg$ / $\lll$.

2.2   Brief Description of SPECK32/64

In 2013, the National Security Agency (NSA) proposed SPECK and SIMON block ciphers, aiming to ensure security on resource-constrained devices [5]. By 2018, both ciphers were standardized by ISO/IEC for air interface communication. The SPECK cipher uses a Feistel-like ARX design, emanating its non-linearity from modular addition and leveraging XOR and rotation for linear mixing. SPECK32/64 is the smallest SPECK variant [5]. Its round function, one of 22 rounds, takes a 16-bit subkey k^i and a state of two 16-bit words, (C_L^i, C_R^i). Its key schedule reuses the round function to generate round keys. With K as a master key and k^i the i-th round key, $K = (l^2, l^1, l^0, k^0)$. The round function's details are in Fig. 1.

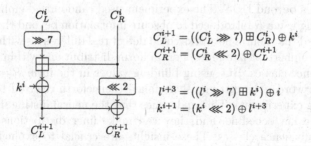

$$C_L^{i+1} = ((C_L^i \ggg 7) \boxplus C_R^i) \oplus k^i$$
$$C_R^{i+1} = (C_R^i \lll 2) \oplus C_L^{i+1}$$

$$l^{i+3} = ((l^i \ggg 7) \boxplus k^i) \oplus i$$
$$k^{i+1} = (k^i \lll 2) \oplus l^{i+3}$$

Fig. 1. The round function and key schedule algorithm of SPECK32/64

2.3   Overview of Differential-Neural Cryptanalysis

The differential-neural distinguisher operates as a supervised model, distinguishing whether ciphertext pairs originate from plaintext pairs with a defined input difference or from random pairs. Given m plaintext pairs $\{(P_j, P_j'), j \in [0, m-1]\}$, the corresponding ciphertext pairs $\{(C_j, C_j'), j \in [0, m-1]\}$ constitute a sample (In [15], $m = 1$). Each training sample is associated with a label Y defined as:

$$Y = \begin{cases} 1, & \text{if } P_j \oplus P_j' = \Delta, j \in [0, m-1] \\ 0, & \text{if } P_j \oplus P_j' \neq \Delta, j \in [0, m-1] \end{cases}$$

The $\mathcal{ND}$ architecture from [15] uses the prevalent ResNet. It comprises an initial input block, several residual blocks, and a prediction output layer.

In [15], three training schemes are proposed: a) Basic training for short-round distinguishers. b) An enhanced method using the KEYAVERAGING simulation and an $(r-1)$-round distinguisher, achieving the optimal 7-round $\mathcal{ND}$ for SPECK. c) A staged training approach evolving a pre-trained $(r-1)$-round distinguisher to an r-round one in stages, yielding the most extended $\mathcal{ND}$ on SPECK, covering 8 rounds. In [15], Gohr also showed how to combine a neural distinguisher with a classical differential and use a Bayesian-optimized key-guessing strategy for key recovery. Later, in [16], the authors provide general guidelines for optimizing Gohr's neural network and diverse optimization approaches across different ciphers, highlighting its efficacy and versatility. The authors also clarify which kind of ciphers the neural network can't learn beyond differential features.

3   Explicitly Explain Knowledge Beyond Full DDT

Studies show differential-based neural distinguishers often outperform DDT-based ones in certain ciphers [3,15,16]. However, what specific knowledge these neural distinguishers learn beyond DDT remains elusive. Prior research suggests that these distinguishers rely on differential distributions in the last two rounds and differential-linear (DL) properties [7,11]. In [15], a "Real Differences Experiment" was conducted to observe how well neural networks could detect real differences beyond DDT. The experiment used randomized ciphertext pairs with a blinding value R introduced to obscure information beyond the difference. Results showed that neural networks could detect real differences without explicit training, and ciphertext pairs have non-uniform distributions within their difference equivalence classes. But, using blinding values in the form $R = aa$ (with a as any 16-bit word), the distinguishers failed (henceforth referred to as Gohr's $aaaa$-blinding experiment). This underlines that the neural distinguishers aren't exploiting the key schedule, and they can make finer distinctions than mere difference equivalence classes. These insights are crucial to explicitly explaining $\mathcal{ND}$'s superior classification mechanism. Based on these studies, this section takes a further step towards fully interpreting the knowledge that an $\mathcal{ND}$ has captured beyond full differential distribution.

We'll initiate by locating the root of the performance improvement, then deduce the specific pattern that causes the improvement, and finally use this pattern to improve the pure DDT-based distinguisher.

3.1   Locating Information Used by $\mathcal{ND}$s of SPECK Beyond DDT

In the following, we start with a generalized definition of information that the differential-neural distinguisher might use.

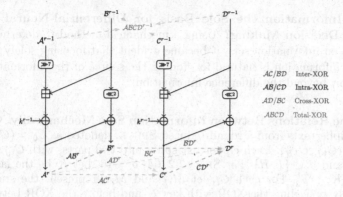

Fig. 2. Definition of XOR information

Table 2. Experimental results detailing the information harnessed by $\mathcal{N}\mathcal{D}$s. Each set comprises both positive and negative samples. The notation $(\mathcal{A}, \mathcal{B}, \mathcal{C}, \mathcal{D})$ denotes ciphertext pairs derived from plaintext pairs with an input difference of (0040,0000), while *Random* signifies pairs generated from random values. $\mathcal{R}_1$ refers to a random value.

Set	Positive Samples	Negative Samples	Acc.
1-1	$(\mathcal{A}, \mathcal{B}, \mathcal{C}, \mathcal{D})$	*Random*	0.7906
1-2	$(\mathcal{A}\mathcal{R}_1, \mathcal{B}\mathcal{R}_1, \mathcal{C}\mathcal{R}_1, \mathcal{D}\mathcal{R}_1)$	*Random*	0.7911
1-3	$(\mathcal{A}, \mathcal{B}, \mathcal{C}, \mathcal{D})$	$(\mathcal{A}\mathcal{R}_1, \mathcal{B}\mathcal{R}_1, \mathcal{C}\mathcal{R}_1, \mathcal{D}\mathcal{R}_1)$	*Fail*

Generalized Definition of XOR Information. In Gohr's differential-neural distinguishers, given SPECK's Feistel-like structure, samples are split into four words: $\mathcal{A}, \mathcal{B}$ (forming the first ciphertext) and $\mathcal{C}, \mathcal{D}$ (forming the second), as depicted in Fig. 2. In subsequent discussions, a symbol's superscript denotes the number of encryption rounds. The absence of a superscript implies r rounds.

Traditional differential distinguishers focus solely on the difference of ciphertext pairs. Yet, as indicated in prior research [13, 22, 27], internal differentials can also be pivotal in cryptanalytic tasks.

We broaden the focus to include the XOR interactions among $\mathcal{A}$, $\mathcal{B}$, $\mathcal{C}$, and $\mathcal{D}$. For brevity, XOR combinations like $\mathcal{A} \oplus \mathcal{B} \oplus \mathcal{C} \oplus \mathcal{D}$ are shortened to $\mathcal{A}\mathcal{B}\mathcal{C}\mathcal{D}$. In other words, beyond the traditionally focused differences like $\mathcal{A}\mathcal{C}$ and $\mathcal{B}\mathcal{D}$, we explore under-emphasized XORs such as $\mathcal{A}\mathcal{B}$, $\mathcal{C}\mathcal{D}$, $\mathcal{A}\mathcal{D}$, $\mathcal{B}\mathcal{C}$, and $\mathcal{A}\mathcal{B}\mathcal{C}\mathcal{D}$. For clarity, we classify these XORs as: **Inter-XOR** ($\mathcal{A}\mathcal{C}$, $\mathcal{B}\mathcal{D}$), **Intra-XOR** ($\mathcal{A}\mathcal{B}$, $\mathcal{C}\mathcal{D}$), **Cross-XOR** ($\mathcal{A}\mathcal{D}$, $\mathcal{B}\mathcal{C}$), and **Total-XOR** ($\mathcal{A}\mathcal{B}\mathcal{C}\mathcal{D}$).

In SPECK, Intra-XOR and Total-XOR relate to values and differences from the prior round. Specifically, Intra-XOR helps deduce the right-half values, and Total-XOR deduces the right-half differences of the preceding round.

Is XOR Information the Sole Basis for Differential-Neural Distinguisher's Decision Making? Using a mechanical method to determine relations between information sets, it became evident that focusing solely on specified XOR information is natural for finding the source of the information that $\mathcal{ND}$s exploit beyond the difference information.

Determine Relations Between Information Sets Mechanically. Consider a pair of ciphertexts from a round-reduced SPECK, denoted as $C_0 = (C_{0L}, C_{0R})$ and $C_1 = (C_{1L}, C_{1R})$. Each ciphertext splits into two parts, with $C_{iJ} \in \mathbb{F}_2^b$ for $i \in \{0, 1\}$ and $J \in \{L, R\}$. For SPECK32/64, $b = 16$. Let K be the last round key, with $K \in \mathbb{F}_2^b$. For each C_i, let M_{iL} and M_{iR} represent the state value immediately preceding the XOR with key K and before the XOR between the left and right branches for $i \in \{0, 1\}$. That is

$$C_{0L} = M_{0L} \oplus K, \; C_{0R} = M_{0L} \oplus M_{0R} \oplus K, \; C_{1L} = M_{1L} \oplus K, \; C_{1R} = M_{1L} \oplus M_{1R} \oplus K$$

The method to determine relations between information sets can be outlined in the following steps: Let $\mathcal{R}_1$ and $\mathcal{R}_2$ be two random values in $\mathbb{F}_2^b$.

1. **Setup:**
   (a) Set up a vector space $\mathcal{V}$ over the field $\mathbb{F}_2$ with dimension 7.
   (b) Define various basis vectors for $\mathcal{V}$, acting as linear masks whose non-zero bits indicate the variable selection from the following vector $[M_{0L}, M_{0R}, M_{1L}, M_{1R}, K, \mathcal{R}_1, \mathcal{R}_2]$. Concretely,

$$\begin{aligned}
\Gamma_{M_{0L}} &= [1,0,0,0,0,0,0] & \Gamma_{M_{1L}} &= [0,0,1,0,0,0,0] \\
\Gamma_{M_{0R}} &= [0,1,0,0,0,0,0] & \Gamma_{M_{1R}} &= [0,0,0,1,0,0,0] \\
\Gamma_K &= [0,0,0,0,1,0,0] & \Gamma_{\mathcal{R}_1} &= [0,0,0,0,0,1,0] \\
& & \Gamma_{\mathcal{R}_2} &= [0,0,0,0,0,0,1]
\end{aligned}$$

Accordingly, $[C_{0L}, C_{0R}, C_{1L}, C_{1R}]$ can be obtained using the following masks:

$$\begin{aligned}
\Gamma_{C_{0L}} &:= \Gamma_{\mathcal{A}} = \Gamma_{M_{0L}} \oplus \Gamma_K & &= [1,0,0,0,1,0,0], \\
\Gamma_{C_{0R}} &:= \Gamma_{\mathcal{B}} = \Gamma_{M_{0L}} \oplus \Gamma_{M_{0R}} \oplus \Gamma_K & &= [1,1,0,0,1,0,0], \\
\Gamma_{C_{1L}} &:= \Gamma_{\mathcal{C}} = \Gamma_{M_{1L}} \oplus \Gamma_K & &= [0,0,1,0,1,0,0], \\
\Gamma_{C_{1R}} &:= \Gamma_{\mathcal{D}} = \Gamma_{M_{1L}} \oplus \Gamma_{M_{1R}} \oplus \Gamma_K & &= [0,0,1,1,1,0,0].
\end{aligned}$$

Besides, we have $\Gamma_{\mathcal{XY}} = \Gamma_{\mathcal{X}} \oplus \Gamma_{\mathcal{Y}}$ for $\mathcal{X}, \mathcal{Y} \in \{\mathcal{A}, \mathcal{B}, \mathcal{C}, \mathcal{D}, \mathcal{AC}, \mathcal{BD}, \mathcal{AB}, \mathcal{R}_1, \mathcal{R}_2\}$.

2. **Subspace Generation:** Create the subspaces from given vectors and combinations:
   - Set-1-1: span of $\{\Gamma_{\mathcal{A}}, \Gamma_{\mathcal{B}}, \Gamma_{\mathcal{C}}, \Gamma_{\mathcal{D}}\}$.
   - Set-1-2: span of $\{\Gamma_{\mathcal{AR}_1}, \Gamma_{\mathcal{BR}_1}, \Gamma_{\mathcal{CR}_1}, \Gamma_{\mathcal{DR}_1}\}$.
   - Set-1-X: span of $\{\Gamma_{\mathcal{AC}}, \Gamma_{\mathcal{BD}}, \Gamma_{\mathcal{AB}}\}$.
   - Set-2-1: span of $\{\Gamma_{\mathcal{AR}_1}, \Gamma_{\mathcal{BR}_2}, \Gamma_{\mathcal{CR}_1}, \Gamma_{\mathcal{DR}_2}\}$.
   - Set-2-2: span of $\{\Gamma_{\mathcal{AR}_1}, \Gamma_{\mathcal{BR}_2}, \Gamma_{\mathcal{CR}_2}, \Gamma_{\mathcal{DR}_1}\}$.
   - Set-2-3: span of $\{\Gamma_{\mathcal{ABCD}}\}$.

Table 3. Experimental results $\mathcal{ND}$ leveraging select XOR information.

Set	Positive Samples	Negative Samples	Acc.
2-1	$(A\mathcal{R}_1, B\mathcal{R}_2, C\mathcal{R}_1, D\mathcal{R}_2)$	*Random*	0.7558
2-2	$(A\mathcal{R}_1, B\mathcal{R}_2, C\mathcal{R}_2, D\mathcal{R}_1)$	*Random*	0.6722
2-3	$(ABCD, ABCD, ABCD, ABCD)$	*Random*	0.6721

Note that `Set-1-2` is the setting of Gohr's *aaaa*-blinding experiment.

3. **Remove randomness:** In light of the observations from [15], where it's determined that $\mathcal{ND}$s in the single-key attack setting don't leverage the key schedule, we can adapt the Speck32/64 key schedule to employ independent subkeys. This means we treat K along with $\mathcal{R}_1$ and $\mathcal{R}_2$ as random variables. Consequently, any vector that has a component of Γ_K, or $\Gamma_{\mathcal{R}_1}$, or $\Gamma_{\mathcal{R}_2}$ is deemed random, and hence, devoid of information. For example, $\Gamma_{C_{iJ}}$ has a linear component Γ_K, thus, a standalone C_{iJ} lacks information, where $i \in \{0,1\}$ and $J \in \{L, R\}$. Accordingly, we do as follows.
   (a) After creating each subspace, randomness is removed from each subspace according to whether a vector has a component from Γ_K, or $\Gamma_{\mathcal{R}_1}$, or $\Gamma_{\mathcal{R}_2}$. Without ambiguity, the sanitized sets are also denoted by `Set-i-j` for $i \in \{1,2\}$ and $j \in \{1,2,3,\text{X}\}$.
4. **Comparison:** The sanitized sets are then compared against each other to determine if one set equals or is a subset of the other.

The result shows that `Set-1-1` equals `Set-1-2` and `Set-1-X`, meaning that the combination of Inter-XOR and Intra-XOR is exactly what an information-theoretically optimal distinguisher accepting ciphertext pairs can use under the assumption that it does not use key-schedule.

As we proceed, we delve deeper to ascertain the specific XOR information that holds significance.

Which of the XOR Information is Significant for Differential-Neural Distinguisher? To isolate the pivotal XOR information, we conducted experiments where a differential-neural distinguisher was given access to only selected XOR data.

All our subsequent experiments were conducted on a 6-round SPECK32/64 with an input difference of (0040, 0000), adhering to the configurations presented in Table 17 in [4]. The differential-neural distinguishers, trained as per Table 2 **Set.1-1** to **Set.1-3**, serve as baselines (**Set.1-2** and **Set.1-3** correspond to Gohr's *aaaa*-blinding experiment)). In the sequel, we use **Set.i-j** to refer to the experimental setup, while `Set-i-j` represents the associated information set for the positive samples, where $i \in \{1, 2\}$ and $j \in \{1, 2, 3\}$.

Defining $\mathcal{R}_1$ and $\mathcal{R}_2$ as two distinct random values, **Set.2-1** in Table 3 retains only Inter-XOR and Total-XOR, while **Set.2-2** keeps only Cross-XOR and Total-XOR. **Set.2-3**, on the other hand, exclusively considers Total-XOR. Firstly, our mechanical analysis of sanitized subspaces reveals the following relations:

– Set-2-1 $\subset$ Set-1-X,   – Set-2-1 $\not\subseteq$ Set-2-2,   – Set-2-3 $\subset$ Set-2-1,
– Set-2-2 $\subset$ Set-1-X,   – Set-2-2 $\not\subseteq$ Set-2-1,   – Set-2-3 $\subset$ Set-2-2.

In Table 3 **Set.**2-1, the differential-neural distinguisher's access is limited to Inter-XOR and Total-XOR – equivalent to what the DDT distinguisher utilizes. Its accuracy aligns closely with the 6-round DDT's accuracy of 0.758, without any noticeable enhancement. This underscores the differential-neural distinguisher's advantage over the DDT arising from its access to extra information. From this observation, we reinforce the subsequent conclusion.

Conclusion 1. *The differential-neural distinguisher $\mathcal{ND}^{\text{SPECK}rR}$'s superiority over $\mathcal{DD}^{\text{SPECK}rR}$ is mainly due to its exploit of Intra-XOR and Cross-XOR.*

This conclusion naturally prompts a more intricate query: How does the differential-neural distinguisher effectively exploit Intra-XOR and Cross-XOR? Upon closer inspection, we can further dismiss the significance of Cross-XOR. Given that Set-2-3 $\subset$ Set-2-2, it's evident that Set-2-3 provides inherently less data than Set-2-2. While in **Set.**2-2, combining Total-XOR with either Intra-XOR or Cross-XOR results in a valid distinguisher, solely using Total-XOR in **Set.**2-3 yields an accuracy identical to the distinguisher in **Set.**2-2. From this, we conclude that Cross-XOR on its own lacks significance. The differential-neural distinguisher likely uncovers new patterns by melding Inter-XOR with either Intra-XOR or Cross-XOR. This line of reasoning culminates in the following conclusion.

Conclusion 2. *Unlike Inter-XOR, neither Intra-XOR nor Cross-XOR independently offers useful information. The differential-neural distinguisher relies on combinations of Inter-XOR with either Intra-XOR or Cross-XOR.*

Remark 1 (On $\mathcal{ND}$ exploiting the key schedule). Gohr's study in [15] indicates that $\mathcal{ND}$s, in a single-key attack on SPECK, do not exploit the key schedule. It naturally raises the question: Do $\mathcal{ND}$s behave similarly in related-key scenarios? Motivated by this, we conduct comparison experiments similar to Gohr's *aaaa*-blinding experiment (comparing $\mathcal{RK}$-$\mathcal{ND}$s in **Set.**1-1 and **Set.**2-1), investigating whether $\mathcal{RK}$-$\mathcal{ND}$s use the same ciphertext equivalence classes as the single-key $\mathcal{ND}$s by [15]. In Sect. 5.1, we delve deep into our $\mathcal{RK}$-$\mathcal{ND}$s and present an interesting observation reinforcing our following $\mathcal{ND}$ explainability in Sect. 3.2.

3.2 Explicitly Rules to Exploit the Information Beyond Full DDT: From a Cryptanalytic Perspective

This section delves into the exact patterns harnessed by the differential-neural distinguisher. Our exploration commences with an intriguing observation from **Experiment** A, as described in [7]. The experiment unfolds as follows:

1. For each 5-round ciphertext pair difference, δ, which results in extreme scores surpassing 0.9 (indicative of a good score) and exhibiting a high frequency of occurrence:

(a) Generate a set of 10^4 random 32-bit numbers.
(b) Utilize the difference δ to construct a dataset encompassing 10^4 data pairs, each bearing the difference δ.
(c) Feed the dataset to the differential-neural distinguisher and count the predicted labels.

While DDT-based distinguishers would predict **Experiment** A's entire data as positive, the differential $\mathcal{ND}$ does not. For $\mathcal{ND}$, the proportion of each difference is consistently at 0.75 (refer to Table 19 in the full version [4]), suggesting that the $\mathcal{ND}$ employs criteria beyond simple differential probability in its classifications. The consistent proportion of 0.75 also implies a discernible pattern linked to two specific bits. If a ciphertext pair aligns with this bi-bit pattern, it's classified as negative, regardless of high output difference probabilities. This observation prompts an investigation into the potential two-bit pattern, motivating us to look into properties of the addition modular 2^n ($\boxplus$) from a cryptanalytic perspective.

Enhancing DDT-Based Distinguishers via Conditional Probabilities.
In the r-round SPECK32/64, denote the input and output differences of the last $\boxplus$ by (α, β, γ), and their respective values by $(x\ y\ z)$ and $(x'\ y'\ z')$. For each output pairs $((C_L, C_R), (C'_L, C'_R))$, one knows the following information: $\gamma = C_L \oplus C'_L$, $\beta = (C_L \oplus C_R \oplus C'_L \oplus C'_R) \ggg 2$, and $y = (C_L \oplus C_R) \ggg 2$. Namely, apart from knowing two differences (*i.e.*, β and γ), one knows a value (*i.e.*, y) around the last $\boxplus$. Besides, the input difference α is unknown but might be biased among positive samples and thus is predictable. Concretely, attributes of the information around the last $\boxplus$ are as follows:

α	unknown but biased	x	unknown and balanced
β	known	y	known
γ	known	z	unknown and balanced

The knowledge of y, which is one of two inputs of the last $\boxplus$, provides additional information apart from the differences. The concrete analysis is as follows.

When conditioned on a fixed y, the differential probability can differ from the average probability over all possible y. For a valid differential propagation $(\alpha, \beta \mapsto \gamma)$ through $\boxplus$, consider each bit position i where $0 \le i < n - 1$: If $\mathsf{eq}(\alpha, \beta, \gamma)_i = 1$, the difference propagation at the $(i + 1)$-th position is deterministic, as elucidated in [20]; Conversely, for $\mathsf{eq}(\alpha, \beta, \gamma)_i = 0$, the $(i+1)$-th bit's difference propagation is probabilistic; for a given $(i+1)$-th bit differences to be fulfilled, the input values at the i-th position (namely, x_i, y_i, c_i – the carry's i-th bit) must satisfy a certain linear constraint, detailed in Observation 1.

Observation 1 ([10]). *Let $\delta = (\alpha, \beta \mapsto \gamma)$ be a possible XOR-differential through addition modulo 2^n ($\boxplus$). Let (x, y) and $(x \oplus \alpha, y \oplus \beta)$ be a conforming*

Table 4. Necessary and sufficient conditions for a one-bit difference from Observation 1

Case No.	Difference	Constraint on values	Known
$\mathrm{Cxy}_{(i+1,i)}$	$\begin{cases} \mathsf{eq}(\alpha,\beta,\gamma)_i = 0, \\ \alpha_i \oplus \beta_i = 0. \end{cases}$	$\mathsf{xor}(\alpha,\beta,\gamma)_{i+1} \oplus \alpha_i = x_i \oplus y_i$	None
$\mathrm{Cxc}_{(i+1,i)}$	$\begin{cases} \mathsf{eq}(\alpha,\beta,\gamma)_i = 0, \\ \alpha_i \oplus \beta_i = 1, \\ \alpha_i \oplus \mathsf{xor}(\alpha,\beta,\gamma)_i = 0. \end{cases}$	$\mathsf{xor}(\alpha,\beta,\gamma)_{i+1} \oplus \alpha_i = x_i \oplus c_i$	None
$\mathrm{Cyc}_{(i+1,i)}$	$\begin{cases} \mathsf{eq}(\alpha,\beta,\gamma)_i = 0, \\ \alpha_i \oplus \beta_i = 1, \\ \alpha_i \oplus \mathsf{xor}(\alpha,\beta,\gamma)_i = 1. \end{cases}$	$\mathsf{xor}(\alpha,\beta,\gamma)_{i+1} \oplus \beta_i = y_i \oplus c_i$	$y_i \oplus c_i$

The column titled "Known" indicates whether the fulfilment of the condition might be known in SPECK's last ⊞.

pair of δ, x and y should satisfy the follows. For $0 \le i < n-1$, if $\mathsf{eq}(\alpha,\beta,\gamma)_i = 0$

$$\left. \begin{array}{ll} x_i \oplus y_i = \mathsf{xor}(\alpha,\beta,\gamma)_{i+1} \oplus \alpha_i, & \\ x_i \oplus c_i = \mathsf{xor}(\alpha,\beta,\gamma)_{i+1} \oplus \alpha_i, & \textit{if } \alpha_i \oplus \mathsf{xor}(\alpha,\beta,\gamma)_i = 0, \\ y_i \oplus c_i = \mathsf{xor}(\alpha,\beta,\gamma)_{i+1} \oplus \beta_i, & \textit{if } \alpha_i \oplus \mathsf{xor}(\alpha,\beta,\gamma)_i = 1, \end{array} \right\} \begin{array}{l} \textit{if } \alpha_i \oplus \beta_i = 0, \\ \\ \textit{if } \alpha_i \oplus \beta_i = 1, \end{array} \right\}$$

where c_i is the i-th carry bit, $x \boxplus y = z$, $\mathsf{eq}(a,b,d) = (\neg a \oplus b) \wedge (\neg a \oplus d)$ (i.e., $\mathsf{eq}(a,b,d) = 1$ if and only if $a = b = d$), and $\mathsf{xor}(a,b,d) = a \oplus b \oplus d$.

In other words, at bit positions i and $i+1$, a valid difference tuple $(\alpha_{i+1,i}, \beta_{i+1,i}, \gamma_{i+1,i})$ that satisfies $\mathsf{eq}(\alpha_i, \beta_i, \gamma_i) = 0$ imposes a 1-bit linear constraint on the tuple (x_i, y_i, c_i). As c_i is determined by lower bits, the freedom for conforming to the constraint comes exclusively from the i-th bits of x and y, independent of constraints at other bit positions. Accordingly, the constraints on (x_i, y_i), (x_i, c_i), or (y_i, c_i) as listed in Observation 1 are necessary and sufficient. Therefore, when the constraint at a bit position is fulfilled, the conditional probability $\tilde{p}$ of a differential whose unconditional probability is p should be calculated as $2 \cdot p$; when unfulfilled, it is 0. In comparison, the conditional probability for random pairs is still at most 2^{-n}. Hence, leveraging conditional probability for classification amplifies the advantage.

To clarify when the fulfilment of the constraints at the last ⊞ can be effectively predicted, we catalog cases from Observation 1 in Table 4, naming them $\mathrm{Cxy}_{(i+1,i)}$, $\mathrm{Cxc}_{(i+1,i)}$, and $\mathrm{Cyc}_{(i+1,i)}$. As above analyzed, in SPECK32/64's last ⊞, among the tuple (x, y, c) (with $c = z \oplus x \oplus y$ and unknown z), only y is known. Hence, exploiting knowledge of y requires examining bit positions with differential constraints fulfilling $\mathrm{Cyc}_{(i+1,i)}$ in Table 4.

In the $\mathrm{Cyc}_{(i+1,i)}$ case, the constraint is on $y_i \oplus c_i$. While c_i may seem unknown, it is determined by lower bits: $c_i = x_{i-1}y_{i-1} \oplus (x_{i-1} \oplus y_{i-1})c_{i-1}$. The knowledge on c_i might be inferred if the $(i-1)$-th bit differences meet the condition $\mathsf{eq}(\alpha_{i-1}, \beta_{i-1}, \gamma_{i-1}) = 0$, as per Observation 1. For example, when

Table 5. Cases for deducing the i-th carry bit c_i

Case No.	Difference	Value	Known
$\mathrm{Cy0c0}_{(i,i-1)}$		$y_{i-1}=0, c_{i-1}=0$	$c_i=0$
$\mathrm{Cy1c1}_{(i,i-1)}$		$y_{i-1}=1, c_{i-1}=1$	$c_i=1$
$\mathrm{Cxy0}_{(i,i-1)}$	$\mathrm{Cxy}_{(i,i-1)}$ and $\mathbf{xor}(\alpha,\beta,\gamma)_i \oplus \alpha_{i-1}=0$	$x_{i-1}\oplus y_{i-1}=0$	$c_i=y_{i-1}$
$\mathrm{Cxy1}_{(i,i-1)}$	$\mathrm{Cxy}_{(i,i-1)}$ and $\mathbf{xor}(\alpha,\beta,\gamma)_i \oplus \alpha_{i-1}=1$	$x_{i-1}\oplus y_{i-1}=1$	$c_i=c_{i-1}$
$\mathrm{Cxc0}_{(i,i-1)}$	$\mathrm{Cxc}_{(i,i-1)}$ and $\mathbf{xor}(\alpha,\beta,\gamma)_i \oplus \alpha_{i-1}=0$	$x_{i-1}\oplus c_{i-1}=0$	$c_i=c_{i-1}$
$\mathrm{Cxc1}_{(i,i-1)}$	$\mathrm{Cxc}_{(i,i-1)}$ and $\mathbf{xor}(\alpha,\beta,\gamma)_i \oplus \alpha_{i-1}=1$	$x_{i-1}\oplus c_{i-1}=1$	$c_i=y_{i-1}$
$\mathrm{Cyc0}_{(i,i-1)}$	$\mathrm{Cyc}_{(i,i-1)}$ and $\mathbf{xor}(\alpha,\beta,\gamma)_i \oplus \beta_{i-1}=0$	$y_{i-1}\oplus c_{i-1}=0$	$c_i=y_{i-1}$
$\mathrm{Cyc1}_{(i,i-1)}$	$\mathrm{Cyc}_{(i,i-1)}$ and $\mathbf{xor}(\alpha,\beta,\gamma)_i \oplus \beta_{i-1}=1$	$y_{i-1}\oplus c_{i-1}=1$	$c_i=x_{i-1}$

Table 6. Cases where the knowledge on y can be used to check the fulfilment of the differential constraints

Case No.	Difference	Known
C1	$\mathrm{Cyc}_{(0,-1)}$	$\mathbf{xor}(\alpha,\beta,\gamma)_1 \oplus \beta_0 = y_0$
C2	$\mathrm{Cyc}_{(2,1)}$ and $\mathrm{Cy0}_{(1,0)}$	$\mathbf{xor}(\alpha,\beta,\gamma)_2 \oplus \beta_1 = y_1$
C3	$\mathrm{Cyc}_{(i+1,i)}$ and $(\mathrm{Cxy0}_{(i,i-1)}$ or $\mathrm{Cxc1}_{(i,i-1)}$ or $\mathrm{Cyc0}_{(i,i-1)})$	$\mathbf{xor}(\alpha,\beta,\gamma)_{i+1}\oplus\beta_i = y_i\oplus y_{i-1}$
C4	$\mathrm{Cyc}_{(i+1,i)}$ and $(\mathrm{Cxy1}_{(i,i-1)}$ or $\mathrm{Cxc0}_{(i,i-1)})$ and $(\mathrm{Cxy0}_{(i-1,i-2)}$ or $\mathrm{Cxc1}_{(i-1,i-2)}$ or $\mathrm{Cyc0}_{(i-1,i-2)})$	$\mathbf{xor}(\alpha,\beta,\gamma)_{i+1}\oplus\beta_i = y_i\oplus y_{i-2}$

$$\begin{cases} (\alpha_i,\beta_i,\gamma_i) = (0,1,0), \\ (\alpha_{i-1},\beta_{i-1},\gamma_{i-1}) = (1,1,0) \end{cases}, \quad \text{one knows that} \begin{cases} \mathbf{eq}(\alpha,\beta,\gamma)_{i-1} = 0, \\ \alpha_{i-1}\oplus\beta_{i-1} = 0, \\ \mathbf{xor}(\alpha,\beta,\gamma)_i \oplus \alpha_{i-1} = 0. \end{cases}$$

From Table 4, one has $x_{i-1}\oplus y_{i-1}=0$. Thus, $c_i = x_{i-1}y_{i-1}\oplus(x_{i-1}\oplus y_{i-1})c_{i-1} = y_{i-1}$. Therefore, $y_i \oplus c_i = y_i \oplus y_{i-1}$. As a consequence, one can predict the fulfilment of constraint in case $\mathrm{Cyc}_{(i+1,i)}$ by observing whether $y_i \oplus y_{i-1} = \mathbf{xor}(\alpha,\beta,\gamma)_{i+1} \oplus \beta_i$. Table 5 lists more cases where c_i might be known.

Incorporating observations from Table 4 and Table 5, one gets Table 6, which lists various cases where the knowledge of y can be used to determine the satisfaction of differential constraints.

Note that apart from the general cases (C3 and C4) at the i-th bit, special cases (C1 and C2) emerge at the two least significant bits due to the carry bit c_0 being 0. For example,

1. at the 0th bit position, observing $\beta_0 = 0$ and $\gamma_0 = 1$ determines $\alpha_0 = 1$ based on Alg. 3 in [4]. From case $\mathrm{Cyc}_{(i+1,i)}$ in Table 4 and given $c_0 = 0$, one knows that $\mathbf{xor}(\alpha,\beta,\gamma)_1 \oplus \beta_0 = y_0 \oplus c_0 = y_0$;
2. at the 1st bit position, $c_1 = x_0 y_0 \oplus (x_0 \oplus y_0)c_0 = x_0 y_0$. Given an observed $y_0 = 0$, one knows $c_1 = 0$. Consequently, in case $\mathrm{Cyc}_{(2,1)}$ and $y_0 = 0$, one knows $\mathbf{xor}(\alpha,\beta,\gamma)_2 \oplus \beta_1 = y_1 \oplus c_1 = y_1$;

3. in general case C3, based on Table 5, c_i is determined as y_{i-1}, leading to the use of $y_i \oplus y_{i-1}$;
4. in general case C4, applying Table 5 to the $(i-1, i-2)$-th bit position, it is inferred that $c_i = c_{i-1} = y_{i-2}$, leading to the use of $y_i \oplus y_{i-2}$;
5. for cases where $c_{i-1} = c_{i-2}$, one can further observe differences at the $(i-2)$-th bit position and continues deducting c_{i-2} by observing bit differences at the $i-3$ position.

Table 7 lists some concrete examples of differential patterns where the observation of y enables prediction of whether differential constraints are met.

Remark 2. These constraints on values for valid differential propagation resonate with established concepts. Specifically, insights derived from Table 6 align with findings on multi-bit constraints from [18,19], quasi-differential trails in [8], and extended differential-linear approximations in [11]. Table 7 exhibits the correspondence between examples of cases in Table 6 and these established concepts. For instance, given a differential propagation $(\alpha_{i+1,i,i-1}, \beta_{i+1,i,i-1} \mapsto \gamma_{i+1,i,i-1}) = (*01, *11 \mapsto *00)$ (for $0 < i < n - 1$),

1. using the 1.5-bit constraints concept and the finite state machines representing the differential properties of modular addition from [18,19], one can get a new constraint and refine the propagation $(\text{--x}, \text{-xx} \mapsto \text{---})$ to $(\text{--x}, \text{->x} \mapsto \text{---})$ (where the notations $\{-, \mathtt{x}, >, <, =, !\}$ are explained below Table 7); more generally, C3 cases correspond to the 1.5-bit constraints $\{>, <, =, !\}$ in [18,19];
2. using the quasi-differential trail concept from [8], the differential trail $(001, 011 \mapsto 000)$ comprises a non-trivial quasi-differential trail with a mask of $(000, 011 \mapsto 000)$. The non-trivial quasi-differential trail has correlation -2^{-1} (*i.e.*, additional weight of 0). Consequently, the "fixed-y" probability of this differential trail is $(1 - (-1)^{y_i \oplus y_{i-1}}) \cdot 2^{-1}$, *i.e.*, the probability equals 1 when $y_i \oplus y_{i-1} = 1$ and 0 in the opposite case;
3. using the extended differential-linear connectivity table (EDLCT) concept from [11], assessing the constraint $y_i \oplus y_{i-1} = \alpha_{i+1} \oplus \beta_{i+1} \oplus \gamma_{i+1} \oplus \beta_i$ aligns with gauging the bias of the linear approximation $(x_{i+1} \oplus x'_{i+1}) \oplus (y_{i+1} \oplus y'_{i+1}) \oplus (z_{i+1} \oplus z'_{i+1}) \oplus (y_i \oplus y'_i) \oplus (y_i \oplus y_{i-1})$ that corresponds to selecting bits $[x_{i+1}, y_{i+1}, z_{i+1}, y_{i-1}]$ and $[x'_{i+1}, y'_{i+1}, z'_{i+1}, y'_i]$.

As noted in [7], $\mathcal{ND}$s rely on differential-linear (DL) properties. We note that pure DL properties do not provide additional information beyond full DDT; the differential-linear distribution can be directly derived from the full differential distribution. It is the *extended* differential-linear distribution [11] (which includes the selection of ciphertext values apart from differences) that contains additional information.

To directly exploit these observations for an r-round SPECK32/64, a preliminary is to effectively predict the input difference α at the last $\boxplus$, which equals $((\delta_R^{r-2})^{\lll 2} \oplus \delta_R^{r-1})^{\ggg 7}$. Given the known δ_R^{r-1} from r-round outputs, the focus shifts to predicting $(\delta_R^{r-2})^{\lll 2}$. Notably, for $r \leq 7$ and input difference $(0040, 0000)$, some bits of $(\delta_R^{r-2})^{\lll 2}$ exhibit bias, as detailed in Table 8, enabling predictions of α for positive samples.

Table 7. Concrete examples of differential patterns where one can predict the fulfilment of the differential constraints by observing the value of y

Case No.	Observation 1			Multi-bit Constraints in [18,19]		Quasi-differential in [8]		Extended DLCT in [11]
	Difference local map	Value	Observations	org	new	diff	mask (add. w)	selected bits
C1	$\alpha_{1,0}$ *1 $\beta_{1,0}$ *0 $\gamma_{1,0}$ *1	$x_{1,0}$ ** $y_{1,0}$ ** $z_{1,0}$ **	$y_0 =$ $\alpha_1 \oplus \beta_1 \oplus \gamma_1 \oplus 0$	-x -- -x	-x -0 -x	01 00 01	00 00 (+2⁰) 00	[x_1, y_1, z_1], [x'_1, y'_1, z'_1, y_0], [x'_2,
C2	$\alpha_{2,1,0}$ *1* $\beta_{2,1,0}$ *0* $\gamma_{2,1,0}$ *1*	$x_{2,1,0}$ *** $y_{2,1,0}$ **0 $z_{2,1,0}$ ***	$y_1 =$ $\alpha_2 \oplus \beta_2 \oplus \gamma_2 \oplus 0$	-x? --0 -x?	-x? -00 -x?	010 000 010	000 000 (+2⁻¹) 000	[x_2, y_2, z_2, y_0], [x'_2, v'_2, z'_2, z'_2, y'_1]
C3	$\alpha_{i+1,i,i-1}$ *01 $\beta_{i+1,i,i-1}$ *11 $\gamma_{i+1,i,i-1}$ *00	$x_{i+1,i,i-1}$ *** $y_{i+1,i,i-1}$ *** $z_{i+1,i,i-1}$ ***	$y_i \oplus y_{i-1} =$ $\alpha_{i+1} \oplus \beta_{i+1} \oplus$ $\gamma_{i+1} \oplus 1$	--x -xx ---	--x ->x ---	001 011 000	000 011 (-2⁰) 000	[x_{i+1}, y_{i+1}, z_{i+1}, y_{i-1}], [x'_{i+1}, y'_{i+1}, z'_{i+1}, y'_i]
C3	$\alpha_{i+1,i,i-1}$ *11 $\beta_{i+1,i,i-1}$ *00 $\gamma_{i+1,i,i-1}$ *11	$x_{i+1,i,i-1}$ *** $y_{i+1,i,i-1}$ *** $z_{i+1,i,i-1}$ ***	$y_i \oplus y_{i-1} =$ $\alpha_{i+1} \oplus \beta_{i+1} \oplus$ $\gamma_{i+1} \oplus 0$	-xx --- -xx	-xx -.- -xx	011 000 011	000 011 (+2⁰) 000	[x_{i+1}, y_{i+1}, z_{i+1}, y_{i-1}], [x'_{i+1}, y'_{i+1}, z'_{i+1}, y'_i]
C4	$\alpha_{i+1,i,i-1,i-2}$ *111 $\beta_{i+1,i,i-1,i-2}$ *010 $\gamma_{i+1,i,i-1,i-2}$ *101	$x_{i+1,i,i-1,i-2}$ **** $y_{i+1,i,i-1,i-2}$ **** $z_{i+1,i,i-1,i-2}$ ****	$y_i \oplus y_{i-2} =$ $\alpha_{i+1} \oplus \beta_{i+1} \oplus$ $\gamma_{i+1} \oplus 0$	-xxx --x- -x-x	-xxx -2x- -x-x	0111 0010 0101	0000 0101 (+2⁰) 0000	[x_{i+1}, y_{i+1}, z_{i+1}, y_{i-2}], [x'_{i+1}, y'_{i+1}, z'_{i+1}, y'_i]

0: $y_i = y'_i = 0$ 1: $y_i = y'_i = 1$ -: $y_i = y'_i$ x: $y_i \neq y'_i$ 2: uncommon 2.5-bit constraint "28000014"
=: $y'_i = y_i = y_{i-1}$!: $y'_i = y_i \neq y_{i-1}$ <: $y'_i \neq y_i = y_{i-1}$ >: $y'_i \neq y_i \neq y_{i-1}$

Table 8. Bit bias towards '0' of $(\delta_R^{r-2})^{\lll 2}$ for $4 \leq r \leq 7$, where the input difference of the plaintext is $\langle 0040, 0000 \rangle$. A positive (resp. negative) value indicates a bias towards '0' (resp. '1').

Position	15	14	13	12	11	10	9	8	7	6	5	4	3	2	1	0
$(\delta_R^3)^{\lll 2}$	0.4689	0.4377	0.3752	0.2498	-0.0002	-0.5000	0.5000	0.5000	0.5000	0.5000	0.5000	0.5000	-0.5000	0.5000	-0.4922	0.4844
$(\delta_R^4)^{\lll 2}$	0.3749	0.2809	0.1247	-0.1241	0.0100	0.4687	0.4451	0.4062	0.3435	0.2498	-0.1251	-0.0000	-0.4922	0.4844	-0.4608	0.4297
$(\delta_R^5)^{\lll 2}$	0.0926	-0.0347	0.0004	-0.0617	0.0028	-0.3709	0.3012	0.2046	-0.0578	-0.0004	0.0312	-0.0009	0.4451	0.4059	-0.2931	0.2035
$(\delta_R^6)^{\lll 2}$	-0.0002	-0.0016	-0.0002	-0.0238	0.0002	0.1531	-0.0243	-0.0001	-0.0034	-0.0011	-0.0076	-0.0001	0.2700	0.1772	-0.0597	-0.0061
$(\delta_R^7)^{\lll 2}$	0.0001	-0.0006	0.0005	0.0103	0.0002	-0.0002	-0.0009	-0.0003	-0.0004	-0.0002	-0.0033	0.0007	-0.0438	-0.0048	-0.0007	-0.0010

A Simple Procedure to Improve the DDT-Based Distinguisher. To improve a DDT-based distinguisher for an r-round SPECK32/64 using its DDT$_{(0040,\,0000)}$, we proceed as follows, resulting in distinguishers named $\mathcal{YD}^{\text{SPECK}_r R}$:

1. Compute the bias (towards 0) of each bit of $(\delta_R^{r-2})^{\lll 2}$,
2. Predict bit values for $(\delta_R^{r-2})^{\lll 2}$ based on their biases: assign a value of 0 if bias ≥ 0 and 1 otherwise,
3. Define the absolute bias of the i-bit of $((\delta_R^{r-2})^{\lll 2})^{\ggg 7}$ as $\epsilon_\alpha(i)$,
4. For each output pair of r-round SPECK32/64, use Alg. 1 to predict its classification.

Results of Improving the DDT-Based Distinguisher. Table 9 presents the performance of $\mathcal{YD}^{\text{SPECK}_r R}$ distinguishers, derived from the described enhancement of $\mathcal{DD}^{\text{SPECK}_r R}$. For rounds $4 \leq r \leq 7$, $\mathcal{YD}^{\text{SPECK}_r R}$ typically shows improvement.

Algorithm 1: A simple procedure to improve the DDT-based distinguisher: $\mathcal{YD}^{\text{SPECK}_r R}$

---

1. Get the differential probability p of $(0040,\ 0000) \mapsto (C_L \oplus C_L', C_R \oplus C_R')$ by looking up the table $\text{DDT}_{(0040,\ 0000)}[(C_L \oplus C_L', C_R \oplus C_R')]$

2. Compute the following information around the last $\boxplus$ from $((C_L, C_R), (C_L', C_R'))$:
   (a) $\gamma \leftarrow C_L \oplus C_L'$, $\beta \leftarrow (C_L \oplus C_R \oplus C_L' \oplus C_R')^{\ggg 2}$,
   (b) $\alpha \leftarrow ((\delta_R^{r-2})^{\lll 2} \oplus \beta)^{\ggg 7}$, $y \leftarrow (C_L \oplus C_R)^{\ggg 2}$.

3. For bit position 0, if $\epsilon_\alpha(1) > \tau$ and $\epsilon_\alpha(0) > \tau$, do:
   (a) If $\text{Cyc}_{(0,-1)}$, do: $p \leftarrow (1 + (-1)^{\text{xor}(\alpha,\beta,\gamma)_1 \oplus \beta_0 \oplus y_0}) \cdot p$.

4. For bit position 1, if $\epsilon_\alpha(2) > \tau$ and $\epsilon_\alpha(1) > \tau$, do:
   (a) If $\text{Cyc}_{(2,1)}$ and $y_0 = 0$, do: $p \leftarrow (1 + (-1)^{\text{xor}(\alpha,\beta,\gamma)_2 \oplus \beta_1 \oplus y_1}) \cdot p$.

5. For each bit position i $(1 < i < n-1)$, if $\epsilon_\alpha(i+1) > \tau$ and $\epsilon_\alpha(i) > \tau$ and $\epsilon_\alpha(i-1) > \tau$, do:
   (a) If $\text{Cyc}_{(i+1,i)}$ and $(\text{Cxy0}_{(i,i-1)}$ or $\text{Cxc1}_{(i,i-1)}$ or $\text{Cyc0}_{(i,i-1)})$, do:
   $$p \leftarrow (1 + (-1)^{\text{xor}(\alpha,\beta,\gamma)_{i+1} \oplus \beta_i \oplus y_i \oplus y_{i-1}}) \cdot p.$$
   (b) If $\text{Cyc}_{(i+1,i)}$ and $(\text{Cxy1}_{(i,i-1)}$ or $\text{Cxc0}_{(i,i-1)})$ and $(\text{Cxy0}_{(i-1,i-2)}$ or $\text{Cxc1}_{(i-1,i-2)}$ or $\text{Cyc0}_{(i-1,i-2)})$ and $\epsilon_\alpha(i-2) > \tau$, do:
   $$p \leftarrow (1 + (-1)^{\text{xor}(\alpha,\beta,\gamma)_{i+1} \oplus \beta_i \oplus y_i \oplus y_{i-2}}) \cdot p.$$

6. If $p > 2^{-n}$, predict $Z \leftarrow 1$; else predict $Z \leftarrow 0$.

In contrast, when applying a similar method to adjust the $\mathcal{ND}^{\text{SPECK}_r R}$ score Z (converting score Z to probability p using $p = Z/(1 - Z) \cdot 2^{-n}$), the accuracy does not get improved. It is unchanged for $\mathcal{ND}^{\text{SPECK}4R}$ and marginally degrades for rounds $5 \leq r \leq 7$ since the threshold τ is set less than 0.5. This suggests that the additional information useful in improving DDT-based distinguishers does not help improve $\mathcal{ND}$'s; thus, the $\mathcal{ND}$'s might have maximally utilized this information already. Thus, we conclude as follows.

Conclusion 3. *By utilizing conditional differential distributions when the input and/or output values of the last nonlinear operation are observable, a distinguisher can surpass pure DDT-based counterparts. Accordingly, if these conditional distributions differ greatly from the averaged differential distribution, and the satisfaction of the conditions is either observable or effectively predictable, then r-round $\mathcal{ND}$s can outperform r-round DDT-based distinguishers.*

For SPECK, one of the two inputs of the last non-linear operation ($\boxplus$) is observable. If conditioned on this input, the conditional differential distribution can diverge significantly from the averaged one. Therefore, an optimal distinguisher can obviously outperform a pure DDT-based counterpart. A similar analysis applies to SIMON. In SIMON, the values that go through the last nonlinear operation are fully observable. Consequently, it is interpretable that in the case of SIMON, an r-round $\mathcal{ND}$ can achieve an accuracy close to the $(r-1)$-round DDT [3].

This conclusion can be further supported by the following experimental result: In a modified r-round SPECK32/64 where the last key XORing is omitted, revealing both z and y (equating to full awareness of the satisfaction of the last round's differential constraints given a predictable input difference α), a well-trained r-round $\mathcal{ND}$ achieves an accuracy close to the $(r-1)$-round $\mathcal{DD}$. Interestingly, subsequent observations on $\mathcal{RK}$-$\mathcal{ND}$s reinforce our conclusion, while the conclusion itself aids in interpreting those observations.

3.3 Distinguishers Using Systematic Computation of Conditional Differential Probability Under Known y

The simple process in Algorithm 1 is fast, but it requires evaluating the bias of each bit of the difference on the right branch of round $r-2$ to estimate the input difference α for the last modular addition. The differential probability can only be adjusted if the estimated bias of the corresponding bit of α exceeds a certain threshold. As a result, it does not make the most of the information in y. Therefore, we further designed a process, described in Algorithm 2, to systematically calculate the differential probability conditioned under the known value of y and predict based on the $(r-1)$-round DDT[1].

In essence, the systematic process involves using β, γ, and y to determine all possible αs and the conditional differential probabilities of the last round. It combines this information with the probabilities of the previous $(r-1)$ rounds to calculate the conditional differential probability for r rounds under the known value of y. Finally, it uses the systematically computed conditional probability for prediction.

More concretely, in the process, we have the following procedures:

1. **Precomputation:** We generate three b-bit conditional DDTs, denoted as $\mathbf{A}_0$, $\mathbf{A}_{\text{next}}$, and $\mathbf{A}_{\text{next}}^c$, of the single modular addition operation ⊞. These resemble Dinur's b-bit filter in [12]:
   (a) $\mathbf{A}_0$ tells all valid b-bit values of α with their associated probability pr for given b-bit inputs β, γ, and y at the first b least significant bits (LSB) where the first carry bits are zeros.
   (b) $\mathbf{A}_{\text{next}}$ tells all valid 1-bit values of α_{next} with their associated probability pr for given b-bit inputs β, γ, y, and $(b-1)$-bit α at intermediate consecutive b bits where the LSB of carry is undetermined.
   (c) $\mathbf{A}_{\text{next}}^c$ is similar to $\mathbf{A}_{\text{next}}$ but serves scenarios with known carry LSBs.
2. **Initialization:** From a received ciphertext pair, we derive the output difference γ, input difference β, and input value y; initialize the to-be-calculated probability p and the last round's probability factor q with 0 and 1.
3. **Generate candidate LSB b-bit of α:**
   (a) Using table $\mathbf{A}_0$, we obtain candidates for the LSB b-bit of α based on the LSB b-bit of β, γ, and y, update q with the associated pr.

---

[1] Please refer to [1] for the implementation codes and experimental results.

(b) For each valid LSB b-bit of α, we invoke 'ComputeCarryNextBit' to determine the carry bits wherever possible according to Table 5.

4. **Iterative Calculation:** For each valid LSB b-bit of α,

(a) Starting from the $(b-1)$-th bit, we invoke 'ComputeAlphaPrNextBit' to sequentially determine α's later bits and the respective augmentation of the probability factor to q; alongside, we use 'ComputeCarryNextBit' to determine the carry bits wherever possible, preparing to be used to derive later bits of α in case of Cyc or be used to look up $\mathbf{A}^c_{next}$.

Within procedure 'ComputeAlphaPrNextBit':

(a) Once α is fully assigned, we calculate the output difference of the penultimate round and use it to look up the $(r-1)$-round DDT. The resultant value, upon multiplied by the last round's probability factor q, yields a contribution term to the final probability p.

(b) At an intermediate bit position i, equal three input/output bits differences facilitate the direct determination of the subsequent α bit.

(c) When input/output bits differences at position $(i+1, i)$ conforms to the $\mathrm{Cyc}_{(i+1,i)}$ condition with an determined value for c_i, the subsequent α bit is deduced using $y_i \oplus c_i$. After determining α_{i+1}, we invoke 'ComputeCarryNextBit' to determine the carry bit c_{i+1} wherever possible.

(d) Otherwise (in the absence of conformity or a determined c_i value), α_{i+1} is enumerated using either $\mathbf{A}_{next}$ or $\mathbf{A}^c_{next}$, depending on whether the carry bit before b bits of the $(i+1)$-th bit is determined.

(e) After obtaining α_{i+1} and its probability pr, we continue to determine the next α bit, updating the probability factor by multiplying pr to q.

The resulting procedure is slower than the simple one; however, the resulting distinguishers, named "$\mathcal{AD}_{\mathbf{YD}}$", have accuracy exceeds not only that of the distinguishers $\mathcal{DD}$s but also the neural distinguishers $\mathcal{ND}$s, comparable to the $r-1$-round DDT-based key-averaging distinguishers $\mathcal{AD}_{\mathbf{KD}}$s [2] (refer to Table 9 and Table 20 in [4]), indicating an exemplary accuracy for $\mathcal{ND}$s.

3.4   Discussion on $\mathcal{ND}$'s Advantages

Based on the above observations and experiments, we can conclude that $\mathcal{ND}$'s advantage over pure differential-based distinguishers comes from exploiting the conditional differential distribution under the partially known value from ciphertexts input to the last non-linear operation. More specifically, $\mathcal{ND}$s exploited the correlation between the ciphertexts' partial value, the ciphertext pair's differences, and the intermediate states' differences. Specifically, when some of the last-round nonlinear operations' inputs and outputs are known (*i.e.*, not XORed with independently randomized key bits), a distinguisher can achieve higher distinguishing accuracy than an r-round pure differential-based distinguisher.

These findings apply not only to the SPECK but also to other block ciphers, such as SIMON and GIFT (refer to Appendix D.1 in [4]), and demonstrate the ability of neural networks to capture and utilize complex relationships between

---

Algorithm 2: Known-y differential distinguishers: $\mathcal{AD}_{\mathbf{YD}}^{\text{SPECK}_r R}$

---

1. $b \leftarrow 6$ // for practical reason, we consider 6-bit conditional DDT of $\boxplus$
2. $\mathbf{A}_0, \mathbf{A}_{\text{next}}, \mathbf{A}_{\text{next}}^c \leftarrow$ GenMultiBitsConditionalDDTs(b)
3. $p \leftarrow 0.0, q \leftarrow 1.0$
4. Compute the following around the last $\boxplus$ from $((C_L, C_R), (C_L', C_R'))$:
   (a) $\gamma \leftarrow C_L \oplus C_L'$, $\beta \leftarrow (C_L \oplus C_R \oplus C_L' \oplus C_R')^{\ggg 2}$, $y \leftarrow (C_L \oplus C_R)^{\ggg 2}$.
5. $\alpha \leftarrow \mathbf{0}, c \leftarrow \mathbf{0}$
6. $\beta_b \leftarrow$ LSB b bits of β, $\gamma_b \leftarrow$ LSB b bits of γ, $y_b \leftarrow$ LSB b bits of y
7. For $(\alpha_b, pr) \in \mathbf{A}_0[\beta_b, \gamma_b, y_b]$
   (a) $\alpha \leftarrow \alpha_b$
   (b) For i in $\{0, 1, \ldots, b-2\}$: ComputeCarryNextBit($c, \alpha, \beta, \gamma, y, i$)
   (c) ComputeAlphaPrNextBit($c, \alpha, \beta, \gamma, y, b-1, q \times pr, p$)
8. If $p > 2^{-n}$, predict $Z \leftarrow 1$; else predict $Z \leftarrow 0$.

ComputeAlphaPrNextBit($c, \alpha, \beta, \gamma, y, i, q, p$) // update c_{i+1}, α_{i+1}, p in-place
   1. If $i = \text{WordSize} - 1$: $p \leftarrow p + q \times \mathcal{DD}^{\text{SPECK}_{r-1}R}(\alpha^{\lll 7} \| \beta)$; return
   2. If $\text{eq}(\alpha_i, \beta_i, \gamma_i)$:
      (a) $\alpha_{i+1} \leftarrow \beta_{i+1} \oplus \gamma_{i+1} \oplus \beta_i$; ComputeCarryNextBit($c, \alpha, \beta, \gamma, y, i$);
      (b) ComputeAlphaPrNextBit($c, \alpha, \beta, \gamma, y, i+1, q \cdot 1, p$); return
   3. Else if $\text{Cyc}_{(i+1,i)}$ and $c_i \neq \bot$:
      (a) $\alpha_{i+1} \leftarrow \beta_{i+1} \oplus \gamma_{i+1} \oplus \beta_i \oplus y_i \oplus c_i$; ComputeCarryNextBit($c, \alpha, \beta, \gamma, y, i$)
      (b) ComputeAlphaPrNextBit($\alpha, \beta, \gamma, y, i+1, q \cdot 1, p$); return
   4. Else:
      (a) $\beta_b \leftarrow \beta_{\{i+1,\ldots,i+2-b\}}$, $\gamma_b \leftarrow \gamma_{\{i+1,\ldots,i+2-b\}}$, $y_b \leftarrow y_{\{i+1,\ldots,i+2-b\}}$, $\alpha_b \leftarrow \alpha_{\{i,\ldots,i+2-b\}}$
      (b) If $c_{i+2-b} \neq \bot$: For $(\alpha_{i+1}, pr) \leftarrow \mathbf{A}_{\text{next}}^c[\beta_b, \gamma_b, y_b, \alpha_b, c_{i+2-b}]$
         – ComputeCarryNextBit($c, \alpha, \beta, \gamma, y, i$)
         – ComputeAlphaPrNextBit($\alpha, \beta, \gamma, y, i+1, q \cdot pr, p$)
      (c) If $c_{i+2-b} = \bot$: For $(\alpha_{i+1}, pr) \leftarrow \mathbf{A}_{\text{next}}[\beta_b, \gamma_b, y_b, \alpha_b]$
         – ComputeCarryNextBit($c, \alpha, \beta, \gamma, y, i$)
         – ComputeAlphaPrNextBit($\alpha, \beta, \gamma, y, i+1, q \cdot pr, p$)

ComputeCarryNextBit($c, \alpha, \beta, \gamma, y, i$) // update c_{i+1} in-place
   1. If $y_i = 0$ and $c_i = 0$: $c_{i+1} \leftarrow 0$
   2. Else if $y_i = 1$ and $c_i = 1$: $c_{i+1} \leftarrow 1$
   3. Else if $\text{Cxy0}_{(i+1,i)}$ or $\text{Cxc1}_{(i+1,i)}$ or $\text{Cyc0}_{(i+1,i)}$: $c_{i+1} \leftarrow y_i$
   4. Else if $\text{Cxy1}_{(i+1,i)}$ or $\text{Cxc0}_{(i+1,i)}$: $c_{i+1} \leftarrow c_i$
   5. Else: $c_{i+1} \leftarrow \bot$. // $\bot$ means unknown

GenMultiBitsConditionalDDTs(b)
   1. $\mathbf{A}_0 \leftarrow$ Generate b-bit conditional DDT of $\boxplus$, each entry is indexed by (b-bit β, b-bit γ, b-bit y), the values are (b-bit α, non-zero pr). // $\mathbf{A}_0$ will be used for the first b bits since one knows that both LSB carry bits are 0.
   2. $\mathbf{A}_{\text{next}} \leftarrow$ Generate b-bit conditional DDT of $\boxplus$, each entry is indexed by (b-bit β, b-bit γ, b-bit y, $(b-1)$-bit α), the values are (1-bit α_{next}, non-zero pr). // $\mathbf{A}_{\text{next}}$ will be used for the intermediate bits when LSB carry c is unknown.
   3. $\mathbf{A}_{\text{next}}^c \leftarrow$ Generate b-bit conditional DDT of $\boxplus$, each entry is indexed by (b-bit β, b-bit γ, b-bit y, $(b-1)$-bit α, 1-bit carry c), the values are (1-bit α_{next}, non-zero pr). // $\mathbf{A}_{\text{next}}^c$ will be used for the intermediate bits when LSB carry c is known.
   4. Output $\mathbf{A}_0, \mathbf{A}_{\text{next}}, \mathbf{A}_{\text{next}}^c$

Table 9. Performance of the improved DDT-based distinguishers ($\mathcal{YD}$s and $\mathcal{AD}_{\mathbf{YD}}$s) on SPECK32/64 and comparisons with pure DDT-based distinguishers ($\mathcal{DD}$s), neural distinguishers ($\mathcal{ND}$s), and DDT-based key-averaging distinguishers ($\mathcal{AD}_{\mathbf{KD}}$s)

#R	Name	ACC	TPR	TNR	Mem (GBytes)	Time (Secs per 2^{20})
4	$\mathcal{DD}^{\text{SPECK}_4 R}$	0.9869	0.9869	0.9870	32.5	$2^{-4.98}$
4	$\mathcal{YD}^{\text{SPECK}_4 R}$	0.9907	0.9887	0.9928	32.5	$2^{-2.37}$
5	$\mathcal{DD}^{\text{SPECK}_5 R}$	0.9107	0.8775	0.9440	32.5	$2^{-4.94}$
5	$\mathcal{YD}^{\text{SPECK}_5 R}$	0.9215	0.8947	0.9484	32.5	$2^{-1.87}$
5	$\mathcal{ND}^{\text{SPECK}_5 R}$	0.9273	0.9011	0.9536	0.0277	$2^{+3.56}$
5	$\mathcal{AD}_{\mathbf{YD}}^{\text{SPECK}_5 R}$	0.9362	0.9173	0.9552	32.5	$2^{+5.46}$
5	$\mathcal{AD}_{\mathbf{KD}}^{\text{SPECK}_5 R}$	0.9364	0.9171	0.9557	32.5	$2^{+7.03}$
6	$\mathcal{DD}^{\text{SPECK}_6 R}$	0.7584	0.6795	0.8371	32.5	$2^{-4.53}$
6	$\mathcal{YD}^{\text{SPECK}_6 R}$	0.7663	0.7118	0.8207	32.5	$2^{-2.05}$
6	$\mathcal{ND}^{\text{SPECK}_6 R}$	0.7876	0.7197	0.8554	0.0277	$2^{+3.54}$
6	$\mathcal{AD}_{\mathbf{YD}}^{\text{SPECK}_6 R}$	0.7949	0.7309	0.8587	32.5	$2^{+5.12}$
6	$\mathcal{AD}_{\mathbf{KD}}^{\text{SPECK}_6 R}$	0.7946	0.7309	0.8583	32.5	$2^{+7.03}$
7	$\mathcal{DD}^{\text{SPECK}_7 R}$	0.5913	0.5430	0.6397	32.5	$2^{-4.49}$
7	$\mathcal{YD}^{\text{SPECK}_7 R}$	0.5962	0.5582	0.6343	32.5	$2^{-2.18}$
7	$\mathcal{ND}^{\text{SPECK}_7 R}$	0.6155	0.5325	0.6985	0.0277	$2^{+3.57}$
7	$\mathcal{AD}_{\mathbf{YD}}^{\text{SPECK}_7 R}$	0.6237	0.5428	0.7048	32.5	$2^{+5.33}$
7	$\mathcal{AD}_{\mathbf{KD}}^{\text{SPECK}_7 R}$	0.6240	0.5435	0.7046	32.5	$2^{+7.04}$
8	$\mathcal{DD}^{\text{SPECK}_8 R}$	0.5116	0.4963	0.5268	32.5	$2^{-4.64}$
8	$\mathcal{YD}^{\text{SPECK}_8 R}$	0.5117	0.4967	0.5268	32.5	$2^{-2.99}$
8	$\mathcal{ND}^{\text{SPECK}_8 R}$	0.5135	0.5184	0.5085	0.0277	$2^{+3.55}$
8	$\mathcal{AD}_{\mathbf{YD}}^{\text{SPECK}_8 R}$	0.5187	0.4914	0.5460	32.5	$2^{+5.51}$
8	$\mathcal{AD}_{\mathbf{KD}}^{\text{SPECK}_8 R}$	0.5194	0.4919	0.5469	32.5	$2^{+7.04}$

- ACC: Accuracy, TPR: True Positive Rate, TNR: True Negative Rate
- For $\mathcal{YD}$s, the thresholds τ's for $\sigma_\alpha(i)$'s in building $\mathcal{YD}^{\text{SPECK}_4 R}$, $\mathcal{YD}^{\text{SPECK}_5 R}$, $\mathcal{YD}^{\text{SPECK}_6 R}$, $\mathcal{YD}^{\text{SPECK}_7 R}$ are 0.50, 0.30, 0.20, and 0.02, respectively. The number of samples for the accuracy testing is 2^{24}.
- The number of samples for benchmark is 2^{20}. Thus, the times are seconds taken by making predictions on 2^{20} samples.
- All DDT-based distinguishers ($\mathcal{DD}$s, $\mathcal{YD}$s, $\mathcal{AD}_{\mathbf{YD}}$s, and $\mathcal{AD}_{\mathbf{KD}}$s) are implemented in C++ (compiled using g++ 9.4.0 with optimization option '-O3'), whereas $\mathcal{ND}$-based distinguishers ($\mathcal{ND}$s) are implemented in Python.
- The benchmark environment is as follows: OS: Ubuntu 20.04; Processor: Intel(R) Xeon(R) Gold 6330 CPU @ 2.00GHz; Memory: 256 GB DDR4 memory; all timings were restricted to run using a single CPU thread.
- We profiled the memory requirements of $\mathcal{ND}$s using the Tracemalloc module in Python. We specifically measured the peak allocated memory, excluding the memory allocated for storing the testing dataset. This was calculated by determining the memory usage when loading the $\mathcal{ND}$ and making predictions, and then subtracting the memory usage when these operations were excluded (for example, 0.246898 GB − 0.219219 GB). For other distinguishers, we assessed memory requirements by referencing the 'RES' column associated with the process in the 'htop' command.

Table 10. The accuracy of differential-neural distinguishers using distinct differences obtained by (0040, 0000) after i rounds of propagation. Prob. represents the probability of the highest probability differential (0040,0000) → "Diff.".

i	Diff.	Prob.	Acc.	i	Diff.	Prob.	Acc.
0	(0040,0000)	1	0.6137	3	(8000,840a)	2^{-3}	0.7394
1	(8000,8000)	1	0.6137	4	(850a,9520)	2^{-7}	0.9166
2	(8100,8102)	2^{-1}	0.6705				

ciphertext values and intermediate state differences. Note that the neural distinguishers are not aware of the specific details of the ciphers, including their non-linear components and structure. Therefore, these neural distinguishers can be used for ciphers that have unknown components.

On the Performance of Various Distinguishers. Experiments showed that $\mathcal{ND}$s can be more efficient while achieving comparable accuracy to sophisticated manual methods (Alg. 2). Please refer to Table 9 for detailed benchmarks. Note that in benchmarks listed in Table 9, all DDT-based distinguishers are implemented in C++, whereas $\mathcal{ND}$-based distinguishers are implemented in `Python Tensorflow`. Although implementations in C++ might be inherently faster than its `Python` counterpart, $\mathcal{ND}^{\text{SPECK}*R}$s in `Python` are still more efficient than $\mathcal{AD}^{\text{SPECK}*R}_{\text{YD}}$ and $\mathcal{AD}^{\text{SPECK}*R}_{\text{KD}}$ in C++ (all restricted to run in a single CPU thread). Therefore, we can conclude that the neural network-based distinguishers provide a good trade-off between efficiency and accuracy.

4 Insights and Improvements on Training Differential-Neural Distinguisher

4.1 Relations Between Distinguisher Accuracy and Differential Distribution

Traditional differential cryptanalysis predominantly utilizes high-probability differentials as distinguishers. However, differential-neural cryptanalysis exploits all output differences for distinguishing while fixing input differences for plaintext pairs. In EUROCRYPT 2021, Benamira *et al.* [7] argued that differential-neural distinguisher is inherently building a very good approximation of the DDT during the learning phase.

Our study delves into the relation between the accuracy of the differential-neural distinguisher and the differential distribution of ciphertext pairs. We modify the input difference of plaintext pairs, inspired by Gohr's staged training method [15]. In [15], while the basic training method can produce a valid 7-round distinguisher, an 8-round distinguisher must be trained using the staged training approach. The core of the staged training method is training a pre-trained 7-round distinguisher to learn 5-round SPECK32/64's output pairs with

Table 11. The accuracy of the differential-neural distinguisher using distinct differences obtained by (0040, 0000) after 2 rounds of propagation. Prob. represents the probability of differential $(0040,0000) \to$ "Diff.". Round $2 + i$ represents the positive sample of the training set is the ciphertext pair obtained by encrypting the plaintext pair that satisfies this difference for i rounds

Diff.	Prob.	Acc. (2+4)	Acc. (2+5)	Acc. (2+6)	Diff.	Prob.	Acc. (2+4)	Acc. (2+5)	Acc. (2+6)
(8100,8102)	2^{-1}	0.8720	0.6811	0.5270	(8f00,8f02)	2^{-4}	0.6746	Fail	Fail
(8300,8302)	2^{-2}	0.8191	0.6218	Fail	(9f00,9f02)	2^{-5}	Fail	Fail	Fail
(8700,8702)	2^{-3}	0.7492	Fail	Fail	(bf00,bf02)	2^{-6}	Fail	Fail	Fail

the input difference (8000,804a) (the most likely difference to appear three rounds after the input difference (0040,0000)). Employing such plaintext pairs aims to concentrate the difference distribution of ciphertext pairs, escalating the output difference's likelihood and simplifying the distinguisher's learning task.

In our work, we first introduce a 4-round highest probability differential trail starting from (0040,0000).

$$(0040,0000) \to (8000,8000) \to (8100,8102) \to (8000,840a) \to (850a,9520)$$

Our experiments (see Table 10) initially employ a 4-round high-probability differential trail starting from (0040,0000), leading to (850a,9520).

By default, we use (0040,0000) as the input difference of the plaintext pair to generate the ciphertext pair. Here, in Table 10, we use the difference of the highest probability of (0040,0000) after i $(1 \leq i \leq 4)$ rounds of propagation as the input difference of the plaintext pair, respectively.

From Table 8, we can observe that the larger i is, the higher the accuracy of the differential-neural distinguisher. As i increases, the difference distribution in the ciphertext becomes more concentrated, and the probability of each difference increases. Therefore, the more significant the difference between the ciphertext and the random number, the accuracy of the differential-neural distinguisher is continuously improved.

To more comprehensively demonstrate the relation between the accuracy of the differential-neural distinguisher and the differential distribution of the ciphertext pairs, we conducted some experiments from another perspective. We fixed the number of rounds of differential but chose multiple 2-round differences with gradually decreasing probabilities. In Table 11, we notice that the higher the fixed probability of the differential, the higher the accuracy of the differential-neural distinguisher obtained. In other words, a lower probability means that after i rounds of encryption, the differential distribution of the ciphertext is more dispersed, and the neural network is more difficult to learn, resulting in a continuous decrease in the number of rounds and accuracy of the differential-neural distinguisher.

In conclusion, controlling differential propagation is imperative to enhance the differential-neural distinguisher's accuracy and the number of rounds. We thus propose a method to control the differential propagation and reduce the diffusion of features, thereby increasing the number of rounds of the differential-neural distinguisher. However, before the formal introduction, we introduce one method that can simplify the training process of high round distinguisher.

4.2 Freezing Layer Method

In existing experiments on SPECK32/64, especially with an input difference of (0040,0000), there has been a notable limitation. Researchers have been able to directly train a differential-neural distinguisher for up to only 7 rounds. Direct training for higher rounds from scratch has been challenging. A potential avenue that has garnered attention is the utilization of various network fine-tuning strategies. Specifically, continuing the training phase from pre-trained models has been proposed to potentially overcome these limitations and expand the distinguisher's round capability. Examples include the staged training method in [15] and the staged pipeline method in [6].

The inability to directly train the 8-round distinguisher likely stems from feature diffusion associated with the input difference (0040,0000) over increasing rounds. This makes the 8-round features considerably challenging for the distinguisher to learn directly from limited data, as compared to lower rounds. One approach is to either mitigate feature diffusion or narrow the distinguisher's solution space. While a technique to constrain feature diffusion is discussed in the subsequent chapter, in this context, we employ the classic network fine-tuning strategy, the freezing layer method, to limit the solution space.

Our distinguishers consist of two parts: the convolutional layers and fully connected layers. In the field of artificial intelligence, all convolutional layers are viewed as feature extractors, while all fully connected layers are viewed as a classifier. We argue that the feature extractor can be reused, and the classifiers are relatively similar in adjacent rounds. Therefore, to train an 8-round distinguisher for SPECK32/64, we can simply load a well-trained 7-round model and freeze all its convolutional layers, meaning that only parameters in fully connected layers can be updated. Then, we can obtain an 8-round distinguisher with accuracy identical to the ones in [6,15], remaining all hyperparameters in the training process unchanged.

Relative to the staged training method [15], our approach maintains the same hyperparameters and does not require more samples in the final stage. In comparison with the method in [6], we only need two training rounds instead of multiple rounds in a row as required by the simple training pipeline in [6]. Besides, the simple training pipeline [6] did not produce $\mathcal{ND}$s with the same accuracy as Gohr's on 8-round SPECK32/64; it needs a further polishing step to achieve similar accuracy, demanding more time and data. Our freezing layer method also speeds up the training process due to the reduction of trainable parameters. Therefore, we recommend trying the freezing layer method once the number of the distinguisher is too high to train directly.

5   Related-Key Differential-Neural Cryptanalysis

The $\mathcal{ND}$ explainability concept serves as a fundamental theoretical underpinning when aiming to enhance and leverage its capabilities. With the outcome being that $\mathcal{ND}$s can effectively capture additional features and provide a better trade-off between efficiency and accuracy, there is substantial motivation for us to continue refining and exploiting their potential.

In this section, we introduce the related-key into differential-neural cryptanalysis, enabling control over differential propagation and facilitating the training of high-round $\mathcal{ND}$s. Furthermore, we enhance the DDT-based distinguisher under the $\mathcal{RK}$ setting by employing the analytical methods and conclusions outlined in Sect. 3. As a result of these advancements, we successfully implement a 14-round key recovery attack for SPECK32/64 using the proposed $\mathcal{RK}$-$\mathcal{ND}$s.

5.1   Related-Key Differential-Neural Distinguisher for SPECK32/64

Here we present the related-key differential-neural distinguishers on SPECK32/64 obtained in this work.

The Choice of the Input Difference. The input difference is a crucial and central component of differential-neural cryptanalysis, and numerous papers delve into the study of the input difference, such as [3,6,15,16,21]. To maximize the number of rounds for both $\mathcal{ND}$ and $\mathcal{CD}$, as well as the weak key space as large as possible to perform the longest key recovery attack, we use the SMT-based method to search for appropriate $\mathcal{RK}$ differential or differential trails. It is important to note that the largest weak key space does not necessarily equate to the largest $\mathcal{ND}$ or $\mathcal{CD}$, thus requiring a compromise between the three factors. In this paper, the choice of the best input difference is given under different compromises. Table 12 lists the $\mathcal{RK}$ differential trails used to constrain the key space in SPECK32/64, where we label each distinguisher with an ID. Specifically, ID_1 is used to restrict the weak key space for the 13-round, ID_2 and ID_3 are used to restrict the 14-round. Note that part of the $\mathrm{ID}_2/\mathrm{ID}_3$ (2-round to 11-round) $\mathcal{RK}$ difference are same as the 10-round optimal $\mathcal{RK}$ differential trail for speck32/64 given in Table 9 of [23]. In addition, the round-reduced of the trails are used to restrict the weak key space for shorter rounds, *e.g.*, ID_2 and ID_3 are used to restrict the weak key space for 13-round starting from the second round.

Network Architecture. Given the success of the neural network consisting of the Inception block and residual network in SPECK, SIMON and SIMECK [25,26], as well as its superior performance in differential-neural distinguisher, we use this neural network proposed in [26] to train $\mathcal{RK}$ differential-neural distinguisher. However, we also made some modifications to the network architecture. In deep learning, odd numbers such as 3, 5, and 7 are often used as the size of the convolution kernel. However, according to the cyclic shift of the round function of SPECK32/64, we choose 2 and 7 as the size of the convolution kernel. Furthermore, using 2 as the convolution kernel size can make the model's accuracy

Table 12. Related-key differential trails used to constrain the key space in SPECK32/64 where we label each distinguisher with an ID. For example, ID_1 represents the 13-round $\mathcal{RK}$ differential trail for the key schedule algorithm with $(\Delta l^2, \Delta l^1, \Delta l^0, \Delta k^0) = (0044, 0011, 4000, 0080)$

	ID_1	ID_1	ID_2/ID_3	ID_2/ID_3
r	Differential in Key	$\log_2 \Pr$	Differential in Key	$\log_2 \Pr$
0	(0044,0011,4000,0080)		(0200,0080,0011,4a00)	
1	(0000,0044,0011,0200)	-1	(2800,0200,0080,0001)	-4
2	(2000,0000,0044,2800)	-2	(0000,2800,0200,0004)	-1
3	(a000,2000,0000,0000)	$--2$	(0000,0000,2800,0010)	-1
4	(0000,a000,2000,0000)	-0	(0040,0000,0000,0000)	-2
5	(0040,0000,a000,0040)	-1	(0000,0040,0000,0000)	0
6	(0100,0040,0000,0000)	-2	(0000,0000,0040,0000)	0
7	(0000,0100,0040,0000)	0	(8000,0000,0000,8000)	0
8	(8000,0000,0100,8000)	0	(8000,8000,0000,8002)	0
9	(8002,8000,0000,8000)	-1	(8002,8000,8000,8008)	-1
10	(8000,8002,8000,8002)	0	(8108,8002,8000,812a)	-2
11	(8102,8000,8002,8108)	-2	(802a,8108,8002,8480)	-4
12	(8408,8102,8000,802a)	-3	(8180,802a,8108,9382)/(8280,802a,8108,9082)	$-3/-4$
13			(8180,8180,802a,cf8a)/(8080,8280,802a,c28a)	$-4/-4$
	$\log_2(P_r(Q_K))$: -14		$\log_2(P_r(Q_K))$: $-22/-23$	

converge faster than 3. In [26], the size of the convolution kernel continues to increase as the depth of the residual network increases. We think it is reasonable to increase the convolution kernel's size to improve the network's receptive field, but it cannot always be increased. Therefore, we will limit the size of the convolution kernel to less than or equal to 7.

The Training of Related-Key Differential-Neural Distinguisher. This work still uses the basic training method to train short-round distinguishers. When the basic training method fails, we train the r-round distinguisher with the $(r - 1)$-round distinguisher by using the freezing layer method. Please refer to Appendix F in [4] for the detailed training method.

Performance Evaluation of the Distinguisher. In artificial intelligence, the model's accuracy is the most critical evaluation indicator. In differential-neural cryptanalysis, it is judged whether the guessed key is correct based on the score of the distinguisher. Therefore, we evaluate the performance of the differential-neural distinguisher regarding both the accuracy and the score.

- *Test accuracy.* We summarize the accuracy of the differential-neural distinguisher in Table 13. The 8, and 9-round distinguishers were trained using the basic training method, while the 10-round distinguishers were trained using the freezing layer method. For more insight on related-key differential-neural distinguishers, please refer to Appendix F.2 in [4].

Table 13. The summary of related-key differential-neural distinguishers on SPECK32/64, where the plaintext difference is (0000,0000).

Diff.	#R	Name	Accuracy	True Positive Rate	True Negative Rate
ID_1	8	$\mathcal{RK}\text{-}\mathcal{ND}^{\text{SPECK8}R}$	0.7584	0.6836	0.8332
ID_1	9	$\mathcal{RK}\text{-}\mathcal{ND}^{\text{SPECK9}R}$	0.5620	0.5212	0.6028
ID_2/ID_3	8	$\mathcal{RK}\text{-}\mathcal{ND}^{\text{SPECK8}R}$	0.9259	0.9063	0.9455
ID_2	9	$\mathcal{RK}\text{-}\mathcal{ND}^{\text{SPECK9}R}$	0.7535	0.7035	0.8036
ID_2	10	$\mathcal{RK}\text{-}\mathcal{ND}^{\text{SPECK10}R}$	0.5643	0.5382	0.5893
ID_3	9	$\mathcal{RK}\text{-}\mathcal{ND}^{\text{SPECK9}R}$	0.7726	0.7247	0.8206
ID_3	10	$\mathcal{RK}\text{-}\mathcal{ND}^{\text{SPECK10}R}$	0.5562	0.5361	0.5765

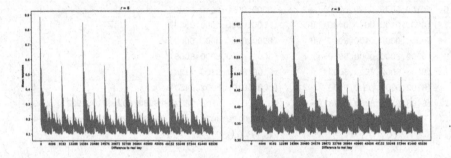

Fig. 3. Wrong key response profile of ID_1

- *Wrong key response profile (WKRP).* In [15], the key search policy depends on the observation that a distinguisher's response to wrong-key decryption varies with the bitwise difference between the guessed and real key. Instead of exhaustive trial decryption, it suggests specific subkeys and scores them. Figure 3 shows the mean response for varying Hamming distances between guessed and actual keys in ID_1. Notably, high scores emerge when differences in keys are small, especially if the difference relates to {16384, 32768, 49152}. This indicates that errors in the 14th and 15th bits of the subkey minimally impact scores, allowing for a reduced key guessing space. This accelerated key recovery in [15]. For WKRPs of ID_2 and ID_3, see Appendix B.2 in [4].

On $\mathcal{RK}\text{-}\mathcal{ND}'$s Explainability. Beyond constructing and comparing various $\mathcal{RK}$ distinguishers (see Appendix F.2 in [4]), we further undertook experiments analogous to Gohr's *aaaa*-blinding experiment. Some $\mathcal{RK}\text{-}\mathcal{ND}$s behaved similarly to single-key setting $\mathcal{ND}$s, while others varied. Refer to $\mathcal{RK}\text{-}\mathcal{ND}^{\text{SPECK9}R}_{\text{ID}_{(2,9182)}}$ and $\mathcal{RK}\text{-}\mathcal{ND}^{\text{SPECK9}R}_{\text{ID}_{(2,9382)}}$ in Table 14 for example for the former and latter case, where the differential trail $ID_{(2,9182)}$ differs from $ID_{(2,9382)}$ only at the last round key, and $ID_{(2,9382)}$ is ID_2 from round 4 to 12. Notably, the behavior of $\mathcal{RK}\text{-}\mathcal{ND}^{\text{SPECK9}R}_{\text{ID}_{(3,9082)}}$ presented intriguing phenomena ($ID_{(3,9082)}$ is ID_3 from round 4 to 12):

Table 14. Experiments detailing the information harnessed by $\mathcal{RK}$-$\mathcal{ND}$s using 9 round $\mathrm{ID}_{(2,9182)}$, $\mathrm{ID}_{(2,9382)}$, and $\mathrm{ID}_{(3,9082)}$, with similar settings in Table 2.

ID	Set	Positive Samples	Negative Samples	Acc.
$\mathcal{RK}$-$\mathcal{ND}^{\text{SPECK9}R}{}_{\mathrm{ID}_{(2,9182)}}$	1–1	$(\mathcal{A}, \mathcal{B}, \mathcal{C}, \mathcal{D})$	Random	0.7531
	1–2	$(\mathcal{AR}_1, \mathcal{BR}_1, \mathcal{CR}_1, \mathcal{DR}_1)$	Random	0.7534
$\mathcal{RK}$-$\mathcal{ND}^{\text{SPECK9}R}{}_{\mathrm{ID}_{(2,9382)}}$	1–1	$(\mathcal{A}, \mathcal{B}, \mathcal{C}, \mathcal{D})$	Random	0.7574
	1–2	$(\mathcal{AR}_1, \mathcal{BR}_1, \mathcal{CR}_1, \mathcal{DR}_1)$	Random	0.7529
$\mathcal{RK}$-$\mathcal{ND}^{\text{SPECK9}R}{}_{\mathrm{ID}_{(3,9082)}}$	1–1	$(\mathcal{A}, \mathcal{B}, \mathcal{C}, \mathcal{D})$	Random	0.7746
	1–2	$(\mathcal{AR}_1, \mathcal{BR}_1, \mathcal{CR}_1, \mathcal{DR}_1)$	Random	0.7539

1. $\mathcal{RK}$-$\mathcal{ND}^{\text{SPECK9}R}_{\mathrm{ID}_{(3,9082)}}$ performed differently on
   Set-1-1 $:= \{\Gamma_\mathcal{A}, \Gamma_\mathcal{B}, \Gamma_\mathcal{C}, \Gamma_\mathcal{D}\}$ and Set-1-2 $:= \{\Gamma_{\mathcal{AR}_1}, \Gamma_{\mathcal{BR}_1}, \Gamma_{\mathcal{CR}_1}, \Gamma_{\mathcal{DR}_1}\}$,
   which, under the assumption of a random last-round key K, defines the same
   information set per Sect. 3.1 (please refer to Table 14).
2. $\mathcal{RK}$-$\mathcal{ND}^{\text{SPECK9}R}_{\mathrm{ID}_{(3,9082)}}$ showed superior performance over $\mathcal{RK}$-$\mathcal{ND}^{\text{SPECK9}R}_{\mathrm{ID}_{(2,9382)}}$ (0.7726
   vs. 0.7535, refer to Table 22 in [4]), while theoretically, if there is no infor-
   mation on the key being revealed beyond the key difference, $\mathcal{RK}$-$\mathcal{ND}^{\text{SPECK9}R}_{\mathrm{ID}_{(3,9082)}}$
   should perform exactly the same as $\mathcal{RK}$-$\mathcal{ND}^{\text{SPECK9}R}_{\mathrm{ID}_{(2,9382)}}$, since the two differential trails differ only at the last round key difference thus the two output
   difference distributions are affine-equivalent.
3. Surprisingly, $\mathcal{RK}$-$\mathcal{ND}^{\text{SPECK9}R}{}_{\mathrm{ID}_{(3,9082)}}$ even outperformed our manually
   enhanced distinguisher $\mathcal{RK}$-$\mathcal{AD}^{\text{SPECK9}R}_{\mathbf{YD}}$ (0.7726 vs. 0.7574, refer to Table 22
   in [4]).

Upon closer examination of the differential trail of $\mathrm{ID}_{(3,9082)}$, we identified the
causative factor. Let's denote input/output differences and values around the
last $\boxplus$ in the key schedule producing the 8-round (counting start from 0) key k^8
as $\alpha, \beta, \gamma, x, y, z$. Then from the differential trail $\mathrm{ID}_{(3,9082)}$, specifically focus on
the 7- and 8-round, we have
$$\begin{cases} \alpha = \text{0x8002}^{\lll 7} & = \text{0b 0000 0101 0000 0000}, \\ \beta = \text{0x8480} & = \text{0b 1000 0100 1000 0000}, \\ \gamma = \text{0x8280} & = \text{0b 1000 0010 1000 0000}, \end{cases}$$
According to Tables 4 and 5, we have follows.

1. The $(8, 7)$-th bit position is in case $\text{Cxc1}_{(8,7)}$, we have $c_8 = y_7$.
2. The $(9, 8)$-th bit position is in case $\text{Cxc0}_{(9,8)}$, we have $c_9 = c_8$.
3. The $(10, 9)$-th bit position is in case $\text{Cxy1}_{(10,9)}$, we have $x_9 \oplus y_9 = z_9 \oplus c_9 = 1$.

Consequently, we have $z_9 \oplus y_7 = 1$. Note that $z_9 \oplus y_7 = 1$ implies that the 9th
bit of the last round key is constantly 1. This does not obscure 1-bit information
of the output of the last $\boxplus$ in the encryption path, allowing for better accuracy
of the resulting distinguisher. This explains all the odds on $\mathcal{RK}$-$\mathcal{ND}^{\text{SPECK9}R}_{\mathrm{ID}_{(3,9082)}}$.

Additionally, for $\mathcal{RK}$-$\mathcal{ND}^{\text{SPECK9}R}_{\mathrm{ID}_{(2,9382)}}$, the 10th bit of the last-round key conforming to the round difference has a bias towards 0 (equals 0 with a probability of

3/4), which could explain its slightly differed accuracy between **Set.**1–1 and **Set.**1–2 (refer to Table 14). After fixing the 10th bit to be 0 and re-training the distinguisher, it achieves almost the same accuracy as $\mathcal{RK}\text{-}\mathcal{ND}_{\text{ID}_{(3,9082)}}^{\text{SPECK9}R}$. When analyzing the probability of related-key pairs under these conditions, we deduced that restricting the 10th bit for $\text{ID}_{(2,9382)}$ still results in a larger weak-key space compared with $\text{ID}_{(3,9082)}$ while achieving the same high $\mathcal{RK}\text{-}\mathcal{ND}$ accuracy.

5.2   Key Recovery Attack on Round-Reduced SPECK32/64

This subsection describes the implementation of $\mathcal{RK}$ differential-neural cryptanalysis using the trained distinguisher. The key recovery framework is similar to [3,15,26]. Since the whole attack is in the $\mathcal{RK}$ setting, we need to specify the difference between each round of subkeys. Specifically, it is unclear how to perform a key recovery attack if only applying a difference to the master key without specifying the difference in the round-key state. In such cases, the guessed one last-round key cannot directly infer the other last-round key in the related pair, as the difference in the last-round key is not specified.

We first introduce some preparatory work before officially implementing the key recovery attack.

Generalized Neutral Bits. We incorporate $\mathcal{CD}$ before $\mathcal{ND}$ to increase the number of rounds for the key recovery attack. Furthermore, to enhance predictive performance, we employ the distinguisher to estimate the scores of multiple ciphertexts with the same distribution (ciphertext structure) and combine them to obtain the scores for the guessed subkey. However, the $\mathcal{CD}$ is probabilistic, and the randomly generated plaintext structure does not retain the same distribution after encryption. Hence, we require neutral bits to generate the plaintext structure, which we encrypt to obtain the ciphertext structure, achieving a successful key recovery attack. Therefore, the $\mathcal{CD}$ should have a high probability and a sufficient number of neutral bits. Appendix B.3 in [4] lists the NBs/SNBSs we used to perform the key recovery attack.

The Parameters for Key Recovery Attack. The attacks follow the framework of the improved key recovery attacks in [15]. An r-round main and an $(r-1)$-round helper $\mathcal{ND}s$ are employed, and an s-round $\mathcal{CD}$ is prepended. The key guessing procedure applies a simple reinforcement learning procedure. The last subkey and the second to last subkey are to be recovered without exhaustively using all candidate values to perform one-round decryption. Moreover, a Bayesian key search employing the *wrong key response profile* will be used. We count a key guess as successful if the last round key was guessed correctly and if the second round key is at the hamming distance at most two of the real keys. The parameters to recover the last two subkeys are indicated below.

Parameter	Definition
n_{cts}	The number of ciphertext structures
n_b	The number of ciphertext pairs in each ciphertext structure, that is, $2^{|NB|}$
n_{it}	The total number of iterations in the ciphertext structures
c_1, c_2	The cutoffs with respect to the scores of the recommended last subkey and second to last subkey, respectively
$n_{byit1/2}$	The number of iterations, the default value is 5
$n_{cand1/2}$	The number of key candidates within each iteration, default value is 32

Complexity Evaluation of Key Recovery Attack. The experiment is conducted by Python 3.7.15 and Tensorflow 2.5.0 in Ubuntu 20.04. The device information is Intel Xeon E5-2680V4*2 with 2.40 GHz, 256GB RAM, and NVIDIA RTX3080Ti 12 GB*7. To reduce the experimental error, we perform 210 key recovery attacks for each parameter setting, take the average running time rt as the running time of an experiment, and divide the number of successful experiments by the total experimental number as the success rate sr of the key recovery attack.

1. *Data complexity.* The data complexity of the experiment is calculated using the formula $n_b \times n_{ct} \times 2$, which is a theoretical value. In the actual experiment, when the accuracy of the differential-neural distinguisher is high, the key can be recovered quickly and successfully. Not all data are used, so the actual data complexity is lower than theoretical.

2. *Time complexity.* We use 2^{32} data to test the speed of encryption and decryption on our device, and each core can perform $2^{26.814}$ rounds of decryption operations per second for SPECK32/64. The formula for calculating the time complexity in our experiments: $2^{26.814} \times rt$.

The Result of Key Recovery Attacks. We list the results of key recovery attacks in multiple differential modes in Table 15. We calculate the corresponding weak key space wks according to the probabilities of ID_1, ID_2, and $ID_{(3,9082)}$. Adv. represents the advantage compared to the time complexity of brute forcing. The time and data complexity can be reduced by reducing n_{cts} and n_{it}, but the success rate sr also decreases accordingly. The first metric for our experiment is to reduce the time complexity.

Remark 3 (The profiling information of the key-recovery attack). To pinpoint the attack's bottleneck, we profiled a 14-round key-recovery attack using ID3. The main result is detailed in Table 16. From the profiling result, the performance of our implementation of the attack is mostly limited by the speed of neural network evaluation (the proportion taken by $\mathcal{ND}$ making the prediction is $79.18\% + 5.17\% = 84.35\%$). The next limiting factor is the speed of computing the weighted Euclidean distance with the wrong key response profile.

Table 15. Summary of key recovery attacks on SPECK32/64

Diff.	#R	Configure	wks	n_{cts}	n_{it}	n_b	c_1	c_2	sr	Time	Data	Advantage
ID_1	13	1+2+9+1	2^{50}	2^7	2^8	2^8	8	5	54.28%	$2^{34.57}$	2^{16}	$2^{15.43}$
ID_2	13	1+2+9+1	2^{46}	2^6	2^7	2^5	5	5	93.33%	$2^{33.95}$	2^{12}	$2^{12.05}$
ID_2	13	1+2+9+1	2^{46}	2^5	2^6	2^5	5	5	72.86%	$2^{33.01}$	2^{11}	$2^{12.99}$
ID_2	13	1+2+9+1	2^{46}	2^4	2^5	2^5	10	1	44.28%	$2^{31.79}$	2^{10}	$2^{14.21}$
ID_2	14	1+3+9+1	2^{42}	2^9	2^{10}	2^6	8	10	75.71%	$2^{35.59}$	2^{16}	$2^{6.41}$
ID_2	14	1+3+9+1	2^{42}	2^9	2^{10}	2^5	8	5	55.71%	$2^{35.32}$	2^{15}	$2^{6.68}$
ID_3	13	1+2+9+1	2^{45}	2^6	2^7	2^5	5	5	95.24%	$2^{34.26}$	2^{12}	$2^{10.75}$
ID_3	13	1+2+9+1	2^{45}	2^5	2^6	2^5	5	5	77.62%	$2^{33.55}$	2^{11}	$2^{11.45}$
ID_3	13	1+2+9+1	2^{45}	2^4	2^5	2^5	10	1	46.67%	$2^{32.20}$	2^{10}	$2^{12.80}$
ID_3	14	1+3+9+1	2^{41}	2^{10}	2^{11}	2^7	10	25	90%	$2^{36.39}$	2^{18}	$2^{4.61}$
ID_3	14	1+3+9+1	2^{41}	2^9	2^{10}	2^7	10	15	71.43%	$2^{35.78}$	2^{17}	$2^{5.22}$
ID_3	14	1+3+9+1	2^{41}	2^9	2^{10}	2^5	5	5	68.57%	$2^{35.40}$	2^{15}	$2^{5.6}$

Table 16. Profiling information of the key-recovery attack

Function	Time (Percentage)
test_bayes	242 s (100 %)
| – bayesian_key_recovery	| – 229.39 s (94.79 %)
| – | – (GPU) net.predict	| – | – 191.62 s (79.18 %)
| – | – (CPU) bayesian_rank_kr	| – | – 28.99 s (11.98 %)
| – verifier_search	| – 12.63 s (5.22 %)
| – | – (GPU) net.predict	| – | – 12.51 s (5.17 %)

– test_bayes: a full run of the attack excluding the generation of the related-key, load models, and generation of ciphertext structures.
– bayesian_key_recovery: the run of the BAYESIANKEYSEARCH algorithm.
– verifier_search: the run of the final improvement [3].
– net.predict: using $\mathcal{ND}$s to score the ciphertext structures decrypted by one round.
– bayesian_rank_kr: computing the weighted Euclidean distance with WKRPs.

Remark 4 (Efficiency measures in symmetric-key cryptanalysis attacks). Assessing the efficiency of distinguishers and key recovery attacks in symmetric-key cryptanalysis poses intricate challenges, particularly when pinpointing computational complexities based on real-time attack timings and then extrapolating these to equivalent primitive evaluations, as done in both $\mathcal{ND}$-based and traditional attacks in [12,14,24] (listed in Table 1).

Factors influencing these complexities include architecture compatibility and algorithmic suitability, varied computation intensity and various operation costs across platforms, memory constraints and flexible trade-offs, and implementation factors. Given these complexities, it is a good idea to have secondary metrics for comparison, for instance, power consumption and cost efficiency (please refer to Appendix E in [4] for detailed discussions). While there's a pressing need for universal metrics, formulating such benchmarks is challenging, warranting caution when interpreting the comparison results and warranting further exploration.

6   Conclusion

This paper provides explicit rules that a distinguisher can use beyond the full differential distribution table to achieve better distinguishing performance. These rules are based on high correlations between values of bits in right pairs of differential propagation through addition modulo 2^n. By leveraging the value-dependent differential probability, which is not typically applied in traditional differential distinguishers, we can equip additional knowledge to DDT-based distinguishers, enhancing their accuracy. These rules or their equivalent form are likely the additional features beyond full DDT that the neural distinguishers exploit. While these rules are not difficult to derive with careful analysis, they rely on non-trivial relations that traditional distinguishers often overlook. This indicates that neural networks help break the limitations of traditional cryptanalysis. Studying this unorthodox model can provide new opportunities to understand cryptographic primitives better.

Another investigation in this paper revealed that controlling differential propagation is crucial to enhance the accuracy of differential-neural distinguisher. It is typically believed that introducing differences into the keys provides chances to cancel differences in the encryption states, thus resulting in stronger differential propagations. However, unlike traditional differential attacks, differential-neural attacks do not specify the output difference and, thus, are not limited to a single differential trail. Therefore, it is unclear whether the difference in a key is helpful in differential-neural attacks. It is also unclear how resistant SPECK is against differential-neural attacks in the $\mathcal{RK}$ setting. This work confirmed that differential-neural cryptanalysis in the $\mathcal{RK}$ setting could be more powerful than in the single-key setting by conducting a 14-round key recovery attack on SPECK32/64.

Acknowledgments. The authors would like to thank anonymous reviewers for their insightful and helpful comments. Special thanks go to the anonymous shepherd, who provided invaluable constructive feedback and patient guidance, which helped us improve the manuscript significantly. This research is partially supported by Nanyang Technological University in Singapore under Start-up Grant 04INS000397C230, and Ministry of Education in Singapore under Grants RG91/20. Zhenzhen Bao was partially supported by the National Key R&D Program of China (Grant No. 2018YFA0704701), the Major Program of Guangdong Basic and Applied Research (Grant No. 2019B030302008), the High Performance Computing Center of Tsinghua University. Jinyu Lu was supported by the National Natural Science Foundation of China (Grant No. 62172427). Liu Zhang was supported by the National Natural Science Foundation of China (Grant No. 62172319), and the Fundamental Research Funds for the Central Universities (Grant No. QTZX23090).

References

1. Source codes in this work (2023). https://www.dropbox.com/sh/yleufeiu0wqwcjv/AADUpM15q86Uk1lM8z99fU2ia?dl=0
2. Bao, Z., Guo, J., Liu, M., Ma, L., Tu, Y.: Enhancing differential-neural cryptanalysis. Cryptology ePrint Archive, Report 2021/719 (2021). https://eprint.iacr.org/2021/719
3. Bao, Z., Guo, J., Liu, M., Ma, L., Tu, Y.: Enhancing differential-neural cryptanalysis. In: Agrawal, S., Lin, D. (eds.) ASIACRYPT 2022, Part I. LNCS, vol. 13791, pp. 318–347. Springer, Heidelberg (2022). https://doi.org/10.1007/978-3-031-22963-3_11
4. Bao, Z., Lu, J., Yao, Y., Zhang, L.: More insight on deep learning-aided cryptanalysis. Cryptology ePrint Archive, Paper 2023/1391 (2023). https://eprint.iacr.org/2023/1391, full version of this paper
5. Beaulieu, R., Shors, D., Smith, J., Treatman-Clark, S., Weeks, B., Wingers, L.: The SIMON and SPECK families of lightweight block ciphers. Cryptology ePrint Archive, Report 2013/404 (2013). https://eprint.iacr.org/2013/404
6. Bellini, E., Gerault, D., Hambitzer, A., Rossi, M.: A cipher-agnostic neural training pipeline with automated finding of good input differences. Cryptology ePrint Archive, Report 2022/1467 (2022). https://eprint.iacr.org/2022/1467
7. Benamira, A., Gerault, D., Peyrin, T., Tan, Q.Q.: A deeper look at machine learning-based cryptanalysis. In: Canteaut, A., Standaert, F.-X. (eds.) EURO-CRYPT 2021, Part I. LNCS, vol. 12696, pp. 805–835. Springer, Cham (2021). https://doi.org/10.1007/978-3-030-77870-5_28
8. Beyne, T., Rijmen, V.: Differential cryptanalysis in the fixed-key model. In: Dodis, Y., Shrimpton, T. (eds.) CRYPTO 2022, Part III. LNCS, vol. 13509, pp. 687–716. Springer, Heidelberg (2022). https://doi.org/10.1007/978-3-031-15982-4_23
9. Biryukov, A., dos Santos, L.C., Teh, J.S., Udovenko, A., Velichkov, V.: Meet-in-the-filter and dynamic counting with applications to speck. IACR Cryptology ePrint Archive p. 673 (2022)
10. Chen, Y., Bao, Z., Shen, Y., Yu, H.: A deep learning aided key recovery framework for large-state block ciphers. Cryptology ePrint Archive, Report 2022/1659 (2022). https://eprint.iacr.org/2022/1659
11. Chen, Y., Yu, H.: Bridging machine learning and cryptanalysis via EDLCT. Cryptology ePrint Archive, Report 2021/705 (2021). https://eprint.iacr.org/2021/705
12. Dinur, I.: Improved differential cryptanalysis of round-reduced speck. In: Joux, A., Youssef, A. (eds.) SAC 2014. LNCS, vol. 8781, pp. 147–164. Springer, Cham (2014). https://doi.org/10.1007/978-3-319-13051-4_9
13. Dinur, I., Dunkelman, O., Shamir, A.: Collision attacks on up to 5 rounds of SHA-3 using generalized internal differentials. In: Moriai, S. (ed.) FSE 2013. LNCS, vol. 8424, pp. 219–240. Springer, Heidelberg (2014). https://doi.org/10.1007/978-3-662-43933-3_12
14. Feng, Z., Luo, Y., Wang, C., Yang, Q., Liu, Z., Song, L.: Improved differential cryptanalysis on speck using plaintext structures. In: Simpson, L., Rezazadeh Baee, M.A. (eds.) ACISP 2023. LNCS, vol. 13915, pp. 3–24. Springer, Cham (2023). https://doi.org/10.1007/978-3-031-35486-1_1
15. Gohr, A.: Improving attacks on round-reduced Speck32/64 using deep learning. In: Boldyreva, A., Micciancio, D. (eds.) CRYPTO 2019, Part II. LNCS, vol. 11693, pp. 150–179. Springer, Cham (2019). https://doi.org/10.1007/978-3-030-26951-7_6

16. Gohr, A., Leander, G., Neumann, P.: An assessment of differential-neural distinguishers. Cryptology ePrint Archive, Report 2022/1521 (2022). https://eprint.iacr.org/2022/1521

17. Lee, H., Kim, S., Kang, H., Hong, D., Sung, J., Hong, S.: Calculating the approximate probability of differentials for ARX-based cipher using sat solver. J. Korea Inst. Inf. Secur. Cryptol. **28**(1), 15–24 (2018)

18. Leurent, G.: Analysis of differential attacks in ARX constructions. In: Wang, X., Sako, K. (eds.) ASIACRYPT 2012. LNCS, vol. 7658, pp. 226–243. Springer, Heidelberg (2012). https://doi.org/10.1007/978-3-642-34961-4_15

19. Leurent, G.: Construction of differential characteristics in ARX designs application to skein. In: Canetti, R., Garay, J.A. (eds.) CRYPTO 2013, Part I. LNCS, vol. 8042, pp. 241–258. Springer, Heidelberg (2013). https://doi.org/10.1007/978-3-642-40041-4_14

20. Lipmaa, H., Moriai, S.: Efficient algorithms for computing differential properties of addition. In: Matsui, M. (ed.) FSE 2001. LNCS, vol. 2355, pp. 336–350. Springer, Heidelberg (2002). https://doi.org/10.1007/3-540-45473-X_28

21. Lu, J., Liu, G., Liu, Y., Sun, B., Li, C., Liu, L.: Improved neural distinguishers with (related-key) differentials: applications in SIMON and SIMECK. Cryptology ePrint Archive, Report 2022/030 (2022). https://eprint.iacr.org/2022/030

22. Peyrin, T.: Improved differential attacks for ECHO and Grøstl. In: Rabin, T. (ed.) CRYPTO 2010. LNCS, vol. 6223, pp. 370–392. Springer, Heidelberg (2010). https://doi.org/10.1007/978-3-642-14623-7_20

23. Sadeghi, S., Rijmen, V., Bagheri, N.: Proposing an MILP-based method for the experimental verification of difference-based trails: application to speck, SIMECK. Des. Codes Crypt. **89**, 2113–2155 (2021)

24. Song, L., Huang, Z., Yang, Q.: Automatic differential analysis of ARX block ciphers with application to SPECK and LEA. In: Liu, J.K., Steinfeld, R. (eds.) ACISP 2016. LNCS, vol. 9723, pp. 379–394. Springer, Cham (2016). https://doi.org/10.1007/978-3-319-40367-0_24

25. Zhang, L., Lu, J., Wang, Z., Li, C.: Improved differential-neural cryptanalysis for round-reduced simeck32/64. arXiv preprint arXiv:2301.11601 (2023)

26. Zhang, L., Wang, Z., Wang, B.: Improving differential-neural cryptanalysis with inception blocks. Cryptology ePrint Archive, Report 2022/183 (2022). https://eprint.iacr.org/2022/183

27. Zhang, Z., Hou, C., Liu, M.: Collision attacks on round-reduced SHA-3 using conditional internal differentials. In: Hazay, C., Stam, M. (eds.) EUROCRYPT 2023, Part IV. LNCS, vol. 14007, pp. 220–251. Springer, Heidelberg (2023). https://doi.org/10.1007/978-3-031-30634-1_8

Author Index

© International Association for Cryptologic Research 2023
J. Guo and R. Steinfeld (Eds.): ASIACRYPT 2023, LNCS 14440, pp. 469–470, 2023.
https://doi.org/10.1007/978-981-99-8727-6

Printed in the United States
by Baker & Taylor Publisher Services